Nutrients in Salmonid Ecosystems: Sustaining Production and Biodiversity

Nutrients in Salmonid Ecosystems: Sustaining Production and Biodiversity

Edited by

John G. Stockner

Fisheries Centre, University of British Columbia,
Vancouver, British Columbia, Canada
and
Eco-Logic Ltd., 2614 Mathers Avenue,
West Vancouver, British Columbia, Canada

American Fisheries Society Symposium 34

Proceedings of the 2001 Nutrient Conference
Restoring Nutrients to Salmonid Ecosystems
Held at Eugene, Oregon, USA
24–26 April 2001

American Fisheries Society
Bethesda, Maryland
2003

Suggested citation formats follow.

Entire book

Stockner, J. G., editor. 2003. Nutrients in salmonid ecosystems: sustaining production and biodiversity. American Fisheries Society, Symposium 34, Bethesda, Maryland.

Chapter within the book

Schoonmaker, P. K., T. Gresh, J. Lichatowich, and H. D. Radtke. 2003. Past and present Pacific salmon abundance: bioregional estimates for key life history stages. Pages 33–40 *in* J. G. Stockner, editor. Nutrients in salmonid ecosystems: sustaining production and biodiversity. American Fisheries Society, Symposium 34, Bethesda, Maryland.

Front cover: photo by Graham Osborne. Back cover: "Bardo 19," by Scott Chambers. Page 287: photos by Richard Grost.

Printed in the United States of America on acid-free paper.

Library of Congress Control Number 2002117151
ISBN 1-888569-44-1
ISSN 0892-2284

American Fisheries Society
5410 Grosvenor Lane, Suite 110
Bethesda, Maryland 20814-2199

Contents

Background and Historic Perspective

Ecosystem Responses

Replacing Lost Nutrients: Stream and Lake Fertilization

Method Refinement

Innovative Ecosystem Management

About This Book

This book represents the concluding efforts of contributors to the 24–26 April 2001 conference in Eugene, Oregon, entitled Restoring Nutrients to Salmonid Ecosystems. Hence, it is instructive to 'wind the clock' back a few years to explain the conference's origins and view its significance in relation to prevailing attitudes in western fisheries and aquatic science.

An enormous amount of scientific effort in the 1960s and early 1970s had been directed at resolving the serious problem of cultural eutrophication or excessive anthropogenic additions of limiting nutrients to water bodies. One of the seminal books of this era, "The Algal Bowl" by Jack Vallentyne (1974), elegantly described the entire eutrophication issue. This clearly was a major environmental problem throughout the developed world, and with confirmation of phosphorus and nitrogen as the primary limiting macronutrients in freshwater, societal efforts through the remainder of the 1960s, 1970s, 1980s, and 1990s focused on reducing nutrient discharges, mainly point-source, to inland waters. Hence, the regulatory and educational mind-set for the last third of the 20th century was cast, and the reduction or elimination of phosphorus discharges to fresh and coastal marine waters became the standing order of the day.

However, starting back in the 1950s in Alaska, and even earlier in Russia, a few astute limnologists and fisheries biologists working around the North Pacific Rim had noted, by observation and experiment, that phosphorus was essential to aquatic life in these harsh environments and that salmon carcass decomposition biogenically recycled phosphorus and nitrogen. The suggestions of success from early fertilization experiments led to a decision in 1968, by the Canadian Department of Fisheries and Oceans (DFO), to add nutrients to Great Central Lake on Vancouver Island, B.C., in an attempt to rebuild a sockeye salmon stock that had been depressed since the turn of the 20th century, yet had failed to recover despite cessation of fishing activities. This was a paradoxical decision, as an agreement was established the same year between the Government of Canada and the Province of Ontario to establish the Experimental Lakes Area (ELA) in northwestern Ontario to study cultural eutrophication and related pollution problems in freshwater! The research conducted at ELA by Dave Schindler and other limnologists, including John Stockner, provided much of the scientific basis for detergent phosphate bans and reduction of phosphorus discharges, mainly from wastewater treatment plants in North America. Meanwhile, in British Columbia, the rapid recovery of Great Central Lake sockeye in 1974 led to the creation of a much larger Lake Enrichment Program (LEP), under the direction of DFO's Salmonid Enhancement Program a few years later, a similar sockeye lake fertilization program in Alaska, and eventually, an experimental stream and reservoir fertilization program in British Columbia in the 1990s. Thus, the limnological duality of phosphorus has always been present: too much phosphorus causes cultural eutrophication; too little phosphorus causes cultural oligotrophication; both conditions create nutrient imbalances that are detrimental to aquatic life. The former message was appropriately acknowledged and acted upon by society, whereas the latter message became lost in the onslaught of phosphorus and nitrogen control efforts and regulations.

Following a series of deficit budget years in the 1990s, DFO decided, in 1997, to close their West Vancouver laboratory, which had acted as the scientific center for B.C.'s Lake Enrichment Program, and at the same time, the senior LEP scientist, John Stockner, chose to leave DFO. Soon afterwards, Dr. Stockner was invited to become a professor and director of the prestigious Institute of Limnology at the University of Uppsala, Sweden. Upon moving to Uppsala in August of 1997, John Stockner teamed up with Goran Milbrink, also at the University of Uppsala, who had conducted innovative fertilization experiments on small, northern Swedish lakes with Staffan Holmgren, who had trained at the ELA in Ontario! The net result of this Canadian–Swedish collaboration was the submission of a proposal to Elforsk (a corporate consortium of Swedish hydroelectric power industries), in December 1997, to host the first international workshop on Restoration of Fisheries by Enrichment of Aquatic Ecosystems. The fact that this conference was held in Sweden and organised by Canadian and Swedish trained limnologists appears, at first glance, to be incongruous, as both countries were leaders in the crusade against cultural eutrophication of their inland waters. However, Sweden, like Canada, has long been a leader in the scientific study of factors influencing the productivity of lakes, from the pioneering studies of Einar Naumann and Wilhelm Rodhe to the later research programs conducted by the Institute of Freshwater Research at Drottingholm and Institutes of Limnology at the University of Uppsala and the University of Lund. Due to the limited budget, only 25 participants from four countries (Canada, the United States, Sweden, and Norway) were able to attend the 30 March–1 April 1998 workshop at the Institute of Limnology, Uppsala. However, the proceedings were published to reach as wide an audience as possible (Stockner and Milbrink 1999).

On the return flight to Vancouver, Pat Slaney, who pioneered the early stream nutrient enrichment experiments on Northern Vancouver Island, and Ken Ashley discussed the concept of holding a similar but larger conference in the Pacific Northwest, where wild salmonid stocks have been in decline for many years. The idea germinated for several months. Meanwhile, two unprecedented restoration programs had begun in the Pacific Northwest. The Presidents Plan, the Clinton Administration's response to the spotted owl/salmon crisis in the Pacific Northwest, became the U.S. Forest Service's (Region 6) watershed restoration plan and was in full swing by 1994. In British Columbia, a similar watershed restoration program began in mid-1994, which was assisted by an international technical exchange agreement between the USFS and B.C.'s Ministry of Environment, had expanded to a $70 million per year program in British Columbia. At the same time, collapsing kokanee stocks in several large interior reservoirs had initiated a large program of reservoir fertilization modelled after the LEP program. Consequently, British Columbia became the center for a variety of lake, stream, and river fertilization experiments with extensive research connections throughout the Pacific Northwest, Alaska, Japan, and Scandinavia. Simultaneously, several researchers in Alaska, British Columbia, Oregon, and Washington were using stable isotope tracers, mainly ^{15}N and ^{13}C, to document the movement of marine-derived nutrients (MDN) through aquatic and terrestrial foodwebs, which further elucidated the role and importance of salmon nutrients in sustaining production and biodiversity of PNW ecosystems.

The idea for the nutrient conference lay dormant throughout 1998 and most of 1999, other than a belief that it should be held in either Washington or Oregon. The reason being that the theory and practice of enrichment had received less exposure there, and given the critical state of many wild salmonid stocks, the greatest MDN deficit was in the U.S. PNW (Gresch et al. 2000). In addition, fertilization practices that had become routine in British Columbia were still illegal in the United States, according to some state and federal laws; hence, a U.S. venue would generate greater interest, perhaps some enlightenment. In August 1999, during a visit by Dave Heller, head of the USFS Region 6 Fisheries Program, to discuss a large-scale northern river fertilisation experiment (Mesilinka River), Heller, Slaney, and Ashley discussed the concept and agreed that a conference seemed like a good idea and that a U.S. venue made sense. Upon returning from the Mesilinka River, John Stockner, who had recently returned from Uppsala, Sweden, concurred with our conclusions and offered to present a keynote address that had been 25 years in the making! In September 1998, the Alaska Chapter of AFS organized a nutrient symposium during their annual meeting, and interest in the 'nutrient' topic continued to build. Given the 12–18 month lead time required to deliver a major conference, April 2001 was selected as the conference date, and the Oregon Chapter of AFS was chosen as the host chapter. The timing could not have been better, as the scientific interest in salmonids and nutrients increased markedly during this period, with four articles appearing in *Fisheries* (Cederholm et al. 1999; Gresch et al. 2000; Stockner et al. 2000; Bilby et al. 2001) plus feature newspaper articles on salmon nutrient research of Mark Wipfli in Alaska and Tom Reimchen and Bruce Ward in British Columbia. The Nutrient Conference website, designed and maintained by Richard Bayley of the Portland Chapter of AFS, even received two awards for content and design, as it contained links to several of these current publications on nutrients and salmonids.

Given this heady atmosphere and recognition that the timing for the conference was near perfect, all of the funds to conduct the conference were raised in advance from a variety of supporting institutions (see Acknowledgements). The five basic tenants of the conference were: low conference fees; concurrent sessions were not permitted; aquatic and terrestrial topics would be accepted; extensive student travel support would be provided; and free refreshments would be available every evening. All of these were achieved, as 17 students were provided with 90% of their travel funding requests, and the free refreshments lasted until the 11th hour on the final evening, as we slightly underestimated the consumption of the conference participants. Attendees to the conference included three Scandinavian members from the Uppsala workshop, many from the Alaska symposium, and a special visit by several people from Japan, including C. W. Nicol whose long interest in environmental issues allowed him to bring a film crew from the Hokkaido Broadcasting Corporation to film the conference. Hence, we felt it fitting that Mr. Nicol, now a Japanese citizen, be given the opportunity to write the preface for the conference proceedings, as his experience around the North Pacific Rim gave him a unique perspective on the topic. The conference went off exceptionally well, including a command performance by anthropologist Brian Chisholm, who, despite excruciating back pain, was able to deliver his presentation from a wheelchair, and an evening screening of the CBC's Nature of Things "The Salmon Forest" with introductions by Tom Reimchen. A festive atmosphere prevailed at the conference, and many in attendance indicated it was one of the best scientific meetings they had ever attended. To show our appreciation to the artists who exhibited their work at the conference, the beautiful carcass photo is by Scott Chambers, while the Richard Grost images on page 287 capture some of the magic of the moment. Hopefully, you will find these proceedings informative and use the information to help protect and restore critical salmonid habitat, so that the nutrient shadow now so attenuated can be restored to its fullest extent to the benefit of aquatic and terrestrial ecosystems that are so vitally dependent upon it. In summary, the conference was truly a wonderful experience, which proves, once again, that a small group of dedicated people can accomplish great things, and in this case, the 'gumboot biologists' had their moment in the sun.

KENNETH ASHLEY
JOHN STOCKNER

Literature Cited

Bilby, R. E., B. R. Fransen, J. K. Walter, C. J. Cederholm, and W. J. Scarlett. 2001. Preliminary evaluation of nitrogen stable isotope ratios to establish escapement levels for Pacific salmon. Fisheries 26:6–14

Cederholm, C. J., M. D. Kunze, T. Murota, and A. Sibatani. 1999. Essential contributions of nutrients and energy for aquatic and terrestrial ecosystems. Fisheries 24:6–15.

Gresh, T. J., J. Lichatowich, and P. Schoonmaker. 2000. An estimation of historic and current levels of salmon production in the Northeast Pacific ecosystem: evidence of a nutrient deficit in the freshwater systems of the Pacific Northwest. Fisheries 25:15–21.

Stockner, J. G., and G. Milbrink, editors. 1999. Restoration of fisheries by enrichment of aquatic ecosystems. Workshop Proceedings, Uppsala University Press, Sweden.

Stockner, J. G., E. Rydin, and P. Hyenstrand. 2000. Cultural oligotrophication. Fisheries 25:7–14.

Vallentyne, J. R. 1974. The algal bowl: lakes and man. Miscellaneous Special Publication 22, Canadian Department of the Environment, Fisheries and Marine Service, Ottawa.

A Few Words in Preface

All of us, who were fortunate enough to be able to attend the International Conference on Restoring Nutrients to Salmonid Ecosystems in Eugene, Oregon, in April of the year 2001, have had our lives deeply touched by the salmon family. This was plainly evident in the intensity and enthusiasm of the participants, the many discussions and arguments that continued on after each session, and, let us admit, the sheer fun of the whole thing. That conference made us all think.

As I sit in my study in Nagano, Japan, I hear the rush of the Torii River, icy cold with the snowmelt from the mountains of Togakushi and Kurohime. This river runs into the Chikuma, which joins the Shinano and empties into the Japan Sea at Niigata. It is the longest river system in Japan. Up until the early decades of the twentieth century, the Torii River had a healthy run of spawning salmon and anadromous char. Dams and other obstructions killed that.

After the conference, when I went on lecture tours from Hokkaido to Okinawa, I made a point of asking my audiences to put up their hands if they had recently eaten salmon. Even down in Okinawa, where there have never been salmonid rivers, more than ninety percent of the Japanese raised their hands. The Japanese appetite for salmon is voracious. We probably consume more salmon than any other modern, industrialized nation on earth.

It is not surprising that salmon is a traditional food in this country. From Hokkaido to Northern Kyushu, there were many, many wonderful salmon and char rivers; yet, nearly all of these have been destroyed by man-made obstructions and pollution. Of all countries, Japan should be taking a responsible, sensible look at the future of anadromous fisheries, both in Japan itself and in all the many nations where Japanese money and industry are affecting economy and environment. This book should be a boost to this.

In 1975, Japan held an international ocean exposition in Okinawa. I was selected to represent Environment Canada at the Canadian pavilion. For very special guests, we had an elegant book, bound in brown cloth with an engraved print of a salmon on the cover, done in black and red by a North Coast native artist. The book was commissioned by the Fisheries and Marine Service of Environment Canada in 1974. It was written by Roderick Haig Brown and "dedicated to the salmons of the Pacific and Atlantic and to all their friends in Canada and other countries who wish to protect them and restore or enhance their abundance. The salmons' return to their rivers of origin is a continuing reminder to us of our duty to preserve, in harmony, their environment and ours."

There you are. That was 1974.

As a boy, growing up in Britain, the only salmon I knew came in a can, and it was treasured. When three young American officers were visiting our house for afternoon tea, just after the end of World War II, one of them asked why the British ate so much canned salmon. My poor mother was aghast. She had been carefully saving that last can for special guests. That, of course, is what so many British housewives and mothers had done, bringing out that precious can for honored visitors.

Between the world wars, British Columbia alone was producing some two million cases of canned salmon a year, with the bulk of it going to Britain. During both world wars, uncounted tons of canned salmon also ended up on the bottom of the ocean due to the activity of the German submarines. Britain had, by this time, sacrificed most of her productive salmonid rivers to industrialization, and the common folk did not know fresh, wild salmon. That was a treat for the rich and privileged only.

I had my first taste of fresh wild salmon at the age of fifteen, when I went to France as an exchange student. The salmon came from the Garonne River and was grilled in the garden over a fire of dried vine twigs. Never had I tasted fish like that! I was seventeen the next time I had wild, fresh salmon. This was on my first long arctic field trip, to Ungava Bay. The salmon was brought to us by an Inuit hunter, Jobi Snowball. Having eaten all the salmon my young stomach could possibly hold, I compiled words in my diary as to what being rich or privileged really meant. I reflected that even though many British at the time might cling to the notion that we were lords of the earth, compared with an Inuit hunter, the average Britisher was underprivileged indeed.

Coming to Japan for the first time in 1962 was an eye opener too. Whenever I could, I traveled in the mountains or to small coastal villages or islands. Even deep in rural Japan, wild trout and char were a regular part of the diet. I recall my delight at having char, taken fresh from a nearby mountain stream, speared on a stick, salted, and grilled over charcoal in the ash-filled fire pit of an old traditional thatched home. As a boy in Britain, the only trout I got were those I learned to poach from a rich man's river.

Then, over these forty years, (during which I have gained Japanese citizenship), I have seen the senseless, terrible destruction of salmonid river systems, mostly sacrificed to a bloated construction industry and corrupt politics. Now, we face an even more insidious threat. There is uncontrolled dumping of industrial and medical waste all through the mountains, all in watershed areas, and mostly carried out by the underworld, while bureaucrats and politicians are either intimidated or corrupted by the huge sums of unaccounted money this garbage generates.

I say this and know it to be true, for I also have been threatened for speaking out; yet, I am glad to say that there is a gradual awakening in Japan, and there are dedicated and honest men like Dr. T. Murota.

At the conference and in travels to see the efforts to restore salmonid ecosystems, I was made aware again of science that at times seemed like sheer magic. Science that took me into the glorious, beautiful, complex, interlocking cycles of life, death, physics, chemistry, history, and human culture. Things like being able to read the history and presence of salmon in tree rings, seeing and knowing the invisible!

After the conference, I was able to do some filming of salmon streams in British Columbia, to see again this miracle of returning salmon, to witness again the dying salmon, their bodies all battered and torn, gasping out their last after spawning. What we learned so well at the conference, though, was that there is no waste in this death. The death of adult salmon sustains not only their own progeny and life in the river, but also the entire biodiversity of the ecosystem, from the smallest microbe and insect to the mighty grizzly and the tallest tree. The tragedy lies not in the death of a wild salmon, but in the loss of salmon ecosystems, especially when this conference has taught us what we can do to bring the salmon and all they support back.

I can not even begin to thank the friends, both old and new, whose efforts went into this conference. The results gave folk like me ammunition and inspiration to forge ahead.

To again quote from that book called *Salmon*, which I mentioned in the beginning, "In prehistoric times most of the rivers in Europe, Asia, and North America, north of the 40th parallel, provided salmon in great quantities to graze the waters of the Atlantic and Pacific oceans and to bring back the wealth of their bodies to the land. The returning salmon have been welcomed, protected and often venerated by their people."

I especially like the notion of veneration for salmonids and their systems. That, in essence, is what the conference was about. What do you think?

C. W. NICOL
Kurohime, Nagano, Japan
5 May 2002

Acknowledgements

A number of agencies and organizations kindly donated funds to sponsor the Eugene Salmon Nutrient Conference. Our sincerest thanks for their important financial and in-kind contributions:

Agrium Inc., Standard, Alberta
American Fisheries Society Chapters—Oregon, Greater Portland, North Pacific International Chapter
Boise-Cascade Corporation
British Columbia Conservation Foundation, Surrey, B.C.
Bureau of Land Management, Oregon and Washington Office
Canadian Department of Fisheries and Oceans, Vancouver, B.C.
David Suzuki Foundation, Vancouver, B.C.
National Marine Fisheries Service, Seattle, Washington
Natural Resources Conservation Service, Oregon
Oregon Watershed Enhancement Board
US Environmental Protection Agency, Corvallis, Oregon
US Forest Service, Portland Office
Washington Department of Natural Resources, Olympia, Washington
Washington Department of Fish and Wildlife (SSHIAP), Olympia, Washington

A conference of this size required a significant number of volunteers to provide Opening and Plenary presentations, chair sessions, organize the registration desk, and assist in the preparation of manuscripts for the conference proceedings. We would like to thank the following individuals for donating their time, as their efforts greatly contributed to the success of the Eugene Conference:

Harvey Forsgren and Hon. John Fraser, Q.C.
Session chairs: Jeff Cederholm, Bob Bilby, Hal Michael, Goran Milbrink, Wayne Minshall, Tom Reimchen, Lisa Thompson, and Mark Wipfli
Panel chairs: Robert Lackey, Bill Bakke
Loretta Brenner, Joan Baker, and about 20 volunteers
The David Suzuki Foundation
C. W. (Nic) Nicol and the Hokkaido Broadcasting Corporation
Richard Bayley—*The WebMaster*

We greatfully acknowledge the work and extra effort of our science editor, John Stockner, who logged many long hours adjudicating submissions and providing a critical and constructive science edit for each chapter of this conference proceedings volume.

A small group of visionary individuals formed the Eugene Conference Steering Committee in 2000. Special thanks for tolerating the innumerable conference calls and discussions. It paid off with one of the best fisheries conferences held in the Pacific Northwest in recent times!

Ken Ashley, BC Fisheries, Vancouver, B.C.
Jeff Cederholm, WA DNR, Olympia, Washington
Rich Grost, RTG Inc., Idleyld Park, Oregon
Dave Heller, US Forest Service, Portland, Oregon
Dave Hohler, US Forest Service, Portland, Oregon
Pat Slaney, Watershed Restoration Program, Vancouver, B.C.

Symbols and Abbreviations

The following symbols and abbreviations may be found in this book without definition. Also undefined are standard mathematical and statistical symbols given in most dictionaries.

A	ampere	ha	hectare (2.47 acres)
AC	alternating current	hp	horsepower (746 W)
Bq	becquerel	Hz	hertz
C	coulomb	in	inch (2.54 cm)
°C	degrees Celsius	Inc.	Incorporated
cal	calorie	i.e.	(id est) that is
cd	candela	IU	international unit
cm	centimeter	J	joule
Co.	Company	K	Kelvin (degrees above absolute zero)
Corp.	Corporation	k	kilo (10^3, as a prefix)
cov	covariance	kg	kilogram
DC	direct current; District of Columbia	km	kilometer
D	dextro (as a prefix)	l	levorotatory
d	day	L	levo (as a prefix)
d	dextrorotatory	L	liter (0.264 gal, 1.06 qt)
df	degrees of freedom	lb	pound (0.454 kg, 454g)
dL	deciliter	lm	lumen
E	east	log	logarithm
E	expected value	Ltd.	Limited
e	base of natural logarithm (2.71828...)	M	mega (10^6, as a prefix); molar (as a suffix or by itself)
e.g.	(exempli gratia) for example		
eq	equivalent	m	meter (as a suffix or by itself); milli (10^{23}, as a prefix)
et al.	(et alii) and others		
etc.	et cetera	mi	mile (1.61 km)
eV	electron volt	min	minute
F	filial generation; Farad	mol	mole
°F	degrees Fahrenheit	N	normal (for chemistry); north (for geography); newton
fc	footcandle (0.0929 lx)		
ft	foot (30.5 cm)	N	sample size
ft³/s	cubic feet per second (0.0283 m³/s)	NS	not significant
g	gram	n	ploidy; nanno (10^{29}, as a prefix)
G	giga (10^9, as a prefix)	o	ortho (as a chemical prefix)
gal	gallon (3.79 L)	oz	ounce (28.4 g)
Gy	gray	P	probability
h	hour	p	para (as a chemical prefix)
		p	pico (10^{212}, as a prefix)

Pa	pascal	USA	United States of America (noun)
pH	negative log of hydrogen ion activity	V	volt
ppm	parts per million	V, Var	variance (population)
qt	quart (0.946 L)	var	variance (sample)
R	multiple correlation or regression coefficient	W	watt (for power); west (for geography)
		Wb	weber
r	simple correlation or regression coefficient	yd	yard (0.914 m, 91.4 cm)
rad	radian	α	probability of type I error (false rejection of null hypothesis)
S	siemens (for electricalconductance); south (for geography)	β	probability of type II error (false acceptance of null hypothesis)
SD	standard deviation	Ω	ohm
SE	standard error	μ	micro (10^{26}, as a prefix)
s	second	$'$	minute (angular)
T	tesla	$''$	second (angular)
tris	tris(hydroxymethyl)-aminomethane (a buffer)	$\circ$	degree (temperature as a prefix, angular as a suffix)
UK	United Kingdom	%	per cent (per hundred)
U.S.	United States (adjective)		

Background and Historic Perspective

American Fisheries Society Symposium 34:3–15, 2003

Salmon Nutrients: Closing the Circle

John G. Stockner

Fisheries Centre, University of British Columbia, 2204 Main Mall
Vancouver, B.C. V6T 1Z4, Canada

Eco-Logic Ltd., 2614 Mathers Avenue
W. Vancouver, B.C. V7V 2J4, Canada

Kenneth I. Ashley

B.C. Fisheries Research Section, Ministry of Fisheries
University of British Columbia, 2204 Main Mall
Vancouver, B.C. V6T 1Z4, Canada

Introduction

The consequences of nutrient loss (oligotrophication) and attendant low productivity on ecosystem biodiversity and fish production have only recently perked the interest of researchers in aquatic science (Ney 1996; Ashley and Slaney 1997; Stockner et al. 2000). Conversely, research on the ecological consequences of 'excess' nutrients (eutrophication) has been a major focus of limnological research for several decades (Forsberg 1998; Vollenweider 1968). Inputs of phosphorus (P) and nitrogen (N) from anthropogenic interventions on the landscape were identified as primary causal factors of eutrophication (Edmondson 1969; Vallentyne 1974). Over the last century, the impact of man, mediated by overfishing, dam construction, and habitat destruction in both coastal and interior regions of the Pacific Rim nations (United States, Canada, Japan, Russia), has led to a marked decline and, in some cases, total loss of adult salmon spawners, which has had a profound impact on the productivity and biodiversity of salmonid ecosystems (Mathisen 1972; Stockner 1987; Larkin and Slaney 1997; Cederholm et al. 2000a; Gresh et al. 2000). Further, the construction of some dams within the Columbia River basin has not only markedly reduced and/or eliminated anadromous salmon runs, but also, in the upper basin within Canada, has had an equally dev-astating impact on kokanee salmon *Oncorhynchus nerka* stocks, due both to reservoir oligotrophication and introductions of exotic species, for example, mysids (Northcote 1973; Ashley et al. 1997; Pieters et al., this volume).

The roots of this discourse were largely developed in 1997 and 1998 in Sweden, a country where, for most of the populace, phosphorus removal from lakes and streams has become the standard, and any thoughts of purposely adding nutrients to lakes or streams to enhance fisheries are deemed unorthodox. Thus, it was time to introduce a new paradigm of global 'oligotrophication' to limnology and fisheries science, and the subject of nutrient deprivation and its impacts on fisheries and food chains became the subject of the opening address for the first international symposium on 'Restoration of Fisheries by Enrichment of Aquatic Ecosystems,' held in March 1998 in Uppsala, Sweden (Stockner and Milbrink 1999). Here, we briefly summarize some of the factors known to cause oligotrophication of lakes and streams worldwide, but our main objective is to focus only on those factors affecting anadromous salmon and land-locked kokanee ecosystems, discussing some of the consequences of the oligotrophic condition on production, biodiversity, and fish. We conclude with a few salient comments on some of the more promising remedial measures that can reverse oligotrophication and hasten ecosystem recovery, notably fertilization and habitat restoration.

Background

Nutrients

The primary nutrients essential for growth and reproduction of all living matter are carbon (C), nitrogen (N), and phosphorus (P), and they usually occur in a ratio of approximately 102:16:1 by atoms or 40:7:1 by mass (Vallentyne 1974). Carbon is an important component of carbohydrates and lipids, while nitrogen is common in amino acids, the building blocks of proteins, and P is a vital component of mitochondria, important in metabolic processes and in nucleic acids (e.g., DNA, RNA). Because both C and N are ubiquitous in their gas phase, in most ecosystems, inputs of plant utilizable forms of C (HCO_3^-, CO_2) and N (NH_4^+, NO_3^-) can be restored by biogenic reductive assimilation. However P, lacking a gas phase, cannot be renewed and, therefore, is commonly the nutrient in shortest supply and most limiting to biotic phototrophic production in freshwater habitats (Schindler 1980; Stockner 1987). If C and N are present in ecosystems in nonlimiting concentrations, then 1 mg P can produce about 500 mg of periphyton or phytoplankton biomass; said another way, each person on average releases about 2 kg P per year to wastewater that is capable of producing more than a ton of living plants (Vallentyne 1974). A returning adult salmon weighing 4 kg contains about 18 g P that, if in soluble, available form, would be capable of producing 7.5 kg of living autotrophic plant biomass. Though globally there is a large supply of phosphate rock, most is burdened with impurities (heavy metals), and supplies of quality high-grade rock available for fertilizer manufacture are rapidly diminishing and are predicted to be exhausted from most sources within the first half of this century (CEEP 1998; Driver et al. 1999). Therefore, we opine that it is imperative that the populace now commences all economically and technologically feasible means of recycling P, not discarding this scarce but essential element for life (Stockner et al. 2000).

Oligotrophication

Oligotrophic ecosystems are nutrient-poor and are characterized by their low annual rates of biogenic production. This nutrient-poor or 'oligotrophic' status is the antithesis of the nutrient-rich or 'eutrophic' condition. Since most actions leading to either nutrient gain or loss (i.e., nutrient 'imbalances') are mediated by anthropogenic causes, it makes sense to term these processes 'cultural' oligotrophication and eutrophication. Though some lakes, rivers, and streams can become oligotrophic from natural events, most of the documented cases originate from cultural oligo-trophication and can be traced to man's activities, some examples of which include the following (after Stockner et al. 2000):

- **Excessive removal of anthropogenic nutrients**. The consequence of the near total elimination or diversion of direct (point) sources of anthropogenic nutrients (e.g., sewage treatment plant [STP] effluents, stormwater, and/or agricultural drainage).
- **Dam construction.** Reservoirs behind dams on rivers or at lake outflows retain water either for irrigation or hydroelectric power generation or both. Dams, by increasing water retention, increase biogenic reduction of organic matter, increase sedimentation rates and excessive water level fluctuations (drawdown), and destabilize the littoral zone, thereby creating effective P-sinks and low production habitat.
- **Drainage of wetlands.** Land drainage schemes result in increased P-export, due to soil erosion, diminished water retention in soil, wetlands, and streams, and lower and enriched ground water. The newly created agrarian lands eventually require annual fertilizer application (P-import) to sustain production, which further exacerbates P-export to streams and lakes.
- **Fish reductions.** When migratory adult fish leave a large lake or ocean rearing ground and migrate to lakes, rivers, and tributary streams to spawn, they become effective conveyers of nutrients from one ecosystem to another. This salmon mediated nutrient transport system or 'nutrient pump' can be an important C, N, and P source for the maintenance of ecosystem productivity and biodiversity in salmonid lakes and streams where most salmon die after spawning, enriching their natal freshwater and riparian habitats with marine-derived nutrients (MDN) (Kline et al. 1990; Kline, Reimchen et al., Schoonmaker et al., all this volume). Overfishing can remove large

quantities of these nutrients and even moderate fishing extracts nutrients from the ecosystem, and in nutrient-limited habitats, the impacts of these lost nutrients are particularly severe.

- **Acidification.** There is growing evidence that acidification of lakes and streams by acidic precipitation leads to oligotrophication (Jansson et al. 1986; Kopacek et al. 1995; Turner et al. 1995). Processes that increase adsorption of P to aluminum and decrease P-recycling from sediments and littoral margins are implicated.

- **Deforestation.** A clear-cut logged coniferous forest can represent a significant loss of P (P-export) from forested landscapes, not only in log (biomass) removal, but also from erosion of humus and mineral soil layers, due to road construction, log skidding, and related activities. Most deforested lands have decreased soil water retention capacities that initially increase run-off and often turbidity (P-export). After vegetative colonization, a vigorous second growth of young trees and shrubs create high P demands that reduce P supplies to streams and lakes.

- **Climate change.** Recent studies suggest that continued climate warming will reduce carbon production in lakes, due to more protracted periods of stratification that will create severe phytoplankton nutrient limitation within the euphotic zone. With the increased likelihood of milder winters with little or no ice-cover, the water circulation period of an increasing number of temperate dimictic lakes will become warm-monomictic and, as a consequence, will be less productive and experience oligotrophication (Schindler et al. 1990; Henderson et al. 1992; Stockner 1987, 1998).

Among the many causes of oligotrophication, those that have most compromised the efficiency and production of food webs of PNW salmonid ecosystems over the past century are fish reductions (overfishing, habitat loss), construction of hydroelectric and irrigation dams, deforestation (logging), and climate change.

Impacts of Oligotrophication

Extinguishing the Salmon Nutrient Source. As smolts young salmon migrating to the Pacific Ocean take some of their natal lake's or stream's nutrients with them to the sea, but as adults migrating back to the ecosystem of birth, they return much larger quantities of marine nutrients from their vast oceanic rearing grounds; as such, they become effective conveyers of marine nutrients into freshwater and estuarine ecosystems. For example, in many coastal B.C. sockeye *O. nerka* lakes, smolt out-migrations represent from less than 1% to 5% of the total annual TP load from the drainage basin, while marine TP in returning adult spawners can return from 15% to 40% of the annual TP load (Stockner 1987). This marine TP 'interest' payment accrues largely to the ecosystem and supports annual autotrophic aquatic and riparian production cycles while promoting species biodiversity (Cederholm et al. 2000a, 2000b; Jauquet, Reimchen et al., both this volume). Some of the largest salmon P inputs accrue to sockeye, chinook *O. tshawytscha*, and coho *O. kisutch* ecosystems, where some migrations reach great distances inland to mountain lakes and streams where freshwater rearing is a requisite to growth and survival of the species (Murota, this volume). Most juvenile chum *O. keta* and pink salmon *O. gorbuscha* have a short freshwater residency and rear mainly in estuaries and nearshore marine waters. As adults, chum salmon spawners travel far shorter migratory pathways to their natal spawning grounds than pinks, but both are eclipsed by sockeye and chinook migrations. Thus, a larger portion of chum and pink salmon nutrients, if not physically removed in carcasses from streams by large salmon consumers (e.g., bear, mink, raccoon, and eagles), often provide greater nutrient supplementation to lower-gradient reaches of rivers and to estuaries and nearshore coastal regions. The large annual influx of marine nutrients from adult salmon carcasses to river estuaries and coastal embayments over many centuries is certainly one of the more compelling reasons why most estuaries of salmonid river ecosystems are considered highly productive and biologically diverse. Clearly, it has been the gradual loss of adult salmon through the past century, the anadromous nutrient pump, that has resulted in the oligotrophication of a vast majority of PNW salmonid ecosystems. Of course, there are exceptions to this generalization, ecosystems that have been compensated, often to excess, for salmon losses by input of nutrients from anthropogenic sources (e.g., sewage, agricultural drainage), often contaminated by suspended sediments, metals, and so on, which can negate nutrient benefits. However, we opine that in the uppermost reaches of river and lake drainage basins, where salmon are able to spawn and their fry rear, annual supplements of marine nutrients in organic and inorganic form become vitally important to the carbon metabolism of these ecosystems because they are inherently nutrient poor and remain exceptionally so today.

There are other sources of marine nutrients uploaded to freshwater and estuarine ecosystems, such as the eulachon *Thaleichthys pacificus* or candlefish along the Pacific Coast, some species of herring, and several species of sea bird, but salmon, by their adult size and population abundance, represent one the most important vectors of marine nutrients to freshwater habitats (Murota, this volume). Though we focus on Pacific salmon in this discourse, we would be remiss not to mention Atlantic salmon *Salmo salar*. Roughly half of adult Atlantic salmon die after spawning, so several centuries ago, Atlantic salmon nutrient uploads must have cast a far-reaching shadow across the northeastern coasts of North America, Northern Europe, Scandinavia, Great Britain, and Ireland that sadly has now been largely extinguished. On the Pacific Coast of North America, in Japan, and in the Kamchatka Peninsula of Russia, commencing in the latter half of the 19th century, the anadromous Pacific salmon nutrient pump (shadow) has also been slowly attenuated by overfishing, dams, and loss of habitat, now to such an extent that in the remotest salmon ecosystems, the shadow has either been obscured or completely extinguished by reduced escapements and/or complete extinction of runs (Larkin and Slaney 1997; Nakajima and Ito, Schoonmaker et al., both this volume). A case in point would be the extinction of all chinook runs to the Upper Columbia Basin in Northeast Washington and all of Northeastern British Columbia in the early 1940s by closure of the Columbia River after construction of the Grand Coulee Dam, extirpating anadromous salmon forever to these vast, wild regions. Notable, also, is the loss of most anadromous chinook and sockeye salmon runs to large portions of eastern Oregon, Idaho, and Nevada by the construction of multiple Snake and Columbia river dams (Griswold et al., Thomas et al., both this volume).

Some sense of how great the nutrient reduction has been to British Columbia's freshwaters, since the inception of commercial fishing and habitat disruption, can be seen by converting the historic record of B.C. salmon catches into phosphorus equivalents (Figure 1). Losses of adult salmon P to catch since the turn of the century have averaged between 225–275 tons, enough phosphorus to produce more than 100,000 tons of living autotrophic plant biomass! Said another way, sufficient nutrients to 'green' the beds of rivers, estuaries, and margins of salmon lakes throughout the province.

But to better view the direct impact of oligotrophication imparted by nutrient loss to salmon ecosystems, it is more realistic to com-

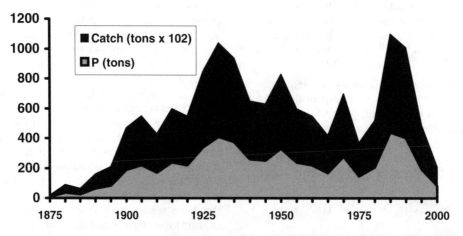

FIGURE 1. British Columbia salmon catch expressed in biomass and phosphorus equivalents (Canadian Department of Fisheries and Oceans, Vancouver, B.C., unpublished data)

pare estimates of early returns and escapement with those of the 20th century (Figure 2).

Sockeye escapements to Chilko Lake in the central interior of British Columbia, expressed as percent of total returns since commercial fishing, illustrates the general trend of salmon nutrient reduction to many of the large, sockeye nursery lakes in the Fraser River system. For nearly a century, adult sockeye returning to Chilko Lake $(0.08–0.25 \times 10^6)$ were less than 15% of estimated historic levels (1.1×10^6), but in recent years, they have improved (1990–2000) $(>0.6 \times 10^6)$ to about 20% of total returns, owing to implementation of lake fertilization in the late 1980s and early 1990s and to restricted harvest policies in the 1990s (Bradford et al. 2000).

Only about one-third of the total Chilko Lake sockeye escapement actually enters the lake from the river below, but when the P content of the lake escapement is normalized to lake surface area, some sense of the impact of oligotrophication by loss of salmon nutrients and its effects, past and present, on lake biogenic production can be seen (Figure 3).

The Keogh River provides an example of changes in salmon nutrient income to a small coho, steelhead, and pink salmon stream prior to and after the onset of 20th century commercial fishing and logging activities (Figure 4).

The Keogh River is typical of small, B.C. coastal salmon rivers, and its loss of salmon nutrients offers some perspective on local impacts of oligotrophication on biotic production potentials of stream and estuary ecosystems common throughout the Pacific Rim. On average, there has been about a 25-fold decline in adult salmon nutrients to the ecosystem with major losses accruing to the mid to lower reaches of the river and to the estuary, due to pink salmon losses. Prior to anthropogenic disturbance in the early 20th century, coho and steelhead P contributions were estimated to be about 1,300 kg P, about 8–10-fold higher than recent returns from these two species (165 kg P). Large declines in salmon nutrients, since the turn of the century, have also been estimated for the larger, interior Salmon River Basin of Idaho (Thomas et al., this volume).

The Freshwater Nutrient Shadow. A less recognized component of biogenic nutrient recycling in the PNW is the freshwater nutrient shadow. In many interior lakes and reservoirs, landlocked kokanee salmon convey thousands of kilograms of lake-derived N and P into tributary streams during autumn spawning migrations. Nutrients, physiologically released during these migrations, temporarily increase tributary nutrient concentrations and stimulate microbial, algal, and invertebrate production (Richey et al. 1975). Upon decomposition, carcasses provide vital carbon, nitrogen, and phosphorus to a variety of terrestrial and aquatic vertebrates and invertebrates dependent on this seasonal supply of kokanee nutrients. A striking example of the keystone role of landlocked salmonids is the case

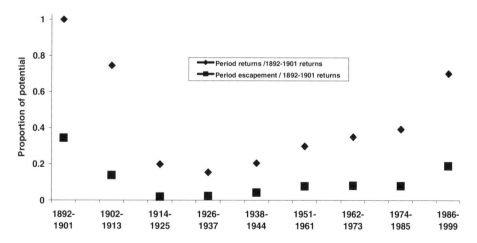

FIGURE 2. Depiction of change in total return and escapement in the 20th century from Chilko Lake 'optimal' potential sockeye return (3+ million) and escapement (1+ million) from 1892–1901 to present (Data from Pacific Salmon Commission, Vancouver, B.C., and J. Hume, Canadian Department of Fisheries and Oceans, Cultus Lake, B.C., unpublished data.)

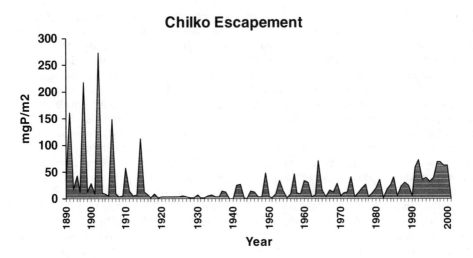

FIGURE 3. Total P content of Chilko Lake sockeye escapement (30% total escapement) from 1890 to present normalized to lake surface area. (Data from Pacific Salmon Commission, Vancouver, B.C., and J. Hume, Department of Fisheries and Oceans, Cultus Lake Laboratory, Cultus Lake, B.C., unpublished data).

study of Flathead Lake, Montana, that once supported large escapements of kokanee and a diverse terrestrial megafauna dependent on their seasonal spawning migrations. Following introduction of mysid shrimp *Mysis relicta*, the kokanee population collapsed, followed by a complete disappearance of bald eagles and grizzly bears from the carcass-deficient tributary drainage basins (Spencer et al. 1989). Although reproductively isolated from their anadromous relatives for thousands of years, kokanee and other landlocked semilparous salmonids represent the inland extension of the anadromous nutrient shadow and provide the same positive ecological benefits of increased production and biodiversity to interior, large-lake ecosystems.

Managing Climate Change

Many have warned of impending global warming with increasing concentrations of greenhouse gases and their potential impacts on terrestrial and aquatic habitats (Schneider 1989). It is clear that changes in circulation patterns and processes that deliver nutrients to euphotic regions of oceans have created large-scale events and that these have affected ocean temperatures, plankton production, and associated salmon population cycles in the past and are likely to continue to do so in the future, perhaps with greater intensity and more profound effects (Venrick et al.

1987; Beamish and Bouillon 1993). So, now superimposed upon documented declines of adult salmon, due to anthropogenic interventions (e.g., overfishing, habitat loss), we must also consider the significance of climate-imposed variability on forage production in the ocean rearing grounds of adult salmon and its impact on their marine survival. To scientifically document such effects is expensive and often imprecise because of scale (i.e., magnitude of the oceanic rearing ground), but thanks to recent paleolimnological studies, we have been given some compelling evidence of long-term, major climate oscillations and their impact on adult sockeye salmon production in some large Alaskan lakes (Finney et al. 2002). Unfortunately, apart from 'riding a bicycle' instead of 'driving an SUV', there is little we can do as fish ecologists or salmon managers to mollify the influence of these global, mesoscale oceanic events on North Pacific salmon production. Nonetheless, it is important that we understand that these ocean events have in the past and will continue in the future to influence salmon populations. A warmer climate is sure to impact salmonid freshwater rearing habitats as well, and preliminary studies suggest potential impacts on juvenile sockeye from warmer nursery lakes (Levy 1992; Henderson et al. 1993). But we must not lose focus on the requirement for further work in fresh water habitat restoration and in creative ecosystem management to rehabilitate salmonid freshwater early life stages. We need, also, to use inno-

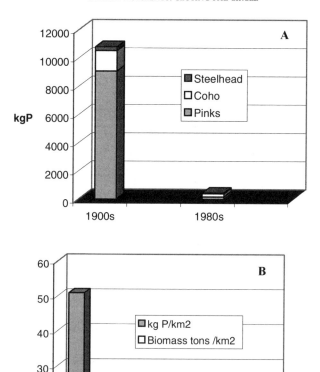

Figure 4. A. Estimated total P contributions from adult salmon accruing to the Keogh River and estuary in the predisturbance early 1900s and in the 1980s. B. Total kg P input and autotrophic biomass production potential in Keogh River normalized to km² wetted area before and after disturbance. (B. Ward, B.C. Ministry of Fisheries, UBC, Vancouver, B.C., personal communication).

vative management approaches that recognize the value of curtailing harvest and allowing sufficient adult salmon escapement to assure that ecosystem production and biodiversity are sustained and/or further enhanced by salmon nutrients (Knudson et al., Michael, both this volume).

Some Hope for the Future

Lake and Stream Fertilization in the Pacific Northwest

In an attempt to reverse the oligotrophication of sockeye salmon nursery lakes and to increase ju-

venile growth and survivals, the Canadian Department of Fisheries and Oceans (DFO) began a large lake enrichment program (LEP) in 1975. Selected sockeye nursery lakes were aerially fertilized to increase primary and secondary production, so as to increase juvenile sockeye forage base and improve growth and survival (Stockner 1981; Stockner and MacIsaac 1996). The lakes chosen for treatment varied from small (<200 ha) warm-monomictic coastal lakes to very large (>15,000 ha) dimictic, interior lakes. Over the last 3 decades, about 25 lakes were fertilized weekly during the growing season with liquid N and P fertilizer at an atomic N:P ratio greater than 25:1. Fertilizer loads to lakes averaged about 3.0–4.5 mg P/m² per week, equivalent to a weekly epilimnetic addition of 0.2–0.7 µg P/L. The treated lakes have shown a positive production response at all trophic levels, with an increase in activity and doubling of bacterial abundance, a 50–60% increase in autotrophic picoplankton abundance and phytoplankton biomass (chlorophyll), and a greater than 2-fold increase in primary production and zooplankton biomass (Stockner and MacIsaac 1996). This enhanced lake production has increased growth and survival of lake-rearing juvenile sockeye and increased the weight of seaward migrant smolts by more than 60%, resulting in improved marine survival and larger adult sockeye returns (Hyatt and Stockner 1985; Bradford et al. 2000). The Alaskan Fisheries Research and Enhancement Division (FRED) followed with a similar program to restore productivity to Alaskan sockeye lakes that were showing signs of decreased fertility caused by several decades of intensive commercial harvest (Kyle et al. 1997). In addition, lake enrichment is a key part of the recovery strategy for the imperiled Redfish Lake, Idaho, sockeye population (Gris-wold et al., this volume).

Many large interior lakes that have been impounded for hydroelectric purposes have experienced major disruptions to kokanee populations and the inland nutrient shadow as a result of hydropower operations (Stockner et al. 2000). The impoundment process initiates a downward spiral in reservoir productivity (oligotrophication), eventually leading to collapse of large piscivores (*Oncorhynchus mykiss* and *Salvelinus confluentus*) heavily dependent on kokanee populations. In 1992, the B.C. Ministry of Environment, Land and Parks (MELP) initiated an experimental reservoir fertilization program to reverse this trend in selected B.C. reservoirs. Kootenay Lake (39,500 ha) was chosen for the initial enrichment experiment, due to concerns about the effect of declining kokanee stocks on their major predator—the famous Gerrard rainbow trout strain (Ashley et al. 1997). The program was expanded in 1997 to include the upper and lower Arrow reservoirs (46,450 ha) and two coastal reservoirs—Wahleach (320 ha) and Alouette (1,670 ha), all of which were experiencing catastrophic declines in kokanee abundance because of a combination of cultural oligotrophication and species introductions (mysid shrimp and three-spine sticklebacks—*Gasterosteus aculeatus*). Each reservoir has been fertilized weekly during the 20-week growing season with a variable N:P ratio loading schedule, starting at 0.67:1 (weight:weight) ratio in late April and incre-

mentally increasing to about 7.5:1 towards the end of the growing season (Ashley et al. 1997). Fertilizer loading averaged 13.6 mg P/m² per week and 60 mg N/m² per week in the large Columbia Basin reservoirs.

All reservoirs have shown strong, positive responses at each trophic level, with significant increases in zooplankton biomass and kokanee populations (Ashley et al. 1999; Wilson et al. 2001; Pieters et al., this volume). For example, in Kootenay Lake, the escapement of North Arm kokanee has increased from a record low of 237,100 in 1991 to 1,204,700 in 1999, after 8 years of enrichment (Ashley et al. 1999 and K. Ashley, B.C. Ministry of Fisheries, Vancouver, unpublished data). A similar recovery has been recorded on the Columbia's upper and lower Arrow reservoirs, where the amount of phosphorus translocated into tributary streams by spawning kokanee has increased from a prefertilization (1989–1998) mean of 130 kg to more than 430 kg (1999 and 2000 average; Figure 5), demonstrating the partial recovery of the long-attenuated freshwater nutrient shadow (Pieters et al., this volume). In Alouette Reservoir, kokanee size has increased from a mean prefertilization weight of 122 g in 1998 to 587 g in 2001, after three years of enrichment, even though hydroacoustic estimates indicate the pelagic fish population has increased from 57,600 in 1998 to 265,500 in 2001 (Wilson et al. 2001; Scholten and Woodruff 2002).

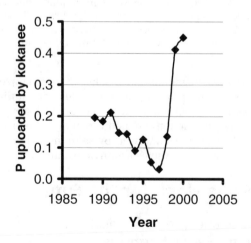

FIGURE 5. Metric tonnes of phosphorus uploaded by spawning kokanee into tributary streams in upper and lower Arrow reservoirs. Note: nutrient enrichment experiment started in 1999.

Research on stream fertilization has occupied a central theme within British Columbia for nearly two decades. Pioneering studies on the Keogh River, in the early 1980s, demonstrated the role of autotrophic production in maintaining the productivty of steelhead *O. mykis* and coho salmon in coastal rivers (Perrin et al. 1987; Johnston et al. 1990). The Keogh River served as the principle research site to investigate various fertilizer loading rates and formulations and habitat restoration techniques (Slaney et al., this volume). Instream mesocosm studies, here, have demonstrated that phosphorus loadings (solu-able P) of 3–5 µg/L were sufficient to restore autotrophic production and maintain high water quality, even though increased insect production was detected at higher nutrient loading rates (Quamme and Slaney, this volume). A multiyear paired watershed experiment at the Keogh River has been intrumental in quantifying the synergistic effect of stream habitat structures and inorganic nutrient treatment on steelhead and coho salmon production, thus providing the scientific rationale for ecologically-based watershed restoration activities (Ward et al., this volume). Knowledge gained from the Keogh River experiments have been applied to several B.C. rivers with similar positive results, demonstrating the importance of nutrient supply and autotrophic production in rebuilding fish populations in nutrient deficient coastal river systems (Slaney et al., Wilson et al., both this volume). Stream studies on the Olympic Pennisula in Washington have convincingly demonstrated the important role of native alder trees *Alnus rubra* in supplementing nutrients in oligotrophic salmonid streams (Volk et al., this volume)

A variety of innovative application systems has been developed to facilitate nutrient application to rivers, including flow proportional fertilizer injection systems using real–time stage-discharge information, and pre-programmed units designed for metering fertilizer into snowmelt dominated river systems (Wilson et al., this volume). The most promising technique has been the development and testing of slow release inorganic nutrient briquettes (Sterling et al. 2000), thus allowing once per year treatments, which are particulary useful in remote regions (Sterling and Ashley, this volume). All of these treatments are designed as *temporary* treatments to restore stream productivity and structure awaiting the return of carcasses to rebuild salmonid populations, thus 'priming' the anadomous nutrient pump.

Management for Ecosystem Production and Biodiversity

Given the overwhelming evidence of the importance of salmon nutrients in maintaining productivity in salmonid ecosystems, it is clearly time for a major paradigm shift in fisheries, forestry, and river basin management. Single species stock-recruitment models that failed to recognize the role of salmon nutrients in maintaining stock productivity dominated the previous fisheries paradigm, and most forest managers did not appreciate the ecological function of salmon nutrients in riparian ecosystems. Hydropower interests advocated single-use river systems, primarily to provide flood protection, irrigation water, and low cost energy to industry and often-subsidized agriculture and/or transportation. Urbanization expanded with little or no regard for salmon habitat. As a consequence, high exploitation rates gradually "mined" centuries of accrued phosphorus "interest" from salmonid ecosystems, while bank-to-bank logging disrupted the riparian habitat, flood plains, and estuaries where terrestrial vertebrates previously transported a majority of the salmon nutrients (Reimchen et al., this volume). The loss of large woody debris (LWD) in streams reduced the retention of carcasses and further accelerated the negative spiral towards cultural oligotrophication (Slaney and Martin 1997; Cederholm et al. 2000a, 2000b). The complete anadromous blockage by some dams such as Grand Coulee forever disrupted the social fabric of First Nations communities dependent for millennia on substantial runs of migrating salmon. The biological extinction of numerous stocks, including the famous "June hogs" chinook of the upper Columbia River, was nothing short of an ecological disaster that should never have happened and must never be repeated again. On the ledger of salmon abundance, the 20th century will be recorded by historians as one of a massive net loss for anadromous salmon, worldwide.

It is now time to replace nonsustainable resource management models and adopt holistic, ecologically-based, basin-scale, multispecies management strategies. Fisheries managers must convert to ecosystem-based escapement models that ensure that annual "interest" payments of MDN are allowed to accrue to the ecosystem (Michael, Knudsen, both this volume). Forest management must establish sufficient riparian reserve zones to ensure that logging does not occur in the riparian corridors and that LWD is allowed to recruit to the rivers to trap gravel, create habitat complexity, and retain salmon car- casses (Slaney and Martin 1997). They also must understand the significance of subsurface stream hyporheic zones and the role they play in nutrient retention (O'Keefe and Edwards, this volume). Future hydropower systems must be designed with near-zero upstream and downstream fish mortalities, as new bypass and turbine systems are developed (Cada 2001). Older hydropower dams can be retrofitted during relicensing to minimize anadromous barriers, while careful enrichment of nutrient deficient reservoirs should become standard practice in oligotrophic reservoirs (Stockner et al. 2000). Society, as a whole, must take greater responsibility for the footprint of urbanization and the endless demands for excessive 'paved' land, often at the expense of 'green-belts' for salmonid habitats. Municipal, provincial, and state zoning regulation and policies can be fish friendly and not significantly impede societal progress (Lackey, this volume). If our populace chooses to ignore these warning signs, the alternatives will be a cumulative wasting of salmonid stocks to the point where they resemble much of those of western Europe, eastern North America, and the Asian Far East, where only remnant stocks remain and most have been extirpated. To date, society has shown scant willingness to adopt the policy changes to reverse the long-term downward trend in wild salmon (Lackey 2001). Time is running out for wild salmon; further extinction of stocks is occurring. Is this what we desire for future generations in the PNW? We do not think so.

Conclusions and Summary

The importance of the adult salmon returns to production cycles of lakes and streams of the PNW, Alaska, Japan, and Russia have been elaborated in this volume. Factors such as overfishing, dams, and habitat destruction have markedly reduced adult salmon migrations and have attenuated the once-extensive nutrient shadow cast on freshwater salmonid habitat, diminishing both production and biodiversity. Many of these now salmonless ecosystems have seen an improvement in their aesthetic appeal (water clarity), but what is visually pleasing but unproductive is not necessarily good for fish production or efficient ecosystem function.

In many lakes and streams maintaining viable salmonid fisheries are important, and managers have now begun to recognize the importance of a balanced source of nutrients to support these fisheries. Nutrient enrichment has proven to be an effective habitat restoration and enhancement tool, increasing fish production in oligotrophic lakes and streams in British Columbia and in Alaska. Properly administered nutrient additions to lakes and streams should be viewed as an effective means of *restoration* of ecosystem production and biodiversity. But implementation will require good limnological knowledge and a better understanding of how important it is to maintain a balanced nutrient supply and suitable habitat to optimize production potentials. More importantly, this will require a change in the way the public views and engineers and resource managers design wastewater discharges, hydroelectric and irrigation dams, logging plans, and atmospheric emissions affecting climate change.

As a life form, salmon have demonstrated they are capable of colonizing and thriving in harsh nutrient-deficient ecosystems during the current and previous interglacial periods, partly because of their unique ability to increase the productivity of their natal streams, rivers, and lakes by recycling phosphorus and other carcass nutrients, thus casting a thin but vast nutrient shadow. The importance of this biogenic phosphorus recycling to the aquatic and terrestrial ecosystems cannot be overemphasized. As noted by Asimov (1975), "Life can multiply until all the phosphorus is gone and then there is an inexorable halt which nothing can prevent." The message is clear: a balanced supply of nutrients, reduced fishing pressure, and restoration/protection of suitable habitat is vital to the recovery of salmonids and ultimately humans in the Pacific Northwest. Thus, it is our conviction that modern society must once again 'close the circle' on phosphorus through efficient use and recycling, or we will ultimately experience the same fate as our salmonid sentinels and struggle to find a meaningful existence in a nutrient deficient world.

Acknowledgements

The authors wish to thank many colleagues at the University of British Columbia, Vancouver, for many fruitful discussions, notably Pat Slaney, Tom Johnson, and Bruce Ward, Fisheries Research Section, Fisheries Centre, and Ken Hall, Institute of Resources and Environment. Jeremy

Hume and Ken Shortreed, DFO, Cultus Lake Laboratory, provided unpublished data from Chilko Lake, and Bruce Ward, Fisheries Research, UBC, provided estimates of Keogh River escapements. Finally, we wish to thank Pat Slaney for his thoughtful comments in review.

References

Ashley, K. I., and P. A. Slaney. 1997. Accelerating recovery of stream, river and pond productivity by low-level nutrient replacement (Chapter 13). Pages 1–341 *in* P. A. Slaney and D. Zaldokas, editors. Fish habitat rehabilitation procedures. Province of British Columbia, Ministry of Environment, Lands and Parks, and Ministry of Forests. Watershed Restoration Technical Circular No. 9.

Ashley, K. I., L. C. Thompson, D. C. Lasenby, L. McEachern, K. E. Smokorowski, and D. Sebastian. 1997. Restoration of an interior lake ecosystem: the Kootenay Lake fertilization experiment. Canadian Journal of Water Quality Re- search 32:192–212.

Ashley, K. I., L. C. Thompson, D. Sebastian, D. C. Lasenby, K. E. Smokorowski, and H. Andrusak. 1999. Restoration of kokanee salmon in Kootenay Lake, a large intermontane lake, by controlled seasonal application of limiting nutrients. Pages 127–169 *in* T. Murphy and M. Munawar, editors. Aquatic restoration in Canada ecovision. Word Monograph Series. Backhuys Publishers, Leiden, Netherlands.

Asimov, I. 1975. Asimov on chemistry. Macdonald and James, London.

Beamish, R. J., and D. R. Bouillon. 1993. Pacific salmon production trends in relation to climate. Canadian Journal of Fisheries and Aquatic Sciences 50:1002–1016.

Bradford, M. J., B. J. Pyper, and K. S. Shortreed. 2000. Biological responses of sockeye salmon to the fertilization of Chilko Lake, a large lake in the interior of British Columbia. North American Journal of Fisheries Management 20:661–671

Cada, G. F. 2001. The development of advanced hydroelectric turbines to improve fish passage survival. Fisheries 26:14–23.

Cederholm, C. J., MD. Kunze, T. Murota, and A. Sibatani. 2000a. Pacific salmon carcasses. Fisheries 24:6–15.

Cederholm, C. J., D. J. Johnson, R. E. Bilby, L. G. Dominguez, A. M. Garrett, W. H. Graeber, E. L. Greda, M. D. Kunze, B. G. Marcot. J. F. Palmisano, R. W. Plotnikoff, W. G. Pearcy, C. A. Simenstad, and P. C. Trotter. 2000b. Pacific salmon and wildlife: ecological contexts, relationships, and implications for management. Pages 1–138 *in* Washington Department of Fish and Wildlife, Special Edition, Technical Report. Olympia, Washington.

CEEP (Centre European d'Etudes des Polyphosphates). 1998. Phosphates a sustainable future in recycling. CEEP, Bruxelles, Belgium.

Driver, J., D. Lijmbach, and I. Steen. 1999. Why recover phosphorus for recycling and how?" Environmental Technology 20:651–662

Edmondson, W. T. 1969. Eutrophication in North America. Pages 124–149 *in* Eutrophication: causes, consequences and correctives. National Academy of Sciences, Publication No. 1700. Washington, D.C.

Finney, B. P., I. Gregory-Eaves, M. S. V. Douglas, and J. P. Smol. 2002. Fisheries productivity in the northeastern Pacific Ocean over the past 2,200 years. Nature 416:729–733

Forsberg, C. 1998. Which policies can stop large-scale eutrophication? Water Science and Technology 37:193–200.

Gresh, T. J., J. Lichatowich, and P. Schoonmaker. 2000. An estimation of historic and current levels of salmon production in the Northeast Pacific ecosystem: evidence of a nutrient deficit in the freshwater systems of the Pacific Northwest. Fisheries 25(1):15–21.

Henderson, M. A., D. A. Levy, and J. G. Stockner. 1992. Probable consequences of climate change on freshwater production of Adams River sockeye salmon (*Oncorhynchus nerka*) GeoJournal 59:51–59.

Hyatt, K. D., and J. G. Stockner. 1985. Responses of sockeye salmon (*Oncorhynchus nerka)* to fertilization of British Columbia coastal lakes. Canadian Journal of Fisheries and Aquatic Sciences 42:320–331.

Jansson, M., G. Persson, and O. Broberg. 1986. Phosphorus in acidified lakes: the example of Lake Gardsjon, Sweden. Hydrobiologia 139:81–96.

Johnston, N. T., C. J. Perrin, P. A. Slaney, and B. R. Ward. 1990. Increased juvenile growth by whole-river fertilization. Canadian Journal of Fisheries and Aquatic Sciences 47:862–872.

Kline, T. C. Jr., J. J. Goering, O. A. Mathisen, P. H. Poe and P. L. Parker. 1990. Recycling of elements transported upstream by runs of Pacific sal-mon: I. $d^{15}N$ and $d^{13}C$ evidence in Sashin Creek, southeastern Alaska. Canadian Journal of Fisheries and Aquatic Science 47:136–144.

Kopacek, J., L. Prochazkova, E. Stuchlik, and P. Blazka. 1995. The nitrogen-phosphorus relationship in mountain lakes: influence of atmospheric input, watershed and pH. Limnology and Oceanography 40:930–937.

Kyle, G. B., J. P. Koenings, and J. A. Edmundson. 1997. An overview of Alaska lake rearing salmon enhancement strategy: nutrient enrichment and juvenile stocking. Pages 205–227 *in* A. Milner and A. Oswood, editors. Freshwaters of Alaska, ecological synthesis. Ecology Studies, Volume 119, Springer Verlag, New York.

Levy, D. A. 1992. Potential impacts of global warming on salmon production in the Fraser River watershed. Canadian Technical Report Fisheries and Aquatic Sciences No. 1889.

Lackey, R. T. 2001. Defending reality. Fisheries 26:26–27.

Larkin, G. A., and P. A. Slaney. 1997. Implications of trends in marine-derived nutrient influx to south coastal salmonid production. Fisheries 22:16–24.

Mathisen, O. A. 1972. Biogenic enrichment of sockeye salmon lakes and stock productivity. Verhandlungen Internationale Vereinigung Limnologie 18:1089–1095.

Naumann, E. 1921. Einige Grundlinien der regionalen Limnologie. Lund Universitets Arsskrift N. F. 17:1–22.

Ney, J. J. 1996. Oligotrophication and its discontents: effects of reduced nutrient loading on reservoir fisheries. Pages 285–295 in L. E. Miranda and D. R. DeVries, editors. Multidimensional approaches to reservoir fisheries management. American Fisheries Society, Symposium 16, Bethesda, Maryland.

Northcote, T. G. 1973. Some impacts of man on Kootenay Lake and its salmonids. Great Lakes Fisheries Committee Technical Report 25.

Perrin, C. J., M. L. Bothwell, and P. A. Slaney. 1987. Experimental enrichment of a coastal stream in British Columbia: effects of organic and inorganic additions on autotrophic periphyton production. Canadian Journal of Fisheries and Aquatic Sciences 44:1247–1256.

Richey, J. E., M. A. Perkins, and C. R. Goldman. 1975. Effects of kokanee salmon (Oncorhynchus nerka) decomposition on the ecology of a subalpine stream. Journal Fisheries Research Board of Canada 32:817–820.

Schindler, D. W. 1980. The effect of fertilization with phosphorus and nitrogen versus phosphorus alone on eutrophication of experimental lakes. Limnology and Oceanography 25:1149–1152.

Schindler, D. W., K. G. Beaty, E. J. Fee, D. R. Cruikshank, E. R. DeBruyn, D. L. Findlay, G. A. Linsey, J. A. Shearer, M. P. Stainton, and M. A. Turner. 1990. Effects of climate warming on lakes of the central boreal forest. Science 250:967–970.

Schneider, S. H. 1989. The changing climate. Scientific American 262:70–79.

Scholten, G., and P. Woodruff. 2002. Results of Alouette Reservoir hydroacoustic surveys: September 2000 and November 2001. Stock Management Report No. 19. Biodiversity Branch, Ministry of Water, Land and Air Protection, Province of British Columbia.

Slaney, P. A., and A. D. Martin. 1997. The watershed restoration program of British Columbia: accel-

erating natural recovery processes. Canadian Journal Water Quality Research 32:325–346.

Spencer, C. N., B. R. McClelland, and J. A. Stanford. 1989. Shrimp stocking, salmon collapse and eagle displacement: cascading interactions in the food web of a large aquatic ecosystem. Bioscience 41:14–21.

Sterling, M. S., K. I. Ashley and A. B. Bautista. 2000. Slow-release fertilizer for rehabilitating oligotrophic streams: a physical characterization. Canadian Journal of Water Quality Research 35:73–94.

Stockner, J. G., 1981. Whole-lake fertilization for the enhancement of sockeye salmon (Oncorhynchus nerka) in British Columbia, Canada. Verhandlungen Internationale Vereinigung Limnologie 21:293–299.

Stockner, J. G. 1987. Lake fertilization: the enrichment cycle and lake sockeye salmon (Oncorhynchus nerka) production. Pages 198–215 in H. D. Smith, L. Margolis, and C. C. Wood, editors. Sockeye salmon (Oncorhynchus nerka): population biology and future management. Canadian Fisheries and Aquatic Sciences, Special Publication Number 96.

Stockner, J. G. 1998. Global warming, picocyano-bacteria and fisheries decline: is there a connection? Pages 29–37 in E. Piccazzo, editor. Proceedings Atti del 12th Congress dell'AIOL, Vol II. Rome, Italy.

Stockner, J. G., and E. A. MacIsaac. 1996. British Columbia lake enrichment program: two decades of habitat enhancement for sockeye salmon. Regulated Rivers: Research and Management 12:547–561.

Stockner, J. G., and G. Milbrink, editors. 1999. Restoration of fisheries by enrichment of aquatic ecosystems. International workshop proceedings, Uppsala University Press, Uppsala, Sweden.

Stockner, J. G., E. Rydin, and P. Hyenstrand. 2000. Cultural oligotrophication. Fisheries 25:7–14.

Turner, M. A., G. G. C. Robinson, B. E. Townsend, B. J. Hann, and J. A. Amaral. 1995. Ecological effects of blooms of filamentous green algae in the littoral zone of an acid lake. Canadian Journal of Fisheries and Aquatic Sciences 52:2264–2275.

Vallentyne, J. R. 1974. The algal bowl: lakes and man. Canadian Department of Environment and Marine Service, Miscellaneous Publication. Ottawa, Ontario, Canada.

Venrick, E. L., J. A. McGowan, D. R. Cayan and T. L. Hayward. 1987. Climate and chlorophyll a: long-term trends in the central North Pacific Ocean. Science 238:70–72.

Vollenweider, R. A. 1968. Scientific fundamentals of the eutrophication of lakes and flowing water, with particular reference to nitrogen and phosphorus as factors in eutrophication. Pages 1–192 in OECD Report DAS/CSI 68. Paris, France.

Wilson, G. A., M. R. McCusker, K. I. Ashley, R. W. Land, J. G. Stockner, G. Scholten, D. Dolecki, and D.

Sebastian. 2001. The Alouette Reservoir fertilization experiment: years 3 and 4 (2000-01) Report, Whole Reservoir Fertilization. British Columbia Ministry of Fisheries, Project Report No. RD 99.

American Fisheries Society Symposium 34:17–31, 2003

The Marine Nutrient Shadow: A Global Comparison of Anadromous Salmon Fishery and Guano Occurence

Takeshi Murota

Department of Economics, Doshisha University, Kyoto 602-8580, Japan

Abstract.—While the ecology of seed dispersal has been widely studied, the ecology of nutrient dispersal has not. Growing concerns about loss of biodiversity has resulted in an increasing number of studies on anadromous fishes as vectors for uploading and dispersing marine nutrients into freshwater and terrestrial ecosystems through various pathways. As an outgrowth of the idea of Lindebroom (1984), who analyzed the penguin-derived "ammonia shadow" over a vigorous plant growth on an Antarctic island, this paper develops the concept of the "nutrient shadow" as the geographical space on terrestrial land that is covered by marine nutrients, due primarily to anadromous fishes, especially Pacific salmon *Oncorhynchus* spp., and secondarily to other animals that have fed upon them. Here, I present a quantitative estimate of the relative position of anadromous salmon as vectors of marine nutrient uploading onto lands compared with those of marine fishery by human hands and of guano (sea birds' feces) occurrences as a final product of upwelling ecosystems. Then, I assess the extent of the nutrient shadow cast by spawning runs of salmon in view of the dynamics of nutrient condensation and dispersal (thinning) and conclude with some speculation about the vastness, albeit thin, of salmon-derived nutrient shadows over wild environments and the effects of anadromous salmon on fertilizing terrestrial ecosystems that may even be larger than those of marine fishery and guano occurrence, if we interpret such fertilization as the material basis for increasing biodiversity.

Introduction

Material cycle is essential to all living beings on the earth (Pomeroy 1974). Recent studies in the United States, Canada, and Japan on anadromous fishes, especially Pacific salmon *Oncorhynchus* spp., strongly suggest that they have been contributing to the activation of the material cycle between the ocean and terrestrial ecosystems. Such studies are opening the door to a new understanding of nutrient transport with global and local environmental implications.

Given this state of science, it is time to renew our recognition of the nature of the material cycle on this planet, from both ontological and epistemological standpoints, following the tradition of Justus von Liebig (1803–1873), one of the founders of the theory of cycles of essential elements (Liebig 1842). Because the earth is approximately closed to outer space in terms of matter, the supply of available matter needed by human beings and all other living beings has to come from the earth system itself, not from outside. At the same time, the universal law of gravity points to the general tendency of relatively heavy substances to sink down from high to low places, or more globally speaking, from lofty mountains to ocean bottoms. If this is the case, mountains must lose nutrients, becoming barren, while the oceans must suffer from super eutrophication, but we know that this picture has not necessarily been the reality of our earth system, so there must be some agents that upload nutrients from the ocean onto terrestrial ecosystems (Murota 1998). This paper explores such agents and pathways through which such uploading takes place.

A clear-cut example is seen in Lindebroom

(1984) who analyzed the "ammonia shadow" over Marion Island in the Antarctic Sea. A large number of penguins roost on the island thanks to the abundance of the surrounding marine fishes. This results in an enormous amount of excreta deposition on the island. The chemical differentiation of such fresh guano (sea birds' feces) was shown to be mainly uric acid, with 20% being protein and ammonia. Further investigations made it clear that uric acid was quickly evaporating as ammonia. The island has been known to entertain the vigorous growth of coprophilous plants, predominantly *Poa cookii* and *Callitriche antarctica*. Lindebroom (1984) concluded that such plant growth under a very severe climate was the product of an ammonia-rich atmosphere hanging over the island. In short, such a bounty of plants comes from the ocean, with penguins being an upwardly running locomotive with full loads of marine nutrients. Herein arises the concept of the "ammonia shadow."

While nitrogen sometimes has this type of volatile pathway from the ocean onto land, the case of phosphorus is more complicated. Phosphorus is one of the elements essential for all living beings on earth. Under standard conditions, however, it rarely forms gaseous compounds. Because of this fact, the dynamics of the phosphorus cycle, both globally and locally, must be analyzed using more "practical" methods. As for the upward movement of phosphorus-rich nutrients from the deep sea to the ocean surface, oceanography and marine biology tell us that their major pathway is the nutrient-rich upwelling of cold seawater (Boje and Tomczak 1978; Lalli and Parsons 1993).

This paper, focusing on phosphorus, examines the relative weights of marine fishery, guano occurrence, and anadromous fishes as the major components of upward transport of marine nutrients onto freshwater and terrestrial ecosystems. Once landed, such nutrients follow sometimes similar but at other times rather different paths to become incorporated into the natural ecosystems and/or human settlements. We call the area covered by the marine-derived nutrients the "nutrient shadow." We then characterize such nutrient shadows depending on which locomotive (humans engaged in marine fishery, guano-forming seabirds, or anadromous fishes) drives nutrients onto land. Concluding remarks will be made to encourage desirable manners of watershed management so as to enhance natural spawning runs of wild salmon and other anadromous fishes.

Method of Study: Quantification of Phosphorus Uploading

To broaden the scope of the theory of material cycles and biogeochemical cycles in a direction that includes the anthropogenic dimension, we classify the major components of the uploading of marine nutrients onto terrestrial ecosystems into the following four categories, from the most visible and tangible to the least obvious to human eyes:

1. Marine fishery by human hands.
2. Guano deposition (eventually forms phosphate rock if deposited on coral reefs).
3. Anadromous behavior of some fish.
4. Geological (plate tectonic) uplift of the ocean floors.

We would like to know quantitatively how many nutrients these activities are pumping up annually from the ocean onto land. To avoid complicated analyses, we focus on phosphorus as a representative indicator of essential elements for terrestrial ecosystems (oceanic ones, as well).

Marine Fishery by Human Hands

Quantitatively speaking, the world total of fishery harvests has been almost steadily increasing since the end of the second world war (Pauly 1996) and reached 112,910,300 metric tons in 1995, of which 91,904,900 metric tons were from marine areas (FAO 1997, p. 93). These figures are of fish, crustaceans, mollusks, and so on, but exclude the catches of whales, seals, and other aquatic mammals, miscellaneous aquatic animal products, and aquatic plants. Regarding aquatic plants, the world total catch of seaweed and other plants also has been increasing and amounted to 7,817,000 metric tons in 1995 (FAO 1997, p. 108). In our analysis, we will consider only these two categories of typical marine fishery products.

We used the following numbers as the phosphorus content in fish, crustaceans, and mollusks: 0.36% P, 0.27% P, and 0.30% P, respectively (Ikeda 1981, p. 212). FAO (1997) gives the break down of the 91,904,900 metric tons of the total catches into 69,822,300 metric tons of fish (84%), 4,942,100 metric tons of crustaceans (6%), and 7,888,500 metric tons of mollusks (10%), with 376,100 metric tons of miscellaneous aquatic animals being a negligible order. Multiplying these numbers by the above P-content factors, we obtain the rough estimations of 251,300 metric tons P, 1 3,300 metric tons P, and 23,600 metric tons P, respectively, the sum of which turns out to be 288,200 metric tons P.

To assess the phosphorus content in seaweed and other aquatic plants, we refer to Yoshikawa and Ashida (1990), who show that the raw seaweed *Undaria pinnatifida*, called wakame in Japanese, with 90.4% water; the seaweed *Gracilaria verrucosa*, called ogonori in Japanese, with 90.0% water; the raw agar-agar or ceylon moss *Gelidium amansii* with 68.1% water; the raw seaweed *Meristotheca papulosa*, called tosakanori in Japanese, with 92.5% water; and so on, contain 0.036% P, 0.021% P, 0.050% P, 0.011% P, and so on, respectively, on a live weight basis. From these numbers, we tentatively assume that the average P content in live seaweed and other aquatic plants is 0.020%; hence, their catch of 7,817,000 metric tons per year in 1995 implies that some 1,500 metric tons P per year is brought up from the sea onto land by human hands.

Table 1 gives the summary of these computations, from which we understand that total phosphorus uploading through marine fishery was 289,700 metric tons P in 1995.

Considering the almost constant increase in the world catch of marine fish and others in the past until today, it may be worthwhile to see what the case was a few decades ago. As for 1960, we find, in FAO (1966), the world total catches of marine fish to be 29,010 thousand metric tons, crustaceans and mollusks combined as 3,460 thousand metric tons, and seaweed and other aquatic plants as 540 thousand metric tons. The corresponding annual P-uploading figures are computed as 104,400 metric tons P, 7,700 metric tons P, and 100 metric tons P, respectively. From these, we have a total of 112,200 metric tons P per year for 1960, which is 38% of the 1995 P uploading.

Guano Occurrence

Guano (sea birds' feces) is a direct product of upwelling ecosystems in many island and coastal parts of the world. The most massive case of its occurrence was the one of Peruvian guano along the Pacific shoreline from northern Chili to Peru, which was recognized to be of the best quality for fertilizer, due to its high content of nitrogen and phosphorus. The word "guano" also means bat guano, depending on the context of the discussion. The diet of some species of bat can partly be of marine origin as well (Brooke 1994), but its amount is very small relative to the sea birds' guano, and, hence, we have chosen to ignore bat guano in the following discussion.

To the author's knowledge, there is a paucity of data on the total amount of guano production from historical and contemporary perspectives. Based on their own interest in the possible relationship between marine fish populations and El Niño events, Schneider and Duffy (1988) give quantitative data on how much guano was produced annually on the coasts along the Peru and Benguela currents, respectively. Needless to say, there is an inverse relationship between guano formation and industrial fishing. For example, if the fishing industry catches a great amount of anchoveta in the Peru Coast for fish meal and/or for fertilizer, the amount of the same fish available to seabirds is much less than otherwise, so that correspondingly, less formation of guano is highly probable. In order to delineate the trends of guano production in those two areas, with such an anthropogenic impact being at a minimum level, Schneider and Duffy show the data from shortly

TABLE 1. Estimation of phosphorus (P) uploading by marine fishery activities.

Type of product	(A) Concentration of P (dry weight basis)	(B) Average water content	(C) P content (adjusted to wet weight	(D) Catch in 1995 (thousand tons)	(E) Phosphorus uploading (tons)
Fish	18,000 ppm	80%	0.36% P	69,822	251,300
Crustaceans	9,000 ppm	70%	0.27% P	4,942	13,300
Mollusks	6,000 ppm	50%	0.30% P	7,888	23,600
Seaweed and other plants			0.02% P	7,817	1,500
Data source	Ikeda (1981, p. 212)	Assumption in this paper	Computed from (A) and (B)	FAO (1997)	(C) × (D)

before 1910 to the early 1960s, when the major industrial fisheries were not there yet. From their graph (Schneider and Duffy 1988, p. 311) for the period 1909–1962, we find that annual guano production along the Peruvian upwelling area was at levels of 0.5–3.3 million metric tons and that the one along the Benguela upwelling area was between 0.8–4.0 thousand metric tons.

How can these figures be evaluated from the viewpoint of nutrient transport from the ocean to terrestrial lands? McConnel (1979) gives the table of chemical contents of excrement of birds and mammals (including bats), in which the total N is 2.86% and 17.41% for guano from the feces of seal and birds in Peru. Corresponding figures of P_2O_5 are 16.80% and 7.14%, respectively. Assuming, based on the above set of partial data, that the annual average of global guano production is somewhere between 1.5 and 2.0 million metric tons of Peruvian birds guano equivalent, the total N supplied by such guano is between 262,500 and 350,000 metric tons per year, and P_2O_5 is between 105,000 and 140,000 tons per year. Cathcart (1980) gives the conversion factor: % P_2O_5 × 0.436 = % P. Using this factor, one can estimate that between 45,700 and 61,000 metric tons P per year are brought up from the world's oceans onto lands in various forms of guano with a marine origin at times prior to the start of the massive industrial fishery along the Peru Coast.

There are, however, smaller quotations of guano-derived phosphorus in other literature. Sandstrom (1982) presents a list of major sinks in the marine geochemical cycle of phosphorus and lists the phosphorus content in guano as 0.32 × 10^{10} mol P per year, which is equal to approximately 9,300 metric tons P per year. Pierrou (1979) quotes a figure for guano equivalent to 10,000 metric tons P per year.

Anadromous Salmon

When a diadromous fish swims from one place to another, nutrients embodied in the fish also move accordingly. In the case of anadromous fish, its spawning run can be considered as an upstream transport of marine-derived nutrients onto terrestrial lands (Cederholm et al. 1999). Among such a group of anadromous fishes, Atlantic salmon *Salmo salar* and Pacific salmon are the major species in terms of size and length or distance of spawning run. The life history of Atlantic salmon is described by Shearer (1992) and Pacific salmon by Groot and Margolis (1991). A particular characteristic of Pacific salmon from the viewpoint of nutrient transport is their semelparity (death within a few days after spawning), which implies that their carcasses will remain near their spawning grounds in their natal habitat.

Terrestrial gains of salmon-derived nutrients in general, or phosphorus in particular, in the past and present, are hard to quantitatively assess due to the lack of escapement data for many salmon-spawning rivers worldwide. But, this does not mean that nothing can be done with the question of what salmon have been doing for terrestrial ecosystems. Larkin and Slaney (1996) show a first attempt at estimating the amounts of ocean-derived nitrogen and phosphorus brought up by spawning runs of Pacific salmon, not in a single river or in several rivers but in much broader areas, including seven salmon spawning areas in the mainland and on Vancouver Island, British Columbia. For each of the seven areas, they first quote the annual escapement data of five species of Pacific salmon (i.e., sockeye *Oncorhynchus nerka*, coho *O. kisutch*, pink *O. gorbuscha*, chum *O. keta*, and chinook *O. tshawytscha*) for the past 42 years (1953–1994). They then compute the average body weight of adults of each of these species and the average percentage content of nitrogen and phosphorus. Combining all these data, they present the nitrogen and phosphorus influxes for each of the areas.

Their analysis is very useful for tentatively but quickly obtaining the estimates of nitrogen and phosphorus influx by Pacific salmon of the entire area (623,000 km^2) of British Columbia. Henderson and Graham (1998) show catch and escapement data for British Columbia in recent years, where annual average escapement was about 35 million or more, out of which sockeye, pink, chum, chinook, and coho salmon were 10 million, 20 million, 1.5–2.5 million, 150,000–200,000, and 200,000–300,000, respectively. Assuming the average body weight per fish for each of the five species of adult salmon and using these data, we find that the annual average for nitrogen uploading was about 2,400 metric tons and for phosphorus was about 300 metric tons in British Columbia (Table 2).

There is not any detailed statistical data of escapements in other regions of the world for Pacific and Atlantic salmon, though the catch data are easily available. Leaving further statistical studies on escapements for future research, we very

TABLE 2. Marine nitrogen (N) and phosphorus (P) uploading onto lands by five species of Pacific salmon in British Columbia (B.C.), Canada (estimates for the annual average for several years around 1990).

Species	Annual average escapements (thousand fish) (a)	Average body weight per fish (kg) (b)	Total weight by species (ton) (c)	Annual average N uploading (ton) (d)	Annual average P uploading (ton) (e)
sockeye	10,000	2.27	22,700	689	81.5
pink	20,000	1.82	36,400	1,105	130.6
chum	1,500–2,500	5.45	8,200–13,600	249–413	29.4–48.5
chinook	500	15.91	8,000	243	28.7
coho	200–300	4.55	900–1,400	27–43	3.2–5.0
B.C. total				2,313–2,493	273–295

Remarks: Data in (a) are taken from Henderson and Graham (1988). Data in (b) are taken from Larkin and Slaney (1996). (d) = (c) × 0.03037, and (e) = (c) × 0.00359. These coefficients are adopted from Larkin and Slaney (1996). Though the numbers in columns (c), (d), and (e) have several digits for computation purposes, their significant digits are two or even one because the ones of numbers in column (a) are at most two.

roughly estimate the world annual phosphorus influx of aquatic and terrestrial ecosystems with all anadromous salmon combined and very wide error ranges. A likely minimum estimate is five times as large as the B.C. total, and a maximum estimate is 10 times as large as the B.C. total; that is to say, a minimum of 1,500 metric tons P and a maximum of 3,000 metric tons P per year, in recent times.

Geological (Plate Tectonic) Uplift of the Ocean Floor

While many sets of quantitative data have been presented and discussed among the specialists of the biogeochemical cycle as to the annual nutrient loss from the terrestrial lands by erosion, weathering, and so on, it is difficult to assess how much sediment at the ocean floor annually rises up beyond sea level in the contemporary age. Geological uplifts of the ocean floor are matters of million years long. Pierrou (1979) states of the global phosphorus cycle that "the turnover rate of this cycle is regulated by the rate of diagenesis of phosphorus-containing sediments into phosphate rock. This process takes 0.1–1 gigayear (Gy) which implies that a period of more than 1 Gy is required for one global cycle of phosphorus to be completed." Therefore, the assessment of the rate of nutrient uptake of land from the ocean, of this nature, however important for the study on the long-run nutrient budgets of the terrestrial ecosystems, does not fit the scope of the present paper, which is primarily concerned

with annual average figures in the contemporary age.

Summary of Quantitative Comparison

In Table 3, we examine the relative position of salmon-derived phosphorus to other components of oceanic phosphorus uploading. Simple numerical comparison tells us that the contribution of anadromous salmon is about 1% of the estimate for ocean fisheries and about 10% of natural guano occurrence prior to the age of massive industrial fishery. Does this then mean that anadromous fishes represented by Pacific and Atlantic salmon are not as important as upstream vectors of marine nutrients onto terrestrial ecosystems? We believe that the simple numerical comparison does not tell the whole story (e.g., ecological implications of marine nutrient uploading). More important is the dynamic question of the spatial distribution patterns such nutrients have on freshwater and terrestrial ecosystems that have seriously been affected by global environmental depredation of various forms.

Enormous amounts of marine fishery products, first, go to the food markets or food processing factories (canneries) in many areas of the world, as food for human beings and, second, are transformed into fish meal, fertilizers, or industrial raw materials. Fish meal is used as the diet for livestock that eventually become food for human beings. Fertilizers made of marine products help increase the productivity of agriculture,

TABLE 3. Marine phosphorus uploading and other characteristics of anadromous salmon in comparison with marine fishery and guano occurrence.

Phosphorus uploading	Annual average tons (year of reference)	Data source	Characteristics of distribution on lands
Marine fishery	112,000 t P (1960) 289,000 t P (1995)	FAO (1966, 1997) This paper, data shown in Table 1	Tendency to concentrate in densely human popu- lated areas
Guano occurrence	9,000 t P (year unspecified) 11,000 t P (year unspecified) 45,700 to 61,000 t P (1909–1962)	Sandstrom (1982) Pierrou (1979) This paper, based on Schneider and Duffy (1988)	Thick accumulation on lim- ited seashore lines, unless removed by human hands
Anadromous salmon	minimum estimate 1,500 t P (1990) maximum estimate 3,000 t P (1990)	This paper, based on assumed min/max of world totals as being five and ten times the B.C. total shown in Table 2.	Creation of vast nutrient on terrestrial ecosystems various pathways to promote

mainly for food production. In summary, oceanic nutrients gained by fisheries tend to stay in human settlements and vicinities. Given the worldwide trend of urbanization, this general tendency is enhanced in such a way that nutrients, coupled with artificially manufactured chemical fertilizers, concentrate within densely populated cities and surroundings and manifest themselves in the form of water pollution or excessive eutrophication of freshwater of rivers and lakes and seawater of bays and inland seas.

Guano occurrences as products of coastal and equatorial upwelling ecosystems have dimensions both different from and similar to those of marine fishery. They stay and accumulate on narrow bands of deserted shorelines where they are originally deposited. In the case of Peruvian guano, its accumulation on the Chincha Islands at the beginning of the 19th century was several tens of meters thick (Murphy 1936). This tendency towards continuing deposition, however, does not exclude the possibility that human beings may extract and transport guano for use as fertilizer in agricultural production. The world history of the political economy of guano extraction and international transport is vividly described in such outstanding works as Levin (1960) and Mathew (1981).

In contrast to these condensation-oriented characteristics of marine fishery and guano occurrence, spawning runs of anadromous salmon coupled with other living beings have the nature of dispersal or dilution (thinning). The dispersal here is a thin dispersal of nutrients over a vast area of landscape. Due to such characteristics, they have a high potential for supporting and even promoting biodiversity in the relatively cold zones of the northern hemisphere. Table 3 includes a brief summary of the qualitative differences in the pattern of nutrient distribution though uploading by major components.

Maximum Ascent of Nutrient Shadow by Salmon

The marine nutrient shadow is the terrestrial area (including the freshwater lakes and streams) that is or could be covered by marine-derived nutrients. Let us, then, imagine a hypothetical tree in the following sense. The roots of this tree stretch deeply into the cold ocean and absorb nutrients in the form of small fishes (prey for salmon) that have fed on zooplankton. Its stem is the returning adult salmon escapement in a river from its mouth open to the ocean up to the spawning ground. Its boughs, twigs, and leaves are mammals and birds that feed on salmon. This tree drops hypothetical seeds (i.e. nutrients, such as excreta of mammals and birds, dissolved nitrogen, phosphorus, and their mineralized forms due to decomposition of salmon carcasses). The area that receives such substances is the "nutrient shadow" of our tree, in the primary sense. The fish-derived inorganic nutrients in the lakes and rivers serve to grow phytoplankton and algae, which in turn grow benthic insects, juvenile salmon, nonanadromous fish, and so on. Adult insects may become prey for birds. These birds may drop excreta on the soil away from the direct watershed of the river. In this case, the nutrient shadow can be widened further than the primary one. Under the shadow of the hypothetical tree, the real, not hypothetical, vegetation may start growing, as the seeds under the seed shadow start germinating.

Keeping this new concept of the nutrient shadow in mind, our immediate concern is the question of how long and how tall the stem of that tree is. In other words, we would like to know the maximum distances and altitudes necessary for salmon to ascend rivers in various parts of the world.

Atlantic Salmon in East Coast of North America and Europe (Figure 1)

MacCrimmon and Gots (1979) made an extensive survey of the historical distribution of Atlantic salmon in North America and Europe. The furthest regions that Atlantic salmon historically had ascended rivers in North America seem to have been the tributaries of Lake Ontario in the St. Lawrence River system, though natural spawning stopped by 1860. The distance of the inland water travel of Lake Ontario's resident fish from the seawater of the Gulf of St. Lawrence was about 1,000 km.

When one considers the nutrient transport from the Atlantic Ocean onto the inlands of North America, other anadromous fishes should not be neglected. With respect to the maximum distances of inland penetration of alewife *Alosa pseudoharengus* and blueback herring *A. aestivalis*, McDowall (1988) cites literatures that suggest 120 km and more than 200 km, respectively.

In the Rhine River (total length 1,320 km) Basin, salmon fishery used to be a common business in Holland and Germany, with an average annual catch of 350,000. Even in Switzerland, the salmon fishery constituted a means of livelihood for some people (Pearce 1993). This means that fish were making inland water travel of nearly 1,000 km, maximum. Their disappearance from the High-Rhine Nasin was rather recent—"the

decline in abundance began with the building of many hydroelectric dams on the Rhine and the Aar rivers between 1898 and 1920 with generally inefficient fish passes, if any" (MacCrimmon and Gots 1979). The Elbe River is 1,290 km long, with the Vltava (Moldau) River included, and its headwaters had spawning runs of Atlantic salmon until 1877, when such runs declined by dams and pollution (MacCrimmon and Gots 1979). This again means that the Atlantic salmon used to ascend almost 1,000 km in Europe before being hindered by anthropogenic intervention.

Pacific Salmon in Yukon River

Describing the chinook salmon in the Yukon River, Mathews (1968) notes, "At some time between 20 May and 15 June, the Yukon Kings begin to ascend the river. Since some races have much farther to go than others, they must begin the upriver journey earlier. Salmon of Nitsulin River must travel nearly two thousand miles, while those of the Anvik merely five hundred. The Nisutlin rises farther from the Yukon's mouth than any other tributary and their altitude > 1,000 m above the sea level, hence some chinook salmon stocks in the Yukon River system are still forming a nutrient shadow of some 3,000 km long." On the other hand, Jarman (1972) notes "The king salmon of the North Pacific, which run in late spring or early summer, have the greatest distance to travel. Their spawning grounds are in Canada's Yukon Territory, near Caribou Crossing and Lake Bennett—a distance of some 2,250 mi from the sea." This record of some 3,500 km may be the world's longest!

Pacific Salmon in Other Rivers in North America

Devine (1992) notes that tens of thousands of sockeye salmon used to manage a 1,400-km journey to reach creeks and lakes as high as 2,100 m above sea level at the Columbia–Snake–Salmon River Watershed in Idaho. This is the highest altitude of historical salmon runs. The current status, however, is so alarming that, in 1991, "only four adult wild sockeye returned to Redfish Lake, Idaho's principal spawning ground. Of the four, only one was a female" (Devine 1992). Gross et al. (1998) also present evidence that the number of wild runs has grown very small, since the spawning ground is as far as 1,450 km from the river mouth and as high as 1,996 m from sea level.

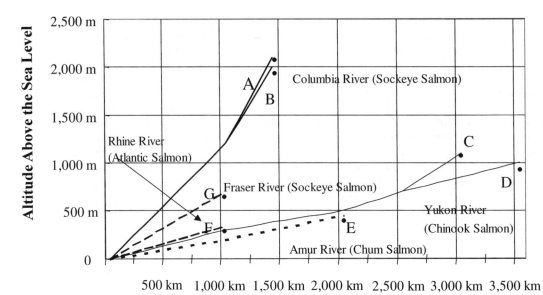

FIGURE 1. Maximum fresh water distance and altitude of spawning runs of salmon. Sources of information: A—Devine (1992), B—Gross et al. (1998), C—Mathews (1968), D—Jarman (1972), E—Smirnov (1976), F—Pearce (1993), and G—Johnston et al. (1997).

As for Canadian streams, it is well known that some of the Fraser River stocks of sockeye salmon ascend more than 1,000 km to reach the Middle River–Stuart Lake System (Johnston et al. 1997). Adams River and Scotch Creek, 450 km upstream from the mouth of the Fraser River in British Columbia, represent a major nutrient shadow, casting well into the interior of the province.

Pacific Salmon in Russian and Japanese Rivers

The Amur River has a total length of more than 4,000 km. This river has spawning runs of chum and pink salmon, and the former has summer and autumn runs. Smirnov (1976) noted that "the autumn form may swim as far as 2,000 km upstream," which suggests that a huge area in the Amur River Drainage Basin may be under the nutrient shadow of mainly chum and partly pink salmon returns. Quantitative information from the rest of Russia is extremely limited, but from various studies, we note that most of the Kamchatka Peninsula has been and still is under the nutrient shadow of Pacific salmon, notably sockeye, chum, pink, and masou. However, it should be noted that the lengths of the major salmon spawning rivers in the peninsula are not as long as many in North America.

As for the Japanese archipelago, historical records of the geographical distribution of spawning run of Pacific salmon are given in Ichikawa (1977). His detailed documentation suggests that chum salmon had ascended close to the headwaters of Shinano River, 350 km in length on Honshui Island. Since it is the longest river in Japan, the furthest run, historically, of salmon, could be beyond 300 km. From Ichikawa (1977) and many other studies, it appears that almost the entire area of Hokkaido Island appears under the nutrient shadow of Pacific salmon, mostly chum and pink. But, it was quite clearly the story of the past. The success of hatchery operations (Sato 1986) has stopped natural spawning runs of once-abundant salmon in most rivers of the archipelago. Water pollution, anthropogenic riverbed changes, and dam construction are other factors with disastrous consequences for salmon. According to Deguchi (1996), there are only a few adult escapements left, and these are mainly pink and chum in several small rivers of the Hokkaido and Honshu Islands.

Figure 1 summarizes the maximum distances and altitudes of fresh water journey of salmon in the northern hemisphere.

Studies on Pathways through which Marine Nutrients are Incorporated into Terrestrial Ecosystems

Thus far, we have been concerned with accounts of the contribution of salmon carcasses to terrestrial lands. In contrast, accounts of adult salmon nutrients to freshwater productivity were initiated by Juday et al. (1932), Donaldson (1966), Mathisen (1972), Krokhin (1957, 1959), and Krokhin (1967, 1968), for sockeye salmon in lakes in Alaska and on the Kamchatka peninsula. After such pioneering studies in the United States and the former Soviet Union, a rapid increase in the number of studies has occurred in the United States and Canada since the 1980s, and these studies have found strong relationships between the spawning run of Pacific salmon from the ocean and the productivity of fresh water ecosystems, in particular terrestrial ecosystems. Studies on the phosphorus budgets of lakes were made by scientists who were concerned that low escapements contributed to the oligotrophication of sockeye nursery lakes and that aerial application of nitrogen and phosphorus fertilizers was effective at enhancing juvenile production and hastening the return of adult sockeye salmon (Stockner 1987; Stockner and MacIsaac 1996).

Many species of mammals, birds, and insects are now known to derive great benefits from the carcasses of spawning runs of Pacific salmon (Frame 1974; Stalmaster and Gessaman 1984; Wood 1987; Cederholm et al.1989; Stalmaster and Kaiser 1997; Ben-David 1997; Minakawa 1997). Given the momentum of research of this field, Willson and Halupka (1995) characterize, from the eyes of ecologists, anadromous fish as a keystone species in vertebrate communities.

Stable Carbon and Nitrogen Analysis

Wada et al. (1981), Peterson et al. (1985), and others have developed a highly skillful method of using stable isotopes of carbon and nitrogen to study the food web structure of aquatic ecosystems. This new method can differentiate the marine nutrients embodied in salmon from those of terrestrial origin. By using this method, the im-

pacts of Pacific salmon as vectors for fertilizing fresh water and terrestrial ecosystems have been described by Mathisen et al. (1988), Kline et al. (1990), Piorkowski (1995), Bilby et al. (1996), Johnston et al. (1997), Ben-David et al. (1997, 1998), and Bilby et al. (2001).

From the viewpoint of the nutrient shadow, the findings of Hilderbrand et al. (1996) are of particular interest. They examine stable isotope analysis of the bone collagen and/or hair taken from museum-stored grizzly bears *Ursus arctus horribilis*, which were known to have been killed in various parts of northwestern states in 1856–1931, to infer their diet composition. The percentage-composition of the diet of these bears was 1. salmon, 2. terrestrially-produced meat, and 3. plant matter. On a map of the northwestern states, Hilderbrand et al. plotted signature points (1, 2, 3). Results show that, near Seattle, we see values of 54, 0, and 46; in west-central Oregon, 87, 0, and 13; in Wyoming, 0, 31, and 69. A total of fifteen points were given; some of them are shown with two signatures, both of bone collagen and hair, others have a single signature. The value for salmon in Montana and Wyoming is 0, clearly indicating that in the late nineteenth and early twentieth centuries, these areas did not have salmon-spawning streams. In contrast, the point corresponding to the Salmon River Watershed in Idaho has the value 1 = 90, with 2 = 0 and 3 = 10 for bone collagen. This map strongly supports the map of salmon-derived nutrient shadow.

Autotrophic Versus Heterotrophic Incorporation of Fish-Derived Nutrients into Aquatic Ecosystems

While direct predation of mammals and birds on live and spawned-out salmon is certainly one of the major pathways of nutrient transfer, there must be other pathways. To find such pathways, a carcass decomposition study is very important. Though not for ocean-going salmon, but instead for resident kokanee salmon, a study was done by Richey et al. (1975) on the manner of carcass decomposition in Taylor Creek, a tributary of Lake Tahoe, California-Nevada border. Minshall and Hitchcock (1991), Parmenter and Lamarra (1991), and Schuldt and Hershey (1995) also conducted similar research.

Given the increased number of studies of this kind, one of the focal points of research now is on the issue of autotrophic versus heterotrophic incorporation of marine-derived nutrients. When ocean-going salmon come back to the fresh waters but are not directly eaten up by mammals and birds, are their nutrients mostly mineralized first to help the growth of phytoplankton, algae, and photosynthetic bacteria (autotrophic incorporation), or are they largely taken up by a variety of macroinvertebrates before mineralization and heterotrophic bacteria (heterotrophic incorporation)? Many of the studies cited above tend to suggest the latter. The results in Bilby et al. (1996) and Johnston et al. (1997) point to a similar possibility for anadromous salmon.

Studies in Japan and Scotland

As for the Japanese salmon fishery, Krogius and Krokhin (1956, 1957) critically state, "In the prewar years (in the second half of the 1930s), in addition to the coastal fishery for sockeye, there was a very intensive Japanese fishery in the open ocean, in the region of Cape Kronotsk and the Kurile Straits. As a result, the numbers became reduced in the beginning of the 1940s." Harris (1987) also raises a similar question about high seas salmon fishery by Japan. While such exploitative salmon fishery was stopped in 1992 under international criticism, Japan has been successful at significantly increasing the salmon catch along its own coasts by means of artificial hatchery techniques (Sato 1986). This success has caused a long delay in the study of nutrient transport by anadromous fishes. However, a new initiative is taking place, and as Sibatani (1992, 1997) points out, spawning runs of Pacific salmon in Amur River and its tributaries may have been fertilizing boreal forests in the Maritime Province, and perhaps beyond, by stressing the intermediate roles of insects and birds. Murota (1995) presented a U.S.–Canadian–Russian literature survey on the upstream transport of marine nutrients by anadromous fishes, the first survey of its kind in Japan. A brief note by Kaeriyama (1998) shows phosphorus budgets in Lake Shikotsu in Hokkaido, Japan, which does not rear anadromous fish, in comparison with the one in sockeye-rearing Kurile Lake in southern Kamchatka, finding a much higher production of biomass in the latter. Saruwatari (1994) presents a hypothesis that some species of Salangidae fish in brackish waters may depend on the nutrients released from salmon carcasses of a previous year.

Ueta et al. (1999) surveyed 19 rivers in November 1995 and 16 rivers in November 1997, all of which are located in northeastern Hokkaido, facing the Sea of Okhotsk. The purpose of their survey was to investigate if there was a relationship between chum salmon carcasses and Stellar' and white-tailed sea eagles *Halieetus pelagicus* and *H. abicilla*. Significant correlations were found between the density of eagles and salmon carcasses, in both years. This result suggests that salmon are an important food item for the endangered eagles in Japan. Studying some other rivers in Hokkaido, Nakajima and Ito (2000) established that chum salmon carcasses were important for a number of species of benthic insects.

Research on the nutrient transport by Atlantic salmon has not been intensive, but there are several pioneering works, especially the work of Hewson (1985) on the River Dee, in Scotland, where he observed birds scavenging salmon carcasses and found that the rate of carcasses fed on was already as high as 76.7% in a four-week period at the beginning of the main spawning season, but rose to 94.4% in the following three months. He also observed mammals, mostly otters *Lutra lutra*, which were identified as the main scavengers. Foxes *Vulpes vulpes* were found to be the secondary scavengers. As for other scavengers, birds such as heron *Ardea cinerea*, great blue-backed gull *Larus marinus*, and goosander *Mergus merganser* were identified as important.

Although Atlantic salmon are not semelparous, their carcasses still may play a significant role in nourishing the drainage basin, depending on how they are preserved. It has been widely known that otters largely feed largely on the salmon along rivers in Scotland (Kruuk 1995). A quantitative account of such predation was given in Carss et al. (1990). Given these results, we realize that many other issues are related to the nutrient shadow cast by anadromous salmon, and here we highlight issues of importance.

Contribution of Anadromous Fishes Other than Salmonid Fishes

Atlantic and Pacific salmon are not the only anadromous fishes. Clupeid fishes *Alosa* spp., such as alewife and blueback herring, are also anadromous. Durbin et al. (1979) found that dead and dying alewife contributed significantly to the enrichment of experimental ponds and that, when expressed on a per unit area or volume basis, their nutrient addition surpassed the values recorded for sockeye salmon by Juday et al. (1932) and Donaldson (1966). Browder and Garman (1994) obtained similar results of nutrient enrichment for alewife and blueback herring in Wards Creek, Virginia.

Conclusion

Liebig (1842) warned of the tendency of modern humans to concentrate nutrients in large cities by letting their own excrements flow into sewerage systems, instead of dispersing them over farmlands. In the modern world, human beings harvest and consume large amounts of marine animals and plants, and these ocean-derived nutrients are not widely dispersed over farms and croplands, but instead are discharged into sewerage systems and deposited into coastal rivers and seas. A tendency similar to this process is manifested in the drastic decline of the number of naturally-spawning anadromous fishes. Only considering a few factors, such as gigantic dam construction for hydroelectric power and irrigation and the careless watershed development that destroys valuable salmon habitat, it is important for us to realize that the last half of the nineteenth century and most of the twentieth century has been an age of grave suffering for salmonids worldwide (MacCrimmon and Gots 1979; Pearce 1993; Brown 1982; Muckleston 1990; Devine 1992). As many types of environmental destruction have deepened at global scales, however, increased attention has been paid to the importance of biodiversity on this water planet Earth as having crucial significance for the sustainability of ecosystems, especially important in connection with humankind's activities, which often play a negative role by diminishing biodiversity. The vast literature on Pacific salmon ecology supports the premise that Pacific salmon have been and still are casting a vast nutrient shadow, albeit thin, over numerous islands and terrestrial lands of the continents facing the Pacific Ocean. Allowing spawning of wild salmon as far upstream as they wish to go is more important now than ever before.

Over the past few decades, new initiatives have been made to restore salmon runs to historic levels in North America. One of the more promising measures was the whole-lake fertilization of sockeye salmon nursery lakes to increase production and produce larger and more numerous smolts (Stockner 1987; Stockner and MacIsaac 1996; Griswold et al., this volume). Recognizing the importance of salmon carcasses as nutrient vectors, another approach is to place carcasses from hatcheries into rivers where spawning runs

are expected (Michael 1996). In Portland, Oregon, such a measure has already been taken by the combined effort of salmon specialists and volunteer workers (Corrarino 1998).

Another important question was raised by Michael (1998), who asked how many adult salmon should be allowed to spawn so as to guarantee the sustainability and proper functioning of freshwater and terrestrial ecosystems at their historic levels, instead of solely focusing research efforts on an analysis of the extent presently supported by the currently low spawning runs of anadromous salmon?

Recent advancements in the studies of nutrient transport by anadromous salmon have caused salmon specialists in Japan to reconsider the hatchery-only policy of managing migratory fishes of Japan. Kaeriyama (1996) warns of the decrease in body size and the delay of maturation of hatchery-reared chum salmon in Japan. With this in mind, Kaeriyama (1998) thinks it worthwhile to now reevaluate the possible merits of natural spawning in Japan.

Watershed Management

Due to the law of gravity, it is theoretically possible for all spawned-out salmon carcasses to flow downstream back to the ocean without noticeably affecting freshwater and terrestrial ecosystems. Though this possibility can occur, the current literature supports carcass retention; most notably, the stream studies of Cederholm and Peterson (1985) show a positive relationship between the number of carcasses retained and the amount of large organic woody debris within the stream. Similar conclusions were reached by Bilby and Bisson (1998) in Pacific Northwest streams.

Anadromous fishes, especially Pacific salmon carcasses, may be contributing significant amounts of nutrients to support riparian vegetation, trees, scavenging insects, birds, and mammals (Bilby et al. 1996; Johnston et al. 1997; Ben-David et al. 1998; Reimchen 2001).

The strength of the interface between anadromous salmon carcasses, birds, mammals, and forest production appears worthy of further exploration.

Acknowledgments

The author benefited from communications with Professor Masahide Kaeriyama, Hokkaido Tokai

University, at various stages of writing this paper. He is also grateful to Professor Eitaro Wada, Center for Ecological Research, Kyoto University, for his encouragement towards this direction of research. The responsibility for any remaining errors belongs solely to the author.

References

Ben-David, M. 1997. Timing of reproduction in wild mink: the influence of spawning Pacific salmon. Canadian Journal of Zoology 75:376–382.

Ben-David, M., R. W. Flynn, and D. M. Schell. 1997. Annual and seasonal changes in diets of martens: evidence from stable isotope analysis. Oecologia 111:280–291.

Ben-David, M., T. A. Hanley, and D. M. Schell. 1998. Fertilization of terrestrial vegetation by spawning Pacific salmon: the role of flooding and predator activity. Oikos 83:47–55.

Bilby, R. E., B. R. Fransen, and P. A. Bisson. 1996. Incorporation of nitrogen and carbon from spawning coho salmon into the trophic system of small streams: evidence from stable isotopes. Canadian Journal of Fisheries and Aquatic Sciences 53:164–173.

Bilby, R. E., and P. A. Bisson. 1991. Enhancing fisheries resources through active management of riparian areas. Pages 201–209 *in* B. White, and I. Guthrie, editors. Proceedings of the 15th Northeast Pacific Pink and Chum Salmon Workshop, Pacific Salmon Commission, Vancouver, B.C.

Bilby, R. E., and P. A. Bisson. 1998. Function and distribution of large woody debris. Pages 324–346 *in* Naiman, R. J., and R. E. Bilby, editors. River ecology and management. Springer, New York.

Bilby, R. E., B. R. Fransen, and J. K. Walter, C. J. Cederholm, and W. J. Scarlett. 2001. Preliminary evaluation of the use of nitrogen stable isotope ratios to establish escapement levels for Pacific salmon. Fisheries 26:6–14.

Boje, R., and M. Tomczak, editors. 1978. Upwelling ecosystems. Springer, Berlin.

Brett, J. R. 1965. The swimming energetics of salmon. Scientific American 213:80–85.

Brooke, A. P. 1994. Diet of the fishing bat, Noctilio Leporinus (*Chiroptera noctilionidae*). Journal of Mammalogy 75:212–218.

Browder, R. G., and G. C. Garman. 1994. Increased ammonium concentrations in a tidal fresh-water stream during residence of migratory clupeid fishes. Transactions of the American Fisheries Society 123:993–996.

Brown, B. 1982. Mountain in the clouds: a search for the wild salmon. Collier Books, New York.

Budy, Luecke, and Wurtsbaugh. 1998. Adding nutrients to enhance the growth of endangered sockeye salmon. Transactions of the American Fisheries Society 127:19–34.

Carss, D. N., H. Kruuk, and J. W. H. Conroy. 1990. Predation on adult Atlantic salmon, *Salmo salar* L., by otters, *Lutra lutra* (L.), within the River Dee system, Aberdeenshire, Scotland. Journal of Fish Biology 37:935–944.

Cathcart, J. B. 1980. World phophate reserves and resources. Pages 1–18 *in* the American Society of Agronomy, Crop Science Society of America, and Soil Science Society of America, editors. The role of phophorus in agriculture. Madison, Wisconsin.

Cederholm, C. J., D. B. Houston, D. L. Cole, and W. J. Scarlett. 1989. Fate of coho salmon (*Oncorhynchus kisutch*) carcasses in spawning streams. Canadian Journal of Fisheries and Aquatic Sciences 46:1347–1355.

Cederholm, C. J., M. D. Kunze, T. Murota, and A. Sibatani. 1999. Pacific salmon carcasses: essential contributions of nutrients and energy for terrestrial and aquatic ecosystems. Fisheries 24:6–15.

Cederholm, C. J., and N. P. Peterson. 1985. The retention of coho salmon (*Oncorhynchus kisutch*) carcasses by organic debris in small streams. Canadian Journal of Fisheries and Aquatic Sciences 42:1222–1225.

Cederholm, C. J., R. E. Bilby, P. A. Bisson, T. W. Bumstead, B. R. Fransen, W. J. Scarlett, and J. W. Ward. 1997. North American Journal of Fisheries Management 17:947–963.

Cederholm, C. J., W. J. Scarlett, and P. Peterson. 1988. Low-cost enhancement technique for winter habitat of juvenile coho salmon. North American Journal of Fisheries Management 8:438–441.

Chanton, J. P., and C. S. Martens. 1987. Biogeochemical cycling in an organic-rich coastal marine basin. 8. A sulfur isotopic budget balanced by differential diffusion across the sediment-water interface. Geochimia et Cosmochimia Acta 1201–1208.

Corrarino, C. 1998. The Oregon story–an overview. Page 55 *in* Abstracts of ecosystem considerations in fisheries management. 16th Lowell Wakefield Symposium and American Fisheries Society joint meeting. 30 September–3 October. Anchorage, Alaska.

DeAngelis, D. L. 1992. Dynamics of nutrient cycling and food webs. Chapman and Hall, London.

Deguchi, A. 1996. Environmental ethnology: people and nature of salmon spawning Ara River of Yechigo. Nagoya, Nagoya University Press. (in Japanese)

Devine, B. 1992. The salmon dammed. Audubon. January/February: 83–889.

Donaldson, J. R. 1966. The phosphorus budget of Iliamna Lake, Alaska, as related to the cyclic abundance of sockeye salmon. Ph.D thesis, submitted to the University of Washington, Seattle.

Durbin, A. G., S. W. Nixon, and C. A. Oviatt. 1979. Effects of the spawning migration of the alewife, *Alosa Pseudoharengus*, on freshwater ecosystems. Ecology 60:8–17.

FAO (Food and Agriculture Organization of the United Nations). 1966. FAO yearbook fishery statistics: catches and landings. Rome.

FAO (Food and Agriculture Organization of the United Nations). 1997. FAO yearbook fishery statistics: catches and landings. Rome.

Folkard, N. F. G., and J. N. M. Smith. 1995. Evidence for bottom-up effects in the boreal forest: do passerine birds respond to large-scale experimental fertilization? Canadian Journal of Zoology 73:2231–2237.

Frame, G. W. 1974. Black bear predation on salmon at Olsen Creek, Alaska. Zeitschrift fur Tierpsychologie 35:23–38.

Groot, C., and L. Margolis, editors. 1991. Pacific salmon life history. UBC Press, Vancouver.

Gross, H. P., W. A. Wurtbaugh, and C. Luecke. 1998. The role of anadromous sockeye salmon in the nutrient loading and productivity of Redfish Lake, Idaho. Transactions of the American Fisheries Society 127:1–18.

Harris, C. K. 1987. Catches of North American sockeye salmon (*Oncorhynchus nerka*) by the Japanese high seas salmon fisheries, 1972–84. Pages 458–479 *in* H. D. Smith, S. L. Margolis, and C. C. Wood, editors. Sockeye salmon (*Oncorhynchus nerka*) population biology and future management. Canadian special publication of fisheries and aquatic science 96. Fisheries and Oceans Canada, Ottawa.

Henderson, M. A., and C. C. Graham. 1998. History and current status of Pacific salmon in British Columbia. North Pacific Anadromous Fish Commission Bulletin 1:13–22.

Hewson, R. 1985. Scavenging of salmon carcasses by birds. Scottish Birds 13:179–182.

Hewson, R. 1995. Use of salmonid carcasses by vertebrate scavengers. Journal of Zoology 235:53–65.

Hilderbrand, G. V., S. D. Farley, C. T. Robbins, T. A. Hanley, K. Titus, and C. Servheen. 1996. Use of stable isotopes to determine diets of living and extinct bears. Canadian Journal of Zoology 74:2080–2088.

Ichikawa, T. 1977. Salmon in Japan–their cultural history and fishery. NHK Books, Tokyo. (in Japanese)

Ikeda, S. 1981. Trace elements in fish and shell fish: their biochemistry and food science. Kouseisha-Kouseikaku, Tokyo. (in Japanese)

Jahnke, R. A. 1992. The phosphorus cycle. Pages 17–34 *in* S. S. Butcher, R. J. Charlson, G. H. Orians, and G. V. Wolfe, editors. Global biogeochemical cycles. Academic Press, London.

Jarman, C. 1972. Atlas of animal migration. William Heinemann, London.

Johnston, N. T., J. S. Macdonald, K. J. Hall, and P. J. Tschaplinski. 1997. A preliminary study of the role of sockeye salmon (*Oncorhynchus nerka*) carcasses as carbon and nitrogen sources for benthic insects and fishes in the 'Early Stuart' stock spawning streams, 1050 km from the ocean. Fisheries Project Report No. RD55. Fisheries Branch, Ministry of Environment, Lands and Parks, Province of British Columbia, Canada.

Juday C., W. H. Rich, G. I. Kemmerer, and A. Mann. 1932. Limnological studies of Karluk Lake, Alaska, 1926–1930. Bulletin of the Bureau of Fisheries (Bureau of Fisheries, U.S. Department of Commerce) 12:407–436.

Kaeriyama, M. 1996. Population dynamics and stock management of hatchery-reared salmons in Japan. Bulletin of National Research Institute of Aquaculture, Supplement 2: 11–15.

Kaeriyama, M. 1998. Salmon: gifts from the ocean–the material cycle and biodiversity by the salmonid fish. Mori to Kawa [Forests and Rivers] 7(8):52–55. Hokkaido, Japan. (In Japanese)

Kline, Jr., T. C., J. J. Goering, O. A. Mathisen, and P. H. Poe. 1990. Recycling of elements transported upstream by runs of Pacific salmon: I. d^{15}N and d^{13}C evidence in Sashin Creek, southeastern Alaska. Canadian Journal of Fisheries and Aquatic Sciences 47:136–144.

Kline, Jr., T. C., J. J. Goering, and R. J. Piorkowski. 1997. The effect of salmon carcasses on Alaskan freshwaters. Pages 179–204 *in* A. M. Milner and M. W. Oswood, editors. Freshwaters of Alaska, ecological syntheses. Springer-Verlag, New York.

Krogius, F. V., and E. M. Krokhin. 1956. English translation 1957. Causes of the fluctuations in abundance of sockeye salmon in Kamchatka. Fisheries Research Board of Canada, Translation Series No. 92. (Translated from Russian by R. E. Foerster)

Krogius, F. V., E. M. Krokhin, and V. V. Menshtkin. 1987. Pacific sockeye salmon in the ecosystem of Lake Dalnee (Kamchatka). Nauka Publishers, Leningrad. (in Russian)

Krokhin, E. M. 1957. English translation 1959. Sources of enrichment of spawning lakes in biogenic elements. Fisheries Research Board of Canada, Translation Series No. 207. (Translated from Russian by R. E. Foerster)

Krokhin, E. M. 1967. English translation 1968. Effect of size of escapement of sockeye salmon spawners on the phosphate content of a nursery lake. Fisheries Research Board of Canada, Translation Series No. 1186. (Translated by R. E. Foerster)

Kruuk, H. 1995. Wild otters: predation and populations. Oxford University Press, Oxford.

Kumazawa, B. 1685/86, English translation. 1938. A discussion of public questions in the light of the great learning. Transactions of the Asiatic Society of Japan, Second Series 16: 259–356. (Translated from Japanese by G. M. Fisher)

Lalli, C. M., and T. R. Parsons. 1993. Biological oceanography: an introduction. Pergamon, Oxford.

Larkin, G. A., and P. A. Slaney. 1996. Trends in marine-derived nutrient sources to south coastal British Columbia streams: impending implications to salmonid production. Watershed Restoration Management Report No. 3. Ministry of Environment, Lands and Parks and Ministry of Forests, British Columbia.

Levin, J. V. 1960. The export economies: their pattern of development in historical perspective. Harvard University Press, Cambridge, Massachusetts.

Liebig, J. 1842. Chemistry in its applications to agriculture and physiology (Second edition). Taylor and Walton, London.

Lindebroom, H. J. 1984. The nitrogen pathway in a penguin rookery. Ecology 65(1):269–277.

MacCrimmon, H. R., and B. L. Gots. 1979. World distribution of Atlantic salmon, *Salmo salar*. Journal of the Fisheries Research Board of Canada 36:422–457.

McConnel, D. 1979. Biogeochemistry of phosphate minerals. Pages 163–210 *in* P. A. Trudinger and D. J. Swaine, editors. Biogeochemical cycling of mineral-forming elements. Elsevier, Amsterdam.

McDowall, R. M. 1988. Diadromy in fishes: migrations between fresh water and marine environments. Croom Helm, London.

Mathew, W. M. 1981. The House of Gibbs and the Peruvian guano monopoly. Royal Historical Society, London.

Mathews, R. 1968. The Yukon. Holt, Reinhart, and Winston, New York.

Mathisen, O. A. 1972. Biogenic enrichment of sockeye salmon lakes and stock productivity. Verh Internat Verein Limnol 18:1089–1095.

Mathisen, O. A., P. L. Parker, J. J. Goering, T. C. Kline, P. H. Poe, and R. S. Scalan. 1988. Recycling of marine elements transported into freshwater systems by anadromous salmon. Verh Internat Verein Limnol 23:2249–2258.

Michael, J. H. 1998. How many salmon should ascend rivers: an extension of Dr. Sibatani's discussion. Selected Papers on Entropy Studies 5:19–24.

Minakawa, N. 1997. The dynamics of aquatic insect communities associated with salmon spawning. A Ph.D. thesis submitted to University of Washington, Seattle.

Minshall, G. W., and E. Hitchcock. 1991. Decomposition of rainbow trout (*Oncorhynchus mykiss*) carcasses in a forest stream ecosystem inhabited only by nonanadromous fish populations. Canadian Journal of Fisheries and Aquatic Sciences 48:191–195.

Muckleston, K. W. 1990. Salmon vs. hydropower: Striking a balance in the Pacific Northwest. Environment 32:10–15, 32–36.

Murota, T. 1995. Upstream transport of oceanic nutrients onto land ecosystems by anadromous fish. Biological Science (Tokyo) 47:124–140. (In Japanese)

Murota, T. 1998. Material cycle and sustainable economy. Pages 120–138 *in* R. Keil, D. V. J. Bell, P. Penz, and L. Fawcett, editors. Political ecology: global and local. Routledge, London.

Murphy, R. C. 1936. Oceanic birds of South America, Volume I. Macmillan, New York.

Nakajima, M., and T. Ito. 2000. Aquatic animal colonization on chum salmon (*Oncorhyncus keta*) carcasses in Hokkaido, northern Japan. Scientific Reports of the Hokkaido Fish Hatchery 54:23–31.

Opsahl, S., and R. Benner. 1997. Distribution and cycling of terrigenous dissolved organic matter in the ocean. Nature 386:480–482.

Parmenter, R. R., and V. A. Lamarra. 1991. Nutrient cycling in a freshwater marsh: the decomposition of fish and waterfowl carrion. Limnology and Oceanography 36(5):976-987.

Pauly, D. 1996. One hundred million tons of fish and fisheries research. Fisheries Research 25:25–38.

Pearce, F. 1993. Greenprint for rescuing the Rhine. New Scientist 138:25–29.

Peterson, B. J., R. W. Howarth, and R. H. Garritt. 1985. Multiple stable isotopes used to trace the flow of organic matter in esturian food webs. Science 227:1361–1363.

Pierrou, U. 1979. The phosphorus cycle: quantitative aspects and the role of man. Pages 205–210 *in* P. A. Trudinger and D. J. Swaine, editors. Biogeochemical cycling of mineral-forming elements. Elsevier, Amsterdam.

Piorkowski, R. J. 1995. Ecological effects of spawning salmon on several southcentral Alaskan streams. Ph.D thesis submitted to University of Alaska, Fairbanks.

Pomeroy, L. R., editor. 1974. Cycles of essential elements, benchmark papers in ecology volume 1. Dowden, Hutchinson and Ross, Strousburg, Pennsylvania.

Reimchen, T. E. 2001. Historical signatures of salmon in tree rings. Page 35 *in* International conference: restoring nutrients to salmonid ecosystems. 24–26 April. Eugene, Oregon.

Richey, J. E., M. A. Perkins, and C. R. Goldman. 1975. Effects of kokanee salmon (*Oncorhynchus nerka*) decomposition on the ecology of a subalpine stream. Journal of the Fisheries Research Board of Canada 32:817–820.

Ridley, H. N. 1930. The dispersal of plants throughout the world. L. Reeve and Co., Ashford, Kent.

Sandstrom, M. W. 1982. Diagenesis of organic phosphorus in marine sediments: implication for the global carbon and phosphorus cycles. Pages 133–141 *in* J. R. Freney and I. E. Galbally, editors. Cycling of carbon, nitrogen, sulfur and phosphorus in terrestrial and aquatic ecosystems. Springer-Verlag, Berlin.

Saruwatari, T. 1994. Salangichthys microdon–shrewd wanderer in brackish water. Pages 74–85 *in* A. Goto, K. Tsukamoto, and K. Maekawa, editors. Diadromous, fresh-water fish–life history and evolution. Tokai University Press, Tokyo. (in Japanese)

Sato, S. 1986. Salmon–a challenge to aquaculture. Iwanami Shoten, Tokyo. (in Japanese)

Schneider, D., and D. C. Duffy. 1988. Historical variation in guano production from the Peruvian and Benguela upwelling. Climatic Change 13:309–316.

Schuldt, J. A., and A. E. Hershey. 1995. Effect of salmon carcass decomposition on Lake Superior tributary streams. Journal of the North American Benthological Society 14(2):259–268.

Shearer, W. D. 1992. The Atlantic salmon: natural history, exploitation and future management. Blackwell Scientific Publications, Cambridge, Massachusetts.

Sibatani, A. 1992. English translation 1996. Why do salmon ascend rivers?: another perspective on biodiversity and the global environment. Selected Papers on Entropy Studies 3:3–12. (Translated from Japanese by R. Davis)

Smirnov, A. I. 1976. Chum salmon. Page 87 *in* Great Soviet Encyclopedia: Volume 7. Macmillan, New York.

Stalmaster, M. V., and J. A. Gessaman. 1984. Ecological energetics and foraging behavior of overwintering bald eagles. Ecological Monographs 54:407–428.

Stalmaster, M. V., and J. L. Kaiser. 1997. Winter ecology of bald eagles in the Nisqually River Drainage, Washington. Northwest Science 71:214–223.

Stockner, J. G. 1987. Lake fertilization: the enrichment cycle and lake sockeye salmon (*Oncorhynchus nerka*) production. Pages 198–215 *in* H. D. Smith, S. L. Margolis, and C. C. Wood, editors. Sockeye salmon (*Oncorhynchus nerka*) population biology and future management. Canadian Special Publication of Fisheries and Aquatic Sciences 96. Fisheries and Oceans Canada, Ottawa.

Stockner and MacIssac, 1996. British Columbia lake enrichment programme: two decades of habitat enhancement for sockeye salmon. Regulated Rivers: Research and Management 12:547–561.

Stockner, J. G., E. Rydin, and P. Hyenstrand. 2000. Cultural oligotrophication: causes and consequences for fisheries resources. Fisheries 25:7–14.

Sugai, S., and D. C. Burrell. 1984. Transport of dissolved organic carbon, nutrients, and trace metals from the Wilson and Blossom rivers to Smeaton Bay, Southeast Alaska. Canadian Journal of Fisheries and Aquatic Sciences 41:180–190.

Tsuchida, A. 1996. The importance of the cycle of matters: a discussion of nutrient cycling in basins, land, and human society from the viewpoint of entropy. Pages 150–170 *in* Proceedings of International Workshop and Symposium on Environmental Restoration for Closed Seas. 27–30 August. Toyohashi, Japan.

Ueta, M., M. Koita, and K. Fukui. 1999. The relationship between the autumn distributions of salmon and of Steller's and white-tailed sea eagles in Hokkaido, Japan. STRIX (A Journal of Field Ornithology), Wild Bird Society of Japan 17:25–29. (in Japanese)

Utekhina, L., E. Potapov, and M. J. McGrady. 2000. Diet of the Stellar' sea eagles in the northern sea of Okhotsk. Pages 71–82 *in* M. Ueta and M. J. McGrady, editors. First symposium on Steller's and white-tailed sea eagles in East Asia. Wild Bird Society of Japan, Tokyo.

Wada, E., R. Shibata, and T. Torii. 1981. 15N Abundance in Antarctica: origin of soil nitrogen and ecological implications. Nature (London) 292:327–329.

Wada, E., Y. Kabaya, and Y. Kurihara. 1993. Stable isotopic structure of aquatic ecosystems. Journal of Bioscience 18:483–499.

Whittaker, R. J., and S. H. Jones. 1994. The role of frugivorous bats and birds in the rebuilding of a tropical forest ecosystem, Krakatau, Indonesia. Journal of Biogeography 21:245–258.

Willson, M. F., and K. C. Halupka. 1995. Anadromous fish as keystone species in vertebrate communities. Conservation Biology 9:489–497.

Wood, C. C. 1987a. Predation of juvenile Pacific salmon by common merganser (*Mergus merganser*) on eastern Vancouver Island. I: Predation during the seaward migration. Canadian Journal of Fisheries and Aquatic Sciences 44:941–949.

Wood, C. C. 1987b. Predation of juvenile Pacific salmon by common merganser (*Mergus merganser*) on eastern Vancouver Island. II: Predation of stream-resident juvenile salmon by merganser broods. Canadian Journal of Fisheries and Aquatic Sciences 44:941–949.

Yoshikawa, H., and M. Ashida. 1990. Dictionary of nutrition: 4th edition. Dobun Shoin, Tokyo. (in Japanese)

American Fisheries Society Symposium 34:33–40, 2003

Past and Present Pacific Salmon Abundance: Bioregional Estimates for Key Life History Stages

PETER K. SCHOONMAKER

Institute for the Northwest, 421 SW Sixth Avenue, Suite 1090, Portland, Oregon 97204, USA

TED GRESH

Parametrix Inc., 700 NE Multnomah Boulevard, Suite 1160, Portland, Oregon 97232, USA

JIM LICHATOWICH

Alder Fork Consulting, P.O. Box 439, Columbia City, Oregon 97018, USA

HANS D. RADTKE

P.O. Box 244, Yahats, Oregon 97498, USA

Abstract.—Pacific salmon *Oncorhynchus* spp. are important components of numerous food webs throughout their life history, yet we know very little about the historic and current abundance of these life history stages. We used past cannery records, recent harvest and hatchery records, and salmon life history information drawn from the literature to construct a simple bioregional model of historic and recent salmon abundance at egg, fry, smolt, ocean adult, and spawning stages for five species of Pacific salmon from Alaska to California. We found a historic-to-recent bioregional decline in salmon biomass in all life history stages. Recent salmon egg, fry, smolt, ocean-going adult, and escapement biomass estimates for northwestern North America are 74%, 55%, 59%, 86%, and 35%, respectively, of historic levels. Recent high productivity in Alaskan waters, however, masks a precipitous decline south of Alaska, where recent egg, fry, smolt, ocean-going adult, and escapement biomass levels are 34%, 23%, 50%, 40%, and 15% that of historic levels. Adult production and harvest levels are no longer sufficient measures of salmon management success. Researchers need to quantify and elucidate the ecosystem effects of historic biomass changes in life history stages of Pacific salmon on a watershed basis. Fisheries managers must set and meet specific targets for salmon life history stage abundance—from egg to spawning adult—to restore and maintain ecosystem function.

Introduction

Pacific salmon *Oncorhynchus* spp. are an important component of freshwater and marine ecosystems from Alaska to central California (National Research Council 1996). Recent studies have shown that 20–40% of the phosphorous, nitrogen, and carbon in freshwater systems may be marine-derived through the carcasses of spawned salmon (Bilby et al. 1996; Johnston et al. 1997; multiple authors, this volume). The role of salmon in freshwater and marine ecosystems is more complex, however, than spawning salmon serving as vectors for nutrient and biomass distribution. The different life history stages of salmon likely play different roles in the various habitats they occupy throughout their life cycle (Willson and Halupka 1995). Salmon eggs are an important food source for numerous aquatic vertebrates, including other salmonids. Salmon fry and smolts are both predators and prey for various species from high order streams to estuaries (Groot and Margolis 1991). Likewise, adult salmon feed on various marine organisms and are, in turn, preyed upon by seals, tuna, killer whales, mackerel, and other predators (Cederholm et al. 1989, 2000). In summary, salmon are important components of numerous food webs throughout their life history.

Only recently have we scaled up our consideration of marine-derived nutrients to consider the significance of spawning Pacific salmon at a bioregional scale (Murota, this volume; Gresh et al. 2000). Furthermore, the abundance of salmon as components of food webs and as nutrient sources at different stages of their life history has received little attention at a broad bioregional scale. There is evidence from catch and cannery records that the overall abundance of Pacific salmon has declined over the past century (Figure 1) and that nutrient inputs to freshwater systems have consequently decreased (Hewes 1947; Gresh et al. 2000; Larkin and Slaney 1997; Stouder et al. 1997).

It follows, then, that the abundance of other life history stages of Pacific salmon has also declined. To examine the magnitude of this deficiency, this paper provides estimates of early 20th century and current abundances of egg, fry, smolt, and adult stages of five Pacific salmon species: coho *O. kisutch*, chinook *O. tshawytscha*, sockeye *O. nerka*, pink *O. gorbuscha*, and chum *O. keta*. We use a simple bioregional-scale model with parameters derived from various life history studies of the five salmon species.

Methods

We used 1988–1997 catch records (PFMC, 1988–1997) to estimate recent harvests of five Pacific salmon species. We used two data sources, as described in Gresh et al. (2000), for estimating salmon abundance prior to the arrival of Euro-Americans (pre-contact): (1) historical cannery records for the Oregon coast, Puget Sound, British Columbia, and Alaska, adjusting for discarded weight, unprocessed fish, and harvest rates; and (2) previously published estimates of historical run abundance for the California coast and central valley, Columbia River Basin, and Fraser River. We applied subregional escapement, fecundity, survivorship, and weight parameters (Table 1) derived from the literature to estimate

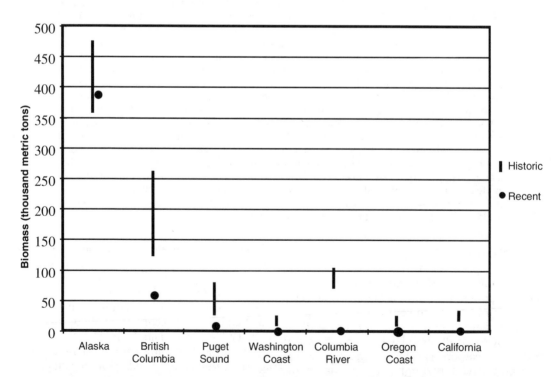

FIGURE 1. Historic salmon biomass estimated from cannery records compared to recent biomass estimated from harvest records, summarized from tables 6 and 7 in Gresh et al. (2000).

TABLE 1. Life history parameters for estimating numbers and biomass of five salmon species.

Historic	Egg#/pair	Egg wt (kg)	Egg>fry	Fry wt (kg)	Fry>smolt	Smolt wt (kg)	Smolt>adult	Adult wt (kg)	Spawn wt (kg)	Esc %
Coho	1,800–4,000	0.000349	0.30	0.005	0.02	0.035	0.07	4.05	3.24	NA
Chinook	2,000	0.000267	0.07	0.005	0.07	0.1	0.13	9.09	7.27	NA
Sockeye	1,500	0.0002753	0.15	0.006	0.15	0.012	0.04	2.70	2.16	NA
Pink	925	0.0002753	0.05	0.0015	0.6	0.002	0.04	1.82	1.64	NA
Chum	1,400	0.0002753	0.05	0.002	0.6	0.003	0.05	5.45	4.91	NA
Recent wild	Egg#/pair	Egg wt (kg)	Egg>fry	Fry wt (kg)	Fry>smolt	Smolt wt (kg)	Smolt>adult	Adult wt (kg)	Spawn wt (kg)	Esc %
Coho	1,800–3,000	0.000349	0.30	0.005	0.035	0.035	0.10	2.70–3.20	1.86–2.88	0.45
Chinook	2,000	0.000267	0.10	0.005	0.1	0.1	0.20	3.31–8.25	2.98–7.43	0.45
Sockeye	1,500	0.0002753	0.15	0.006	0.1	0.012	0.08	2.55	2.30	0.45
Pink	900	0.0002753	0.07	0.0015	0.7	0.002	0.06	1.45	1.30	0.45
Chum	1,400	0.0002753	0.08	0.002	0.35	0.003	0.09	3.29–4.84	2.96–4.36	0.45
Recent hatchery	Egg#/pair	Egg wt (kg)	Egg>fry	Fry wt (kg)	Fry>smolt	Smolt wt (kg)	Smolt>adult	Adult wt (kg)	Spawn wt (kg)	Esc %
Coho	1,800–4,000	0.000349	NA	NA	NA	0.020–0.035	0.003–0.05	1.77–3.20	1.59–2.88	0.25
Chinook	2,000	0.000267	NA	NA	NA	0.035	0.01–0.03	3.31–8.25	2.98–7.43	0.25
Sockeye	1,500	0.0002753	0.20	0.003	0.15	0.003	0.02–0.03	2.55	2.30	0.25
Pink	900	0.0002753	0.07	0.0015	0.7	0.002	0.02	1.45	1.30	0.25
Chum	1,400	0.0002753	0.08	0.0015	0.35	0.003	0.02	3.29–4.84	2.96–4.36	0.25

salmon abundance and biomass in egg, fry, smolt, and adult stages for current and historic wild salmon (Groot and Margolis 1991; Bradford 1995). We used the last five years of fry and smolt releases from west coast hatcheries to estimate hatchery-produced fry, smolt, and adult biomass. We also applied subregional escapement, fecundity, survivorship, and weight parameters derived from the literature to estimate hatchery salmon abundance and biomass in egg, fry, smolt, and adult stages (Groot and Margolis 1991, Bradford 1995, Bigler et al. 1996, United States Army Corps of Engineers, Walla Walla District 2002).

Results

As would be expected, biomass of ocean-going and escaping salmon is considerably higher than that of salmon at the egg, fry, and smolt stages, both historically and presently. Historically, 80 million kg of eggs transformed into 179 million kg of fry, which developed into 77 million kg of smolts, which then grazed marine pastures to increase to 874 million kg of adult biomass (Table 2). We found a historic-to-recent bioregional decline in salmon biomass in all life history stages. Including 86 million kg of hatchery fish, we estimate that recent adult salmon biomass is 754 million kg or 86% that of historic levels. Excluding hatchery fish drops this estimate to 668 million kg or 76% of historic levels. Recent salmon egg, fry, smolt, and adult escapement biomass estimates for northwestern North America are 74%, 55%, 59%, and 35%, respectively, of historic levels, if hatchery fish are included, and 73%, 54%, 41%, and 32%, if they are excluded. However, recent high productivity in Alaskan waters (583 million kg recently versus 446 million kg historically) masks a precipitous decline in adult biomass of salmon that spawn south of Alaska. Recent egg, fry, smolt, ocean-going adult, and escapement biomass levels south of Alaska are 34%, 23%, 50%, 40%, and 15% that of historic levels, if hatchery fish are included (Table 3). Excluding hatchery fish, recent egg, fry, smolt, ocean-going adult, and escapement biomass levels are 32%, 21%, 20%, 31%, and 13% of historic levels south of Alaska.

The trend of declining salmon biomass from north to south is apparent on a state-to-state basis for most life history stages. In Alaska, recent biomass exceeds historic levels for egg and adult stages, whereas fry and smolt biomass are some-what lower than historic, and escapement is less than half of historic estimates. The recent/historic biomass ratio declines from Alaska to British Columbia across all life history stages, with further decreases for Washington, Oregon, and California. Recent salmon biomass as a percentage of historic biomass is lowest in California across all life history stages. One exception to this trend is the recent/historic smolt ratio for the Columbia River. Recent hatchery practices have pushed this ratio up to 82%; yet ocean adult and escapement recent/historic biomass ratios are 15% and 5%, respectively.

Discussion

Our results are based on extrapolating egg, fry, smolt, and adult numbers from regionally broad, recent and historical catch/escapement estimates and applying mean per fish weights to those estimates. We intend this to be the first step in building a heuristically useful model that compares current and historic salmon biomass at several life history stages. Clearly, our estimates will benefit from more geographically and temporally precise harvest, escapement, and life history parameter information. Nevertheless, this first iteration indicates that the biomass of salmon eggs, fry, and smolts is considerable and in the same order of magnitude as that of escaping adult salmon. Our results also support the conclusion of Gresh et al. (2000) that the biomass of salmon escaping to northwest coast river systems has declined overall, most precipitously in the southern portion of the salmon's range. We attribute the difference between our estimates and those of Gresh et al. to the different methodologies used. Gresh et al. used historic cannery records and recent escapement records to estimate current escapement at 5–7% of historic escapement, whereas we used Gresh et al.'s estimates as inputs for our *model* that *predicts* current escapement to be 15% of the biomass that our model of historic escapement predicts. Regardless, both studies indicate that Pacific Northwest/British Columbia salmon escapement has declined an order of magnitude. Furthermore, wild egg, fry, and smolt biomass have declined nearly two orders of magnitude in California, Oregon, and parts of Washington.

The effects of these declines on aquatic ecosystems are unknown at this point. Clearly, spawning salmon are important nutrient and carbon sources for Pacific river systems (Ceder-

TABLE 2. Biomass of egg, fry, smolt, adult, harvest, and escapement for five species of Pacific salmon, estimated for the period from 1880 to 1920, 1988 to 1997 (for wild salmon), and 1993 to 1997 (for hatchery salmon).

Historic	Egg (kg × 1,000)	Fry (kg × 1,000)	Smolt (kg × 1,000)	Adult (kg × 1,000)	Catch (kg × 1,000)	Escapement (kg × 1,000)
California	2,124	4,886	3,030	34,234	2,000	32,234
Oregon	1,548	5,560	1,153	12,585	2,000	10,585
Columbia River	5,424	10,815	7,628	89,823	16,000	73,823
Washington	11,345	23,281	10,881	117,556	10,000	107,556
British Columbia	17,061	40,676	16,976	173,999	10,000	163,999
Alaska	42,554	93,361	37,004	446,140	10,000	436,140
Total	80,056	178,578	76,671	874,337	50,000	824,337

Recent wild	Egg (kg × 1,000)	Fry (kg × 1,000)	Smolt (kg × 1,000)	Adult (kg × 1,000)	Catch (kg × 1,000)	Escapement (kg × 1,000)
California	48	87	180	1,896	1,043	421
Oregon	284	920	631	4,483	2,466	1,227
Columbia River	NA	NA	NA	NA	NA	NA
Washington	2,563	4,351	2,078	28,011	15,406	10,409
British Columbia	9,153	14,394	4,982	98,753	54,314	39,357
Alaska	47,345	76,780	23,255	534,375	293,906	216,556
Total	59,392	96,532	31,126	667,518	367,135	267,970

Recent hatchery	Egg (kg × 1,000)	Fry (kg × 1,000)	Smolt (kg × 1,000)	Adult (kg × 1,000)	Catch (kg × 1,000)	Escapement (kg × 1,000)
California	45	NA	1,373	2,082	1,562	468
Oregon	18	NA	786	558	418	126
Columbia River	171	0	6,301	12,187	9,140	2,742
Washington	43	39	1,195	1,521	1,141	342
British Columbia	594	225	2,138	21,514	15,980	4,794
Alaska	1,503	1,988	2,512	48,791	33,471	10,041
Total	2,373	2,252	14,303	86,653	61,712	18,514

| Present total | 61,766 | 98,785 | 45,429 | 754,171 | 428,847 | 286,484 |

TABLE 3. Comparison of biomass estimates for Alaska versus British Columbia and the Pacific Northwest states.

Alaska	Egg (kg × 1,000)	Fry (kg × 1,000)	Smolt (kg × 1,000)	Adult (kg × 1,000)	Catch (kg × 1,000)	Escapement (kg × 1,000)
Historic	42,554	93,361	37,004	446,140	10,000	436,140
Recent wild	47,345	76,780	23,255	534,375	293,906	216,556
Recent hatchery	1,503	1,988	2,512	48,791	33,471	10,041

Pacific Northwest including B.C.	Egg (kg × 1,000)	Fry (kg × 1,000)	Smolt (kg × 1,000)	Adult (kg × 1,000)	Catch (kg × 1,000)	Escapement (kg × 1,000)
Historic	37,502	85,218	39,667	428,197	40,000	388,197
Recent wild	12,048	19,752	7,871	133,143	73,229	51,414
Recent hatchery	871	265	11,793	37,862	28,241	8,472

Recent as percent of historic	Egg M	Fry (%)	Smolt (%)	Adult (%)	Catch (%)	Escapement (%)
Alaska	115	84	70	131	NA	52
PNW including B.C.	34	23	50	40	254	15

holm et al. 2000; multiple authors, this volume). It is likely that the 80 million kg of salmon eggs delivered to freshwater systems each year are also an important nutrient source for numerous aquatic organisms, including other salmonids. Salmon eggs also extend the marine-derived biomass available to aquatic systems through winter months, when ecosystem productivity is low, and thus may play an important role in increasing the winter survivorship of metabolically active organisms, as well as providing a food source for organisms that emerge in the spring before ecosystem productivity has reached a seasonal peak. Fry and smolts are both food source and consumer. The increase in biomass from egg to fry stage indicates that fry play more of the consumer role on an ecosystem basis. The decrease in biomass from fry to smolt stage indicates that mature fry and smolts are a net source of nutrients for northwest coast ecosystems.

The role that salmon play in ecosystem trophic webs is beginning to be appreciated for certain portions of aquatic systems (Cederholm et al. 2000; Bilby et al. 1996). It is incumbent upon researchers to further explore the role that the various life history stages of salmon play in aquatic systems and to further elucidate the possible effects of declining salmon biomass in these systems (Willson and Halupka 1995). Especially critical are the numerous smaller streams in the bioregion that are home to a great diversity of stocks whose low numbers put them at risk of extinction, thus eliminating the ecosystem function of salmon in these areas. Sustained production for harvest is no longer a sufficient measure of salmon managers' performance. Habitat and fisheries managers are equally responsible for the contribution that salmon make to the overall health and function of aquatic systems (Lichatowich 1996). Resource managers must protect habitat and set harvest and escapement targets that result in salmon life history stage abundances sufficient to ensure the ecological integrity of aquatic systems. This has not been the case historically or recently, and it must become so if watersheds in the bioregion are to recover their normative function.

Acknowledgments

This paper is one of four studies addressing the ecological and economic status of Pacific salmon initiated by Ecotrust and in cooperation with Institute for the Northwest. The authors wish to acknowledge financial support from the Compton, Ford, and Mead foundations and the M. J. Murdock Charitable Trust that has made this work possible. The authors thank Ted Wolf for his invaluable support and input in the evolution of this paper.

References

Bigler, B. S., D. W. Welch, J. H. Helle. 1996. A review of size trends among North Pacific salmon. (*Oncorhynchus* spp.). Canadian Journal of Fisheries and Aquatic Science 53:455–465.

Bilby, R. E., B. R. Fransen, and P. A. Bisson. 1996. Incorporation of nitrogen and carbon from spawning coho salmon into the trophic system of small streams: evidence from stable isotopes. Canadian Journal of Fisheries and Aquatic Sciences 53(1):164–173.

Bradford, M. J. 1995. Comparative review of Pacific salmon survival rates. Canadian Journal of Fisheries and Aquatic Sciences 52:1327–1338.

Cederholm, C. J., D. H. Johnson, R. E. Bilby, L. G. Dominguez, A. M. Garrett, W. E. Graeber, E. L. Greda, M. D. Kunze, B. G. Marcot, J. F. Palmisano, R. W. Plotnikoff, W. G. Pearcy, C. A. Simonstad, and P. C. Trotter. 2000. Pacific salmon and wildlife–ecological contexts, relationships, and implications for management. Special Edition Technical Report, prepared for D. H. Johnson and T. A. O'Neil, Managing Directors, Wildlife-Habitat Relationships in Oregon and Washington. Washington Department of Fish and Wildlife, Olympia, Washington.

Cederholm, C. J., D. B. Houston, D. L. Cole, and W. J. Scarlett. 1989. Fate of coho salmon (*Oncorhynchus kisutch*) carcasses in spawning streams. Canadian Journal of Fisheries and Aquatic Sciences 46(8):1347–1355.

Gresh, T., J. Lichatowich, and P. K. Schoonmaker. 2000. An estimation of historic and current levels of salmon production in the northeast Pacific ecosystem: evidence of a nutrient deficit. Fisheries 25(1):15–21.

Groot, C., and L. Margolis. 1991. Pacific salmon life histories. UBC Press, Vancouver, British Columbia.

Hewes, G. W. 1947. Aboriginal use of fishery resources in northwest North America. Ph.D. dissertation, Department of Anthropology, University of California, Berkeley, California.

Johnston, N. T., J. S. MacDonald, K. J. Hall, and P. J. Tschaplinski. 1997. A preliminary study of the role of sockeye salmon (*Oncorhynchus nerka*) as carbon and nitrogen sources for benthic insects and fishes in the 'Early Stuart' stock spawning streams, 1050 km from the ocean.

Province of British Columbia Fisheries Project Report No. RD55.

Larkin, G. A., and P. A. Slaney. 1997. Implications of trends in marine-derived nutrients flow to south coastal British Columbia salmonid production. Fisheries 22(11):16–24.

Lichatowich, J. A. 1996. Evaluating the performance of salmon management institutions: the importance of performance measures, temporal scales and production cycles. Pages 69–87 *in* D. J. Stouder, P. A. Bisson, and R. J. Naiman, editors. Pacific salmon and their ecosystems. Chapman and Hall, New York.

National Research Council (NRC). 1996. Upstream: salmon and society in the Pacific Northwest. Committee on Protection and Management of Pacific Northwest Anadromous Salmonids. National Academy of Science, Washington, D.C.

Stouder, D. J., P. A. Bisson, and R. J. Naiman, editors. 1997. Pacific salmon and their ecosystems. Chapman and Hall, New York.

Willson, M. F., and K. C. Halupka. 1995. Anadromous fish as keystone species in vertebrate communities. Conservation Biology 9:3489–3497.

American Fisheries Society Symposium 34:41–55, 2003

Assessing the Historic Contribution of Marine-Derived Nutrients to Idaho Streams

STEVEN A. THOMAS*

Biology Department, Virginia Tech, Blacksburg, Virginia 24061-0406, USA

TODD V. ROYER

Department of Natural Resources and Environmental Sciences
University of Illinois, Urbana, Illinois 61801, USA

G. WAYNE MINSHALL

Department of Biological Sciences, Idaho State University, Pocatello, Idaho 83209, USA

ERIC SNYDER

Department of Biological Sciences, Central Michigan University
Mount Pleasant, Michigan 48859, USA

Abstract.—Recent studies have shown that anadromous fish deliver ecologically significant quantities of marine-derived nitrogen (N), phosphorus (P), and organic carbon (C) to lakes, rivers, and streams of the Pacific Northwest. These marine-derived nutrients (MDN) can influence the ecological functioning of receiving streams through nutrient release and food availability. In Idaho, populations of anadromous salmon have declined dramatically with many formerly salmon-bearing streams now receiving no MDN supplementation. In order to assess how the loss of MDN may influence Idaho streams and rivers, we examined the current nutrient status of streams and rivers in Idaho with particular emphasis on the limiting role of N and P. We also generated a range of estimates of the historic and current affects of MDN on selected basins of the Salmon River, Idaho. Our analysis indicates that 25–50% of Idaho's streams are potentially nutrient limited. Further analysis suggests that N and P limitation occurred in an approximately equal number of streams. Historic contributions of MDN to the Salmon River had varying potential to influence N and P availability, ranging from undetectable to resulting in a doubling of N availability. The level of influence depended upon location within the basin and the choices made regarding some simplifying assumptions. Finally, we discuss the effectiveness of artificial fertilization as a means of compensating for lost MDN and suggest that a spiraling approach be used to design and monitor fertilization treatments.

Introduction

Production rates in freshwater ecosystems often are limited by the availability of specific nutrients, particularly nitrogen (N) and phosphorus (P). Both detrital processing and autotrophic production respond to changes in the availability of N and P (e.g., Elwood et al. 1981; Grimm and Fisher 1986; Peterson et al. 1993; Francoeur et al. 1999). Nutrient delivery to streams and lakes is primarily a physical phenomenon, with N and P moving from terrestrial sources to aquatic habitats via

*To whom correspondance should be addressed. Current address: Eco-Metrics, Inc, 322 SW 3rd St., Pendleton, Oregon 97801. Email: sthomas@eco-metrics.com

litter fall, groundwater discharge, precipitation, weathering, and, in many cases, direct additions of anthropogenic N and P. However, there are exceptions to this generic pattern. For example, in aquatic habitats with abundant cyanobacteria, fixation of atmospheric nitrogen may be a significant source of biologically available N (e.g., Grimm and Petrone 1997). Similarly, it has long been recognized that salmon decomposition contributes N and P to stream and lake ecosystems (Juday et al. 1932). However, only recently has research illustrated that anadromous salmonids deliver ecologically significant quantities of marine-derived N, P, and organic C to rivers and streams (e.g., Kline et al. 1990; Larkin and Slaney 1997; Cederholm et al. 1999; Gresh et al. 2000; Bilby et al. 2001). In this paper, we examine the extent to which salmon declines occurring within the last century have influenced the nutrient budgets of Idaho streams.

As in other ecosystems, the relative demand for N and P in streams by primary producers (e.g., algae and vascular macrophytes) and heterotrophic organisms (e.g., bacteria, fungi, and secondary consumers) results from the stoichiometric demands of resident biota. Because demand and delivery are rarely in balance, often N or P alone limits the production of freshwater ecosystems when nutrients are in short supply, although co-limitation has been documented (e.g., Rosemond et al. 1993. Tank and Webster 1998, Francoeur 2001). As a first approximation, the stoichiometry of organisms is estimated by the Redfield ratio (Redfield 1956; C:N:P in organisms is 106:16:1). From this ratio, it follows that nutrient limitation should be predictable from the molar ratio of various available forms of N and P in stream water (Lohman et al. 1991; Schanz and Juon 1983). The appropriate species of N or P used in this ratio depends upon the types of organisms present in the community of interest. Dissolved inorganic forms of N and P are often used because they are more readily available to stream microbes than are organic or particulate forms. The most commonly used ratios are total, dissolved inorganic N to soluble, reactive P (DIN:SRP) and DIN to total P (DIN:TP). In the assessment below, we begin by characterizing the current nutrient status of Idaho streams (concentrations, fluxes, and N:P ratios) in order to provide the background information necessary to assess the historical significance of MDN.

There is a growing literature base on the effects of anadromous salmon on their nursery streams. Recent research has demonstrated that nutrients released from salmon carcasses enhance stream and riparian productivity (Wipfli et al. 1999; Helfield and Naiman 2001), and the isotopic signature of marine-derived nitrogen is evident in both stream and riparian biota near salmon-spawning habitat (e.g., Kline et al. 1990; Ben-David et al. 1998; Bilby et al. 1996, 2001). Ironically, salmonid losses may be accelerated by a negative feedback loop, where declining returns impoverish the biological habitat of successive generations. Nutrient amendments that mimic historical delivery of marine-derived nutrients (in magnitude and timing) may stimulate juvenile salmon production (Slaney and Ward 1993) and increase overwintering (Scrivener and Brown 1993) and ocean survival rates (Ward et al. 1989). These observations have led to the development and application of fertilization as a remediation technique for salmon stocks in both lakes (Stockner and MacIssac 1996) and streams (Ashley and Slaney 1997).

Current field research on the effect of spawners on stream ecosystems is necessarily limited to regions where salmon populations remain abundant. Anadromous salmon once returned to central and southern Idaho in large numbers with significant populations throughout the Salmon, Clearwater, Snake, Payette, Boise, Bruneau, and Lemhi river basins (Evermann 1895, 1896). Commercial harvest, dam construction, and habitat loss have resulted in dramatic reductions in salmon stocks in Idaho (see Hassemer et al. 1997, for a review), and most stocks have been eliminated or listed as threatened or endangered pursuant to the federal Endangered Species Act. The loss of salmon and accompanying changes in nutrient loading beckon ecologist and resource managers to question whether nutrient conditions in Idaho's wilderness streams reflect historical levels and how the loss of marine-derived nutrients has affected the trophic structure of these streams. In this paper, we (1) examine the current nutrient status of streams and rivers across Idaho, including the potential for nutrient limitation; (2) provide a range of estimates of the historical contribution of MDN to the Salmon River, Idaho; and (3) briefly discuss stream fertilization in the context of nutrient spiraling.

Methods

Nutrient Concentrations and N:P Ratios in Idaho Streams

Water quality records were obtained through the USEPA-STORET database. The data query consisted of NH_4, $NO_3 + NO_2$, total phosphorus (TP), soluble reactive phosphorus (SRP), total alkalinity, and discharge. Samples from a single location, but different times, were averaged for each location. However, multiple locations from a single stream do exist and may inflate the relative importance of streams with multiple sampling stations. Further, the geographic distribution of samples is heterogeneous and, in some cases, discontinuous. Despite these caveats, the data cover much of the state and permit an initial statewide assessment of nutrient conditions in Idaho.

NH_4 values are not reported here because of the rarity of this variable in the database relative to $NO_2 + NO_3$ and because it is not expected to be abundant in the well-oxygenated, relatively high quality waters characteristic of Idaho. Therefore, DIN and $NO_2 + NO_3$ are presumed equivalent in this manuscript, for the sake of N:P calculations. In calculating N:P, both SRP and TP were used such that N:P will be referred to as either DIN:SRP or DIN:TP. In each case, the nutrient ratios were calculated as molar ratios. The predictions of nutrient limitation made with N:P ratios are commonly tested in situ with nutrient diffusing substrata (NDS; e.g., Francoeur 2001). The use of NDS to assess limitation in Idaho streams is published elsewhere (Snyder et al. 2001) and only briefly reviewed in this paper (see Discussion).

Historical Contribution of MDN to the Salmon River Basin from Chinook Salmon

We estimated the number of adult chinook salmon *Oncorhynchus tshawytscha* that returned to the Salmon River Basin in central Idaho during a 34-year period, from 1957 to 1990. This was a period of precipitous decline for chinook salmon in Idaho, and even the early portions of this period are not likely to reflect the presettlement number of fish, which were reported to "litter the banks" of central Idaho rivers by the thousands (Evermann 1895). Therefore, we feel the

1957–1990 data can be used to estimate the minimal impact of MDN on the Salmon River basin. We focus here on the Salmon River because it is the largest free-flowing, salmon-bearing system in the state, historical records are relatively complete, and its ecological condition in recent times is well documented (e.g., Minshall et al. 1992). Although other species of anadromous salmon occurred in the Salmon River, including sockeye *O. nerka*, coho *O. kisutch*, and steelhead *O. mykiss*, our analysis is limited to chinook because it was the most abundant species and has the best historical records.

Matthews and Waples (1991) reported redd counts from 1957 to 1990 for the South Fork Salmon, Middle Fork Salmon, and Upper Salmon rivers. These data were used to estimate the number of adult fish by assuming that each redd represented one female salmon. The number of males was then calculated using female:male sex ratios of 0.5:1, 1:1, and 1:1 for the South Fork Salmon, Middle Fork Salmon, and Upper Salmon rivers, respectively (Howell et al. 1985, cited in Matthews and Waples 1991). The number of adult chinook was converted to biomass by assuming a live mass of 7 kg for each fish (Fulton 1968). The amount of N and P delivered by the returning fish was calculated using a live-mass composition of 3% N and 0.36% P (Vinogradov 1953; Donaldson 1967). These are conservative estimates of the number of adult chinook salmon returning to these basins because only selected index streams were used for the redd counts reported by Matthews and Waples (1991). In addition to the main stem of each river segment, the index streams included Johnson Creek, Secesh River, and Lake Creek in the South Fork Salmon River Watershed; Loon Creek, Bear Valley Creek, Elk Creek, Marsh Creek, Sulfur Creek, and Upper Big Creek in the Middle Fork Salmon River Watershed; and Valley Creek, East Fork Salmon River, Alturas Lake Creek, Lemhi River, and the Upper Yankee Fork in the Upper Salmon River Watershed.

We evaluate the potential for marine-derived nutrients to influence nutrient concentrations in these basins by comparing the N and P loads from the decaying carcasses to DIN and SRP loads in selected Salmon River basins (August – September). STORET data and discharge from a typical hydrological year (1997) were used to calculate the increase in nutrient concentrations for the mean salmon returns during two 4-year periods, 1957–1960 and 1987–1990. For both N and P, three comparisons were made. In the most liberal approach, all salmon-derived N and P were assumed to directly enter DIN and SRP pools, respectively. In addition, all loading was assumed to occur during the August and September spawning period. In an intermediate approach, 20% of salmon N and P were assumed to enter the dissolved inorganic pools, while the remaining 80% was lost in other forms (e.g., as dissolved organic N and P). In the most conservative estimate, the 20% loading rate of N and P was assessed with respect to the annual flux of DIN and SRP, rather than that occurring during the spawning period only.

Results

The water quality records used in this study were not evenly distributed within Idaho (Figure 1), but rather emphasize economically important basins and/or river sections (e.g., Snake River, Boise River) while underrepresenting locations with limited access. One consequence of this sampling distribution is that summary statistics (e.g., mean and median) are likely to be greater than values generated from a random sampling of Idaho rivers. Therefore, we suggest that values presented in this manuscript be viewed as liberal with respect to current nutrient concentrations and fluxes, but conservative with respect to the historic contribution of MDN to river nutrient budgets.

As expected, nutrient concentrations were not distributed normally, but rather, were skewed toward higher concentrations due to the influence of a few extreme values. For NO_3, SRP, and TP, the skewedness resulted in mean values greater than or equal to the 75th percentile (Figure 2). The mean and the median were more similar in the alkalinity dataset, possibly due to the larger number of sampling locations for this variable. N and P concentrations were unrelated to discharge, but variability tended to be highest in streams with discharge less than 1 m^3/s.

Spatial Patterns in Nutrient Concentrations and Nutrient Provinces

The USEPA STORET database provided adequate coverage ($N = 746$) of alkalinity conditions in Idaho to identify a clear gradient in conditions across the state. In southeastern Idaho, total al-

kalinity was consistently above 100 mg $CaCO_3/L$ and often exceeded 200 mg $CaCO_3/L$. Alkalinity values consistently decline northward with values rarely exceeding 50 mg $CaCO_3/L$ in northern Idaho. In central Idaho, there was a tendency for higher values (>50 mg $CaCO_3/L$) along the western edge of Idaho and lower values in the central and eastern third of this region.

In contrast, spatial patterns were less apparent in N and P concentrations. In part, this was a result of fewer sites where NO_3, SRP, and TP concentrations were available. It also may result from susceptibility of these variables to loading changes associated with human activities. The lack of clear spatial patterns inhibited our ability to partition Idaho into distinct provinces based on water chemistry alone. Thus, we established provinces of nutrient status (Figure 3; Table 1) based on the available data for water chemistry and on geographic, vegetation, and land-use criteria. Of the nine provinces, anadromous salmon historically occurred in large numbers in provinces II, III, IV, VII, and at least the Bruneau River in Province VI. This combined area contains a substantial portion of the stream and river systems in Idaho. Streams of this area quite likely received marine-derived nutrients, whether the contribution of MDN constituted a significant nutrient supplement is dependent on discharge, ambient nutrient concentration, and number of spawning salmon (see below).

Nutrient Limitation in Idaho

Both mean and median concentrations of DIN and SRP are above levels previously shown to limit biotic processes in streams (e.g., Davis and Minshall 1999; Lohman et al. 1991; Grimm and Fisher 1986; Manuel-Faler et al. 1984; Elwood et al. 1981; Figure 2; Table 2). Assuming N saturation at 100 mg DIN/L, approximately one quarter of all water quality records suggest N limitation. A similar proportion of sites have SRP values below those considered to be limiting (10 mg P/L). These data indicate that 25–50% of the sites we used in this analysis were potentially nutrient-limited. Nitrogen limitation is expected when the ratio of DIN to SRP is less than 16, and P limitation is indicated when that ratio exceeds 20. In the current database, approximately 55% and 36% of all sites were predicted to be N- and P-limited, respectively (Table 2), assuming light, grazing, or some other factor is not limiting production. Re-

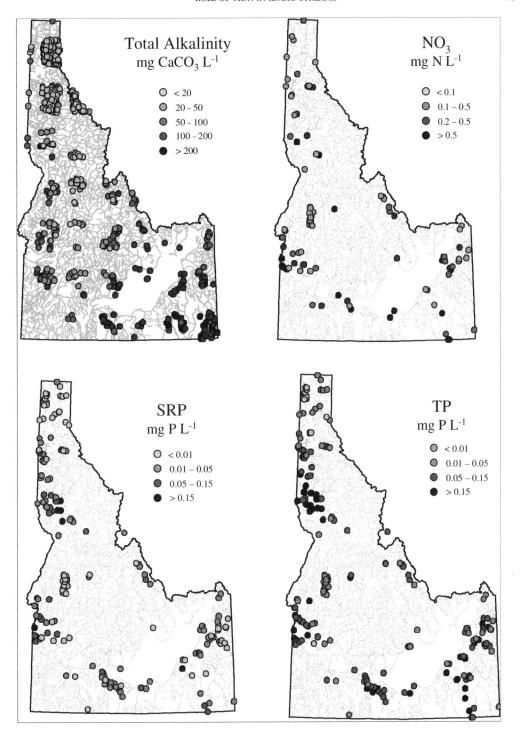

FIGURE 1. Total alkalinity (as mg /L CaCO₃), NO₃, soluble reactive phosphorus, and total phosphorus in Idaho streams. Symbols represent the mean off all data collected from a single location. Sample number (*N* size) ranged from 5 to more than 100. Data are from the USEPA-STORET database, the Idaho Department of Environmental Quality's Beneficial Use Reconnaissance Program (IDEQ-BURP), and other literature sources.

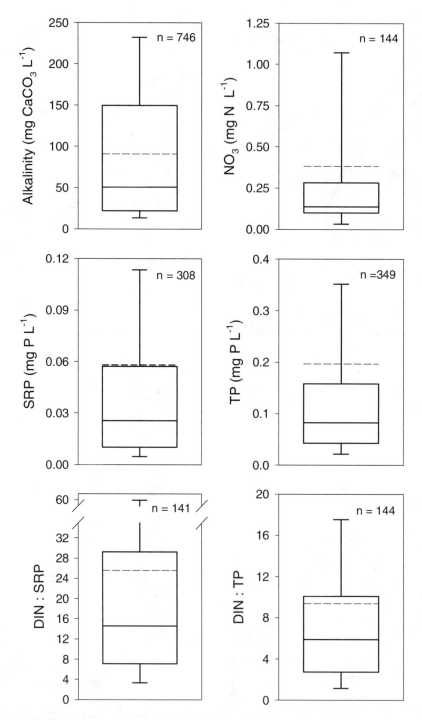

Figure 2. Box plots of alkalinity, nitrate (NO_3), soluble reactive phosphorus (SRP), total phosphorus (TP), NO_3:SRP, and NO3:TP values in Idaho. The dotted line represents the mean; the solid lines indicate the median; and the top and bottom of the box equal the 75th and 25th percentiles, respectively. The top and bottom of the whiskers equal the 90th and 10th percentiles, respectively. Data are from the USEPA-STORET database, the Idaho Department of Environmental Quality's Beneficial Use Reconnaissance Program (IDEQ-BURP), and other literature sources.

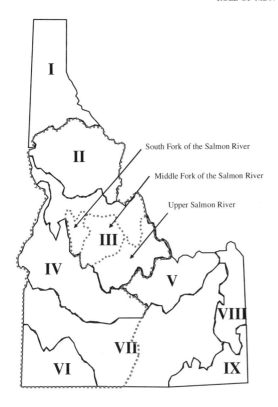

South Fork of the Salmon River

Middle Fork of the Salmon River

Upper Salmon River

FIGURE 3. Map of the geographic provinces described in Table 1. The dashed line delineates the region historically accessed by anadromous fish. The dotted lines identify the different subbasins of the Salmon River for which we assess the influence of marine derived nutrients.

stricting the analysis to sites with data on both nutrients and with at least one nutrient below a limiting concentration indicated that 30% and 31% of those sites are N- and P-limited, respectively. Spatially, neither DIN:SRP nor DIN:TP display a recognizable pattern across Idaho. At more local scales, it appears that N:P approaches or exceeds 20 in sites from larger and topographically lower watersheds, likely reflecting the influence of agriculture in these regions.

Historical Contribution of MDN to the Salmon River Basin from Chinook Salmon

From 1957 to 1990 the amount of N and P estimated to have been delivered to the Salmon River basin in the form of chinook biomass declined sharply (Figure 4). The greatest input of marine-derived nutrients occurred in the first year of the period, 1957, with nearly 6 metric tons of N returned to the basin in the form of chinook carcasses. In our most liberal analysis (100% mineralization, spawning period), DIN and SRP concentrations in the SF Salmon basin increased 16.8 and 1.9 mg/L, respectively, for the first period of analysis, 1957–1960 (Table 3). These loadings translate to 129% and 27% increases in DIN and SRP, respectively (using mean nutrient concentrations during the spawning period). The increase was not as dramatic in the other basins (Table 3), and when calculated for the entire Salmon River Basin, the increase was only 5% and 1% for DIN and SRP, respectively, during 1957–1960. Both intermediate and conservative approaches indicated minor enrichment during this time period (Table 3). The number of spawners was considerably reduced by the second period of analysis (1987–1990), and even our liberal approach suggested little nutrient enrichment is occurring under current spawning densities (Table 3).

Discussion

Nutrient Conditions in Idaho Streams

Our analysis indicated a spatial pattern in nutrient status across the state of Idaho. The pattern was most evident in the data for alkalinity (Figure 1), although this may be an artifact of the less extensive spatial coverage of the N and P dataset. The relative ease in which alkalinity is measured should make alkalinity robust to analytical variation. Therefore, we suggest that the data reflect a real pattern in bedrock geology. In general, nutrient status increases from northern and central Idaho to southeastern Idaho. Within the spatial gradient, local influences can lead to higher than expected nutrient concentrations. This was the case for SRP and TP in agricultural regions in the northern portion of the state (Figure 1).

Across the state as a whole, we expect many streams to be nutrient-limited particularly those in the central and northern areas of Idaho. Using nutrient diffusing substrata (see Francoeur 2001, for review), primary productivity in a variety of Idaho streams has been found to be limited by N, P, or, occasionally, by both elements (Snyder et al. 2001). Snyder et al. (2001) found amendment with N to stimulate primary production in the Clearwater, Lochsa, and Selway rivers, all of which are located in Province II (Figure 3) and were formerly major salmon-bearing systems. Province III, the

TABLE 1. Hydrological provinces of Idaho. Nutrient ranges are based on the USEPA STORET database, salmonid presence is based on available literature (see text), and MDN influences are inferred.

Province	Name	Rivers	Vegetation and land-use characteristics	Nutrient condition	Fish characteristics	MDN influence
I	North Idaho Panhandle	Couer d' Alene R. St. Joe R. St. Maries R. Clark Fork R.[1] Kootenai R.[1]	Montane forest High precipitation Timber production Mining	Alkalinity: <20 mg CaCO$_3$/L Nutrients: <150 µg DIN/L, Limitation: frequent, N and P limitation equally likely	Kokanee (land-locked *Oncorhynchus nerka*)	None: no connection to the ocean Lake-run kokanee in the Kootenai R. and Clark Fork R.
II	Clearwater River System	Clearwater R. Lochsa R. Selway R.	Montane forest Moderate precipitation Largely wilderness and national forests	Alkalinity: low in headwaters, higher in lowlands near Lewiston, Idaho. Nutrients: typically >100 µg DIN/L Limitation: infrequent, N and P limitation equally likely	Chinook (*Onchorynchus tshawytscha*) Steelhead (*Onchorynchus mykiss*) Coho (*Oncorhynchus kisutch*)–extinct	Historical runs of Snake R. chinook and steelhead. Current stocks of chinook are low and access is limited by Dworshak reservoir.
III	Salmon River	Salmon R. SF Salmon R. MF Salmon R. Lemhi R. Pahsimeroi R. Panthor Cr.	Semiarid Largely wilderness and national forests Timber production Agriculture Mining	Alkalinity: generally <50 mg CaCO$_3$/L Nutrients: little N and P data, available data suggest that DIN < 100 µg N/L, SRP < 50 µg P/L, TP < 100 µg P/L Limitation: frequency poorly represented, available data suggest N limitation most likely	Chinook Sockeye (*Onchorynchus nerka*) Steelhead Coho–extinct	Sole sockeye stock in Idaho Historically large chinook and steelhead runs Modern stocks have been severely reduced
IV	Lower Snake River Tributaries	Wood R. Boise R. Payette R. Weiser R.	Large tracks of national forests Semiarid Timber production Livestock grazing Irrigated agriculture Urbanization	Alkalinity: 20–100 mg CaCO$_3$/L Nutrients: <300 µg DIN/L (often <100), <10 µg SRP/L, <100 µg TP/L Limitation: common and N limitation indicated	Chinook Coho Steelhead	Historical: extinct Current: none; blocked by Hells Canyon dams

TABLE 1. continued.

Province	Name	Rivers	Vegetation and land-use characteristics	Nutrient condition	Fish characteristics	MDN influence
V	The Lost Rivers	Big Lost R. Little Lost R. Birch Cr. Camas Cr.	Large tracts of national forest Semiarid to arid Livestock grazing Irrigated agriculture	Alkalinity: 100–200 mg CaCO$_3$/L Nutrients: little data available, available data suggest 100–300 µg DIN/L, <10 µg SRP/L, <100 µg TP/L Limitation: insufficient data	Native and hatchery trout	None: no connection to the ocean
VI	Desert Rivers of SW Idaho	Bruneau R. Jarbridge R. Owyhee R.	Arid Livestock grazing	No data	Extinct chinook and coho	Historical: unknown Current: none
VII	Snake River Plain	Snake R. Wood R. Salmon Falls Cr.	Arid to semi-arid Extensive grazing Extensive agriculture Urbanization	Alkalinity: 50–200 mg CaCO$_3$/L Nutrients: >100 µg DIN/L (often >300 µg TP/L Limitation: rare, N:P ratios suggest N limitation	Extinct chinook and coho Steelhead (Oncorhynchus mykiss)	Historical: unknown Current: none; blocked by Hells Canyon dams
VIII	Upper Snake River Highlands	Henry's Fork and the Middle Fork of the Snake R. Falls R. Teton River Blackfoot R.	Large tracks of national forest Semiarid Moderate livestock grazing Irrigated agriculture in lowlands	Alkalinity: 20–300 mg CaCO$_3$/L Nutrients: <100 µg DIN/L in highlands, elevated in lowlands, <10 µg SRP/L in highlands, 10–100 in lowlands, 100–500 µg TP/L Limitation: N limitation frequently suggested	Native and hatchery trout	None: blocked by Salmon Falls and other natural obstructions
IX	Great Basin	Bear River	Basin and Range topography Moderate tracts of national forest Irrigated agriculture Extensive livestock grazing	Alakalinity: 100–500 mg CaCO$_3$/L Nutrients: <100 µg DIN/L, 10–100 µg Limitation: rare, high P suggests N limitation likely	Native and hatchery trout	None: no connection to ocean

[1] Rivers that originate elsewhere but flow through a specific region.

TABLE 2. Alkalinity, nitrogen, and phosphorus concentrations and DIN:SRP and DIN:TP in Idaho streams. Data are from 1984 to 1998 and obtained from the USEPA-STORET database.

	Total alkalinity (mg CaCO$_3$/L)	Nitrate + Nitrite (µg N/L)	Total phosphorus (µg P/L)	P – PO$_4$ (µg P/L)		DIN/SRP	DIN/TP
n size	746	144.0	349.0	308.0		141.0	144.0
median	50	137.0	82.0	26.0		14.6	5.9
mean	91	384.0	196.0	57.0		25.6	9.6
25th percentile	22	100.0	43.0	10.0		7.1	2.8
75th percentile	150	282.0	158.0	57.0		29.2	10.5
% limited* by N or P		24.3	3.7	24.4	% <16	55.3	86.1
% saturated* by N or P		75.7	96.3	75.6	% >20	35.5	8.3
					% 16–20	9.2	5.6

* The threshold between limitation and saturation is assumed to occur at DIN and SRP concentrations of 100 µg N/L and 10 µg P/L, respectively.

Salmon River basin, was the other major salmon producing area in Idaho, but unfortunately is an area with few data on stream nutrients. Given the proximity of provinces II and III and the data on water chemistry that do exist, we expect streams in the Salmon River Basin to also be N-limited. The other provinces contain numerous local impacts, primarily agriculture, grazing, mining, and urbanization, which confound broad-scale predictions of nutrient limitation.

The Role of Marine-Derived Nutrients in Idaho Streams

Our analysis for the Salmon River Basin indicates that nutrient delivery by anadromous salmon may have been ecologically significant under historical spawning densities. However, this analysis is not definitive, and our conclusion should be viewed as speculative for it relies on several assumptions. For example, we assume that the

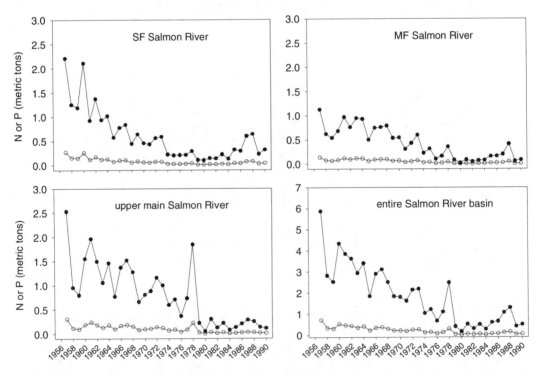

FIGURE 4. Trends in marine derived nutrient (MDN) loading from 1957 to 1990 in various subbasins of the Salmon River.

TABLE 3. Loading of N and P and subsequent enrichment in basins of the Salmon River, Idaho. Estimates are based on mean salmon returns occurring between 1957–1960 and 1987–1990. To control for annual variation in discharge (Q), all estimates were calculated using a standard hydrograph (1997) representing a 'typical' water year for the Salmon River basin. Aug.–Sept. is the presumed spawning duration for Salmon River chinook salmon. Discharge during Aug.–Sept was 12.3% of annual Q during 1997. The percent mineralization refers to the amount of N and P assumed to directly enter dissolved inorganic pools. Δ Concentration = change in concentration.

River	Period	Total delivery from carcasses (metric tons)		Δ Concentration: 100% mineralization Aug.–Sept. (μg/L)		Δ Concentration: 100% mineralization Aug.–Sept. (μg/L)		Δ Concentration: 100% mineralization Annual (μg/L)	
		N	P	DIN	SRP	DIN	SRP	DIN	SRP
SF Salmon	1957–1960	1.69	0.20	16.80	1.90	3.36	0.38	0.41	0.05
River	1987–1990	0.44	0.05	4.40	0.50	0.88	0.10	0.11	0.01
MF Salmon	1957–1960	0.74	0.09	3.30	0.40	0.66	0.08	0.08	0.01
River	1987–1990	0.19	0.02	0.80	0.10	0.16	0.02	0.02	0.00
Upper main	1957–1960	1.46	0.17	8.20	1.00	1.64	0.20	0.20	0.02
Salmon River	1987–1990	0.20	0.02	1.10	0.10	0.22	0.02	0.03	0.00
Entire Salmon	1957–1960	3.89	0.47	6.10	0.70	1.22	0.14	0.15	0.02
River basin	1987–1990	0.83	0.10	1.30	0.10	0.26	0.02	0.03	0.00

vast majority of MDN enters local food webs either through mineralization and uptake, direct consumption of the particulate carcass, or assimilation of leached constituents (dissolved organic carbon). We also assume that entry of MDN into lotic food webs occurs prior to spring snowmelt, thus avoiding direct loss from receiving basin by export during spring runoff. This is to say we believe that the nutrient comparisons based on 100% mineralization during the spawning period best represent actual conditions, even though entry of MDN may into lotic food webs may not first pass through inorganic forms of N or P.

Despite the observation that much of the annual flux of N and P may be in organic forms (Gross and Wurtsbaugh 1994), we suspect that salmon organic matter is highly labile, rapidly exploited by local communities, and, therefore, unlikely to be exported directly from the basin during periods of base flow. Rapid entry of MDN into lotic food webs (via assimilation of mineralized N and P or direct consumption of organic forms) may quickly result in increased food availability to juvenile salmon and increase overwintering survival (Scrivener and Brown 1993). These predictions are supported by rapid carcass decay rates (0.02–0.04/d; Minshall 1991) and considerable documentation of the rapid assimilation of inorganic N (see Thomas et al. 2001) and P (e.g., Mulholland et al. 1997) in streams. Little information is available on the longitudinal dynamics (e.g., export) of dissolved and fine particulate organic matter derived directly from carcasses. However, existing data on FPOM (Min-

shall et al. 2000; Thomas et al. 2001) and DOM (Hall 1995) transport in streams suggest that this material is rapidly lost from the water column through deposition and assimilation, respectively. If most organic forms of N and P that are not derived from salmon carcasses are refractory by comparison, then inorganic N and P fluxes should approximate the relative amounts of biologically available N and P in that system. Together, the arguments above suggest that the ecological significance of MDN loadings is best assessed by comparing those loads to inorganic fluxes during the spawning period, represented by 100% mineralization during August–September (Table 3).

The assumptions made above are liberal, but several other aspects of our analysis are conservative and provide further support for our conclusion regarding the significance of MDN in Idaho rivers. For example, chinook returns had already declined substantially by 1957–1960, the earliest years for which data were available. Presettlement salmon densities (Everman 1896) may have been as much as twice those reported by Matthews and Waples (1991). In addition, our analysis was based on the mixing of MDN export into the total hydrological flux of specific basins, when in fact, the distribution of spawners, and thus carcasses, would not have been evenly distributed. Rather, particular streams and specific stream reaches would have received the majority of the marine-derived N and P, and these local areas would have experienced nutrient amendments well above those suggested by our analysis. Also, only chinook salmon are included in our analysis despite the historical presence of other salmon species (e.g., sockeye and coho) in these river systems.

One documented avenue of MDN loss from stream channels that we have yet to discuss is loss via foraging by mammals and birds. Helfield and Naiman (2001) documented considerable movement of salmon derived nitrogen into riparian vegetation. However, lateral losses of MDN differ from hydrological export in that materials remain within the stream-riparian corridor and are likely to reenter the stream at a later date. Therefore, we consider lateral movement of MDN into riparian habitats an internal process rather than a loss from the system.

Although this analysis has focused on the role of marine-derived N and P, salmon carcasses represent a potentially significant source of labile organic carbon to streams. Though an assessment of the relative importance of this energy supplement is beyond the scope of this paper, the role of carcasses as food may be as significant or more significant than the delivery of N and P into receiving streams. In summary, our analysis and the arguments presented above suggest that historical rates of primary and secondary productivity, and the timing of that activity, may have been substantially different from those observed today, especially in the Salmon River Basin where human activities may not have replaced the historical delivery of N and P by salmon.

The Role of Artificial Fertilization

Because eutrophication is such a prevalent issue, invoking fertilization as a remediation tool is likely to be met with widespread skepticism. Therefore, it seems likely that fertilization will be permitted only when (a) salmon decline in a specific basin has reached a threshold level of concern; (b) nutrient limitation is clearly indicated; (c) the historical contribution of MDN has been documented, or at least strongly suspected, to be substantial; and (d) current knowledge of nutrient dynamics is used to predict nutrient fate. Much of this paper addresses points (a–c), and we now turn to a brief discussion of (d). Nutrient dynamics in streams are currently described using a conceptual and numerical framework referred to as nutrient spiraling. Originally coined by Webster (1975), the term spiraling refers to the successive downstream displacement of a nutrient as it cycles through individual ecosystem compartments. Stated another way, spiraling is simply a spatially explicit approach to the study of nutrient cycling. Newbold et al. (1981, 1983, 1992) developed a variety of empirical relationships that describe specific aspects of nutrient spiraling. For example, the distance traveled by the average atom of an inorganic nutrient is defined as the uptake length (S_W: m) and equals the flux of a given nutrient (F_W; mg/s) divided by the product of uptake rate (U; mg, m^{-2} s^{-1}) and stream width (w; m). Not surprisingly, S_W is strongly influenced by Q (Peterson et al. 2001). One method of removing the influence of stream size on S_W, and thereby generating a more conservative parameter, is to convert S_W to an uptake velocity (v_i: mm/s) using

$$v_i = (v_{wat}*z*1000)/S_W,$$

where v_{wat} is mean water velocity (m/s) and z equals mean stream depth (m). Published values of v_i range from 0.03 to 0.13 mm/s, 0.006 to 0.16 mm/s, and 0.007 to 0.18 mm/s for NH_4, NO_3, and PO_4, respectively. The application of the spiraling framework to fertilization experiments should be obvious. The values presented above can be used to derive first approximations of the longitudinal distance over which elevated nutrient conditions should exist during a fertilization treatment. For example, in a stream with Q = 1.0 m^3/s and z = 0.30 m, w = 8.0 m and v_{wat} = 0.42 m/s, the mean travel distance of NH_4 (S_W) is expected to be between 1–4 km. When predicting S_W, we suggest using the upper end of these ranges when a nutrient is expected to be limiting and values toward the lower limits in non-limiting cases. The scenario above predicts the distance of nutrient enrichment during the early stages of nutrient additions. As the biotic community adjusts to elevated nutrient availability, we predict that the longitudinal profile of nutrient enrichment will change, initially becoming steeper due to greater biotic demand (increasing U), but ultimately elongating due to mineralization of assimilated nutrients. However, temporal changes in the longitudinal profile of nutrient concentrations that accompany long-term nutrient additions (greater than one month) are poorly understood and represent an arena in which fishery biologists and stream ecosystem ecologists could collaborate in a mutually beneficial context.

In summary, understanding the ecological consequences of declining MDN imports to Idaho rivers and others in the Pacific Northwest is a pursuit that will require collaboration between representatives of various fields of aquatic science (e.g., fisheries biology and aquatic biogeochemistry) that are frequently isolated from one another. Often thought of as an applied issue, the ecological implications of salmon loss and the responses of stream ecosystems to artificial fertilization can provide a test of our theoretical understanding of streams and, thereby, provide an opportunity for basic and applied researchers to interact and mutually benefit.

References

APHA (American Public Health Association). 1996. Standard methods for the examination of water and wastewater. 19th Edition. American Public Health Association, Washington, D.C.

Ashley, K. E., and P. A. Slaney. 1997. Accelerating recovery of stream, river and pond productivity by low-level nutrient replacement. Chapter 13 *in* P. A. Salney and D. Zaldokas, editors. Fish habitat rehabilitation procedures. British Columbia Ministry of Environment, Lands and Parks. Watershed Restoration Technical Circular No. 9.

Baker, M. A., C. N. Dahm, and H. M. Valett. 1999. Acetate retention and metabolism in the hyporheic zone of a mountain stream. Limnology and Oceanography 44:1530–1539.

Ben-David, M., T. A. Hanley, and D. M. Schell. 1998. Fertilization of terrestrial vegetation by spawning Pacific salmon: the role of flooding and predator activity. Oikos 83:47–55.

Bilby, R. E., B. R. Fransen, and P. A. Bison. 1996. Incorporation of nitrogen and carbon from spawning coho salmon into the trophic system of small streams: evidence from stable isotopes. Canadian Journal of Fisheries and Aquatic Sciences 53:164–173.

Bilby, R. E., B. R. Fransen, J. K. Walter, and W. J. Scarlett. 2001. Preliminary evaluation of the use of nitrogen stable isotopes to establish escapement levels for pacific salmon. Fisheries 26(1):6–14.

Cederholm, C. J., M. D. Kunze, T. Murota, and A. Sabatani. 1999. Pacific salmon carcasses: essential contributions of nutrients and energy for aquatic and terrestrial ecosystems. Fisheries 24(10):6–15.

Davis, J. C., and G. W. Minshall. 1999. Nitrogen and phosphorus uptake in two Idaho (USA) headwater wilderness streams. Oecologia 119:247–255.

Donaldson, J. H. 1967. The phosphorus budget of Iliamna Lake, Alaska as related to the cyclic abundance of sockeye salmon. Doctoral dissertation, University of Washington, Seattle.

Elwood, J. W., J. D. Newbold, A. F. Trimble, and R. W. Stark. 1981. The limiting role of phosphorus in a woodland stream ecosystem: effects of P enrichment on leaf decomposition and primary producers. Ecology 62:146–158.

Evermann, B. W. 1895. A preliminary report upon salmon investigations in Idaho in 1894. Bulletin of the US Fish Commission XV:253–284.

Evermann, B. W. 1896. A report upon salmon investigations in the headwater of the Columbia River, in the state of Idaho, in 1895, together with notes upon the fishes observed in that state in 1894 and 1895. Bulletin of the US Fish Commission XVI:151–202.

Francoeur, S. N., B. J. F. Biggs, R. A. Smith, an R. L. Lowe. 1999. Nutrient limitation of algal biomass accrual in streams: seasonal patterns and a comparison of methods. Journal of the North American Benthological Society 18:242–260.

Fulton, L. A. 1968. Spawning areas and abundance of chinook salmon (*Oncorhynchus tshawyt-scha*) in the Columbia River basin–past and present. US Fish and Wildlife Service Special Scientific Report–Fisheries No. 571, Washington, D.C.

Francoeur, S. N. 2001. Meta-analysis of lotic nutrient amendment experiments: detecting and quantifying subtle responses. Journal of the North American Benthological Society 20:358–368.

Gresh, T., J. Lichatowich, and P. Schoonmaker. 2000. An estimation of historic and current levels of salmon production in the northeast Pacific ecosystem. Fisheries 25(1):15–21.

Grimm, N. B., and K. C. Petrone. 1997. Nitrogen fixation in a desert stream ecosystem. Biogeo-chemistry 37:33–61.

Grimm, N. B., and S. G. Fisher. 1986. Nitrogen limitation in a Sonoran desert stream. Journal of the North American Benthological Society 5:2–15.

Gross, H. P., and W. Wurtsbaugh. 1994. Water and nutrient budgets of the Sawtooth Valley Lakes. Pages 7–29 *in* D. Teuschner and D. Taki, editors. Snake River sockeye salmon habitat and limnological research. U.S. Department of Energy DE-B179–91BP22548.

Hall, R. O., and J. L. Meyer. 1998. The trophic significance of bacteria in a detritus-based stream food web. Ecology 79(6):1995–2012.

Helfield, J. M., and R. J. Naiman. 2001. Effects of salmon-derived nitrogen on riparian forest growth and implications for stream productivity. Ecology 82:2403–2409.

Hassemer P. F., S. W. Kiefer, and C. E. Petrosky. 1997. Idaho's salmon: can we count every last one? Pages 113–126 in D. J. Stouder, P. A. Bisson, and R. J. Naiman, editors. Pacific salmon and their ecosystems: status and future options. Chapman and Hall, New York.

Juday, C. W. H. Rich, G. I. Kemmerer, and A. Mann. 1932. Limnological studies of Karluk Lake, Alaska, 1926–1930. Bulletin of the Bureau of Fisheries 57:407–436.

Kline, T. C., J. J. Goering, O. A. Mathison, P. H. Poe, and P. L. Parker. 1990. Recycling of elements transported upstream by runs of Pacific salmon: I. d^{15}N and d^{13}C evidence in Sashin Creek, Southeastern Alaska.

Larkin, G. A., and P. A. Slaney. 1997. Implications of trends in marine-derived nutrient influx to south coastal British Columbia salmonid production. Fisheries 22:16–24.

Lohman, K., J. R. Jones, and C. Baysinger-Daniel. 1991. Experimental evidence for nitrogen limitation in a northern Ozark stream. Journal of the North American Benthological Society 10:14–23.

Manuel-Faler, C. Y., G. W. Minshall, R. W. Dunn, and D. A. Bruns. 1984. *In situ* nitrogen enrichment experiments in two Idaho (USA) streams. Environmental Monitoring and Assessment 4:67–79.

Matthews, G. M., and R. S. Waples. 1991. Status review for Snake River spring and summer chinook salmon. NOAA Technical Memorandum NMFS F/NWC-200, Portland, Oregon.

Minshall, G. W., 1992. Stream ecosystem dynamics of the Salmon River, Idaho: an 8th-order system. Journal of the North American Bentho-logical Society 11:111–137.

Minshall, G. W., E. Hitchcock, and J. R. Barnes. 1991. Decomposition of rainbow trout (*Oncorynchus mykiss*) carcasses in a forest stream ecosystem occupied by nonanadromous fish populations. Canadian Journal of Fisheries Aquatic Sciences 48:191–195.

Minshall, G. W., S. A. Thomas, J. D. Newbold, M. T. Monaghan, and C. E Cushing. 2000. Physical factors influencing fine organic particle transport and deposition in streams. Journal of the North American Benthological Society 19:1–16.

Newbold, J. D., J. W. Elwood, R. V. O'Neill, and W. VanWinkle. 1981. Measuring nutrient spiralling in streams. Canadian Journal of Fisheries and Aquatic Sciences 38: 860–863.

Newbold, J. D., J. W. Elwood, R. V. O'Neill, and A. L. Sheldon. 1983. Phosphorus dynamics in a woodland stream ecosystem: a study of nutrient spiralling. Ecology 64:1249–1265.

Newbold, J. D. 1992. Cycles and spirals of nutrients. Pages 370–408 *in* P. Calow and G. E. Petts, editors. The rivers handbook. Blackwell Scientific Publications, Oxford.

Peterson, B. J., L. Deegan, J. Helfrich, J. E. Hobbie, M. Hullar, B. Moller, T. E. Ford, A. Hershey, A. Hiltner, G. Kipphut, M. A. Lock, D. M. Fiebig, V. McKinley, M. C. Miller, J. R. Vestal, R. Ventullo, and G. Volk. 1993. Biological responses of a tundra river to fertilization. Ecology 74:653–672.

Peterson, B. J., W. M. Wollheim, P. J. Mulholland, J. R. Webster, J. L. Meyer, J. L. Tank, E. Marti, W. B. Bowden, H. M. Valett, A. E. Hershey, W. H. McDowell, W. K. Dodds, S. K. Hamilton, S. Gregory, and D. J. Morrall. 2001. Control of nitrogen export from watersheds by headwater streams. Science 292:86–90.

Redfield, A. C. 1956. The biological control of chemical factors in the environment. American Scientist 46:205–221.

Rosemond, A. D., P. J. Mulholland, and J. W. Elwood. 1993. Top-down and bottom-up control of stream periphyton: effects of nutrients and herbivores. Ecology 74:1264–1280.

Schanz, F., and H. Juon. 1983. Two different methods of evaluating nutrient limitation of periphyton bioassays, using water from the River Rhine and eight of its tributaries. Hydro-biologia 102:187–195.

Scrivener, J. C., and T. G. Brown. 1993. Impact and complexity from forest practices on streams and their salmonid fisheries in British Columbia. Pages 41–49 in G. Schooner and S. Asselin, editors. Le developpement du saumon Atlantique au Quebec: connaitre les regles du jeu pour reussir. Colloque international de la Federation Quebe-coise pour le saumon Atlantique, Quebec.

Slaney, P. A., and B. R. Ward. 1993. Experimental fertilization of nutrient deficient streams in British Columbia. Pages 128–141 in G. Schooner and S. Asselin, editors. Le developpement du saumon atlantique au Quebec: connaitre les regles du jeu pour reussir. Colloque international de la Federation quebecoise pour le saumon Atlantique, Quebec.

Snyder, E. B., C. T. Robinson, G. W. Minshall, and S. R. Rushforth. In press. Regional patterns in periphyton accrual and diatom assemblage structure in a heterogeneous nutrient landscape. Canadian Journal of Fisheries and Aquatic Sciences.

Stockner, J. G., and E. A. MacIssac. 1996. British Columbia lake enrichment programme: two decades of habitat enhancement for sockeye salmon. Regulated Rivers: Research and Management 12:547–561.

Tank, J. T., and J. W. Webster. 1998. Interaction of substrate and nutrient availability on wood biofilm processes in streams. Ecology 79:2168–2179.

Thomas, S. A., J. D. Newbold, M. T. Monaghan, G. W. Minshall, T. Georgian, and C. E. Cushing. 2001. The influence of particle size on seston deposition in streams. Limnology and Oceanography 46:1415–1424.

Vinogradov, A. P. 1953. The elementary chemical composition of marine organisms. J. Efron and J. K. Setlow, translators. Yale University Press, New Haven, Connecticut.

Ward, B. R., P. A. Slaney, A. R. Facchin, and R. W. Land. 1989. Size-biased survival in steelhead trout (*Oncorhynchus mykiss*)–back calculated lengths from adults scales compared to migrating smolts at the Keough River, British Columbia. Canadian Journal of Fisheries and Aquatic Sciences 46:1853–1858.

Webster, J. R. 1975. Analysis of potassium and calcium dynamics in stream ecosystem on three southern Appalachian watersheds of contrasting vegetation. Doctoral dissertation. University of Georgia, Athens, Georgia.

Wipfli, M. S., J. P. Hudson, D. T. Chaloner, and J. P. Caouette. 1999. Influence of salmon spawner densities on stream productivity in Southeast Alaska. Canadian Journal of Fisheries and Aquatic Sciences 56:1600–1611.

Ecosystem Responses

American Fisheries Society Symposium 34:59–69, 2003

Isotopic Evidence for Enrichment of Salmon-Derived Nutrients in Vegetation, Soil, and Insects in Riparian Zones in Coastal British Columbia

THOMAS E. REIMCHEN, DEANNA D. MATHEWSON, MORGAN D. HOCKING, AND JONATHAN MORAN

Department of Biology, University of Victoria
P.O. Box 3020, Victoria, B.C. V8W 3N5, Canada

DAVID HARRIS

Stable Isotope Facility, 122 Hunt Hall,
University of California, Davis, California 95615, USA

Abstract.—Anadromous fishes such as salmonids link marine and terrestrial ecosystems in coastal watersheds of western North America. We examine here the extent of isotopic enrichment of salmon-derived nutrients in soil, vegetation, and terrestrial insects among six watersheds from coastal British Columbia that differ in the density of salmon. Results demonstrate a direct relationship between the salmon spawning density and ^{15}N enrichment in humus soil, in riparian vegetation (*Tsuga heterophylla, Vaccinium parvifolium, Rubus spectabilis*), and in riparian insects including herbivorous and carnivorous Carabidae (*Pterostichus, Scaphinotus, Zacotus*). The results suggest broad cycling of salmon-derived nutrients into multiple trophic levels of terrestrial ecosystems. We also describe for the first time the detection of salmon-derived nitrogen in wood samples extracted from old-growth riparian conifers. This result suggests new opportunities for assessing relative nutrient transfer and salmon abundance in past centuries.

Introduction

Recent studies have begun to quantify the ecological role of salmon to coastal watersheds of western North America. These anadromous fish provide direct nutrients to a diverse assemblage of predators and scavengers (Willson and Halupka 1995; Cederholm et al. 2000), ecologically comparable to the migrating herds of wildebeest in the Serengetti (Reim-chen 1995). Salmon carcasses, which are considerably enriched in the stable isotopes ^{15}N and ^{13}C, also contribute to primary production in estuaries, freshwater streams, and lakes (Stockner 1987; Cederholm et al. 1989, 2000; Kline et al. 1990, 1993; Bilby et al. 1996; Wipfli et al. 1998) and are incorporated into riparian vegetation (Ben-David et al. 1997, 1998) and terrestrial predators (Hilderbrand et al. 1999a).

Some of the most common and widely distributed large terrestrial carnivores are bears, and salmon represent a major yearly source of nutrients for these foragers (Gilbert and Lanner 1995, Hilder-brand et al. 1999b). The congregation of bears during the two months of salmon spawning and their extensive diurnal and nocturnal foraging activity results in a major transfer of salmon carcasses from the stream into the forest (Reimchen 1992, 1994, 2000). This can lead to high densities of abandoned carcass remnants reaching 4,000 kg/ha in the near-stream riparian zone and high densities of secondary vertebrate and invertebrate scavengers (Reimchen 1994). Furthermore, there is recent evidence (Hilderbrand et al. 1999a) that the salmon foraging activity of brown bears in Alaska can lead to a major input of nitrogen-enriched urine and feces on bear trails in riparian zones that is subsequently utilized by vegetation.

The extent of the bear-mediated nutrient pulse into forests and the utilization by vegetation and terrestrial insects remains poorly understood. In this paper, we provide preliminary analyses of the ^{15}N levels in soils and three common species of riparian vegetation, as well as ^{15}N and ^{13}C levels in selected terrestrial invertebrates from six British Columbia watersheds varying in salmon density. We also present evidence that the signature of salmon-derived nutrients is detectable in wood samples extracted from tree cores and this offers new opportunities for historical assessment of nutrient cycling.

Study Area

We studied six coastal watersheds in Clayoquot Sound, on the west side of Vancouver Island, British Columbia. These watersheds, Warn Bay, Bulson, Moyeha, Megin, Watta, and Sidney, are some of the least affected by the extensive deforestation in the region. Up to seven species of salmonids occur in the watersheds comprising chinook *Onchorynchus tshawytscha*, chum *O. keta*, coho *O. kisutch*, pink *O. gorbuscha*, sockeye *O. nerka*, cutthroat trout *O. clarki*, and steelhead *O. mykiss*. The area is located within the Coastal Western Hemlock biogeoclimatic zone (CWHvh1) and is characterized by dense forests of western hemlock *Tsuga heterophylla*, Amabilis fir *Abies amabilis*, and Sitka spruce *Picea sitchensis* (Green and Klinka 1994; Pojar and MacKinnon 1994). Western red cedar *Thuja plicata*, though less common, is also present in the low elevation forests. Shrubs such as salmonberry *Rubus spectabilis*, false azalea *Menziesia ferruginea*, and red huckleberry *Vaccinium parvifolium* dominate understory vegetation along streams. Salal *Gaultheria shallon*, deer fern *Blechnum spicant*, and sword fern *Polystichum munitum* are also locally abundant. The climate of this region is influenced primarily by westerly air masses moving onshore from the Pacific Ocean (Harcombe 1990). It is cool and perhumid, receiving more than 2,500 mm precipitation per year, mainly in the form of rain at lower elevations with an annual temperature range of ca. 10°C (Schaefer 1978). Due to moderate temperatures and high precipitation, soils retain moisture throughout most of the year and rarely freeze, resulting in a prolonged growing season. However, excessive amounts of soil moisture and high leaching lead to low levels of nutrients available for plant growth and a heavy dependence on decomposi-tion of organic material and nutrient recycling (Harcombe 1990). In a wet, cool climate such as this, decomposition is slow, resulting in large accumulations of deep organic soil horizons (Harcombe 1990).

The soils are ferrohumic podzols (Lord and Valentine 1978) overlying granitic intrusions of Jurassic Age and are characterized by an often substantial, darkly stained organic (humus) layer above siliceous, base-poor mineral horizons. Organic matter, aluminum and iron typically accumulate in the B horizon (Valentine and Lavkulich 1978). This soil type under CWH forest is generally N- and P-deficient (Prescott et al. 1993), and the soil climate is classed as cold cryoboreal (mean annual temperature 2–8°C) and perhumid (i.e., no significant water deficit throughout the year; Lavkulich and Valentine 1978).

Warn Bay Creek (49° 15' 46.14" N, 125° 43' 31.6" W) and Bulson Creek (49° 15' 48.8" N, 125° 43' 40.79" W) are located in adjacent valleys and both feed into Warn Bay through a common estuary. Warn Bay Creek, with a stream length of four km, is a narrow, shallow system, which supports four species of anadromous salmonids (chum, coho, cutthroat, and steelhead). The Department of Fisheries and Oceans escapement counts show an average of 3,700 salmon entering Warn Bay Creek each year during the period 1990–1999. These are primarily chum salmon with a small number of coho. Bulson Creek is 20 km in length and has a high gradient canyon near the mouth of the creek that appears to be impassable to salmon. Although the riparian zones of both Warn Bay and Bulson Creek appeared undisturbed and intact during original field surveys, on subsequent field surveys we observed that the sampling site at Bulson Creek had evidence of past human disturbance (3–4 decades), including localized removal of trees.

Moyeha River (49° 24' 58.62" N, 125° 54' 45.87" W) at the north end of Herbert Inlet is 28 km in length and supports runs of chinook, chum, coho, pink, sockeye, cutthroat, and steelhead. Escapement records show a yearly average of about 9,000 salmon, mainly chum, coho, and sockeye, enter this stream over the period 1990–1999.

Megin River (49° 26' 12.20" N, 126° 5' 5.40" W), located on the north side of Shelter Inlet, is the largest of the six study sites, extending more than 33 km to the southwest from the headwaters. Fish species recorded in this system include chinook, chum, coho, pink, and sockeye salmon, resident and sea-run cutthroat trout, rainbow trout *O. mykiss*, steelhead, and Dolly Varden *Salvelinus malma*. An average of 6,600 salmon, mainly chum, coho, and chinook, enter the river yearly (1990–1999).

Watta Creek (49° 27' 29.42" N, 126° 1' 38.77" W) flows into the northern end of Herbert Inlet and is 10 km in length, supporting runs of chinook, chum, coho, pink, and steelhead. Average yearly runs during 1990–1999 were approximately 2,400 salmon, with chum comprising the vast majority of these.

Sydney River (49° 30' 47.71" N, 126° 17' 48.28" W) is 11 km long with the majority of spawning activity occurring in a braided region at the lower 2 km. This river supports chinook, chum, coho, pink, and sockeye salmon, as well as cutthroat trout, steelhead, and sculpins (Cottidae). On average, 793 salmon (mainly chum) per year have been recorded in this river between 1990 and 1999.

We observed salmon carcasses or their remnants in the riparian zone of all watersheds apart from the control site (Bulson Creek). As well, black bears were present in each watershed and, based on carcass characteristics, appeared to be the predominant transfer agent of salmon carcasses into the riparian zone. Wolf *Canus lupis*, river otter *Lutra canadensis*, and bald eagle *Haliaeetus leucocephalus* are also present in all watersheds and will be contributing transfer agents. Gulls *Larus* spp. occurred in the estuaries and in the lower reaches of the rivers and, while their fecal droppings were uncommon in the riparian zone, these birds can be expected to also contribute to the nitrogen transfer.

Methods

For each of the rivers where salmon spawning occurred, we made general field notes of the distribution of carcasses, but quantified total carcass abundance only at Warn Bay Creek. We also estimated average salmon density based on average salmon escapement (1990–1999) and total spawning area (m²; Table 1).

We obtained wood samples from five Western Hemlock at Warn Bay Creek and from two hemlocks at the adjacent control site at Bulson Creek. The former were located at 100 m and 500 m upstream from the mouth adjacent to spawning gravels and at variable distances into the riparian zone (4 m to 34 m). Those from Bulson Creek were 600 m upstream from the mouth and 4 m and 28 m into the riparian zone. Trees chosen for augering ranged in size from 30 cm to 50 cm diameter at breast height. Wood samples were extracted using an auger bit (2.5 cm diameter, 12 cm length) drilled at breast height. We collected the wood chips separately from each incremental 1 cm depth into the trees. This yielded 20 to 30 wood samples for each tree. We also used a standard increment borer (5 mm) and extracted a 40-cm core 2 cm above the auger hole, and this allowed us to cross-reference auger depth with an approximate time frame.

Soil sampling was conducted in July and August 1998. At each watershed, collection sites were initially chosen near the stream adjacent to areas of suitable spawning gravel for salmon and where there was evidence of carcass transfer into the forest. At each stream, sampling sites were fairly consistent with respect to general morphological features, slope, and vegetation cover. A 40-m transect was established at each site running perpendicular to the stream edge into the adjacent forest. At 10, 20, 30, and 40 m distance from the stream edge, sampling lines were established perpendicular to the transect line. Ten soil samples, 1 m apart, were collected along each of the four sample lines. The top 10 cm of soil below the litter (L) layer was collected, corresponding to the zone of maximum fine root density

TABLE 1. Average salmon escapement (1990–1999), spawning area and salmon densities for study watersheds in Clayoquot Sound.

Stream	Escapement	Potential spawning area (m²)	Maximum salmon density (salmon/m²)
Bulson Creek	130	65,025	0.002
Sydney River	1627	109,000	0.015
Megin River	8975	367,200	0.024
Moyeha River	7000	264,000	0.026
Watta Creek	2683	21,760	0.123
Warn Bay Creek	3128	10,400	0.301

(and, therefore, maximum potential nutrient up-take). In most cases, the collection zone comprised the humus (F/H) horizon, although the mineral (Ae) horizon and, less frequently, decayed wood from fallen trees, were also included.

Foliar tissues of red huckleberry and salmonberry were sampled in August 1998 and again in April and July 1999 at each watershed. Vegetation sampling sites coincided with soil plots in relatively flat areas, with moderate to dense understory cover and evidence of bear-mediated carcass transfer. Initial collection sites occurred within approximately 15 m of streams and also included steeply sloping sites further into the forest (up to 120 m from stream). Foliage samples were collected from one to five individual plants at each site and stored separately in envelopes.

In May 2000, common carabid beetles (*Pterostichus, Scaphinotus,* and *Zacotus*) were collected from all six watersheds through pitfall trapping and hand collection from the forest floor. Five pitfall arrays were constructed on each watershed within a 40 × 40 m area adjacent to the stream. Pitfall arrays were arranged in a three-way branching fashion with a central pitfall connected via three 50 cm by 15 cm aluminum drift fences to a pitfall at the end of each fence. Hand collection occurred more randomly as individual beetles were encountered in the riparian area. All beetles were stored in 70% ethanol. In the spring of 1999, pre-emergent blowfly pupae (Calliphoridae) were hand-collected from the soil and coarse woody debris within five to ten meters of the Moyeha River. Two pupae were dried and the remainder ($N = 5$) was transferred to rearing containers until adult emergence. Adult blowflies were then stored in 70% ethanol until processing in March 2001.

Sample Preparation

Wood samples were oven-dried at 67°C for 3 weeks and then coarsely ground. Foliar samples were oven-dried in their envelopes at 67°C for three days. Soil samples were sieved to remove roots and stones, oven-dried at 105°C for 48 h, then ground and homogenized using mortar and pestle. Whole flies and beetles were dried at 60°C for at least 48 h. All of the samples were ground to a fine homogeneous powder using a Wig-L-Bug grinder (Crescent Dental Co., Chicago, Illinois). Soil and vegetation samples (1 mg) were assayed for total N and ^{15}N, while invertebrate samples (1 mg) were assayed for total N, ^{15}N, total C, and ^{13}C, at the

University of Saskatchewan Stable Isotope Facility, by continuous-flow isotope ratio mass spectrometry (CF-IRMS). Natural abundances of ^{15}N (d^{15}N) and ^{13}C (d^{13}C) are expressed in ppt (‰) and calculated as $(R_{sample}/R_{standard})-1) \times 1,000$, where R = the ratio of ^{15}N/^{14}N or ^{13}C/^{12}C. Isotopic standards include N_2 in air for nitrogen isotope analyses and Pee-Dee Belemnite (PDB) limestone for carbon isotope analysis. Measurement precision is approximately ± 0.35‰ and ± 0.10‰ for ^{15}N and ^{13}C, respectively.

Delta^{15}N values from powdered wood were determined after online combustion of 30 mg samples in an elemental analyzer (PDZEuropa, ANCA-Hydra 20–20). Sample combustion was achieved at 1050°C with a 40 mL oxygen injection and a Cr_2O_3 catalyst. Reproducibility of ^{15}N values on replicated samples averaged ± 1.0‰.

Mean d^{15}N and d^{13}C values in salmon are known to range from +11.2 to +12.3‰ and –23.5 to –19.6‰, respectively, based on variations in species, spawning condition, and body tissue fractionation (Mathisen et al. 1988; Kline et al. 1993).

Statistical Analyses

Analysis of variance (ANOVA) tests were employed to test for differences in d^{15}N values among vegetation and soil samples with varying levels of salmon density and also among carcass categories (i.e., present, absent, control) for vegetation species. Paired and unpaired *t*-tests were used to examine d^{15}N levels in vegetation species. We used Spearman's rank correlation analyses to test whether increasing distance from stream within each watershed and salmon density values among watersheds had significant effects on isotope values in sample types (soil, foliar tissues, and insects). Linear regression was used to examine relationships between d^{15}N values in plants and soil fractions in relation to salmon densities. Assumptions of normality and homoscedasticity were met.

Results

Wood samples extracted from western hemlock yield reproducible isotopic signatures (±1‰) and were highly variable among the seven trees (range minus 2.5‰ to + 2.5‰). The two control trees at Bulson Creek, where salmon were absent, both had d^{15}N values near –2.5‰, and this was independent of their distance from the stream ($F = 0.0$, $P = 1.0$). Trees from the adjacent watershed at Warn Bay, where salmon are present, have $d^{15}N$ values ranging from −2.4‰ to +2.5‰, dependent on the distance from the stream (Figure 1). The lowest value (−2.4‰) occurs in the tree furthest from the stream (34 m) and intermediate values (−1.5‰ to −0.5‰) occur in the two trees 10–15 m from the stream, while the highest values (1.5‰, 2.5‰) occur in the two trees closest to the stream (7 m, 4 m, respectively; $F = 89.4$, $P < 0.001$).

Delta ^{15}N values for each of the soil fractions and vegetation species differ significantly among watersheds (ANOVA; $P < 0.01$ for each; Table 2). Humus soil, huckleberry, and salmonberry all show highest mean values of $d^{15}N$ at Warn Bay Creek, where salmon carcass density is highest. In contrast, mineral soil has the highest ^{15}N enrichment at Bulson Creek, where salmon are largely absent, although sample size is small ($N = 2$). Sydney River, with a very low salmon density, shows consistently negative $d^{15}N$ values for all species, and Megin River demonstrates positive values for soil fractions and negative values for veg-

etation samples. Mean values at Moyeha, Watta, and Warn Bay creeks are positive for all samples. Each factor (humus, mineral, huckleberry, salmonberry) shows significant positive relationships between values of $d^{15}N$ and carcass density at each watershed ($P < 0.05$ for each; Figures 2A, 2B). No significant differences in mean $d^{15}N$ values of foliage were detected between spring and summer collections for either of the two species of plants ($P = 0.27$ and 0.15, respectively).

Shrub species, carcass category (i.e., salmon carcasses present or no evidence of carcasses nearby), and distance from stream were tested for associations with $d^{15}N$ values. Species differ in $d^{15}N$, with salmonberry having a higher mean value for all watersheds ($t = 3.51$, df = 247, $P < 0.01$). Within watersheds, the species effect occurs only at Warn Bay ($t = 2.38$, df = 38, $P = 0.02$). Proximity to carcasses is associated with isotopic signature, as both huckleberry and salmonberry collected near carcasses had a marginal but nonsignificant trend of higher $d^{15}N$ values than in plants where salmon carcasses were absent. However, this comparison was only possible at

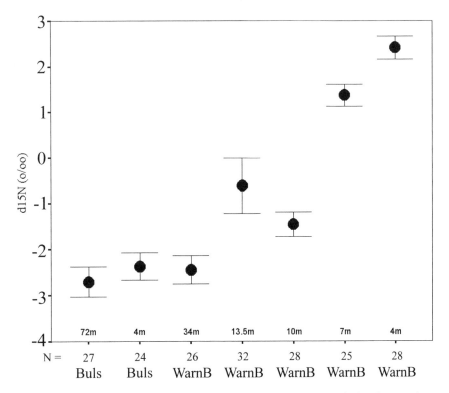

FIGURE 1. Mean $d^{15}N$ values (±1 SE) in wood samples from western hemlock taken at the control site without salmon (Bulson Creek–Buls) and the site with salmon (Warn Bay Creek–WarnB) in Clayoquot Sound. Tree distances (m) from stream shown on horizontal axis. N = number of separate wood samples.

TABLE 2. Values of $d^{15}N$ (mean±SD) of soil fractions and vegetation species from each watershed. Results of ANOVA testing for effects of salmon density on $d^{15}N$ values of each sample type are also shown.

	Mineral		Humus		Huckleberry		Salmonberry	
	n	$d^{15}N$ (‰)	n	$d^{15}N$ (‰)	n	$d^{15}N$ (‰)	n	$d^{15}N$ (‰)
Bulson	2	4.80±1.13	30	0.87±1.33	16	−0.94±1.92	15	−0.10±2.45
Sydney	26	−0.03±1.96	13	−1.95±0.76	21	−0.82±2.05	17	−1.13±1.38
Megin	10	3.79±1.77	29	1.09±0.79	13	−0.38±1.98	14	−0.18±1.12
Moyeha	10	1.57±2.17	30	0.32±1.58	20	1.12±1.89	11	1.30±3.42
Watta	35	2.15±1.97	5	0.60±1.37	7	0.49±2.95	17	1.88±2.90
Warn Bay	1	3.80	35	1.46±1.25	13	1.58±2.89	18	3.18±2.46
df	4		5		5		5	
F	9.62		15.85		3.65		7.55	
P	<0.001		<0.001		<0.01		<0.001	

the Sydney and Moyeha rivers, where sample numbers are high enough for comparisons. Proximity to stream also influences $d^{15}N$ values (Table 3). At Bulson River, which is the control site and has the most depleted $d^{15}N$ values for foliar tissues among watersheds, samples of humus soil, huckleberry, and salmonberry collected near stream have lower ^{15}N values than those collected further from the stream ($P < 0.01$). In contrast, at the adjacent site of Warn Bay, which has high salmon runs and high $d^{15}N$ values in soil and vegetation, humus soil and huckleberry each exhibit a significant reduction in $d^{15}N$ values at increased distances from the stream. The remaining localities show no significant associations apart from Sydney River, which exhibits a reduction in $d^{15}N$ values of mineral soil at increased distance from the stream ($P < 0.05$).

Invertebrates also exhibited isotopic differences with a gradient in salmon density among watersheds. In carabid beetles, $d^{15}N$ was positively correlated to spawning density ($r^2 = 0.43$; $P < 0.001$; Figure 3). Mean $d^{15}N$ values in each beetle species ranged from 3.13‰ in *Scaphinotus* to 4.65‰ in *Pterostichus* to 6.87‰ in *Zacotus*. However, $d^{13}C$ values decreased with increasing salmon spawning density ($r^2 = 0.120$, $P = 0.029$), which was contrary to prediction. Mean $d^{13}C$ values ranged from −26.16‰ in *Zacotus* to −26.04‰ in *Scaphinotus*. Collections of blowfly adults and pupae (Calliphoridae) from the riparian zone at Moyeha River demonstrated substantial isotopic enrichment. Mean $d^{15}N$ and $d^{13}C$ values were +16.55 ± 0.72‰ ($N = 7$) and −20.20 ± 0.37‰ ($N = 5$), respectively.

Discussion

Previous studies of ^{15}N enrichment in salmon watersheds rivers have yielded direct evidence for nutrient cycling between marine and terrestrial habitats (Ben-David et al. 1998; Hilderbrand et al. 1999a). Our results indicate that the levels of ^{15}N enrichment in riparian soils, vegetation, and ground-dwelling insects differ among watersheds and are directly related to the density of salmon in the spawning reaches of each stream. As we observed the greatest extent of bear-mediated transfer of salmon into the riparian zone at Warn Bay, where $d^{15}N$ values were highest, and no transfer at Bulson, where salmon were absent, we infer that salmon is the predominant source of ^{15}N enrichment, at least in the humus soil, vegetation, and insects. We are unable to account for the isotopic enrichment in the mineral soil at Bulson, but this might be associated with human disturbance of the site during the middle part of the 20th century. Additional factors, such as rainfall, have been shown to affect the $d^{15}N$ values in soil and vegetation (Handley et al. 1999), but due to the narrow geographical range of the samples taken in this study, in particular between the adjacent watersheds of Warn Bay Creek and Bulson Creek, differences in precipitation will be negligible. Species differences in $d^{15}N$ levels also occur, as was evident between huckleberry and salmonberry sampled within close proximity to each other. Differences in rooting depths or mycorrhizal associations between co-existing species can lead to different levels of $d^{15}N$ in plant tissues (Schulze et al. 1994; Nadelhoffer and Fry 1994).

As the number of salmon carcasses and scavenger activity decreases with increased distance from the stream, we expected to see a concordant reduction in $d^{15}N$ levels in soil and vegeta-

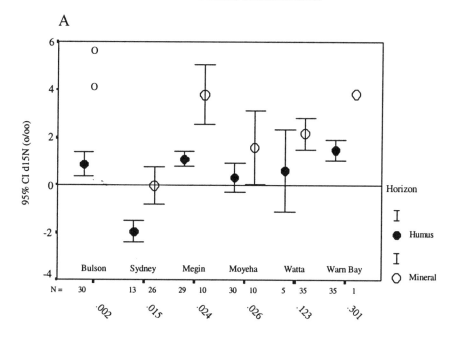

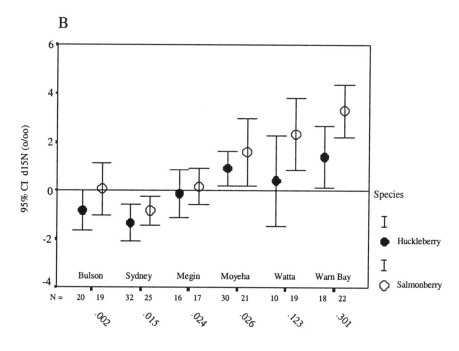

FIGURE 2. Δ^{15}N values of mineral soil and humus (A) and huckleberry and salmonberry (B) plotted against salmon density values for six watersheds. Symbols show mean and 95% confidence intervals. N = number of samples. All sample types show significant positive relationships between d^{15}N values and carcass density. Results of Spearman's rank correlation analyses are HS: r = 0.23, $P < 0.01$; MS: r = 0.26, P = 0.02; HB: r = 0.39, $P < 0.001$; SB: r^2= 0.48, $P < 0.001$.

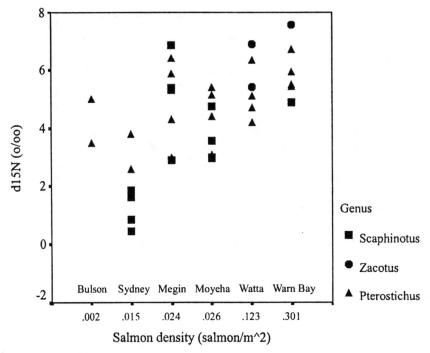

FIGURE 3. d[15]N isotopic signatures in three genera of common coniferous forest dwelling carabid beetles (Coleoptera: Carabidae) in six Clayoquot Sound watersheds ranked (left to right) by increasing salmon spawning density ($r^2 = 0.43$, $P < 0.001$).

tion. This was observed at Warn Bay among wood samples extracted from western hemlock trees that differed in stream proximity, as well as in foliar tissue of both species of understory vegetation and humus soil. However, within the other watersheds with regular returns of spawning salmon, the decline occurred to a very limited extent in soil and foliar tissues, at least over the 50-m riparian zone that we sampled. One possible explanation for this is that a reduction in levels of ^{15}N with increased distance from stream may be proportional to the density of spawning salmon in the river. Low salmon abundance at the Sydney, Megin, Moyeha, and Watta rivers, relative to Warn Bay, could result in less bear activity and, subsequently, less transfer of carcasses to the streamside forests. Another suggestion is that substantive horizontal cycling of salmon-derived nutrients within forest habitats is occurring through carcass transfers and animal waste, and we may have not sampled over a zone of sufficient width. In Alaska, Ben-David et al. (1998) observed enrichment throughout a 200-m riparian zone for fruits or seeds of *Rubus*, skunk cabbage *Lysichitum americanum*, and devil's club

Oplopanax horridus. Furthermore, Hilderbrand et al. (1999a) document ^{15}N enrichment in vegetation 800 m from the stream along bear trails.

It has been well established that higher returns of salmon in coastal streams benefit aquatic organisms through additions of nutrient-rich biomass from decomposing carcasses (Kline et al. 1990, 1993; Bilby et al. 1996). Transfer of salmon carcasses onto the forest floor surrounding coastal streams should also benefit terrestrial organisms where soils are nitrogen deficient. In coastal forests of the Pacific Northwest where precipitation and nutrient leaching rates are high, evidence of utilization of salmon-derived nitrogen by terrestrial vegetation (Bilby et al. 1996, Ben-David et al. 1998, this study) is consistent with this hypothesis. Our results also demonstrate a direct relationship between salmon density and levels of d[15]N in soil and vegetation, suggesting further support for these associations, as plants in N-limited systems utilize virtually every available source of nitrogen (Nadelhoffer and Fry 1994).

The influence of salmon carcass and nutrient pulses may also benefit terrestrial invertebrates, although this has received only limited attention. Dipterans have been found to be dominant carrion consumers in a diverse range of habitats (Lord and Burger 1984; Tomberlin and Adler 1998) and support a wide variety of secondary consumers from predators to parasites (Ulrich 1999). Blowflies (Calliphoridae) dominate salmon carrion communities in forests adjacent to streams, as large numbers of their larvae consume the majority of the salmon carcass tissue and then disperse to the forest floor for pupation (Reimchen 1994; Cederholm et al. 2000). Blowfly maggots consumed about 90% of the 4,000 kg of salmon carcasses abandoned by bears in the riparian zone of a small chum salmon stream on the Queen Charlotte Islands (Reim-chen 1994). Whole insect isotope values in Calliphorids, collected as pupae from the soil adjacent to the Moyeha River in Clayoquot Sound, were enriched by approximately 4.5‰ for $d^{15}N$ and 0.5‰ for $d^{13}C$ over the known isotopic signature of salmon. Blowfly $d^{15}N$ and $d^{13}C$ values are within bounds predicted by the trophic enrichment factor of a single trophic step of 3.4 ± 1.1‰ for $d^{15}N$ (DeNiro and Epstein 1981; Minigawa and Wada 1984) and 0.4 ± 1.4‰ for $d^{13}C$ (DeNiro and Epstein 1978; Gearing et al. 1984), suggesting 100% consumption of salmon carcass tissue. In watersheds with high transfer of salmon biomass into the forest, production of Calliphorid flies may be substantive, representing a significant food source for an unknown array of invertebrate and vertebrate predators and parasites, and requiring further investigation.

Carabid beetles (*Pterostichus, Scaphinotus, Zacotus*) are common coniferous forest dwelling arthropods and are thought to be generalist forest floor predators on a variety of soil invertebrates, including gastropods, millipedes, isopods, annelids, and springtails (Collembola; Hatch 1953; LaBonte 1998). We observed $d^{15}N$ enrichment in beetles and a positive relationship between enrichment in these litter-based omnivores and salmon spawning density among watersheds, suggesting a direct trophic association between carabids and salmon carcasses. However, the absence of a positive relationship between salmon spawning density and $d^{13}C$ among watersheds suggests that salmon is not a direct component to carabid diets, but rather, that $d^{15}N$ enrichment is derived indirectly through trophic cycling from the consumption of other $d^{15}N$ enriched invertebrates or vegetation (for example, Ponsard and Arditi 2000; Hocking and Reimchen 2002).

The use of soil, leaves, and invertebrates provides direct information on current or very recent uptake of marine-derived nitrogen, but these results are of limited application to any historical assessment of these processes. Tree rings potentially offer insight into historical trends. Because of the low levels of total nitrogen in wood (ca. 0.05%), natural abundance levels of $d^{15}N$ in tree rings have not been determined apart from Poulson et al. (1995), who were able to characterize $d^{15}N$ values by combusting large quantities of wood from individual rings (400 mg) extracted from two fallen hemlock trees in the eastern United States. Our studies are the first to detect the signature of marine-derived nitrogen in small samples (30 mg) of wood tissues augered from standing trees and show enrichment comparable to that found in the foliar tissues, soil, and insects from the same habitat. There are substantive limitations, such as vertical and horizontal movement of nitrogen in xylem, that may blur any yearly signature of nitrogen isotopes (Sheppard and Thompson 2000). However, our observation that wood $d^{15}N$ values among adjacent trees increase with increased access to salmon suggests new opportunities for assessing the relative transfer of marine-derived nitrogen into riparian zones in past centuries in localities where ancient trees still persist.

We conclude that significant relationships of $d^{15}N$ values in soil, wood, foliar, and insect tissues with salmon density in the streams provide evidence of the influence of salmon on the nutrient budget of riparian habitats and demonstrate the broad-scale ecosystem-level cycling of marine nitrogen from salmon into riparian vegetation and invertebrates occupying multiple trophic levels. This raises the possibility that productivity and carrying capacity in the riparian zone will be directly correlated with the abundance of salmon returning to streams and with the subsequent transfer of these nutrients by bears and other vectors into riparian zones. If so, the widespread decline in salmon abundance throughout most regions of coastal western North America over the last 100 years will translate into ecosystem-level declines in carrying capacity (i.e., cultural oligotrophication; Stockner et al. 2000).

Acknowledgments

We are grateful to J. B. Foster and R. A. Ring for discussion, to B. Hawkins and N. Livingston for shared laboratory space and equipment, to S.

Robin and P. Nosil for technical assistance, and to D. Klinka, I. Jacobs, C. Brinkmeier, and L. Hale for field assistance. We are grateful to the David Suzuki Foundation for the principle financial support of this project. Additional financial support was received from Friends of Ecological Reserves, Victoria, B.C., and from a Natural Sciences and Engineering Research Council of Canada (NSERC) operating grant to T. E. Reimchen and an NSERC-DSF industrial partnership award to M. Hocking.

References

Ben-David, M., R. W. Flynn, and D. M. Schell. 1997. Annual and seasonal changes in the diet of martens: evidence from stable isotope analysis. Oecologia 111:280–291.

Ben-David, M., T. A. Hanley, and D. M. Schell. 1998. Fertilization of terrestrial vegetation by spawning Pacific salmon: the role of flooding and predator activity. Oikos 83:47–55.

Bilby, R. E., B. R. Fransen, and P. A. Bisson. 1996. Incorporation of nitrogen and carbon from spawning coho salmon into the trophic system of small streams: evidence from stable isotopes. Canadian Journal of Fisheries and Aquatic Sciences 53:164–173.

Cederholm, C., D. Houston, D. Cole, and W. Scarlett. 1989. Fate of coho salmon (*Oncorhynchus kisutch*) carcasses in spawning streams. Canadian Journal of Fisheries and Aquatic Sciences 46:1347–1355.

Cederholm, C. J., D. H. Johnson, R. E. Bilby, L. G. Dominguez, A. M. Garrett, W. H. Graeber, E. L. Greda, M. D. Kunze, B. G. Marcot, J. F. Palm-isano, R. W. Plotnikoff, W. G. Pearcy, C. A. Simenstad, and P. C. Trotter. 2000. Pacific salmon and wildlife–ecological contexts, relationships, and implications for management. Special Edition Technical Report, prepared for D. H. Johnson and T. A. O'Neil. Wildlife-habitat relationships in Oregon and Washington. Washington Department of Fish and Wildlife, Olympia, Washington.

DeNiro, M. J, and S. Epstein. 1978. Influence of diet on the distribution of carbon isotopes in animals. Geochimica et Cosmochimica Acta 42:495–506.

DeNiro, M. J, and S. Epstein. 1981. Influence of diet on the distribution of nitrogen isotopes in animals. Geochimica et Cosmochimica Acta 45:341–351.

Handley, L. L., A. T. Austin, D. Robinson, C. M. Scrimgeour, J. A. Raven, T. H. E. Heaton, S. Schmidt, and G. R. Stewart. 1999. The ^{15}N natural abundance (d^{15}N) of ecosystem samples reflects measures of water availability. Australian Journal of Plant Physiology 26:185–199.

Gearing, J. N., P. J. Gearing, D. T. Rudnick, A. G. Requejo, and M. J. Hutchins. 1984. Isotopic variability of organic carbon in a phytoplankton-based estuary. Geochimica et Cosmochi-mica Acta 48:1089–1098.

Gilbert, B. K., and R. M. Lanner. 1995. Energy, diet selection and restoration of brown bear populations. Pages 231–240 *in* Proceedings of the 9th International Conference of Bear Research and Management. Pateris: French Ministry of the Environment and the Natural History Museum of Grenoble, Grenoble, France.

Green, R. N, and K. Klinka. 1994. A field guide to site identification and interpretation for the Van-couver forest region. Land Management Handbook No. 28. British Columbia Ministry of Forests, Victoria, British Columbia.

Harcombe, A. P. 1990. Vegetation resources of Van-couver Island, volume 1. Forest zonation. B.C. Ministry of Environment, Victoria, Canada.

Hatch, M. H. 1953. The beetles of the Pacific Northwest. Part 1: introduction and adephaga. University of Washington Publications in Biology 16(1). University of Washington Press, Seattle, Washington.

Hilderbrand, G. V., T. A. Hanley, C. T. Robbins, and C. C. Schwartz. 1999a. Role of brown bears (*Ursus arctos*) in the flow of marine nitrogen into a terrestrial ecosystem. Oecologia 121:546–550.

Hilderbrand, G. V., C. C. Schwartz, C. T. Robbins, M. E. Jacoby, T. A. Hanley, S. M. Arthur, and C. Servheen. 1999b. The importance of meat, particularly salmon, to body size, population productivity, and conservation of North American brown bears. Canadian Journal of Zoology 77:132–138.

Hocking, M. D, and T. E. Reimchen. 2002. Salmon-derived nitrogen in terrestrial invertebrates from coniferous forests of the Pacific Northwest. BMC Ecology 2:4.

Kline, T. C., J. J. Goering, O. A. Mathisen, and P. H. Poe. 1990. Recycling of elements transported upstream by runs of Pacific Salmon: I. d^{15}N and d^{13}C evidence in the Sashin creek, Southeastern Alaska. Canadian Journal of Fisheries and Aquatic Sciences 47:136–144.

Kline, T. C., J. J. Goering, O. A. Mathisen, P. H. Poe, P. L. Parker, and R. S. Scalan. 1993. Recycling of elements transported upstream by runs of Pacific salmon: II. d^{15}N and d^{13}C evidence in the Kvichak River watershed, Bristol Bay, Southwestern Alaska. Canadian Journal of Fisheries and Aquatic Sciences 50:2350–2365.

LaBonte, J. R. 1998. Terrestrial riparian arthropod investigations in the Big Beaver Creek research natural area, North Cascades National Park Service Complex, 1995–1996: part II, Coleoptera. Technical Report NPS/NRNOCA/NRTR/98–02. United States Department of the Interior, National Park Service, Pacific West Region.

Lavkulich, L. M, and K. W. G. Valentine. 1978. The Canadian system of soil and soil climate classification. Pages 59–65 *in* K. W. G. Valentine, P. N. Sprout, T. E. Baker, and L. M. Lavkulich, editors. The soil landscapes of British Columbia. B.C. Ministry of Environment, Victoria, Canada.

Lord, T. M, and K. W. G. Valentine, K. W. G. 1978. The soil map of British Columbia. Pages 99–100 *in* K. W. G. Valentine, P. N. Sprout, T. E. Baker, and L. M. Lavkulich, editors. The soil landscapes of British Columbia. B.C. Ministry of Environment, Victoria, Canada.

Lord, W. D, and J. F. Burger. 1984. Arthropods associated with herring gull (*Larus argenatus*) and great black-backed gull (*Larus marinus*) carrion on islands in the gulf of Maine. Environmental Entomology 13:1261–1268.

Mathisen, O. A., P. L. Parker, J. J. Goering, T. C. Kline, P. H. Poe, and R. S. Scalan. 1988. Recycling of marine elements transported into freshwater by anadromous salmon. Verhandlungen. Internationale Vereinigung fur theoretische und angewandte Limnologie 18:1089–1095.

Minigawa, M, and E. Wada. 1984. Stepwise enrichment of 15N along food chains: further evidence and relation between d^{15}N and animal age. Geochimica et Cosmochimica Acta 48:1135–1140.

Nadelhoffer, K. J, and B. Fry. 1994. Nitrogen isotope studies in forest ecosystems. Pages 22–44 *in* K. Lajtha and R. H. Michener, editors. Stable isotopes in ecology and environmental science. Blackwell, Boston.

Pojar, J, and A. MacKinnon, editors. 1994. Plants of coastal British Columbia. Lone Pine Publishing, Vancouver, British Columbia.

Ponsard, S, and R. Arditi. 2000. What can stable isotopes (d^{15}N, and d^{13}C) tell about the food web of soil macro-invertebrates? Ecology 81:852–864.

Poulson, S. R., C. P. Chamberlain, and A. J. Friedland. 1995. Nitrogen isotope variation of tree rings as a potential indicator of environmental change. Chemical Geology 125:307–315.

Prescott, C. E., M. A. McDonald, and G. F. Weetman. 1993. Availability of N and P in the forest floors of adjacent stands of western red cedar-western hemlock and western hemlock-Amabilis fir on northern Vancouver Island. Canadian Journal of Forest Research 23:606–610.

Reimchen, T. E. 1992. Mammal and bird utilization of adult salmon in stream and estuarine habitats at Bag Harbour, Moresby Island. Canadian Parks Service Report.

Reimchen, T. E. 1994. Further studies of black bear and chum salmon in stream and estuarine habitats at Bag Harbour, Gwaii Haanas. Canadian Parks Service Report.

Reimchen, T. E. 1995. Estuaries, energy flow and biomass extraction in Gwaii Haanas. Sea Wind 9:26–28.

Reimchen, T. E. 2000. Some ecological, and evolutionary aspects of bear-salmon interactions in coastal British Columbia. Canadian Journal of Zoology 78:448–457.

Schaefer, D. G. 1978. Climate. Pages 3–10 *in* K. W. G. Valentine, P. N. Sprout, T. E. Baker, and L. M. Lavkulich, editors. The soil landscapes of British Columbia. B.C. Ministry of Environment, Victoria, Canada.

Schulze, E.-D., F. S. Chapin III, and G. Gebauer. 1994. Nitrogen nutrition and isotope differences among life forms at the northern treeline of Alaska. Oecologia 100:406–412.

Sheppard, P. R, and T. L. Thompson. 2000. Effect of extraction pretreatment on radial variation of nitrogen concentration in tree rings. Journal of Environmental Quality 29: 2037–2042.

Stockner, J. G. 1987. Lake fertilization: the enrichment cycle and lake sockeye salmon (*Oncorhynchus nerka*) production. Pages 198–215 *in* H. D. Smith, L. Margolis, and C. C. Wood, editors. Sockeye salmon (*Oncorhynchus nerka*) population biology and future management. Canadian Special Publications Fisheries and Aquatic Sciences.

Stockner, J. G., E. Rydin, and P. Hyenstrand. 2000. Cultural oligotrophication: causes and consequences for fisheries resources. Fisheries 25:7–14.

Tomberlin, J. K, and P. H. Adler. 1998. Seasonal colonization and decomposition of rat carrion in water and on land in an open field in South Carolina. Journal of Medical Entomology 35:704–709.

Ulrich, W. 1999. Species composition, coexistence and mortality factors in a carrion-exploiting community composed of necrophagous diptera and their parasitoids (Hymenoptera). Polish Journal of Ecology 47:49–72.

Valentine, K. W. G, and L. M. Lavkulich. 1978. The soil orders of British Columbia. Pages 67–96 *in* K. W. G. Valentine, P. N. Sprout, T. E. Baker and L. M. Lavkulich, editors. The soil landscapes of British Columbia. B.C. Ministry of Environment, Victoria, Canada.

Willson, M. F, and K. C. Halupka. 1995. Anadromous fish as keystone species in vertebrate communities. Conservation Biology 9:489–497.

Wipfli, M. S., J. Hudson, and J. Caouette. 1998. Influence of salmon carcasses on stream productivity: response of biofilm and benthic macroinvertebrates in southern Alaska, USA. Canadian Journal of Fisheries and Aquatic Sciences 55:1503–1511.

American Fisheries Society Symposium 34:71–88, 2003

Observations of Chum Salmon Consumption by Wildlife and Changes in Water Chemistry at Kennedy Creek during 1997–2000

JOSEPH JAUQUET

Washington Department of Fish and Wildlife, Habitat Division
600 Capitol Way North, Olympia, Washington 98501-1091, USA

NED PITTMAN

Washington Department of Fish and Wildlife, Olympia, Washington, USA

JEFFREY A. HEINIS

Department of Natural Resources, Skokomish Nation 98584, USA

STEVEN THOMPSON

Washington Department of Transportation, Olympia, Washington, USA

NUI TATYAMA

Evergreen State College, Olympia, Washington, USA

JEFF CEDERHOLM

Washington Department of Natural Resources, Olympia, Washington, USA

Abstract.—During 1997–2000, chum salmon *Oncorhynchus keta* spawners and their predators and scavengers were observed in lower Kennedy Creek, a small south Puget Sound, Washington stream. Chum salmon occupy 5.2 km of main Kennedy Creek and a small tributary called Fiscus Creek. Spawning escapements within this stream averaged 39,000 fish annually during this study. Active spawning began in late October and was over by mid-December. Direct consumption of live and dead salmon was observed or inferred from animal signs over the spawning period. Salmon carcasses and tissue fragments could be found scattered along the streambed from October through March, and bones remained year round. Live spawners, carcass flesh, and eggs were consumed by 30 species of birds, mammals, invertebrates, and fungi, including 9 previously undocumented species. High carcass densities allowed selective feeding for some consumers and opportunistic feeding for others. Apparent preferences for eggs by several consumers suggested another important role for naturally spawning salmon. Varied thrush *Ixoreus naevius*, otter *Lutra canadensis*, and song sparrow *Melospiza melodia* showed preferences for salmon eggs, and a cougar *Felis concolor* killed live salmon and fed on them. Some consumers coordinate successive utilization of carcasses, such as the gull *Larus* spp., terrestrial beetle *Agyrtidae*, raccoon *Procyon lotor*, fly maggots, and mice. Water samples taken from the anadromous areas of these creeks and from the estuary in Totten Inlet showed elevated levels of dissolved ammonium, nitrate, and nitrite. Benefits to chum fry were inferred.

Introduction

On 17 October 1906, the Russian explorer-scientist Vladimir Arseniev reported numerous forest mammals and birds feeding on "dog salmon or keta" in the Sanhobe River, which empties into the North Pacific in northeastern Manchuria (Arseniev 1941).

Juday et al. (1932) reported some of the earliest North American studies of salmon carcass nutrient subsidy on Kodiak Island, Alaska, where they estimated that 400,000 kg of protein and 5,000 kg of phosphorous resulted annually from 2,000,000 kg of sockeye salmon *Oncorhynchus nerka* carcasses in Karluk Lake.

Observers in North America have noted the importance of salmon carcasses as food for a variety of terrestrial and aquatic animals. Studies of salmon consumption have focused on their use by high profile wildlife species like bald eagles *Haliaeetus leucocephalus* (Stalmaster and Gessaman 1984; Hansen et al. 1984) and grizzly bears *Ursus arctos* (Hilderbrand et al. 1996). Another study on the Olympic Peninsula of Washington (Cederholm et al. 1989) documented salmon carcass use by many lesser known consumers, including the red-tailed hawk *Buteo jamaicensis*, ravens *Corvus corax*, crow *Corvus* spp., American dippers *Cinclus mexicanus*, jays *Perisoreus canadensis* and *Cyanocitta stelleri*, winter wren *Troglodytes troglodytes*, shrews *Sorex* spp., deer mice *Peromyscus maniculatus*, squirrels *Tamiasciuris douglasii* and *Glaucomys sabrinus*, skunk *Mephitis mephitis*, raccoons *Procyon lotor*, weasel *Mustela* spp., mink *Mustela vison*, river otters *Lutra canadensis*, bobcats *Lynx rufus*, coyote *Canis latrans*, and black bears *Ursus americanus*.

The growth and condition factor of juvenile coho salmon *O. kisutch* and steelhead trout *O. mykiss* has been found to increase with the addition of salmon carcasses to western Washington streams. Juvenile coho that had access to these carcasses fed on them nine times more often than those in two other streams (Bilby et al. 1998).

Pacific Northwest estuaries act as traps for many of the nutrients washed downstream from watersheds. The importance of estuaries as nursery zones for several species of anadromous salmon is well documented (Healey 1982; Myers and Horton 1982; Macdonald et al. 1987; Pearcy 1992; Seliskar and Gallagher 1983; Hayman et al. 1996). The role that salmon carcasses play in maintaining the productivity of estuaries may be critically important (Fujiwara and Highsmith 1997; Reimchen 1994); however, little is known about the effect of salmon carcasses on estuarine nutrient dynamics and trophic productivity. This is important because some salmon species, such as juvenile chinook *O. tshawytscha* and chum *O. keta* typically use estuaries as rearing areas.

Japanese scientists studying the material cycle (Sibatani 1996; Murota 1998) emphasized the importance of salmon in transporting marine-derived inorganic salts (nitrates and phosphates) from the sea to the land. Sibatani points out that these numbers of salmon deliver a significant level of ocean nutrients along rivers, calling them a "powerful means of supporting the material cycle for the way they work against the earth's gravity, a necessity for supporting life" (Sibatani 1996).

We suggest that salmon provide an important source of nutrient and energy for both aquatic and terrestrial inhabitants and that the eventual breakdown of the carcasses subsidizes primary and secondary productivity in the estuary. Migrating chum fry feed on secondary producers in estuaries, such as harpactacoid copepods (Simenstad et al. 1980), and these organisms benefit from the nutrients provided by salmon spawners.

This study focuses on consumption of chum salmon in lower Kennedy Creek by various wildlife species. Emphasis is placed on consumption by previously undocumented species and their feeding behaviors. Investigation was also made into the changes in water chemistry in Kennedy Creek and its estuary.

Methods

Study Area

Kennedy Creek is a third-order tributary of Totten Inlet in southern Puget Sound, Washington (Figure 1). This forested watershed has a range of elevations, from sea level to 700 m, over its 16 km length. Slopes are moderately steep and underlain by marine volcanics of the Crescent formation. The mainstem valley is mantled with undifferentiated glacial till and recessional outwash materials deposited during episodic continental glaciation (Schuett-Hames et al. 1994).

There is an impassable waterfall on Kennedy Creek that restricts salmon to the lower 4.4 km of mainstem and 0.8 km of a small tributary called Fiscus Creek. Channel confinement down-

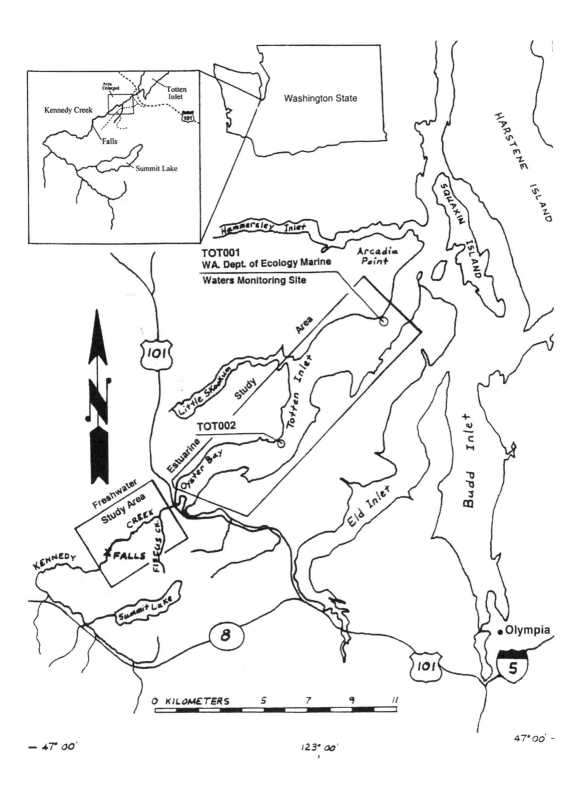

FIGURE 1. Kennedy Creek and Totten Inlet study area.

stream of the Kennedy Creek falls grades from steep bedrock canyons to a broad alluvial floodplain toward the mouth. Fiscus Creek is a small right bank tributary entering Kennedy approximately 1 km above its mouth. Kennedy Creek averages 10–15 m wide and Fiscus averages 1–1.5 m wide during the spawning season.

The Kennedy Creek watershed was originally logged in the early 20th century and is now composed of a mixed timber stand of Douglas fir *Pseudotsuga menziesii*, Western Red Cedar *Thuja plicata*, red alder *Alnus rubra*, and large leaf maple *Acer macrophylum*. Logging is presently underway in the basin, and riparian buffer strips of varying width have been left along the stream and the tributaries.

The local climate is maritime, with relatively wet, mild winters and cool dry summers. Annual precipitation averages 147 cm. The mean monthly discharge of Kennedy Creek ranges from 0.1 m³/s in August to 4.8 m³/s in January, with a mean annual flow of 1.7 m³/s. The highest recorded flow between 1960 and 1979 was 39.1 m³/s (USGS gaging station).

Kennedy Creek salmon runs are composed of large numbers of wild chum salmon and relatively few chinook, coho, steelhead, and coastal cutthroat trout *O. clarki clarki*. Male chums average 74 cm in length and females average 65 cm. Chums start entering Kennedy Creek in mid- to late-October, usually reaching the peak of spawning activity between the first and third weeks of November. Spawning is usually complete by the middle of December.

Chum spawning escapements have ranged from 1,200 in 1979 to 85,000 in 1996 (Figure 2; Washington Department of Fish and Wildlife, Olympia, Washington, unpublished data). Escapements in Kennedy Creek declined significantly between 1976 and 1982 (Figure 2), probably due to intensive fisheries in mid-Puget Sound and Totten Inlet (Tim Tynan, Washington Department of Fish and Wildlife, personal communication). As a result of declines in escapement, commercial fisheries were reduced and the escapement increased up to present times (Figure 2).

Salmon Consumption

In 1997–1998, observations of chum salmon carcass consumption were made in Kennedy Creek and in its tributary, Fiscus Creek. Two intensive survey sections of 100 m in length were established in Kennedy Creek, and the entire 600 m of

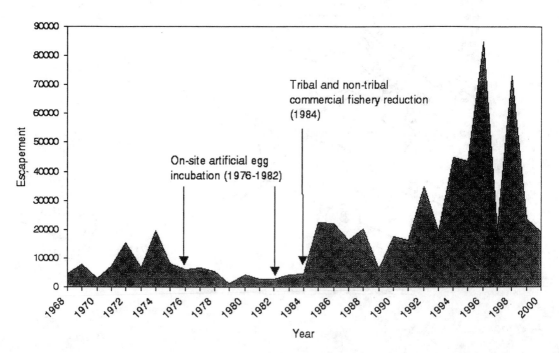

FIGURE 2. Chum salmon spawning escapements in Kennedy Creek, 1968–2000. Source: Washington Department of Fish and Wildlife, Olympia, Washington, unpublished data.

Fiscus Creek was surveyed. Observers made weekly or biweekly surveys of these streams between November and March to note carcass location, percent consumption, and evidence of scavenging.

In 1998–1999, seven study sites were established along Kennedy Creek and Fiscus Creek, based on carcasses distribution (Table 1), to facilitate discreet viewing of wildlife from blinds. Three study sites (K3, F1, F3) were subdivided into quadrants and mapped to aid in data organization, and the four remaining sites received only occasional attention. Weekly observation days were selected at random, always maintaining at least 3 d per week between December 1998 and March 1999 (totaling 193 observation hours). Observations of scavenging and predatory activity were made only during daylight hours.

Carcass consumers were primarily determined by direct observation or inferred from tracks or other sign. Observations from blinds were the primary tactic for observing wildlife consumers, and these observations were supple-

mented with regular stream walks. Additional weekly foot surveys were conducted within study-sites to assess tracks and other sign; sandbars within the study sites were raked following these foot surveys.

Birds and mammals were identified and counted both within and outside of the intensive study sites, while those within the study sites were tallied separately. Aquatic and terrestrial invertebrates were collected when observed on carcasses and identified to the lowest reliable taxa. For further documentation, a Pentax© model Zoom 90-WR camera set for automatic exposure at 10–20 min intervals (83 samples) was also employed.

Field data included the following: time, date, location within site, consumer species, method of consumption, and the condition and final disposition of particular carcasses. Precipitation and air temperature information was acquired from the National Oceanic and Atmospheric Administration, and stream flow data were provided by the Washington Department of Ecology in Olympia.

TABLE 1. Description of 7 study sites on Kennedy and Fiscus creeks, winter 1998–1999.

Creek	Site	Description
Kennedy	K1	Includes the area immediately upstream and downstream of the Old Pacific Highway bridge. Receives frequent human disturbance. Narrowly buffered by primarily hardwoods with moderate canopy closure.
	K2	A large lateral sandbar near river km 1. LWD and riparian vegetation retained carcasses here. Canopy is open over the stream channel.
	K3	Blind site with 90m × 50m observation view. Tree stand blind located at upstream end on a high terrace riser. Channel morphology is complex including 2 protected backwaters and 2 log-jams. Adjacent topography includes low alluvial deltas, large gravel bars, and abandoned channels. Forest age ranges from relatively young second growth (left bank) to mature stands (right bank).
	K4	Includes a large gravel point-bar and a large lateral sandbar. Woody debris and sediment burial retained carcasses here.
Fiscus	F1	The confluence of Kennedy and Fiscus creeks, this 50m × 50m blind site mostly includes the alluvial plain deposited at the mouth of Fiscus Creek. A small off-channel pond is also included in this site. The blind was located on an old terrace riser overlooking the area. Canopy closure is open over the Kennedy Creek channel and dense over the Fiscus Creek channel.
	F2	A sinuous and slightly incised reach of Fiscus Creek below the first culvert (facing upstream). Forest type is primarily hardwoods and is relatively open for a mature stand.
	F3	Blind site with 50m × 50m observation view. Located in a relatively dense mixed forest near a small clear cut and a decommissioned road. The blind was located on the upslope of the old road and overlooked the site.

Observations were organized into species observation days (SODs) for statistical frequency analysis. An SOD was defined as follows: for each observation of one or more individuals of a given species, a single tally was assigned relative to the study area (Figure 1) or particular study site (Table 1) where the observation was made. This made it possible for any given species to receive as many as eight SODs per study day, depending on the location(s) that they were observed.

Due to large numbers of carnivorous species and high stream flows in 1998–1999, eight relatively fresh carcasses were transported to site K3 on study day 30. We moved three of these carcasses to a high terrace riser near a blind and removed their heads for identification. Another carcass was wired to a log in an overflow eddy area near the blind. The other four (two loose and two wired to vegetation) were placed on a large gravel bar in open view. When carnivores appeared to reject the wired carcasses, their fastening apparatus was changed to wooden stakes.

During 1999–2000, the second period of observation from the blinds, observations were made from 6 December 1999 to 29 March 2000. These observations were carried out two days per week at each site, from 7:00 to 11:00 a.m. and 1:00 to 4:00 p.m. Periodic stream walks were made in Fiscus Creek, and supplemental stream walks were conducted in Kennedy Creek during the entire spawning period of October and November of 1999.

Annual live spawner counts were made throughout the anadromous area of Kennedy Creek by the Washington Department of Fish and Wildlife.

Water Chemistry

In 1998–1999, we measured the nutrient contribution of chum salmon spawners in lower Kennedy Creek, Fiscus Creek, and the estuary in Totten Inlet and compared them to the upstream nonanadromous areas. Freshwater samples were collected from the anadromous and nonanadromous areas of Kennedy and Fiscus creeks. Multiple samples were taken along the stream cross-section (i.e., four in Kennedy and two in Fiscus). Seawater samples were collected in Totten Inlet using a Van Dorn bottle at depths of 0.4 m, 3.0 m, and 4.5 m. Two to four seawater samples were filled at each depth and were analyzed in the field within a few minutes after collection to avoid sample degradation. Water samples were ana-

lyzed for dissolved nitrate, nitrite, and ammonium. Other measurements of water temperature, pH, conductivity, and flow were taken. Nutrient samples were analyzed at the water chemistry laboratory at Evergreen State College in Olympia and in the field. Additional nutrient samples for Totten Inlet were provided by the Washington Department of Ecology in Olympia.

Results

Carcass Consumers 1997–1998

Observations in the intensive study sections during the fall/winter of 1997–1998 showed a progression of salmon consumption from the arrival of spawners in the fall to their disappearance the following winter. In the initial stages of the run (late October), most salmon were alive, but by mid-November, many carcasses began to appear. Figure 3 shows the counts of live and dead salmon in Kennedy Creek from the third week in October 1997 to the second week in December 1997. Dead counts in the study sections increased from the third week in November and peaked in the first week of December, then gradually declined as they were utilized or washed downstream in freshets (Figure 3). Carcass tissue in Kennedy Creek was almost completely consumed or buried during storms by the end of January 1998.

At the peak of spawning, in November, approximately 7,000 live chums were counted in a single day in Kennedy Creek (Figure 3). Assuming an average weight of 4.5 kg per adult and an overall escapement of 19,900, we estimate that 90 metric tons of salmon flesh were present in Kennedy Creek during this season.

In Fiscus Creek, however, tissue and carcass material remained visible for a longer period of time (Figure 4). Comparisons of carcasses on the bank and in the stream showed that those remaining in the creek disappeared quickly after 3 January 1998, while those on the bank persisted well into March. This difference in carcass persistence can be explained by the flushing effects of high stream flow on the carcasses remaining in the stream. The carcasses on the banks of Fiscus Creek were fed upon by wildlife consumers more frequently than those in the stream.

The consumption of carcasses in Fiscus Creek, as a percent of total wet weight, was observed from the first week of January 1998 to the

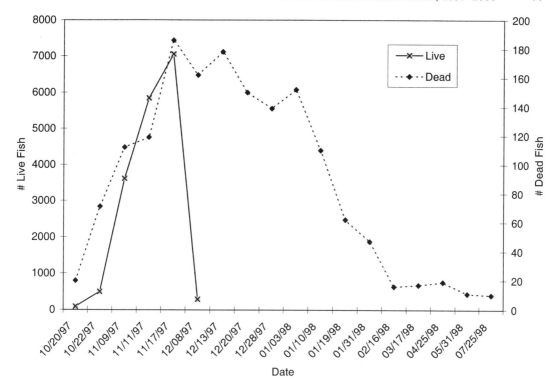

FIGURE 3. The arrival and disappearance of live and dead chum salmon in Kennedy Creek, 1997–1998 (Live chum: total count of Kennedy Creek; Dead chum: counts in two intensive study areas).

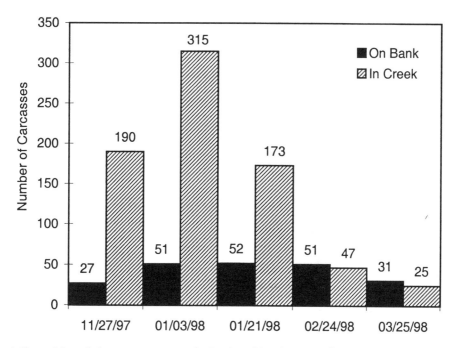

FIGURE 4. Deposition of chum carcasses on the bank and in Fiscus Creek, 1997–1998.

fourth week of March. As shown in Figures 5A–D, carcass tissue was nearly totally gone by the end of March. At this time, the remaining carcass material in Fiscus and Kennedy Creeks consisted of bones, small pieces of skin, and some tough vertebral connective tissue. We found that carcasses were dismantled in several ways, including the breakdown caused by fungus *Sphaeratellis natans*, disintegration caused by the current, and direct consumption by mammals, birds, insects, and earthworms.

Fungus covered approximately half the carcasses in any given area, with a thick coating that most terrestrial animals seemed to avoid. As the carcasses decomposed and disintegrated, the fungus fragmented and disappeared.

The most numerous insects observed were fly maggots; however, their species was unknown. These maggots were most often found on or in the heads of carcasses. Concentrations of small humpbacked flies (Phoridae) were observed flying from under skeletal material, especially spinal columns resting on sand and grass.

Earthworms were observed under head bones resting on sand and gravel and were presumed to be feeding on the carcass remains.

The observation of carcass consumption by birds and mammals included the use of carcasses in the stream, and some deposited more than 5 m beyond the high water mark. Evidence of feeding activity often appeared as holes made by consumers in the skin or head of carcasses, and an estimated 98% of the carcasses had the up-facing eye removed.

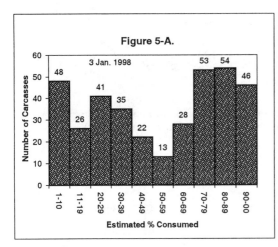

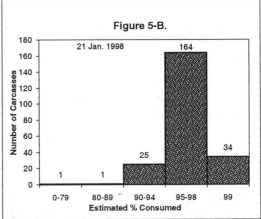

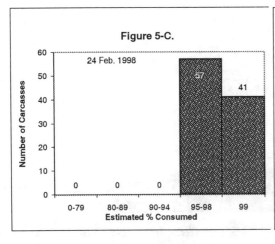

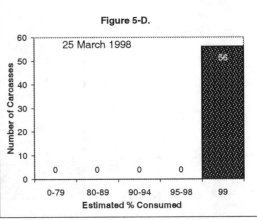

FIGURE 5. Estimated percent carcass wet weight consumed at Fiscus Creek, January–March 1998.

The most numerous terrestrial scavenger observed in the intensive study sections was the raccoon. Other frequent consumers included the osprey, gull, crow, and river otter. Based on inference from clear tracks in the sand, there was even evidence of a black-tailed deer *Odocoileus hemionus columbianus* feeding on a carcass vertebrae. Intensive observation of four carcasses along Kennedy Creek using photographic techniques revealed a chronological progression of four consumers that included raccoon, maggots, mice, and deer.

Carcass Consumers 1998–1999

In 1998–1999, we identified 73 species of mammals, birds, fish, amphibians, invertebrates, and fungus. From this group of species, 27 (37%) were directly observed as consumers (Table 2), and we observed a mean consumer abundance of 9 species within each of the study-sites (range 5–16), or about 35% of species present within all sites. Generally, the sites had similar consumer species. Scavenging was observed by nine previously undocumented species, including cougar *Felis concolor*, song sparrow *Melospiza melodia*, spotted towhee *Pipilo maculatus*, terrestrial beetle and larvae Agyrtidae, ground beetle *Scaphinotus* spp., false clown beetle *Sphaerites politus*, marsh fly (Diptera: Family Sciomyzidae), winter crane fly (Diptera: Family Trichoceridae), and springtail (Collembola: Family Sminthuridae).

Birds were the most frequently observed consumers at Kennedy Creek, totaling 10 different species. A possible exception may have been one intensive study site (F3) where relatively dense forest appeared to deter many of the avian consumers. Bird consumers were observed 3.7 times more frequently at the study sites than mammalian consumers. Gulls *Larus* spp., raccoon, and river otter utilized large amounts of carcasses of different decay classes, while bobcat and mink preferred fresh carcasses.

Cougar, a previously undocumented salmon consumer, was positively identified as a predator of chum salmon in main Kennedy Creek during the fall of 1999 (Table 2). The cougar moved fifteen chum salmon to gravel bars away from the wetted channel over approximately 2 km of stream. Eight "caches" by this mammal averaged about two fish each (range 1–4) and were easily identified by tracks. All cougar kills were on male salmon, and each was deeply punctured by canine teeth and some by incisors. One specimen displayed claw marks on one side of its body.

Raccoon were inferred as a predator in Kennedy Creek during October 1999 when a large raccoon was seen consuming a male chum salmon that appeared to be a fresh kill by the presence of arterial blood on snow. A similar pattern of predation was observed at Fiscus Creek where several male chum salmon, heavily covered with teeth marks and punctures, had been removed to the stream banks. Based on tracks and bite-mark evidence, we inferred that these fish had been killed by raccoons. In situations of

TABLE 2. Mammals present (P) and observed consuming (C) salmon carcasses and/or eggs at the Kennedy Creek study area and 7 subsites, winter 1998–1999.

Species	Site:	K1	K2	K3	K4	F1	F2	F3
Cougar *Felis concolor*[a]					C			
Bobcat *Lynx rufus*[b]				P				
River otter *Lutra canadensis*		P		C	P	C		C
Black-tailed deer *Odocoileus hemionus*		P	P	P		P	P	P
Coyote *Canis latrans*		P	P	P				
Douglas squirrel *Tamiasciurus douglasii*						P	P	
Mole *Scapanus* spp.						P		
Jumping mouse *Zapus trinotatus*					P			
Beaver *Castor canadensis*		P		P				
Raccoon *Procyon lotor*		C	C	C	C	C	C	C
Mink *Mustela vison*		P	P	C		P	P	C
Weasel *Mustela frenata*			P	P	P			
Cottontail rabbit *Sylvilagus floridanus*[c]								

[a] Observed taking live spawners during fall 1999.
[b] Consumed outside the 7 subsites.
[c] Observed outside the 7 subsites.

carcass abundance, raccoons preferred the gills and eyes of recently dead salmon.

At site K3 (Table 1), river otters deposited salmon eggs in the riparian zone in their scat. A lack of salmon bones and large numbers of undigested eggs in these scats suggested that the otters favored eggs over flesh, even when live spawners were present. The undigested eggs in the scats were later scavenged by unknown species within four days.

Many birds were present in the study areas, and some were observed consuming salmon carcasses (Table 3). The varied thrush *Ixoreus* *naevius* was the most frequently observed avian consumer in Kennedy Creek (46 SODs), observed at all sites except one. They typically accessed the gravel bars on foot from locations in riparian vegetation and swallowed eggs whole. They were often seen digging through silts, sandbars, and organic debris to locate eggs buried during high flows and would sometimes take advantage of erosion of gravel bars to search laterally in the bar. This digging involved the feet and the bill and sometimes covered a relatively extensive area (about 5 m^2). Once a thrush was observed recovering a salmon egg from the aquatic drift, then

TABLE 3. Birds present (P) and observed consuming (C) salmon carcasses and/or eggs at the Kennedy Creek study area and 7 subsites, winter 1998–1999.

Species	Site:	K1	K2	K3	K4	F1	F2	F3
Spotted towhee *Pipilo maculatus*		P	P	P		P	C	
Song Sparrow *Melospiza melodia*				C		P		C[a]
Northern harrier *Circus cyaneus*[b]								
Varied thrush *Ixoreus naevius*		C	C	C	P	C	C	
Common merganser *Mergus merganser*			P	C	P	P		
Hooded merganser *Lophodytes cucullatus*				C[a]	P	C[a]		
American dipper *Cinclus mexicanus*				C	C			
Winter wren *Troglodytes troglodytes*		P	C[a]	P	P	P	P	C[a]
Red-tailed hawk *Buteo jamaicensis*		P	C	P		P		C
Kinglets *Regulus* spp.				P	P	P	P	P
Raven *Corvus corax*			P	P		P		P
Belted kingfisher *Ceryle alcyon*				P				
Ruffed grouse *Bonasa umbellus*							P	P
Great blue heron *Ardea herodius*		P				P		
Gold-crowned sparrow *Zonotrichia atricapilla*		P						
Bald eagle *Haliaeetus leucocephalus*		P		C		P		
Downy woodpecker *Picoides pubescens*				P				
Hairy woodpecker *Picoides villosus*[b]								
Steller's jay *Cyanocitta stelleri*		C	P	C		P		
Chickadees *Parus* spp.				P				
Red-breasted sapsucker *Sphyrapicus ruber*		P				P		
Northern flicker *Colaptes auratus*							P	
Starling *Sturnus vulgaris*[b]								
Brown creeper *Certhia americana*						P		
Hutton's vireo *Vireo huttoni*						P		
Dark-eyed junko *Junco hyemalis*		P				P	P	
Sharp-shinned hawk *Accipiter striatus*				C[c]				P
Fox sparrow *Passerella iliaca*		P	P	C[a]	P	P	C[a]	P
American crow *Corvus brachyrynchus*		C	P	P		P	P	
American robin *Turdus migratorius*		P				C[a]		
Mallard *Anas platyrynchos*						P		
Common goldeneye *Bucephala clangula*				P				
Gulls *Larus* spp.[d]		C	C	C	P	C		
Pileated woodpecker *Dryocopus pileatus*				P				

[a] Suspected consumer; based on tracks or direct observation.

[b] Observed outside the 7 subsites.

[c] Secondary consumer; killed and consumed known consumer species

[d] Predominately juvenile *L. occidentalis*.

quickly tilting its head upwards, swallowing the egg, and continuing with digging. Varied thrush seemed to prefer eggs to flesh, with the exception of a cold period (-18°C) when carcasses were frozen. During this cold period, they were observed feeding on carcasses thawed by stream waters, when they were seen standing on carcasses and dipping their heads into the water to retrieve the softer flesh available below.

Two previously unreported avian species observed during this study were the song sparrow and the spotted towhee. They were often seen eating eggs and carcass flesh in both Kennedy and Fiscus creeks. At site F2, on Fiscus Creek, a single spotted towhee was observed feeding on a salmon carcass retained by woody debris, hopping directly onto the carcass, and tearing flesh free with its bill.

Similar to the varied thrush, song sparrows were observed in Kennedy Creek recovering loose chum salmon eggs that had been deposited on gravel bars during high flow events. However, these birds typically flew to gravel bars from riparian vegetation, quickly grasped a single egg with their bill, and then returned to their original position. The actual consumption of these eggs was not directly observed; however, empty egg chorions were photographed in the vegetation that may be attributable to this species.

The American robin *Turdus migratorius* and fox sparrow *Passerella iliaca* were also observed digging in sandbars high in egg deposition; however, neither was directly observed consuming salmon eggs.

A juvenile sharp-shinned hawk *Accipiter striatus* was noted as a secondary consumer of chum salmon at one site where it killed and consumed two American dippers *Cinclus mexicanus*, a known consumer of salmon eggs. This hawk captured these prey in flight over the stream channel and returned to the coniferous forest where it consumed them.

The terrestrial beetle *Agyrtidae* and its larvae were observed at three of seven sites. The adult form of this beetle was observed under carcasses and often within the salmon carcass eye sockets. Adult beetles were observed primarily during the first four weeks of the study, and their larvae (appearing by week 4) were observed until no flesh remained on the carcasses they occupied. Similar in abundance, the humpbacked fly, a Dipteran of the family Phoridae, was often observed in aggregations around puddles of fluid accumulated on carcasses that they occupied.

The ground beetle was often observed consuming the exposed gills of a dead salmon and was the only terrestrial insect observed at a carcass within the normal highwater marks. The majority (79%) of observed invertebrate species were of terrestrial origin, often seen at carcasses deposited outside the bankfull channel.

During the 1998–1999 spawning season, fungus could be seen "blooming" in Fiscus Creek during a period of low flow. It was attached to roots on the outside of meanders and to gravel substrate at riffles. This fungus was more abundant in the swifter flowing water and quickly disappeared during a subsequent freshet.

Approximately 1,500 carcasses were counted over the accessible length of Fiscus Creek in 1998–1999, providing a rich dissolved organic carbon load to the stream.

Water Chemistry 1998–1999

As the first salmon carcasses appeared in lower Kennedy Creek in mid-October 1998, when stream flows were low, the water chemistry of lower Kennedy Creek showed a clear increase in nutrients, especially ammonium (Figure 6). However, when the autumn freshets came in mid-November, the nutrient concentrations became diluted with high flows. Despite the dilution, ammonium concentrations remained significantly high in the anadromous area of Kennedy Creek compared with the upstream nonanadromous zone. This trend continued long after spawning was completed, at least until early February 1999.

From 4 to 14 November 1998, nitrite concentrations showed a statistically significant difference between the anadromous and nonanadromous areas, and between 25 October and 4 November 1998, nitrate concentrations showed a statistically significant difference between the two areas. After 14 November, nitrite and nitrate concentrations no longer showed a statistically significant difference between the anadromous and nonanadromous areas because floodwaters diluted the concentrations. Nitrate concentrations were elevated during the floods, presumably because of the nitrate leached from eroded soils.

Baseline sampling in September 1998, prior to salmon entry, showed no significant difference in the water chemistry between the anadromous and nonanadromous areas of Kennedy Creek. Nitrite, however, was slightly higher in the downstream sampling location. For several weeks fol-

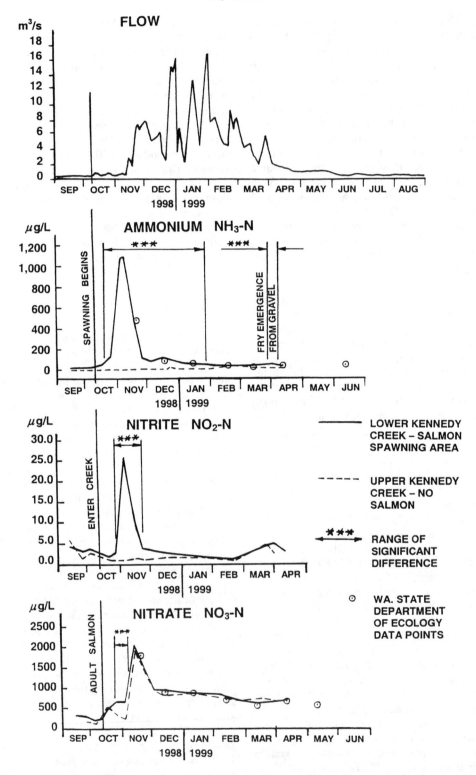

FIGURE 6. Stream flow and three dissolved nutrients during and after chum spawning in Kennedy Creek, 1998–1999. Significance level $p > 0.05$.

lowing 13 September, nitrite concentrations were low at both sampling locations in Kennedy Creek.

During late summer, prior to the entry of chum salmon, ammonium measurements ranged from nondetectable limits to 30 µg/L; nitrite measured from 2 to 8 µg/L, and nitrate + nitrite levels measured from 100 to 350 µg/L. At this time, there were no significant differences in water chemistry between the anadromous and nonanadromous areas.

After spawning activity was underway, the highest nutrient concentrations were recorded on 8 November 1998, at a time when stream flows were relatively low, around 0.7 m^3s, and chum salmon in the stream numbered more than 15,000. Ammonium measured 1,080 µg/L in the anadromous zone, while the ammonium concentration in the nonanadromous zone was below detectable limits, 0 µg/L. Other nutrient concentrations measured on 8 November were 25.3 µg/L for nitrite and 915 µg/L for nitrate + nitrite in the anadromous zone. These concentrations contrasted with 2.0 µg/L for nitrite on 4 November and 220 µg/L for nitrate + nitrite on 14 November in the nonanadromous zone. We assumed that these increases in nutrient concentrations in the anadromous area were coming from the presence of abundant spawners and carcasses.

A large storm occurred on 11 November, the first in a record-breaking series of 80 consecutive days of measurable precipitation (Figure 6). High stream flows diluted nutrient concentrations and flushed many carcasses downstream into the estuary.

Once the flows increased, the salmon were able to access Fiscus Creek for the first time and began to spawn. Water samples from Fiscus Creek followed the same pattern as main Kennedy Creek (Figure 6) for ammonium concentrations, showing a significant increase in the anadromous area. However, in Fiscus Creek, there were no significant differences in the concentrations of nitrite or nitrate between the anadromous and nonanadromous areas. We observed the last live chum salmon in Fiscus Creek on 18 December. Water samples in Kennedy Creek and Fiscus Creek continued to show high levels of ammonium in the anadromous area through December and January, even after high flows had either disintegrated the carcasses or flushed them to downstream areas.

The estuary of Kennedy Creek was sampled during the first few weeks of spawning in late October 1998. The surface ammonium measurement was 120 µg/L (Figure 7), and the combined nitrate + nitrite measurement was 70 µg/L. At this time, Kennedy Creek was releasing high concentrations of ammonium, presumably from salmon carcasses. This evidence further indicates that ammonium from Kennedy Creek salmon carcasses entered the estuary. With increasing distance from the Kennedy Creek mouth, ammonium was either gradually diluted by the saline waters of Totten Inlet or was reduced through denitrification. Collaborative evidence was provided by the Washington Department of Ecology that documented a steady decline of ammonium concentrations with increasing distance from the mouth of Kennedy Creek.

Additional samples were collected at high tide in early November, when Kennedy Creek stream flows were low and the saltwater/freshwater wedge was not well developed. Surface ammonium averaged 70 µg/L, and combined nitrate + nitrite averaged 140 µg/L. At a depth of 3 m, ammonium measured 90 µg/L, and combined nitrate + nitrite measured 100 µg/L. Lower Kennedy Creek remained high in ammonium concentrations in December and January. During this period, salinities ranged from 28 ppt on the surface to 29 ppt near the bottom.

Discussion

This study supports the work of Willson and Halupka (1995) and Cederholm et al. (1999, 2000), who point out the importance of Pacific salmon as a source of nutrient and energy for a wide variety of fish and wildlife species in the Pacific Northwest ecosystem. Willson and Halupka (1995) concluded that Pacific salmon are a "keystone" species. Similarly, the annual return of chum salmon at Kennedy Creek distributes nutrients throughout the stream system, including the estuary, where it benefits many ecosystem inhabitants.

Nehlsen et al. (1991) identified 49 of Washington's naturally spawning salmon stocks either at high risk of extinction or already extinct. The effect this may have on other ecosystem inhabitants has been discussed by others (Cederholm et al. 1989, 2000; Willson et al. 1998). Diminished wildlife populations have been attributed to the collapse of salmon populations in other parts of western North America (Spencer et al. 1991).

The role that salmon play in maintaining overall ecosystem productivity is not currently

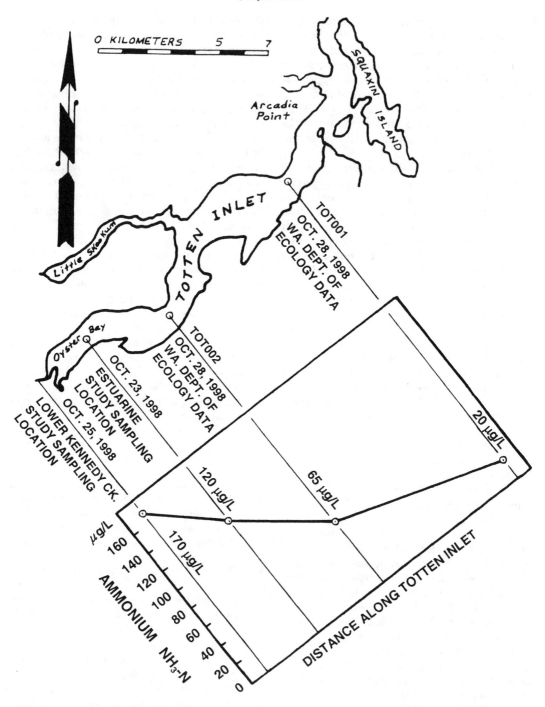

FIGURE 7. Ammonium concentrations in Totten Inlet during chum salmon spawning in Kennedy Creek, 1998.

considered when managing salmon runs (Bilby et al. 1998a; Michael 1995, 1998). While enlightened management of Kennedy Creek chum stocks has led to healthy adult returns and likely benefited many wildlife species, the future of many other Pacific Northwest ecosystems remains in doubt.

This study compliments the existing scientific literature. Of 23 species previously documented as salmon carcass consumers on the Olympic Peninsula (Cederholm et al. 1989), 16 (70%) were also observed consuming salmon flesh and eggs at Kennedy Creek. In addition, the work at Kennedy Creek has documented nine additional, previously undocumented salmon consumers.

Bilby et al. (1998a) suggested that the selection of salmon eggs over other food sources is energetically efficient, citing the high caloric content of sockeye salmon *O. nerka* eggs. While we saw several avian consumers feeding on loose eggs in this study, only the varied thrush was observed digging for eggs.

As high water moves carcasses or covers and re-exposes their deposition sites, this nutrient load is actively deposited and distributed. This temporal and spatial movement pattern seems to ensure that nutrients are more evenly distributed throughout the stream corridor. Many salmon carcasses in the upper anadromous zone of Kennedy Creek that were entrained in woody debris were gradually torn apart by the current, sending pieces of flesh to downstream consumers. Carcasses often lodged on the stream margin, where they were covered with sediment. Later in the winter, some carcasses were uncovered by the stream current and provided a source of nutrients for aquatic insects and other scavengers. Occasionally, buried carcasses would reappear in relatively fresh condition, often protruding from the gravel bottom, where they were made available to a variety of consumers.

All live salmon preyed upon by mammals during 1999 were males. Two possible explanations are, first, that the apparent high commercial demand for chum salmon eggs may lead to a disproportionate catch and removal of females from the population and, second, that during low flow conditions, the larger and deeper bodied male salmon seemed to be more vulnerable to predation when they swam across shallow riffles.

Flies and fly maggots were important consumers of salmon carcasses in 1998. In 1999, the Diptera species *Sciomyzidae* was positively identified as a scavenger. This agrees with an auxiliary survey on a nearby stream where a carrion beetle (Coleoptera: Family Silphidae) and a yellow jacket (Hymenoptera: Family Vespinae) were observed feeding on a dead chinook salmon (Pittman, personal communication). All carcass-consuming insects identified in this study, except *Scaphinotus* spp., were only observed on carcasses deposited outside the normal highwater mark.

Johnson and Ringler (1979) identified the consumption of blowfly (Diptera: Family Calliphoridae) larvae by juvenile coho and steelhead where they occurred on carcasses at a Lake Ontario tributary. In Alaska, Kline et al. (1997) report that diptera (Calliphoridae) maggots became entrained in the aquatic drift during variable streamflow conditions, but only the egg-laying adult form of Calliphoridae were observed, due to colder temperatures during this study. The Agyrtidae larvae found on Kennedy Creek carcasses may play a similar role to fly maggots. The presence of high numbers of insects like Calliphoridae and Agyrtidae on salmon carcasses may further provide food sources to several insectivorous vertebrate species, such as some birds, during the winter months when other food items may be scarce. During our study, no avian or mammalian species were associated with carcasses known to contain insects.

Secondary consumption of salmon carcass consumers may allow for nutrient enrichment of species that do not feed directly on salmon carcasses. While Bilby et al. (1996) observed this phenomenon among the functional class of aquatic insects called shredders, in western Washington streams, Minigawa and Wada (1984) further recognized the stepwise enrichment of ^{15}N along food chains. A sharp-shinned hawk was directly observed as a secondary consumer, and evidence suggested that other predatory species, such as the mink and Coleoptera (Family Staphylinidae and Cantharidae), may also benefit from secondary consumption.

The exceptional high-water year of 1998 probably reduced carcass availability to many consumers. Fragmented carcasses added to the aquatic drift (Bilby et al. 1998), but utilization was probably decreased for strictly terrestrial species while carcasses were submerged during high flow events. Carcass burial in the streambed was probably frequent during the winter, due to extensive bed-load movement and sediment deposition. The digging activities of raccoon, gull and varied thrush suggested that consumers tolerated shallow burial of carcass flesh and eggs, and burial of carcasses and eggs may have functioned as storage for later consumption. Removal and burial of live and dead salmon by wildlife consumers from the wetted channel may also function as a nutrient storage vehicle for later consumption. Carcasses observed outside the normal high-water mark were available for wildlife consumption for a significantly longer time than those in the channel.

The ammonium produced by salmon carcasses may be functionally linked to the production of harpacticoid copepods, the primary estuary prey of chum salmon fry (Fujiwara and Highsmith 1997). This apparent indirect linkage could be especially significant in the fjord-like systems of South Puget Sound. We found evidence linking nutrients from salmon carcasses to the productivity of har-pacticoid copepods. Harpacticoid copepods either directly consume diatoms or they consume bacteria associated with detritus from diatoms, riparian plants, and marsh grasses that previously may have benefited from salmon carcass nutrients such as ammonium.

Our study has documented a significant contribution of dissolved nitrogen, primarily ammonium, from the decomposition of chum salmon carcasses (Figures 6 and 7). Ammonium concentrations in Totten Inlet were highest near the mouth of Kennedy Creek, and the ammonium concentrations decreased as a function of distance away from Kennedy Creek (Figure 7). Ammonium concentrations near the mouth of Kennedy Creek were also relatively higher than concentrations typically found in more open marine waters. This ammonium gradient shows the influence that Kennedy Creek chum salmon carcasses have on the estuarine ecosystem. Published data from the Washington Department of Ecology shows that high concentrations of ammonium existed in Totten Inlet well after the spawning season, demonstrating that, in winter, dissolved ammonium can reside in the estuary for extended periods.

Brickell and Goering (1970) noted similar findings in the fjords of Southeast Alaska. They sampled less saline water, collected near the surface of the saltwater wedge in Iliuliuk Bay at the mouth of a salmon spawning stream, and compared it with more saline marine water entering the fjord from Captains Bay. Ammonium concentrations of the surface water measured 250 µg/L when salmon were spawning, and the comparison sample from the outside marine waters entering the fjord measured 10 µg/L. The time required for these nutrients to cycle through different trophic levels in the estuary could explain the timing of carcass nutrient availability to the next generation of salmon fry.

Kline et al. (1993) found incompletely decomposed salmon carcasses at depths of 20–50 m in Iliamna Lake, Alaska, suggesting carcass nutrient input for longer than eight months after the end of spawning.

The factors that control chum fry emergence are independent of the factors that control primary production in the estuary (C. Simenstad, University of Washington, personal communication). Solar radiation and nutrient input control primary production, while the egg incubation rate is mainly controlled by water temperature. Intuitively, the same solar radiation that controls primary production also controls temperature in streams; however, Leach (1970), found that the correlation between solar radiation and water temperature was not strong ($r = 0.62$).

These study results suggest that nutrients released from salmon carcasses in the fall can persist in the system until spring. In Totten Inlet (Figures 6 and 7), a relatively high (greater than 20 µg/L) concentration of ammonium persisted from the beginning of salmon spawning in Kennedy Creek until late March and April, when chum fry entered the estuary. Ammonium concentrations lower than 20 µg/L (January and March 1999) corresponded with high flows when concentrations were diluted by floodwater. However, despite this dilution effect of surface water samples, the deeper estuarine samples of ammonium measured in the 60–70 µg/L range.

The role of winter and spring phytoplankton production may be underestimated in the estuary food web of benthic primary producers, especially in fjord-like estuaries similar to Totten Inlet. Fjord-like estuaries have limited tidal exchange with the open ocean and retain high concentrations of ammonium for long periods of time. This enhances diatom production during the winter months. Salmon carcass nutrients could play a major role in maintaining the base populations of estuary food webs during winter months when production is otherwise low. In the spring, population increases of zooplankton would be enhanced if winter populations of diatoms remained high.

Estimates of escapement goals made by fish management agencies assume that too many salmon returning to spawn creates a negative impact on future salmon runs. Supposedly, when too many salmon are allowed to spawn, the result is excessive competition for spawning space and can lead to loss of eggs due to redd superimposition. During redd superimposition, females dig up the eggs of other females to make room for their own. Some managers view this as a waste of salmon that could have otherwise been caught in the fishery. We suggest that in nature's econ-omy, nothing is wasted. During mass spawning and co-incidental redd superimposition, some egg mortality is inevitable; however, this is all part of the chum salmon's highly successful life history strategy. Competition for spawning space insures full utilization of the available spawning area and survival that favors the strongest individuals, and this maximizes the potential fitness of the stock (Miller and Brannon 1982). Excess spawners and eggs result in greater nutrient capitol and consequent supplementation of the ecosystem into which their progeny will emerge.

We hypothesize that chum salmon carcasses may be supplying a critically important nutrient source for a broad community of watershed inhabitants, whether they live in the watershed or in the estuary. It has been shown that the longer chum fry reside in estuaries, the better their chances for marine survival (Simenstad et al. 1980). Therefore, it follows that the nutrients that benefit chum fry prey (harpacticoid copepods) also benefit chum fry and, in turn, benefit overall stock productivity. This suggests a feedback loop between adult chum salmon spawners and harpacticoid copepods. If this feedback loop exists, then a decline in the spawning escapement could result in reduced estuarine survival of juvenile chum salmon and ultimately have a negative impact on stock productivity.

References

Arseniev, V. K. 1941. Dersu the Trapper. English edition translated by Malcolm Burr. McPherson, New York.

Bilby, R. E., B. R. Fransen, P. A. Bisson, and J. W. Walter. 1998. Response of juvenile coho salmon (*Oncorhynchus kisutch*) and steelhead (*Oncorhynchus mykiss*) to the addition of salmon carcasses to two streams in southwestern Washington, U. S. A. Canadian Journal of Fisheries and Aquatic Sciences 55:1909–1918.

Bilby, R. E., C. J. Cederholm, B. R. Fransen, W. Scarlett, and J. W. Walter. 1998a. Establishing spawner escapement goals to maintain stream ecosystem productivity. Abstract. 16th Lowell Wakefield fisheries symposium and 1998 joint meeting of the American Fisheries Society Western Division, Alaska Chapter, and North Pacific International Chapter 30 September–3 October, Anchorage, Alaska.

Bilby, R. E., B. R. Fransen, and P. A. Bisson. 1996. Incorporation of nitrogen and carbon from spawning coho salmon into the trophic system of small streams: evidence from stable isotopes. Canadian Journal of Fisheries and Aquatic Sciences 53:164–173.

Brickell D. C., and Goering J. J. 1970. Chemical effects of salmon decomposition on aquatic ecosystems. Pages 125–138 *in* R. S. Murphy R, editors. Proceedings of the symposium on water pollution control in cold climates. U.S. Government Printing Office, Washington D.C.

Cederholm, C. J., D. H. Johnson, R. E. Bilby, L. G. Dominguez, A. M. Garrett, W. H. Graeber, E. L. Greda, M. D. Kunze, B. G. Marcot, J. F. Palmisano, R. W. Plotnikoff, W. G. Pearcy, C. A. Simenstad, and P. C. Trotter. 2000. Pacific salmon and wildlife–ecological contexts, relationships and implications for management. Pages 628–684 *in* D. H. Johnson and T. A. O'Neil, managing directors. Wildlife-habitat relationships in Oregon and Washington. Oregon State University Press, Corvallis, Oregon.

Cederholm, C. J., M. D. Kunze, T. Murota, and A. Sibatani. 1999. Pacific salmon carcasses: essential contributions of nutrients and energy for aquatic and terrestrial ecosystems. Fisheries 24(10):6–15.

Cederholm, C. J., D. B. Houston, D. L. Cole, and W. J. Scarlett. 1989. Fate of coho salmon (*Oncorhynchus kisutch*) carcasses in spawning streams. Canadian Journal of Fisheries and Aquatic Sciences 46:1347–1355.

Fujiwara, M., and R. C. Highsmith. 1997. Harpacticoid copepods: potential trophic link between inbound adult salmon and outbound juvenile salmon. Marine Ecology Progress Series 158:205–216.

Hansen, A. J., E L. Boeker, J I. Hodges, and D R. Cline. 1984. Bald eagles of the Chilkat Valley, Alaska: ecology, behavior, and management. National Audubon Society, New York.

Hayman, R. A., E. M. Beamer, and R. E. McClure. 1996. Fiscal year 1995 Skagit River chinook restoration research. Final project performance report. National Marine Fisheries Service, Contract No. 3311 for FY 1995. Skagit System Cooperative, La Conner, Washington.

Healey, M. C. 1982. Juvenile Pacific salmon in estuaries: the life support system. Pages 315–341 in V. S. Kennedy, editor. Estuarine comparisons. Academic Press, New York.

Hilderbrand, G. V., S. D. Farley, C. T. Robbins, T. A. Hanley, K. Titus, and C. Servheen. 1996. Use of stable isotopes to determine diets of living and extinct bears. Canadian Journal of Zoology 74:2080–2088.

Johnson, J. H., and N. H. Ringler. 1979. The occurrence of blowfly larvae (Diptera: Calliphoridae) on salmon carcasses and their utilization as food by juvenile salmon and trout. Great Lakes Entomology 12:137–140.

Juday, C. W., H. Rich, G. I. Kemmerer and A. Mean. 1932. Limnological studies of Karluk Lake, Alaska 1926–1930. U. S. Bureau of Fisheries Bulletin 47:407–436.

Kline, T. C., Jr., J. J. Goering and R. J. Piorkowski. 1997. The effect of salmon carcasses on Alaskan freshwaters. Pages 179–204 in A. M. Milner and M. W. Oswood, editors. Freshwaters of Alaska: ecological syntheses. Springer-Verlag, Inc., New York.

Kline, T. C., Jr., J. J. Goering, O. A. Mathisen, P. H. Poe, P. L. Parker, and R. S. Scalan. 1993. Recycling of elements transported upstream by runs of Pacific salmon: II. d^{15}N and d^{13}C evidence in the Kvichak River watershed, Bristol Bay, southwestern Alaska. Canadian Journal of Fisheries and Aquatic Sciences 50:2350–2365.

Leach, J. H. 1970. Epibenthic algal production in an intertidal mudflat. Limnology and Oceanography 15:514–521.

Macdonald, J. S., I. K. Birtwell, and G. M. Kruzynski. 1987. Food and habitat utilization by juvenile salmonids in the Campbell River estuary. Canadian Journal of Fisheries and Aquatic Sciences 44:1233–1246.

Michael, J. H., Jr. 1998. Pacific salmon spawner escapement goals for the Skagit River watershed as determined by nutrient cycling considerations. Northwest Science 72:239–248.

Michael, J. H., Jr. 1995. Enhancement effects of spawning pink salmon on stream rearing juvenile coho salmon: managing one resource to benefit another. Northwest Science 69:229–233.

Miller, R. J., and E. L. Brannon. 1982. The origin and development of life history patterns of Pacific salmon. Pages 296–309 in E. L. Brannon and E. O. Salo, editors. Proceedings of the salmon and trout migratory behavior symposium. 3–5 June 1981, First International Symposium, School of Fisheries, University of Washington, Seattle.

Minigawa, M., and E. Wada. 1984. Stepwise enrichment of ^{15}N along food chains: further evidence and the relation between d^{15}N and animal age. Geochimica et Cosmochimica Acta 48:1135–1140.

Murota, T. 1998. Material cycle and sustainable economy. Pages 120–138 in D. Bell, L. Fawcett, R. Keil, and P. Penz, editors. Political ecology. Routledge, London and New York.

Myers, K. W., and H. F. Horton. 1982. Temporal use of an Oregon estuary by hatchery and wild juvenile

salmon. Pages 377–392 in V. S. Kennedy, editor. Estuarine comparisons. Academic Press, New York.

Nehlson, W., J. E. Williams, and J. A. Lichatowich. 1991. Pacific salmon at the crossroads: stocks at risk from California, Oregon, Idaho, and Washington. Fisheries 16:4–21.

Pearcy, W. G. 1992. Ocean ecology of North Pacific salmonids. Seattle, Washington Sea Grant Program, distributed by University of Washington Press. Seattle, Washington.

Reimchen, T. E. 1994. Further studies of predator and scavenger use of chum salmon in stream and estuarine habits at Bag Harbor, Gwaii Haanas. Island Ecological Research, Queen Charlotte City, B.C. Prepared for Canadian Parks Service.

Schuett-Hames, D., N. P. Peterson, and T. P. Quinn. 1994. Incubation environment of Chum salmon (Oncorhynchus keta) in Kennedy Creek. Part C: patterns of scour and fill in a low gradient alluvial channel. Pages 42–55 in T. P. Quinn and N. P. Peterson, editors. The effects of forest practices on fish populations.

Seliskar, D. M., and J. L. Gallagher. 1983. The ecology of tidal marshes of the Pacific Northwest Coast: a community profile. U.S. Fish and Wildlife Service, Division of Biological Services, Washington, D.C. FWS/OBS-82/32.

Sibatani, A. 1996. (English translation by R. Davis). Why do salmon ascend rivers? Selected Papers on Entropy Studies 3:3–11.

Simenstad, C. A., W. J. Kinney, S. S. Parker, E. O. Salo, J. R. Cordell, and H. Buechner. 1980. Prey community structure and trophic ecology of out-migrating juvenile chum and pink salmon in Hood Canal, Washington: a synthesis of three years' studies, 1977–1979. Fisheries Research Institute, University of Washington College of Fisheries. FRI-UW-8026.

Spencer, C. N., B. R. McClelland, and J. A. Stanford. 1991. Shrimp stocking, salmon collapse, and eagle displacement. Bioscience 41:14–21.

Stalmaster, M. V., and J. A. Gessaman. 1984. Ecological energetics and foraging behavior of overwintering bald eagles. Ecological Monographs 54:407–428.

Willson, M. F., S. M. Gende, and B. H. Martson. 1998. Fishes and the forest: expanding perspectives on fish-wildlife interactions. Bioscience 48:455–463.

Willson, M. R., and K. C. Halupka. 1995. Anadromous fish as keystone species in vertebrate communities. Conservation Biology 9:489–497.

American Fisheries Society Symposium 34:89–97, 2003
© Copyright by the American Fisheries Society 2003

Aquatic Animal Colonization of Chum Salmon Carcasses in Hokkaido, Northern Japan[1]

MIYUKI NAKAJIMA AND TOMIKO ITO

Hokkaido Fish Hatchery, Kitakashiwagi 3-373, Eniwa, Hokkaido 061-1433, Japan

Abstract.—We observed that the aquatic animals, especially macroinvertebrates, colonized chum salmon *Oncorhynchus keta* carcasses in six rivers of five coastal districts in Hokkaido, northern Japan, 1997–2000. Fifty-six taxa of aquatic macroinvertebrates were found with the carcasses. Taxa and number of the macroinvertebrates were different among rivers and districts. Three taxa, Gammaridea (Amphipoda), *Hydatophylax* spp. (Trichoptera: Limnephilidae), and Chironomidae (Diptera), were widely and abundantly found. *Hydatophylax* larvae were more abundant on the carcasses, in comparison with the streambed, in some sites. The maximum number of macroinvertebrates colonizing a carcass was observed near an estuary site of the Shiretoko District, 747 on average of *Eogammarus* spp. (Gammaridea).

Introduction

Chum salmon *Oncorhynchus keta* is the most important salmonid for fisheries in Hokkaido. In the past several decades, almost all of the adult chum salmon, which return to spawn, were captured in the lower reaches for artificial breeding in Hokkaido hatcheries. However, from the mid-1990s, the adult catches have been reduced in many rivers early in the salmon season. At the present time, some parts of adult salmon spawn in upper reaches, so that many salmon carcasses are present there in fall and winter.

The contribution of salmonid carcasses to stream macroinvertebrates is mainly studied in North America. Piorkowski (1995) reported that salmon carcasses increased the number of insect taxa and their diversity, and 11 families of aquatic insects, including four families of Trichoptera, colonized the salmon carcasses. Minakawa (1997) showed that insect densities and biomass increased in boxes with added salmon tissue, and some species of Limnephilidae (Trichoptera), which associate with salmon carcasses, grew on

the diet of salmon flesh. Limnephilidae were also known as consumers of dead pikeminnow (squawfish; Brusven and Scoggan 1969). Wipfli et al. (1998) reported that total macroinvertebrate densities increased in carcass-enriched areas of artificial channels, and Chironomidae, two genera of Ephemeroptera, and *Zapada* (Plecoptera) were abundant with carcasses. Minakawa and Gara (1999) reported that even shredders, two genera of Plecoptera, and three genera of Trichoptera, directly fed on salmon flesh in a laboratory. Kline, Jr. et al. (1990) and Bilby et al. (1996), using stable isotope analyses, found that aquatic insects ingested the marine nutrients from carcasses.

In addition to the carcass studies in North America, the aquatic animal colonization and eagle consumption of carcasses were reported in Hokkaido, northern Japan (Nakajima and Ito 2000; Ueta et al. 1999). The aim of the present study is to clarify the variety of colonization by animals, especially macroinvertebrates, among rivers and coastal districts in Hokkaido.

Study Sites and Methods

The aquatic animal colonization was observed on the island of Hokkaido (Figure 1). The climate of Hokkaido (temperature, snowfall, and sunlight)

---

[1]The small part of results in two rivers was reported in Japanese (Nakajima and Ito 2000) .

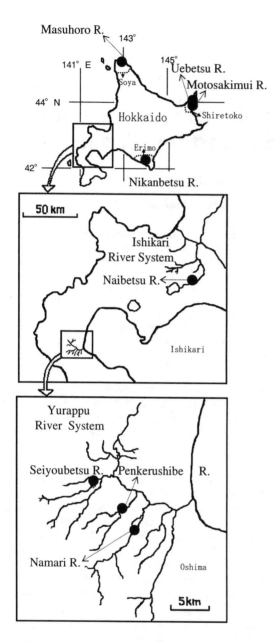

FIGURE 1. Study sites (solid circles) in five districts of Hokkaido.

is remarkably different between the northern part and southern part, and also between the east and the west (HKK 1953–1999). In this study, we investigated the animal colonization in five coastal districts of Hokkaido in 1997–2000 (Figure 1). Features of the study sites are shown in Table 1. We observed all carcasses in the study sites of the

Naibetsu, Namari, Penkerushibe, and Motosakimui rivers. We conducted sampling only once at the Erimo and Shiretoko districts and in the Namari and Penkerushibe rivers of the Oshima District, but revisited the other sites 3–13 times (Table 1). At each study site, we measured carcass fork length, the length from the pointed skull to the center of tail curve, and wet weight. The average sizes of carcasses were 59.2–70.8 cm in length and 1.8–3.9 kg in wet weight (Table 2). The carcasses were usually present in shallow (<32 cm, on average) and slow (<24 cm/sec, on average) sites near the stream edge. We also noted the presence of water fungi cover for each carcass (Table 2).

To collect colonized animals, the carcass was put into a 1-mm mesh bag in water. Then, the animals were washed down in the bag and gathered into small bottles. The carcass was returned to the position where it was found. The measurement and collecting of animals were carefully and rapidly done to prevent the destruction of the carcass. The carcasses observed previously were repeatedly observed in the second and following visits in a season, if they were still present in the study site.

We also collected macroinvertebrates from the pebble streambed by Surber type sampler to compare them with carcasses in all sites, except the Namari and Penkerushibe rivers. We classified the pebble samples into two types, with leaf litter (more than 15 g dry weight/m of CPOM, abbreviated as "with," below and in Figure 2) and without leaf litter (not exceeding 15 g dry weight/ m^2 of CPOM, abbreviated as "without"), since leaf litter might strongly influence macroinvertebrate taxa and density. Collecting replicates from "with" and "without" pebble beds were 12 and 12 in the Naibetsu River (sampler frame 100 cm^2), 9 and 14 in the Masuhoro River (sampler frame 625 cm^2), 3 and 26 in the Seiyoubetsu River (sampler frame 625 cm^2), and 3 and 3 in each of the Nikanbetsu and Moto-sakimui rivers and the upper substream of the Uebetsu River (sampler frame 100 cm^2). In the lower reach of the Motosakimui River, sampling of leaf litter was impossible, due to very scare accumulations. Relative abundance, as a percentage of each of three taxa (Gammaridea, *Hydatophylax* spp., and Chironomidae), was examined between carcass and streambed "with" and "without" leaf litter, respectively, by a comparison of the two proportions. For appropriate comparison with macro-

TABLE 1. General feature of rivers and study sites and research methods.

District	Ishikari	Soya		Oshima		Erimo	Shiretoko		
River	Naibetsu	Masuhoro	Namari	Penke-rushibe	Seiyou-betsu	Nikanbetsu	Motosakimui upper substream	Motosakimui lower reach	Uebetsu
Stream type[1]	S	M	M	M	M	M	S	M	M
Stream order[2]	1	3	3	4	2	4	1	3	4
Catchment area[2] (km²)	6.9	120	60.4	32.5	77.2	54	25.7	25.7	61.9
Total length of the stream[2] (km)	3.0	23.6	20.9	13.6	12.5	13	9.0	9.0	22.3
Distance from sea[2] (km)	65.0	13.0	10.1	12.8	16.2	0.2	10.5	0.2	0.2
Width of site on average (m)	6.0	6.0	36.0	36.0	11.0	–	2.0	15.0	15.0
Length of site (m)	200.0	100.0	27.3	100.0	42.0	–	–	–	–
Substrate[3]	p, s, cc	b, c, p	b, c, p, s	b, c, p, bd	c, p	c, p	c, p	b, c, p, s	b, c, p, s
Habitat	plane-riffle, pool	riffle, backwater pool	plane-riffle	riffle, backwater pool	riffle, backwater pool	riffle, backwater pool	riffle, backwater pool	riffle, backwater pool	riffle, backwater pool
Type of research[4]	A	P	A	A	P	P	A	A	A
Year	1999–2000	2000	1997	1997	1997,1998,1999	1999	1999	1999	1999
Month	Oct.–Mar.	Oct.–Dec.	Oct.	Oct.	Oct.–Dec.	Nov.	Oct.	Oct.	Oct.
Replicate	13	4	1	1	1, 1, 3	1	1	1	1

[1] S: spring stream; M: mountain stream.
[2] Based on the topographical map (1:50000).
[3] b: boulder; c: cobble; p: pebble; s: sand; cc: crowfoot colony, bd: bedrock
[4] A: all submarged carcasses was observed; P: a part of carcasses was observed.

TABLE 2. Size of carcasses and their positions in streams. –: no data.

District	River		Year	Number of carcasses observed	Size of carcasses				Positions of carcasses in streams					
					Fork length (cm)		Wet weight (kg)		Distance from stream edge (m)		Velocity (cm/sec)		Water depth (cm)	
					average	SE	average	SE	average	SE	average	SE	average	SE
Ishikari	Naibetsu		1999–2000	20	60.3	1.27	2.37	0.254	1.4	0.24	14.6	6.32	27.4	3.31
Soya	Masuhoro		2000	109	64.6	0.58	2.92	0.292	0.8	0.08	11.3	6.37	10.6	0.94
Oshima	Namari		1997	20	70.8	1.06	3.77	0.170	–		–		–	
	Penkerushibe		1997	3	67.6	4.73	3.94	1.137	–		–		–	
	Seiyoubetsu		1997	20	65.9	1.23	3.09	0.209	–		24.2	5.65	12.0	1.18
			1998	15	67.4	1.04	2.78	0.233	0.1	0.11	11.6	2.42	1.6	1.09
			1999	46	70.0	0.91	3.87	0.154	0.6	0.12	20.5	8.14	7.0	1.15
Erimo	Nikanbetsu		1999	20	66.5	0.70	2.87	0.193	1.5	0.40	8.9	7.22	12.8	4.06
Shiretoko Peninsula	Motosakimui	upper	1999	8	66.4	2.50	3.01	0.258	0.3	0.19	8.6	7.90	25.8	9.56
		lower	1999	10	63.3	0.98	2.78	0.139	0.4	0.16	9.8	6.81	9.2	1.42
	Uebetsu		1999	21	64.8	1.91	2.83	0.316	1.5	0.38	10.7	6.87	32.8	4.69

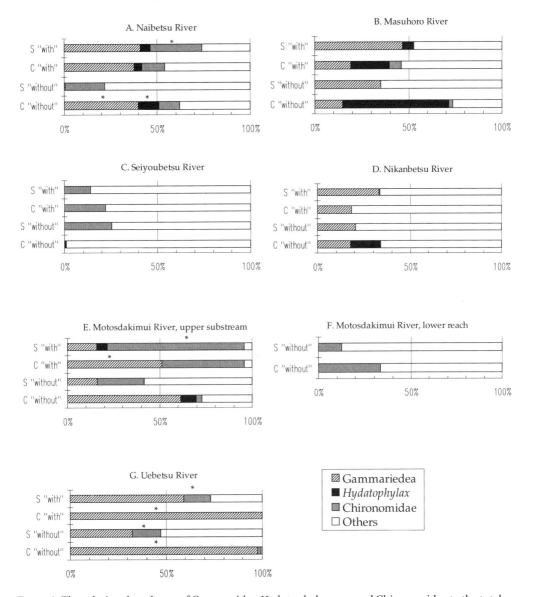

FIGURE 2. The relative abundance of Gammaridea *Hydatophylax* spp. and Chironomidae to the total number of macroinvertebrates on the four substrates. S "with": streambed with leaf litter; C "with": carcass with leaf litter; S "without": streambed without leaf litter; C "without" carcass without leaf litter. * statistical significance by text for the comparison of two propotions in relative abundance of the taxon between carcass and streambed to the total population, in two cases, "with" and "without," respectively.

invertebrates of pebble streambed, we treated only the carcasses located on pebbles. The alpha level of 0.05 was used for statistical significance.

All collected animals were preserved in 5% formalin. In the laboratory, the animals were identified into taxa, using Kawai (1985) and Nakabo (1993).

Results

The total number of macroinvertebrate taxa colonizing carcasses and average density (± SE) are shown in Table 3. Besides the abundant taxa, Hirudinea, Oligochaeta, Gastropoda, Isopoda, Plecoptera, and other taxa of Ephemeroptera,

TABLE 3. Total number of taxa and number on average ±SE of abundant taxa colonizing salmon carcasses.

District	Ishikari	Soya	Oshima (Yurappu River System)					Erimo	Shiretoko		
River	Naibetsu	Masuhoro	Seiyoubetsu			Namari	Penkeru-shibe	Nikan-betsu	Motosakimui upper substream	Motosakimui lower reach	Uebetsu
Year	1999–2000	2000	1997	1998	1999	1997	1997	1999	1999	1999	1999
Number of carcasses	20	109	20	15	46	20	3	20	8	10	21
Total number of taxa	32	20[1]	0[1]	0[1]	16	17	11	13	9	2	5
Turbellaria	0.50±0.96	0.00	0.00	0.00	0.00	0.00	0.00	0.00	4.13±3.85	0.10±0.10	0.00
Gammaridea	13.87±4.30	0.46±0.13	0.00	0.00	0.00	0.00	0.00	7.30±6.01	6.25±3.09	0.00	746.7±244.9
Ameletus spp.	0.00	0.00	0.00	0.00	0.00	0.00	0.00	4.55±1.73	0.00	0.00	0.00
Ephemerellidae	0.26±0.26	0.07±0.03	0.00	0.00	2.58±1.41	1.85±1.09	0.00	0.00	0.00	0.00	0.00
Hydatophylax spp.	3.08±1.13	0.81±0.20	0.00	0.00	0.02±0.02	0.00	0.67±0.67	0.20±0.20	0.88±0.52	0.00	0.00
Apatania spp.	0.50±0.19	0.09±0.03	0.00	0.00	0.00	0.00	0.00	1.00±0.65	0.00	0.00	0.00
Goerodes spp.	0.33±0.129	0.28±0.07	0.00	0.00	0.49±0.40	0.00	2.33±0.88	4.35±1.50	0.00	0.00	0.00
Elminae	1.50±0.76	0.06±0.02	0.00	0.00	0.00	0.00	0.00	0.00	0.38±0.26	0.00	0.00
Chironomidae	2.50±0.96	0.13±0.04	0.00	0.00	0.00	1.45±0.58	0.00	0.05±0.05	3.13±2.58	0.00	0.43±0.15

[1]Salmon carcasses were wholly covered with water fungi.

Trichoptera, Coleoptera, and Diptera were also collected. A gobiid fish *Gymnogobius urotaenia* was collected with a carcass at a lower reach near an estuary of the Motosakimui River, Shiretoko. The number of taxa colonized was variable among rivers and districts. The largest number of taxa was 32 observed in Naibetsu River, Ishikari. The number of taxa near estuary sites was different among districts. Density was low (2) in Shiretoko, in the lower reach of the Motosakimui River, and only 5 in the Uebetsu River, but moderate (13) in the Nikanbetsu River, Erimo. No animal colonized the carcasses in the Seiyoubetsu River (in 1997 and 1998), Oshima, where all carcasses were completely covered with water fungi. But 20 taxa of macroinvertebrates colonized in Masuhoro River, Soya, in spite of a dense cover of fungi. In the Seiyoubetsu River, each carcass was partly (<50% of the surface) covered with fungi and colonized with 16 taxa of macroinvertebrates, in 1999.

Gammaridea (Amphipoda) were the most abundant colonizer, except in Oshima (Yurappu River System) and in the lower reach of the Motosakimui River (Table 3). Species were different at specific elevations in rivers and in districts: *Jesogammarus jesoensis* and *Eogammarus kygi* (Anisogammaridae) in the Naibetsu River; *Eogammarus* spp. in the Masuhoro River, Soya, Motosakimui River, and Uebetsu River, Shiretoko; and *Sternomoera rhyaca* (Eusiridae) in the Nikanbetsu River, Erimo. In the Uebetsu River, *Eogammarus* spp. was extremely numerous, ranging from 2 to 3,624 and averaging 747 per carcass. *Hydatophylax* larvae were observed on carcasses in almost all sites, except near the estuary in Shiretoko, and Chironomidae (Diptera) were also widely observed in all rivers. Turbellaria colonized the carcasses in some origin streams, the Naibetsu River, and upper substream of the Motosakimui River. Ephemerellidae (Ephemeroptera) abundantly colonized carcasses in the Yurappu River System, Oshima. *Ameletus* spp. (Ephemeroptera: Siphlonuridae) and *Goerodes satoi* (Trichoptera: Lepidostomatidae) were abundant in the Nikanbetsu River, Erimo.

The relative composition of three abundant taxa (Gammaridea, *Hydatophylax*, and Chironomidae) to total number of all macroinvertebrates is shown in Figure 2, for each of four types of substrates: carcasses with and without leaf litter and streambed with and without leaf litter. The ratio of Gammaridea was significantly higher on the carcass than in the streambed, in four

cases: without litter in the Naibetsu River (Figure 2A), with litter in upper substream of the Motosakimui River (Figure 2E), and both cases in the Uebetsu River (Figure 2G). *Hydatophylax* larvae seemed to be more abundant on carcass than in the streambed in the Masuhoro River (Figure 2B) and without litter in the Naibetsu River (Figure 2A), Nikanbetsu River (Figure 2D), and upper substream of the Motosakimui River (Figure 2E). The relative composition of Chironomidae was more than 10% of total macroinvertebrates in the streambed, in five out of seven sites: the Naibetsu River (Figure 2A), the Seiyoubetsu River (Figure 2C), and two sites in the Motosakimui (Figure 2E, F) and Uebetsu rivers (Figure 2G). The ratio of Chironomidae was significantly lower on the carcass than in the streambed with leaf litter in the Naibetsu River (Figure 2A), upper substream of the Motosakimui River (Figure 2E) and the Uebetsu River (Figure 2G), and 'without' litter in the Uebetsu River (Figure 2G). But, in other rivers, no significant difference was detected in the ratio of Chironomidae between carcasses and streambed.

Discussion

Fifty-six taxa of macroinvertebrates and a gobiid fish colonized the chum salmon carcasses in Hokkaido. The gobiid fish was attracted to the carcasses because of the density of macroinvertebrates colonizing the carcasses, since the fish is a typical aquatic insect feeder. Gammaridea, *Hydatophylax*, and Chironomidae larvae widely colonized most chum carcasses in Hokkaido (Table 3). The taxa and number of macroinvertebrates were different among rivers and districts, and the relative composition of the three abundant taxa was also different among rivers (Figure 2).

Several researchers reported the macroinvertebrate taxa colonizing salmon carcasses (Kline, Jr. et al. 1990, 1997; Minakawa 1997; Minakawa and Gara 1999; Minshall et al. 1991; Piorkowski 1995; Schuldt and Hershery 1995; Wipfli et al. 1998) and nonsalmonid carcasses (Brusven and Scoggan 1969). Some genera of Trichoptera, including *Hydatophylax*, were listed in these studies, but the Gammaridea reported have not been seen before. Chironomidae colonization was reported for salmon carcasses in Alaska (Wipfli et al. 1998) and also for mammal carrion (Haskell et al. 1989; Keiper et al. 1997).

The taxon that colonized carcasses most densely was *Eogammrus* spp. in the Uebetsu River: 3,624 (maximum) and 747 (average) on a single carcass (Table 3). High colonization on salmon carcasses has been observed by others: more than 1,000 Trichoptera larvae on a carcass head (Piorkowski 1995) and 3,379 Chironomidae larvae on a carcass (Chaloner and Wipfli 1998).

Aquatic animals did not colonize carcasses in the Seiyoubetsu River in 1997 and 1998, but 16 taxa colonized carcasses in 1999 (Table 3). Carcasses were completely covered with fungi in 1997 and 1998, but only partly covered in 1999, in the Seiyoubetsu River. Thus, the occurrence of water fungi and aquatic animal colonization to the carcasses showed considerable variance among rivers and even among seasons within a river (Table 3). Some Trichoptera larvae graze the fungi directly (Minakawa 1997). The effects of fungi cover on the rate of macroinvertebrate colonization should be further studied.

Relative proportions of the three taxa Gammaridea, *Hydatophylax*, and Chironomidae were different among rivers and substrates (Figure 2). The composition of Gammaridea and *Hydatophylax*, which abundantly colonized carcasses in many study sites (Table 3), was higher on the carcasses than in streambed in some rivers, but did not differ between the two substrates in other rivers. The positive effects of leaf litter were distinct in some sites, but not necessarily clear in others. Thus, further quantitative research would be needed to clarify the selective colonization of Gammaridea and *Hydatophylax* on carcasses.

Jesogammarus jesoensis, an abundant Gammaridea in the Naibetsu River, grew fast on a diet of leaves fertilized with carcass leachate (Ito, in press), and *Eogammarus kygi*, another abundant Gam-maridea in the Naibetsu River, grows effectively on diets of carcasses only (T. Ito, unpublished data). Thus, salmon carcasses are available as soluble nutrient sources for *J. jesoensis* and, directly, as edible foods for *E. kygi*, but the effects of carcasses on growth and maturation are not as clear for other species of Gammaridea.

Almost all *Hydatophylax* were final instar larvae of *Hydatophylax festivus*, in October and November, and young instar larvae of *H. soldatovi*, in December. *Hydatophylax festivus* has an annual life cycle with an adult flight period in spring and early summer in Hokkaido; the larvae born in early summer grow up to the final instar in fall and develop to pupae in early spring (Zhang 1996; Ito et al. 2000). So, *Hydatophylax*

eagerly take carcasses as food in fall and early winter, required for growth and preparation of metamorphosis in spring. The larvae of *H. festivus* usually take leaf litter (Zhang 1996), but may take carcasses if they are available, since they readily take salmon flesh and grow as fast as on leaf litter in the laboratory (M. Nakajima unpublished data). Minakawa (1997) observed the direct ingestion of salmon flesh in several species of Limnephilidae (Trichoptera) in streams and the fast growth of *Ecclisomyia conspersa* larvae with salmon flesh in the laboratory. *Ecclisomyia conspersa* has a one-year life cycle with an early flight period, April to July, in Oregon (Anderson 1976), so it is likely that it may be a heavy carcass eater in fall and early winter, just like *H. festivus*.

Chironomidae colonized carcasses in 6 out of the 8 rivers (Table 3). The relative abundance of this family was significantly lower on the carcass than in the streambed in three rivers (Figure 2A, E, G), but not different between the two substrates ("with" vs "without") in other rivers. Food habits are widely diverse in Chironomidae, with many genera and species being detritivores or herbivores, and others being predators or scavengers (Oliver 1971). More detail identification would be necessary to clarify the status of Chironomidae colonization to chum salmon carcasses in Hokkaido rivers.

In this study, the aquatic animals colonizing salmon carcasses were reported for almost all coastal districts of Hokkaido. Taxa and number of the aquatic animals were different among rivers and districts. Further studies are needed to detect the effects of the carcasses on each taxon's population and on stream community dynamics and productivity.

Acknowledgments

We are deeply thankful to Takeshi Murota, Doshisha University, who recommended the nutrient conference and provided valuable information, and to Noboru Minakawa, State University of New York at Buffalo, who gave us literature and many suggestions. We thank the late Kenichi Suzuki, Hokkaido Fish Hatchery; Kazutoshi Hieda, Yakumo, Hokkaido; and Hideyuki Kamei, Shibetsu, Hokkaido, for their help on our research; Harumi Kusano, Tama Zoo, Tokyo, for her kind help on amphipod identification; and Akira Goto, Hokkaido University, for providing the scientific name and ecology of the gobiid fish.

References

Anderson, N. H. 1976. The distribution and biology of the Oregon Trichoptera. Technical Bulletin 134. Agricultural Experiment Station, Oregon State University.

Bilby, R. E., B. R. Fransen, and P. A. Bisson. 1996. Incorporation of nitrogen and carbon from spawning coho salmon into the trophic system of small streams: evidence from stable isotopes. Canadian Journal of Fisheries and Aquatic Sciences 53:164–173.

Brusven, A. M., and A. C. Scoggan. 1969. Sarcophagous habits of Trichoptera larvae on dead fish. Entomological News 80:103–105.

Chaloner, D. T., and M. S. Wipfli. 1998. Aquatic invertebrates colonizing salmon carcasses in southeastern Alaskan streams (abstract). Bulletin of the North American Benthological Society 15:210–211.

Haskell, N. H., D. G. McShaffrey, D. A. Hawley, R. E. Williams, and J. E. Pless. 1989. Use of aquatic insects in determining submersion interval. Journal of Forensic Science 34:622–632.

HKK (Hokkaido Kisho Kyokai, Hokkaido Meteorological Association). 1953–1999. Hokkaido no kisho (Weather of Hokkaido), 1-43. HKK, Sapporo. (In Japanese).

Ito, T., A. Ohkawa, and N. Kuhara. 2000. Trichoptera fauna of Eniwa City, Hokkaido, northern Japan. Annual Report of Eniwa Historical Museum 6:16–46. (In Japanese with English abstract).

Ito, T. In press. Indirect effect of a salmon carcass on growth of a freshwater amphipod, *Jesogammarus jesoensis* (Gammaridea): an experimental study. Ecological Research 18.

Kawai, T., editor. 1985. An illustrated book of aquatic insects of Japan. Tokai University Press, Tokyo. (In Japanese).

Keiper, J. B., E. G. Chapman, and B. A. Foote. 1997. Midge larvae (Diptera: Chironomidae) as indicators of postmortem submersion interval of carcasses in a woodland stream: a preliminary report. Journal of Forensic Science 42:1074–1079.

Kline Jr., T. C., J. J. Goering, O. A. Mathisen, and P. H. Poe. 1990. Recycling of elements transported upstream by runs pacific salmon: I. ä[15]N and ä[13]C evidence in Sashin Creek, Southeastern Alaska. Canadian Journal of Fisheries and Aquatic Sciences 47:136–144.

Kline Jr., T. C., J. J Goering, and R. J. Piorkowski. 1997. The effect of salmon carcasses on Alaskan freshwaters. Pages 179–204 *in* A. M. Milner and M. W. Oswood, editors. Freshwaters of Alaska ecological syntheses. Springer-Verlag, New York.

Minakawa, N. 1997. The dynamics of aquatic insect communities associated with salmon spawning. Ph.D. Thesis, University of Washington, Seattle.

Minakawa, N., and R. I. Gara. 1999. Ecological effects of a chum salmon (*Oncorhynchus keta*) spawning run in a small stream of the Pacific Northwest. Journal of Freshwater Ecology 4:327–335.

Minshall, G. W., E. Hitchcock, and J. R. Barns. 1991. Decomposition of rainbow trout (*Oncorhynchus mykiss*) carcasses in a forest stream ecosystem inhabited only by nonanadromous fish populations. Canadian Journal of Fisheries and Aquatic Sciences 48:191–195.

Nakabo, T., editor. 1993. Fishes of Japan with pictorial keys to the species. Tokai University Press, Tokyo. (In Japanese).

Nakajima, M., and T. Ito. 2000. Aquatic animal colonization of chum salmon (*Oncorhynchus keta*) carcasses in Hokkaido, northern Japan. Scientific Reports of the Hokkaido Fish Hatchery 54:23–31. (In Japanese with English abstract).

Oliver, P. R. 1971. Life history of Chironomidae. Annual Review of Entomology 16:211–230.

Piorkowski, R. J. 1995. Ecological effects of spawning salmon on several southcentral Alaskan streams. Ph.D Thesis, University of Alaska, Fairbanks.

Schuldt, J. A., and A. E. Hershery. 1995. Effect of salmon carcass decomposition on Lake Superior tributary streams. Journal of North American Benthological Society 14:259–268.

Ueta, M., M. Koita, and K. Fukui. 1999. The relationship between the autumn distributions of salmon and of steller's and white-tailed sea eagles in Hokkaido, Japan. Strix, a Journal of Field Ornithology 17:25–29. (In Japanese with English abstract).

Wipfli, M. S., J. Hudson, and J. Caouette. 1998. Influence of salmon carcasses on stream productivity: response of biofilm and benthic macroinvertebrates in southern Alaska, U.S.A. Canadian Journal of Fisheries and Aquatic Sciences 55:1503–1511.

Zhang, Y. P. 1996. Life History of *Hydatophylax intermedius* (Trichoptera, Limnephilidae) in Hokkaido, northern Japan. Aquatic Insects 18:223–231.

American Fisheries Society Symposium 34:99–107, 2003

Evidence for Hyporheic Transfer and Removal of Marine-Derived Nutrients in a Sockeye Stream in Southwest Alaska

THOMAS C. O'KEEFE

School of Aquatic and Fishery Sciences,
University of Washington, Seattle, Washington 98195, USA

RICK T. EDWARDS

Aquatic and Land Interactions Program, Pacific Northwest Research Station,
USDA Forest Service, 2770 Sherwood Lane, Suite 2A, Juneau, Alaska 99801, USA

Abstract.—Evidence for the importance of marine-derived nutrient (MDN) inputs from spawning salmon to terrestrial and freshwater ecosystems is rapidly accumulating, but the mechanisms by which MDN inputs are transferred and stored within spawning streams and their catchments are poorly understood. Presumed marine isotope signals have been found in riparian vegetation, suggesting that marine nutrients may impact terrestrial plant communities. Studies have suggested that MDN increases stream productivity both immediately after spawning and during the following spring. The peak of many spawning runs occurs at the end of the summer growing season, suggesting that overwinter storage of MDN must be occurring. A potential location for lateral nutrient transfers and overwinter MDN storage is the hyporheic zone within stream channels or in adjacent riparian floodplains. Within Lynx Creek, a sockeye-spawning stream in the Wood River Lake drainage in southwestern Alaska, extensive floodplain hyporheic zones occur along spawning reaches. Surface water moves into the floodplain hyporheic zone and flows downstream 70–80 m before returning to the stream. Ambient nutrient concentrations within the surface and hyporheic zone indicate that marine-derived nitrogen and phosphorus entered hyporheic flow paths, where they were rapidly removed from the water during the spawning run. Some marine-derived ammonium was remobilized as nitrate and continued to move, but marine-derived phosphorus was stored for at least the duration of the spawning run. Hyporheic sediments are not scoured by winter floods and contain active heterotrophic biological communities that are capable of storing and transforming various forms of MDN. Thus, it seems likely that hyporheic storage and re-release of marine-derived nutrients is an important mechanism by which salmon-derived nutrients are retained over winter within stream ecosystems and subsequently made available to primary producers the following growing season.

Introduction

Pacific salmon feeding in the nutrient-rich North Pacific Ocean incorporate carbon, nitrogen, and phosphorus into their body tissues along with other micronutrients that provide an important nutrient and energy subsidy to the oligotrophic streams where they spawn (Cederholm et al. 1999; Kline et al. 1997; Larkin and Slaney 1997). This nutrient subsidy can enhance insect and fish growth (Bilby et al. 1996; Chaloner and Wipfli 2002). Marine-derived nutrients are also an important source of energy for numerous riparian wildlife species (Ben-David 1997; Cederholm et al. 2000; Hilderbrand et al. 1999a, 1999b). Marine stable isotopes signatures have been found within leaves of riparian vegetation, suggesting that salmon products can potentially influence terrestrial productivity and community composition (Ben-David et al. 1998; Helfield and Naiman 2001).

Although we have greatly expanded our understanding of the potential significance of these marine nutrients in recent years, many questions remain regarding the mechanisms of transport to the riparian zone and where nutrient inputs may be stored within the ecosystem. Animals are one potentially important transfer vector from stream to riparian zone. Where present, bears remove significant numbers of salmon from streams and transfer nutrients through their urine and deposition of carcass remains that they do not consume (Hilderbrand et al. 1999a; Reimchen 2000). Numerous other species of wildlife and birds (Ben-David 1997; Cederholm et al. 2000) as well as insects (Wipfli et al. 1998) feed on salmon carcasses and distribute the nutrients throughout the stream and adjoining riparian forest. Within the stream, aquatic biota incorporate salmon nutrients directly into their own tissue, retaining it within biota (Bilby et al. 1996; Kline et al. 1990, 1993; Mathisen et al. 1988). Physical processes such as accumulation in pools or entrainment on woody debris can retain carcasses in the stream beyond the spawning period (Cederholm and Peterson 1985). Whereas consumption of carcasses by biota is one mechanism for the transfer and storage of salmon-derived nutrients, we also know that salmon release inorganic nutrients through active metabolism while on the spawning grounds and through decomposition of carcasses that remain in the stream channel (Richey et al. 1975; Schuldt and Hershey 1995).

Although many studies indicate that these biological and physical mechanisms are important, the role of the hyporheic zone in the transport and storage of salmon-derived nutrients has remained largely unexplored. Hyporheic zones are subsurface, saturated zones containing some proportion of water that previously ran within the surface stream channel (Edwards 1998; Harvey and Wagner 2000). For purposes of this study, we have focused on the floodplain hyporheic zone, which is an area of hydraulically conductive substrate beneath the overlying soil and vegetation of the riparian terrace. From studies in non-salmon streams, we know that nutrients entering the hyporheic zone from surface water can be rapidly taken up through physical sorption

and biological uptake by biofilm communities within the hyporheic zone and that the hyporheic zone can, thus, serve as a transient storage zone for these nutrients (Triska et al. 1989, 1994). Where hyporheic waters are near the soil surface, the roots of riparian vegetation may transfer nutrients from hyporheic water to their leaves. Our study objectives were to 1) delineate hyporheic flow-paths along a designated reach of Lynx Creek, southwestern Alaska; 2) determine whether the hyporheic zone could act as a vector for transfer of nutrients from spawning salmon to riparian vegetation; and 3) explore the likelihood that hyporheic storage of marine derived nitrogen (N) and phosphorus (P) could be occurring.

Methods

We conducted our study at the University of Washington's facilities in the Wood River Lakes System in southwestern Alaska (59°20'N latitude, 158°40'W longitude), where spawning sockeye salmon *Oncorhynchus nerka* have been studied since 1946 (Rogers and Rogers 1998). The Wood River system is a series of four interconnected lakes (425 km^2) that drain into Bristol Bay, which in turn supports the world's largest commercial sockeye salmon fishery.

Our study took place on Lake Nerka (201 km^2), which is the largest lake in the Wood River Lakes system. Lake Nerka is bordered by mountains (800-m elevation) at its western end and flat muskeg areas at its eastern end. The lake's watershed is characterized by a boreal forest association of white spruce *Picea glauca* interspersed with balsam poplar *Populus balsamifera* and willow *Salix* spp. along riparian zones, moist tundra communities at low elevations, and extensive stands of green alder *Alnus crispa* at higher elevations (J. Helfield and K. Bartz, unpublished data). Very little alder is found in riparian areas. In addition to Lake Nerka's primary inlet and outlet, approximately 60 surface water streams enter along its shores. Our study stream, Lynx Creek, has a summer base flow discharge of approximately 500 L/s. The stream supports runs of 600–18,000 sockeye salmon with a mean run size of 3,040 fish over the last 55 years (Rogers and Rogers 1998). The salmon run during the summer reported here (2000) was approximately 9,910 fish, the largest run over the past 20 years (Rogers and Rogers 1998).

We installed a rectilinear grid of 130 piezometers on a meander bend of Lynx Creek (Figure

1). For results presented here, we selected a subset of 15 wells that were located along discrete flow paths (determined by using NaCl as a conservative tracer and a conductivity meter to map the flow of water). Piezometers were 2.5 cm schedule 40 PVC pipe, open on the bottom end. These piezometers enabled us to measure water surface elevation and collect samples for water chemistry analysis. Hyporheic water was sampled with a battery driven peristaltic pump. A manifold holding sampling probes was fitted to the pump tubing, so that temperature, dissolved oxygen, and electrical conductance could be measured simultaneously with portable field meters (YSI). Because gravel hydraulic conductivities were high, it was impossible to empty the wells. Water was withdrawn from the pipe bottom until about 4 standing volumes were withdrawn; then, the pump rate was lowered to ensure that new water flowing into the pipe bottom was sampled. Temperature, electrical conductance, and oxygen concentrations in the sample stream were monitored to confirm that remaining standing water was not contaminating samples.

Surface water samples were collected at sites upstream from, adjacent to, and downstream from the piezometer grid. All samples for inorganic water chemistry were collected during mid-day and filtered in the field with syringe-mounted GF/F filters. Samples for dissolved inorganics were fixed with chloroform, and samples for both dissolved inorganics and total dissolved nutrients were frozen within 8 h of collection. These samples were collected through the summer field season (May to September) every 3–10 d, depending on the rate of change for parameters of interest (samples were generally measured within a few days of collection so that the sampling interval could be adjusted accordingly). Inorganic nitrate was measured by the cadmium reduction method (Mulvaney 1996) in the field laboratory with a Spectronic 20 Genesys and a 1-cm cell yielding a detection limit of 10 μg NO_3-N/L. SRP was measured by the ascorbic acid method (Kuo 1996) in the field laboratory with a Spectronic 20 Genesys and a 5-cm cell yielding a detection limit of 8 μg/L soluble reactive phosphorus (SRP). The P-detection limits in the field laboratory were unusually high for

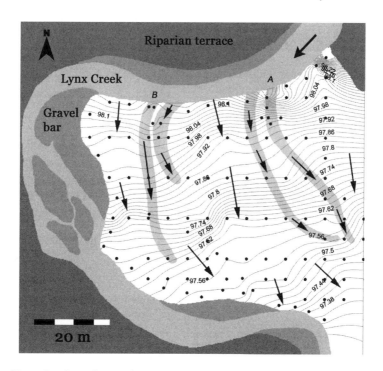

FIGURE 1. Map of Lynx Creek study site showing elevation (m) of groundwater above an arbitrary datum within the riparian hyporheic zone. Filled circles are piezometer locations. Water flow is across head contours. Shaded areas depict major flow paths delineated with salt tracer. Data from flow paths A and B are plotted in Figure 2. Arrows illustrate major flow directions. Contour interval is 2 cm.

SRP, and water samples checked by the analytical laboratory at the University of Washington, Seattle, confirmed that actual background concentrations were in the range of 1–3 µg/L. Ammonium samples were measured in the field laboratory by the fluorometric technique (Protocol A) in Holmes et al. (1999) with a detection limit of 1 µg NH_4^+-N/L. Samples for total dissolved nutrients were digested using the alkaline persulfate method (Valderrama 1981) and analyzed as described above for N nitrate and P.

To estimate the potential importance of spawning sockeye in the nutrient budget of Lynx Creek, nitrogen and phosphorus imported by returning adults was compared with estimates of total system losses (concentration × discharge). Discharge from Lynx Creek was estimated by prorating discharge measured during the summer over the year using a hydrograph from Elva Creek (USGS station 15302840), which is located less than 15 km away and has a watershed area 10% smaller than Lynx Creek. To estimate input from fish, we assumed the average salmon contained 73 g N and 12 g P (Mathisen et al. 1988), and we multiplied this by the run size to calculate annual total fish N and P input to the system.

Results and Discussion

A hydraulic head contour plot (Figure 1) and tracer injections confirmed the existence of an extensive hyporheic zone that is 30–150 cm below the soil surface and, thus, potentially within the rooting zone of riparian vegetation. The total depth of the water mass actively exchanging with surface water is unknown but exceeds the 20–40 cm our piezometers penetrated the saturated zone. Temperature and electrical conductance values from piezometers were always similar to surface water values and showed little spatial variation that would indicate mixing with other water masses. Groundwater temperatures (4°C) were never detected within the grid, suggesting that the upper layer of the hyporheic zone that we sampled was derived entirely from advecting surface stream water. Dissolved oxygen concentrations within the grid varied from near saturation (>11 mg/L) at the head of the flow field to less than 1 mg/L further down the flow paths. Although concentrations decreased along the direction of flow, only a few anaerobic pockets were observed; most sites had DO concentrations greater than 3 mg/L.

Surface water ammonium concentrations increased dramatically when salmon entered Lynx Creek. Values that were less than 2 µg N/L before the entrance of salmon began to increase immediately upon salmon entry and peaked at the height of the run at 147 µg N/L. The rapid increase in ammonium is likely due to excretion by nonfeeding salmon metabolizing body protein for energy (Hendry and Berg 1999). The proportion of total inorganic N as ammonium increased from less than 2% to more than 17% when fish were present. The increase began as salmon were holding in the stream and before individuals began to die. Upon death, which occurs approximately 1 week after entry to this stream, decomposition of salmon tissue in the stream further increased concentrations of ammonium. Increased ammonium concentrations were observed in other streams that we sampled within the area (a total of 23 additional streams). Ammonium increased from near zero in streams with salmon runs with no significant increase in those without salmon runs, supporting the interpretation that the ammonium increase is attributable to salmon inputs.

In Lynx Creek, this ammonium entered the hyporheic zone where we detected elevated levels up to 82 µg N/L in piezometers in the upper section of the flow paths where surface water entered the hyporheic zone (Figure 2). This increase in hyporheic ammonium concentration began at the same time stream concentration increased. Ammonium concentrations along the flow paths declined to near zero background concentrations within 3–5 m along the transect from where surface water entered the hyporheic zone (Figure 2a). These results are consistent with experimental ammonium additions we performed in 1999 and previous work showing high uptake potential for ammonium within the hyporheic zone.

Stream surface water nitrate concentrations decreased from a high of 482 µg N/L in June to a low of 290 µg N/L just prior to the entry of fish. This reduction occurred as stream discharge progressively decreased through the summer and likely reflects the reduced movement of nitrate from valley wall alder forests as soil moisture in the watershed decreased. When spawners entered the stream, there was a small increase of about 50 µg N/L in stream nitrate concentration, suggesting that some of the ammonium released by fish was nitrified within the channel. Within the hyporheic zone, nitrate concentrations in the

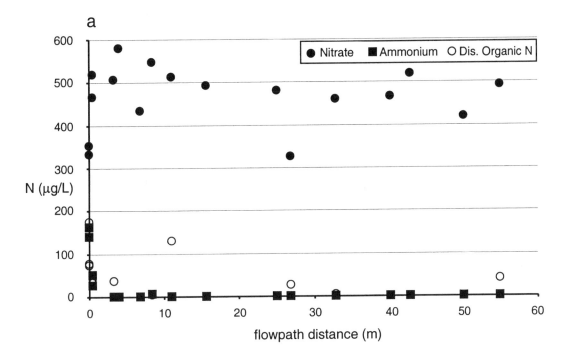

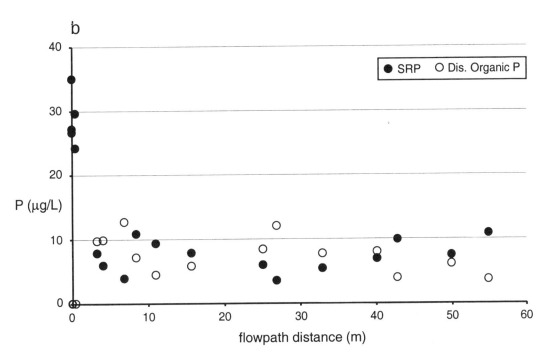

FIGURE 2. Longitudinal plots of dissolved inorganic and dissolved organic forms of N and P along flow paths A and B at the dates of maximum concentration within the upper flow path. a) ammonium, nitrate, and dissolved organic N from 21 August 2000. b) SRP and dissolved organic P from 3 September 2000. Distance 0 values are surface water concentrations at three sites adjacent to the location at which water enters the upper flow field.

first 3 m of the flow paths increased by 150–250 µg N/L from the initiation of spawning to peak spawning densities. This increase is about the same magnitude as the increase in surface water ammonium concentration, suggesting that ammonium entering the hyporheic zone was nitrified. However, longitudinal plots of nitrate along the studied flow paths do not exhibit an obvious increase in nitrate that can be attributed to progressive nitrification (Figure 2a). Instead, nitrate values remained high throughout the flow paths, and any contribution by nitrification was undetectable in the high background variability. Conceivably, ammonium could have been incorporated into dissolved organic or particulate forms within the hyporheic zone and lost in those forms rather than being stored. However, 60 m of sand and gravel is an effective filter, and it is unlikely that particles move very far. Dissolved organic nitrogen values dropped from 31 to 37 µg/L in the first few meters to below detection and remained low along the lower section; thus, we see no evidence for immediate loss in that form.

Soluble reactive phosphorus increased from background levels of less than 8 µg P/L before salmon entered the stream to 45 µg P/L by the end of August, just after the peak of the salmon run. Although phosphorus may also be released from living salmon through metabolism during spawning, the surface concentration increase began two weeks later than that of ammonium. As salmon began to die, SRP concentrations in the upstream section of the hyporheic zone increased from below detection limits to a peak of 33 µg P/L. Similar to ammonium, values decreased to background concentration 3–5 m along the flow paths (Figure 2b). For the duration of our sampling, we saw no indication that phosphorus was re-entering the flow stream as SRP. Likewise, dissolved organic P remained at detection limits in the lower flow path sections, indicating no immediate losses in that form (Figure 2b).

In reference to our study objectives, we conclude that hyporheic transport of salmon-derived nutrients to riparian vegetation is a feasible mechanism. Advecting surface water flowed up to 60 m into the riparian terrace, carrying N and P that appears to be derived from spawning salmon and lies within the rooting zone of riparian vegetation. Whether vegetation actually takes these nutrients up remains to be shown; however, actual uptake of salmon-derived products has not been documented for any known transport

vector; inference of uptake has been based solely on presence of presumed marine isotopic signatures. Our data suggest that the relative importance of N and P as a nutrient source from salmon to riparian vegetation differs in this catchment.

Salmon seem to be a minor source of nitrogen in the Lynx Creek watershed, and most of the nitrogen entering the saturated riparian zone appears to be derived from other sources, most likely alder-dominated soils on the valley walls. A simple annual flux budget for nitrogen based on export of total dissolved nitrogen indicates that even in a year with a large fish run, as we observed in 2000, the salmon are still only supplying 6% of nitrogen discharged from the system, and the long term average is less than half that. Thus, although ammonium and nitrate from salmon are clearly present in the hyporheic zone during spawning, the bulk of nitrogen flowing beneath the riparian terrace enters before spawning and is unrelated to salmon. In contrast, salmon-derived phosphorus appears to be potentially much more important as a source for riparian vegetation. Summer-long SRP values are low, and the increase coinciding with spawning is much more pronounced. A flux budget for phosphorus export relative to potential input from salmon indicated that marine phosphorus made up 38% of the inorganic phosphorus discharged from the stream. Clearly, the rapid removal of SRP within the upper flow field may reduce the distance P penetrates into the riparian zone and thereby its availability to riparian vegetation throughout the flow field. Whether this P is subsequently released into the water and moved farther down the flow path requires further study. In regard to the question of storage of MDN within hyporheic zones, the differences between N and P must also be considered. Although ammonium, the dominant form of marine-derived N input into the hyporheic zone, is efficiently removed from solution (Triska et al. 1994), there is evidence that nitrification is converting some to nitrate, which continues to move down the flow paths. Denitrification is also occurring in the terrace soils (Gilles Pinay, personal communication), which could further reduce long-term storage of nitrogen. Nonetheless, advecting marine-derived N is physically retarded by entrainment within the hyporheic zone and is exposed to biological and physical uptake mechanisms that can retain it for periods exceeding the hydrologic residence time; so, overwinter storage of some proportion remains a possibility. Definitive testing of overwinter nutrient retention will require research in a system that can be studied year round and some manipulative experiments. Phosphorus storage appears more likely because little export of SRP was observed during spawning, there are no pathways for gaseous loss, and conversion to more mobile forms is unlikely. However, how long the P is stored and how long it takes to work its way down the flow field and re-enter the surface stream remains to be demonstrated. The question is an important one for Lynx Creek because nutrient diffusing substrate studies indicate that benthic algae are strongly P-limited (R. T. Edwards, unpublished data).

The elevated nitrate concentrations we measured both before and during spawning likely result from extensive stands of nitrogen-fixing green alder that dominate the uplands of many of the watersheds. Our study site was characteristic of streams in southwestern Alaska where large stands of alder can dominate watersheds. This alder-derived nitrogen could be an important source of nutrients and must be considered when examining the flux of nutrients, especially N, in these systems. Alder covers approximately 44% of the Lynx Creek watershed, and in a survey of 23 additional watersheds in this area, dissolved nitrogen was highly correlated ($r^2 = 0.75$) with percent alder coverage (authors' unpublished data). This suggests that stream nitrogen budgets in this area are strongly influenced by alder coverage.

Summary

We have documented hyporheic flow beneath the riparian terrace in a sockeye spawning stream. Because the physical characteristics of the porous gravel substrate used by salmon for spawning also create ideal conditions for hyporheic flow, we believe that extensive subsurface flow is a characteristic feature of all salmon spawning streams. We have also documented elevated ammonium and SRP concentrations in surface water during the period of spawning and the intrusion of these nutrients into the hyporheic zone. These nutrients are rapidly removed from solution upon entering the metabolically active upstream edge of the hyporheic zone, demonstrating the potential for these areas to serve as storage areas for salmon-derived nutrients. In systems or years with few salmon relative to the capacity of wildlife to remove carcasses from the stream, we predict that hyporheic transfer and storage will be relatively small. In contrast, during larger runs when animal consumption is saturated and many fish decompose within the stream, hyporheic transfer and storage may process an ecologically significant mass of N and P. The net effect of hyporheic processes on stream productivity depends upon the ultimate fate of N and P removed. If the bulk of ammonium is converted to mobile forms or lost via denitrification and if phosphorus is ultimately irreversibly bound to minerals, then hyporheic zones are a sink for MDN. If, on the other hand, nutrient spiraling within the saturated zone allows nutrients to slowly migrate down flow paths and re-enter the surface channel after some delay, hyporheic zones can function to buffer the seasonal pulse of limiting nutrients and increase stream productivity. Other sources of nutrients within the watershed, such as alder, need to be considered when interpreting the importance of salmon nutrients at any given location throughout the geographic range of salmon.

Acknowledgments

Research was supported with National Science Foundation Grant DEB9806575 to R. J. Naiman and the Aquatic and Lands Interaction Program, PNW Research Station, USDA Forest Service. We gratefully acknowledge our collaboration with and field assistance from K. Bartz, J. S. Bechtold, J. Helfield, K. Overberg, G. Pinay, and R. J. Naiman. This manuscript benefited by comments from Dom Chaloner and Beth Sanderson. We also thank T. Rogers, D. Schindler, and staff from the University of Washington's Alaska Salmon Program for their assistance and support at the field site.

References

Ben-David, M. 1997. Timing of reproduction in wild mink: the influence of spawning Pacific salmon. Canadian Journal of Zoology 75:376–382.

Ben-David, M., T. A. Hanley, and D. M. Schell. 1998. Fertilization of terrestrial vegetation by spawning Pacific salmon: the role of flooding and predator activity. Oikos 83:47–55.

Bilby, R. E., B. R. Fransen, and P. A. Bisson. 1996. Incorporation of nitrogen and carbon from spawning coho salmon into the trophic system of small streams: evidence from stable isotopes.

Canadian Journal of Fisheries and Aquatic Sciences 53:164–173.

Cederholm, C. J., and N. P. Peterson. 1985. The retention of coho salmon (*Oncorhynchus kisutch*) carcasses by organic debris in small streams. Canadian Journal of Fisheries and Aquatic Sciences 42:1222–1225.

Cederholm, C. J., M. D. Kunze, T. Murota, and A. Sibatani. 1999. Pacific salmon carcasses: essential contributions of nutrients and energy for aquatic and terrestrial systems. Fisheries 24:6–15.

Cederholm, C. J., D. H. Johnson, R. E. Bilby, L. G. Dominguez, A. M. Garrett, W. H. Graeber, E. L. Greda, M. D. Kunze, B. G. Marcot, J. F. Palmisano, R. W. Plotnikoff, W. G. Pearcy, C. A. Simenstad, and P. C. Trotter. 2000. Pacific salmon and wildlife-ecological contexts, relationships, and implications for management. Special edition technical report, prepared for D. H. Johnson and T. A. O'Neil (managing directors), Wildlife-Habitat Relationships in Oregon and Washington. Washington Department of Fish and Wildlife, Olympia, Washington.

Chaloner, D. T., and M. S. Wipfli. 2002. Influence of decomposing Pacific salmon carcasses on macroinvertebrate growth and standing stock in southeastern Alaska streams. Journal of the North American Benthological Society 21:430–442.

Edwards, R. T. 1998. The hyporehic zone. Pages 399–429 *in* R. J. Naiman and R. E. Bilby, editors. River ecology and management. Springer-Verlag, New York.

Harvey, J. W. and B. J. Wagner. 2000. Quantifying hydrologic interactions between streams and their subsurface hyporheic zones. Pages 3–44 *in* J. A. Jones and P. J. Mulholland, editors. Streams and ground waters. Academic Press, San Diego, California.

Helfield, J. M., and R. J. Naiman. 2001. Fertilization of riparian vegetation by spawning salmon: effects on tree growth and implications for long-term productivity. Ecology 82:2403–2409.

Hendry, A. P., and O. K. Berg. 1999. Secondary sexual characters, energy use, senescence, and the cost of reproduction in sockeye salmon. Canadian Journal of Zoology 77:1663–1675.

Hilderbrand, G. V., T. A. Hanley, C. T. Robbins, and C. C. Schwartz. 1999a. Role of brown bears (*Ursus arctos*) in the flow of marine nitrogen into a terrestrial ecosystem. Oecologia 121:546–550.

Hilderbrand, G. V., C. C. Schwartz, C. T. Robbins, M. E. Jacoby, T. A. Hanley, S. M. Arthur, and C. Servheen. 1999b. The importance of meat, particularly salmon, to body size, population productivity, and conservation of North American brown bears. Canadian Journal of Zoology 77:132–138.

Holmes, R. M., A. Aminot, R. Kérouel, B. A. Hooker, and B. J. Peterson. 1999. A simple and precise method for measuring ammonium in marine and freshwater ecosystems. Canadian Journal of Fisheries and Aquatic Sciences 56:1801–1808.

Kline, T. C., J. J. Goering, O. A. Mathisen, P. H. Poe, P. L. Parker. 1990. Recycling of elements transported upstream by runs of Pacific salmon: I. Δ15N and Δ13C evidence in Sashin Creek, southeastern Alaska. Canadian Journal of Fisheries and Aquatic Sciences 47:136–144.

Kline, T. C., J. J. Goering, O. A. Mathisen, P. H. Poe, P. L. Parker, R. S. Scalan. 1993. Recycling of elements transported upstream by runs of Pacific salmon: II. Δ15N and Δ13C evidence in the Kvichak River watershed, Bristol Bay, southwestern Alaska. Canadian Journal of Fisheries and Aquatic Sciences 50:2350–2365.

Kline, T. C., J. J. Goering, R. J. Piorkowski. 1997. The effect of salmon carcasses on Alaskan freshwaters. Pages 179–204 *in* A. M. Milner and M. W. Oswood, editors. Freshwaters of Alaska. Springer-Verlag, New York.

Kuo, S. 1996. Phosphorus. Pages 869–919 *in* J. M. Bigham, editor. Methods of soil analysis part 3: chemical methods. Soil Science Society of America, Inc., Madison, Wisconsin.

Larkin, G. A., and P. A. Slaney. 1997. Implications of trends in marine-derived nutrient influx to south coastal British Columbia salmonid production. Fisheries 22:16–24.

Mathisen, O. A., P. L. Parker, J. J. Goering, T. C. Kline, P. H. Poe, and R. S. Scalan. 1988. Recycling of marine elements transported into freshwater systems by anadromous salmon. Internationale Vereinigung für Theoretische und Angewandte Limnologie 23:2249–2258.

Mulvaney, R. L. 1996. Nitrogen–inorganic forms. Pages 1123–1184 *in* J. M. Bigham, editor. Methods of soil analysis part 3: chemical methods. Soil Science Society of America, Inc., Madison, Wisconsin.

Reimchen, T. E. 2000. Some ecological and evolutionary aspects of bear-salmon interactions in coastal British Columbia. Canadian Journal of Zoology 78:448–457.

Richey, J. E., M. A. Perkins, and C. R. Goldman. 1975. Effects of kokanee salmon (*Oncorhynchus nerka*) decomposition on the ecology of a subalpine stream. Journal of the Fisheries Research Board of Canada 32:817–820.

Rogers, D. E., and B. J. Rogers. 1998. Spawning ground surveys in the Wood River lakes. Fisheries Research Institute, University of Washington. FRI-UW-9803.

Schuldt, J. A., and A. E. Hershey. 1995. Effect of salmon carcass decomposition on Lake Superior tributary streams. Journal of the North American Benthological Society 14:259–268.

Triska, F. J. V. C. Kennedy, R. J. Avanzino, G. W. Zellweger, and K. E. Bencala. 1989. Retention and transport of nutrients in a third-order stream in northwestern California: hyporheic processes. Ecology 70:1893–1905.

Triska, F. J., A. P. Jackman, J. H. Duff, and R. J. Avanzino. 1994. Ammonium sorption to channel and riparian sediments: a transient storage pool for dissolved inorganic nitrogen. Biogeochemistry 26:67–83.

Valderrama, J. C. 1981. The simultaneou analyis of total nitrogen and total phosphorus in natural waters. Marine Chemistry 10:109–122.

Wipfli, M. S., J. Hudson, and J. Caouette. 1998. Influence of salmon carcasses on stream productivity: response of biofilm and benthic macroinvertebrates in southeastern Alaska, USA. Canadian Journal of Fisheries and Aquatic Sciences 55:1503–1511.

Replacing Lost Nutrients:
Stream and Lake Fertilization

American Fisheries Society Symposium 34:111–126, 2003

Experimental Nutrient Addition to the Keogh River and Application to the Salmon River in Coastal British Columbia

PATRICK A. SLANEY AND BRUCE R. WARD

Ministry of Water, Land and Air Protection, 2204 Main Mall, Fisheries Centre
University of British Columbia, Vancouver, B.C. V6T 1Z4, Canada

JAMES CRAIG WIGHTMAN

Ministry of Water, Land and Air Protection, 2080-A Labieux Road
Nanaimo, B.C. V9T 6J9, Canada

Abstract.—Oligtrophic streams are ubiquitous throughout coastal British Columbia, and thereby, significant nutrient influx can be provided externally via salmon carcasses. At the Keogh River on northern Vancouver Island, experimental nutrient addition was conducted from 1983 to 1986 to examine if potential increases in trophic productivity may augment growth and production of salmonid smolts. Subsequently, an applied treatment was conducted over the past decade at the infertile Salmon River to offset intensive logging impacts and to accelerate colonization of steelhead trout *Oncorhynchus mykiss* of headwater reaches above a hydroelectric diversion. The two rivers were treated with agricultural (dry, later liquid) fertilizers, while upstream control reaches were untreated. At Keogh, inorganic P and N were introduced to produce target soluble phosphorus concentrations of 10–15 mg per L, and N loadings of 50–100 mg per L over the four years of nutrient addition. Average peak algal biomass as chlorophyll *a* increased 5–10-fold in response to nutrient addition. Geometric mean weights of steelhead trout and coho salmon *O. kisutch* fry within several treated reaches were 1.4–2.0-fold higher than the control, and mean weights of steelhead parr were 30–130% greater in the three treated reaches. Average steelhead smolt yield in three brood years increased 62% (peak, 2.5-fold in 1987) over prefertilization years; yet there was no increase in average smolt size because mean smolt age was reduced by about one year. There were corresponding increases in returning adults and reported catches by steelhead anglers at the Keogh River, compared with trends at an adjacent river fishery. The response of coho smolts to nutrient addition was less marked, or a suggested 21% increase in numbers ($P < 0.1$) with no change in size, although results were moderated by production of coho smolts from several untreated tributaries and small lakes. At the upper Salmon River, where nutrient targets were reduced to one-third that of the Keogh, nutrient addition was associated with 3–7-fold higher benthic insect density in treated reaches than controls, and 2–3-fold greater mean weights and biomass of steelhead and rainbow trout in treated index sites than upstream, unfertilized sites. Over the decade, estimated numbers of steelhead parr and smolt migrants at the Salmon River diversion increased from about 1,500 to 8,000. The results at the Salmon River confirmed those of the Keogh and indicated that lower-level nutrient addition can produce a similar positive trophic response.

Introduction

Food abundance functions through territory size as a major factor affecting the abundance and growth of salmonids and, thus, the carrying capacity of streams (Chapman 1966; Slaney and Northcote 1974; Dill et al. 1981). Additions of inorganic nutrients to oligotrophic streams increase periphyton production (Stockner and Shortreed 1978; Peterson et al. 1985; Perrin et al. 1987) at the base of the food chain, and thereby augment insect growth, abundance (Milbrink and Holmgren 1981; Peterson et al. 1985; Johnston et al. 1990; Perrin and Richardson 1997), and survival (Mundie et al. 1991). Accordingly, fish growth is increased, as documented in steelhead trout *Oncorhynchus mykiss*, coho salmon *O. kisutch* (Slaney et al. 1986; Johnston et al. 1990), and Arctic grayling *Thymallus arcticus* (Deegan and Peterson 1992). Thus, nutrient augmentation has the potential to be beneficial, particularly where nutrient influxes from Pacific salmon carcasses are depressed as a result of low escapement.

Research on nutrient addition to streams has been conducted for several years on northern Vancouver Island in British Columbia. Primary objectives were to determine the effect of nutrient additions on the growth and abundance of anadromous salmonids in oligotrophic streams,

and to determine if controlled release of nutrients during the growing season is a viable option for restoration or habitat mitigation. In this paper, we follow the effects of whole-river nutrient addition in 1983–1986 through to the production of salmonid smolts and returns of adult steelhead trout at the Keogh River. We then describe subsequent results from similar studies in the Salmon River, Vancouver Island.

Methods

Study Sites

Keogh River. Nutrient manipulations were conducted at the Keogh River (127°25'W by 50°35'N) on northeastern Vancouver Island near the town of Port Hardy (Figure 1), first as a pilot experiment within the uppermost reach of the river (km 28 to km 31) in 1981, as described in Perrin et al. (1987) and Johnston (1990), and sub-

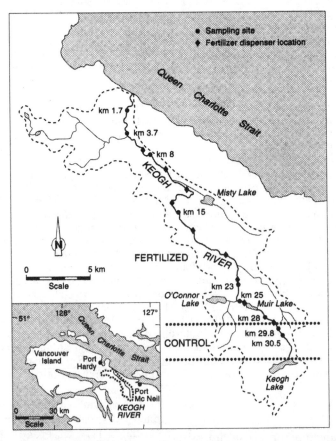

FIGURE 1. Keogh River watershed and locations of fertilizer dispenser sites and sampling stations in 1984.

sequently as whole-river treatments from 1983 to 1986. Detailed descriptions of the study areas and methods are given in Slaney et al. (1986), Perrin et al. (1987), Johnston et al. (1990), and Slaney and Ward (1993). Briefly, the stream is 32 km long within a 130-km² watershed, and the wetted mean width at average summer flows is 8.1 m (range 5–15 m). The stream is composed of a diverse distribution of gradients and hydraulic habitats in the main stem: riffles (36%, by area), runs (14%), flats (24%), and pools (26%). Mean annual discharge is 5.3 m³/s, with a minimum flow of 0.1 m³/s (midsummer) and an estimated maximum flow of 254 m³/s (fall 1975). Mean summer flows at km 28 in the upper river and km 3 near the mouth are about 0.5 m³/s and 1.6 m³/s, respectively. Annual precipitation, mainly as rainfall, averages 173 cm. Water temperature averages about 12°C in spring and 16°C in summer and is 1–2°C higher in the upper river in summer because of warmer water from a headwater lake. Total dissolved solids and total alkalinity in spring to summer are low; 30 mg/L and 7 mg/L $CaCO_3$, respectively, and the water is stained with tannins and lignins (1–2 mg/L). Nutrient concentrations in spring to summer are extremely low: orthophosphorus, <1 mg/L; total dissolved phosphorus, 5 mg/L; nitrate nitrogen, usually <15 mg/L. At low flow in summer, there is a slight increase in inorganic phosphorus and up to a 4-fold increase in nitrate nitrogen (Perrin et al. 1987).

Forest harvesting of Sitka spruce *Picea sitchensis*, western hemlock *Tsuga heterophylla*, and red cedar *Thuja plicata* is active in the watershed, and about 35% of the area was logged to 1983. In riparian zones where red alder *Alnus rubra* is common, canopy closure is about 30% in the headwaters and 60–70% elsewhere; 55–60% of riparian areas were logged historically to streambanks until restricted in 1988.

The Keogh River supports runs of pink salmon *O. gorbuscha* (about 50,000 spawners in the 1980s with even years dominant), coho salmon (1,000–7,000 spawners), and steelhead trout (200–2,000 fish). Anadromous Dolly Varden char *Salvelinus malma* and resident cutthroat trout *O. clarki* also inhabit the river, the latter mainly in tributaries. In contrast to coho, few steelhead inhabit the tributaries and small lakes in the system. Steelhead trout migrate seaward in spring as smolts at ages 2–4, and coho salmon migrate as age-1 smolts (>90%). Hatchery steelhead smolts (Keogh stock: 3,100–30,400, all with a clipped adipose fin) were released into the Keogh River near the ocean, from 1979 to 1990.

Salmon River. The headwater reaches of the Salmon River are located about 30 km west of the city of Campbell River, British Columbia, on the east coast of Vancouver Island, and about 130 km southeast of the Keogh River (Figure 2). Wetted stream width is similar to the Keogh River, but the Salmon has a steeper gradient and higher minimum summer flows and lacks the organic staining of the Keogh. Mean annual flow of the Salmon River at a gauging site (Water Survey of Canada) located 15 km downstream of a hydroelectric water diversion is about 13 m³/s, declining in spring to summer from 12 m³/s to 3 m³/s. In a main tributary, Grilse Creek, average flow from early May to midsummer declines from 3 m³/s to 0.5 m³/s. Water temperatures are lower than the Keogh River, increasing at the diversion from 6°C to 9°C in May to 9–12°C in June to 12–16°C in July and August, and are about 1°C higher on average in Grilse Creek than the Salmon River. Nutrient concentrations are similar to the Keogh River: soluble reactive phosphorus (SRP), <1 mg/L; total dissolved phosphorus (TDP), 5 mg/L; and nitrate nitrogen (NO_3-N) 15 mg/L, the latter increasing several-fold with declining flows by midsummer (Perrin 1991a). In contrast to the Keogh River watershed, steep hill slopes dominate much of the Salmon River watershed. Also, Douglas fir *Pseudotsuga menziesii* and western hemlock dominate the latter, except in most riparian areas where alder is common because of the historical logging of mature conifers. Channel instability, including widening and high bed load, are common in the boulder-dominated Salmon River, in contrast to the Keogh River.

The Salmon River is utilized by Pacific salmon, Dolly Varden char, cutthroat trout, and steelhead trout, the latter renown for trophy-sized fish (10–15 kg) that supported an estimated 1,200 angler-days with an average catch of 1,000 fish annually in the 1980s. The headwater streams of the Salmon River, where nutrients were added, are inhabited by resident rainbow trout *O. mykiss*, as well as a sparse population of Dolly Varden char, both typically maturing at a small size in the high-gradient and unproductive waters. During the late 1970s, a barrier to fish passage was removed by blasting a boulder obstruction in a canyon, and anadromous fish were once again able to migrate upstream for several kilometers to a hydroelectric diversion dam (Figure 2). Thereafter, a fish screen was installed in the diversion canal in 1986 and operated to return parr and smolts to the Salmon River. These headwater streams have been stocked with

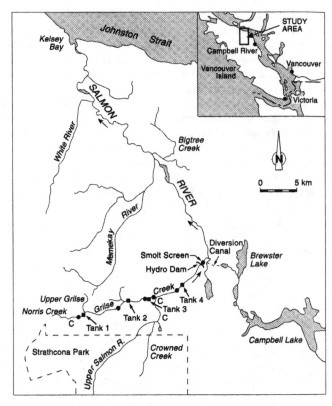

FIGURE 2. Salmon River, Grilse Creek, and tributaries, showing locations of liquid fertilizer tanks in 1992. Dots (treated) and C (control) indicate sampling sites.

steelhead trout fry in either late summer (1986–1989; 4–7 g) or mid-July (1990–1998; 1.1–1.4 g) to extend their distribution beyond the hydroelectric diversion and into 8 km of main stem and about 20 km of streams within Grilse Creek and the upper Salmon River. Coho fry were also stocked into ponds and small lakes to develop a run of adult coho salmon in the upper watershed. Stocking of steelhead fry was ceased after an adult fishway was constructed at the diversion in 1992, when increasing numbers of adults migrated into the upper river. Nutrients were added to Grilse Creek in 1989 to speed colonization by steelhead and to offset the hydrologic and geomorphic impacts of intensive clear-cut logging in this mountainous watershed.

Fertilizer Treatments

Keogh River. Nutrient treatments during 1983–1986 at the Keogh River were described in detail in Johnston et al. (1990). Briefly, target nutrient concentrations were selected to saturate P-limited periphyton production, with N added to ensure that nitrogen did not become limiting after P was replete. One exception was during spring and summer in 1983 when applications of a coated slow-release fertilizer sporadically introduced inorganic N and P and, thus, the seasonal treatment was not continuous. Although several concentrations of fertilizer were applied at the Keogh River, we regard these as one treatment of "inorganic fertilization" because most changes were in loadings of nitrogen. Inorganic P and N were added from mid-spring to summer in 1983–1986 to produce a "whole-river treatment" of target concentrations of 10–15 mg/L over a distance of 29 km, while maintaining a 2-km section of similar gradient as a control reach. Target concentrations of N varied to reduce costs of application to that needed to obtain a strong periphyton response. In 1983, a solid coated fertilizer (Osmocote, Sierra Chemicals Ltd., Milpitas, California) was spread on three occasions by helicopter to attempt to produce concentrations of 10 mg/L P and 100 mg/L N from late March to late July. In 1984, the 29 km were continuously fertilized with inorganic P and N from early May to late September. A more thickly coated Osmocote prill was spread by hand in the upper 3 km of the 29-km treated length to produce P and N concentrations of 15 mg/L. The other 26 km were fertilized continuously with 10–55–0 and 34–0–0 fertilizers dispensed from fish feeders at 3 km intervals. These were set to provide target concentrations of 15 mg/L of P and N in the upper 3 km, and 15 mg/L P and 150 mg/L N in the remaining 23 km. In 1985, 29 km were fertilized continuously with the dispensers at 5-km intervals from mid-April to late September to produce concentrations of 10 mg/L P and 100 mg/L N. From late April to early September in 1986, this treatment was repeated, except 34–0–0 was not added in the upper 3 km, and N was reduced to a target of 50 mg/L in the lower 26 km.

Salmon River. Following the technique developed at the Keogh River, nutrients were added to Grilse Creek in 1989 by dispensing dry fertilizer (10–55–0 and 34–0–0) continuously with fish feeders at two sites, including a tributary near the confluence with upper Grilse Creek and at Grilse Creek, 6.5 km from the upper dispenser. Target concentrations were reduced by about one-half of that used at Keogh, and results similar to that documented at Keogh are presented elsewhere (Perrin 1991).

In 1990, nutrient formulations were shifted to liquid agricultural fertilizers to improve efficiency in adjusting inputs to changing flows. Ammonium polyphosphate (10–34–0, composed of 50% polyphosphate and 50% monophosphate molecules) and ammonium nitrate (34–0–0) were metered into the stream using gravity flow from 1.4-m^3 polyethylene tanks secured at the streambank. Tank one was placed about 600 m upstream of the Norris-Grilse creeks confluence, tank two was about 6 km downstream at Grilse Creek, and tank three was 4 km further downstream or almost 1 km upstream of the confluence with the upper Salmon River (Figure 2). Target concentrations were 5 mg/L P and 15 mg/L N as dissolved nitrogen, with some variability resulting from periodic clogging of valves. The timing of the treatment was mid-May to early September. The targets at the upper site were augmented to adjust for flow from Grilse Creek. Commencing in 1991, the seasonal treatment was repeated for a fourth year, but was terminated by 1 August. In 1992, nitrate inputs were terminated because N concentrations were sufficient to maintain a molar N:P high enough to prevent N-deficiency of the benthic biofilm. A fourth tank was also in-

stalled 5 km downstream from the third tank, or about 4 km below the confluence of Grilse Creek and the upper Salmon River (Figure 2). Thus, in 1992, only ammonium polyphosphate was metered into the stream from mid-May until late July. Nitrogen was again added in 1993 because of low ambient N concentrations the previous spring, which could have induced N-limitation in algae. Also, the third tank (lower Grilse) was removed and reset at 25 km to add fertilizer to the Salmon River to near its confluence with Memekay River (km 50).

Study Design

Determination of treatment effects of whole-stream nutrient addition is largely based on multiple lines of evidence of effects on three trophic levels in salmonid food chains. In addition, to unequivocally separate treatment from location effects, a before-and-after controlled impact (BACCI; Stewart-Oaten et al. 1986) design was utilized for comparisons of fry sizes at Keogh River, as described by Johnston et al. (1990). The magnitude of differences in treated and untreated reaches can provide convincing evidence of treatment effects (Hurlbert 1984); large differences are supportive of inferences that whole-stream fertilization has had profound effects on fish growth or abundance.

Food Chain Response

To assist in interpreting the effects of nutrient addition on salmonids, ancillary data were collected on water chemistry, periphyton accrual, and benthic insect biomass in riffles. Water samples were collected at the Keogh and Salmon rivers and processed as described in Perrin et al. (1987). More recently, at the latter stream, samples were shipped and analyzed (within three days) either by Zenon Laboratories Ltd. (Burnaby) or Cantest Laboratories Ltd. (Vancouver), using the analyses described in APHA (1985). Detection limits for SRP and NO_3-N were usually 1 mg/L and 5 mg/L, respectively. Periphyton accrual on Styrofoam substrates (30 cm × 30 cm × 0.6 cm, elevated on concrete blocks) was measured in monthly time series within the control sites and at treatment sites during the season of fertilization, following the procedures described in Perrin et al. (1987). Periphyton standing crop was measured as chlorophyll *a* at the control site and at several treatment sites at approximately 5-km intervals. Chlorophyll-*a* results were also available from both rivers before nutrient addition, as described by Perrin (1989) and Johnston et al. (1990). At the Salmon River, additional sampling sites were established in 1993 at 9 km and 25 km downstream of the fourth nutrient dispenser.

Benthic invertebrate density and biomass were also sampled within treated and untreated (upstream) reaches of the two rivers. Large differences in measures of benthos abundance may be expected, thus providing additional lines of potential evidence to discriminate treatment effects. Within control and fertilizer sections of the upper Keogh River, during the 1981 "pilot," benthos samples were collected monthly in riffles with a Hess sampler (Johnston et al. 1990), but sampling was not repeated during the 1983–1986 whole-river treatment. However, at the Salmon River, more intensive sampling during nutrient addition was conducted. In 1992, six cylindrical benthic baskets (22 cm in diameter by 13 cm in depth; 0.04 m² in area and 0.005 m³ in volume) containing gravel (size 1–3 cm) were installed in mid-June within riffles in each of four reaches: a control site 50 m above the first fertilizer dispenser; within Grilse Creek, about 300 m downstream of the second dispenser; at the diversion site, 8 km downstream of the fourth dispenser; and 25 km downstream of the fourth dispenser. The latter was included to detect if there was distant translocation of the effects of nutrient addition. The baskets of gravel were left to colonize with invertebrates for eight weeks. A Surber sampler (0.2-mm mesh net) was used to collect insects and detritus from the gravel baskets that were washed into the net, collected, and preserved. Sample means were compared with the controls by *t*-tests. In 1993, similar sampling of both benthic insects, as well as periphyton chlorophyll *a*, was conducted at these and six additional sites to confirm earlier results to a distance of 38 km. These matched sampling sites for juvenile fish in Grilse Creek and the Salmon River.

Effects on Salmonids

Keogh River. We assessed the effects of nutrient addition on the growth and abundance of young steelhead trout and coho salmon within the stream. A before-after control-impact design (Stewart-Oaten et al. 1986) was used by Johnston et al. (1990) to test for treatment effects on steelhead and coho fry, comparing differences in paired measurements of fry size in control and fertilized reaches during several treated and untreated years. This design was not repeated with steelhead parr because size data in late summer was unavailable from most unfertilized reaches. Rather, analyses of parr were restricted to comparisons of the upstream control to the three fertilized reaches. Regardless, weight-at-age sam-ples from 1980, before enrichment, provide a useful benchmark for upper, middle, and lower reaches of the river. Sample means were compared with the control by *t*-tests at the *P* = 0.05 level (Wilkinson 1988).

Instream fish sampling was conducted from 1983 to 1986 at multiple sites (4–10) within each of four reaches: the control, an upper reach, a middle reach, and a lower river reach. Population estimation was stratified by habitat unit, except in 1983 when only sampling for fish size was conducted. In deep and complex pools, Peterson mark–recapture estimates were completed by use of a combination of seining and electrofishing. A small fin clip (caudal) was used to mark fish. Because of few replicated sample sites per reach, estimates of parr densities were crude and limited to 1984 and 1985. Age-classes were separated by length frequencies and by extensive aging from scales, using methods described in Ward and Slaney (1988).

A fish-counting fence, located 300 m from the river mouth, was used to determine the effect on the size, age, and numbers of smolts migrating from the Keogh River. Methods were outlined in Ward and Slaney (1988, 1993). Briefly, smolts were enumerated from early April to mid-June from 1977 to 1991 by passing smolts over a large horizontal screen trap and Wolfe traps, the latter during peak flow events. To obtain total numbers of smolts, a series of trapping efficiency tests, using marked smolts, were conducted annually to correct smolt yields. Trapping efficiency was typically 90% (range 70–100%), and fish were randomly sampled for fork length and weight, and subsampled for scales. Aging was carried out as described in Ward and Slaney (1988, 1993). Because smolts migrate in mixed year-classes at ages 1–5, numbers migrating per brood year were examined to detect the effects of nutrient addition in 1983–1986.

Adult steelhead returning to the river after two or three years at sea (rarely one year), were trapped as upstream migrants during winter to spring since 1975 (Ward and Slaney 1988, 1993). Because adult coho salmon typically migrate into the river during autumn freshets, adult coho were not enumerated. Total numbers of adult male and female steelhead were estimated separately by mark and recapture using the adjusted Peterson estimate, by marking upstream migrant adults and recovering kelts during their downstream migration through the trap from March to June. On average, from 1976 to 1986, 62% of the estimated population was handled either as upstream migrants or unmarked downstream migrant kelts; the average rate of recapture of marked adults as kelts was 23% and 42% for males and females, respectively (Ward and Slaney 1988). Smolts from fertilizer-treated brood years returned as adults in 1986–1990.

Salmon River. Several sampling sites were located in the Salmon River and its tributaries to compare the size and abundance of juvenile steelhead and rainbow trout in sections with and without nutrient addition (Figure 2). In 1990–1992, 6 to 10 cobble-boulder "index" riffles, were established, including two spatial control sites in the upper Salmon River, one directly upstream of the confluence with Grilse Creek and a second about 3 km upstream, below a small lake (Figure 2). One to three index sites were in the fertilizer section of Grilse Creek near the second dispenser, and 2–4 index sites were situated in the mainstem Salmon River downstream about 5 and 10 km from the third (1990) and fourth dispensers (1992) described earlier. In 1992, an additional two sites were sampled up to 50 km downstream to provide index sites that were likely to be unaffected by fertilization. Sampling and enumeration techniques were similar to methods described in the Keogh, except a 2-step removal method was used to estimate numbers of fry and parr within enclosed 20–30 m sections (Seber and Le Cren 1967).

Migrant parr and smolts from the upper Salmon were also enumerated from the screened hydro diversion (20 km downstream of tank 1 in Grilse Creek), using a bypass trap and releases of marked smolts from April to June each year from 1988 to 1998.

Results

Water Chemistry and Periphyton Accrual

Changes in nutrient concentrations and periphyton biomass in the Keogh River were described for pretreatment and fertilized years (1975–1986) in Johnston et al. (1990). During fertilizer addition, nutrients were detectable at all sampling sites because of the high loading rates. In the control reach and within the treated reaches prior to nutrient addition, mean summer concentrations of dissolved inorganic nitrogen (DIN; nitrate + nitrite + ammonia) and soluble inorganic phosphorus were low, at 10–30 mg/L DIN and 1–3 mg P/L. During fertilizer addition in the treated reaches, mean concentrations were elevated 10–20 fold (1981) and 2–12 fold (1983–1986). The lowest increase was in 1983 when the slow-release prill was introduced, releasing rapidly then slowly. Periphyton accrual, as chlorophyll a, increased substantially as a result of nutrient addition, except in 1983. Peaks were in spring, averaging 100 mg/m^2 initially during whole-stream fertilization, with lesser peak accrual (60–70 mg/m^2) by the fourth year in 1986. In contrast, peak accrual in the control reach was 10 mg/m^2, or an order of magnitude less. Responses to the slow-release prill in 1983 (km 0–25) and in 1984 (km 28) peaked at lower levels, 20–50 mg/m^2, and were not sustained in 1983. In all treatments, diatoms dominated the algal community, but chlorophytes became evident in fertilized sections by late summer (Johnston et al. 1990).

Results at Grilse Creek and the Salmon River from nutrient and periphyton sampling in 1988, 1990, and 1991 are described in detail by Perrin (1989, 1991). Briefly, dissolved inorganic phosphorus concentrations at the Grilse Creek sampling sites in 1990 and 1991 were one-third to one-half of the target 5 mg P/L, and nitrate nitrogen was 2–4 times the target of 15 mg N/L, except in the Salmon mainstem, where nitrate was near the target. In 1992 from mid-May to late July, when only ammonium polyphosphate was added, inorganic phosphorus concentrations in Grilse Creek and the Salmon River were mainly less than the detection limit. In 1988, before fertilizer addition, peak chlorophyll a in Grilse Creek during early and late summer was 18.6 mg/m^2 and 5.4 mg/m^2, respectively, and in the upper Salmon River, it was 8.2 mg/m^2 and 2.5 mg/m^2, respectively. In contrast, during 1990 and 1991, peak periphyton responses were several-fold greater, or similar to those recorded at the Keogh River. In May, June, and July of 1990 and 1991, chlorophyll a at the treated sites and downstream in the mainstem at the diversion peaked 5–10 times the level in the control section (10 mg/m^2; Perrin 1991). However, by 1992, at the fertilized site in Grilse Creek and at the Salmon River diversion site (9 km downstream of the fourth nutrient dispenser), peak chlorophyll *a* was only moderately elevated during July to 42 and 37 mg/m², respectively, whereas the peaks in the control and 25 km downstream of the fertilizer dispenser in the Salmon River were low in July (9 and 8 mg/m²). Similar moderation was evident in 1993; chlorophyll *a* averaged 36 mg/m² at seven stations versus 14 mg/m² at two control sites (Figure 3).

Benthic Insects

At Keogh River, in 1981, by late summer, there was 5-fold higher mean biomass of benthic insects in the high nutrient section than the upstream control section (Johnston et al. 1990). Likewise, at the Salmon River, the abundance and composition of insects differed markedly within treated and untreated reaches. Treated reaches of Grilse Creek and Salmon River were 3–4-fold greater in chlorophyll *a* in 1991. Accordingly, mean densities of benthic insects were 2.5-fold and 7-fold higher there than both the upstream control and the sampling site located 25 km downstream from the fourth fertilizer dispenser at km 38 (*t*-tests, P < 0.05). More intensive sampling in 1993 indicated that, on average, there was a 3.7-fold greater benthic insect biomass within the eight treated sites than the two control sites (Figure 3). In contrast to 1991, the km 38 site in 1993 was

treated (from the tank added at km 25), which accounts for the 5-fold greater benthic density there in 1993 than in 1991. Numerical composition of insects in 1991 varied among the four sites, with mayflies dominating the control (52%) and the fertilizer site (50%) in the Salmon River, with slightly less at the lower Salmon site (40%), and much less in Grilse Creek (20%). Dipterans, which were mainly composed of chironomids, dominated the composition at the Grilse Creek site (75%) but were also evident at the other sites (29–36%). Stone flies and caddis flies were sparse (<10%), although caddis comprised 14% of insects at the Salmon diversion, and both groups made up 13–14% of benthic insects in the lower Salmon River.

Salmonid Response to Nutrient Addition

Keogh River Fry and Parr. Based on eight years of data from untreated years and five years of data from treated years, geometric weights of underyearling coho salmon and steelhead trout increased on average by 1.4-fold and 2.0-fold, respectively, as a result of fertilization (*t*-tests on the log-transformed differences of mean weights before and after fertilization within the control and treatment; P < 0.05; Table 1 in Johnston et al. 1990). The growth response was weakest in 1983,

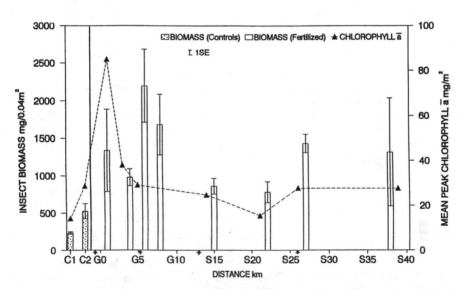

FIGURE 3. Mean benthic insect biomass in gravel colonization baskets and peak chlorophyll *a* in summer 1993, in control sites (C), Grilse Creek (G), and the Salmon River (S) (vertical bars on mean insect biomass are 1 standard error; *n* = 6/site).

when nutrient release from coated fertilizer prills was sporadic. Yet densities of fry in the reaches were similar in most years. Average densities of coho fry in 1984–1986 were variable in midsummer; 50 fry·100/m² in treated and untreated reaches in 1984; 158 and 41 fry·100/m², respectively, in 1985; and 43 fry·100/m² within the treated reaches in 1986. Mean steelhead fry densities were 86 fry·100/m² (1984) and 77 fry·100/m² (1985) in the control reach, and 116, 108, and 120 fry·100/m² in the treated reaches in the three respective years.

Larger size-at-age of steelhead parr within treated sections than the untreated control was evident during whole-river treatments from 1984 to 1986 in late summer (Figure 4); yet before nutrient addition in 1980, parr weight-at-age was similar in upper, middle, and lower reaches (age 1+, 8.1, 9.7, and 8.0 g; age 2+, 21.4, 20.2, and 19.9 g). In 1984, mean weights of parr at-age did not differ statistically between the upper treated reach and the control. However, in the other two reaches in 1984 and within the three treated reaches in 1985 and 1986, age-1+ parr were 30–130% greater in mean weight than parr in the upstream control reach (t-tests; P < 0.05; Figure 4). Age-2+ parr were 41–63% larger in the treated reaches than the control, in 1985 and 1986. In addition, Age-2+ parr comprised only 12.5% of all parr in the fertilized reaches, yet made up 40% of parr in the control reach, suggesting earlier seaward migration in the former. Mean estimated parr densities in the control and treated reaches

were 3 and 10 parr·100/m², respectively, in 1984 and 10 parr·100/m² in both reaches in 1985.

Keogh River Smolts and Adults. Large numbers of coho smolts were produced within 17 small tributaries and 6 small lakes, which were untreated, and thus confounded coho production from the main stem. On average, there was a suggested 21% increase in the numbers of coho smolts resulting from fertilization, based on a comparison of eight years with little or no nutrient addition versus four smolt cohorts emigrating during treatment years (t-test; P < 0.1 > 0.05; Table 1). There was no detectable shift in mean length of smolts of 104 mm.

There were greater numbers of steelhead smolts, with younger smolt age, and more adults from years associated with fertilizer treatment. Peak numbers of smolts increased 2.5-fold to 14,000, once all age-classes were affected by nutrient addition, by 1997 (Figure 5). However, variable age composition of the multiple year-classes increased annual variability (especially in 1981), thus requiring analysis by fry brood year to examine treatment effects. On average, numbers of steelhead smolts by brood year increased by 62% over the three broods affected by whole-river treatment, compared with seven years with little or no treatment (Figure 6; Table 1; t-test; P < 0.05). Before fertilizer addition, age-3 steelhead smolts dominated annual smolt yields from the river (Ward and Slaney 1988), but after three years of treatment, age-2 smolts were dominant (Figure 5), a trend that became more evident each year (Slaney et al. 1986). Also, age-4 smolts became rare,

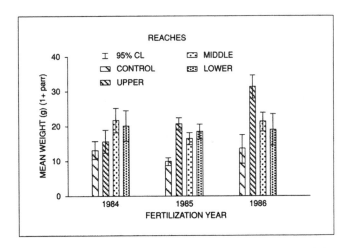

FigurE 4. Mean weights of age-1+ steelhead parr in the upper control reach and three treatment reaches (upper, middle, and lower river) in the Keogh River in 1984–1986.

TABLE 1. Mean yield of steelhead trout smolts (by brood year) and coho salmon smolts from the Keogh River during nutrient treated and untreated years (sample size in parenthesis as years).

	No. coho smolts	No. steelhead smolts
Nutrient treated	77,607	9,691
	(4)	(3)
Untreated	64,222	5,972
	(8)	(7)
Percent mean change	+21%[1]	+62%[2]

[1]significant at $p < 0.1$
[2]significant at $p < 0.05$

and age-1 smolts comprised a significant proportion (12%) of the migration for the first time by 1987. Mean smolt age was negatively correlated with mean weight of fry in midsummer ($y = 3.11 - 0.48x$; $r^2 = 0.45$; $P < 0.05$). Of note, there was not an increase in mean size of steelhead smolts migrating seaward. Mean smolt length in 1985, 1986, and 1987 was 175, 160, and 170 mm, respectively, or, in two of three years, near the 1977–1983 average size of 173 mm, and all three within the historical range of variation (Figure 7). Adult steelhead originating from smolt cohorts of treated years returned to the river from 1986 to 1990. Their numbers and catch in the sport fishery corresponded with the increased numbers and size-at-age of smolts; yet catch of wild steelhead at a similar river 10 km away showed little change (Figure 8). Immediately after nutrient addition, smolt yield declined to about 4,000 from 1988 to 1990, then increased to near the historical average of 5,000–6,000 in 1991–1992 (Ward and Slaney 1993).

Salmon River Trout Size and Abundance. In 1990, the mean weights of trout fry were 3-fold greater, on average, in sites associated with liquid fertilizer addition than in the spatial control, both within Grilse Creek and the Salmon River (Figure 9). In 1992, without nitrate addition, there was still a 2-fold greater size of fry in fertilizer reaches, on average, also about two-fold larger than sites more than 25 km downstream, where peak periphyton chlorophyll *a* was not elevated in 1992. Mean weights of age-1+ parr were 2–3-fold greater in 1990 and 1992 at the treated sites. The total standing crop of rainbow and steelhead trout varied among sites, ranging from 40 to 130 kg/ha in the treated sections versus 15–30 kg/ha in the upstream control, thus suggesting that carrying capacity was 3-fold greater in the treated reaches (Slaney and Ward 1993).

The addition of nutrients at the Salmon River was effective over a large distance at a low cost. Fish size was affected for at least 30 km of stream in 1992 (Figure 9), using liquid ammonium

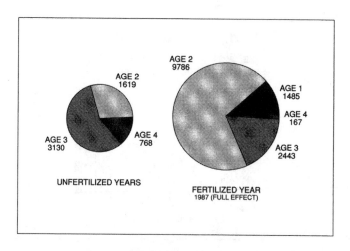

FIGURE 5. Age composition and numbers of steelhead smolts before (1977–1983) and during (1987; full effect) whole-river nutrient addition at the Keogh River.

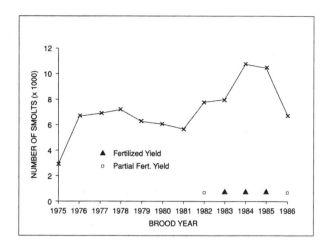

FIGURE 6. Numbers of steelhead smolts by brood year migrating from the Keogh River, from 1975 to 1986. Broods completely (all year-classes) and partially (1 year-class) affected by whole-river fertilization are indicated above the x-axis.

polyphosphate from mid-May to late July. Cost of the fertilizer was about $2,000 ($65 per km) or about $4,500 ($150 per km) when both liquid polyphosphate and nitrate were introduced. The effective distance of fertilization, based on the locations of the third (1990) and fourth (1992) tanks, was km 10 to km 27, in 1990, and km 15 to at least km 27, in 1992, or, on average, 15 km (range 12–17 km; Figure 9). The response dissipated rapidly thereafter, with average weights at km 38 and km 50 similar to the upstream control sites. Thus, further recycling or spiraling of nutri-

ents downstream from km 38 to km 50 was not indicated by increased fish size, which also corresponds with low chlorophyll a and low insect abundance at km 38 in 1992.

Overall, there was a marked increase in the estimated numbers parr and smolts migrating downstream past the diversion screen at the Salmon R, increasing from about 1,500 in 1989–1991 to 5,000–9,500 in 1994–1998 (Table 2). Smolt age shifted to a high proportion (80% by 1998) of age-2 smolts, from an earlier dominance of age-3 smolts, similar to the Keogh River.

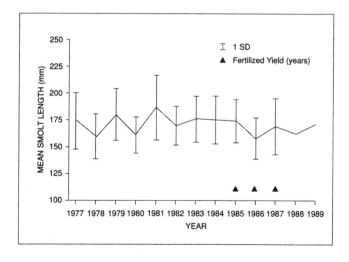

FIGURE 7. Mean length, with one standard deviation, of steelhead smolts migrating from the Keogh River from 1977 to 1989; smolts are affected by nutrient addition in 1985–1987.

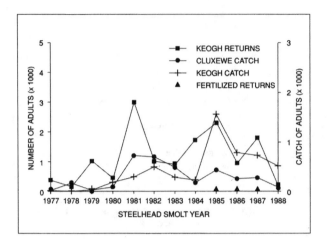

FIGURE 8. Estimated numbers of adult wild steelhead returning to the Keogh River and estimated catch of wild steelhead in the Keogh River and the adjacent and untreated Cluxewe River. Years on the x-axis are smolt years from 1977 to 1990, and those affected by nutrient addition are indicated by triangles.

Discussion

Food Chain Responses

The response of periphyton at the Keogh and Salmon rivers is in general agreement with other field studies as well as with experiments conducted in artificial channels. Addition of nutrients to the Kuparuk River resulted initially in a similar order of magnitude increase in periphyton accrual as indicated by chlorophyll a (Peter-son et al. 1985). Similarly, at the Nechako River, enrichment for two months with N and P resulted in 10-fold increases in peak chlorophyll a (Perrin 1989; Slaney et al. 1991). Smaller increases in chlorophyll were detected within sections of a deciduous woodland stream after P enrichment, which was attributed to grazing by invertebrates and possibly co-limitation with nitrogen (Elwood et al. 1981). By 1992 and 1993, at the Salmon River, the effect of

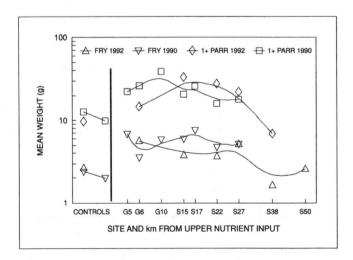

FIGURE 9. Trends in mean weights fry and parr of steelhead and rainbow trout within upstream control (2 sites), nutrient treated, and downstream sampling sites at Grilse Creek (G) and Salmon River (S) during 1990 and 1992. Distances are numbers of kilometers from the uppermost nutrient input site at Grilse Creek.

TABLE 2. Number of steelhead parr and smolt migrants enumerated from a diversion trap at the screened hydroelectric canal at the Salmon River from 1988 to 1998 (trap not operated in 1997 and 1999—diversion closed).

Migrants	Year									
	1988[1]	1989[2]	1990	1991	1992[1]	1993	1994	1995	1996	1998
Parr	500	763	447	490	718	1,357	5,593	5,312	3,403	6,014
Smolt	150	902	1,041	1,128	2,265	1,379	2,414	3,446	1,931	3,718
Total	650	1,665	1,488	1,618	2,983	2,736	8,007	8,758	5,334	9,732

[1]Efficiency of smolt screen estimated at <50%
[2]Trapping and enumeration later than usual

nutrient addition on the peak chlorophyll-a response was moderated to 2–4-fold that of untreated sites; yet earlier treatment with ammonium phosphate (as P_2O_5) alone caused a larger sevenfold increase in chlorophyll in the upper Keogh River. Low chlorophyll in 1993 at the Salmon River, increased to 5 mg P/L, was probably related to increased grazing by abundant benthic insects (Figure 3). This was examined experimentally at the Kuparuk River under constant enrichment with phosphorus, and by the third year, chlorophyll a was no longer significantly increased. Thereafter, it was confirmed that benthic insects increased sufficiently to graze periphyton to near control levels (Peterson et al. 1985). These field results are consistent with experiments conducted in artificial channels, where algal chlorophyll a was augmented several-fold when nitrogen and phosphorus were continuously added (Stockner and Shortreed 1978; Mundie et al. 1991). In this and most other field studies, diatoms and, to a lesser extent, chloro-phytes dominated the algal composition, with blue greens typically sparse (Johnston et al. 1990).

Coinciding with increased algal biomass, the abundance of benthic insects was substantially higher by late summer in treated sections of the Salmon River, which was similar to results at the upper Keogh River (Johnston et al. 1990), and in mesocosm experiments (Perrin and Richardson 1997). Insect biomasses from the colonization baskets at the Salmon River were similar to that measured by standard benthic sampling in the upper Keogh River. These results were consistent with those of Murphy et al. (1986), who detected a strong positive correlation between density of benthic insects and algal biomass in several reaches of logged and unlogged coastal streams in South East Alaska. Mundie et al. 1991 also found that benthic insects and emergent adult insects increased 2-fold when chlorophyll a was

elevated 3–4 times in meso-cosms. Additional experiments conducted in mesocosms at the Keogh River, in 1991, confirmed similar increases in insect abundance, including mayflies, stoneflies, and caddisflies, at nutrient concentrations ranging from 2.5 mg P/L to 50 mg P/L. There, nutrient saturation for benthic and emergent insects was suggested at 2.5 mg/L P to 5 mg/L P (Quamme and Slaney, this volume). Insect composition was dominated by either mayflies or chironomids at the Salmon River and by chironomids and caddis earlier in the Keogh River, which is consistent with other whole-stream enrichments (Peterson et al. 1985) and mesocosm experiments (Mundie et al. 1991; Perrin and Richardson 1997).

Salmonid Responses

Similar to Johnston et al. (1990) for steelhead and coho fry, we attribute the larger size-at-age of parr to increased aquatic insects, resulting from increased periphyton biomass, in turn resulting from nutrient addition. At the Keogh River, both coho and steelhead fry fed primarily on benthic insects, particularly mayflies and chironomids (Johnston et al. 1990). In our analysis, much higher mean weights of steelhead parr were also evident in the fertilizer reaches, than the control. Also, older age-2+ parr were rare in the treated reach, in contrast to the control reach, which corresponds with the observed earlier smolt age after fertilization.

The response of coho smolts was confounded by production from untreated tributaries and small lakes, and thus, the response was moderated. Earlier studies suggest there were 2,000–3,000 smolts produced from each main tributary and small lake (Irvine and Ward 1989). Because there are 17 tributaries and 6 lakes, it is probable that 50–60% of smolts originated from unfertilized tributary waters, based on numbers of smolts per kilometer of stream. During nutrient addition, numbers of coho smolts appeared to increase by 21%, but adjustment for smolts produced in tributaries and small lakes suggests that the yield of mainstem coho smolts may have increased by 40–50%. Overwinter survival of juvenile coho salmon is a function of fry size at the end of the growing season (Scrivener and Brown 1992), which could explain an increase in numbers of coho smolts in spring without a detectable change in smolt size.

The response of steelhead smolts to nutrient addition was a marked increase in numbers of smolts migrating to the ocean, which was reflected in greater numbers of returning adults. Sixty-two percent more steelhead smolts were produced on average and peaked at 2.5-fold in 1997. Yet, the average size of smolts overall did not change. This anomaly was readily explained by aging because smolts were about a year less in age than before whole-river treatment. As described by Slaney et al. (1986), there was a gradual decrease in age of steelhead smolts over the four years of whole-river enrichment, and by 1987, age-4 smolts were sparse and some age-1 smolts were evident for the first time. Before treatment, age-3 and 4 smolts dominated the migration, but during treatment, age-2 smolts dominated. Thus, mean smolt age was negatively correlated with mean fry weight in summer (Slaney and Ward 1993). There is compelling evidence that survival of salmonids in coastal streams is positively size-related (Scrivener and Brown 1992; Ward and Slaney 1993). These striking shifts in smolt age are strong evidence of a shift in productivity because steelhead are known to smolt at a minimum size range (Ward and Slaney 1988). A 62% increase in the average numbers of smolts was reflected in 50% greater numbers of adults returning to the Keogh River in at least two of three years. A marked expansion in the reported catch of wild steelhead occurred at the Keogh River, yet there was no change evident in the trend at the untreated and adjacent Cluxewe River. However, the relation between run size and catch may not be robust, as in 1981 when a large run of steelhead returned from a strong output of large older smolts in 1979, yet catch of adults was only moderate.

It is unlikely that the increase in steelhead smolts was related to natural variability or some extraneous factor. Cessation of nutrient addition resulted in a rapid return from 1988 to 1990 of near-average smolt yields. Also, during treatment, there was a striking shift in smolt-age composition that was unlikely related to chance, and

there were also no corresponding changes in stream temperature (data on file). At the Quinsam River, located 170 km southeast, there was no corresponding sharp increase in yields of wild steelhead smolts. Estimated yields of smolts at the Quinsam River, where age-2 smolts are dominant, was 7,800 (1979–1983) and 8,500 (1984–1987) or, on average, only 9% greater during the same years when the Keogh River was affected by fertilizer, although accuracy of estimates was low (data on file). Hatchery steelhead could also affect production of Keogh smolts because of greater egg deposition, and thereby high fry densities, which were evident by 1986. Yet, hatchery steelhead, produced in local net-pens, returned in abundant numbers both during and after fertilizer addition (1987 and 1988). Also, returns of wild adults increased after treatment (1987–1989), yet smolt abundance still declined rapidly to the pretreatment level (Figure 5; Slaney and Ward 1993), regardless of high egg deposition. Also, there is further evidence from before treatment that smolt yield is not increased at high fry densities. Rather, the output reaches an asymptote at relatively low numbers of spawners and low densities of fry (20–30 fry·100/m^2), and during the two periods of comparison, there were adequate densities of fry in the river (Ward and Slaney 1993).

It is possible that the influx of even-year pink salmon affected the whole-river treatment, but their carcasses would have added to nutrient loading of 1984 and 1986 during the fall, after nutrient addition had ceased. Similar increased nutrient concentrations in fall could be expected from the decay of 50,000 carcasses over the length of the river in two of the four years of treatment. Ward and Slaney (1988) detected larger size steelhead smolts in spring after the even-year run of pink salmon, some of which was likely caused by parr feeding on dislodged salmon eggs. However, river productivity would also be augmented from nutrient influx, although winter floods and cool temperatures would be expected to depress the response. Regardless, the before-and-after controlled-impact analysis that was applied to weights of salmonid fry by Johnston et al. (1990) confirms overriding treatment effects of fertilization during spring and summer periods.

Results from the Salmon River treatment confirmed the pattern of faster growth of fish with nutrient addition. Average fry and parr weights were 2–3-fold greater in treated sites, and age of smolts shifted from a dominance of age 3 to age 2. Yet, weights of fry and parr before treatment were roughly similar in Grilse Creek (later treated) and control sites in the upper Salmon River (Perrin 1989). As at the Keogh and Kuparuk rivers, the response in trout at the Salmon River was associated with increases in both periphyton accrual and benthic insects. Although it is not possible to separate effects of colonization of habitat from effects of nutrient addition at the Salmon River, similar trends in increasing smolt production were not evident at other rivers on the east coast of Vancouver Island. For example, there was a striking decline in numbers of smolt migrants during the mid-1990s at the Keogh River during untreated years, suggesting greater survivals of steelhead at the Salmon River than other monitored rivers on the east coast of Vancouver Island.

Summary

The stimulative responses of nutrient addition to periphyton, benthic insects, and salmonids at both the Keogh and Salmon rivers confirm the inherent nutrient deficiency of the salmonid food chains of coastal oligotrophic streams. Small seasonal additions of inorganic nutrients as low as 5 mg/L P were capable of stimulating primary production. Through increases in benthic insects, the size and abundance of salmonids including smolts were increased, culminating in greater numbers of adults, as was evident in steelhead trout at the Keogh River (by about 50%, or 15 adults per kilometer). Because nutrient addition affected production for a considerable distance downstream (15 km), and at low cost, it should be effective as a habitat restoration option. Potentially, depressed influxes of nutrients from salmon carcasses could be offset or the recovery of degraded habitat could be accelerated during rehabilitation, provided further land-use impacts have ceased. These results provide further evidence of "bottom-up" control of the productivity of stream ecosystems, from algae to fish, similar to findings from the Kuparuk River in Alaska by Deegan and Peterson (1992).

Acknowledgments

Research at the Keogh and Salmon rivers was supported by the Salmonid Enhancement Program and the Habitat Conservation Trust Fund, respectively. Preparation of this paper was supported by the Watershed Restoration Program. Numerous individuals were involved at the Keogh River in fish sampling or enumeration and deserve thanks. Tom Johnston and, especially, Chris Perrin were closely involved with nutrient addition at the Keogh River, and the latter again at the Salmon River until 1990. Loreta Hansen and Daiva Zaldokas, among others, deserve thanks for their efforts at the Salmon River.

References

APHA (American Public Health Association). 1985. Standard methods for the examination of water and wastewater. 16th edition. American Public Health Association, Washington, D.C.

Chapman, D. W. 1966. Food and space as regulators of salmonid populations in streams. American Naturalist 100:345–357.

Deegan, L. A., and B. J. Peterson. 1992. Whole-river fertilization stimulates fish production in an Arctic tundra river. Canadian Journal of Fisheries and Aquatic Sciences. 49:1890–1901.

Dill, L. M., R. C. Ydenberg, and A. H. G. Fraser. 1981. Food abundance and territory size in juvenile coho salmon (Oncorhynchus kisutch). Canadian Journal of Zoology 59:1801–1809.

Egglishaw, H. J. 1968. The quantitative relationship between bottom fauna and plant detritus in streams of different calcium concentrations. Journal of Applied Ecology 5:731–740.

Elwood, J. W., J. D. Newbold, A. F. Trimble, and R. W. Stark. 1981. The limiting role of phosphorus in a woodland stream ecosystem: effect of P enrichment on leaf. decomposition and primary producers. Ecology 62:146–158.

Huntsman, A. G. 1948. Fertility and fertilization of streams. Journal of Fisheries Research Board of Canada 7:248–253.

Hurlbert, S. H. 1984. Pseudoreplication and the design of ecological field experiments. Ecological Monographs 54:187–211.

Hyatt K. D., and J. G. Stockner. 1985. Responses of sockeye salmon (Oncorhynchus nerka) to fertilization of British Columbia coastal lakes. Canadian Journal of Fisheries and Aquatic Sciences 42:320–331.

Hynes, H. B. 1971. The biology of polluted waters. University of Toronto Press.

Irvine, J. R., and B. R. Ward. 1989. Patterns of timing and size of wild coho salmon (Oncorhynchus kisutch) smolts migrating from the Keogh River watershed on northern Vancouver Island. Canadian Journal of Fisheries and Aquatic Sciences 46:1086–1094.

Johnston, N. T., C. J. Perrin, P. A. Slaney, and B. R. Ward. 1990. Increased juvenile growth by whole-river fertilization. Canadian Journal of Fisheries and Aquatic Sciences 47:862–872.

McFadden, J. T., and E. L. Cooper. 1962. An ecological comparison of six populations of brown trout (*Salmo trutta*). Transactions of American Fisheries Society 91:53–62.

Milbrink, G., and S. Holmgren. 1981. Addition of artificial fertilizers as a means of reducing the negative effects of "oligotrophication" in lakes after impoundment. Drottningholm Reports 59:121–127.

Minshall, G. W. 1978. Autotrophy in stream ecosystems. Bioscience 28:767–771.

Mundie, J. H., K. S. Simpson, and C. J. Perrin. 1991. Responses of stream periphyton and benthic insects to increases in dissolved inorganic phosphorus in a mesocosm. Canadian Journal of Fisheries and Aquatic Sciences 48:2061–2072.

Murphy, M. L., J. Heifetz, S. W. Johnson, K. V. Koski, and J. F. Thedinga. 1986. Effects of clear-cut logging with and without buffer strips on juvenile salmonids in Alaskan streams. Canadian Journal of Fisheries and Aquatic Sciences 43:1521–1533.

Perrin, C. J. 1989. The feasibility of inorganic fertilization for salmonid enhancement in the Salmon River, Vancouver Island. Habitat Conservation Report. Limnotek Research and Development Inc., Vancouver, B.C.

Perrin, C. J. 1991. Steelhead enhancement by nutrient addition to the Salmon River, Vancouver Island: monitoring in the second and third year of treatment. Habitat Conservation Report. Limnotek Research and Development Inc., Vancouver, B.C.

Perrin, C. J., M. L. Bothwell, and P. A. Slaney. 1987. Experimental enrichment of a coastal stream in British Columbia: effects of organic and inorganic additions on autotrophic periphyton production. Canadian Journal of Fisheries and Aquatic Sciences 44:1247–1256.

Perrin, C. J., and J. S. Richardson. 1997. N and P limitation of benthos abundance in the Nechako River, British Columbia. Canadian Journal of Fisheries and Aquatic Sciences 54:2574–2583.

Peterson, B. J., J. E. Hobbie, A. E. Hershey, M. A. Lock, T. E. Ford, J. R. Vestal, V. L. McKinley, M. C. Miller, R. M. Ventullo, and G. S. Volk. 1985. Transformation of a tundra stream from heterotrophy to autotrophy by addition of phosphorus. Science 229:1383–1386.

Scrivener, J. C., and T. G. Brown. 1992. Impacts and complexity of forest practices on streams and their salmonid fishes in British Columbia. Pages 41–49 *in* G. Shooner and S. Asselin, editors. Le developpement du saumon Atlantique au Quebec; connaitre les regles du jeu pour reussir. Colloque international de la Federation Quebe-coise pour le saumon Atlantique. Quebec, decembre 1992. Collection *Salmo salar* No. 1.

Seber, G. A. F., and E. D. Le Cren. 1967. Estimating population parameters from catches large relative to the population. Journal of Animal Ecology 36:631–643.

Slaney, P. A., and T. G. Northcote. 1974. Effects of prey abundance on density and territorial behavior of young rainbow trout (*Salmo gairdneri*) in laboratory stream channels. Journal of Fisheries Research Board of Canada 31:1201–1209.

Slaney, P. A., C. J. Perrin, and B. R. Ward. 1986. Nutrient concentration as a limitation to steelhead smolt production in the Keogh River. Proceedings of the Annual Conference of the Western Association of Fish and Wildlife Agencies 66:146–157.

Slaney, P. A., W. O. Rublee, C. J. Perrin, and H. Goldberg. 1991. Debris structure placements and whole-river fertilization for salmonids in a large regulated stream in British Columbia. Bulletin of Marine Science 55:1160–1180.

Slaney, P. A., and B. R. Ward. 1993. Experimental fertilization of nutrient deficient streams in British Columbia. Pages 128–141 *in* G. Shooner and S. Asselin, editors. Le developpement du saumon Atlantique au Quebec; connaitre les regles du jeu pour reussir. Colloque international de la Federation quebecoise pour le saumon Atlantique. Quebec, decembre 1992. Collection *Salmo salar* No. 1.

Stewart-Oaten, A. W. W. Murdoch, and K. R. Parker. 1986. Environmental impact assessment "pseudoreplication" in time? Ecology 67:929–940.

Stockner, J. G., and K. R. S. Shortreed. 1978. Enhancement of autotrophic production by nutrient addition in a coastal rainforest stream on Vancouver Island. Journal of Fisheries Research Board of Canada 35:28–34.

Ward, B. R., and P. A. Slaney. 1988. Life history and smolt-to adult survival of Keogh River steelhead trout (*Salmo gairdneri*) and the relationship to smolt size. Canadian Journal of Fisheries and Aquatic Sciences 45:1110–1122.

Ward, B. R., and P. A. Slaney. 1993. Egg-to-smolt survival and fry-to-smolt density dependence of Keogh River steelhead trout. Canadian Special Publication of Fisheries and Aquatic Sciences 118:209–217.

Wilkinson, L. 1988. SYSTAT: the system for statistics. SYSTAT Inc, Evanston, Illinois.

American Fisheries Society Symposium 34:127–147, 2003

Evaluation of the Addition of Inorganic Nutrients and Stream Habitat Structures in the Keogh River Watershed for Steelhead Trout and Coho Salmon

BRUCE R. WARD

Ministry of Water, Land and Air Protection, Fisheries Research and Development
2204 Main Mall, University of British Columbia, Vancouver, B.C. V6T 1Z4, Canada

DONALD J. F. MCCUBBING

InStream Consultants, 223 - 2906 West Broadway, Vancouver, B.C. V6K 2G8, Canada

PATRICK A. SLANEY

Ministry of Water, Land and Air Protection, Watershed Restoration Program
2204 Main Mall, University of British Columbia, Vancouver, B.C. V6T 1Z4, Canada

Abstract.—Positive numerical responses in steelhead *Oncorhynchus mykiss* and coho salmon *O. kisutch* juvenile abundance and size, smolt yield, and smolts per spawner were obtained from watershed restoration in the Keogh River on northern Vancouver Island, British Columbia. Annual increases coincided with treatment and were compared with data from an untreated neighboring watershed (Waukwaas River). The steelhead population, now apparently capable of thriving, was below replacement recruitment prior to the addition of inorganic nutrients and instream habitat structures, the key components of several restoration activities. Annual increases in summer densities of steelhead juveniles were recorded as the rehabilitation treatments progressed from 1997 to 2000. Estimation of steelhead parr densities indicated a 3.8-fold increase over pretreatment or internal untreated values; increases in sites with both inorganic nutrient briquettes and habitat structure additions were 2.5–1.9 times higher than sites with nutrient additions or habitat structures alone. Average size-at-age of juvenile salmonids, by autumn, significantly increased through the years of rehabilitation treatment and compared with fish in the Waukwaas River. Steelhead smolt yield in 2000 increased to 2,338 fish, the highest yield since 1993, but lower than the historical average (>6,000) due to low escapement. Current yield was an improvement over the historic low (<1,000 steelhead smolts, 1998). Coho smolt yield increased to 74,500 or 20% above the historic average (62,000 smolts; 1975–1999), well above the record low counts of 1998 (22,000), but below the historic maximum yield (105,000; 1981). A significant increase in steelhead smolt recruitment at low escapement, from less than 2 to greater than 50 smolts per spawner, was observed over the last four brood years (1995–1998). The assessment now shifts to further benefits to smolt yield, which will require evaluation to 2004.

Introduction

Efforts at diligent habitat protection, restoration, and mitigation to augment the survival of salmonids in freshwater have been proposed as a means to assist salmonid populations experiencing the current low rates of survival during their Pacific Ocean life stage (Ward 2000a). Numerically depressed salmonid stocks could benefit from efforts that improve productivity and capac-

ity of the freshwater stream environment to levels where spawners produce recruits above replacement. This increase could compensate for
declines in the survival rate experienced during
the marine life stage.

Steelhead *Oncorhynchus mykiss* abundance
in southern British Columbia suddenly, dramatically, and persistently declined after a climate
regime shift in 1989 (Welch et al. 2000; Smith and
Ward 2000; Smith et al. 2000), the reasons for
which are poorly understood. Ward (2000a) demonstrated that reductions in smolt-to-adult survivals were to levels where spawners were producing smolt recruits below replacement, and
indicated that declines in survival during the
freshwater life stage of steelhead also accompa-
nied the ocean climate shift. The freshwater decline, it was speculated, was due to increased frequency and intensity of summer drought and
winter storm events, potentially lower fecundity
of returning adults, and lowered stream productivity. A continuing decline in important stream
habitat elements, such as large woody debris recruitment to the stream, was a result of past
streambank logging practices (Slaney and Martin 1997). In part, this reduction in productivity
may also have been due to lower salmonid escapement and, thus, fewer salmon carcasses, as
observed throughout the decade of the 1990s in
many of the watersheds of the west coast of North
America. Reductions in escapement to levels estimated at 6% to 7% of historic abundance have
seriously depleted the level of marine-derived
nutrients transported to freshwater (Stockner
1987; Larkin and Slaney 1997; Gresh et al. 2000).

Efforts to increase salmonid survival in freshwater, mitigating for the past damages of logging,
carcass reduction, and other related habitat impacts, are being attempted as a key part of the
British Columbia Watershed Restoration Program (WRP; Slaney and Martin 1997). The Keogh
River, on northern Vancouver Island, was selected early in the program to evaluate the effectiveness of watershed restoration treatments,
particularly fish habitat rehabilitation. The first
experiments that examined the effects of stream
nutrient addition on salmonids on the west coast
of Canada occurred at this site in the early to mid-
1980s (Johnston et al. 1990; Slaney and Ward
1993). That work was preceded by experimental
habitat manipulation for juvenile steelhead trout
and coho salmon *O. kisutch* (Ward and Slaney
1979, 1981, 1993a). No habitat rehabilitation work

or nutrient treatment occurred at the Keogh River
from the mid-1980s to the mid-1990s.

The objective of this study was to determine
the benefits of stream habitat restoration (i.e., the
addition of inorganic nutrients and stream habitat structures) on steelhead trout and coho
salmon using a study design that accounted for
the impacts of natural environmental variations
on fish populations during the study period. We
assessed the fish response to stream habitat rehabilitation techniques through instream sampling in representative treated and untreated sections and by comparison of steelhead and coho
juvenile densities and smolt yield from the neighboring and untreated Waukwaas River. Here, we
summarize these results and further evaluate the
number of steelhead smolts produced per
spawner.

In-river treatments to the Keogh watershed
were incrementally added over a five-year period,
along with hillslope stabilization, road deactiva-
tion and storm-proofing, riparian treatment, and
side-channel pond constructions. An interim report on the assessment of improved productivity and capacity for salmonids in freshwater is
presented. Here, we present evidence that suggests steelhead recruitment has been reversed
from an extinction trajectory and will slowly rebuild as long as ocean conditions do not worsen.

Methods

Study Area

The Keogh and Waukwaas rivers are neighboring fourth-order streams at the northern end of
Vancouver Island, British Columbia, in the
coastal western hemlock biogeoclimatic zone,
draining to the northeast and west, respectively
(Figure 1). Further description of the watersheds,
including their logging history, river size, salmonid species present, and low-level nutrient background, can be found in Irvine and Ward (1989)
and Slaney et al. (2002, this volume); reach defi-
nitions and sample site locations are further described in McCubbing and Ward (1997).

Restoration Treatments

In 1997, Watershed Restoration Program (WRP)
structures consisting of large logs and boulders
(i.e., treated habitat sites; Ward 1997; Slaney et

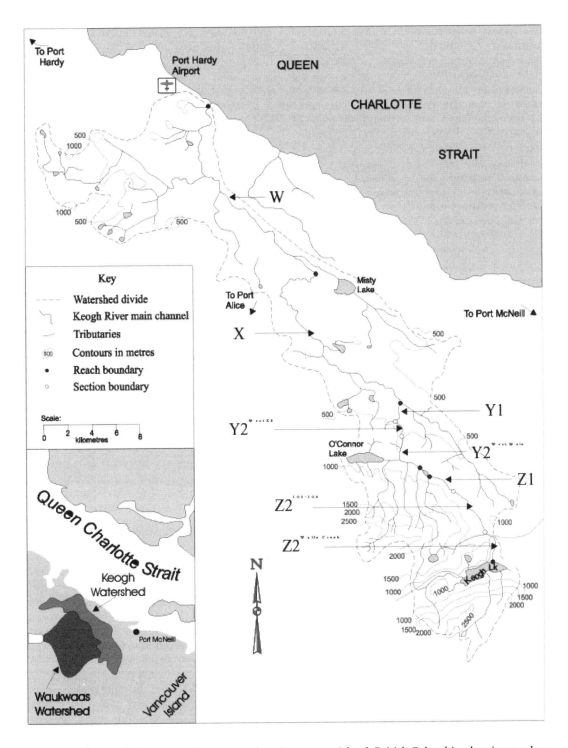

FIGURE 1. The Keogh River watershed on northern Vancouver Island, British Columbia, showing reaches examined that were treated with the addition of inorganic nutrients and habitat structures from 1997 to 2000. The inset indicates the location on the B.C. coast and the neighboring untreated watershed, the Waukwaas River.

al. 1997) were placed in the upper Keogh River over 5.4 km (Potyrala 1999a). In 1998, additional restoration structures were placed, for a total treated length of 6.8 km (Potyrala 1999b, 1999c). Further structures were placed in the middle reaches of the mainstem Keogh over a length of 3.0 km, in 1999 (Zaldokas et al. 1999), and in over 1.0 km of the lower river in 2000 (Burroughs et al. 2001). Thus, habitat restoration was undertaken on large sections of reaches Y, Z, X, and a small area of Reach W by the summer of 2000 (Figure 1) with more than 10 km and 475 habitat structures in place. Reach W was partially treated in 2000 with structures in the west tributary area, but was not sampled in 2000. Several off-channel ponds and side-channels have been completed, including three in the lower reach (W) and one in the middle portion of the watershed (Reach Y). A wetland was expanded in 2000, approximately 3.5 km upstream of the river mouth. A total of approximately 2 ha of new wetland habitat was restored or created by these off-channel developments to offset losses in overwinter habitat caused by a reduction in large woody debris by past logging practices.

Inorganic nutrients can substitute for declines in marine-derived nutrients from salmon carcasses in streams when salmon escapement has declined as a result of past disturbance (Cederholm et al. 1989) and ocean conditions (Welch et al. 2000), as in the Keogh River. Nutrient addition in the form of slow-release fertilizer briquettes composed of magnesium ammonium phosphate (Lesco Inc., Ohio), as described in Ashley and Slaney (1997), was applied to the Keogh River from 1997 to 2000. Inorganic nutrients as a once-annual manual application of briquettes were added in May to riffle sections at about 3-km intervals, with a target concentration of 5 g/L P as soluble phosphate. Application of briquettes included the lowermost 19 km of the Keogh River mainstem and approximately 10 km of tributary stream length in 1997 for a total weight of 908 kg. In 1998, 1,110 kg were added over a total length of 27.5 km of the Keogh River mainstem, from the river mouth to Muir Lake (Figure 1), as well as to 11 km of key tributaries entering the mainstem from Muir Lake to the river mouth (Potyrala 1999a). Inorganic nutrients (1,190 kg in 1999 and 840 kg in 2000; Zaldokas et al. 1999; Burroughs et al. 2000) were again added in 1999 and 2000 as a once-annual spring application. A total length of 36.5 km of the Keogh River mainstem, from the river mouth to 4 km

upstream of Keogh Lake (Figure 1), was treated with fertilizer, as well as 11 km of key tributaries entering the mainstem from Keogh Lake to the river mouth.

Experimental Design

The design was described in detail by McCubbing and Ward (1997). Briefly, the experiment considers two treatment types, habitat structures, and slow-release fertilizer application. The plan of restoration was adapted to the experimental design with structure placement commencing in the upper reaches, nutrient addition beginning in lower reaches, and both treatments expanded annually until, by 2000, the whole watershed was treated. Density and growth of salmonid juveniles as well as smolt yield comparisons were analyzed with analysis of variance (ANOVA) on the difference between rivers among years and among reaches within rivers; differences were considered significant at the $p < 0.05$ level. Changes to smolts-per-spawner values were examined with analysis of covariance (ANCOVA), with treatment and level of spawners as the covariates. Since slopes significantly differed, nonparametric statistical methods were also used (chi-square). Spawner levels during the study period were at historic lows (outside the range of previous values). The linear relationship between ln(smolts-per-spawner) and number of spawners was examined and used as a predictor of expected smolt recruits at low spawner abundance, compared with that observed from brood years 1997–1999.

Measurement of the Fish Response

To evaluate the effectiveness of rehabilitation techniques, stream sampling and smolt yield methods were utilized. First, salmonid juvenile density in freshwater was assessed by mark–recapture electrofishing and seine-netting techniques in summer and fall (McCubbing and Ward 1997). Second, smolt yield was assessed through operation of a full-river counting fence near the mouth of the Keogh River (since 1976; Ward 2000a) and by mark–recapture estimates using rotary screw traps on two locations within the Waukwaas River (Melville 1997; McCubbing 1998, 1999, 2000b). Finally, we assessed the smolt recruitment per spawner in the Keogh River as a function of the number of spawners, comparing previous production regimes with the restored condition. Thus, we examined data on steelhead and coho fry densities, steelhead parr densities and smolt yield, steelhead smolt age and size, and the smolts produced per spawner as a function of the number of steelhead spawners in the brood year.

Each summer, from 1997 to 2000, four reaches in each river were sampled by electro-fishing to obtain juvenile salmonid population estimates. Reaches in the Waukwaas River were compared with reaches within the Keogh River, according to similarity in stream gradients (i.e., sampled sections in reaches 1–4 of the Waukwaas River were of equal gradient to sample sections in reaches W, X, Y, and Z of the Keogh River, re-spectively). Sample sites were randomly chosen as representative of the composition of habitat types (riffles, runs, pools, and flats) within that reach, based on annual surveys of habitat as de-scribed in Hankin and Reeves (1988) and Ward and Slaney (1993a). Order of sampling of stream reaches varied from year to year, dependent on river height and temperature. In general, lower reaches of the Keogh River were sampled in early July, followed by lower Waukwaas reaches. Up-per Keogh reaches and upper Waukwaas reaches were sampled in early August and late August, respectively. In 2000, a year of high flow during July, sampling was altered to allow work to be completed; upper river sites were sampled in early July to allow river flow to subside. In all years, sampling was completed between early July and early September.

Fish abundance among four stream reaches from each of the Keogh and Waukwaas rivers was collated, as described in McCubbing and Ward (1997), as average numbers per 100 m of stream-bank length within a reach (statistically adjusted for replicate habitat sites and relative habitat fre-quency) and as population densities per 100 m^2 of habitat type and structure type (average of rep-licate habitat sites). Utilization of habitat struc-tures by steelhead fry, coho fry, and steelhead parr was tested for any preference (ANOVA) among six main structure types.

Sampling by electrofishing and minnow trapping during the fall provided data on fish size and growth when compared with summer samples. All sampling occurred in late October or November once the river had experienced at least one autumn flood and water temperatures were less than 6°C. Sampling was undertaken in open areas of representative habitat in each

sample reach with a minimum sample target of 25 fish of each species and age-class.

Smolt yield from the Keogh River was mea-sured, as described in Ward et al. (1990), as total counts. Fish captured in the smolt trap near the river mouth from early April to mid-June were counted daily. Efficiency at smolt capture was estimated annually by marking and releasing coho smolts upstream, as described in Ward and Slaney (1988, 1990, 1993a). Scale samples were taken from above the lateral line and behind the dorsal fin on coho and steelhead smolts in a sam-pling regime that was stratified according to fish size and migration time (Ward et al. 1989). Fork lengths (mm) were taken from all fish in a subsample (~15% of the total) every day during the smolt run. Weights were recorded once per week using an Acculab v400 electronic scale and a bowl of water (correcting for its weight) in which the fish were placed. Fish were partially anesthetized with clove oil (dissolved in ethanol) during length and weight measurement only.

Smolt yield from the Waukwaas River from 1996 to 2000 was estimated based on mark–re-capture estimates derived through operation of two rotary screw traps, similar to methods de-scribed in Dempson and Stansbury (1991). Two 5-ft rotary traps (E.G. Solutions Inc., Corvallis, Oregon) were spaced about 500 m apart with the lower trap approximately 500 m upstream of the river's tidal limit. The upper trap was used only as a marking trap, while the lower trap was used as an enumerator and biological sampling sta-tion as described in Frith et al. (1995a, 1995b). Both traps were operated commencing mid-April and continued 24 h per day until the smolt run was completed by mid-June. The traps were checked once daily, in the morning. As at the Keogh River, coho salmon less than 70 mm and steelhead trout less than 130 mm were defined as parr when parr marks were evident. Smolts were determined by their silver bright coloration and by size. All fish caught in the downstream recapture trap were released more than 200 m downstream to deter fish from reentering. Fish caught in the upstream trap were marked and released 25 m downstream of it. Every day, 25 coho smolts or the total day's catch (whichever was less) and 15% to 20% of all other species (steelhead and cutthroat) were sampled from the downstream trap for length, weight, and scales, as at the Keogh fence.

Marks (unique to a release group) were a combination of caudal fin marks (upper caudal, lower caudal, or upper-lower caudal) and the subdermal injection of a colored dye using a jet inoculator (Hart and Pitcher 1969). Prior to dye marking, smolts were anesthetized in a bath of dilute clove oil dissolved in ethanol. Smolts that were clipped only were not anesthetized. The caudal fin was cut dorso-ventrally at a point approximately one-fourth the distance from the tip of the lobe to the caudal peduncle. Blue (alcian blue) colored dye was applied either to the upper or lower caudal peduncle or the pectoral fin. The mark was a line on the fin rays approximately 3–4 mm long. Potential stress due to temperature (always <10°C) was minimized by marking as fast as possible in the morning and in a shady area. The anesthetic bath and recovery water was changed frequently during the procedure.

The Petersen population estimation method was used, as described in Frith et al. (1995a, 1995b), where estimated catch efficiency (ECE) was used to estimate weekly and total smolt emigration. A second population estimate was derived using the SPAS program (Arnason et al. 1996), which generated a pooled estimate. Chapman's adjustment for bias was applied to the ECEs (Ricker 1975). Overall recapture rates for steelhead and coho smolts averaged 6% and 8%, and overall capture rates averaged 13% and 14% of the population estimates, respectively.

Methods of estimating adult steelhead abundance at the Keogh River are described in detail elsewhere (Ward 1996, 2000a; McCubbing et al. 1999; Ward et al. 1989; Ward and Slaney 1988, 1990). Briefly, the total numbers of adult males and females were estimated separately by mark and recapture using the adjusted Petersen estimate, by marking upstream migrant adults (operculum punch) and capturing and examining kelts during their downstream migration. During 1998, 1999, and 2000, the fence was not operated in the period December through March for capture of upstream migrants, as it previously and partially had been (combined with marking by angling; Ward 2000a). Instead, electronic counting was undertaken using the Logie 2100C resistivity fish counter (Aquantic Ltd; McCubbing et al. 1999). Fish passing through the counter channels during this time were enumerated and sized, although some fish may have bypassed these channels during the highest spring tides or highest flood conditions (the frequency and duration of these events was low and varied). Counter efficiency of fish passing over the channels has been estimated as 90% during enumeration of adult

coho salmon in the fall (McCubbing et al. 1999). Sampling and marking by angling upstream of the fence provided a comparison and check of the escapement estimated by the counter, based on the mark–recapture estimate and from the relationship between catch per unit effort and population size (Smith and Ward 2000), as reported in McCubbing (2000a).

Keogh smolt recruitment was calculated based on the total number of smolts manually counted, their age based on scale analyses, and tabulation into brood year of origin. These data were used to estimate the smolts per spawner in comparison to the number of spawners that contributed to their recruitment (Ward and Slaney 1993a; Ward 2000a).

Results

Steelhead and Coho Fry Densities

Fish were not distributed equally between rivers and among reaches within rivers when we compared their densities using ANOVA. Steelhead fry densities were higher overall in the Waukwaas River (mean, 310 fry/100 m versus 146 fry/100 m over all years in the Keogh; Figure 2). Due to high variance, there was no significant difference between watersheds ($p = 0.08$). From 1997 to 2000, Waukwaas had higher steelhead fry densities, but only significantly so in 1999, and that mainly due to a high abundance in Reach 2 (Figure 2). Within the Keogh River, there were no significant differences among years or reaches ($p = 0.07$). Steelhead fry were observed at highest densities in Reach X (fertilizer and structures) in 1999 and 2000 (mean, 251 and 444 fry/100 m, respectively; Figure 2). This differed from 1997 and 1998, when steelhead fry were found in greatest abundance in the lower Keogh, treated with fertilizer only (Reach W; 180 and 287 fry/100 m, respectively). The middle reaches of the Waukwaas (reaches 2 and 3) consistently had the greatest steelhead fry densities (average, 660 and 469 fry/100 m) throughout the four years of investigation; densities among years were not significantly different ($p > 0.05$).

Coho fry were more abundant in the Keogh River (mean, 270 versus 66 fry/100 m in the Waukwaas) throughout the study period (Figure 2). In 1999, average coho fry densities among all reaches of the Keogh River were significantly higher than in the Waukwaas River ($p = 0.04$). How-

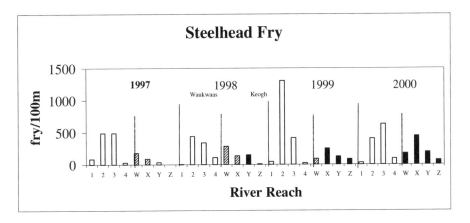

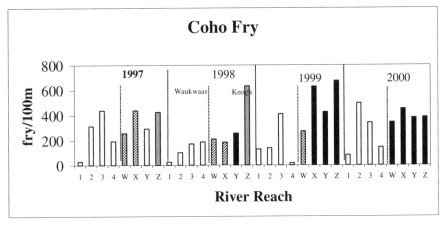

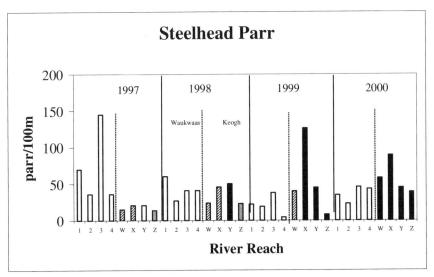

FIGURE 2. Densities of steelhead fry, coho fry, and steelhead parr among years and reaches of the Keogh and Waukwaas rivers from 1997 to 2000. Open columns = control; columns with diagonal stripe = reaches with fertilizer addition; grey columns = structures; and black columns = fertilizer and structures. Numbers 1 to 4 and letters W to Z refer to reaches of similar gradient, respectively, on the Keogh and Waukwaas rivers.

ever, coho densities were similar among reaches between rivers in 1997, 1998, and 2000. Within the Keogh River, differences in abundance among reaches were not significant (ANOVA, $p = 0.051$); greatest density occurred in 1999 in Reach Z (675 fry/100 m). There was a significant effect of treatment in the Keogh River on coho fry abundance, where reaches treated with both structures and fertilizer and the one reach with structures and no fertilizer (Reach Z, 1998) had higher values than reaches with nutrient addition only ($p = 0.04$). On the Waukwaas River, differences in abundance of coho fry were not significant among years, but were significant among reaches ($p < 0.05$) where, again, the middle reaches generally had the highest average values. As observed with steelhead fry, the results were highly variable.

Steelhead Parr Densities

Steelhead parr (1+ and older) were numerically more abundant in Reach X (treated with structures and fertilizer) of the Keogh River in 1999 and 2000 than in the other three reaches within the Keogh, but differences were not statistically significant among the four years ($p = 0.101$) or reaches ($p = 0.061$). Likewise, Waukwaas River steelhead parr showed no trend among years or reaches that was significant ($p = 0.08$ and 0.13, respectively). Waukwaas parr were at highest densities in Reach 1 in 1998 and Reach 3 in 1997 and 1999. Mean parr densities were not significantly different in 2000 than on the neighboring Keogh River (average overall, 42 parr/100 m), despite higher fry densities in the Waukwaas in the previous year (1999, $p < 0.05$).

Fish Utilization of Habitat Structures

The favored habitat types and structures for each species and age-class were examined and previously reported by McCubbing and Ward (2001, 2002). The mean densities of fish (No./100 m) for all structure sites and for each structure type were compared, including steelhead fry, steelhead parr, and coho fry, from 1997 to 2000. The variability in mean density was broad among common structure types in 2000, as in other sample years (coho fry, 26–102 fry/100 m²; steelhead parr, 2–10 parr/100 m²). This was similar to the range in values observed in 1998 and 1999, which were an improvement on 1997 densities. Highest steelhead parr densities in 2000 were re-

corded in boulder clusters (BC) and lateral debris jams (LDJ). There was no statistically significant difference among six main structure types owing to high variance. Over all years, steelhead fry were most abundant in boulder clusters (Figure 3). Coho fry were most abundant in double deflector logs (DDL) and lateral debris jams, although results were highly variable, with no indication of preference for any particular type of habitat structure.

Combined Response to Instream Structure Placement and Nutrient Addition

Data on fish density collected from sampling within stream habitats on the Keogh River and the untreated sections on the Waukwaas River provided the average response to treatments (i.e., no treatment, fertilizer only, structure placement only, and fertilizer plus structure placement). Steelhead fry densities in areas treated with fertilizer and structures on the Keogh River were, on average, five-fold greater than those in a control section (Reach Y, 1997) of the same watershed, but not significantly different from densities in the untreated Waukwaas River. Areas with nutrient addition (but without structures, $N = 5$) also, on average, exhibited greater abundance of fry than areas with structure placement only ($N = 2$), but not significantly so. Average levels of fry abundance in areas treated with both fertilizer and structures in the Keogh River were 26% lower than average reach densities on the Waukwaas River, but differences were not significant ($p > 0.05$).

The response in coho fry abundance to nutrient addition only in the Keogh River was not statistically significant (10% lower abundance than Keogh River control reaches). The addition of habitat structures appeared as an effective restoration technique in at least one reach, as well as at sites where structures were combined with nutrient addition. Reaches treated with structures (and, in some cases, fertilizer) supported an abundance of coho fry, up to three-fold higher than untreated sections (Figure 2). Untreated and fertilized-only reaches on the Keogh River had higher (30–40%) coho fry abundance than that observed in the untreated Waukwaas River.

Steelhead parr densities were, on average, nearly twice as abundant in areas treated with both fertilizer and structures on the Keogh River than in sections treated with only fertilizer or

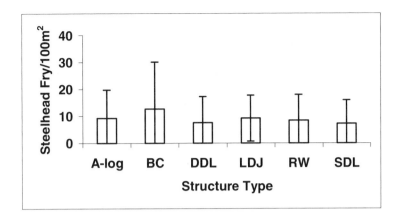

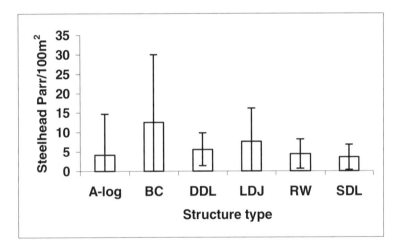

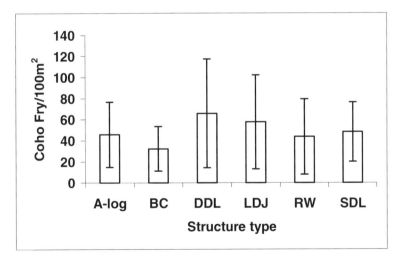

FIGURE 3. The utilization of habitat structures by steelhead fry, steelhead parr, and coho fry (mean and 95% CL) in the Keogh River, 1997 to 2000, within six of the main habitat structure types: A-log debris bundles, boulder clusters (BC), doubled deflector logs (DDL), lateral debris jams (LDJ), root wads (RW), and single deflector logs (SDL).

structures (mean in sites with structures, 19 parr/ m; with fertilizer, 34; with structure and fertilizer, 57; Figure 4), but the difference was not statistically significant (low power to the analysis; $p = 0.2$). Average levels of parr abundance in areas treated with both fertilizer and structures in the Keogh River by 2000 exceeded average reach densities on the Waukwaas River by more than 30%, and a further increase by 10% over combined data from 1997 to 1999 (Figure 4). Nevertheless, differences in 2000 within the Keogh River were also not statistically significant ($p = 0.14$). Parr densities on the Keogh River were relatively high despite low fry densities in the previous year (i.e., fry densities in 1999 and parr densities in 2000). Lower parr densities on the Waukwaas River were despite previous fry densities there that were numerically greater than at Keogh, suggesting that fry-to-parr survival was higher within the Keogh River than in the Waukwaas River.

Effect of Fertilizer Addition on Fish Growth

We compared fish weight (g) among reaches of the Keogh River and between the Keogh and Waukwaas rivers. Significant differences in steelhead fry weights during sampling in July and Au-gust were not apparent either among reaches or years for the Keogh River ($p = 0.41$ and 0.93) or on the Waukwaas River ($p = 0.78$ and 0.20). However, sampling during late autumn was concentrated over a much shorter period of time at temperatures when growth was limited (4–6°C). Steelhead fry sampled after two to three months in all reaches of the Keogh (fertilized) exhibited changes in weights and lengths significantly greater than in unfertilized reaches of the Waukwaas River ($p < 0.005$, anova). The average weight of steelhead fry in the Keogh, by autumn 2000, exceeded those in the Waukwaas River by more than 50% (Figure 5). Coho fry weights were significantly different among years on both rivers; highest mean weights during summer were observed in 1998 ($p < 0.05$ for both watersheds). By autumn, mean weights of coho fry were significantly greater in the Keogh River in 2000, by 38% on average, than in the untreated Waukwaas River (Figure 5; $p < 0.005$).

Smolt Yield

Twenty-six years of results of smolt monitoring at the Keogh River and 6 years of study at the Waukwaas River provided information on steelhead and coho smolt abundance. Coho smolt

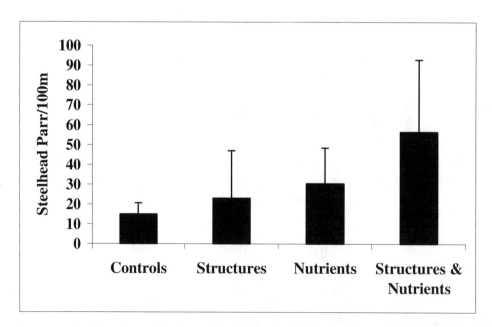

FIGURE 4. Average density (and 95% CL) of steelhead parr within treatment areas of the Keogh River from 1997 to 2000, including controls, sites with instream structure placement, sites where nutrients were added, and sites with both nutrient addition and habitat structures.

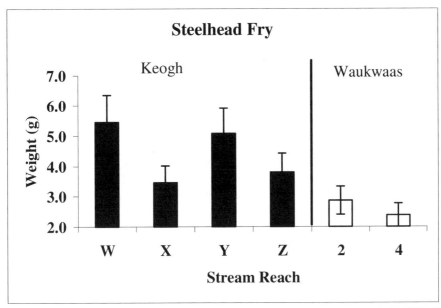

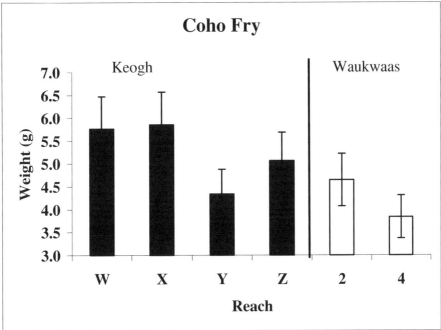

FIGURE 5. Average weight (and 95% CL) of steelhead trout and coho salmon fry in reaches W, X, Y, and Z of the Keogh River and reaches 2 and 4 of the Waukwaas River, by autumn 2000.

numbers rose steadily for both watersheds through the first three years of investigation (1995–1997), but fell sharply in the Keogh River in 1998 (prior to any expected response from treatments), while continuing to increase in 1998 in the Waukwaas River. A marked increase (>2 × 1998 values) of coho smolt counts was observed in 1999 from the Keogh River, with more than 53,000 migrants recorded (Figure 6). This trend continued in 2000, when 74,459 smolts were captured, the highest smolt yield on this watershed since 1987. From the Waukwaas River, a reduction in smolt yield observed in 1999 was followed by a further 10% decrease in yield in 2000. The total estimated

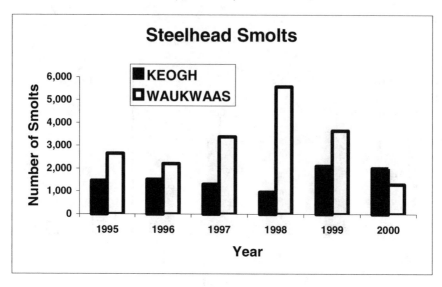

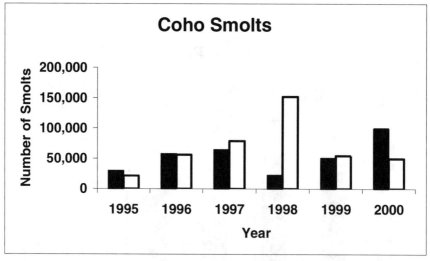

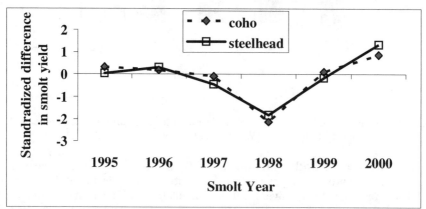

FIGURE 6. Steelhead trout and coho salmon smolt yield and standardized difference in smolt yield from the Keogh and Waukwaas rivers from 1995 to 2000.

yield of 48,898 coho smolts from the Waukwaas River was the second lowest on record (Figure 6). Steelhead smolt yield increased to 2,338 fish on the Keogh River in 2000, a further increase over 1999 counts. In comparison, estimated yield on the Waukwaas River in 2000 was reduced to 1,791 steelhead smolts, the lowest estimate of yield in the six sample years (Figure 6).

Tests of the annual difference in either coho or steelhead smolt yield from the two rivers indicated no statistically significant change. Of interest, however, was the parallel trend in the standardized difference in smolt yield of coho and steelhead in the two watersheds (Figure 6), suggesting that the differences may be due to a common cause in both species (e.g., the 1998 coho and steelhead smolt yield was dramatically reduced at the Keogh River, yet there was a positive trend in steelhead and coho smolt numbers in 1999 and 2000). Meanwhile, improvements in smolt yield in both species in 1998 on the Waukwaas River were followed by declines in 1999 and 2000. This perhaps indicates a preliminary response to Keogh treatments as well as the effect of spawner density on smolt yield described below.

Our design also allows for a before-and-after treatment response, with an external reference river. We considered 1995–1998 as pretreatment years at Keogh and 1999 and 2000 as a partial post-treatment response (years spent in rearing under at least partial restoration treatment). Steelhead smolt yield on the Keogh River improved significantly ($p < 0.02$), but coho smolt yield did not ($p > 0.28$). No significant difference for either species was detected from the Waukwaas smolt yields for the equivalent time period ($p > 0.5$, both species).

Steelhead Smolt Length and Age

Scale-age data derived from the sampling of steelhead smolts indicated a dramatic response to nutrient addition. Results from the sampling of lengths and ages of smolts from the Keogh River in the spring of 1997–2000 indicated no significant increase in length-at-age or mean smolt size in years where nutrient addition (1999, 2000) was a component of the juvenile rearing experience, compared with years without nutrient addition. When all years (1977–2001) of data on age-2 smolt length from the Keogh River were tested, the difference in average length of these age-2 smolts was highly significant and greater ($p <$

0.005) from years that included rearing under conditions of nutrient addition ($n = 7$; mean, 165 mm; SD, 8.5) than otherwise ($n = 18$; mean, 157 mm; SD, 5.3). Smolts from 1999 and 2000 displayed a shift in age structure, from predominantly 3-year-old smolts (mean age, 2.8 years; Ward and Slaney 1988, 1993a) to an average age of 2.6 years in 1999 and 2.2 years by 2000. Numerically, the number of age-2 smolts from all years with and without nutrient addition was significantly different (mean without nutrient added, 1,403; with nutrients, mean 4,363; $p < 0.004$; Figure 7). The combination of these factors (i.e., positive numerical, age structure, and smolt length-at-age changes) indicated a translation of improved growth during stream rearing through to benefits in the smolt stage. These positive changes were despite increased density of fish during in-stream rearing.

Coho smolt weights were also significantly greater in the Keogh River ($n = 6$; mean, 12.7 g; SD, 5.1) than in the untreated Waukwaas River ($n = 6$; mean, 9.4; SD, 2.1) among sample years 1996–2001 ($p < 0.002$), but not significantly different among years within watersheds ($p = 0.06$). Scales for aging are archived although not analyzed for all years, but partial results indicate similar distributions of one and two year old coho smolts (80–90% spend one year in freshwater) for both watersheds.

Smolts Per Spawner

Smolt yield per spawner from the Keogh River is incomplete for year-classes where steelhead trout juveniles were produced under partial or totally restored conditions. The steelhead smolt response is expressed two to four years after restoration treatment, whereas the coho smolt response requires one to two years. Partial (lower river) treatment with nutrients commenced in 1997, while structures were installed only in the upper reaches. Full-river habitat restoration including nutrient addition was near completion by 1999. A response in smolt yield that encompassed the whole river was therefore not anticipated until smolts of 2002 and 2003. Pretreatment data indicated very low recruitment during the freshwater life stage (Ward 2000a); less than 2 smolts per spawner were produced from the 1995 brood year, well below the level required for population replacement (i.e., at 4% smolt-to-adult survival, each spawner must produce 25 smolts to generate 1 adult recruit). This at-risk level was exceeded

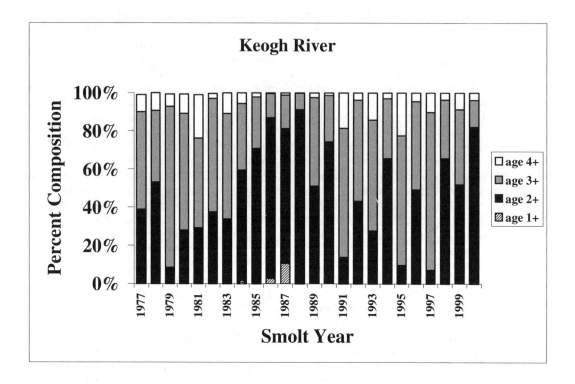

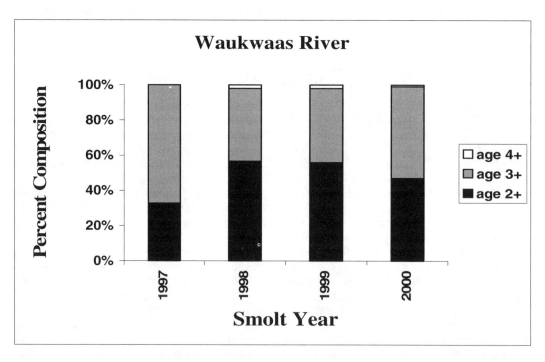

FIGURE 7. Age structure (percent composition) of steelhead smolts of the Keogh River from 1977 to 2000 and from the Waukwaas River from 1997 to 2000.

after partial restoration treatment; more than 14 smolts per spawner were produced from the 1996 brood year, where smolts aged 3+ and 4+ had reared under whole-river nutrient addition conditions for their last one and two years in the river. Further improvement to 42 and 53 smolts per spawner from 1997 and 1998 broods, respectively (Figure 8), have since been observed. We require the counts of age-3+ smolts of 2002 to add to the smolt recruits from the 1999 brood; the smolt-per-spawner value from 1999 brood is as yet only a partial result.

Since smolt yield is density dependent (Ward and Slaney 1993a), the smolts produced per spawner was considered as a function of the number of spawners (Figure 8). That relationship was linearized by natural log transformation of the smolts-per-spawner values, which provided clear indication of different production regimes from the decade of the 1980s versus the 1990s. The benefits of nutrient addition experiments on smolt yield during the mid-1980s and the initial (partial) response to restoration treatments was clear (Figure 8). Slopes for regimes and restoration results were significantly different (treat-ment and spawner interaction; $p < 0.002$). Further statistical comparison of the recruitment as a result of restoration efforts was not possible using standard parametric regression techniques, because the new values from 1997 to 1999 broods were outside the range of production values from the 1980s or 1990s regimes (i.e., much lower numbers of spawners). We used the predicted values of smolts per spawner based on the production regimes of the 1980s and 1990s (Figure 8) and compared observed values with the chi-squared statistic. These differences were highly significant for the 1997 and 1998 broods ($p < 0.01$). Intercepts in these relationships (Ricker a; Ward 2000a) for the 1980s, 1990s, and fertilizer-addition years indicated maximum yields of 24.5, 13.5, and 27.0 smolts per spawner, respectively. From restoration, an average of 30 smolts per spawner was obtained; the true maximum is likely much higher and greater than previous production regimes. We could not, however, obtain a reliable intercept from these three data points.

Coho smolt-per-spawner data were only available for the 1998 and 1999 brood years. Coho

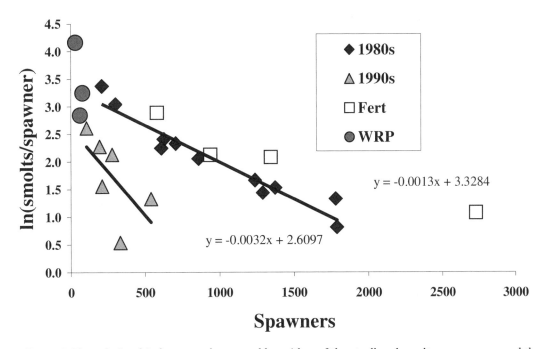

FIGURE 8. The relationship between the natural logarithm of the steelhead smolts per spawner and the number of spawners in the Keogh River during the production regimes of the 1980s (black diamonds) and the 1990s (grey triangles), during nutrient experiments in the mid-1980s (open squares), and preliminary results from the period of watershed restoration treatments (dark grey circles).

smolt counts were conducted each spring since 1977, but adults have been counted during their fall migration using the resistivity counter only since 1998 (McCubbing et al. 1999). The preliminary estimate was 9 and 20 smolts per spawner, respectively, assuming 90% of smolts were one year in age, with higher smolt-per-spawner values at lower spawner densities due to density-dependent effects.

Discussion

Steelhead smolt yield was improved by the addition of inorganic nutrients and habitat structures. Nutrient addition was interpreted as a key variable in the Keogh River from 1997 to 2000, based on trends in steelhead fry, steelhead parr, and coho fry abundance and growth, through to the smolt stage (cf. Johnston et al. 1990; Slaney and Northcote 1974). We could not statistically separate the synergistic effects to smolts from nutrient addition and habitat structures or from other watershed restoration works on hillslopes or riparian areas. Habitat structure placement appeared to be a more important component to the increased density of coho fry. The positive response by steelhead fry and parr, coho fry, as well as steelhead and coho smolts varied, but was generally in agreement with habitat restoration as it progressed on the Keogh River, while changes at the Waukwaas River represented natural variation.

In general, we found that the response of steelhead smolt size and age structure to nutrient addition confirmed results documented earlier by Slaney and Ward (1993) and Slaney et al. (this volume). The analysis was confounded by low numbers of both steelhead and coho spawners and subsequent fry distribution and abundance. Ideally, experiments such as this should be conducted during conditions of fry seeding to capacity, but due to poor marine survival conditions and low adult returns, fry recruitment in this study was generally low. Steelhead fry abundance was variable but higher at Wauk-waas than Keogh, yet subsequent parr abundance was higher at Keogh in treated years. Trends of instream juvenile abundance and smolt yield from the untreated Waukwaas River, draining to the west coast of Vancouver Island, may be attributed to adult spawning escapements that were relatively high compared with the Keogh River. There, conditions for survival in the ocean may have been better

than at Keogh (Smith and Ward 2000; Welch et al. 2000). Yet, Waukwaas smolt yields declined recently, indicating that relatively harsher instream conditions had prevailed.

The highly variable nature of data on both the instream abundance and smolt yield further demonstrates the difficulty of relying on only a single pair of streams and detailed life stage sampling for restoration effectiveness evaluations (Keeley and Walters 1994). An effective evaluation using the Keogh and Waukwaas will require several more years of analysis (at least to 2004) due to high variability in Waukwaas smolt yields, low spawner density at Keogh, and the time required to follow the control or treatment response through to the smolt stage and smolts-per-spawner. The latter has proven to be the better response variable. Steelhead parr represent the key response variable of the instream studies, since they integrate effects over more years in freshwater than coho and since they have passed the main density-dependant fry-to-parr stage (Ward and Slaney 1993a; Ward 1996). Abundance of steelhead parr in reaches treated with the addition of nutrients and habitat structures was highest and exceeded that observed in the untreated Waukwaas River. Densities of parr on the Keogh River were similar to historic densities recorded in their preferred habitat—boulder clusters in riffles and runs (Facchin and Slaney 1977; Ward and Slaney 1979, 1981, 1993a, 1993b). Coho fry abundance in the Keogh River exceeded that on the Waukwaas River, with densities in preferred habitats exceeding those in previous surveys (Johnston et al. 1990; Ward and Slaney 1979, 1981, 1993a, 1993b), further indicating a positive response to restoration measures.

When fry and parr abundance was examined according to treatment type, nutrient addition appeared as a very positive factor. Reaches on the Keogh River treated with nutrients had steelhead fry abundance more than 10 times that in untreated areas. Nevertheless, abundance was lower than that observed in the untreated Waukwaas River. Fry densities in the Keogh River were low in 2000 compared with historic values (Ward and Slaney 1993a), yet they were the highest observed in the four years of this study. Our interpretation is that the increase in fry density was at least partly a treatment response confounded by spawner numbers. In general, structures associated with higher velocity water (riffles and runs) exhibited higher steelhead parr abundance, as previously observed by Ward and Slaney (1981, 1993b). Complex debris structures associated with low velocity water (pool and flat habitat) contained a greater abundance of coho fry, similar to observations of Peters et al. (1992), House and Boehme (1986), and Ward and Slaney (1979). Thus, a variety of structure types and placements within a range of habitat types seems to provide a diversity of niches for these stream-dwelling salmonids, such that a specific structure type may be less important than a wide range of habitat designs that provide a greater diversity of habitats.

Marine-derived nutrients (MDN) from carcasses of adult salmon can account for as much as 40% of the nitrogen and carbon input to streams (Bilby and Ward 1996), and for orthophosphate input as well (Stansby and Hall 1965). This input is depleted where salmon runs are reduced (Larkin and Slaney 1997) or when large woody debris (LWD) is limited and carcass retention within the river is reduced (Cederholm et al. 1989). Coastal streams like the Keogh River are typically phosphate limited (Ashley and Slaney 1997), thus declining runs of pink *O. gorbuscha* and coho salmon and reductions of instream LWD through past forest practices (Potyrala 1997) potentially result in a downward spiral of MDN levels. Recent declines in the abundance of pink salmon at the Keogh River have been dramatic, from more than 60,000 in even years to less than 10,000 in 1998, and from more than 30,000 in odd years to less than 1,000 in 1999. Thus, nutrient supplementation was experimentally attempted, and direct observations of algal response indicated increased accrual, moderated by the increases in grazing by invertebrates, especially by abundant dipteran larvae and mayfly (Ephemeropterae) and stonefly (Plecopterae) species in riffles of the Keogh River (Johnston et al. 1990). The nutrient addition was effectively transferred through the ecosystem to provide significant increases in growth of steelhead and coho fry. In steelhead, at least, this was reflected in changes in age structure of the smolts, to a full year younger. Inorganic nutrient addition led to significant increases in average weights of steelhead and reduced smolt age compared with earlier data from the Keogh River and the untreated Waukwaas River. These increases in mean weight and condition factor on the Keogh River observed throughout the current study cannot be attributed to density-dependant factors because steelhead numbers were generally increasing at the same time.

Steelhead smolt yields were higher than expected for the numbers of spawners based on the 1990s recruitment model (Ward 2000a). Steelhead smolt yield increased again in 2000 with further changes to a predominance of two-year-old smolts. Similar changes in age structure were attained during pilot whole-river nutrient replacement studies in the mid-1980s (Slaney and Ward 1993). Improved yield was the combined result of increased growth rates due to nutrient addition as well as increased overwinter survival. These changes were perhaps also due to the increased availability of winter refuge habitat (habitat structures and off-channel developments) as well as reduced residence time in freshwater. Further improvements in steelhead yield might be expected based on the observed increase in steelhead parr abundance and distribution, increased adult escapement from at least one year of improved ocean survival, and increases in smolt yield per spawner. The effects of full-river nutrient supplementation and habitat construction will not be fully realized as smolt yield until 2004. Meanwhile, steelhead smolts from the Waukwaas River showed a reduction in steelhead smolt yield in 1999 with further decreases in 2000, as predicted from summer parr densities in 1999, with no change in length-at-age or in the age composition of smolts.

Coho smolt yield increased again on the Keogh River in 2000 to the highest count since 1987 over the historically poor yield observed in 1998, to the highest count since 1987. This was partially related to the large escapement of adults in 1998. Coho smolts were, on average, slightly larger (10% increase in length) for their age than in previous unfertilized years or in the untreated Waukwaas River, despite density increases. Overwinter survival rates may have been better than average because of larger fry size. Improved diversity of habitat, both instream and off-channel, may also be responsible for the observed improvements in fry survival and for the recent differences (increase at Keogh, decrease at Waukwaas) in smolt yield from the two river systems.

The goal of most habitat restoration projects is to increase instream production and the capacity for salmonids to produce higher yields of smolts per spawner, yet rarely is this variable ever measured. Initial results for steelhead trout indicate that smolts produced per spawner in the Keogh River have risen from at-risk levels of less than 3 smolts per spawner from the 1996 brood to at least 50 smolts per spawner from the 1998 brood. This is the highest smolt production per spawner of the Keogh record. Low numbers of spawners and reduced competition for resources by fry and parr may in part be responsible for these observations, yet the cumulative evidence from initial results suggests recruitment of steelhead smolts from spawners at the Keogh River was in positive response to watershed restoration, with nutrient addition a major factor.

The preliminary results presented here on the recruitment response suggest that stream habitat restoration, nutrient addition, and off-channel habitat creation will buffer negative environmental factors. Further reprieve may be possible through means of supplementation, including the use of wild smolts as broodstock, an experiment now in progress at the Keogh River (Ward 2000b). Supplementation and habitat restoration combined with occasional years of improved ocean survival may be sufficient to maintain salmonid populations in coastal streams against generally poor ocean conditions. Continued experimentation to increase yield, monitoring of salmonid survival during their freshwater and marine life stages, and examination of the smolt migration along the coast may assist towards understanding and sustaining salmonid populations.

Acknowledgments

We are especially grateful to the many field crews that have operated the Keogh River fish fence and that have conducted electrofishing during summer over many years. In particular, we thank Cheryl Burroughs, Lloyd Burroughs, Caroline Melville, and the Northern Vancouver Island Salmonid Enhancement Association for recent efforts. We also thank the habitat assessment, prescription and restoration team, especially Mark Potyrala, Lloyd Burroughs, and Rheal Finnigan. Funding for this evaluation was through the auspices of the Watershed Restoration Program (WRP) for Forest Renewal B.C. Fish fence operations were supported with funds from B.C.'s Habitat Conservation Trust Fund and the Fisheries and Oceans Canada Habitat Restoration and Salmon Enhancement Program. Support from many individuals within B.C. Fisheries and the Watershed Restoration Programmes is gratefully appreciated.

References

Arnason, A. N., C. W. Kirby, C. J. Schwarz, and J. R. Irvine. 1996. Computer analysis of data from stratified mark-recovery experiments for the estimation of salmon escapements and other populations. Canadian Technical Report of Fisheries and Aquatic Sciences 2106.

Ashley, K. I., and P. A. Slaney. 1997. Accelerating recovery of stream, river and pond productivity by low-level nutrient replacement. Chapter 13 in P. A. Slaney and D. Zaldokas, editors. Fish habitat rehabilitation procedures. Province of British Columbia, Ministry of Environment, Lands and Parks, and Ministry of Forests. Watershed Restoration Technical Circular No. 9.

Bilby, R. E., and J. W. Ward. 1996. Incorporation of nitrogen and carbon from spawning coho salmon into the trophic system of small streams: evidence from stable isotopes. Canadian Journal of Fisheries and Aquatic Sciences 53:164–173.

Burroughs, L. E., P. A. Slaney, and J. S. Cleary. 2001. The Keogh River watershed restoration: 2000/2001 fish habitat rehabilitation. Province of British Columbia, Ministry of Environment, Lands and Parks, and Ministry of Forests. Watershed Restoration Progress Report No. 17.

Cederholm, C. J., D. B. Houston, D. L. Cole, and W. J. Scarlett. 1989. Fate of coho salmon (Oncorhynchus kisutch) carcasses in spawning streams. Canadian Journal of Fisheries and Aquatic Sciences 46:1347–1355.

Dempson, J. B., and D. E. Stansbury. 1991. Using partial counting fences and a two-sample stratified design for mark-recapture estimation of an Atlantic salmon smolt population. North American Journal of Fisheries Management 11:27–37.

Facchin, A., and P. A. Slaney. 1977. Management implications of substrate utilization during summer by juvenile steelhead trout (Salmo gairdneri) in the South Alouette River. Province of British Columbia, Ministry of Recreation and Conservation. Fisheries Technical Circular No. 32.

Frith, H. R., T. C. Nelson, and B. L. Nass. 1995a. Assessment of rotary traps for monitoring and enumerating populations of migratory juvenile salmonids. Province of British Columbia Ministry of Environment, Lands and Parks. Watershed Restoration Contract Report from LGL Ltd., March 1995.

Frith, H. R., T. C. Nelson, and C. J. Schwarz. 1995b. Comparison of rotary trap mark-recapture outmigration estimates with fence counts for coho and steelhead smolts in the Keogh River, 1995. Province of British Columbia Ministry of

Environment, Lands and Parks. Watershed Restoration Contract Report from LGL Ltd., September 1995.

Gresh, T., J. Lichatowich, and P. Schoonmaker. 2000. An estimation of historic and current levels of salmon production in the northeast Pacific ecosystem. Fisheries 25(1):15–21.

Hankin, D. G., and G. H. Reeves. 1988. Estimating total fish abundance and total habitat area in small streams based on visual estimation methods. Canadian Journal of Fisheries and Aquatic Resources 45:834–844.

Hart, P. J., and T. J. Pitcher. 1969. Field trials of fish marking using a jet inoculator. Journal of Fish Biology 1:383–385.

House, R. A., and P. L. Boehme. 1986. Effects of instream structures on salmonid habitat and populations in Tobe Creek, Oregon. North American Journal of Fisheries Management 6:283–295.

Irvine, J. R., and B. R. Ward. 1989. Patterns of timing and size of wild coho salmon (*Oncorhynchus kisutch*) smolts migrating from the Keogh River watershed on northern Vancouver Island. Canadian Journal of Fisheries and Aquatic Sciences 46:1086–1094.

Johnston, N. T., C. J. Perrin, P. A. Slaney, and B. R. Ward. 1990. Increased juvenile salmonid growth by whole river fertilization. Canadian Journal of Fisheries and Aquatic Sciences 47:862–872.

Keeley, E. R., and C. J. Walters. 1994. The British Columbia Watershed Restoration Program: summary of the experimental design, monitoring and restoration techniques workshop. Province of British Columbia, Ministry of Environment, Lands and Parks and Ministry of Forests. Watershed Restoration Project Report No. 4.

Larkin, G. A., and P. A. Slaney. 1997. Implications of trends in marine-derived nutrients flow to south coastal British Columbia salmonid production. Fisheries 22(11):16–24.

Melville, C. 1997. Keogh River enumeration fence spring 1997. Province of British Columbia, Ministry of Environment, Lands and Parks, Fisheries Research and Development. Contract Report by the British Columbia Conservation Foundation, August 1997.

McCubbing, D. J. F. 1998. A report on the assessment of the 1998 smolt output from the Waukwaas River, North Vancouver Island, using rotary traps. Province of British Columbia. Contract Report by the Northern Vancouver Island Salmonid Enhancement Association.

McCubbing, D. J. F. 1999. A report on the assessment of the 1999 smolt output from the Waukwaas River, North Vancouver Island, using rotary traps. Province of British Columbia Ministry of Environment, Lands and Parks. Fisheries Research and Development Section Contract Report by the Northern Vancouver Island Salmonid Enhancement Association.

McCubbing, D. J. F 2000a. Adult steelhead trout and salmonid smolt migration at the Keogh River during spring 2000. Province of British Columbia Ministry of Environment, Lands and Parks. Fisheries Research and Development Section Contract Report by the Northern Vancouver Island Salmonid Enhancement Association.

McCubbing, D. J. F. 2000b. Assessment of salmonid smolt yield from the Waukwaas River, North Vancouver Island, 2000. Province of British Columbia Ministry of Environment, Lands and Parks. Fisheries Research and Development Section Contract Report by the Northern Vancouver Island Salmonid Enhancement Association.

McCubbing, D. J. F., and B. R. Ward. 1997. The Keogh and Waukwaas rivers paired watershed study for B.C.'s Watershed Restoration Program: juvenile salmonid enumeration and growth 1997. Province of British Columbia, Ministry of Environment, Lands and Parks, and Ministry of Forests. Watershed Restoration Project Report No. 6.

McCubbing, D. J. F., and B. R. Ward. 2001. Stream rehabilitation in British Columbia's Watershed Restoration Program: juvenile salmonids in the Keogh River compared to the untreated Waukwaas River in 2000. Province of British Columbia, Ministry of Environment, Lands and Parks. Watershed Restoration Project Report No. 17.

McCubbing, D. J. F., and B. R. Ward. 2002. Stream rehabilitation in British Columbia's Watershed Restoration Program: juvenile salmonids in the Keogh River compared to the untreated Waukwaas River in 2001. Province of British Columbia, Ministry of Environment, Lands and Parks. Watershed Restoration Project Report No. 20.

McCubbing, D. J. F, B. R. Ward, and L. Burroughs. 1999. Salmonid escapement enumeration on the Keogh River: a demonstration of a resistivity counter in British Columbia. Province of British Columbia Fisheries Technical Circular No. 104.

Peters, R. J., E. E. Knudsen, C. J. Cederholm, W. J. Scarlett, and G. B. Pauley. 1992. Preliminary results of woody debris use by summer-rearing juvenile coho salmon (*Oncorhynchus kisutch*) in the Clearwater River, Washington. Pages 323–339 *in* L. Berg and P. W. Delaney, editors. Proceedings of the coho workshop, Nanaimo, British Columbia, 26–28 May, 1992.

Potyrala, M. 1997. Summary of the 1996/97 fish habitat assessment and overview riparian assessment of the Keogh River watershed. Province of British Columbia Ministry of Environment, Lands and Parks, Watershed Restoration Program Contract Report by the British Columbia Conservation Foundation.

Potyrala, M. 1999a. Summary of the 1997/1998 Keogh River Watershed Restoration Program. Province of British Columbia Ministry of Environment, Lands and Parks, Watershed Restoration Program Contract Report by the British Columbia Conservation Foundation.

Potyrala, M. 1999b. Summary of the 1998/1999 Keogh River Watershed Restoration Program. Province of British Columbia Ministry of Environment, Lands and Parks, Watershed Restoration Program Contract Report by the British Columbia Conservation Foundation.

Potyrala, M. 1999c. Preliminary restoration plan for the 1999/2000 Keogh River Watershed Restoration Program. Province of British Columbia Ministry of Environment, Lands and Parks, Watershed Restoration Program. Contract Report by the British Columbia Conservation Foundation.

Ricker, W. E. 1975. Computation and interpretation of biological statistics of fish populations. Fisheries Research Board of Canada Bulletin 191.

Slaney, P. A., and T. J. Northcote. 1974. Effects of prey abundance on density and territorial behaviour of young rainbow trout (Salmo gairdneri) in laboratory stream channels. Journal of the Fisheries Research Board of Canada 31:1201–1209.

Slaney, P. A., and B. R. Ward. 1993. Experimental fertilization of nutrient deficient streams in British Columbia. Pages 128–141 in G. Shooner and S. Asselin, editors. Le développement du saumon Atlantique au Québec: connaître les règles du jeu pour réussir. Colloque international de la Fédération québécoise pour le saumon atlantique. Québec, décembre 1992. Collection Salmo salar n°1.

Slaney, P. A., R. J. Finnigan, and R. G. Millar. 1997. Accelerating recovery of log-jam habitats: large woody debris-boulder complexes. Chapter 9 in P. A. Slaney and D. Zaldokas, editors. Fish habitat rehabilitation procedures. Province of British Columbia, Ministry of Environment, Lands and Parks, and Ministry of Forests, Watershed Restoration Technical Circular No. 9.

Slaney, P. A., and A. D. Martin. 1997. Planning fish habitat rehabilitation: linking to habitat protection. Chapter 1 in P. A. Slaney and D. Zaldokas, editors. Fish habitat rehabilitation procedures. Province of British Columbia, Ministry of Environment, Lands and Parks, and Ministry of Forests, Watershed Restoration Technical Circular No. 9.

Smith, B. D., and B. R. Ward. 2000. Trends in adult wild steelhead (Oncorhynchus mykiss) abundance for coastal regions of British Columbia support the variable marine survival hypothesis. Canadian Journal of Fisheries and Aquatic Sciences 57:271–284.

Smith, B. D., Ward, B. R., and Welch, D. W. 2000. Trends in wild adult steelhead (Oncorhynchus mykiss) abundance in British Columbia as indexed by angler success. Canadian Journal of Fisheries and Aquatic Sciences 57:255–270.

Stansby, M. E., and A. S. Hall. 1965. Chemical composition of commercially important fish of the United States. Fishery Industrial Research 3:29–46.

Stockner, J. G. 1987. Lake fertilization: the enrichment cycle and lake sockeye salmon (Oncorhynchus nerka) production. Pages 198–215 in H. D. Smith, L. Margolis, and C. C. Wood, editors. Sockeye salmon (Oncorhynchus nerka) population biology and future management. Canadian Special Publication of Fisheries and Aquatic Sciences 96.

Ward. B. R. 1996. Population dynamics of steelhead trout in a coastal stream, the Keogh River, British Columbia. Pages 308–323 in I. Cowx, editor. Stock assessment in inland fisheries. Fishing News Books, Blackwell Scientific Publications, Oxford.

Ward, B. R. 1997. Using boulder clusters to rehabilitate juvenile salmonid habitat. In P. A. Slaney and D. Zaldokas, editors. Fish habitat rehabilitation procedures. Province of British Columbia, Ministry of Environment, Lands and Parks, and Ministry of Forests, Watershed Restoration Technical Circular No. 9.

Ward, B. R. 2000a. Declivity in steelhead trout recruitment at the Keogh River over the past decade. Canadian Journal of Fisheries and Aquatic Sciences 57:298–306.

Ward, B. R. 2000b. Canadian supplementation and captive broodstock programs. Page 19 in Independent Multidisciplinary Science Team. 2000. Conservation hatcheries and supplementation strategies for recovery of wild stocks of salmonids. Report of a workshop. Technical Report 2000–1 to the Oregon Plan for Salmon and Watersheds. Oregon Watershed Enhancement Board, Salem, Oregon.

Ward, B. R., and McCubbing, D. J. F. 1998. Adult steelhead trout and salmonid smolts at the Keogh River during spring 1998 and comparison to the historic record. Province of British Columbia Fisheries Technical Circular No. 102.

Ward, B. R., and P. A. Slaney. 1979. Evaluation of insteam enhancement structures for the production of juvenile steelhead trout and coho salmon in the Keogh River: progress 1977 and 1978. Province of British Columbia, Ministry of Environment, Lands and Parks. Fisheries Technical Circular No. 45.

Ward, B. R., and P. A. Slaney. 1981. Further evaluation of structures for the improvement of salmonid rearing habitat in a coastal stream in British Columbia. In T. J. Hassler, editor. Proceedings: propagation, enhancement, and reha-bilitation of anadromous salmonid populations and habitat symposium. American Fish- eries Society, Western Division, Humboldt Chapter, Arcata, California.

Ward, B. R., and P. A. Slaney. 1988. Life history and smolt-to-adult survival of Keogh River steel-head trout (*Salmo gairdneri*) and the relation-ship to smolt size. Canadian Journal of Fisher-ies and Aquatic Sciences 44:1110–1222.

Ward, B. R., and P. A. Slaney. 1990. Returns of pen-reared steelhead trout from riverine, estuarine, and marine releases. Transactions of the Ameri-can Fisheries Society 119:492–499.

Ward, B. R., and P. A. Slaney. 1993a. Egg-to-smolt survival and fry-to-smolt density dependence of Keogh River steelhead trout. Pages 209–217 *in* R. J. Gibson and R. E. Cutting, editors. Pro-duction of juvenile Atlantic salmon, *Salmo salar*, in natural waters. Canadian Special Pub-lication Fisheries and Aquatic Sciences 118.

Ward, B. R., and P. A. Slaney. 1993b. Habitat manipula-tions for the rearing of fish in British Columbia. Pages 142–148 *in* G. Shooner and S. Asselin, edi-tors. Le développement du saumon Atlan-tique au Québec: connaître les règles du jeu pour réussir. Colloque international de la Fédé-ration québécoise pour le saumon Atlantique. Québec, décembre 1992. Collection *Salmo salar* n°1.

Ward, B. R., J. A. Burrows and D. L. Quamme. 1990 Adult steelhead population size and salmonid mi-grants of the Keogh River during the spring, 1990. Province of British Columbia Fisheries Techni-cal Circular No. 89.

Ward, B. R., P. A. Slaney, A. R. Facchin, and R. W. Land. 1989. Size-biased survival in steelhead trout: back-calculated lengths from adults' scales compared to migrating smolts at the Keogh River, B. C. Canadian Journal of Fisher-ies and Aquatic Sciences 46:1853–1858.

Welch, D. W., B. R. Ward, B. D. Smith, and J. P. Eveson. 2000. Temporal and spatial responses of Brit-ish Columbia steelhead (*Oncorhynchus mykiss*) populations to ocean climate shifts. Fisheries Oceanography 9:17–32.

Zaldokas, D. O., L. Burroughs, and M. Potyrala. 1999. The Keogh River watershed restoration project. 1999/2000 fish habitat restoration major works. Province of British Columbia, Ministry of Envi-ronment, Lands and Parks, and Ministry of For-ests, Watershed Restoration Project, Unpub-lished Report.

American Fisheries Society Symposium 34:149–162, 2003
© Copyright by the American Fisheries Society 2003

Experimental Enrichment of Two Oligotrophic Rivers in South Coastal British Columbia

GREGORY A. WILSON, KENNETH I. ASHLEY, AND ROBERT W. LAND

Fisheries Research and Development Section, Province of British Columbia
2204 Main Mall, University of British Columbia, Vancouver, B.C. V6T 1Z4, Canada

PATRICK A. SLANEY

Watershed Restoration Program, Province of British Columbia
2004 Main Mall, University of British Columbia, Vancouver, B.C. V6T 1Z4, Canada

Abstract.—Big Silver Creek and the Adam River are oligotrophic (conductivity < 45 $\mu\Omega$/cm; TDP < 2–5 μg/L; NO_{2+3}-N < 45 μg/L), mid-sized coastal rivers in southwestern British Columbia. They were treated with inorganic P (phosphorus) and N (nitrogen) to examine the feasibility of low-level inorganic fertilization as a method of increasing resident fish populations in rivers subject to habitat loss by historical logging practices. Both rivers have low numbers and sizes of resident salmonids (<20/ha, >20 cm fork length), despite extensive suitable habitat. Water temperatures in summer average 12°C and 14°C with summer discharge averaging 12 and 4 m^3/s in Big Silver Creek and the Adam River, respectively. In 1992–1997, physical, chemical, and biological assessments took place from May to September in three reaches of each river. Liquid agricultural fertilizer was added to the lower reach(es) of each river from June to September of 1994–1997, while upstream reaches were monitored as controls. Fertilizer addition methods evolved from dripping through a hose and valve system, to a more dependable preprogrammable injection system, with the merits of each system discussed. In each river, chlorophyll-*a* accrual and benthic invertebrate biomass and density increased, on average, two to four-fold in the fertilized reaches. There was an average four-fold increase in rainbow trout abundance in each river following four summers of fertilization, with a large increase in mountain whitefish *Prosopium williamsoni* (Big Silver Creek) and a smaller increase in brown trout *Salmo trutta* (Adam River). The experimental treatments confirmed that low-level fertilization augmented productivity, resulting in a significant response of resident trout in two oligotrophic streams. The technique can be applied to aquatic systems with reduced fish populations resulting from habitat loss, overfishing, or to anadromous populations caught in the negative feedback loop of decreasing escapement and associated losses of marine-derived nutrients.

Introduction

Coastal drainages in the Pacific Northwest (PNW) are dominated by nutrient-poor, oligotrophic waters (Northcote and Larkin 1966) resulting from a combination of erosion-resistant granitic bedrock overlaid by shallow soils and high rainfall (Stockner 1981, 1987; Cannings and Cannings 1996). These streams have some of the lowest nutrient and net production values ever recorded (Stockner and Shortreed 1976). Gross et al. (1988)

suggest that diadromous migrations of Pacific salmon evolved to take advantage of the productivity differential between the oligotrophic freshwater environment and the more productive marine environment.

A combination of environmental factors limit the growth and abundance of salmonids in streams, including physical habitat limitations (Ward and Slaney 1979, 1981), water temperature regimes (Holtby and Hartman 1982; Egglishaw and Shackley 1985), winter freshets, droughts, and poor egg survival resulting from sedimentation or bedload movement (Parkinson and Slaney 1975), or instream food supply (Egglishaw 1968). Food availability directly impacts territory size and, thus, abundance, growth, carrying capacity, and production of juvenile fish per unit of stream area (Slaney and Northcote 1974; Grant et al. 1998).

Primary production forms the basis of the food chain in large streams (Minshall 1978), and the addition of inorganic nutrients to oligotrophic streams has been shown to increase periphytic production (Stockner and Shortreed 1978; Peterson et al. 1985; Perrin et al. 1987) and thereby insect growth and abundance (Milbrink and Holmgren 1981; Peterson et al. 1985; John-ston et al. 1990; Mundie et al. 1991; Peterson et al. 1993) and the growth of steelhead trout *Oncorhynchus mykiss*, coho salmon *O. kisutch* (Slaney et al. 1986; Johnston et al. 1990), and Arctic grayling *Thymallus arcticus* (Deegan and Peterson 1992) in smaller streams. Additionally, small increases in juvenile and smolt size often result in significant increases in overwinter and ocean survival in anadromous species (Ward et al. 1989). Thus, controlled addition of limiting nutrients during the optimal growth period in oligotrophic rivers should result in increased growth, abundance, and production of fish per unit area. Fertilization could be a useful management tool to compensate for habitat loss from historical logging practices that significantly degraded instream fish habitat and to compensate for interruption in the nutrient cycle of PNW watersheds resulting from declines in anadromous fish returns (Stockner 1987; Kline et al. 1993).

Methods of nutrient addition to streams have evolved since Huntsman (1948) placed bags of fertilizer streamside or since Mason (1976) hand-fed coho in stream with marine euphausiids. Stockner and Shortreed (1978) demonstrated the significant nutrient limitation of autotrophy in a PNW ecosystem using concentrated solutions of $NaNO_3$ as a nitrogen (N) source and Na_2HPO_4 for phosphorus (P). Experimental instream fertilization experiments began in earnest in 1981 when organic (barley) and inorganic (dry agricultural) fertilizers were added to different reaches of the oligotrophic Keogh River (Vancouver Island); the latter increased autotrophic periphyton production an order of magnitude (Perrin et al. 1987). Other inorganic nutrient sources used include a slow-release fertilizer added to the Keogh River (Johnston et al. 1990) and liquid phosphoric acid

added to the Kuparuk River, Alaska (Peterson et al. 1985). Liquid agricultural fertilizer, ammonium poly-phosphate (10–34–0; % by weight N-P_2O_5-K_2O), and ammonium nitrate (34–0–0), were tested in the early 1990s on the Salmon River, Vancouver Island (Slaney and Ward 1993), the benefits of which included low cost, availability, and safe handling (Ashley, this volume).

Nutrient stimulation of primary and secondary productivity has been demonstrated in smaller streams, but the effects of fertilization on productivity in larger rivers and associated resident salmonid populations remain uncertain. Dependable and cost-effective methods of nutrient addition are also required, if this restoration technique is to be extended to other/larger aquatic ecosystems. We examined the effects of low-level inorganic P and N additions, using liquid agricultural fertilizer in two medium-to-large coastal rivers (mean annual flow > 15 m³/s) in southwest British Columbia, some of the largest streams yet fertilized. We assessed the effects on water chemistry, periphyton accrual, zoobenthos standing crop, and size and density of juvenile and adult fish, while developing and testing dependable liquid fertilizer application methods. A more detailed presentation of the following can be found in Wilson et al. (1999a, 1999b).

Methods

Study Area

The Adam River (50°40'W by 126°20'N) is located 12 km northwest of Sayward on Vancouver Island and originates from the Vancouver Island Mountain Range, flowing northwest for 50 km into Johnstone Straight (Figure 1). Waterfalls located at River km 4 (upstream from river mouth) are a barrier to fish migration. Watershed area and mean annual flow are 320 km² and 14–15 m³/s, respectively, with summer water temperatures averaging 14°C. Wild rainbow *Oncorhynchus mykiss* and introduced brown trout *Salmo trutta* inhabit the river above the falls, with low densities of cutthroat trout *O. clarki*, and Dolly Varden *Salvelinus malma*. Most rainbow trout are small (<20 cm), with densities 10–20/ha (30–45/km) before fertilization. Densities of brown trout in the main stem ranged from less than 0.5 to 5/ha (1–14/km) prior to fertilization, with most of catchable size, but only a few (<1/ha, 1–2/km) more than 40 cm in length.

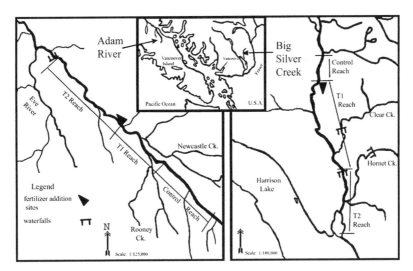

FIGURE 1. Study area showing the three experimental reaches in the Adam River and Big Silver Creek and points of fertilizer addition.

Big Silver Creek (49°40'W by 121°51'N), located 35 km north of Harrison Hot Springs, originates in the Lillooet Range of the Coast Mountains and flows west for 40 km into Harrison Lake (Figure 1). Waterfalls at River km 6 limit migrant fish, with the possible exception of a few summer run steelhead trout *O. mykiss*, to the lower river. Below the falls several anadromous species are found, in addition to fluvial or lacustrine-adfluvial populations of rainbow trout, cutthroat trout *O. clarki*, Dolly Varden *Salvelinus malma*, and mountain whitefish *Prosopium williamsoni*. Upstream of the km-6 barrier, rainbow trout are relatively abundant but depressed in size with a density of 10/ha (43/km) for fish less than 20 cm in length. No fish have been found upstream of River km 15, where steep canyons appear to limit fish distribution. Steelhead parr (<5 g mean size) have been stocked annually (4–12,000 per year) above the barrier at River km 6, since 1993 (except 1995), and all were clipped for differentiation from wild fish. Historical flow records are not available for Big Silver Creek, but spring flows during 1992–1993 averaged 50–60 m³/s from May to June, then declined to summer lows of about 10 m³/s in August and September, with water temperatures averaging 12°C during summer.

The predominant human activity in the watershed of both rivers, for the past 40 years, has been intensive logging. Little old growth remains on the lower slopes, but secondary growth is well established with riparian vegetation of western red cedar *Thuja plicata*, western hemlock *Tsuga heterophylla*, alder *Alnus rubra*, and Douglas fir *Pseudotsuga menziesii* along the Adam River and Douglas fir, western hemlock, maple, alder, and some cottonwood along Big Silver Creek.

Both rivers are extremely oligotrophic, with alkalinity less than 20 mg/L, conductivity less than 45 μΩ/cm (<20 μΩ/cm in Big Silver Creek), total reactive phosphorus (TRP) concentrations less than 1 mg/L, and total phosphorus (TP) less than 3–5 mg/L. Nitrogen concentrations are also low, with dissolved nitrate + nitrite-nitrogen (NO_{2+3}-N) levels typically dropping to 35–45 mg/L in Big Silver, and less than 15 mg/L in the Adam River during summer. The rivers contain good fish habitat with a positive riffle-to-pool ratio ranging from 3:1 to 1:1 in assessed sections, many large bedrock-controlled pools and runs, and substrate of gravel and cobble. The abundance of favorable fish habitat suggests that mean size and abundance of trout are limited by very low biological productivity rather than physical habitat.

Experimental Design and Data Analysis

The lower portion of each river was divided into three contiguous reaches, 3–8 km in length. Proceeding downstream, the reaches were designated as control reach, treatment 1 (T1) reach, and treatment 2 (T2) reach (Figure 1). In each reach, chemical and biological sampling took place during the growing seasons (May to September) of 1992–1993 for the prefertilization assessment, and in 1994–1997 during fertilization of the downstream reach(es). To test for significant effects, we used a BACI experimental design (Stewart-Oaten et al. 1986), which relies on a temporal series of data taken before and after (or during) a perturbation, simultaneously at both a control and impact site. Inferential statistics (t-tests) were applied to the difference in values from the control and impact sites, during the prefertilization and fertilization periods. Data were log-transformed to improve normality and homogeneity of variances. The additivity and independence assumptions were tested using the Tukey test for nonadditivity (Tukey 1949) and the von Neumann ratio test (Stewart-Oaten et al. 1986), respectively. Assumptions were met and variation given as ± SE of untransformed data, unless otherwise noted.

Nutrient additions were conducted during 1994–1997, when liquid agricultural grade ammonium polyphosphate (10–34–0; % by weight $N-P_2O_5-K_2O$) was added to each river between June and September. In Big Silver Creek, fertilizer was added at the junction of the control and T1 reaches (Figure 1). This allowed examination of the nutrient addition on both the isolated resident (T1 reach) and the lacustrine-adfluvial (T2 reach) salmonid populations, while ensuring a long fertilized section to determine effective distance. In the Adam River, fertilizer was added at the junction of the T1 and T2 reaches. In both rivers, addition rates were adjusted to increase concentrations of instream dissolved inorganic phosphorus by 5 µg/L P, at the point of addition. The nitrogen component of the ammonium polyphosphate added 3.5 µg/L N to the rivers at target phosphorus loadings. In the Adam River, additional nitrogen was added using liquid agricultural grade urea-ammonium nitrate (28–0–0; % by weight $N-P_2O_5-K_2O$) added at target concentrations of 5 µg/L N. In 1994, fertilizer was gravity fed into the river through a hose and valve systems with rates adjusted manually on each site visit, usually 10–14 d apart, to flow conditions in the stream at that time determined using stage-discharge relationships. Drip rates usually declined between site visits as changes in ambient temperatures caused viscosity changes in the fertilizer, sedimentation (crystallized fertilizer) tended to clog the valves, and tank head pressure declined. As a result, nutrient loading rates

were usually below target concentrations. A similar system was in use on the Mesilinka River Fertilization Experiment, where nutrient loading rates were usually 40% below target concentrations (Larkin et al. 1999).

A battery-driven flow-proportional injection system was developed and installed during the 1995 field season, which automatically changed addition rates to match changes in river level (Ashley, this volume). The system generally functioned well, but the four 12-V deep-cycle batteries had to be changed every two weeks, and loading rates between site visits were not recorded. Nutrient loading rates recorded during site visits ranged between 4.8 and 8.5 µg/L P and 3.4–6.0 µg/L N to Big Silver Creek and averaged 4.6 µg/L P and 7.6 µg/L N to the Adam River. A preprogrammable injection system was developed for the 1997 field season, which was gravity fed, eliminating the need for the large batteries and contained other improvements to prevent clogging in the hoses (Larkin et al. 1997). It decreased fertilizer addition rates once per day to match the flow in the descending limb of a spring-summer hydrograph, which were found to follow exponential decay curves in snow and glacier-headed systems (Larkin et al. 1997). Loading rates measured on site visits averaged 5.1 µg/L P and 7.6 µg/L N to the Adam and 5.2 µg/L P and 3.6 µg/L N to the Big Silver. While loading rates were often below target concentrations, rates were almost always above the levels demonstrated, to saturate lotic diatoms at the cellular level and produce exponential growth at the community level (2 µg/L P; Bothwell 1988, 1989). Therefore, the four annual treatments are referred to as the 'fertilization period' with no distinction made between years.

Concurrent field testing of solid 'slow-release' fertilizer briquettes ($MgNH_4-PO_4-H_2O$; 7–40–0; % by weight $N-P_2O_5-K_2O$) for small stream restoration was conducted on the Adam River tributaries of the Rooney and Newcastle creeks and on the Big Silver tributary of Clear Creek (Figure 1), starting in 1994 (Ashley and Slaney 1997; Sterling et al. 2000).

Sampling Procedures

Water temperatures were recorded hourly in summer with Ryan RTM 200 temperature loggers installed in the T1 reach of the Adam River and the control reach of Big Silver Creek. Daily maximum, minimum, and average temperature readings were calculated based on hourly measurements. A stage–discharge relationship was developed for each river. Discharge was determined by dividing the streams into 1-m cross-sectional areas; the flow within each was determined, then summed for total flow. Water velocity was determined using a Marsh-McBirney (Frederick, Maryland) Model 201 electromagnetic velocity meter and stage by measuring the distance from a permanent mark on a logging bridge to the water surface. Mainline logging bridges at River km 14 and km 4 on the Adam River and Big Silver Creek, respectively, were used.

Water samples were collected at two week to monthly intervals and transported on ice within 24 h to Zenon Environmental Laboratories, Vancouver (1993–1995) or to the Pacific Environmental Science Center, North Vancouver, British Columbia (1996–1997). Samples were analyzed for TRP, TP, total dissolved phosphorus (TDP), NO_{2+3}-N, ammonia ($NH_4^+ + NH_3$-N), and total nitrogen (TN) using standard methods of analysis as described in APHA et al. (1992).

Periphyton biomass was estimated at 2–3 sites within each reach by extracting chlorophyll *a* on open-cell Styrofoam substrata. At each site, a pair of Styrofoam blocks (19 cm × 39 cm × 1.25 or 0.075 cm) were attached to concrete blocks and placed in the river, as described in Perrin et al. (1987). At approximately two-week intervals, duplicate core samples of Styrofoam substrata (5.7 cm^2) were extracted from each block. Cores were placed in an opaque desiccator until delivery to the laboratory, followed by extraction in 90% acetone and spectrophotometric determination of chlorophyll *a*. Styrofoam substrata were replaced after six weeks or three sampling periods. Thus, each replicated set of chlorophyll *a* determinations indicated periphyton biomass accumulation over fixed incubation periods referred to as early (late May to June) or middle (July to early August), with a late (August to September) incubation period in some years. The values from all sites within a reach were averaged to indicate periphyton biomass.

Benthic invertebrate populations were assessed using artificial substrate, by placing two groups of five gravel baskets in each reach. Each of the cylindrical baskets (22 cm in diameter, 13 cm in depth; 0.04 m^2 in area, and 0.005 m^3 in volume) was filled with 1–3 cm diameter clean gravel, placed in approximately 0.4 m of water with a velocity of 0.3–0.4 m/s, surrounded by cobbles, and left to colonize with invertebrates for six weeks. In the Adam River, baskets were placed for two six-week periods each summer, June–July and July–August, while in the Big Silver, they were placed for July–August. Baskets were removed using a Surber sampler (0.15-mm mesh net) with samples preserved in 80% alcohol. Invertebrates collected from each basket were stained with Rose Bengall, separated from detritus, and allowed to air dry for 2–3 min before the total wet-weight of invertebrates in each basket was determined. Four samples from each reach, in each year, were randomly chosen for taxonomic identification to at least the family level using McCafferty (1981), Stehr (1987), Pennak (1989), and Merritt and Cummins (1996). Periphyton plates and invertebrate baskets were moved as river levels changed, to maintain constant physical conditions, but invertebrate baskets remained undisturbed for a minimum of two weeks prior to removal.

Underwater fish counts were conducted annually in both rivers to estimate the abundance and size distribution of fish. Groups of 3–4 snorkelers swam the rivers when temperatures were 12–14°C (typically 1100–1600 hours) and visibility was 3–6 m (determined with Secchi disk between swimmers). Fish were counted using standardized methods described in Gardiner (1984) and Slaney and Martin (1987). Counts in each lane were expanded to cover the wetted width determined for each reach. The methodologies for swims remained standard, but swim dates and portions of each reach enumerated varied slightly, and only swims conducted under moderate summer flows (4–8 and 7–17 m^3/s in Adam River and Big Silver Creek, respectively) were included in the analysis. Counts were conducted in early September of 1993–1997 on Big Silver Creek and in June of 1993 and 1994, July of 1995, and September of 1996 and 1997 on the Adam River. In Big Silver Creek, fish less than 20 cm in length were excluded to avoid confusion with the stocked steelhead.

Sampling of juvenile fish for size-at-age data were conducted between 17 September and 5 October in 1992–1996 from each reach of the Adam River and on 26 August, 10 September, 23 September, 2 November, and 2 October of 1993–1997, respectively, from Big Silver Creek (except no T2 reach sampling). Samples were captured with a Smith Root Type VII backpack electrofisher from established sites along the shorelines and out to a depth of approximately 1 m. In the Adam River, rainbow and cutthroat trout were grouped (most were rainbow) to avoid confusion due to their similar appearance and possible hybridization. In Big Silver Creek, only wild (unclipped) rainbow were included. All fish captured were anesthetized, measured to the nearest millimeter, and weighed to the nearest 0.1 g on an electronic balance, with scale samples taken, processed, and read, as described in Ward and Slaney (1988). Captured fish were then revived with song and released.

Results

Physicochemical

Adam River flows typically declined from a May/June average of 12 m³/s, to summer lows averaging 4 m³/s in July to September (Figure 2). Lowest flows were recorded in 1996, and highest in 1997, with July to September averages of 1.5 and 6 m³/s, respectively. Spring flows in Big Silver Creek were relatively high, averaging 55 m³/s in May/June, declining to summer lows averaging 12 m³/s from August to September (Figure 2). At Big Silver Creek, lowest flows were recorded in 1994 and highest in 1996, with August to September averages of 10 and 16 m³/s, respectively. Wetted widths in the study reaches measured during the September snorkel surveys averaged 22 m and 33 m in the Adam River and Big Silver Creek, respectively.

Adam River water temperatures ranged from 7°C to 23°C during summer (June to September), averaged 14°C, and were usually more than 10°C from July to mid-September (Figure 2). Average summer temperatures ranged from 16°C in 1993 to 13°C in 1995. Big Silver Creek temperatures were slightly lower, ranging from 7°C to 17°C during summer, averaged 12°C, and were usually more than 8°C from July to September. Summer averages ranged from 13°C in 1994 to 11°C in 1996.

Both rivers showed no elevated nutrient concentrations downstream of the fertilizer inputs, indicating complete uptake by primary producers. Nitrogen and phosphorus co-limitation of attached algae was suggested in the fertilized reaches of both rivers during 1995–1997, when NO_{2+3}-N concentrations in Big Silver Creek decreased to 15 µg/L in July, and in the Adam River, concentrations usually decreased to detection limit levels of 5 µg/L during June, despite the addition of 3–8 µg/L N with the fertilizer (Figure 3).

Periphyton

Periphyton biomass in the Adam River was similar in all unfertilized sections, with maximum chlorophyll *a* concentrations averaging 12 mg/m² and ranging from 3 to 22 mg/m² (Figure 4A). Values peaked in July or early August, just before maximum temperatures and a month before low flows. Unfertilized chlorophyll *a* biomass was slightly lower in Big Silver Creek, averaging 8 mg/m² with a peak of 15 mg/m² in the T1 reach in 1993 (Figure 4B). Concentrations peaked between August and September, during low flows but after peak temperatures. There was no significant difference (*t*-test, $p > 0.1$) in maximum values between incubation periods in either river prior to fertilization. Values were within the range reported for streams at this latitude in the PNW (Stockner and Shortreed 1976, 1978; Perrin et al. 1987; Slaney and Ward 1993).

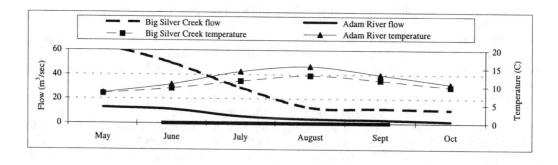

FIGURE 2. Average monthly flows and water temperatures of the Adam River and Big Silver Creek, 1993–1997. Dark bar on *x*-axis indicates approximate time of liquid fertilizer additions to the Adam River T2 reach and Big Silver Creek T1 and T2 reaches.

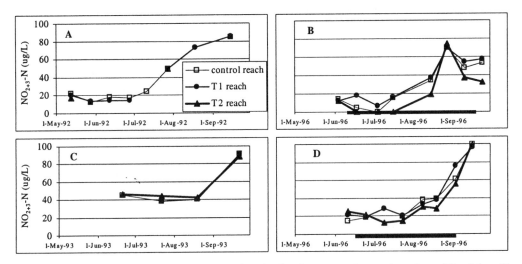

FIGURE 3. Nitrate + nitrite nitrogen concentrations in the three experimental reaches of the Adam River and Big Silver Creek during prefertilization and representative fertilization years. Adam River prefertilization in 1992 (A) and during fertilization in 1996 (B); Big Silver Creek prefertilization in 1993 (C) and during fertilization in 1996 (D). Dark bars on x-axes indicate fertilization periods.

Chlorophyll a concentrations increased 5-fold and 3-fold in the fertilized Adam River T2 reach during the early and late incubations periods, respectively, to an average of 32 mg/m² (Figure 4A). Values increased through the second year of fertilization (1995), then declined, with an intriguing increase, but of lower magnitude, in the unfertilized T1 reach. During September 1996, fertilizer addition rates to the Adam River were intentionally increased 3.5-fold, which resulted in a 10-fold increase in chlorophyll a concentrations to 70–100 mg/m² in the T2 reach (data not shown). In the fertilized reaches of Big Silver Creek, peak concentrations increased an average 2-fold, with significant increases in the T1 ($p = 0.009$) and T2 ($p = 0.036$) reaches during the August–September

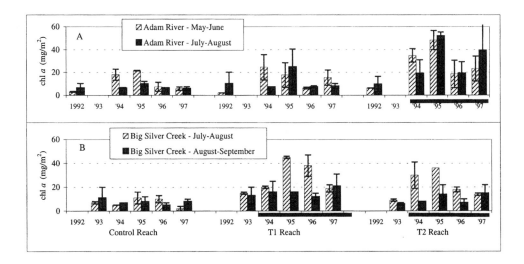

FIGURE 4. Peak chlorophyll a concentrations (±SD) in the three experimental reaches of the Adam River (A) and Big Silver Creek (B) during 2 incubation periods 1992–1997. Dark bars on x-axes indicate fertilization periods.

incubation periods (Figure 4B). Chlorophyll *a* values also increased through the second year of fertilization, then declined, and were significantly (*t*-test, p < 0.05) higher in the July–August incubation period compared with the August–September period, in Big Silver Creek.

Benthic Invertebrates

Benthos populations in unfertilized sections of each river were similar and dominated by chironomid and tipulid dipterans, hepatgeniid and baetid ephemeropterans, chloroperlid plecopterans, and hydropsychid tricopterans. Overall, dipterans were the most numerous in Big Silver Creek and ephemeropterans in the Adam River. Control reach populations were relatively consistent in each river during the study, with total average biomass values of 155 (±27), 228 (±26), and 151 (±17) mg/basket in Big Silver Creek (August), Adam River (July), and Adam River (August) incubation periods, respectively (Figure 5), and density values averaging 180 (±14), 150 (±31), and 151 (±33) individuals/basket during the same time periods (Figure 6). Prefertilization (1993) populations in the lower reaches of the Adam River were similar, but density increased downstream in Big Silver Creek to 429/basket in the T2 reach, resulting from the presence of more dipterans (Figure 6A).

After nutrient additions began, a few large changes were evident in each river, with maximum yearly increases in density and biomass of 5 to 10-fold, but average increases closer to 2-fold. In Big Silver Creek, the mean biomass of benthic invertebrates increased 2-fold and 5.7-fold in the fertilized T1 and T2 reaches, respectively. There was

no change in density in the T1 reach (Figure 6A), but on average, there was a 1.8-fold increase in density in the T2 reach associated with significant increases in family Chironomidae abundance (p = 0.005). There were also smaller increases in the Baetidae, Simuliidae, and Capniidae families. The largest responses were recorded during the first year of fertilization (Figure 6A).

In the Adam River, mean benthos density in the fertilized T2 reach increased 2.4-fold compared with prefertilization values during the July colonization period, with a significant increase in family Chironomidae density (p = 0.047) resulting in significant increases in both dipteran (p = 0.045) and total (p = 0.005) densities. There was also a smaller but significant increase in the family Baetidiae (p = 0.006). The largest responses were recorded in the second or third years of fertilization (Figure 6B). In the August colonization period, density and biomass increased, on average, 1.4-fold and 2.5-fold, respectively, in the fertilized reach resulting from an increase in chironomids (Figure 6C), but the results were not statistically significant (p = 0.092).

Fish Populations

Young-of-the-year (age-0) rainbow trout in the control reaches of both rivers were similar in size and did not change during the study. Adam River annual size averages ranged from 1.7 g to 2.5 g and 55–60 mm in 1992–1997, while in Big Silver Creek, they ranged from 2.0 g to 2.7 g and 53–61 mm (Table 1). Prefertilization sizes of age-0 fish in the lower reaches were similar. In the Adam River fertilized T2 reach, the age-0 fish increased to an average 4.1 g and 69 mm during

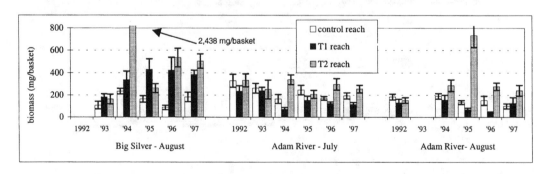

FIGURE 5. Biomass (wet-weight) of benthic invertebrates (±SE) in the three experimental reaches of the Adam River and Big Silver Creek, collected during August in Big Silver Creek and July and August from the Adam River, 1992–1997. Note: Adam T2 reach and Big Silver T1 and T2 reaches fertilized summers of 1994–1997.

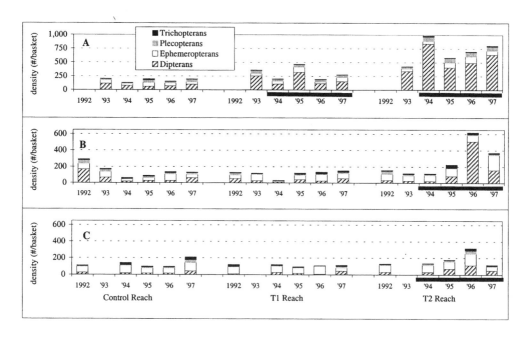

FIGURE 6. Benthic invertebrate density in the three experimental reaches of Big Silver Creek in August (A), Adam River in July (B) and August (C), 1992–1997 colonization periods. Dark bars on x-axes indicate fertilization periods.

TABLE 1. The average weight (g) and length (mm) of age-0 rainbow trout (± SD) in the Adam River and Big Silver Creek, 1992–1997. Values averaged from all sites within a reach. Adam River T2 reach and Big Silver T1 and T2 reaches fertilized summers 1994–1997. * denotes significant difference from prefertilization values by BACI analysis, $p < 0.05$.

reach	year	Adam River			year	Big Silver Creek		
		weight	length	ratio		weight	length	ratio
control	1992 prefert	1.7 ±0.5	55 ±1	0.031	1992 prefert	–	–	
	1993 prefert	2.0 ±1.0	57 ±8	0.035	1993 prefert	2.0 ±0.9	58 ±8	0.034
	1994 unfert	2.5 ±0.6	60 ±5	0.042	1994 unfert	2.4 ±1.3	59 ±9	0.041
	1995 unfert	2.1 ±0.5	57 ±5	0.037	1995 unfert	2.7 ±1.0	61 ±8	0.044
	1996 unfert	2.3 ±0.8	57 ±7	0.040	1996 unfert	2.4 ±0.6	56 ±6	0.043
	1997 unfert	–	–		1997 unfert	2.0 ±0.0	53 ±0	0.038
	mean unfert	**2**	**58**	**0.034**	**mean unfert**	**2.4**	**57**	**0.042**
T1	1992 prefert	1.7 ±0.5	55 ±5	0.031	1992 prefert	–	–	
	1993 prefert	2.4 ±0.8	59 ±5	0.041	1993 prefert	1.8 ±0.3	52 ±4	0.035
	1994 unfert	2.8 ±0.9	61 ±6	0.046	1994 fert	3.3 ±1.4	64 ±12	0.052
	1995 unfert	2.9 ±0.9	63 ±7	0.046	1995 fert	3.9 ±1.4	68 ±8	0.057
	1996 unfert	3.3 ±1.7	64 ±5	0.051	1996 fert	2.5 ±1.0	56 ±8	0.045
	1997 unfert	–	–		1999 fert	2.7 ±0.0	58 ±0	0.047
	mean unfert	**3.0**	**63**	**0.048**	**mean fert**	**3.1**	**62***	**0.050**
T2	1992 prefert	–	–		1992 prefert	–	–	
	1993 prefert	3.0 ±0.9	65 ±6	0.046	1993 prefert	–	–	
	1994 fert	4.7 ±1.5	73 ±7	0.064	1994 fert	–	–	
	1995 fert	3.3 ±1.3	66 ±7	0.050	1995 fert	–	–	
	1996 fert	4.2 ±1.4	69 ±7	0.061	1996 fert	2.3 ±0.7	57 ±5	0.040
	1997 fert	–	–		1997 fert	–	–	
	mean fert	**4.1**	**69**	**0.059**	**mean fert**	–	–	

fertilization, a 1.4 fold increase in weight. Big Silver Creek T1 reach age-0 fish increased to an average 3.1 g and 62 mm, a 1.7-fold increase in weight. The largest size increases were within the first two years of fertilization (Table 1), with maximum average sizes of 4.7 g and 73 mm in the Adam T2 reach in 1994 and 3.9 g and 68 mm in the Big Silver T1 reach in 1995. However, the only significant increase was length in the Big Silver T1 reach ($p = 0.045$). There was also an increase in weight per unit length in the fertilized reaches, particularly in the first year of fertilization, indicating an increase in condition factor (Table 1).

In the unfertilized Adam River T1 reach, the size of the age-0 fish increased consistently from an average 1.7 g and 55 mm in 1992 to 3.3 g and 64 mm in 1996 (Table 1). Rooney Creek, which joins the Adam River in the vicinity of the site where the samples were collected, was fertilized annually since 1993 as part of the experimental testing of slow release fertilizer previously mentioned, as was Newcastle Creek just downstream (Figure 1). Direct nutrient loading to the Adam River would have been very low, as flow contributions from these tributaries were small, approximately 3% and 10% of Adam River flow, respectively, and slow release fertilizer loading rates were below 3 μg/L P (Mouldey Ewing and Ashley 1998). However, there were increases in periphyton and benthos biomass in the tributaries, and movement of fish between systems was possible.

Density of adult rainbow trout (>20 cm length) in Big Silver Creek was initially similar throughout the river, averaging 10/ha (±3) in the control reach, with prefertilization densities of 12 and 10/ha in the T1 and T2 reaches, respectively (Figure 7A). Following the first summer of fertilization, density in the T1 reach increased to 37/ha and averaged 38/ha (±11) for a 3-fold increase during fertilization. Rainbow from 20 cm to 30 cm in length increased 2.8-fold from 12 to 33/ha (±10), and those 30–40 cm increased 20-fold from 0.2 to 4/ha (±1.5). The density of both size-classes reached a maximum in 1997, the fourth year of fertilization and the final year of evaluation. Below the waterfalls barrier, rainbow trout density in the T2 reach showed no perceptible change, although these fish are migratory and larger fish may have migrated to the lake or ocean, but mountain whitefish increased from 53/ha in 1993 to an average of 129/ha (±29) during fertilization, including a high of 204/ha in 1995 (Figure 7B). Whitefish 10–20 cm in length showed the largest increase, from 8/ha in 1993 to an average 48/ha (±13) during fertilization.

Fish populations in the Adam River exhibited a slower response compared with Big Silver Creek, but initial densities were much lower. Numbers of fish in the control reach were consistent through the study period (Figure 8): rainbow trout (>10 cm in length) averaged 10/ha (±1.5); brown trout 0.5/ha (±0.2); and rainbow, more than 20 cm in length, just 1.5/ha (±0.4). The density of both species increased in the unfertilized T1: the rain-

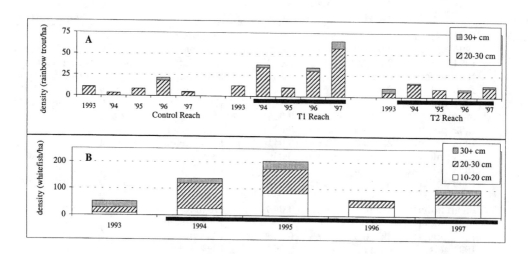

Figure 7. Density of different size classes of rainbow trout in the three experimental reaches of Big Silver Creek (A), and mountain whitefish in the T2 reach (B), from snorkel surveys during early September 1993–1997. Dark bars on x-axes indicate fertilization periods.

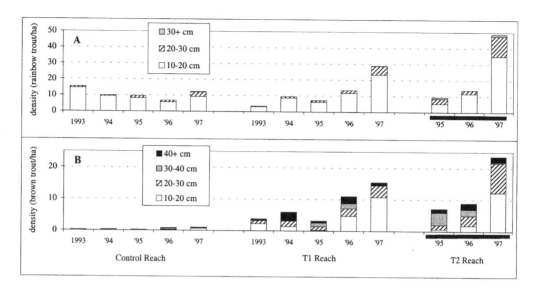

FIGURE 8. Density of different size classes of rainbow trout (A), and brown trout (B) in the three experimental reaches of the Adam River, from snorkel surveys during June 1993 and 1994, July 1995, and September 1996 and 1997. Dark bars on x-axes indicate fertilization periods.

bow from 3.5/ha in 1993 to a high of 29/ha in 1997 and brown trout from 3.8 to 15/ha, at the same time (Figure 8). In the fertilized T2 reach, no data were available for 1993–1995, but there were 3-fold and 5-fold increases in rainbow and brown trout density, respectively, between 1995 and 1997, when their densities peaked at 49/ha and 24/ha, respectively (Figure 8).

Discussion

The addition of phosphorus and nitrogen-based fertilizer stimulated growth (increased biomass) at all trophic levels analyzed, indicating that this restoration method is applicable to larger nutrient-deficient streams. We could not investigate specific rates or food chain links, but increases in autotrophic periphyton growth following nutrient addition and subsequent translocation of carbon and nutrients through the food chain to fish has been demonstrated on smaller systems (Peterson et al. 1985; Perrin et al. 1987; Peterson et al. 1993) that produced standing crop/biomass/size responses similar to our study.

Peak periphyton values attained in the Adam River and Big Silver Creek were 50% those reported for the Kuparuk, Nechako, Keogh, and Salmon rivers (Perrin et al. 1987; Slaney and Ward 1993; Peterson et al. 1993; Slaney et al. 1994). How-

ever, phosphorus-loading rates in the previous studies were at least double our target concentration of 5 µg P/L, which often was not attained. Additionally, when fertilizer addition rates to the Adam River were intentionally increased 3.5-fold (in September 1996), periphyton values increased almost 10-fold to values that were comparable with the other rivers.

The average 2-fold increase in benthos population over four years in both the Adam River and Big Silver Creek, including peak annual increases of 4-fold, are similar to the 3 to 5-fold increases on the Salmon and Keogh rivers (Slaney and Ward 1993). Increases on all rivers were limited to large increases in the same few families: collectors/gatherer dipterans (family Chironomidae) and ephemeropterans (Family Baetidae) and some predatory stoneflies (family Perlodidae). Additionally, the 1.5-fold increase in weight of age-0 rainbow was similar to results found in the Keogh (Johnston et al. 1990) and Salmon rivers (Slaney and Ward 1993), as well as to increases in age-0 Arctic grayling in the Kuparuk River (Peterson et al. 1993).

The delayed response of benthos and fish populations in the Adam River was likely related to their initial depressed populations. The prefertilized benthic density of 100 individuals per basket was low compared with values of 200 per basket in Big Silver Creek and 250 per basket in the Salmon River (Slaney and Ward 1993). Adult rainbow (>20 cm length) initially averaged 10/ha in Big Silver Creek, but only 1.5/ha on the Adam River. Additionally, low initial (1994) fertilizer loading rates and nitrogen limitation of the periphyton likely influenced response patterns. The increase in fish density and the size of age-0 fish in the unfertilized Adam River T1 reach is attributable to several factors. Rooney and New-castle creeks, which flow into the lower half of the T1 reach (Figure 1), were fertilized annually in 1993–1997. Therefore, the lower part of this reach was essentially fertilized at a very low level. The fertilized tributaries would provide good rearing habitat for the juveniles, some of which probably move into the main stem. The lower portion of this reach also contains good fish habitat, so there could easily be movement of adult fish between the fertilized and unfertilized reaches of the main stem as well.

The differential response in the two fertilized Big Silver reaches are likely a result of life history differences in fish stocks or strains because fish of the lower reach are largely migratory, making use of the large Harrison Lake or ocean (salmon and steelhead) for rearing from juveniles or smolt stages to adult.

The effective distance of the nutrient enrichment was estimated at 8–11 km in our study, based on a doubling of periphyton biomass, which was limited by the downstream extent of assessment. In comparison, the effective enrichment distance in the Salmon River and larger Mesilinka River was 15 km and at least 20 km, respectively, and the Mesilinka River was also N and P co-limited (Slaney and Ward 1993; Larkin et al. 1999). An earlier study at the larger Nechako River suggested 50 km, but nutrients were delivered in 5-min pulses, and the river was also N and P co-limited (Slaney et al. 1994).

Many of the periphyton and insect responses were not statistically significant using the BACI method because of only one or two years of prefertilization data and fertilization responses which were cumulative, delayed, and often highly variable. However, the increasing trend over time, particularly of fish abundance when supported by responses in both periphyton and insect communities in both rivers, strongly suggests that nutrient additions stimulated overall productivity of the rivers. The maximum fish densities in each river were attained in the final year of assessments, suggesting populations had not reached equilibrium. Longer-term investigations

are needed, especially in rivers with low populations and/or water temperatures. Ideally, several years of prefertilization assessments would be followed by a multiyear transition period after fertilization begins, followed by several years of fertilization assessment. Additional nitrogen should also be added to ensure that nitrogen does not become limiting.

Nutrient enrichment of oligotrophic rivers would be a cost-effective and ecologically sound method of increasing fish populations, provided habitat is intact, compared with the current practice of stocking hatchery-reared fish. Annual fertilizer costs for the larger of the two rivers, Big Silver Creek, were modest, less than $4,000CDN (9.5 metric tons of fertilizer at $400/ton) for 10 km of river. More importantly, the genetic or behavioral viability of the wild fish are not compromised, as there are no interactions between wild and stocked fish, thus preserving biodiversity.

Acknowledgments

This project was funded by the Provincial Fisheries Branch (1992) and by the Habitat Conservation Trust Fund (HCTF). Encouragement and good advice was offered by A. Martin, S. Rimmer, C. Wightman, and Trout Unlimited Canada. Field work was conducted by S. Biancolin, S. Carswell, P. Davidson, T. Godin, Loreta Hansen, S. Jennings, W. Koning, S. Moldey, M. Neilsen, E. Standen, M. Stanford, B. Toth, K. Tsumura, C. Warren, and D. Zaldokas. A noble spirit embiggins the smallest man. Staff and volunteers of the Fraser Valley Trout sorted the benthos samples. Thanks to Jordan Rosenfeld, Megan McCusker, and two anonymous reviewers who graciously provided very helpful comments on drafts of this paper.

References

APHA (American Public Health Association), American Water Works Association, and Water Environment Federation. 1992. Standard methods for the examination of water and waste water. 18th edition. APHA, Washington, D.C.

Ashley, K. I., and P. A. Slaney. 1997. Accelerating recovery of stream, river and pond productivity by low-level nutrient replacement. Chapter 13 *in* P. A. Slaney and D. Zaldokas, editors. Fish habitat rehabilitation procedures. British Columbia Ministry of Environment, Lands and Parks and Ministry of Forests, Watershed Restoration Program. Watershed Restoration Technical Circular No. 9. Vancouver.

Bothwell, M. L. 1988. Growth rate responses of lotic periphyton diatoms to experimental phosphorus enrichment: the influence of temperature and light. Canadian Journal of Fisheries and Aquatic Sciences 45:261–270.

Bothwell, M. L. 1989. Phosphorus-limited growth dynamics of lotic periphyton diatom communities: areal biomass and cellular growth rate responses. Canadian Journal of Fisheries and Aquatic Sciences 46:1293–1301.

Cannings, R., and S. Cannings. 1996. British Columbia–a natural history. Greystone, Vancouver.

Deegan, L. A., and B. J. Peterson. 1992. Whole-river fertilization stimulates fish production in an Arctic tundra river. Canadian Journal of Fisheries and Aquatic Sciences 49:1890–1901.

Egglishaw, H. J. 1968. The quantitative relationship between bottom fauna and plant detritus in streams of different calcium concentrations. Journal of Applied Ecology 5:731–740.

Egglishaw, H. J., and P. E. Shackley. 1985. Factors governing the production of juvenile Atlantic salmon in a Scottish stream. Journal of Fish Biology 27(Supplement A):27–33.

Gardiner, W. R. 1984. Estimating populations of salmonids in deep water in streams. Journal of Fish Biology 24:41–49.

Grant, J. W. A., S. O. Steingrimsson, E. R. Keely, and R. A. Conjak. 1998. Implications of territory size for the measurement and prediction of salmonid abundance in streams. Canadian Journal of Fisheries and Aquatic Sciences 55(Supplement 1):181–190.

Gross, M. R., R. M. Coleman, and R. M. McDowall. 1988. Aquatic productivity and the evolution of diadromous fish migration. Science 239:1291–1293.

Holtby, L. B., and G. F. Hartman. 1982. The population dynamics of coho salmon (*Oncorhynchus kisutch*) in a west coast rain forest stream subjected to logging. Pages 308–347 in G. F. Hartman, editor. Proceedings of the Carnation Creek workshop, a ten year review. Pacific Biological Station, Nanaimo, British Columbia.

Huntsman, A. G. 1948. Fertility and fertilization of streams. Journal of Fisheries Research Board of Canada 7:248–253.

Johnston, N. T., C. J. Perrin, P. A. Slaney, and B. R. Ward. 1990. Increased juvenile growth by whole-river fertilization. Canadian Journal of Fisheries and Aquatic Sciences 47:862–872.

Kline, T. C. Jr., and five coauthors. 1993. Recycling of elements transported upstream by runs of Pacific salmon: II. 15N and 13C evidence in the Kvichak River watershed, Bristol Bay, southwestern Alaska. Canadian Journal of Fisheries and Aquatic Sciences 50:2350–2365.

Larkin, G. A., and five coauthors. 1997. Recent advances in liquid fertilizer injection technology for stream and river restoration. Watershed Restoration Program, Government of British Columbia. Watershed Restoration Project Report No. 5.

Larkin, G. A., and five coauthors. 1999. Development of a premier northern river fishery: Mesilinka River, the fourth year of fertilization (1997). Government of British Columbia, Fisheries Project Report No. RD70.

Mason, J. C. 1976. Response of underyearling coho salmon to supplemental feeding in a natural stream. Journal of Wildlife Management 40(4):775–788.

McCafferty, W. P. 1981. Aquatic entomology. Science Books International, Boston, Massachusetts.

Minshall, G. W. 1978. Autotrophy in stream ecosystems. Bioscience 28:767–771.

Milbrink, G., and S. Holmgren. 1981. Addition of artificial fertilizers as a means of reducing the negative effects of "oligotrophication" in lakes after impoundment. Swedish Board of Fisheries, Institute of Freshwater Research, Drottningholm Report No. 59:121–127.

Merritt, R. W., and K. W. Cummins. 1996. Aquatic insects of North America. Kendall/Hunt Publishing Company, Dubuque, Iowa.

Mouldey Ewing, SE, and K. I. Ashley. 1998. Development and testing of slow release fertilizer for restoring salmonid habitat: 1996 progress report. Watershed Restoration Program, British Columbia Ministry of Environment, Lands and Parks and Ministry of Forests. Watershed Restoration Project Report No. 9. Victoria.

Mundie, J. H., K. S. Simpson, and C. J. Perrin. 1991. Responses of stream periphyton and benthic insects to increases in dissolved inorganic phosphorus in a mesocosm. Canadian Journal of Fisheries and Aquatic Sciences 48:2061–2072.

Northcote, T. G., and P. A. Larkin. 1966. Western Canada. Pages 451–485 in D. G. Frey, editor. Limnology in North America. University of Wisconsin Press, Madison.

Parkinson, E. A., and P. A. Slaney. 1975. A review of enhancement techniques applicable to anadromous gamefishes. Province of British Columbia, Fisheries Management Report No. 66.

Pennak, R. W. 1989. Fresh-water invertebrates of the United States. John Wiley and Sons, Inc., New York.

Peterson, B. J., and nine coauthors. 1985. Transformation of a tundra stream from heterotrophy to autotrophy by addition of phosphorus. Science 229:1383–1386.

Peterson, B. J., and sixteen coauthors. 1993. Biological Response of a tundra river to fertilization. Ecology 74:653–672.

Perrin, C. J., M. L. Bothwell, and P. A. Slaney. 1987. Experimental enrichment of a coastal stream in British Columbia: effects of organic and inorganic additions on autotrophic periphyton production. Canadian Journal of Fisheries and Aquatic Sciences 44:1247–1256.

Slaney, P. A., and A. D. Martin. 1987. Accuracy of underwater census of trout populations in a large stream in British Columbia. North American Journal of Fisheries Management 7:117–122.

Slaney, P. A., and T. G. Northcote. 1974. Effects of prey abundance on density and territorial behaviour of young rainbow trout in laboratory stream channels. Journal of the Fisheries Research Board of Canada 31:1201–1209.

Slaney, P. A., C. J. Perrin, and B. R. Ward. 1986. Nutrient concentration as a limitation to steelhead smolt production in the Keogh River. Proceedings of the annual conference of Western Association Fish and Wildlife Agency 66:146–147.

Slaney, P. A., W. O. Rublee, C. J. Perrin, and H. Goldberg. 1994. Debris structure placements and whole-river fertilization for salmonids in a large regulated stream in British Columbia. Bulletin of Marine Sciences 55:1160–1180.

Slaney, P. A., and B. R. Ward. 1993. Experimental fertilization of nutrient deficient streams in British Columbia. Pages 128–141 in G. Shooner and S. Asselin, editors. Le développement du saumon Atlantique au Québec: connaître les règles du jeu pour réussir. Colloque international de la Fédération quebécoise pour le saumon Atlantique. Québec, décembre 1992. Collection *Salmo salar* No. 1.

Stehr, F. W. 1987. Immature insects. Kendall/Hunt Publishing Company, Dubuque, Iowa.

Sterling, M. S., K. I. Ashley, and A. B. Bautista. 2000. Slow release fertilizer for rehabilitating oligotrophic streams: a physical characterization. Water Quality Research Journal of Canada 35:73–94.

Stewart-Oaten, A., W. W. Murdoch, and K. R. Parker. 1986. Environmental impact assessment: "pseudoreplication" in time? Ecology 67:929–940.

Stockner, J. G. 1981. Whole-lake fertilization for the enhancement of sockeye salmon (*Oncorhychus nerka*) in British Columbia, Canada. Verhandlungen Internationale Veriningung fur Theoretische und Angewandte Limnologie 21: 293–299.

Stockner, J. G. 1987. Lake fertilization: The enrichment cycle and lake sockeye salmon (*Oncorhynchus nerka*) production. Pages 198–215 in H. D. Smith, L. Margolis and C. C. Wood, editors. Sockeye salmon (*Oncorhynchus nerka*) population biology and future management. Canadian Special Publications Fisheries and Aquatic Sciences 96.

Stockner, J. G., and K. R. S. Shortreed. 1976. Autotrophic production in Carnation Creek, a coastal rainforest stream on Vancouver Island, British Columbia. Journal of the Fisheries Research Board of Canada 33:1553–1563.

Stockner, J. G., and K. R. S. Shortreed. 1978. Enhancement of autotrophic production by nutrient addition in a coastal rainforest stream on Vancouver Island. Journal of the Fisheries Research Board of Canada 35:28–34.

Tukey, J. W. 1949. One degree of freedom for nonadditivity. Biometrics 5:232–242.

Ward, B. R., and P. A. Slaney. 1979. Evaluation of instream enhancement structures for the production of juvenile steelhead trout and coho salmon in the Keogh River: progress 1977 and 1978. Province of British Columbia, Fisheries Technical Circular No. 45. Victoria.

Ward, B. R., and P. A. Slaney. 1981. Further evaluations of structures for the improvement of salmonid rearing habitat in coastal streams of British Columbia. Pages 99–108 in T. J. Hassler, editor. Proceedings: propagation, enhancement and rehabilitation of anadromous salmonid populations and habitat symposium. American Fisheries Society, Western Division, Humbolt Chapter, Arcata, California.

Ward, B. R., and P. A. Slaney. 1988. Life history and smolt-to-adult survival of Keogh River steelhead trout (*Salmo gairdneri*) and the relationship to smolt size. Canadian Journal of Fisheries and Aquatic Sciences 45:1110–1122.

Ward, B. R., P. A. Slaney, A. R. Facchin, and R. W. Land. 1989. Size-based survival in steelhead trout: back-calculated lengths from adults' scales compared to migrating smolts at the Keogh River, B.C. Canadian Journal of Fisheries and Aquatic Sciences 46:1853–1858.

Wilson, G. A., K. I. Ashley, S. Mouldey Ewing, P. Slaney, and R. W. Land. 1999a. Development of a resident trout fishery on the Adam River through increased habitat productivity: final report of the 1993–97 project. British Columbia Ministry of Fisheries Project Report No. RD68.

Wilson, G. A., K. I. Ashley, S. Mouldey Ewing, P. Slaney, and R. W. Land. 1999b. Development of a premier river fishery: the Big Silver Creek fertilization experiment, 1993–97: final project report. British Columbia Ministry of Fisheries, Project Report No. RD69.

American Fisheries Society Symposium 34:163–175, 2003

The Relationship between Nutrient Concentration and Stream Insect Abundance

Darcie L. Quamme

Integrated Ecological Research, 924 Innes Street, Nelson, B.C. V1L 5T2, Canada

Patrick A. Slaney

Ministry of Water, Land and Air Protection, Watershed Restoration Program
2204 Main Mall, University of British Columbia, Vancouver, B.C. V6T 1Z4, Canada

Abstract.—The relationship between added soluble nutrient concentration and the abundance and taxonomic composition of stream insects was determined in an experiment using streamside troughs. Target phosphorus (P) concentrations were 0, 0.5, 2.5, 5, 10, and 50 µg/L at a N:P ratio of 1:1 (wt.:wt.). All treatments were replicated three times except 50 µg/L, which was unreplicated. Peak algal biomass (PB) increased with nutrient concentration linearly to 7.4 mg/m² at 2.5 mg P/L and reached an asymptote at 9.2 mg/m² (2.7× the controls) at 10 µg P/L. Adult baetid mayflies increased 2- and 4-fold when caught in drift nets and emergent insect traps, respectively, at a phosphorus concentration of 10 µg/L compared with controls. Numbers of benthic baetids, nemourid, and perlodid stoneflies and hydroptilid and polycentripodid trichopterans increased 1.6, 2.3, 2.9, 2.8, and 1.2-fold, respectively, at 10 µg P/L compared with controls. Adult and nymphal baetids and benthic nemourids, perlodids, and hydroptilids initially increased rapidly at nutrient concentrations of 0–2.5 µg P/L and reached asymptotes at concentrations of 2.5–10 µg P/L. Exclusion of insects from a single unfertilized trough suggested that grazing limited peak biomass of periphyton to low levels. Increased abundances of aquatic insects resulted from greater periphyton availability at relatively low dissolved-nutrient additions ranging from 0.5 to 10 µg P/L.

Introduction

Low-level nutrient addition to oligotrophic streams is a technique that has been investigated by fisheries researchers as a means to restore salmonid populations in nutrient-deficient coastal streams (Johnston et al. 1990; Slaney and Ward 1993), particularly where availability of salmon carcasses is reduced (Ashley and Slaney 1997). Nitrogen and phosphorus augmentation can increase areal biomass of benthic algae (Bothwell 1989) and microbial growth in streams (Peterson et al. 1993; Hullar and Vestal 1988), providing high quality food for many aquatic insect grazers (Lamberti and Moore 1984). The increased availability of periphyton food may in turn determine the abundance or biomass of insect algal grazers in streams (Johnston et al. 1990; Mundie et al. 1991; Peterson et al. 1993).

Studies have shown that the biomass of stream-rearing insects (Johnston et al. 1990; Mundie et al. 1991) and insectivorous fish (Slaney and Ward 1993; Peterson et al. 1993; Peterson et al. 2001) may be increased by additions of inorganic phosphorus and nitrogen through increases in autotrophic production.

Whole river fertilization has been shown to increase sizes of fry and parr and smolt-at-age (Johnston et al. 1990; Slaney and Ward 1993; Ashley and Slaney 1997) as a result of improved freshwater survival of juvenile salmonids. Increased adult returns from the ocean have been reported for coho salmon *Oncorhynchus kisutch* (Hager and Noble 1976) and steelhead trout *O.*

mykiss (Ward and Slaney 1988) with greater smolt size.

Despite the growing body of knowledge on stream fertilization, information concerning insect response to nutrient addition in terms of abundance, composition, and timing of response is limited (Mundie et al. 1991). The relationship between ambient nutrient concentration in streams and insect abundance, biomass, and composition has never been quantified experimentally over a broad range of nutrient concentrations in a regression-type analysis.

The objectives of this study were to quantify the relationships between (1) nutrient concentration and the areal biomass of periphytic algae, and (2) nutrient concentration and the abundance and composition of stream insects using stream mesocosms.

The establishment of the above relationships is important in order to guide studies of low-level stream fertilization that aim to restore salmonid populations in British Columbia (Ashley and Slaney 1997). The present study will also improve our understanding of trophic interactions and pathways in oligotrophic streams.

Methods

Study Site

The experiment was carried out on the Keogh River (127°25′W by 50°35′N), a third-order coastal stream on northeastern Vancouver Island, near the town of Port Hardy in southwestern British Columbia. The experimental mesocosms were located 31 km upstream of the river mouth, approximately 1 km downstream from Keogh Lake outlet (see Ward et al., this volume, for map of the watershed). Ambient nutrient concentrations of the Keogh River in spring to summer are very low. Johnston et al. (1990) reported that soluble reactive phosphorus (SRP) levels were less than 1 μg/L; total dissolved phosphorus, 5 μg/L; nitrate nitrogen, less than 15 μg/L; and total ammonia, less than 5 μg/L. At this experimental site, the wetted width ranged from 6.0 m to 7.0 m, and the flows ranged from 0.14 to 0.39 m^3/s over the course of the experiment (10 May–8 July 1991). Water temperatures at the study site ranged from 12.5–21°C over the 9-week duration of the experiment. Detailed descriptions of the Keogh River are given in Ward and Slaney (1988), Perrin et al. (1987), and Johnston et al. (1990).

Description of Mesocosms

Seventeen flow-through Plexiglas troughs (each 1.52 m × 0.20 m × 0.20 m) were assembled at the streamside. Water and drift from the Keogh River were delivered to the mesocosms by gravity through a 300 m long (15.2 cm inside diameter) plastic pipeline fitted to a head tank. Water flow from the head tank to each of the troughs was adjusted to approximately 1 L/s by the use of rotating polyvinyl chloride (PVC) standpipes and flexible nylon tubing, similar to Mundie et al. (1991). High rates of hydraulic flushing through the troughs (nine-second residence time) ensured that trough water was similar in quality to river water and that the concentration of added nutrients remained constant over the trough length.

The trough environment was designed to simulate the characteristics of a stream riffle, including a fast current, coarse substrates, some sand content, and a low accumulation of organic matter. Each trough was filled with gravel to a depth of 7 cm over an area of 0.30 m^2. The size of the trough gravels consisted of 17% (by mass) coarse sand and gravel passed through a sieve size of 7.9 mm, 43% that ranged from 7.9 to 19.1 mm, and 40% of 19.1–50.8 mm. Four baskets (each 10 cm × 10 cm × 7 cm) filled with gravel were placed at the downstream end of the gravel for purposes of subsampling benthic insects. Water in the troughs covered the gravel to a depth of 3.0 cm, and surface velocities of the troughs averaged 21.3 cm/s. The bottom of the trough, downstream of the gravel, was fitted with a sheet (320 cm^2) of open cell Styrofoam DB, which was used to colonize and monitor algal biomass.

A funnel trap for emerging adult insects covered the length and completely sealed the top of each trough, similar to Mundie et al. (1991). Nitex drift nets (100-mm mesh) were used to monitor insect immigration to and emigration from the troughs by filtering the inflowing or outflowing stream water. The inflow nets prevented insect immigration and colonization of the troughs one day a week during the experimental period. Experiments were simplified by excluding insectivorous fish from the mesocosm.

Nutrient Treatments

Previous work has shown that phosphorus is the primary limiting nutrient to productivity at this reach of the Keogh River (Perrin et al. 1987). Six target levels of total phosphorus (0, 0.5, 2.5, 5, 10, and 50 µg/L) were selected to enhance growth rates of cells within the algal mat. Each treatment was randomly assigned and replicated three times except for the 50 µg/L treatment, which was unreplicated.

Nitrogen was added to troughs at a constant ratio of 2:1 N:P (atomic weight) or 1:1 (wt:wt). Levels of dissolved inorganic nitrogen (<20 µg N/L) at the Keogh River are generally considered sufficient to permit maximum algae cellular growth rates (Perrin et al. 1987).

The source of nutrients (supplied by Coast-Agri, Abbotsford, British Columbia) used in the present study was a liquid agricultural fertilizer blend of 32–0–0 (50% urea, 25% ammonium, and 25% nitrate, by mass) and 10–34–0 (10% ammonium and 34% total phosphorus as P_2O_5). Total phosphorus was 100% water soluble and available as 25–35% orthophosphate and 65–75% 4–12 chain polyphosphates. The ammonium polyphosphate fertilizer (10–34–0) also contained micronutrients. These included boron (0.01% B, by mass), calcium (0.07% CaO), copper (0.0005% CuO), iron (0.56% Fe_2O_3), magnesium (0.5% MgO), manganese (0.015 MgO), potassium (0.12% K_2O), sulfate (1.8% SO_4), and zinc (0.10% ZnO). This fertilizer blend was used because it is easily applied in whole-stream applications (Ashley and Slaney 1997).

Beginning 27 April 1991, water from the stream was run through the troughs for 21 d to allow colonization by stream macroinvertebrates. Nutrient additions began 18 May 1991 and ran until 8 July 1991. Fertilizer was dripped into the head of the artificial stream troughs via microbore tubing using a Technicon autoanalyzer pump powered by two 12-V batteries. A Plexiglas baffle at the head of each trough created water turbulence and ensured the complete mixing of stream water and added nutrient solution.

Samples for water chemistry were taken at weekly intervals from all trough outlets in order to check computed nutrient additions. Because of limited sensitivity of analytical methods for phosphorus, only higher levels of phosphorus additions (2–50 mg/L) could be accurately verified. Water samples were collected and analyzed within 24-h analyses of $NO_3 + NO_2$-N, NO_2-N, total phosphorus, soluble total phosphorus, and soluble orthophosphorus were performed according to modified procedures of Taras et al. (1971), described in McQuaker (1976). Analyses

of NH_4-N were performed according to modified procedures of Greenberg et al. (1980), described in McQuaker (1989).

Algal Community

Algal biomass was sampled weekly from 2 April to 8 July as chlorophyll a, by removing two periphyton cores (6.2 cm^2) from Styrofoam plates in each trough. As expected, the algal biomass on the plates showed an initial exponential increase in biomass due to colonization of the algae on the plates. This increase in biomass was followed by a plateau and then a decline, which resulted from sloughing of the algae off the plate (similar to Bothwell 1989). As a result, two sets of plates were used over the course of the experiment. Plates that were placed in the troughs on 2 April were replaced on 31 May, following a decline in algal biomass. The new plates were then monitored until 8 July.

Chlorophyll-a analyses followed the procedure of Parsons et al. (1984) with a correction made for phaeophytin. Duplicate cores from each trough were averaged for each date, and coefficients of variation among duplicates averaged 14% before treatment. Peak algal biomass (PB) was used to describe the relationship between P concentration and areal algal biomass (Bothwell 1989). Peak algal biomass was estimated by averaging chlorophyll-a values observed on the Styrofoam sheets for the final two collection dates (3 and 8 July).

Periphyton adhering to gravel was sampled on 8 July for taxonomic identification and cell counts. Two stones per trough were removed and preserved in Lugol's solution. Later, algae was scraped from both stones, and distilled water was added to a standard volume of 25 mL. Quantitative cell counts were made from subsamples of the standard volume at 500× magnification in Utermóhl chambers. A minimum of 100 individuals of the predominant species and at least 500 cells in total were counted. The areas of the rocks were calculated with a planimeter after obtaining an impression of the surface with aluminum foil in order to calculate cell counts per unit area of rock.

Insect Community

Adult insects were collected weekly from emergence traps and preserved in 90% ethanol. Drift nets that collected emigrating insects from the outflow of the troughs were emptied twice a week. Once a week, drift nets were placed on the inflow of the troughs for 24 h to assess the immigration of insects to each trough. One pipe from the head tank was monitored for immigrating insects three times per week (two 3-d and one 24-h collection period). As a result, drift nets excluded drifting insects from a single trough after the initial 21-d insect colonization period.

Benthic insects from two of the baskets in each trough (200 cm²) were sampled at the end of the experiment (8 July) using drift nets (100-μm mesh) to capture released insects. Samples were handpicked at 10× magnification. Benthic insects greater than 650 μm were identified and enumerated. Generally, drifting insects greater than 1,000 μm were enumerated and identified. However, all sizes of drifting insects sampled near the beginning of the experiment (31 May and 3 June) were examined. Insect taxonomy followed Merritt and Cummins (1984). Generally, insects were not subsampled, except that a gridded petri dish was used to subsample drifting Baetidae. In this case, variance-to-mean ratio tests for agreement with a Poisson series were performed, according to Elliott (1971).

Data Analysis

Poisson regression was used to determine whether invertebrates displayed a positive response to increases in nutrient concentration. A positive response was detected by a positive and significant β_1 term in an exponential equation where y is insect counts and x is the corresponding fertilizer concentration. Poisson regression was used because count data are usually distrib-uted as Poisson (not normal), especially when counts are low, and the variance in count data are usually proportional to the mean violating assumptions of parametric linear regression techniques (McCullough and Nelder 1989). This exponential curve is similar to log transforming the y-axis and conducting a linear regression.

The variance functions of the distributions were scaled by the square root of the deviance, divided by the degrees of freedom (DSCALE option in PROC GENMOD). The regression parameter estimates were tested for significance using likelihood ratio statistics in a Type 1 analysis. The P-values were calculated by comparison of the log likelihoods to the asymptotic chi-square distribution (SAS Institute 1997). An α level of 0.05 was used for tests.

In addition, a simple deterministic growth curve (Monomolecular model):

$$y = \left(a - e^{\beta_x}\right) + d$$

was fitted to the relationships determined to be linearly significant by Poisson regression. The Monomolecular model has been used to model populations with limits on growth (Brown and Rothery 1993). SAS PROC NLIN was used to fit the data using a standard least-squares procedure.

Results

Nutrient Treatments and Algal Community Response

Increases in phosphorus addition to troughs led to measured increases in total dissolved phosphorus (Table 1), which, on average, were ap-

TABLE 1. Dissolved inorganic phosphorus (P) and nitrogen (DIN) concentrations (μg/L) measured for each target treatment.

Target		Measured			
Total P	DIN	Total P[a]	Dissolved P[b]	Ortho-P[b]	DIN[b]
0.0	0.0	4.6(0.6)	<3³–3	<1[c]	16–23
0.5	0.5	4.6(0.4)	<3³–3	<1[c]	14–23
2.5	2.3	5.1(0.1)	<3³	<3[c]	<25[c]–25
5.0	4.5	6.3(0.2)	4–6	<3[c]	<25[c]–26
10.0	9.0	9.4(0.4)	5–6	<3[c]–4	<25[c]–29
50.0	45.1	38.3	32	32	60

[a]Mean of three replicates with standard error in brackets (June 18,25 and July 2,91).
[b]Ranges of three replicates collected on above dates.
[c]Values are below detection limits.

proximately one-third lower than the target concentrations of phosphorus for treatments of 2.5–10 mg/L. This difference may have represented flow variability to the mesocosms, uptake from the water column, or sorption to sediments. Thus, measured nutrients were elevated up to 8 and 3–4 times the controls for total phosphorus and dissolved inorganic nitrogen, respectively

(Table 1). Measured N:Total P ratios ranged from 1.5 to 5 in experimental and control troughs.

A significant increase in chlorophyll *a* with increasing nutrient concentration was observed after only 6 d of treatment ($p = 0.001$). There was an exponential increase in chlorophyll *a* for all treatments over time (Figure 1.1). In addition, the removal of in-migrating insects from one trough

(1.1) By target total phosphorus treatment ($n = 3$, except at 50 μg P/L where $n = 1$). The following treatments are indicated by symbols in brackets: controls (open squares), 0.5 μg P/L (open diamonds), 2.5 μg P/L (open circles), 5.0 μg P/L (closed squares), 10.0 μg P/L (close diamonds), and 50.0 μg P/L (closed circles).

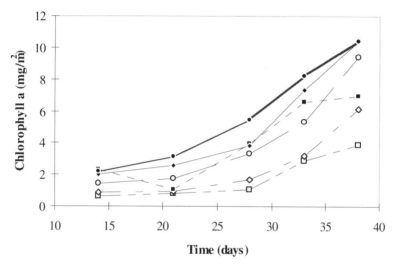

(1.2) Comparison of trough with grazers removed and no nutrient addition ($n = 1$, indicated by closed diamonds) compared with the controls ($n = 3$, indicated by open squares).

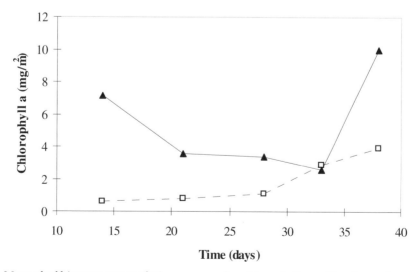

FIGURE 1. Mean algal biomass accumulation measured as chlorophyll *a* on Styrofoam plates versus number of days after placement of plates in troughs.

with no nutrient addition in the study resulted in up to a seven-fold increase in chlorophyll-*a* levels on the Styrofoam plates, compared with the controls (Figure 1.2).

Peak algal biomass increased rapidly with phosphorus concentrations of 0–2.5 µg/L but showed diminishing effects at 2.5–10 µg/L, peaking at about 11 mg/m² at 10 and 50 µg P/L (Figure 2). A significant relationship was observed between algal biomass and log phosphorus concentration ($p = 0.001$).

Algal cell composition sampled from the trough gravel substrate collected at the end of the experiment showed that cyanophytes, especially *Oscillatoria* spp., predominated at lower nutrient treatments, while at higher concentrations, *Achnanthes minutissima* made up a greater percentage of the total cell number (Table 2). In addition, total cell numbers collected from the trough gravel showed a negative relationship with nutrient addition ($p < 0.01$).

Insect Response

Baetid mayflies showed strong responses to nutrient additions. Significant results were obtained with increasing nutrient additions for adult baetids caught in emergence traps and outflow drift nets and baetid nymphs collected from the benthos and outflow drift nets. In addition, adult and larval hydroptilid caddisflies collected from

drift nets and the benthos showed a similar positive response. Finally, other families, including perlodids, polycentripodids, and nemourids, collected from the benthos, also increased in abundance with higher nutrient treatments. The results of the Poisson regression for significant relationships are shown in Table 3.

Adult Insects

Five to six weeks after the treatment initiation, total adult insects reached peak numbers for all nutrient concentrations. Adult insect taxa from the emergent insects traps were composed largely of Chironomidae (51–61%), Baetidae (18–33%), Simuliidae (3–12%), and Trichoptera (5–8%). Adult Baetidae caught in emergence traps and outflow drift nets increased in number by four- and two-fold, respectively, at 10 µg P/L, when compared with controls at the end of the experiment (Figures 4 and 5.1).

The mean number of adult Baetidae immigrating to troughs in the drift was very low and averaged 1.3 per trough per day. Thus, adult Baetidae trapped in drift nets largely originated from trough gravel. The number of baetid adults increased rapidly with increasing phosphorus concentrations of 0–2.5 µg/L, but showed diminishing increases at 2.5–10 µg/L.

Numbers of adult Hydroptilidae caught in the drift also showed a three-fold increase at 10

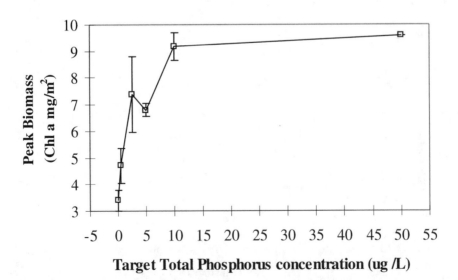

FIGURE 2. Mean peak algal biomass measured as chlorophyll *a* on Styrofoam plates target total phosphorus concentration. Error bars indicate the standard error ($n = 3$, except at 50 µg P/L where $n = 1$).

TABLE 2. Taxonomic composition of algal cell numbers by target phosphorus concentration (ug P/L) collected from trough gravel at the end of the experiment.

Taxon	0[a]	0.5[a]	2.5[a]	5.0[a]	10[a]	50[b]
Cyanophyta						
Oscillatoria spp.	60.3	83.3	71.5	74.1	38.1	16.4
Lyngbya spp.	2.0	3.5	7.6	5.5	6.9	0.0
Chrysophyta-Bacillariophyceae						
Achnanthes mimutissima	16.8	8.4	7.7	9.3	26.2	42.7
Eunotia spp.	0.6	0.3	1.1	0.7	3.1	7.3
Synedra ulna	1.2	0.4	1.5	1.8	1.3	8.2
Tabellaria fenestra	2.2	0.0	4.3	1.5	2.6	5.5
Chlorophyta						
Oedogonium spp.	0.1	1.4	1.3	0.8	1.1	0.0

[a]Based on pooled counts from three replicate troughs.
[b]From one unreplicated trough.

μg P/L, when compared with controls at the end of the experiment (Table 3; Figure 5.2). No significant treatment effects were observed on the total number of Plecoptera, Simuliidae, Chironomidae, Leptophlebiidae, Heptageniidae, Plecoptera, Coleoptera, or other Trichoptera collected in the emergence traps.

Benthic Invertebrates

Numbers of benthic Baetidae, Hydroptilidae, Nemouridae, Perlodidae, Hydroptilidae, and Polycentripodidae significantly increased with increasing nutrient concentrations (Table 3; Figures 6.1–6.5). Densities of baetids, nemourids, perlodids, and hydroptilids initially increased rapidly at nutrient additions of 0–2.5 μg P/L and reached asymptotes at concentrations of 2.5–10 μg P/L. However, perlodids showed a slower increase in response to nutrient concentration and reached an asymptote at approximately 5 μg P/L. Other major insect taxa from the benthos showed no significant response to fertilization ($p > 05$). The number of taxa per sample (taxonomic richness) of the trough benthos was not influenced by treatment.

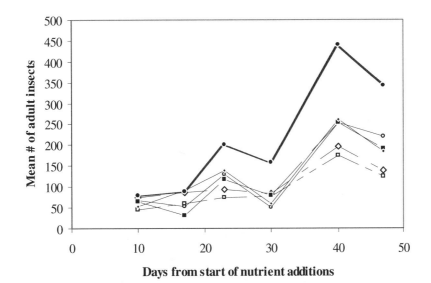

FIGURE 3. Mean number of adult insects captured in emergent insect traps over time by nutrient concentration ($n = 3$, except at 50 μg P/L where $n = 1$). The following treatments are indicated by symbols in brackets: controls (open squares), 0.5 mg P/L (open diamonds), 2.5 μg P/L (open circles), 5.0 μg P/L (closed squares), 10.0 μg P/L (close diamonds), and 50.0 μg P/L (closed circles).

TABLE 3. Equations and tests for significant responses of insects to treatments.

Taxa	Life Stage	Sample type	Sample date	χ^2	df[a]	p
Baetidae	Adult	Emergence trap	1 July	8.82	13	0.004
		Outflow drift	24 June	15.25	13	<0.001
	Nymph	Benthos	8 July	3.96	12	0.050
		Outflow drift	3 June	9.49	13	0.002
			24 June	11.15	13	0.001
Hydroptilidae	Adult	Outflow drift	24 June	6.71	13	0.010
	Larvae	Benthos	8 July	4.05	12	0.049
Perlodidae	Nymph	Benthos	8 July	6.71	12	0.011
Polycentripodidae	Larvae	Benthos	8 July	5.56	12	0.021
Nemouridae	Nymph	Benthos	8 July	3.56	12	0.063

[a] degrees of freedom for likelihood ratio tests were the same as deviance tests.

Drifting Nymphs and Larvae

The composition of immigrating nymphs and larvae was largely made up of Baetidae (42.3%), Chironomidae (15.9%), Simuliidae (10%), Trichoptera (10%), and Leptophlebiidae (5%). Perlodidae and Nemouridae had very low immigration rates and made up only 0.02 and 0.01%, respectively, of the total insects collected. Emigration rates were only assessed for families that showed a significant response in the benthos sampling. The effect of nutrient concentration on emigration rates of large baetid nymphs (>1 mm) was not significant for dates 6 and 13 June and 1 July 1991. However, on 3 and 24 June (p = 002; p = .001), emigration rates of large baetids showed a significant positive response to increasing nutrient concentration (Table 3). Emigration rates of other families including Hydroptilidae, Nemour-idae, and Perlodidae were not assessed because of very low numbers in the drift.

Discussion

Effect of Nutrient Additions on Periphyton

Peak algal biomass collected from Styrofoam substrates and plotted as a function of target nutrient concentrations showed saturation kinetics similar to that found by Bothwell (1989). About 70% of the maximum chlorophyll-a value

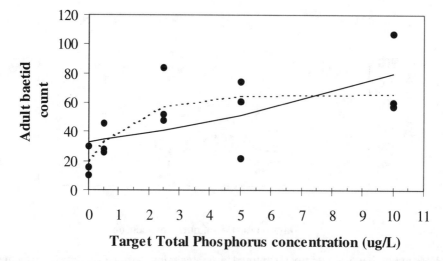

FIGURE 4. Number of adult Baetidae captured in emergent traps at the end of the experiment (4 July) as a function of target total phosphorus concentration. Equations fit by Poisson regression are symbolized as whole lines. The Monod model curves are symbolized as dashed lines.

was achieved at low phosphorus additions (between 0.5 and 2.5 μg/L).

However, the levels of chlorophyll *a* from the Styrofoam substrates were lower than other studies conducted in British Columbia (Bothwell 1989 and Mundie et al. 1991) in troughs. There is compelling evidence that higher grazing rates by invertebrates in the present experiment may have accounted for this discrepancy. The mean density of insects in the controls (47,350 insects/m²) and 10 μg P/L troughs (66,965 insects/m²) were 2.1- and 1.7-fold higher, respectively, than the mean density of invertebrates at the same treatments in Mundie's study. Also, this relative difference in densities is underestimated because invertebrates in our study were only sampled to 630 mm, whereas in Mundie's study, they were sampled to 50 μm.

The removal of insects from one unfertilized trough resulted in up to a seven-fold increase in chlorophyll-*a* levels on the Styrofoam plates compared with the controls. In addition, total cell numbers collected from the trough gravel

(5.1) Adult baetidae. Monod model did not converge and is not shown.

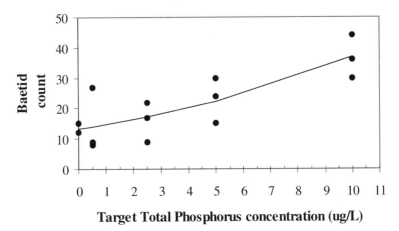

Target Total Phosphorus concentration (ug/L)

(5.2.) Adult Hydroptilidae.

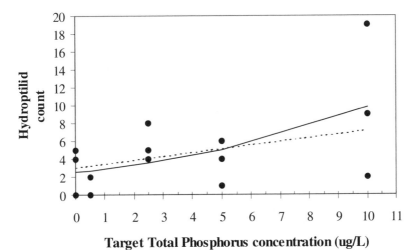

Target Total Phosphorus concentration (ug/L)

FIGURE 5. Number of adults captured in drift nets at the end of the experiment (24 June) as a function of target total phosphorus concentration. Equations fit by Poisson regression are symbolized as whole lines. The Monod model curves are symbolized as dashed lines.

showed a negative relationship with increasing nutrient addition, likely due to higher grazing pressures on the gravel compared with the Styrofoam. This suggests that grazers may have had a significant controlling influence on the biomass of algae similar to Peterson et al. (1993) on the Kuparuk River in Alaska. In the Kuparuk River study, insect grazing clearly reduced chlorophyll-*a* biomass during fertilization by more than 90%. Other studies involving nutrient augmentation clearly show that high abundances of grazers can control periphyton levels (McCormick and Stevenson 1991; Bothwell and Culp 1993; Slaney and Ashley 1998).

Diatoms and cyanophytes made up more than 89.6% of the total cell numbers collected from the trough gravel in our experiment. Diatoms are high quality food for grazing insects, while cyanophytes are thought to be poorer quality (Lamberti and Moore 1984). However, Mundie et al. (1991) showed that an increase in total insect number occurred with increased phosphorus concentration, despite an increase in the percentage of cyanophytes making up the algae in their artificial stream troughs. In our study, cyanophytes made up a decreasing percentage of the total cell number at the higher concentrations of nutrient.

Effects of Nutrient Additions on the Abundance of the Insect Community

The families of insects that showed the greatest increases in density with nutrient enrichment were Baetidae, Nemouridae, Perlodidae, Hydroptilidae, and Polycentripodidae. The numbers of adult and nymphal baetids and benthic nemourids, perlodids, and hydroptilids initially increased rapidly at nutrient concentrations of 0–2.5 µg P/L and reached asymptotes at concentrations of 2.5–10 µg P/L. Nymphal perlodids showed a slower response to nutrient concentration and reached an asymptote at approximately 5 µg P/L.

Positive responses of baetid density to increasing nutrient concentration were observed for adults in the emergence traps and drift nets (Figure 5), as well as for nymphs collected from the benthos (Figure 6). Increased survival of baetid nymphs due to increases in food availability was thought to account for the higher numbers of adults and benthic nymphs. The periphytic community is known to provide high quality food for baetid nymphs (Chapman and Demory 1963; Kohler 1985). Aggregation of baetids at higher nutrient treatments did not account for the increases in abundance because emigration rates did not decrease with fertilization.

Numbers of baetid mayflies emerging from the troughs peaked at the end of the experiment. The synchrony of nutrient enrichment, algal response, and nymphal development probably resulted in strong positive responses of Baetidae to treatment observed in emergence traps, drift nets, and benthos. A number of short-term food-enrichment studies conducted in artificial streams have found that insects like baetids with short generation times may be able to exploit increased food abundance (Mundie et al. 1991; Richardson and Neill 1991).

The benthic nymphs of two plecopteran families, Perlodidae and Nemouridae, also showed a positive response to enrichment. Increased biomass at the consumer trophic level may have resulted in increased available prey for perlodid stoneflies. The food abundance of nemourids, which includes fine or coarse particulate organic matter (Merritt and Cummins 1984), may have been directly enhanced, if the amount of dead and decaying algae increased with fertilization. Alternatively, increases in the numbers of grazers correlated with increasing nutrient may have facilitated an increase in abundance of fine particulate organic matter (FPOM) through feeding and defecation activities (Merritt et al. 1984).

Benthic trichopteran larvae—hydroptilid and polycentripodid—also increased in abundance with increasing nutrient concentration. Hydroptilids are piercer-herbivores, scrapers, or collector gatherers, while polycentripodids are predators, collectors, and shredders (Merritt and Cummins 1984). Their numbers may have been enhanced by increased food abundance through direct fertilization effects on periphyton biomass or indirect effects on the availability of FPOM or prey. The mechanisms by which plecopteran or trichopteran numbers increased were not examined because of low numbers in the drift.

The mesocosm approach used in this study is powerful because it allowed for experimental comparisons with replication and appropriate controls, whereas whole stream manipulations are difficult, and replication is not always possible. However, the generality of the observed insect responses and the effects of long term biotic and abiotic interactions should also be

(6.1.) Benthic Baetidae nymphs.

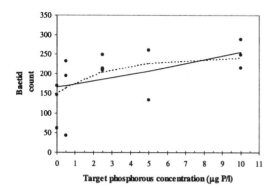

(6.2.) Benthic Nemouridae nymphs.

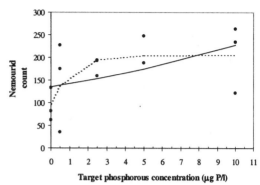

(6.3.) Benthic Perlodidae nymphs.

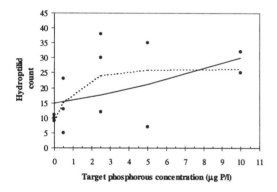

(6.4.) Benthic Hydroptilidae nymphs.

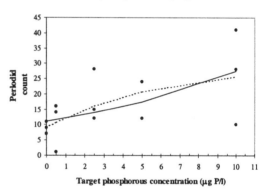

(6.5.) Benthic Polycentripodidae larvae.

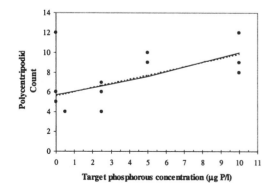

FIGURE 6. Number of insects collected from the benthos at the end of the experiment (8 July) as a function of target total phosphorus concentration. Equations fit by Poisson regression are symbolized as whole lines. The Monod model curves are symbolized as dashed lines.

assessed in controlled larger-scale conditions and whole rivers. It will be especially important to establish how temporal lags in trophic interactions (Peterson et al. 1993) affect the insect response in whole river experiments and translate into improved adult salmon returns.

The most important management implication of the present study is that some insect groups may increase numerically, even at relatively low levels of nutrient additions. In this study, the numerical responses of several macroinvertebrate taxa (baetid, nemourid, perlodid, hydroptilid, polycentripodid) to fertilization were nonlinear with asymtotes at 2.5–10 µg P/L. Most of these groups, particularly baetid mayflies, are important food items for juvenile salmonids (Johnston et al. 1990). Thus, small target concentrations of added nutrients may be effective in accelerating stream restoration and maintaining the productivity of anadromous salmon populations in oligotrophic streams. In addition, positive macroinvertebrate responses were observed at nutrient levels similar to natural inputs (<5 µg P/L) from salmon carcasses (Schuldt and Hershey 1995). The use of low levels of nutrients at these levels in stream restoration projects is important in order to prevent shifts in the composition of the biological community (Wiederholm 1984) and possible changes in the age of maturity of salmonids or degree of anadromy resulting from eutrophic conditions. This may be particularly important in streams where external cultural sources of nutrients are a concern downstream.

Acknowledgments

I would like to thank the thesis advisory committee, which included the co-authors M. L. Bothwell, Dr. T. G. Northcote, J. D. McPhail, G. G.E. Scudder, and C. J. Walters. I also appreciated the helpful reviews by N. T. Johnston and H. A. Quamme. C. J. Perrin of Limnotek Research and Development Inc. provided the Plexiglas set of troughs. J. H. Mundie made suggestions on experimental techniques, and John Boulanger provided valuable statistical advice. This work was supported by an NSERC operating grant to T. G. Northcote and funding from the British Columbia Ministry of Environment, Fisheries Research Branch, and the Nechako Fisheries Conservation Fund.

References

Ashley, K. I. And P. A. Slaney. 1997. Accelerating recovery of stream, river and pond productivity by low-level nutrient replacement. In P. A. Slaney and D. Zaldokas, editor. Fish habitat rehabilitation procedures. Watershed Restoration Technical Circular No. 9. Produced by British Columbia Watershed Restoration Program, Ministry of Environment, Lands and Parks and Ministry of Forests.

Bothwell, M. L. 1989. Phosphorus-limited growth dynamics of lotic periphytic diatom communities: area biomass and cellular growth rate responses. Canadian Journal of Fisheries and Aquatic Sciences 46:1293–1301.

Bothwell, M. L., and J. M. Culp. 1993. Sensitivity of the Thompson River to phosphorus: studies on trophic dynamics. National Hydrology Research Center, Contribution No. 93006. Saskatoon, Saskatchewan, Canada.

Brown, D., and P. Rothery. 1993. Models in biology: mathematics, statistics and computing. Wiley, Toronto.

Chapman, D. W., and R. Demory. 1963. Seasonal changes in the food ingested by aquatic insect larvae and nymphs in two Oregon streams. Ecology 44:140–146.

Elliott, J. M. 1971. Some methods for the statistical analysis of samples of benthic invertebrates. Freshwater Biological Association, Scientific Publication 25.

Greenberg, A. E., J. J. Conners, D. Jenkins. 1980. Standard methods for the examination of water and wastewater. American Public Health Association, Washington, D.C. 1134.

Hager, R. C., and R. E. Noble. 1976. Relation of size at release of hatchery-reared coho salmon to age, size, and sex composition of returning adults. Progressive Fish-Culturist 38:144–147.

Hullar, M. A. J., and J. R. Vestal. 1988. The effects of nutrient limitation and stream discharge on the epilithic microbial community in an oligotrophic Arctic stream. Hydrobiologia 172:19–26.

Johnston, N. T., C. J. Perrin, P. R. Slaney and B. R. Ward. 1990. Increased juvenile salmonid growth by whole-river fertilization. Canadian Journal of Fisheries and Aquatic Sciences 47:862–872.

Kohler, S. L. 1985. Identification of stream drift mechanisms: an experimental and observational approach. Ecology 66:1749–1761.

Lamberti, G. A., and J. W. Moore. 1984. Aquatic insects as primary consumers. Pages 164–195 in V. H. Resh and D. M. Rosenberg, editors. The ecology of aquatic insects. Praeger Publishers, New York.

McCormick, P. V., and R. J. Stevenson. 1991. Grazer control of nutrient availability in the periphyton. Oeciologia 86:287–291.

McCullough P. and J. A. Nelder. 1989. Generalized linear models. Chapman and Hall, New York.

McQuaker, N. E. 1976. A laboratory manual for the chemical analysis of waters, wastewaters, sediments and biological materials. 2nd edition. British Columbia Ministry of Environment.

McQuaker, N. E. 1989. A laboratory manual for the chemical analysis of waters, wastewaters, sediments and biological materials. 3rd edition. British Columbia Ministry of Environment.

Merritt, R. W., and K. W. Cummins. 1984. An introduction to the aquatic insects of North America. 2nd edition. Kendall/Hunt Publishing Company, Dubuque, Iowa.

Merritt, R. W., K. W. Cummins and T. M. Burton. 1984. The role of aquatic insects in the processing and cycling of nutrients. Pages 134–163 *in* V. H. Resh and D. M. Rosenberg, editors. The ecology of aquatic insects. Praeger Publishers, New York.

Mundie, J. H., K. S. Simpson, and C. J. Perrin. 1991. Responses of stream periphyton and benthic insects to increases in dissolved inorganic phosphorus in a mesocosm. Canadian Journal of Fisheries and Aquatic Sciences 48:2061–2072.

Parsons, T. R., Y. Maka and C. M. Lalli. 1984. A manual of chemical and biological methods of seawater analysis. Pergamon Press, New York.

Perrin, C. J., M. L. Bothwell, and P. A. Slaney. 1987. Experimental enrichment of a coastal stream in British Columbia: effects of organic and inorganic additions on autotrophic periphyton production. Canadian Journal of Fisheries and Aquatic Sciences 44:1247–1256.

Richardson, J. S., and W. E. Neill. 1991. Indirect effects of detritus manipulations in a montane stream. Canadian Journal of Fisheries and Aquatic Sciences 48:776–783.

Peterson, B. J., L. Deegan, J. Helfrich, J. E. Hobbie, M. Hullar, B. Moller, T. E. Ford, A. Hershey, A. Hiltner, G. Kipphut, M. A. Lock, D. M. Fiebig, V. McKinley, M. C. Miller, J. R. Vestal, M. C. Miller, J. R. Vestal, R. Ventullo, and G. Volk. 1993. Biological responses of a tundra river to fertilization. Ecology 74(3):653–672.

Peterson, B. J., W. M. Wolheim, P. J. Mulholland, J. R. Webster, J. L. Meyer, J. L. Tank, E. Martt, W. B. Bowden, M. H. Valett, A. E. Hershey, W. H. McDowell, W. K. Dodds, S. K. Hamilton, S. Gregory, and D. D. Morrall. 2001. Control of nitrogen export from watersheds by headwater streams. Science 292:86–90.

SAS Institute. (1997). SAS/STAT Software: changes and enhancements through release 6.12. SAS Institute, Cary, North Carolina.

Schuldt, J. A., M. A. Perkins, and C. R. Goldman. 1995. Effect of salmon carcass decomposition on Lake Superior tributary streams. Journal of the North American Benthological Society 14(2):259–268.

Slaney, P. A., and B. R. Ward. 1993. Experimental fertilization of nutrient deficient streams in British Columbia. In G. Shooner and S. Asselin, editors. Le développement du saumon Atlantique au Québec: connaître les règles du jeu pour réussir. Colloque international de la fédération Québé-coise pour le saumon Atlantique. Québec, décembre 1992. Collection *Salmo salar* No. 201.

Slaney, P. A., and K. I. Ashley. 1998. Case studies of whole-stream fertilization in British Columbia. Restoration of fisheries by enrichment of aquatic ecosystems. In J. G. Stockner and G. Milbrink, editors. Proceedings of international workshop at Uppsala University, March 30–April 1, 1998.

Taras, M. J., A. E. Greenberg, M. C. Rand. 1971. Standard methods for the examination of water and wastewater. American Public Health Association, 13th edition. Washington, D.C.

Ward, B. R., and P. A. Slaney. 1988. Life history and smolt-to-adult survival of Keogh River steelhead trout (*Salmo gairdneri*) and the relationship to smolt size. Canadian Journal of Fisheries and Aquatic Sciences 45:1110–1122.

Wiederholm, T. 1984. Responses of aquatic insects to environmental pollution. Pages 508–557 *in* V. H. Resh and D. M. Rosenberg, editors. The ecology of aquatic insects. Praeger Publishers, New York.

American Fisheries Society Symposium 34:177–196, 2003

Restoration of Kokanee Salmon in the Arrow Lakes Reservoir, British Columbia: Preliminary Results of a Fertilization Experiment

ROGER PIETERS AND SHANNON HARRIS

Department of Civil Engineering and Department of Earth and Ocean Sciences
University of British Columbia, Vancouver, B.C. V6T 1Z4, Canada

LISA C. THOMPSON

Wildlife, Fish, and Conservation Biology Department
University of California, Davis, California 95616-8751, USA

LIDIJA VIDMANIC, MEGHAN ROUSHORNE, AND GREG LAWRENCE

Department of Civil Engineering
University of British Columbia, Vancouver, B.C. V6T 1Z4, Canada

JOHN G. STOCKNER

Eco-Logic Ltd., 2614 Mathers Avenue, West Vancouver, B.C. V7V 2J4, Canada

HARVEY ANDRUSAK

Redfish Consulting Ltd., 5244 Highway 3A, Nelson, B.C. V1L 6N6, Canada

KENNETH I. ASHLEY

Fisheries Research and Development Section,
Ministry of Fisheries, Province of British Columbia
University of British Columbia, Vancouver, B.C. V6T 1Z4, Canada

BOB LINDSAY

Ministry of Water, Land and Air Protection, Province of British Columbia
333 Victoria Street, Suite 401, Nelson, B.C. V1L 4K3, Canada

KEN HALL

Institute for Resources and Environment
University of British Columbia, Vancouver, B.C. V6T 1Z3, Canada

DARCY LOMBARD

Fisheries Centre, 2204 Main Mall
University of British Columbia, Vancouver, B.C. V6T 1Z4, Canada

Abstract.—The Upper and Lower Arrow lakes have undergone major anthropogenic changes. Dams were built below (Grand Coulee 1942), at the outlet (Keenleyside 1967), and above (Mica 1973 and Revelstoke 1983) the Arrow Lakes, and *Mysis relicta* were introduced in 1968. The reservoirs created behind the upstream dams act as nutrient traps, reducing the already naturally low levels of nutrients in the Arrow Lakes Reservoir. The objective of nutrient additions to the Arrow Lakes Reservoir was to replace nutrients trapped upstream and was driven by rapidly declining stocks of kokanee, a native land-locked sockeye salmon *Oncorhynchus nerka* and keystone species of this aquatic ecosystem. In the late 1980s and early 1990s, Upper and Lower Arrow tributaries supported between 600,000–800,000 kokanee salmon spawners, but the numbers declined steadily through the 1990s to a low of 97,000 in 1997. As the number of kokanee decreased, no increase in size was observed, consistent with nutrient-limited conditions. Unlike its neighbor, Kootenay Lake, which is one of the most studied in British Columbia, the Arrow Lakes Reservoir had received little limnological attention. After an initial study of the limnology and trophic status in 1997 and 1998, a 5-year fertilization experiment was initiated in 1999 with seasonally adjusted nutrient (phosphorus and nitrogen) additions to the Upper Arrow Reservoir, in an effort to restore historic kokanee populations. Preliminary data from the first two years of fertilization, 1999 and 2000, show positive and encouraging trends in primary productivity, phytoplankton succession, zooplankton biomass, and the number, size, and fecundity of kokanee spawners. No significant changes have been observed in the water quality parameters measured, consistent with immediate utilization of nutrients in an oligotrophic system.

Introduction

A fundamental problem occupying the center of limnological attention over the past 40 years has been the excess supply of nutrients or eutrophication (e.g., Vallentyne 1974; Schindler 1974; Vollenweider 1976). However, the opposite, namely a reduction in nutrient supply or oligotrophication, is being recognized as a companion problem (Ney 1996; Stockner et al. 2000). Oligotrophication can result from the trapping of nutrients behind upstream impoundments or from the blockage of the anadromous nutrient pump by overfishing or downstream dams (Stockner and MacIsaac 1996; Cederholm et al. 2000). Large water level variation in reservoirs has been implicated in nutrient loss by enhanced transport of littoral nutrients to the profundal sediments (Milbrink and Holmgren 1981), and large changes to the pattern of the seasonal hydrograph may also affect nutrient pathways.

The Arrow Lakes Reservoir, part of the Columbia River system (Figures 1 and 2), exemplifies the process of oligotrophication, having undergone major anthropogenic changes. Prior to dam construction, anadromous runs of chinook salmon, sockeye salmon, and steelhead trout were found in and above the Arrow Lakes (Sebastian et al. 2000). This anadromous nutrient pump to the upper Columbia was blocked by the Grand Coulee Dam, built on the Columbia River in the late 1930s. The Upper and Lower Arrow

lakes were converted to a large reservoir with the completion of the Keenleyside Dam at the outlet of the Lower Arrow Lake in 1967. This increased the mean water level of the resulting Arrow Lakes Reservoir by 12.6 m and flooded both the narrows between the Upper and Lower Arrow lakes and the river between Beaton Arm and Revelstoke (Figure 3). In 1973 and 1983, the Mica and Revelstoke dams were completed on the Columbia River above the Arrow Reservoir (Figures 1, 2). Operation of these dams for flood control and hydroelectric generation changed the timing of the Columbia River inflow to the Arrow Lakes Reservoir. Another major perturbation was the introduction of *Mysis relicta* in 1968 (Lasenby et al. 1986), a small, exotic crustacean that is a highly effective competitor for the zooplankton species preferred as a food source by kokanee.

Dramatically declining kokanee numbers, with no compensating density-driven increase in size, resulted in a two-year baseline study of the trophic status of the Arrow Lakes Reservoir in 1997 and 1998 (Pieters et al. 1998, 1999). Kokanee *Oncorhynchus nerka* spend their entire life cycle in the lake and are one of the keystone species within the ecosystem, supporting large piscivorous sport fish such as rainbow trout *Oncorhynchus mykiss*, white sturgeon *Acipenser transmontanus*, and bull trout *Salvelinus confluentus*. In the late 1980s to the early 1990s, Upper and Lower Arrow tributary streams supported spawning populations of 600,000–800,000 kokanee, but the

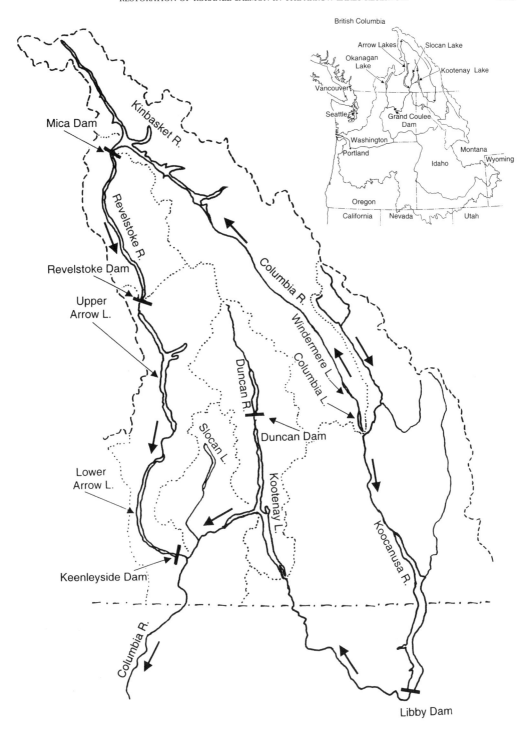

FIGURE 1. Upper Columbia River. Inset: Columbia River drainage. The source water of the Columbia River at Columbia Lake flows northwest into the Kinbasket Reservoir. At Mica Dam, the Columbia River turns south, flowing through Revelstoke Reservoir and into the north end of the Upper Arrow Lakes Reservoir. The outflow at the south end of Upper Arrow passes through a shallow, formerly riverine, narrows and then through the Lower Arrow Lakes Reservoir.

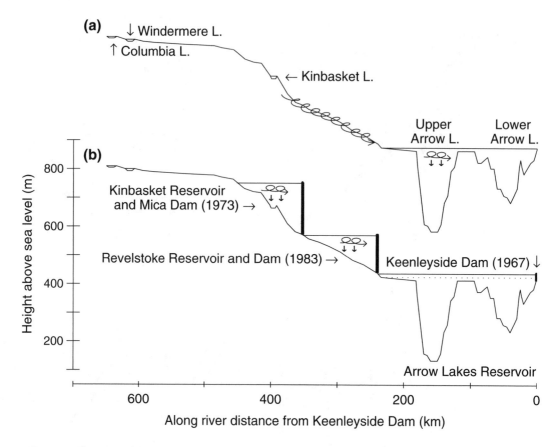

FIGURE 2. Elevation of the Upper Columbia River (a) before and (b) after construction of impoundments.

numbers declined steadily through the 1990s to a low of 97,000 in 1997. In response to these rapidly declining kokanee stocks, experimental fertilization of the Arrow Lakes Reservoir was initiated to replace nutrients lost in the upstream impoundments. A five-year fertilization experiment was started in 1999, modeled on the adaptive management approach used for Kootenay Lake (Ashley et al. 1997, 1999a, 1999b). Summarized here are the results of two years of baseline monitoring (1997, 1998) and the preliminary results of the first two years of the fertilization experiment (1999, 2000).

The first objective of this paper is to describe the Arrow Lakes Reservoir and to assess its trophic status. Large aquatic ecosystems such as the Arrow Lakes Reservoir are sustained by complex physical, chemical, and biological interactions. These include, among many others, the physical role of river inflows to deliver nutrients to the euphotic zone, the adsorption of nutrients to sinking particulates, the recycling of nutrients in the

microbial food web, and the transfer of nutrient-limited productivity through the traditional food web of phytoplankton, zooplankton, plankti-vorous fishes, and the large piscivores. Because of these interactions, it is unwise to base an assessment of the trophic status of an aquatic system on any given trophic level. With this in mind, a variety of data are reported here to assess the trophic status of the Arrow Lakes Reservoir.

The second objective is to describe the fertilization experiment and the initial response of the system to the nutrient additions. Two controls are considered, both with limitations. First, the untreated years, 1997 and 1998, act as a control. As will be discussed, two extremes in climate were observed in these years, pointing to the problem of interannual variability inherent in both this short two-year control record and the short two-year record of fertilization described here. The only long-term record on the Arrow Lakes Reservoir is that for kokanee salmon,

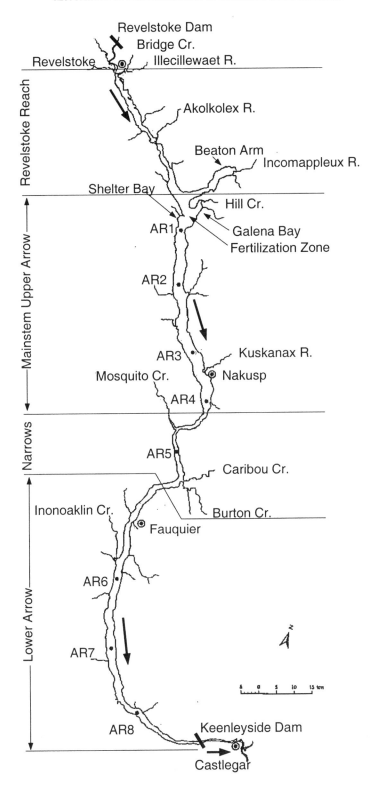

FIGURE 3. Arrow Lakes Reservoir with sampling stations AR1–8.

which has shown a steady decline through the 1990s. The second control is the Lower Arrow Reservoir. However, the Lower Arrow is downstream of the fertilization zone at the top of the Upper Arrow and may benefit from nutrient additions as the residence time of the top 50 m of the main-stem Upper Arrow is approximately two months. The absence of an ideal control is inherent in large-scale experiments of this type.

Background

The Columbia River drains from seven states of the United States and the southeastern corner of British Columbia, Canada (Figure 1). In the Canadian component, the terrain is mountainous, dominated by deep valleys trending north to south, in which five large natural lakes are found: Okanagan, Upper and Lower Arrow, Slocan, and Kootenay. These lakes occupy long, narrow, deep, steep-sided, and glacially carved basins. While representing only 5% of the Columbia River's total drainage area, the discharge from the Arrow Lakes Reservoir contributes 16% of the total flow. The Arrow Lakes Reservoir has a length of 240 km, a mean width of 1.8 km, and a mean and maximum depth of 83 and 287 m, respectively. With a surface area of 465 km² at mean water level, the Arrow Lakes Reservoir represents one of the largest to undergo experimental fertilization.

The elevation of the Columbia River above the Arrow Lakes outlet is shown in Figure 2. Before the construction of upstream dams, nutrients would spiral through the riverine sections. While these nutrients might be utilized in the river, they would nevertheless be recycled as they moved downstream. The river-borne nutrients would then contribute to productivity in the Upper and Lower Arrow lakes, which were two separate basins connected by a riverine narrows (Figure 2a). With the construction of upstream dams, nutrients are now utilized in the upstream impoundments, and most settle to the impoundment sediments, thereby reducing the available nutrients to the Arrow Lakes Reservoir. In effect, the potential for productivity is moved upstream.

The construction of an upstream dam results in a 'boom and bust' nutrient response (Horne and Goldman 1994; Ney 1996; Stockner et al. 2000). On filling the impoundment, the decomposition of organic materials in the basin releases a pulse of nutrients that can last 5–10 years. However, after this period, the impoundment acts as a settling basin, where entering nutrients are used and sedimented rather than being passed for downstream use. Both the Mica Dam (1973) and, more recently, the Revelstoke Dam (1983) were built above the oligotrophic Arrow Lakes Reservoir. These resulted in a marked reduction in the naturally low level of nutrients in the Arrow Lakes Reservoir.

Methods

Methods are only briefly summarized here. For greater detail see Pieters et al. (1998, 1999, 2000, 2001).

Fertilizer Application

From late April to early September, in 1999 and 2000, 1,060 t (metric tons) of agricultural grade fertilizer were applied to the north end of Upper Arrow between Galena Bay and Shelter Bay (Figure 3), 5 km above the first sampling station (AR1). Fertilizer was dispensed from the Ministry of Transportation and Highways' ferry, the *DEV* Galena. This diesel electric ferry (Figure 4a) is 50 m long, has a draft of 2.4 m, and is powered by two Voith-Schnieder cycloidal propellers with 1.6 m blades. A truck and tank were driven onto the ferry and connected to a 3.6 m diffuser pipe (with 0.6 cm holes every 30 cm) bolted to the side of the ferry. Once away from shore, fertilizer was pumped through the diffuser into the propeller wash (Figure 4). Approximately 3,900 L of fertilizer were delivered per trip, with 2–15 trips per day and a total of ~215 trips from April to September.

The fertilizer consisted of a seasonally adjusted blend of liquid ammonium polyphosphate (10–34–0; % by weight equivalent of N-P_2O_5-K_2O) and urea-ammonium nitrate (28–0–0; % by weight equivalent of N-P_2O_5-K_2O; 14% urea N, 7% ammonium N and 7% nitrate N). This delivered 52.8 t of phosphorus and 232 t of nitrogen per year. The seasonal loading and timing of the fertilizer application (Figure 5) was modeled on the Kootenay Lake fertilization experiment (Ashley et al. 1997, 1999a, 1999b). Phosphorus additions followed the preimpoundment freshet flow pattern, increasing to early June and then declining. The ratio of nitrogen (N) to phosphorus (P) is critical to prevent blooms of undesirable blue-

FIGURE 4. (a) The ferry *DEV* Galena crossing Upper Arrow. (b) Truck and fertilizer tank on the *DEV* Galena (c) dispensing from the diffuser (arrow) into the ferry propeller wash. [Photo credits: (a) C. Stevens, (b) Columbia Basin Fish and Wildlife Compensation Program, and (c) R. Pieters]

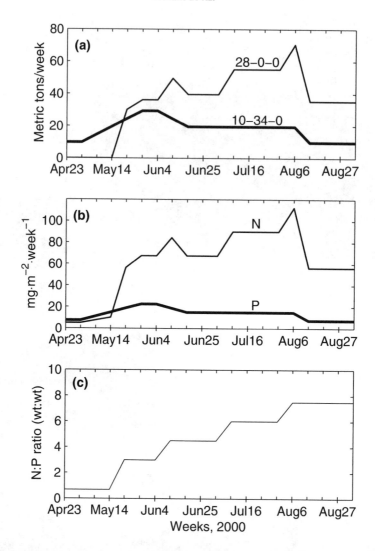

FIGURE 5. (a) Load of liquid ammonium polyphosphate (10–34–0) and urea-ammonium nitrate (28-0-0) fertilizer to the Upper Arrow Lakes Reservoir in 2000, (b) resulting load of phosphorus (P) and nitrogen (N) to the main-stem Upper Arrow (192 km²), and (c) N:P ratio (wt:wt) for fertilizer applied.

green algae (cyanobacteria), which can fix nitrogen in low N:P ratio conditions (Smith 1983). As a result, increased levels of nitrogen are added through the summer.

Water Chemistry

Eight stations along the reservoir (AR 1–8; Figure 3) were sampled 10 months per year (January, March–November) beginning in May 1997. Two types of samples were taken. First, an integrated 0–30 m sample was taken with a 2.54 cm (ID) tube sampler. This depth range was chosen for con-

sistency with prior work on Kootenay Lake. Integrated 0–30 m samples included water from both epilimnion and metalimnion. Second, a deep sample, approximately 5 m above bottom, was collected with a Niskin sampler. In June and August or September, a series of hypolimnetic depths were also sampled—50, 100, 150, 200, and 250 m, as depth allowed.

The main inflow (Columbia River at Revelstoke) and outflow (Columbia River below the Keenleyside Dam) were monitored monthly throughout the year. Eight local rivers and streams (Illecillewaet, Akolkolex, Incomappleux,

Kuskanax, Mosquito, Caribou, Burton, and Inonoaklin) were sampled monthly from April to October, through the freshet and into the fall. For all, two additional samples were taken during freshet (May and June). An additional ten streams and rivers were sampled twice during freshet. All water samples were analyzed by the Environment Canada Laboratories, Pacific Environmental Science Centre, North Vancouver, British Columbia, Canada. Analysis included low-level orthophosphate (OP), total dissolved phosphorus (TDP), which excludes particulates by filtration through a 0.45-μm filter, total phosphorus (TP) determined from an unfiltered sample, ammonia (NH_3), nitrite and nitrate (predominately nitrate, NO_3^-), and chlorophyll *a* (for the 0–30 m samples). Samples for orthophosphate (a.k.a. soluble reactive phosphorus) were field filtered (0.45 μm mesh) and measured with the colorimetric molybdate method using ascorbic acid (Pieters et al. 1998–2000).

Nutrient Load

The flow into the Arrow Lakes Reservoir is composed of the main inflow of the Columbia River at the Revelstoke Dam with the balance being the local inflow from smaller rivers and streams along the length of the reservoir. The daily local flow to the Arrow Lakes Reservoir was computed from the Revelstoke inflow, Keenleyside outflow, water elevation, and a storage-elevation curve (K. Ketchum, B.C. Hydro, Burnaby, British Columbia, Canada). The local flow and stream nutrient data (from eight intensively monitored streams) were apportioned to four regions (Revelstoke Reach, Beaton Arm, Upper Arrow, and Lower Arrow with narrows; Figure 3). The local flow to these regions was 40%, 19%, 23%, and 18% of the total local flow, respectively. The local flow was apportioned to the four regions using the drainage area to each region multiplied by the estimated yield (precipitation per unit area per year) based on historic gauged stream data in each region. Nutrient data (TP, TDP) were interpolated to daily values, and using the daily main and local inflows, the daily nutrient load was estimated and this daily load was summed over the hydrologic year. The hydrologic year was defined to start on 21 November.

Determining the historic nutrient load directly requires nutrient data from before the completion of Mica Dam in 1973, but these data are sparse. Instead, the historic load was esti-mated by working back, using the impoundment retentions and mean 1997–2000 load from the Columbia River at Revelstoke. The data examined suggest a TP retention of 90% for both Kinbasket and Revelstoke Reservoirs and a TDP retention of 50% and 25% for Kinbasket and Revelstoke, respectively. These are comparable to the retentions determined from extensive data collected in 1994–1995 for the nearby Duncan Reservoir of 90% and 52% for TP and TDP, respectively (Perrin and Korman 1997).

Primary Productivity

Primary productivity was determined monthly at AR2 in Upper Arrow Reservoir and at AR7 in Lower Arrow Reservoir from May to September 1998, April to September 1999, and April to October 2000. The April–September rates, as available, were averaged for each year to allow for interannual comparison of production. Primary productivity was measured in situ at depths of 0, 1, 2, 5, 10, and 15 m. Water samples were transferred directly from an opaque Van Dorn bottle to 300-mL acid-clean BOD bottles, using a silicon filling tube. Samples were inoculated with 0.185 MBq (5 μCi) of $NaH^{14}CO_3$ New England Nuclear (NEC-086H) and incubated at the original sampling depths for 4 h, generally between 10:00 a.m. and 2:00 p.m.

The incubations were terminated by filtration onto a 0.2-μm polycarbonate filter using less than 100 mm Hg vacuum differential (Joint and Pomroy 1983) and placed in a scintillation vial. Each vial had 200 μL of 0.5 N HCl added and was left uncapped in the fumehood until the filters were dry (approximately 48 h). To each vial, 5 mL of Ecolite® scintillation cocktail was added and stored in the dark for more than 24 h before the samples were counted for 10 min in a Beckman liquid scintillation counter model #LS 6500 operated in an external standard mode to correct for quenching. Alkalinity was determined using the potentiometric method of APHA (1976) and converted to dissolved inorganic carbon for use in primary productivity calculations.

Primary productivity was determined from the amount of ^{14}C incorporated into particulate organic carbon retained on a filter (Steemann-Nielsen 1952) and was calculated according to Parsons et al. (1984). Solar radiation was collected from April to November using a Kipp and Zonen CM5 and a Rimco SP440 pyranometer in Upper and Lower Arrow, respectively, and was used to convert hourly to seasonally averaged, daily productivity rates.

Phytoplankton

A depth-integrated (0–20 m) sample from each of the eight monitoring stations (AR1–8; Figure 3) were obtained monthly from May to October in 1997 and monthly from April to October with two samples in June and August for 1998–2000. Samples for phytoplankton identification were fixed with acidic Lugol's iodine preservative (Parsons et al. 1984). The samples were stored in the dark until identification and enumeration were performed using inverted microscopy following Utermöhl (1958) procedures.

Zooplankton

Macrozooplankton (length >150 μm) were sampled monthly from May to October 1997 and April to October 1998–2000, using a flume-calibrated Clarke-Bumpus sampler (153-μm mesh), which was hauled obliquely at approximately 1 m/s from 40 to 0 m at each of six stations (AR1–3, 6–8) during the day. Tow duration was 3 min, with approximately 2,500 L of water filtered per tow. Samples were preserved in 70% ethanol. Zooplankton samples were analyzed for species density and biomass, as described in Pieters et al. (1998–2001) or Ashley et al. (1997, 1999a, 1999b).

Mysids

Mysids *M. relicta* were sampled monthly from May to December 1997, January to December 1998–2000. Sampling was done at night, around the time of the new moon, to decrease the chance that mysids would see and avoid the net. Three vertical hauls were done at each of six stations (AR1–3, 6–8), with the boat stationary, using a 1 m² square-mouthed net with a 1,000-μm primary mesh net, 210-μm terminal, and 100-μm bucket. The net was raised from the lake bottom with a hydraulic winch at 0.3 m/s. Samples were preserved in 95% ethanol and analyzed for density and biomass, as described in Pieters et al. (1998–2001) or Ashley et al. (1997, 1999a, 1999b).

Kokanee Salmon Escapements

Kokanee escapements to some Arrow Reservoir tributaries have been estimated periodically since 1966 and annually since 1988 (Sebastian et al. 2000). The kokanee salmon run generally occurs between late August and late September, with the peak of spawning usually occurring in the third week of September.

Adult kokanee returning to spawn in the Hill Creek and Bridge Creek spawning channels are enumerated annually using permanent fish fences (Andrusak 1999). Kokanee salmon at both channels are subsampled at the lower channel fence site for length, sex ratio, and fecundity. Fish downstream of the Hill Creek spawning channel were estimated by ground counts. Up to sixteen additional tributaries to Upper Arrow and ten to Lower Arrow had spawner returns estimated, to approximate a peak spawner count (Sebastian et al. 2000). Estimates were made from helicopter or on foot, due to canopy cover. Flight counts were periodically ground truthed by walking short sections of the larger streams. The index streams represent the vast majority of the total stream-spawning habitat available.

Results

Water Flow and Level

Besides trapping nutrients upstream, the dams have also had a large impact on both inflow and water level (Figure 6). The average annual inflow to the Arrow Lakes Reservoir is 1,080 m³/s, of which 69% passes through the Revelstoke Dam. Before impoundment, the inflow at Revelstoke was a single peak dominated by snowmelt in spring to early summer and sustained by glacial melt in late summer to early fall. After impoundment, the main inflow is more uniform with two broad peaks, the first from the tail of the freshet after upstream reservoirs fill in summer and the second from release of water for power generation in winter (Figure 6b).

As a result of impoundment, the mean water level of the Arrow Lakes rose by 12.6 m, and mean water level variation doubled from 8 to 15.5 m with peak variations of 20 m (Figure 6c). Before impoundment, water levels remained near the low water level through the year with a brief peak in spring. In contrast, after impoundment, water levels remain near the high-water level with a drop in water level during late winter–early spring. Before impoundment, water covered a partially vegetated flood zone in the spring; now, winter release exposes a large and unvegetated drawdown zone in late winter to early spring (Figure 6d).

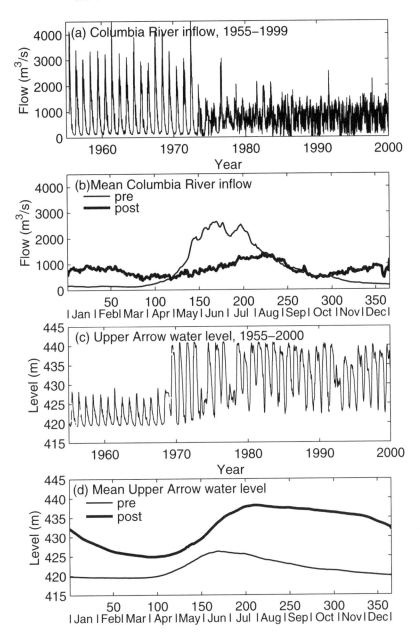

FIGURE 6. (a) Columbia River inflow from 1955 to 2000 showing the change in hydrograph on completion of the Mica Dam in 1973. (b) Mean pre- (light line, 1955–1964) and post-impoundment (heavy line, 1986–1994) inflow. (c) Water level of Upper Arrow at Nakusp from 1955 to 2000. Note the increase in water level variation on filling of the Keenleyside Dam in 1969. (d) Mean pre- (light line, 1930–1965) and post-impoundment (heavy line, 1970–1994) water level.

Weather and Hydrological Conditions

The global climate during the study period was dominated by ENSO (El Niño/Southern Oscillation) events, with an exceptionally strong El Niño in 1997–1998 followed by La Niña in 1998–1999. In 1997, flows were high (local flow 25% above average) in contrast to 1998, when flows were low (local flow 20% below average). Unlike the extremes of 1997 and 1998, in 1999 and 2000, the

mean annual local flows were moderate, being
10% and 1% above average, respectively. In addition to low flow, spring and summer in 1998
were characterized by above average sunlight, air,
and water temperatures (surface water temperatures were 23–26°C in the Upper Arrow in July
1998 in contrast to the usual 16–20°C).

Water Quality

Selected water quality parameters for the reservoir are summarized in Table 1 for the two
prefertilization (1997, 1998) and two postfertilization (1999, 2000) years. Mean Secchi depths
were less than 7 m, and mean chlorophyll a values were less than or equal to 2.2 µg/L, consistent with the oligotrophic character of the reservoir with no significant change after fertilization. Nitrogen levels were high with nitrate averaging 145 µg/L. Ammonia (NH_3), the form of
nitrogen preferred by phytoplankton, was low
and near the detection limit (5 µg/L), as would
be expected. In contrast to nitrogen, phosphorus levels were low, and the N:P ratio ($NO_2 + NO_3$
+ NH_3:TDP) was 60:1 (wt:wt), clearly indicating
phosphorus limitation of organic production. Orthophosphate (OP) was at or near the detection
limit. Note that all samples, including surface
samples immediately downstream of the fertilization zone, were at or below the detection limit
of OP (1 µg/L) during fertilization. Consequently,
fertilization has not resulted in a detectable
change in water quality with the measures used.
As would be expected in an oligotrophic system,
all of the added phosphorus is immediately utilized (Stockner and MacIsaac 1996).

As observed in the reservoir, annual average
ammonia in all river and stream inputs was at or
near detection level (5 µg/L). Mean nitrate over
the study period ranged from 2 to 400 µg/L for
the various rivers and streams. Again, as observed
in the reservoir, rivers and streams had orthophosphate (OP) levels near the detection limit
(1 µg/L). Values of total dissolved phosphorus
(TDP) were low, with means over the study period ranging from 1 to 22 µg/L in the different
streams, compared with a mean of 2.6 µg/L in
the reservoir. As in the reservoir, TDP concentrations were highest in 1997. Total phosphorus (TP)
in the streams was relatively high and variable
as a result of a large particulate fraction, in contrast to the reservoir where TP was relatively low
and uniform as a result of particle settling. The
high nitrogen/low phosphorus loading is consistent with the phosphorus-limited nutrient ratios
observed in the reservoir.

Nutrient Load

Traditionally, work on the trophic status of lakes
(e.g., Vollenweider 1976) has been done using total phosphorus (TP) in order to include the phosphorus sequestered in cell biomass (Wetzel 1983).
However, in the Arrow Lakes Reservoir, the large
particulate load contributes to a large and variable TP load, most of which is likely of low biological availability (e.g., in the form of glacial flour,
such as apatite) and most of which settles on entering the reservoir. The mean TP load is 1,100 mg/
m² per year, whereas the historic load was estimated to be 4,000 mg/m² per year. While little can
be said of the trophic status based on this TP load
because of the large inorganic particulate component, a fraction of the historic TP load was biologically available and would have contributed to
the productivity of the old Arrow lakes.

The load of total dissolved phosphorus
(TDP) varied considerably between years, with
changes in stream flow volume and concentration. TDP load was highest in 1997, lowest in

TABLE 1. Mean value for all (both integrated surface and deep) water samples from Arrow Lakes Reservoir
for calendar years, 1997–2000. Included are the detection limit for the method of analysis and the average
standard deviation for the annual means. Nutrient values are in µg/L of N or P, chlorophyll a is in µg/L, and
Secchi depth is in m.

Year	Nitrogen		Phosphorus			Chl a	Secchi
	NH_3	$NO_2 + NO_3$	OP	TDP	TP		
1997	5.7	143	1.2	3.2	4.8	2.2	7.1
1998	5.4	147	1.1	2.3	3.2	1.4	9.8
1999	5.8	146	1.0	2.4	4.1	1.4	8.7
2000	6.6	144	1.0	2.5	4.3	1.6	7.8
Detection limit	5.0	2	1.0	2.0	2.0	–	–
Average SD of annual means	±2.9	±23	±0.2	±0.9	±2.1	±1.3	±3.1

1998, and intermediate in 1999 and 2000 (Figure 7). The estimated historic mean load of TDP was 400 mg/m² per year, indicating that current TDP loads to Arrow are reduced to about two-thirds of historic values. The fertilizer increased the total loading in 1999 and 2000 by approximately 40%. Care must be taken in comparing TDP to fertilizer loadings, as the fertilizer consists of phosphorus in a highly biologically available form while the bioavailability of the natural TDP load is lower.

Primary Productivity

Primary productivity in Upper Arrow increased 1.5-fold, from 131 mg C·m⁻² per day in the unfertilized year (1998) to 192 and 201 mg C·m⁻² per day in the fertilized years, 1999 and 2000, respectively (Figure 8). In contrast to the increases measured in Upper Arrow, the primary production in Lower Arrow decreased from 131 mg C·m⁻² per day in 1998 to 115 and 102 mg C·m⁻² per day in

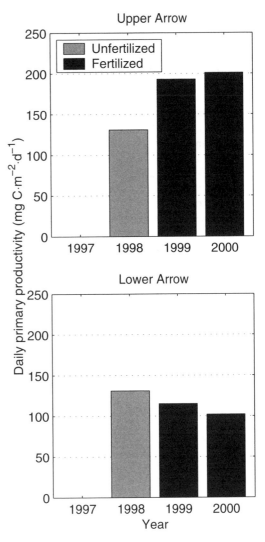

Figure 8. Seasonally-averaged daily primary productivity (mg C·m⁻² per day) in the Upper and Lower Arrow Reservoir from 1998 to 2000. No data collected in 1997.

1999 and 2000, respectively. During the two years of fertilization, primary productivity measured in Upper Arrow was, on average, 1.8-fold greater than that measured in Lower Arrow, likely due in part to the effects of fertilization.

Phytoplankton

Phytoplankton enumeration in the postfertilization years 1999 and 2000 confirm the 1998 and 1997 observations of a community made up

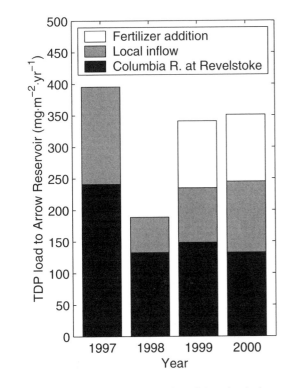

Figure 7. Estimated load of total dissolved phosphorus (TDP) to the entire Arrow Lakes Reservoir (498 km²) from the Columbia River at Revelstoke, the local inflow and from fertilizer addition.

of small species typical of an oligotrophic lake and of a community with very low mean abundance and biomass lacking clear spring and fall blooms. These characteristics provide a clear signal of the oligotrophic status of Arrow Lakes Reservoir. The mean phytoplankton abundance for the Arrow Lakes Reservoir was 5,700, 4,000, 4,800, and 5,000 cells per milliliter in 1997–2000, respectively. The mean biovolume was 0.46, 0.31, 0.29, and 0.46 mm^3/L in 1997–2000, respectively. Note that the abundance and biovolume in the second treated year (2000) remain comparable to that of the first control year (1997).

While no unusual changes in species composition were observed, changes in relative community composition and seasonal succession were noted in the fertilized years. In 1999, abundance peaks were higher than in the previous two years, especially at Station AR1, where high densities of the picoplankter *Synechococcus* spp. were observed. In 2000, the increases in picoplankters were not as apparent; instead, increased densities of microflagellates were observed (two-fold increase in abundance in fall) together with very large populations of colonial diatoms in late summer to late autumn (>6-fold increase in abundance at AR1–3 in September and October 2000).

Zooplankton

During each successive year of the study period, the total zooplankton biomass increased in both Upper and Lower Arrow with the exception of Upper Arrow in 2000 (Figure 9). During all sampling years, Lower Arrow had higher zooplankton biomass than Upper Arrow. During fertilized years, zooplankton biomass increased more in Lower Arrow than Upper Arrow. The zooplankter *Daphnia* spp. is the preferred food of both kokanee and mysids (Thompson 1999), and biomass of *Daphnia* spp. as well as the proportion of total biomass that is composed of *Daphnia* spp. increased in each successive year, to 1999. In 2000, a change was noted; while the total zooplankton biomass in Lower Arrow continued to increase and the proportion of *Daphnia* spp. to total zooplankton biomass remained constant, in Upper Arrow, *Daphnia* spp. biomass declined. It is likely that, in 2000, *Daphnia* spp. biomass was extensively cropped by increased mysid and kokanee populations.

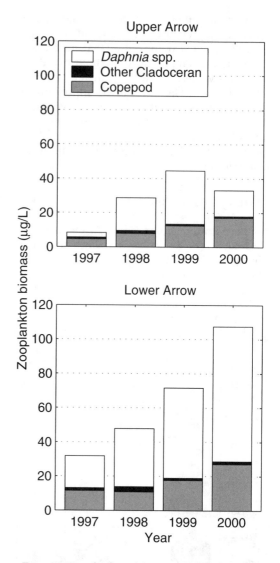

FIGURE 9. Zooplankton biomass (μg/L) in the Upper and Lower Arrow from 1997 to 2000. Values are total annual average biomass of samples collected from May to October 1997 and April to October 1998–2000.

Mysids

Mysis relicta population density increased progressively from 1997 to 2000 in both the Upper and Lower Arrow (Figure 10). In Upper Arrow, the annual average density increased six-fold from 32 individuals/m^2 in 1997 to 195 individuals/m^2 in 2000. Over the same period, density in Lower Arrow increased 3.5-fold from 63 individuals/m^2 to 223 individuals/m^2. The annual average mysid density was consistently higher in Lower Arrow

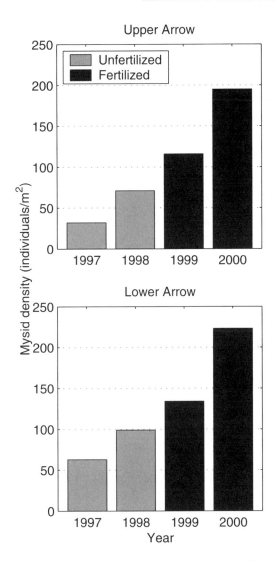

FIGURE 10. Mysid *Mysis relicta* density (individuals/m²) in the Upper and Lower Arrow Lakes Reservoir from 1997 to 2000. Values are annual averages of deepwater samples collected from May to December 1997 and January to December 1998–2000.

than in Upper Arrow during all sampling years (based on data from deep stations from January to December, except for 1997 when sampling began in May). The mean mysid weight was approximately 4.5 mg/individual, similar in both basins and for all years.

Kokanee

Since the late 1980s, kokanee numbers had been steadily decreasing through their 4-year cycles

(Figure 11). Even the modest increase in total numbers in 1998 represents a decline from its parent cycle in 1994. The recruit:spawner ratio for the Hill Creek and Bridge Creek spawning channels portrays the decline for 1992–1998, with values less than the replacement ratio of 1.0 (Figure 12).

Kokanee data suggest that a change occurred in the kokanee population after fertilization was initiated in 1999, with higher escapements, increased size at maturity, increased fecundity, and a recruit:spawner ratio of greater than one. Escapements for Upper Arrow index streams had trended downward through the 1990s to a record low of 47,000 in 1996. Upper Arrow escapements in 1999 and 2000 were 147,000 and 193,000, respectively (Figure 11). At the same time, the size of mature fish at the Hill Creek and Bridge Creek spawning channels, in 1999 and 2000, increased considerably compared with mean size in the 1990s (Figure 13). Mean sizes in 1999 and 2000 were the largest for the years on record for both channels. Fecundity recorded at the spawning channels also increased in 1999 and 2000. Compared with means that have usually been less than 300 eggs per female, the fecundity levels in 1999 and 2000 were among the largest on record (Hill Creek, 394 and 469 eggs/female in 1999 and 2000, respectively).

Arrow Reservoir kokanee return to spawn predominantly at age 4 (Sebastian et al. 2000). Based on otolith readings, the age of kokanee spawners at Hill Creek in 1999 was determined to be primarily 4 years. However, in 2000, a significant shift in age of Hill Creek spawners occurred, in which 52% of the spawners returned as age-3 fish. This shift is also reflected in the size-frequency data with two modes evident rather than one (Pieters et al. 2000, 2001). Because of the change in age at maturity in 2000, and to provide an estimate of the recruit:spawner ratio for 2000, it was assumed that all age-4 fish and 50% of age-3 fish contributed to the spawner numbers in 2000. In 1999 and again in 2000, the recruit:spawner ratios at Hill Creek and Bridge Creek were greater than one for the first time since 1992. While analysis of further data is ongoing, the substantial shift in the recruit:spawner ratio suggests a change in the kokanee population structure has occurred.

Discussion

Apart from a modest record of kokanee data, very little was known about the Arrow Lakes Reservoir

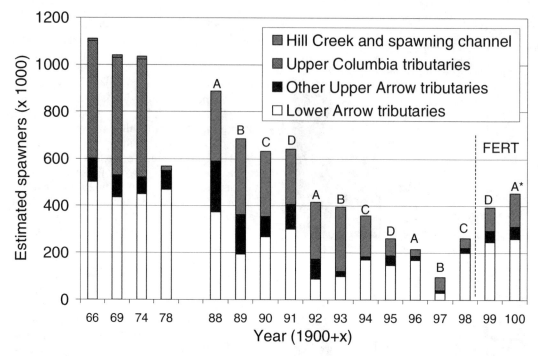

FIGURE 11. Kokanee spawner escapement for the Upper and Lower Arrow Reservoir, 1966–2000. As returning spawners are predominantly 4 years old, the year cycles are labeled A, B, C, or D for 1988–2000. In 2000 (*), returns include spawners of 3 years of age; see text. Number of spawners shown for the Lower Arrow in 1993 and 1994 are estimated. The Upper Columbia tributaries were above the Revelstoke Dam accessible before 1983. The Hill Creek spawning channel was completed in 1980 and was designed to replace the spawning habitat above the Revelstoke Dam.

prior to the present study. This lack of information is somewhat surprising in relation to its size and local importance, but not that unusual in comparison to the many other large lake/reservoir systems throughout the interior of British Columbia. Two years of baseline monitoring were completed in 1997 and 1998, and a 5-year fertilization experiment to replace limiting nutrients trapped upstream began in 1999, with preliminary results for 1999 and 2000 reported here. To many, the term 'fertilization' connotes high levels of nutrient additions, as in a fishpond where water quality is sacrificed for productivity. In contrast, the goal of the nutrient additions to the Arrow Lakes Reservoir has not been enhancement, but the maintenance of natural kokanee populations to avoid either their extinction or population decline to a level no longer genetically viable. Unlike the dangers associated with most exotic species introductions, experience with the relatively light addition of nutrients to coastal lakes indicates that the effects of fertilization are reversible (Stockner and MacIsaac 1996).

In Arrow Lakes Reservoir, observations from all trophic levels in both the pre- and post-treatment years are consistent with a system experiencing low levels of productivity. This is supported by the reservoir water chemistry and nutrient loading data, which shows a very high N:P ratio and phosphorus limitation. The phosphorus load from river and stream inflows has varied significantly between years, but the trapping of nutrients behind upstream dams has reduced TP to approximately one-quarter and TDP to approximately two-thirds of historic levels, based on an estimate of historic pre-impoundment nutrient loads.

In 1999 and 2000, the system was treated with a seasonally adjusted load of phosphorus and nitrogen at a high N:P ratio to prevent blooms of nitrogen-fixing blue-green algae. During fertilized years, levels of orthophosphate in the lake remained at or below detection limits, even at the station just below the fertilization zone. No obvious changes in TP, TDP, or other water quality parameters were apparent during fertilization.

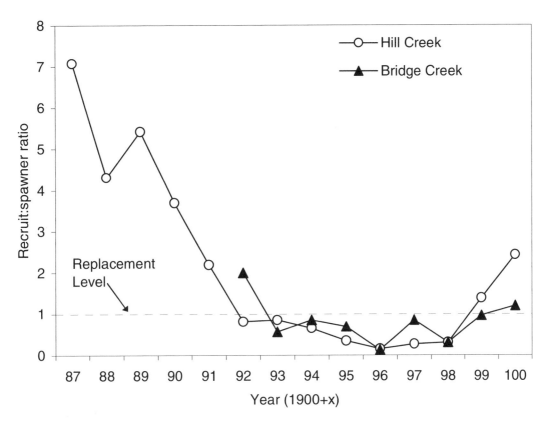

FIGURE 12. The kokanee recruit:spawner ratio, 1987–2000, for Hill Creek and Bridge Creek. The recruit:spawner ratio of, for example, 1997 is the number of spawners that returned in 1997 divided by the number of spawners that returned in 1993. This assumes that all spawners were aged 4. For computation of the 2000 ratio, see text. Replacement occurs when the ratio is above one.

Unlike abundance and biomass at a given trophic level, primary productivity provides a direct measure of the rate of production and is an important key to monitoring the effect of nutrient additions (Stockner and MacIsaac 1996). Primary productivity in Upper Arrow showed an increase in the fertilized years of 1.5-fold over that in 1998. In contrast, Lower Arrow productivity was reduced in 1999 and 2000 compared to that in 1998. If Lower Arrow were considered a control, then the change in the Upper Arrow primary productivity is likely due to the nutrient additions. Note, however, that primary productivity was not measured in 1997 and that the single untreated year, 1998, was characterized by warm surface waters, low flow, and a low load of natural nutrients.

While no unusual changes in phytoplankton species composition were observed, changes in the relative community composition and seasonal succession were noted in the fertilized years, changes that suggest the system was shifting from ultra-oligotrophic to oligotrophic conditions. In 1999, increased abundance peaks and high densities of the picoplankter *Synechococcus* spp. were observed, especially at the northernmost station (AR1). Though this minute picoplankter did not contribute substantially to phytoplankton biomass, it is a vital base for the microbial food webs that dominate the plankton communities and is a strong indicator of the oligotrophic condition of the reservoir. Blooms of *Synechococcus* spp. have been observed in almost all whole-lake fertilization experiments conducted in both coastal and interior regions of British Columbia (Stockner 1987; Stockner and MacIsaac 1996). In 2000, the increases in picoplankters were not as conspicuous; instead, increased densities of microflagellates were observed along with very large, late summer to late autumn populations of diatoms. A response in diatoms of this size has not been observed be-

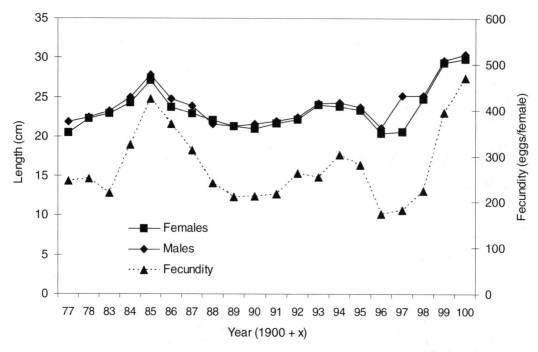

Figure 13. Mean length (cm) and fecundity (eggs/female) of Hill Creek kokanee spawners, 1977–2000.

fore in fertilized coastal or interior subalpine lakes (Stockner and MacIsaac 1996; Stockner and Shortreed 1994). The presence of more diatoms in the pelagic zone of Arrow Reservoir should be viewed as a positive sign, indicating that the system is likely increasing its trophic efficiency and forage production through shorter food chains (Stockner and Porter 1988).

Beside increases in primary productivity and changes in the seasonal succession of phytoplankton, increases have also been observed both in total zooplankton biomass, particularly that of *Daphnia* spp., and in mysid density. Early modeling work on Kootenay Lake indicated that mysids may out-compete kokanee for preferred food sources such as *Daphnia* spp. (Walters et al. 1991). While mysid populations appear relatively stable in Kootenay Lake (Ashley et al. 1997, 1999b) this potential problem in Arrow Reservoir will continue to be monitored.

As kokanee numbers in the Arrow Reservoir declined through the 1990s, their size and fecundity showed little change with no density-dependent response, strongly suggesting a productivity problem. During fertilization in 1999 and 2000, the large size at maturity of kokanee further suggested that a density dependent growth response has yet to occur. A decrease in size

would be expected once the lake's carrying capacity has been reached, and this will likely occur in Arrow, similar to the response of kokanee salmon in the North Arm of Kootenay Lake (Andrusak 2000).

The 5-year experimental fertilization of Arrow Reservoir (1999–2003) is well underway and full evaluation is pending completion. Results collected during 1999 and 2000 suggest that Arrow Reservoir is responding favorably to nutrient additions with more efficient carbon (energy) flows within the pelagic community. The documented increase in kokanee size, numbers, and the improvement in the recruit:spawner ratio from values below to above replacement levels are particularly encouraging.

Acknowledgments

Funding was provided by the Columbia Basin Fish and Wildlife Compensation Program (CBFWCP), with additional funding from the Columbia Power Corporation, the B.C. Ministry of Fisheries, the B.C. Ministry of Water, Land and Air Protection (MWLAP), the National Sciences and Engineering Research Council of Canada, and the University of British Columbia (UBC).

This work was initiated by Jay Hammond (Fisheries Section Head, Nelson, MWLAP) and Ken Ashley (B.C. Ministry of Fisheries). The authors acknowledge that none of this project would have been possible without the tireless work of Mark Young, Don Miller, Adam Croxall, and Gary Monroe (Kootenay Wildlife Service); Grant Thorpe, Diana Koller, Bob Millar, Les Fleck, John Bell and Melvin Wong (MWLAP); Karen Bray, Harold Manson, Steve Arndt (CBFWCP). We also acknowledge the help of Gary Birch, Don Druce, Kelvin Ketchum, Dan Nixon, Ric Olmsted, Brian Gadbois, Dean de Biesen, Chris Madland (B.C. Hydro); the town of Nakusp; and Sabine and Ulf Burmeister (Kokanee Bay Resort). We are grateful for laboratory equipment made available by Paul Harrison (UBC) and for field equipment made available by Douw Steyn and Tim Oke (UBC). We thank the many UBC student volunteers who have helped with the productivity sampling, and thanks to M. Derham, C. Sewell, A. Eskooch, and L. Zaremba for their help in data processing. We also gratefully acknowledge discussions with Dale Sebastian and George Scholten. We thank the reviewers for their helpful suggestions.

References

APHA (American Public Health Association), 1976. Standard methods for the examination of water and wastewater. 14th editor. American Public Health Association, American Water Works Association, and Water Pollution Control Federation, Washington, D.C.

Andrusak, H. 1999. Performance evaluation of six kokanee spawning channels in British Columbia. Report for Ministry of Fisheries, Province of British Columbia, Victoria, B.C.

Andrusak, H. 2000. Response of North Arm Kootenay Lake kokanee in 1999 to experimental fertilization. Prepared for Columbia Basin Fish and Wildlife Compensation Program, Nelson, B.C.

Ashley, K., L. C. Thompson, D. C. Lasenby, L. McEachern, K. E. Smokorowski, and D. Sebastian. 1997. Restoration of an interior lake ecosystem: the Kootenay Lake fertilization experiment. Water Quality Research Journal of Canada 32:295–323.

Ashley K., L. C. Thompson, D. Lombard, Y.-R. Yang, F. R. Pick, P. B. Hamilton, D. C. Lasenby, K. E. Smokorowski, D. Sebastian, and G. Scholten. 1999a. Kootenay Lake fertilization experiment–year 5 (1996/97) report. RD 65, Fisheries Branch, Ministry of Environment, Lands and Parks, Province of British Columbia.

Ashley, K., L. C. Thompson, D. Sebastian, D. C. Lasenby, K. E. Smokorowski, and H. Andrusak. 1999b. Restoration of kokanee salmon in Kootenay Lake, a large intermontane lake, by controlled seasonal application of limiting nutrients. Pages 127–169 in T Murphy and M. Munawar, editors. Aquatic restoration in Canada. Backhuys, Leiden, Netherlands.

Cederholm, C. J., D. H. Johnson, R. E Bilby, L. G. Domiguez, A. M. Garette, W. H. Graeber, E. L. Graeber, E. L. Greda, M. D. Kunze, B. G. Marcot, J. F. Palmisano, R. W. Plotnikoff, W. G. Pearcy, C. A Simenstad, and P. C. Trotter. 2000. Pacific salmon and wildlife–ecological contexts, relationships, and implications for management. Special Edition Technical Report. Prepared for D. H. Johnson and T. A O'Neil (managing directors), Wildlife-Habitat Relationships in Oregon and Washington. Washington Department of Fish and Wildlife, Olympia, Washington.

Horne, A. J., and C. R. Goldman, 1994. Limnology, 2nd edition. McGraw-Hill, New York.

Joint, I. R., and A. J. Pomroy. 1983. Production of picoplankton and small nanoplankton in the Celtic Sea. Marine Biology 77(1):19–27.

Milbrink, G., and S. Holmgren. 1981. Addition of artificial fertilizers as a means of reducing negative effects of "oligotrophication" in lakes after impoundment. Report 59, Swedish Board of Fisheries, Institute of Freshwater Research, Drottningholm.

Ney, J. 1996. Oligotrophication and its discontents: effects of reduced nutrient loading on reservoir fisheries. Pages 285–295 in L. E. Miranda and D. R. DeVries, editors. American Fisheries Society, Symposium 16, Bethesda, Maryland.

Lasenby, D. C., T. G. Northcote, and M. Furst. 1986. Theory, practice and effects of *Mysis relicta* introductions to North American and Swedish lakes. Canadian Journal of Fisheries and Aquatic Sciences 43:1277–1284.

Parsons, T. K., Y. Maita, and C. M. Lalli. 1984. A manual of chemical and biological methods for seawater analysis. Pergamon, New York.

Perrin, C. J., and J. Korman. 1997. A phosphorus budget and limnological descriptions of Duncan Lake Reservoir, 1994–1995. Prepared by Limnotek for B.C. Hydro, Kootenay Generation Area, Castlegar, B.C.

Pieters, R., L. C. Thompson, L. Vidmanic, S. Pond, J. Stockner, P. Hamblin, M. Young, K. Ashley, B. Lindsay, G. Lawrence, D. Sebastian, G. Scholten, and D. L. Lombard. 1998. Arrow Reservoir limnology and trophic status, year 1 (1997/98) report. RD 67, Fisheries Branch, Ministry of Environment, Lands and Parks, Province of British Columbia.

Pieters, R., L. C. Thompson, L. Vidmanic, M. Roushorne, J. Stockner, K. Hall, M. Young, S. Pond, M. Derham, K. Ashley, B. Lindsay, G.

Lawrence, D. Sebastian, G. Scholten, F. Mc-Laughlin, A. Wüest, A. Matzinger, and E. Carmack. 1999. Arrow Reservoir limnology and trophic status, year 2 (1998/99) report. RD 72, Fisheries Branch, Ministry of Environment, Lands and Parks, Province of British Columbia.

Pieters, R., L. C. Thompson, L. Vidmanic, M. Roushorne, J. Stockner, K. Hall, M. Young, M. Derham, S. Pond, K. Ashley, B. Lindsay, G. Lawrence, H. Andrusak, D. Sebastian, and G. Scholten. 2000. Arrow Reservoir fertilization experiment, year 1 (1999/2000) report. RD 82, Fisheries Branch, Ministry of Environment, Lands and Parks, Province of British Columbia.

Pieters, R., L. C. Thompson, L. Vidmanic, S. Harris, J. Stockner, H. Andrusak, M. Young, K. Ashley, B. Lindsay, G. Lawrence, K. Hall, A. Eskooch, D. Sebastian and G. Scholten. 2001. Arrow Reservoir fertilization experiment, year 2 (2000/2001) report. RD 87, Fisheries Branch, Ministry of Environment, Lands and Parks, Province of British Columbia.

Schindler, D. W. 1974. Eutrophication and recovery in experimental lakes: implications for lake management. Science 184:897–899.

Sebastian, D., H. Andrusak, G. Scholten, and L. Brescia. 2000. Arrow Reservoir fish summary. Stock Management Report 2000, Fisheries Management Branch, Ministry of Fisheries, Province of British Columbia, Victoria, B.C.

Smith, V. H. 1983. Low nitrogen to phosphorus ratios favour dominance by blue-green algae in lake phytoplankton. Science 221:669–671.

Steemann-Nielsen, E. 1952. The use of radioactive carbon (^{14}C) for measuring organic production in the sea. Journal du Conseil Permanent International Pour L' Exploration de la Mer 18:117–140.

Stockner, J. G. 1987. Lake fertilization: the enrichment cycle and lake sockeye salmon (*Oncorhynchus nerka*) production. Pages 198–215 *in* H. D. Smith, L. Margolis and C. C. Woods, editors. Sockeye salmon (*Oncorhynchus nerka*) population biology and future management. Canadian Special Publication of Fisheries and Aquatic Sciences 96.

Stockner, J. G., and K. G. Porter. 1988. Microbial food webs in fresh-water planktonic ecosystems. Pages 69–83 *in* S. R. Carpenter, editor. Complex interactions in lake communities. Springer-Verlag, New York.

Stockner, J. G., and K. S. Shortreed. 1994. Picoplankton population dynamics in Chilko Lake, a pre-alpine lake in British Columbia. Canada Hydrobiologia 274:133–142.

Stockner, J. G., and E. A. MacIsaac. 1996. British Columbia lake enrichment program: two decades of habitat enhancement for sockeye salmon. Regulated Rivers: Research and Management 12:547–561.

Stockner, J. G., E. Rydin, and P. Hyenstrand. 2000. Cultural oligotrophication: causes and consequences for fisheries resources. Fisheries 25:7–14.

Thompson, L. C. 1999. Abundance and production of zooplankton and kokanee salmon (*Oncorhynchus nerka*) in Kootenay Lake, British Columbia, during artificial fertilization. Doctoral dissertation. University of British Columbia, Vancouver.

Utermöhl, H. 1958. Zur vervollkommnung der quantitativen phytoplankton methodik. Internationale Vereinigung Fur Theoretische Und Angewandte Limnologie, Mitteilungen 9:1–39.

Vallentyne, J. R. 1974. The algal bowl: lakes and man. Miscellaneous Special Publication 22, Department of the Environment, Fisheries and Marine Service, Ottawa, Canada.

Vollenweider, R. A. 1976. Advances in defining critical loading levels of phosphorus in lake eutrophication. Memorie dell'Istituto italiano di idrobiologia dott Marco De Marchi 33:53–83.

Walters, C. J., J. Digisi, J. Post, and J. Sawada. 1991. Kootenay Lake fertilization response model. Fisheries Management Report No. 98, Ministry of Environment, Province of British Columbia.

Wetzel, R. G.1983. Limnology. 2nd edition. Harcourt Brace, Fort Worth, Texas.

American Fisheries Society Symposium 34:197–211, 2003

Redfish Lake Sockeye Salmon: Nutrient Supplementation as a Means of Restoration

ROBERT G. GRISWOLD

Biolines Environmental Consulting, HC-64 Box 9965, Stanley, Idaho 83278, USA

DOUG TAKI

Shoshone-Bannock Tribes, Fisheries Department, P.O. Box 306, Fort Hall, Idaho 83203, USA

JOHN G. STOCKNER

Eco-Logic Ltd., 2614 Mathers Avenue, West Vancouver, B.C. V7V 2J4, Canada

Abstract.—Snake River sockeye salmon *Oncorhynchus nerka* once inhabited five pre-alpine lakes in the Sawtooth Valley, Idaho, but are presently reduced to the Redfish Lake stock. Declining returns to Redfish Lake in the 1980s prompted the National Marine Fisheries Service to list Snake River sockeye salmon as endangered under the Endangered Species Act, and a multi-agency effort was initiated in 1991 to prevent their extinction. The recovery effort focused on the development of a captive broodstock coupled with evaluation and enhancement of nursery lake habitats. Large populations of nonendemic kokanee salmon *O. nerka* and the oligotrophic conditions of these lakes raised concerns about overstocking sockeye salmon and causing the collapse of macrozooplankton populations. To minimize these risks and to improve sockeye salmon forage production, the Shoshone-Bannock Tribes initiated a 4-year nutrient enrichment program in Redfish Lake. Liquid fertilizer (20:1, N:P by wt) was added weekly during the growing season from 1995 to 1998 to the surface of Redfish Lake with Stanley Lake (unfertilized) acting as a control. During the fertilization of Redfish Lake, Secchi depth decreased by 13% and compensation depth by 24%, while increases were observed for surface chlorophyll *a* (106%) and primary production (117%). Uniformity of phytoplankton communities throughout the experiment indicated that the Redfish Lake food web was efficient (without major carbon sinks) and improved forage conditions for macrozooplankton. Total macrozooplankton biomass increased 31%, and *Daphnia* spp. biomass increased by 225%, simultaneous to a 26% increase in *O. nerka* density. Also, during fertilization, overwinter survival of supplemented sockeye salmon increased 192% in Redfish Lake. However, meteorological conditions were partly responsible for these changes. In unfertilized Stanley Lake, during the same time periods, Secchi depth declined 27%, and compensation depth was reduced by 28%; chlorophyll *a* increased 16%, primary production increased 14%, and zooplankton biomass was stable. These changes highlight the importance of climate (meteorological forcing) and the need for a control when attempting to identify impacts from lake fertilization. Disproportionately larger increases in Redfish Lake chlorophyll *a*, primary productivity, and zooplankton biomass relative to observed changes in Stanley Lake provide evidence for the efficacy of nutrient supplementation in Redfish Lake.

Introduction

For nearly a decade, efforts have been underway to restore Snake River sockeye salmon *Onco-rhynchus nerka* to a portion of their former range. Historically, sockeye salmon returned to several lake systems in the Snake River drainage but are presently reduced to a remnant population in

Redfish Lake, Idaho. Declining adult returns to Redfish Lake prompted the Shoshone-Bannock Tribes to petition the National Marine Fisheries Service to list Snake River sockeye salmon under the U.S. Endangered Species Act. In November 1991, Snake River sockeye salmon were listed as endangered (56 FR 58619; Waples et al. 1991). As a result of the listing, the Sawtooth Valley Project was initiated to conserve and rebuild sockeye salmon populations in Redfish Lake and several other Sawtooth Valley lakes using the Redfish Lake stock. As an emergency measure, the last remaining individuals of this stock were brought into a captive broodstock program to increase population size and preserve genetic diversity (Flagg et al. 1998). Since 1993, progeny from the broodstock program have been released into Redfish Lake each year using a variety of strategies including releases of eyed eggs, presmolts, and prespawning adults. These stocking efforts raised concerns that the carrying capacity of Redfish Lake would be exceeded, resulting in density-dependent impacts on zooplankton size, biomass and species composition (Goodlad et al. 1974), and reductions in sockeye salmon growth and survival (Hyatt and Stockner 1985; Kyle et al. 1988).

To reduce this risk, supplemental nutrients were added during 1995–1998 to Redfish Lake to increase carrying capacity and maintain or improve growth and survival of juvenile sockeye salmon (Stockner 1981; Stockner and MacIsaac 1996). Baseline limnological monitoring of Redfish Lake began in 1992; sockeye salmon from the broodstock program were first stocked into Redfish Lake in 1993, and supplemental nutrients were added during the growing season each year from 1995 to 1998. Stanley Lake was also monitored to identify natural interannual variation of limnological metrics in the Sawtooth Valley during this time but has received no sockeye salmon stocking or nutrient enhancement. The study objectives were to assess the impact of nutrient supplementation on water quality parameters such as Secchi and compensation depths, increase primary production in Redfish Lake, and determine whether enhanced carbon flows (new production) affected rearing *O. nerka* overwinter survival.

Study Area

The Sawtooth Valley lakes are located in south-central Idaho at the headwaters of the Salmon River (latitude 44°, longitude 115°; Figure 1). The lakes are glacially formed and located within the Sawtooth National Recreation Area (SNRA). The majority of their watersheds are federally designated wilderness, administered by the U.S. Forest Service (U.S. Department of Agriculture). The SNRA receives over 1 million visitors per year, primarily summer recreationists. The Sawtooth Valley lakes and Redfish Lake in particular are common destinations and are highly valued for their scenic qualities and clear water.

The Sawtooth Mountains are part of the Idaho batholith, made up of granite-like rock, consisting of granodiorite, quartz diorite, and quartz monzonite (Emmett 1975). Sockeye salmon that return to the Sawtooth Valley from the Pacific Ocean migrate farther than any other sockeye salmon population in the world, a total of 1,445 km, 825 km in the mostly impounded Columbia and Snake rivers and an additional 620 km in the free-flowing Salmon River. Redfish Lake is the only lake that Snake River sockeye salmon have returned to in the past decade, although historically, they returned to three or four other lakes in the Sawtooth Valley. During the 1990s, between zero and eight fish returned each year. The lake is 1996 m above mean sea level, generally ice-covered from January to May, and classified as ultra-oligotrophic (Budy et al. 1998). Redfish Lake has a surface area of 6.15 km², a maximum depth of 91 m, a mean depth of 44 m, and a water residence time of 3 years (Gross et al. 1998). Stanley

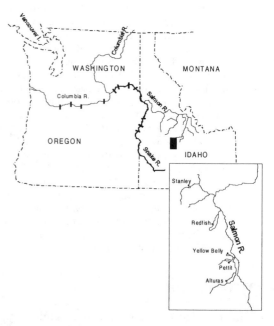

FIGURE 1. Map of study area.

Lake, another subalpine lake located in the Sawtooth Valley, was monitored to identify interannual variation in limnological metrics. Stanley Lake has a surface area of 0.81 km^2, a maximum depth of 26 m, a mean depth of 13 m, and a water residence time of 0.3 years (Gross and Wurtsbaugh 1994). Although not similar in size, Stanley Lake was chosen as a reference, since other candidate lakes in the Sawtooth Valley were receiving supplemental nutrients and being stocked with Redfish Lake stocks of sockeye salmon.

Three distinct forms of *O. nerka* reside in Redfish Lake: anadromous sockeye salmon, residual sockeye salmon, and kokanee salmon. The anadromous form of *O. nerka* spends one or two years in freshwater, emigrates in May, and typically resides in the Pacific Ocean for two years before returning to spawn during October on the shores of Redfish Lake. Residual sockeye salmon are genetically similar to the anadromous form but remain in the lake for their entire life cycle; these fish also spawn on lake shoals during October. Redfish Lake anadromous sockeye salmon and residual sockeye salmon are designated as ecologically significant units (E.S.U.) and classified as endangered (Waples et al. 1991). Kokanee salmon spend their entire lifecycle in Redfish Lake but spawn during August in Fishhook Creek, a major tributary to Redfish Lake. The Redfish Lake kokanee salmon population is believed to be admixed, based on the relatively large number of dominant haplotypes (Madison Powell, University of Idaho, personal communication) and the numerous known stockings of kokanee salmon from out-of-basin stocks (Winans et al. 1996). Kokanee salmon are not listed under the endangered species act. In this discussion, the collective term *O. nerka* is used when kokanee salmon and sockeye salmon cannot be distinguished.

Stanley Lake was chemically treated with Fish-Tox, a rotenone/toxaphene powder, during the 1950s, and a fish barrier was constructed on the outlet stream (Stacy Gebhards, Idaho Department of Fish and Game, personal communication). As a result of these efforts, native *O. nerka* were extirpated from Stanley Lake. Subsequent plantings of out-of-basin kokanee salmon have since established an early stream-spawning population.

Other native fish species found in the nursery lake system include steelhead/rainbow trout *O. mykiss*, chinook salmon *O. tshawytscha*, westslope cutthroat trout *O. clarki lewisi*, bull trout *Salvelinus confluentus*, mountain whitefish *Prosopium williamsoni*, sucker *Catastomus* spp., redside shiner *Richardsonius balteatus*, dace *Rhinichthys* spp., northern pikeminnow *Ptychocheilus oregonensis*, and sculpin *Cottus* spp. Two nonnative species, brook trout *S. fontinalis* and lake trout *S. namaycush*, are present in Stanley Lake.

Methods

Liquid ammonium phosphate (10–34–0) or (20–5-0) and ammonium nitrate (28–0-0–0) fertilizer was applied weekly to Redfish Lake by Shoshone-Bannock tribal personnel during the 1995–1998 growing seasons. Nutrients were applied at a ratio of approximately 20:1 N:P by weight (45:1 molar) to compensate for a low ambient N:P ratio and to avoid the possibility of enhancing populations of nitrogen-fixing, blue-green algae (Cyanophytes). The quantity of nutrients applied each week was variable, intended to simulate the natural hydrograph. Thus, initial applications were relatively small, rapidly increased to a peak in mid to late July, and then gradually declined until late September. The applications were made from a 6.7 m boat equipped with a portable plastic tank and electric pump. The fertilizer was sprayed into the boat's wake following 20 predetermined transect lines using a global positioning system (GPS), compass, and local landmarks to evenly disperse the nutrients over the surface of the lake. Permission to add supplemental nutrients was obtained in the form of a consent order issued by the Idaho Division of Environmental Quality (DEQ). The consent order required weekly monitoring of Secchi depth and biweekly monitoring of total phosphorus (TP) and chlorophyll *a* concentrations. Nutrient additions were allowed as long as Secchi depths were greater than 8 m, chlorophyll *a* was less than 3 µg/L in the epilimnion and 6 µg/L in the metalimnion, and TP concentrations remained less than 15 µg/L in the epilimnion and metalimnion.

Limnological monitoring was conducted once or twice per month from May through November 1992–1998. Detailed methodologies are available in Budy et al. 1995; Luecke et al. 1996; and Griswold 1997. Water temperature (°C), dissolved oxygen (mg/L), conductivity (µ S/cm), Secchi depth (m), compensation depth (m), nutrient concentrations (µg/L), chlorophyll *a* concentration (µg/L), phytoplankton biovolume (mm³/L), primary productivity (mg C · m⁻² · day⁻¹) and zooplankton density (No./L), and biomass (µg/L) were sampled near the middle of each lake. Additional zooplankton samples were collected from two additional stations in each lake.

Water for nutrient analysis, chlorophyll a, and phytoplankton samples were collected from the epilimnion during stratification. Three discrete samples were collected with a 3-L Van Dorn bottle and mixed in a churn splitter. When lake strata could not be delineated, surface water was collected from 0 to 6 m with a 25 mm diameter, 6 m long lexan tube.

Temperature (°C), dissolved oxygen (mg/L), and conductivity (µ S/cm) profiles were collected at the main station of each lake using a Hydrolab Surveyor3 equipped with a Hydrolab H20 submersible data transmitter. Temperature, dissolved oxygen, and conductivity were recorded at 1-m intervals from the surface to 10 m, 1–2 m intervals from 10 m to the thermocline, then at 2–10 m intervals to the bottom. Secchi depth was measured with a 20-cm Secchi disk, and light attenuation was measured with a LiCor Li-1000 data logger equipped with a Li-190SA quantum sensor deck cell and a Li-193SA spherical sea cell. Photosynthetically active radiation (400–700 nm) was measured at 2-meter intervals from the surface to 2–4 m below the compensation depth (1% light level).

Water was collected for nutrient analysis once or twice per month in January, March, May, June, July, August, September, and October. The University of California Davis, Tahoe Research Group Laboratory and the Limnology Laboratory processed nutrient samples. Both facilities are certified by the U.S. Geological Survey and employ standard QA/QC protocols (APHA 1995). NH_4 was assayed with the indophenol method, NO_3+NO_2 with the hydrazine method, organic nitrogen (TKN) using kjeldahl nitrogen; the calorimetric method was used to determine soluble reactive phosphorus (SRP), and TP was assayed by persulfate digestion (APHA 1995). Total nitrogen (TN) concentrations were estimated by adding TKN and NO_3+NO_2.

Chlorophyll a samples were stored at 4°C in the field and then filtered onto 0.45-µm cellulose acetate membrane filters with 130 mm Hg vacuum pressure. Filters were placed in centrifuge tubes and frozen (-25°C). The filters were then placed in methanol for 12–24 h to extract the chlorophyll pigments. Chlorophyll a concentrations

were measured with a Turner model 10-AU fluorometer calibrated with chlorophyll standards. Samples were run before and after acidification to correct for phaeophytin (Holm-Hansen and Rieman 1978).

Phytoplankton samples were fixed in Lugol's iodine solution and total cell abundance and biovolume determined at 1,560 × magnification using a Zeiss Inverted Plankton microscope, following the protocol of Utermohl (1958). Detailed phytoplankton counts began in 1995, the first year that Redfish Lake received nutrient supplementation, which limits our ability to make quantitative comparisons of phytoplankton biovolume and species composition between the prefertilization and fertilization time periods.

Primary productivity was evaluated within the photic zone (1% light level) using the ¹⁴C light–dark bottle method (APHA 1995). Primary production was estimated in Redfish Lake once per month for 4–5 months during the growing season, except in 1997 when only two dates were sampled. Sampling was even more sporadic in Stanley Lake, with between zero and four dates sampled each year and only one estimate during the years prior to fertilization of Redfish Lake. Discrete primary productivity estimates were made at eight depths in Redfish Lake and six depths in Stanley Lake.

Zooplankton were sampled with a 0.35 m diameter, 1.58 m long, 80 µm mesh conical net, equipped with a removable bucket, release mechanism, and flowmeter. Diurnal casts were retrieved by hand at a rate of approximately 1 m/s. Hauls were made in Redfish Lake from 10 to 0 m, 30 to 10 m, and bottom (~60 m) to 30 m, and at the deep main station, an additional haul was made from approximately 85 to 60 m. Stanley Lake was sampled at 10 to 0 m and bottom (~26 m) to 10 m. Samples were preserved in 10% buffered sugar formalin. Techniques used to subsample, count, and measure zooplankton were adopted from Utah State University (Steinhart et al. 1994) using techniques and length–weight relationships developed by McCauley (1984) and Koenings et al. (1987).

Mean values for limnological variables were calculated for the Redfish Lake prefertilization period (1992–1994) and the fertilized years (1995–1998) using data collected during June–September. Raw data were obtained from Utah State University for the early years of this study (1992–1995) and reanalyzed using one or two measurements per month from June through September each year to assure consistency with data collected since 1995.

Total *O. nerka* abundance was estimated in September each year using hydroacoustic techniques. Echo-sounding data were collected with a Hydroacoustic Technology, Inc. Model 240 split-beam system. We used a 15-degree transducer, and the echo-sounder criteria were set to a pulse width of 0.4 milliseconds, a time-varied gain of 40 log(R) + 2 r, and six pings/s for Redfish Lake and four pings/s in Stanley Lake. Data were recorded on a Panasonic SV-3700 digital audio tape recorder. Transects were established in 1994 in a zigzag pattern across the lakes, using a GPS; 14 and 8 transects were established on Redfish and Stanley lakes, respectively. Target strengths and fish densities were processed using a Model 340 digital echo processor and plotted with a Model 402 digital chart recorder. Fish densities were computed by using adjacent transects as replicates within a stratum (lake). Population estimates and variance for individual size classes were estimated by equations found in Gunderson (1993).

Results

We remained in full compliance with DEQ water quality criteria, and nutrient supplementation proceeded uninterrupted in Redfish Lake during 1995–1998. Visual impacts such as reductions in

water clarity and changes in color were imperceptible to the casual observer.

Climatic and Hydrologic

Mean annual discharge for the Salmon River at Salmon, Idaho, was at or below average during the prefertilized years (1990–1994) and above average during the fertilized years (1995–1998; USGS gauge 13302500; Figure 2).

Redfish Lake (Prefertilization, 1992–1994)

Physicochemical. Redfish Lake was identified as a good candidate for nutrient supplementation based on evidence of strong epilimnetic stratification with seasonal depletion of nitrate nitrogen, lack of evidence of light limitation, and loss of marine-derived nutrients. Redfish Lake is a clear water lake with mean Secchi depths of 13.6 m, conductivities of 25–30 μ S/cm, and pH values between 7.0 and 8.0. The lake is exceptionally clear with a compensation depth that averaged 28.4 m. Low nutrient concentrations were typical with mean summer epilimnetic TP concentrations of 6.8–8.5 μg/L (mean = 7.9 μg/L), average TN concentrations less than 70 μg/L, and mean NO_3+NO_2 concentrations of 4.8 μg/L. During stratification, NO_3+NO_2, NH_4, and SRP were typically below method detection levels.

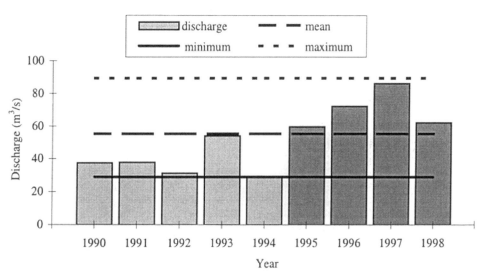

FIGURE 2. Mean annual discharge for the Salmon River at Salmon, Idaho, 1990 through 1998. Mean, minimum, and maximum are for period of record, 1913–1998. Darker gray bars denote fertilized years.

Natural annual TP loading to Redfish Lake was estimated to be 272 mg P · m^{-2}· year^{-1} using the empirical-based equations of Vollenweider (1976) and mean spring overturn TP concentration. Gross et al. (1998) calculated nutrient loading using water budget and nutrient concentration data and estimated natural loading to be 150 mg P · m^{-2}· year^{-1} in 1993, the first normal water year following six years of drought.

Biological. Phytoplankton production was low with seasonal mean surface chlorophyll *a* concentrations of 0.4–0.6 µg/L (mean = 0.5 µg/L) and phytoplankton biovolume less than 0.2 mm^3/L (Table 1). In 1993, Budy et al. (1995) reported that spring phytoplankton biovolume was dominated by *Dinobryon* spp., Bacillariophytes, and Chlorophyceans and that 60–82% of the phytoplankton was of a grazable size (<30 µm). Picoplankton were present and sometimes abundant but were not identified (Budy et al. 1995). In 1993, primary productivity estimates ranged from 25 to 126 mg C · m^{-2}· day^{-1}, and the seasonal average was 92 mg C · m^{-2}· day^{-1}. Macrozooplankton populations consisted of *Daphnia*

rosea, Bosmina longirostris, Holopedium gibberum, Polyphemus pediculus, Epischura nevadensis, and several species of cyclopoid copepods (Budy et al. 1995). Total zooplankton biomass averaged 7.9 µg/L, and *Daphnia* biomass was 0.8 µg/L prior to nutrient supplementation. Total *O. nerka* density was 240 fish/ha in 1994, prior to nutrient supplementation. Estimated overwinter survival of presmolt sockeye salmon released in 1994 was 6.7% (Idaho Department of Fish and Game, unpublished data).

Redfish Lake (Fertilization Response, 1995–1998)

Physicochemical. Nutrient supplementation rates were variable with annual TP applications ranging from 8.3 to 42.4 mg P · m^{-2}· year^{-1} (51–261 kg/year; Table 2). Supplementation increased TP loading by 3–16% (Vollenweider equations) or 6–28% (nutrient budget). Phosphorus supplementation was converted to sockeye salmon carcass equivalents using Larkin and Slaney's (1997) value of 0.36% TP by mass for sockeye salmon

TABLE 1. Mean values, sample size, and percent change for selected variables before and during fertilization of Redfish Lake, Idaho. Stanley Lake (unfertilized) data corresponds to the time periods before and during fertilization of Redfish Lake.

Lake	Variable	Before fertilization		During fertilization		% change
		mean	*n*	mean	*n*	
Redfish	Secchi depth (m)	13.6	(19)	11.8	(31)	−13%
	Compensation depth (m)	28.4	(14)	21.6	(28)	−24%
	Total phosphorus (TP) (µg/L)	7.9	(24)	6.7	(25)	−15%
	Nitrate (NO$_3$+NO$_2$-N) (µg/L)	4.8	(14)	4.4	(25)	−8%
	Ammonia (NH$_4$-N) (µg/L)	3.0	(5)	4.3	(19)	43%
	Chlorophyll *a* (µg/L)	0.5	(22)	1.0	(30)	106%
	Phytoplankton volume (mm^3/L)	–	–	0.24	(14)	–
	Primary production (mgC · m^{-2} day^{-1})	92.4	(4)	200.4	(26)	117%
	Daphnia biomass (µg/L)	0.8	(14)	2.6	(32)	225%
	Zooplankton biomass (µg/L)	7.9	(14)	10.3	(32)	31%
	O. nerka density (fish/ha)	239.8	(1)	301.4	(4)	26%
	Sockeye overwinter survival (%)	6.7	(1)	19.7	(4)	192%
Stanley	Secchi depth (m)	8.4	(21)	6.1	(18)	−27%
	Compensation depth (m)	16.6	(13)	11.9	(19)	−28%
	Total phosphorus (TP) (µg/L)	7.7	(18)	7.7	(12)	0%
	Nitrate (NO$_3$+NO$_2$ − N) (µg/L)	3.5	(8)	2.1	(8)	−39%
	Ammonia (NH$_4$-N) (µg/L)	13.8	(4)	4.3	(8)	−69%
	Chlorophyll *a* (µg/L)	0.7	(22)	0.9	(19)	16%
	Phytoplankton volume (mm^3/L)	–	–	0.13	(4)	–
	Primary production (mgC · m^{-2} day^{-1})	110.2	(1)	125.3	(10)	14%
	Daphnia biomass (µg/L)	8.3	(14)	7.9	(23)	−5%
	Zooplankton biomass (µg/L)	24.7	(14)	24.3	(22)	−2%

TABLE 2. Supplemental nutrient loading rates for Redfish Lake, Idaho, 1995–1998. Sockeye salmon carcass equivalents were calculated based on phosphorous content.

Year	P (kg)	N (kg)	mg P/m²	mg N/m²	TN:TP	Carcass equivalents
1995	260.6	4,622.8	42.4	751.7	17.7	32,500
1996	51.1	933.5	8.3	151.8	18.3	6,300
1997	190.0	3,695.0	30.9	600.8	19.4	23,500
1998	189.8	3,701.7	30.9	601.9	19.5	23,500

and a mean sockeye salmon weight of 2.24 kg. Supplemental TP loading rates were equivalent to an escapement of 6,300–32,500 adult sockeye salmon to Redfish Lake.

During nutrient supplementation, water transparency declined, as evidenced by reductions in mean Secchi depth, to 11.8 m and mean compensation depth to 21.6 m (Table 1). Nutrient concentrations remained low with mean summer epilimnetic TP concentrations of 6.7 µg/L, average TN concentrations less than 70 µg/L, and mean NO_3+NO_2 concentrations of 4.4 µg/L. NO_3+NO_2, NH_4, and SRP remained below method detection levels during stratification.

Biological. Surface chlorophyll *a* increased to 1.0 µg/L (range 0.5–1.5 µg/L), and primary production amplified to 200.4 mg C · m⁻² · day⁻¹. Primary production was positively related to nutrient supplementation ($r^2 = 0.59$, $p = 0.075$; Figure 3). Phytoplankton communities remained typically oligotrophic and were dominated by small, grazable microflagellate taxa. During fertilization, total phytoplankton densities ranged from 1,399 to 6,010 cells/mL (mean 3,144 cells/mL), and total phytoplankton biovolume ranged from 0.08 to 0.53 mm³/L (mean 0.24 mm³/L). Generally, Chryso- and Cryptophycean nano-flagellates and autotrophic picoplankton (Cyanophyceae) were numerically dominant, while Chryso- and Cryptophycean nanoflagellates and Dinophycean dinoflagellates had the highest biovolume of any phytoplankton taxa. Diatoms (Bacillario-

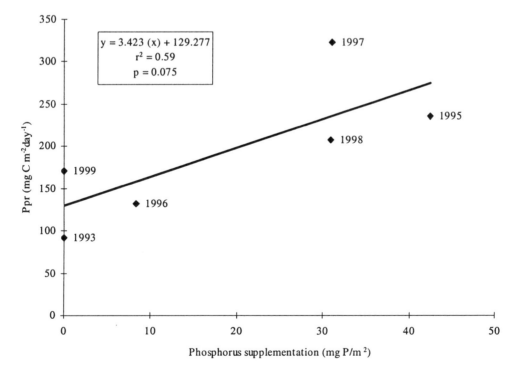

FIGURE 3. Relationship between primary productivity (Ppr) in mg C · m⁻² · day⁻¹ and annual phosphorus supplementation (mg P/m²; $r^2 = 0.59$, $p = 0.075$) in Redfish Lake, Idaho.

phytes) were common during June and July and Chlorophyceans during August and September. Total zooplankton biomass increased to 10.3 μg/L, and Daphnia biomass increased to 2.6 μg/L during nutrient supplementation. *O. nerka* density was 301.4 fish/ha, and *O. nerka* overwinter survival increased to an average of 19.7% (Idaho Department of Fish and Game, unpublished data).

Stanley Lake (Untreated Reference Lake, 1992–1994)

Physicochemical. During 1992–1994, years that correspond to the prefertilized years in Redfish Lake, Stanley Lake had mean Secchi depths of 8.4 m, compensation depth averaged 16.6 m, conductivity was less than 35 μ S/cm, and pH values were between 7.0 and 7.5. Nutrient concentrations were low with mean summer epilimnetic TP concentration of 7.7 μg/L; average TN concentrations were approximately 80 μg/L, and mean NO_3+NO_2 concentration was 3.5 μg/L (Table 1). Like Redfish Lake, NO_3+NO_2, NH_4, and SRP were typically below method detection levels during stratification in Stanley Lake.

Biological. Phytoplankton standing crop was higher than in Redfish Lake, as evidenced by mean seasonal surface chlorophyll *a* concentrations of 0.5–1.1 μg/L (mean 0.7 μg/L) and primary productivity of 110 mg C · m^{-2} · day^{-1}. Zooplankton biomass was much higher in Stanley Lake relative to Redfish Lake, with seasonal mean total zooplankton biomass of 24.7 μg/L and *Daphnia* biomass of 8.3 μg/L

Stanley Lake (Untreated Reference Lake, 1995–1998)

Physicochemical. During 1995–1998, years that correspond to the fertilized years in Redfish Lake, Stanley Lake also had reduced water transparency. Mean Secchi depth declined to 6.1 m, and compensation depth was reduced to 11.9 m (Table 1). Mean summer epilimnetic TP concentration was 7.7 μg/L, average TN concentration was 74 μg/L, and mean NO_3+NO_2 concentration was 2.1 μg/L. Similar to the early years of the study, epilimnetic NO_3+NO_2, NH_4, and SRP concentrations were below method detection levels during stratification.

Biological. Phytoplankton standing crop was lower than in Redfish Lake. Phytoplankton den-

sities ranged from 1,470 to 7,010 cells/mL (mean 3,776 cells/mL), and biomass estimates ranged from 0.07 to 0.15 mm³/L (mean 0.13 mm³/L). Mean seasonal surface chlorophyll *a* concentrations increased to 0.8–1.0 μg/L (mean 0.9 μg/L), and primary productivity was 125.3 mg C · m^{-2} · day^{-1}. Zooplankton biomass was stable in Stanley Lake and still high relative to Redfish Lake, with seasonal mean total zooplankton biomass of 24.3 μg/L and *Daphnia* biomass of 7.9 μg/L. Hydroacoustic estimates of kokanee salmon densities are limited in Stanley Lake, but the population appears to be relatively low and stable based on kokanee salmon spawning escapement estimates (Lewis et al. 2000; in press).

Redfish and Stanley Lakes (Relative Changes)

Comparisons of mean values for the prefertilization period (1992–1994) and the fertilization time period (1995–1998) in Redfish Lake show smaller reductions in Secchi depth and compensation depth and larger increases in surface chlorophyll *a*, primary productivity, and zooplankton biomass than occurred during the same time periods in unfertilized Stanley Lake (Figure 4). In Redfish Lake, mean seasonal Secchi depth declined by 13%, compensation depth decreased by 24%, surface chlorophyll *a* increased by 106%, and mean daily primary productivity increased by 117%. Total zooplankton biomass increased by 31%, and *Daphnia* spp. biomass increased 225%. It is important to note that these increases in zooplankton biomass occurred under increased grazing pressure, as evidenced by the 26% increase in *O. nerka* density, and that overwinter survival of sockeye salmon increased by 192%.

For the same time periods in unfertilized Stanley Lake, mean Secchi depth declined 27%, compensation depth decreased 28%, surface chlorophyll *a* increased 16%, primary production increased 14%, and macrozooplankton biomass was unchanged at approximately 24 μg/L (Figure 4).

Discussion

Rationale for Nutrient Additions to Redfish

Enrichment of oligotrophic lakes has been used to increase primary and secondary production

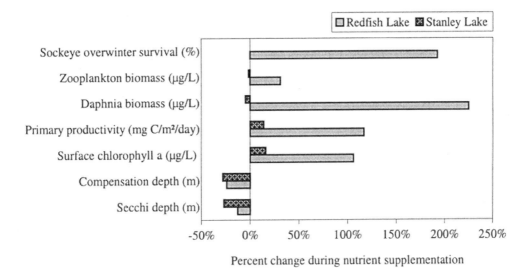

FIGURE 4. Percent change of selected limnological variables for unfertilized (1992–1994) and fertilized (1995–1998) time periods in Redfish Lake and Stanley Lake, Idaho.

(macrozooplankton) and to improve rearing habitat for young planktivorous sockeye salmon in British Columbia and Alaska (Stockner 1987; Kyle 1994). Lake fertilization programs typically replace lost marine-derived nutrients (MDN) from decaying salmon carcasses with inorganic fertilizer to boost production in nutrient-limited systems with low adult escapements (LeBrasseur et al. 1979; Stockner and MacIsaac 1996). In British Columbia and Alaska, new production from lake fertilization has been associated with increased survival and growth of juvenile sockeye salmon (LeBrasseur et al. 1978; Robinson and Barraclough 1978; Hyatt and Stockner 1985; Kyle 1994) and elevated adult escapement (LeBras-seur et al. 1979; Stockner and MacIsaac 1996). The relationship between *O. nerka* population abundance and available forage in a nursery lake can be manipulated with nutrient applications resulting in higher lake carrying capacities and greater in-lake juvenile growth and survival (Stockner and MacIsaac 1996).

Role of Interannual Climatic Variability (Physical Forcing)

Numerous studies have reported effects of nutrient additions by sampling before, during, and after fertilization treatments. However, some of these studies are subject to misinterpretation, if annual variation caused by meteorological forc-

ing or other impacts was not accounted for (Schindler 1987). Gross (1995) modeled nutrient loading into Redfish Lake during the record low water year of 1992 and during the normal water year of 1993 and found a positive correlation between discharge and nutrient loading. Thus, evaluation of the Redfish Lake nutrient supplementation program was confounded by changes in meteorological conditions in the Sawtooth Mountain basin. Prior to fertilization of Redfish Lake, snowpack and subsequent discharge in the drainage was at or below normal, but since fertilization began in 1995, snowpack and discharge has been above average in the basin. As a result, we expected these climatic changes to impact the limnological characteristics of Redfish Lake and complicate our assessment of impacts from nutrient supplementation. Assuming that nutrient loading is positively related to discharge in both our study lakes, we would expect declines in Secchi depth and compensation depth and increases in chlorophyll *a* concentrations, primary productivity, and potentially zooplankton biomass during the wetter years, which corresponded with fertilization of Redfish Lake. Data from Stanley Lake, which has stable kokanee salmon populations and did not receive nutrient supplementation, supports that assumption. However, the disproportionately larger increases in chlorophyll *a*, primary productivity, and zooplankton biomass in Redfish Lake, relative to observed changes in Stanley Lake, provides clear evidence that nutrient supplementation stimulated carbon production of Redfish Lake. However, Stanley Lake should only be considered a gross indicator of variable conditions, since the lake is morphologically dissimilar to Redfish Lake. Stanley Lake has a drainage area 48.6 times the size of the lake, compared with a ratio of 17.6 for Redfish Lake. This results in a much shorter water retention time in Stanley (0.3 years, compared with 3.0 years in Redfish Lake), which should result in higher nutrient input (Gross 1995), but the shorter retention time increases flushing and amplifies 'washout' of nutrients, phytoplankton, resting stages, and eggs, compared with Redfish Lake, especially during high water years (Goldman et al. 1989). If Stanley Lake is more susceptible to washout, then nutrient supplementation impacts may be overestimated in Redfish Lake. The relatively large decreases in Secchi and compensation depths observed in Stanley Lake were primarily caused by suspended particulate matter, a large fraction of which is biologically unavailable.

Top-Down or Bottom-Up?

The strong 'bottom-up' control of production processes in nutrient-limited Pacific coastal and Alaskan oligotrophic sockeye salmon nursery lakes has been well documented from several decades of nutrient addition experiments and limnological research (Koenings and Burkett 1987; Stockner 1987; Stockner and MacIsaac 1996). However, some attempts to increase lake productivity with nutrient additions have been unsuccessful because inedible phytoplankters were stimulated (i.e., energy sinks resulted in inefficient trophic transfers and diminished carbon flows to rearing juvenile sockeye salmon; Stockner and Hyatt 1984; Stockner and Shortreed 1988). Although phytoplankton data for our study lakes prior to nutrient supplementation are limited, it appears phytoplankton populations have remained stable during years of fertilization with assemblages dominated by species typically found in oligotrophic conditions (Stockner and Shortreed 1994). Small grazable autotrophic picoplankton, nanoflagellates, and diatoms dominate phytoplankton species assemblages in the study lakes. The predominance of these phytoplankton and the absence of accumulations of nongrazable taxa (sinks) are good indicators of efficient energy transfers between trophic levels, albeit through longer food-chains, which should result in improved forage production and growth

and survival for endangered sockeye salmon (Stockner 1987; Stockner and MacIsaac 1996).

Top-down trophic interactions, or 'cascades,' are also known to influence primary productivity of lakes (Carpenter et al. 1985; Carpenter and Kitchell 1987, 1988). Trawl and hydroacoustic estimates of *O. nerka* populations in nearby Alturas and Pettit lakes have shown large fluctuations in kokanee salmon abundance and/or biomass (Teuscher and Taki 1996; Taki and Mikkelsen 1997; Taki et al. 1999). During these peaks in kokanee salmon population cycles, intense grazing pressure on macrozooplankton can cause striking shifts in species composition and abrupt declines in zooplankton biomass and size. An excellent example is found in nearby Pettit Lake where in 1995 kokanee salmon density increased to approximately 534 fish/ha, zooplankton biomass dramatically declined, and species composition shifted from a *Daphnia* spp. dominated system to a *Bosmina* spp. dominated macrozooplankton community (Figure 5), a response similar to that noted in Alaskan sockeye lakes under intense sockeye grazing pressure (Koenings and Kyle 1997).

Our nutrient supplementation program was aimed at minimizing the risk of a similar collapse in Redfish Lake. In 1997, *O. nerka* density in Redfish Lake increased to 462 fish/ha, yet macrozooplankton biomass and species composition remained relatively stable (Figure 6). Even with increased *O. nerka* density, mean overwinter survival improved from 6.7% to 19.7%. However, several changes occurred in the hatchery program around the time that nutrient supplementation was initiated, which could account for some of these differences (i.e., utilization of chilled water during maturation resulted in the production of higher quality fish for stocking; Paul Kline, Idaho Department of Fish and Game, personal communication).

Several potential problems can be associated with lake fertilization, including effects of lake eutrophication, increased numbers of residual sockeye salmon, and increased intraspecific competition between kokanee salmon and sockeye salmon. Declines in water quality were virtually nonexistent, leading us to believe that supplementation levels could be increased significantly in the future. Numbers of residual beach spawners were monitored annually and appear to be declining, evidence that nutrient supplementation efforts have not caused sockeye salmon to residualize.

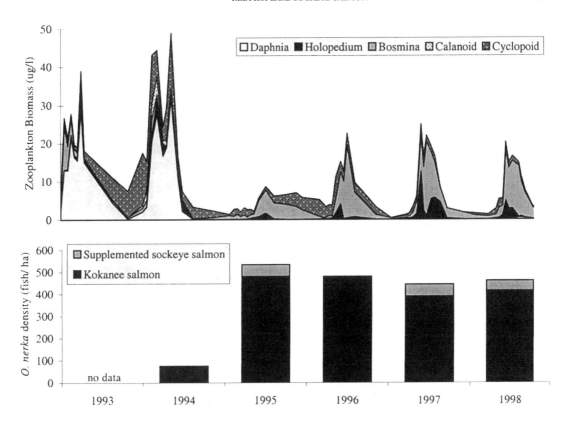

FIGURE 5. Zooplankton biomass (μg/L) and *O. nerka* density (fish/ha) in Pettit Lake, Idaho, 1993–1998.

Habitat use and foraging behavior of kokanee salmon are similar to sockeye salmon (Rieman and Myers 1992), so potential benefits to sockeye salmon from fertilization may be offset by increases in growth, survival, and fecundity of kokanee salmon. A positive response by kokanee salmon to lake fertilization could result in increased competition with sockeye salmon in future years. This was the primary reason that Redfish Lake did not receive supplemental nutrients in 1999, when a smaller number of sockeye salmon presmolts were available for stocking. The authors of this report and the Stanley Basin Sockeye Technical Oversight Committee believed that nonnative kokanee salmon populations would disproportionately benefit from the nutrient additions, which could ultimately increase competition with endangered sockeye salmon.

Summary and Conclusions

Meteorological conditions influence lake productivity and should be monitored in any future attempts to identify nutrient supplementation impacts. The data set for Stanley Lake was incomplete because the need for a reference lake was not foreseen at the initiation of this project; regardless, the available data proved invaluable in discerning impacts from nutrient supplementation in light of the variable climatic conditions that prevailed.

Trophic cascades were difficult to track beyond primary producers because of variable *O. nerka* population densities (top-down effects); however, zooplankton biomass increased by 31%, and *Daphnia* spp. biomass increased by 225% in Redfish Lake simultaneous to a 26% increase in *O. nerka* density, evidence that bottom–up forces may have affected zooplankton and planktivorous fish. These findings are consistent with the results of more than 20 years of lake fertilization efforts in Canada and Alaska that have demonstrated that lake fertilization has been a very cost-effective enhancement technique for sockeye salmon, leaving a 'soft' and imperceptible ecological footprint.

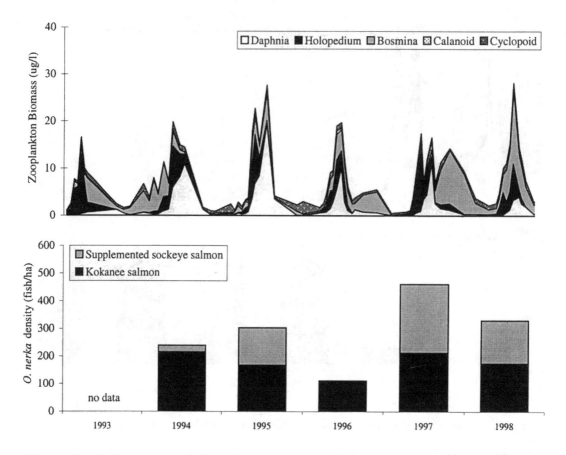

FIGURE 6. Zooplankton biomass (μg/L) and *O. nerka* density (fish/ha) in Redfish Lake, Idaho, 1993–1998.

Concerns for esthetic values (clear water) resulted in relatively light applications of fertilizer to Redfish Lake that sometimes resulted in subtle, hard-to-detect increases in production at the higher trophic levels, especially in light of climatic and cohort variability. However, increased carbon flows, lack of evidence of bottlenecks, and a risk adverse approach to recovery of endangered sockeye salmon lead us to conclude that nutrient supplementation is a useful tool during years when forage resources may be overutilized in the Sawtooth Valley lakes. Future research will attempt to clarify the role of the microbial food webs that are currently thought to be the predominant pathways of carbon flux in the metabolism of Sawtooth Valley lakes. More aggressive (higher) loading rates and selection of a reference lake more similar to Redfish may improve our ability to detect impacts from nutrient supplementation efforts in the future.

Acknowledgments

Kim Gilliland and JeNelle McEwan collected limnology data. Kenneth Ariwite and Rob Trahant fertilized Redfish Lake and assisted with data collection. Deborah A. Hunter, Patricia Bucknell, and Mark Palmer, limnologists with the University of California at Davis, provided technical assistance and assayed nutrient samples. Ellie Stockner processed phytoplankton samples, and Odette Brandt identified and enumerated macrozooplankton samples. Lance Hebdon and Paul Kline (Idaho Department of Fish and Game) provided sockeye salmon overwinter survival estimates. Don Zaroban and Tom Heron (DEQ) provided fertilization consent orders. Jeff Anderson (Shoshone-Bannock Tribes), Lisa Thompson (University of California, Davis), Richard Axler (University of Minnesota-Duluth), and John J. Ney reviewed this manuscript. We would also like to extend our appreciation to the members, past and present, of the Stanley Basin Technical Oversight Committee for their guidance and to the Bonneville Power Administration for funding this effort.

References

APHA (American Public Health Association). 1995. Standard methods for the examination of water and wastewater, 19th edition. APHA, Washington D.C.

Budy, P., G. Steinhart, C. Luecke, and W. A. Wurtsbaugh. 1995. Limnological investigations of Sawtooth Valley lakes. Pages 54–64 *in* D. Teuscher, D. Taki, W. A. Wurtsbaugh, C. Luecke, P. Budy, and G. Steinhart, editors. Snake River sockeye salmon habitat and limnological research. Annual Report 1994. United States Department of Energy, Bonneville Power Administration, Division of Fish and Wildlife, Portland, Oregon. Project Number 91–71, DOE/BP-22548-3.

Budy, P., C. Luecke, and W. A. Wurtsbaugh. 1998. Adding nutrients to enhance the growth of endangered sockeye salmon: trophic transfer in an oligotrophic lake. Transactions of the American Fisheries Society 127:19–34.

Carpenter, S. R., and J. F. Kitchell. 1987. The temporal scale variance in limnetic primary production. American Naturalist 129:417–433.

Carpenter, S. R., and J. F. Kitchell. 1988. Consumer control of lake productivity. BioScience 38:764–769.

Carpenter, S. R., J. F. Kitchell, and J. R. Hodgson. 1985. Cascading trophic interactions and lake productivity. BioScience 35:634–639.

Emmett, W. W. 1975. The channels and waters of the Upper Salmon River, Idaho: Hydrologic evaluation of the upper Salmon River area, Idaho. U. S. Geological Survey professional paper, Paper 870A. Washington, D.C.

Flagg, T. A., W. C. McAuley, M. R. Wastel, D. A. Frost, C. V. W. Mahnken, and J. C. Gislason. 1998. Redfish Lake sockeye salmon captive broodstock program, NMFS. Pages 1–9 *in* Proceedings of the 48th Northwest Fish Culture Conference. Glenden Beach, Oregon.

Goldman, C. R., A. Jassby, and T. Powell. 1989. Interannual fluctuations in primary production: meteorological forcing at two subalpine lakes. Limnology and Oceanography 34(2):310–323.

Goodlad, J. C., T. W. Gjernes, and E. L. Brannon. 1974. Factors affecting sockeye salmon *Oncorhynchus nerka* growth in four lakes of the Fraser River system. Journal of the Fisheries Research Board of Canada 31:871–892.

Griswold, R. G. 1997. Limnology of the Sawtooth Valley lakes. Pages 33–83 *in* D. Taki and A. Mikkelsen, editors. Snake River sockeye salmon habitat and limnological research. Annual Report 1996. United States Department of Energy, Bonneville Power Administration, Environment, Fish and Wildlife. Portland, Oregon. Project Number 91–71. DOE/BP-22548–5.

Gross, H. P., and W. A. Wurtsbaugh. 1994. Water and nutrient budgets of the Sawtooth Valley lakes. Pages 7–29 *in* D. Teuscher, D. Taki, W. A. Wurtsbaugh, C. Luecke, P. Budy, H. P. Gross, and G. Steinhart, editors. Snake River sockeye salmon habitat and limnological research. Annual Report 1993. United States Department of Energy, Bonneville Power Administration, Division of Fish and Wildlife, Portland, Oregon. Project Number 91–71, DOE/BP-22548-2.

Gross, H. P. 1995. Evaluation of lake fertilization as a tool to assist in the recovery of the Snake River sockeye salmon *Oncorhynchus nerka*. Master's Thesis, Utah State University, Logan, Utah.

Gross, H. P., W. A. Wurtsbaugh, and C. Luecke. 1998. The role of anadromous sockeye salmon in the nutrient loading and productivity of Redfish Lake, Idaho. Transactions of the American Fisheries Society 127:1–18.

Gunderson, D. R. 1993. Surveys of fisheries resources. Wiley, New York.

Holm-Hansen, O., and B. Rieman, 1978. Chlorophyll *a* determination: improvements in methodology. Oikos 30:438–447.

Hyatt, K. D., and J. G. Stockner. 1985. Responses of sockeye salmon *Oncorhynchus nerka* to fertilization of British Columbia coastal lakes. Canadian Journal of Fisheries and Aquatic Sciences 42:320–331.

Koenings, J. P., and R. D. Burkett. 1987. Population characteristics of sockeye salmon *Oncorhynchus nerka* smolts relative to temperature regimes, euphotic volume, fry density, and forage base within Alaskan lakes. Pages 216–234 *in* H. D. Smith, L. Margolis, and C. C. Woods, editors. Sockeye salmon *Oncorhynchus nerka* population biology and future management. Canadian Special Publication of Fisheries and Aquatic Sciences 96.

Koenings, J. P., and G. P. Kyle. 1997. Consequences of juvenile sockeye salmon and the zooplankton community resulting from intense predation. Alaska Fishery Research Bulletin 4:120–135.

Koenings, J. P., J. A. Edmundson, G. B. Kyle, and J. M. Edmundson. 1987. Limnology field and laboratory manual: methods for assessing aquatic production. Alaska Department of Fish and Game, Division of Fisheries Rehabilitation, Enhancement and Development. Juneau, Alaska.

Kyle, G. B. 1994. Nutrient treatment of 3 coastal Alaskan lakes: trophic level responses and sockeye salmon production trends. Alaska Fishery Research Bulletin 1(2):153–167.

Kyle, G. B., J. P. Koenings, and B. M. Barrett. 1988. Density-dependent, trophic level responses to an introduced run of sockeye salmon *Oncorhynchus nerka* at Frazer Lake, Kodiak Island, Alaska. Canadian Journal of Fisheries and Aquatic Sciences 45:856–867.

Larkin, G. A., and P. A. Slaney. 1997. Implications of trends in marine-derived nutrients flow to south coastal British Columbia salmonid production. Fisheries 22(11):16–24.

Lebrasseur, R. J., C. D. McAllister, W. E. Barraclough, O. D. Kennedy, J. Manzer, D. Robinson, and K. Stephens. 1978. Enhancement of sockeye salmon *Oncorhynchus nerka* by lake fertilization in Great Central Lake: summary report. Journal of the Fisheries Research Board of Canada 35:1580–1596.

LeBrasseur, R. J., C. D. McAllister, and T. R. Parsons. 1979. Addition of nutrients to a lake leads to greatly increased catch of salmon. Environmental Conservation 6(3):187–190.

Lewis, B., D. Taki and R. G. Griswold. In press. Snake River sockeye salmon habitat and limnological research. Annual Report 1998. United States Department of Energy, Bonneville Power Administration, Environment, Fish and Wildlife. Portland, Oregon. Project Number 91–71, DOE/BP-22548-7.

Luecke, C., M. Slater, and P. Budy. 1996. Limnology of Sawtooth Valley lakes in 1995. Pages 76–91 *in* D. Teuscher and D. Taki, editors. Snake River sockeye salmon habitat and limnological research. Annual Report 1995. United States Department of Energy, Bonneville Power Administration, Environment, Fish and Wildlife, Portland, Oregon. Project Number 91–71, DOE/BP-22548-4.

McCauley, E. 1984. The estimation of the abundance and biomass of zooplankton in samples. Pages 228–265 *in* J. A. Downings and F. Rigler, editors. A manual on methods of secondary productivity in freshwaters, 2nd edition. Blackwell Scientific Publications Scientific Publishing, Oxford, UK.

Rieman, B. E., and D. L. Myers. 1992. Influence of fish density and relative productivity on growth of kokanee in ten oligotrophic lakes and reservoirs in Idaho. Transactions of the American Fisheries Society 121:178–191.

Robinson, D. G., and W. E. Barraclough. 1978. Population estimates of sockeye salmon *Oncorhynchus nerka* in a fertilized oligotrophic lake. Journal of the Fisheries Research Board of Canada 35:851–860.

Schindler, D. W. 1987. Detecting ecosystem responses to stress. Canadian Journal of Fisheries and Aquatic Sciences 44:6–25.

Steinhart, G., H. P. Gross, P. Budy, C. Luecke, and W. A. Wurtsbaugh. 1994. Limnological investigations and hydroacoustic surveys of Saw-tooth Valley Lakes. Pages 30–61 *in* D. Teuscher, D. Taki, W. A. Wurtsbaugh, C. Luecke, P. Budy, H. P. Gross, and G. Steinhart, editors. Snake River sockeye salmon habitat and limnological research. Annual Report 1993. United States Department of Energy, Bonneville Administration, Division of Fish and Wildlife. Project Number 91–71, DOE/BP-22548-2.

Stockner, J. G. 1981. Whole-lake fertilization for the enhancement of sockeye salmon *Oncorhynchus nerka* in British Columbia, Canada. Verhandlungen der Internationalen Vereinigung fuer Theoretische und Angewandte Limnologie 21:293–299.

Stockner, J. G. 1987. Lake fertilization: the enrichment cycle and lake sockeye salmon *Oncorhynchus nerka* production. Pages 198–215 *in* H. D. Smith, L. Margolis, and C. C. Woods, editors. Sockeye salmon *Oncorhynchus nerka* population biology and future management. Canadian Special Publication of Fisheries and Aquatic Sciences 96.

Stockner, J. G., and K. D. Hyatt. 1984. Lake fertilization: state of the art after 7 years of application. Canadian Technical Report of Fisheries and Aquatic Sciences Number 1324.

Stockner, J. G., and E. A. MacIsaac. 1996. British Columbia Lake Enrichment program: two decades of habitat enhancement for sockeye salmon. Regulated Rivers: Research and Management 12:547–561.

Stockner, J. G., and K. S. Shortreed. 1988. Response of Anabaena and Synechococcus to manipulation of nitrogen: phosphorus ratios in a lake fertilization experiment. Limnology and Oceanography 33(6):1348–1361.

Stockner, J. G., and K. S. Shortreed. 1994. Autotrophic picoplankton community dynamics in a pre-alpine lake in British Columbia, Canada Hydrobiologia 274:133–142.

Taki, D., and A. Mikkelsen. 1997. Snake River sockeye salmon habitat and limnological research. Annual Report 1996. United States Department of Energy, Bonneville Power Administration, Environment, Fish and Wildlife. Portland, Oregon. Project Number 91–71, DOE/BP-22548-5.

Taki, D., B. Lewis, R. G. Griswold. 1999. Snake River sockeye salmon habitat and limnological research. Annual Report 1997. United States Department of Energy, Bonneville Power Administration, Environment, Fish and Wildlife. Portland, Oregon. Project Number 91–71, DOE/BP-22548-6.

Teuscher, D., and D. Taki. 1996. Snake River sockeye salmon habitat and limnological research. Annual Report 1995. United States Department of Energy, Bonneville Power Administration, Environment, Fish and Wildlife. Portland, Oregon. Project Number 91–71, DOE/BP-22548–4.

Vollenweider, R. A. 1976. Advances in defining critical loading levels for phosphorus in lake eutrophication studies. Memorie dell'Istituto italiano di idrobiologia dott Marco De Marchi 33:53–83.

Waples, R. S., O. W. Johnson, and R. P. Jones, Jr. 1991. Status review for Snake River sockeye salmon. United States Department of Commerce, National Oceanic and Atmospheric Administration. Technical Memo. NMFS F/NWC-195.

Winans, G. A., P. B. Aebersold, and R. S. Waples. 1996. Allozyme variability of *Oncorhynchus nerka* in the Pacific Northwest, with special consideration to populations of Redfish Lake, Idaho. Transactions of the American Fisheries Society 125:645–663.

Utermohl, H. 1958. Zur Vervollkommmnung der quantitativen phytoplankton methodik. International Vereinigung fuer Theoretische und Angewandte Limnologie und Verhandlugen. Mitteilungen No. 9.

American Fisheries Society Symposium 34:213–225, 2003

Role of Riparian Red Alder in the Nutrient Dynamics of Coastal Streams of the Olympic Peninsula, Washington, USA

CAROL J. VOLK

Ecosystem Sciences Division, College of Forest Resources, Box 352100
University of Washington, Seattle, Washington 98195, USA

PETER M. KIFFNEY

National Marine Fisheries Service, Mukilteo Biological Field Station
10 Park Avenue, Building B, Mukilteo, Washington 98275, USA

ROBERT L. EDMONDS

Ecosystem Sciences Division, College of Forest Resources, Box 352100
University of Washington, Seattle, Washington 98195, USA

Abstract.—One result of clear-cut logging in the Pacific Northwest is that many watersheds are now dominated by riparian stands of red alder *Alnus rubra* (Bong). This species colonizes disturbed areas quickly and can limit the establishment of coniferous forest species. In the Northwest, inputs of nutrients from decaying salmon carcasses have been reduced with declining salmon runs, and nitrogen-rich red alder litter may provide a critical source of nutrients to streams. We hypothesized that high-nutrient inputs from red alder forests would translate into more productive and nutrient-rich stream ecosystems, compared with streams bordered by coniferous species. Leaf litter inputs and chemistry, surface water chemistry, and seston and periphyton nutrient dynamics were measured in six streams in the Hoh River Watershed on the western Olympic Peninsula, Washington, during 1999–2000; three streams were dominated by riparian red alder and three in old-growth coniferous forest. Litter inputs to a red alder–dominated stream were three times greater than litter into an old-growth stream. Although total carbon concentration was similar, nitrogen concentration of red alder litter was approximately three times greater than coniferous litter. Alder litter concentrations of other limiting elements, such as Ca, Cu, Mg, K, P, and Zn, were also significantly higher than conifer needles. Phosphorus and Mg concentrations of suspended particulate matter were significantly higher in streams dominated by red alder. Periphyton biomass was significantly higher in streams dominated by alder and had increased levels of magnesium. These data suggest that red alder forests may provide important subsidies of limiting elements that fuel food webs in Pacific Northwest streams. This might be especially important in stressed systems, such as those that have experienced drastic resource removal through forest harvesting or reduced salmon runs.

Introduction

Natural and anthropogenic disturbances are dominant landscape processes in the Pacific Northwest. Landslides, fires, floods, clear-cutting, and urbanization modify the landscape and, in some cases, result in high habitat complexity across terrestrial and aquatic environments. Red alder *Alnus rubra* (Bong.) is a pioneer species that can dominate disturbed landscapes, is important in establishing forest structure, and provides limiting elements to forests and streams.

Red alder has been an important component of the landscape in the Pacific Northwest for thousands of years. Pollen records date red alder as a dominant species across the Northwest about 13,500 years ago (Worona and Whitlock 1995); therefore, red alder has likely played an important historical role in the ecology of streams and rivers in the Pacific Northwest. Red alder's symbiotic relationship with a nitrogen-fixing endophyte enriches the soils with nitrogen. This can be a significant source of nitrogen for terrestrial ecosystems (Tarrant and Miller 1983; Binkley et al. 1992; Bormann et al. 1994). Large amounts of nitrogen derived from red alder can be transported into aquatic ecosystems via ground and surface waters, becoming accessible to biota in both subsurface and active channels (Goldman 1961; Stottlemeyer 1992).

Historically, most Washington coastal streams received supplemental marine-derived nutrients (MDN) from decaying salmon carcasses after freshwater spawning events. Salmon carcasses can contribute large amounts of organic matter to freshwater and terrestrial P and N pools, and can also provide other macronutrients to these ecosystems (Bilby et al. 1996). Declining salmon runs in the past century, however, have resulted in reduced nutrient inputs to some freshwater systems. Although many northwestern streams are deficient in available physical habitat for fish populations, nutrient resources may be equally limiting (Bilby and Bisson 1992).

Leaves from riparian plants have been recognized as an essential component of lotic organic matter dynamics (Vannote et al. 1980; Webster and Meyer 1997). Nutrient resources from broadleaf species, such as red alder, are predominantly added to stream systems during autumn, while conifer needles can fall year round. Leaf litter is an important direct food source for shredding aquatic macroinvertebrates, as well as fungal and bacterial populations (Cummins 1974; Barlocher 1992). As a result, riparian red alder litterfall can provide a critical source of nitrate (NO_3^-) and ammonium (NH_4^+) to invertebrate shredders, bacterial and fungal decomposers, and other detrivores within the stream. The introduction of other associated macronutrients, such as P, Mg, and Ca from red alder, is also coupled with the inputs of organic matter from red alder, offering a suite of nutrients to terrestrial and aquatic ecosystems.

Nitrogen leached from alder litter (from N-fixation) or transported via groundwater from alder forests can also indirectly provide nutrient resources to stream communities, such as periphyton or filter-feeding invertebrates (Goldman 1961). Aquatic vertebrates in streams dominated by red alder may benefit from increased nutrient inputs from alder litter. For example, population size, growth rates, or nitrogen content of vertebrates might be greater in alder-dominated streams compared with conifer dominated systems, as elevated nitrogen levels can greatly increase the production of stream food webs (Perrin and Richardson 1997). This is particularly important in streams deficient in nutrients (primarily P and N). For example, water chemistry data from West Twin, a long-term ecological research site on a headwater stream in the Hoh River Valley of western Washington, has very low dissolved P levels (Edmonds et al. 1998), indicating fast uptake rates coupled with limited P sources from bedrock material. Despite the important ecological role red alder likely plays in aquatic ecosystems, a popular restoration strategy in the Pacific Northwest (PNW) is to remove riparian red alder and plant conifers. This is because mature conifers provide an important source of pool-forming large woody debris to streams. These pools provide important habitat for juvenile fishes (Connolly 1997).

In this paper, we describe the nutrient contributions of red alder to stream ecosystems and the potential implications for aquatic food webs in headwater streams. We hypothesize that streams bordered by red alder are enriched with nitrogen and other nutrients, which translates into higher levels of productivity for these streams compared with streams bordered by coniferous species. Furthermore, nutrient deficiencies may be alleviated in streams with extensive red alder cover in comparison to riparian areas made up of coniferous species.

Methods

Study Sites

Six second-order headwater streams in the Hoh River watershed on the Olympic peninsula, Washington, were selected as study sites. Within Olympic National Park (ONP), three streams, West Twin, Twin, and Snider, with riparian corridors dominated by western red cedar *Thuja plicata* (Don.), western hemlock *Tsuga heterophylla* (Raf.) Sarg.), and Douglas fir *Pseudotsuga menziesii* (Mirb.) Franco) represented coniferous old-growth sites. Alder, Canyon, and Lindner creeks on Department of Natural Resources (DNR) land just outside of ONP were selected as red alder sites. These DNR watersheds were logged about 30–40 years ago and are currently dominated by 30–40 year old stands of red alder. Streams are tributaries to the north fork of the Hoh River; they have similar aspects, geology, gradients and topography. The Canyon, Lindner, Snider, Twin, and West Twin study sites are all located upstream of anadromous salmon barriers. Alder Creek is not located upstream of a salmon barrier, but only three carcasses have been witnessed on the creek during fall spawning season in the past two years, suggesting a very limited salmon run at the study site. The study was designed to compare the following endpoints: litterfall, water chemistry, seston, and periphyton of two sets of replicated streams (3 alder-dominated and 3 conifer-dominated) to be analyzed by single factor analysis of variance (ANOVA). Litterfall nutrient and seston biomass and nutrient data were only available for West Twin and Lindner creeks.

One hundred meter reaches at similar elevations (~100 m) and gradients (~15%) were selected for sample collections on each stream. Red alder riparian densities were estimated from canopy cover measurements to be 70% and 100% coverage within 20 m of the stream channel. Old-growth streams had limited (<10%) coverage of deciduous species. Annual stream discharge averaged 0.02–0.15 m³/s on all streams, but was seasonally variable.

Sample Collection

Leaf litter, water, seston, and periphyton were collected every 28 days from May 1999 to December 2000 (West Twin and Lindner creeks). Additional leaf litter, periphyton, and water samples were collected from Alder, Canyon, Snider, and Twin creeks from September to December 2000 and March to June 2001. Litterfall collected monthly from Lindner and West Twin creeks for one year was used as an estimate of annual litterfall inputs for all streams. Litterfall inputs from each alder and conifer stream was compared with Lindner and West Twin litterfall biomass, respectively, to ensure consistency across

sites. A single water sample was collected each month from each stream, kept on ice in the field, and frozen-stored prior to nutrient analyses. Eight mesh-covered baskets (0.22 m²) placed within 5 m of the active channel were used to collect leaf litterfall from each site each month during the sampling season. Litterfall was sorted by tree (alder or conifer) and tissue type (leaf, woody material, or reproductive), dried (60°C) to constant mass, and ground with Wiley and ball mills. Periphyton was scrubbed from eight preconditioned ceramic tiles (144 cm²) at each of the six sites. Five wood blocks (red alder, western red cedar, and maple) were placed in West Twin Creek and Lindner Creek to compare algae growth on three types of wood prevalent in the watershed. The five alder, cedar, and maple wood blocks placed in West Twin and Lindner creeks were used as substrates for periphyton in addition to ceramic tiles. Tiles and wood blocks were placed in the stream six weeks prior to initial sampling to precondition and allow algae colonization. Each month during the sampling period, tiles and wood blocks were scraped with a toothbrush; periphyton was rinsed with de-ionized water into dark containers and frozen until processed as a biomass measurement of periphyton. Samples were extracted with acetone (90%) overnight, and chlorophyll *a* was measured using a fluorometer to quantify algal biomass. A 2–4 L water sample was collected each month from West Twin and Lindner creeks from December 1999 to 2001 and frozen until filtered for biomass and nutrient analyses. Seston samples from the other four streams were not monitored until June 2001; as a result, nutrient composition data were only available for West Twin and Lindner creeks. Seston samples were filtered onto pre-ashed and weighed Whatman GF/F filters, and biomass was determined by dry weight after filtering. Dried algae and seston filters were then used for Ca, Cu, Fe, K, Mg, Mn, Na, P, Zn, C, and N analyses.

Nutrient Analysis

Leaf litter, seston, and periphyton samples designated for macronutrient (Ca, K, P, Mg) and micronutrient (Cu, Fe, Mn, Na, and Zn) analyses were acid-digested (modified EPA Method 3050) and analyzed with an ICAP (Inductively Coupled Argon Plasma analyzer; ThermoJarrellAsh Corp, model 61-E) at the Northwest Fisheries Science Center Analytical Laboratory, National Marine

Fisheries Service (Seattle, Washington). Carbon and nitrogen were analyzed using a CE440 Elemental Analyzer (Leeman Laboratories, Inc.) at the Fisheries and Oceanography Analytical Laboratory, University of Washington (Seattle, Washington). Water samples were analyzed for dissolved NH_4^+, NO_3^-, NO_2^-, DOC, and PO_4^{2-} and total kjehldal N and P (Valderrama 1981; UNESCO 1994).

Statistics

Independent sample t-tests were used for comparing monthly means of litterfall ($n = 8$) and seston nutrients ($n = 14$) for Lindner and West Twin creeks. We assumed that alder and conifer litterfall composition was consistent across sites; only litterfall from West Twin and Lindner creeks was analyzed for nutrient composition ($n = 27$ for nutrient analyses). Seston collections were collected from West Twin and Lindner creeks from June 1999 to June 2001 and from Alder, Canyon, Snider, and Twin creeks from April to June 2001. We used independent sample t-tests ($n = 5$) to determine differences in nutrient composition of seston from West Twin and Lindner creeks. We note that these are not true replicates but consider the seston and litterfall nutrient comparisons worthwhile as a pilot study for our sites. Log transformations were used to adjust for normal distributions on litterfall biomass. One-way ANOVA was used to test whether seston and litter nutrient concentrations, periphyton biomass, and surface water nutrient concentrations differed by riparian forest type (alder versus conifer). Periphyton, litterfall, and seston biomass samples from 2000 and 2001 were grouped according to season to facilitate the interpretation of monthly collection data. Streams were used as replicates for one-way ANOVA tests ($n = 6$). Leaf litter and periphyton biomass variables were compared using the nonparametric Mann–Whitney test, due to nonnormal distributions. Discharge and canopy cover were used as covariates in the univariate analyses. In addition, a Tukey's HSD multiple comparison test (post one-way ANOVA) was used to categorize periphyton nutrients on wood blocks (alder, cedar, and maple comparison). Statistical differences were noted at $p < 0.05$. All statistics were done with SPSS software (SPSS 10.0 for Windows).

Results

Biomass

Litterfall and periphyton biomass were significantly higher in alder than conifer sites. Annual litterfall data from West Twin and Lindner creeks were used as representative samples of all alder and conifer streams, since annual litterfall data (monthly sampling for 12 months) were not available at all six study sites. Litterfall from all alder and conifer sites was not significantly different within the fall sampling period, suggesting that annual litterfall inputs from West Twin and Lindner are representative of all six sites. The total annual litterfall biomass on alder-dominated streams (348 g/m²) was significantly higher ($p < 0.01$) than coniferous (104 g/m²) riparian areas and averaged more than three times as much input per year (Figure 1). Monthly chlorophyll a measurements used to determine standing stock algal biomass from benthic periphyton samples indicated that alder sites averaged 0.32 µg/cm² of chlorophyll a and 0.13 µg/cm² for conifer sites from September 1999 to December 2000. Chlorophyll a measurements were significantly different between alder and conifer sites, when discharge was used as a covariate ($p = 0.027$). Periphyton biomass also varied among seasons for both sites (fall, winter, spring, summer; Figure 2). Our initial comparisons of seston biomass in Lindner and West Twin creeks for 2000 suggest similarities between winter, spring, and summer seasons, but additional replicated collections will be necessary to determine any seasonal effects.

Nutrients

Carbon and Nitrogen. Increased concentrations of NO_3^-, NH_4^+, and total kjeldahl nitrogen (TKN) were observed in Lindner Creek after the first seasonal rains in September and October of 2000. Similarly, NO_3^- and TKN in Alder and Canyon creeks were almost twice as high as concentrations found in Twin and West Twin creeks, both old-growth coniferous streams (Table 1).

Carbon to nitrogen ratios were used to compare nutrient richness between litter types. Alder leaf and conifer needle C:N ratios were about 20 and 60, respectively ($p < 0.001$). Similarly, almost twice as much particulate C and N (C: 15.8% and 8%, $p = 0.016$; N: 1.03% and 0.45%, $p = 0.094$)

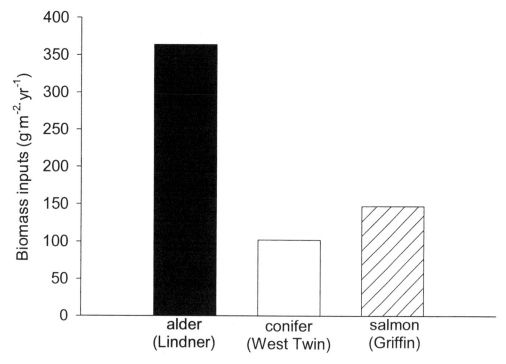

FIGURE 1. Total annual biomass inputs into streams calculated from litter (West Twin conifer and Lindner red alder) and salmon carcass data (Griffin salmon; R. E. Bilby, Weyerhaeuser Inc., unpublished data).

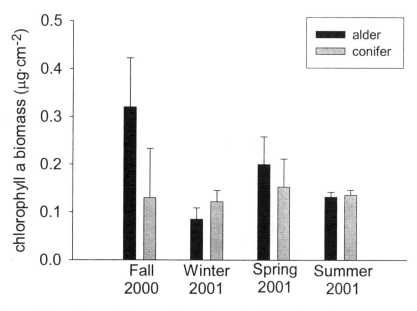

FIGURE 2. Seasonal standing stock biomass of periphyton in alder and conifer headwater streams. Bars indicate standard errors.

TABLE 1. Concentrations of N and P (µg/L) in Hoh River Valley headwater streams in Fall 2000 (Sept.–Dec.). Standard error is shown in parentheses ($n = 3$ for both alder and conifer).

Element	Mean concentration		p value
	Alder	Conifer	
$NH_4^+ - N$	6.9 (0.005)	6.8 (0.003)	0.951
$NO_3^- - N$	180.5 (0.063)	69.1 (0.034)	0.024
TN	264.9 (0.081)	148.5 (0.050)	0.023
$PO_4^{-2} - P$	6.8 (0.003)	4.5 (0.001)	0.195
TP	21.3 (0.007)	15.5 (0.003)	0.019

were detected in seston samples from Lindner compared with West Twin Creek (Figure 3). Periphyton C concentrations were significantly higher in conifer streams, while seston C. concentrations were high in alder streams (Table 2). However, N percent concentrations were similar between stream types, and neither C to N ratios for seston nor periphyton were significantly different (periphyton C:N: alder 7.3, conifer 7.8; seston C:N: alder 18.0, conifer 22.2).

Macronutrients: N, P, K, Mg, and Ca. Macronutrient concentrations in leaf litter varied with vegetation type. Concentrations of N, P, Ca, K, and Mg were significantly higher ($p < 0.05$) in al-

der leaf detritus than coniferous needles (see Figures 4 and 5, for Ca and Mg comparison). Seston particulate matter from Lindner Creek (red alder) was significantly higher in Mg ($p = 0.07$; Figure 5) and P ($p = 0.019$; Figure 6) than West Twin Creek (conifer). Magnesium concentrations in periphyton tended to be higher in red alder-dominated streams than conifer streams, but these differences were not significant. Concentrations of P and K concentrations in periphyton from wood blocks were significantly higher in Lindner than in West Twin Creek, regardless of block type (P: $p = 0.023$, K: $p = 0.093$). Concentrations of P, Ca, and K content in periphyton on cedar blocks was also

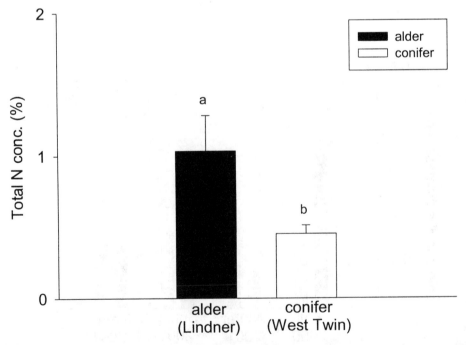

FIGURE 3. Total nitrogen concentrations in suspended particulate matter (seston) in Lindner (alder) and West Twin (conifer) creeks. Bars indicate standard error. Different letters indicate that alder is significantly higher than conifer ($p < 0.05$).

TABLE 2. Carbon and nitrogen concentrations (%) of periphyton and seston from headwater streams in fall 2000. $n = 3$, except for alder seston ($n = 2$).

Material + Element	Alder	Conifer	p value
Periphyton			
C	22.56 (2.02)	27.67 (0.83)	0.080
N	3.09 (0.19)	3.53 (0.35)	0.323
Seston			
C	14.90 (1.00)	8.10 (0.45)	0.006
N	0.67 (0.36)	0.45 (0.09)	0.526

significantly higher than on alder and maple blocks ($p = 0.01$, $p = 0.024$, and $p = 0.034$, respectively; Figure 7).

Micronutrients: Zn, Fe, Cu, Na, Mn. Concentrations of Cu and Zn were significantly higher in alder litterfall than coniferous needles (Table 3). Zinc concentrations were also higher in periphyton from Lindner than from West Twin Creek ($p = 0.048$). Periphyton collected from cedar blocks had significantly more Cu ($p = 0.002$) and Zn ($p = 0.020$) than periphyton from alder and maple blocks. Concentrations of Fe and Mn were not significantly different in litterfall, seston, and periphyton from tiles or in periphyton from wood blocks.

Discussion

Higher concentrations of both macro- and micronutrients were found in leaf litter, seston, and periphyton from alder-dominated streams than in streams bordered by coniferous vegetation. Although periphyton from alder streams was not overly rich in nutrients, the significantly higher biomass suggests that algae responded to nutri-

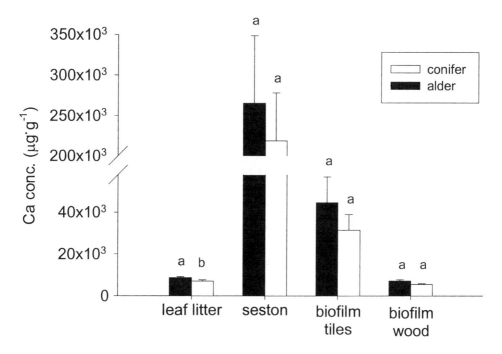

FIGURE 4. Calcium concentrations in leaf litter, seston, and periphyton (biofilm). Data averaged from samples collected monthly. Bars indicate standard error. Note the axis break from 58,000 to 200,000 mg/L. For each material, bars followed by a different letter are significantly different ($p < 0.05$).

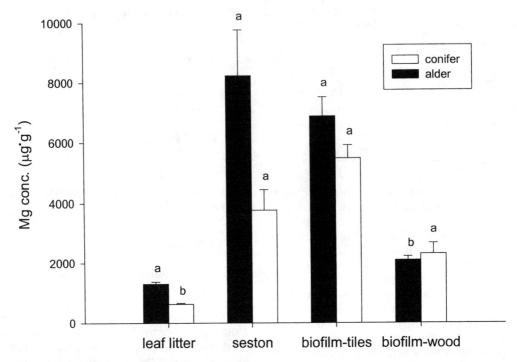

FIGURE 5. Magnesium concentrations in leaf litter, seston, and periphyton (biofilm) in conifer and alder streams. Data averaged from samples collected monthly. Bars indicate standard error. Bars followed by a different letter are significantly different ($p < 0.05$).

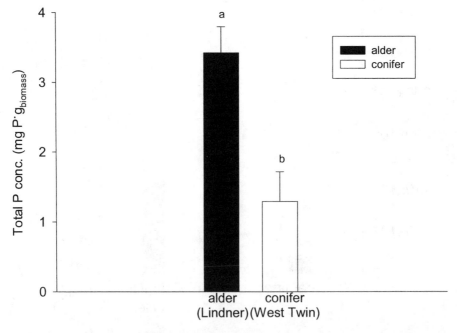

FIGURE 6. Total phosphorus concentrations from suspended particulate matter collected from Lindner (alder) and West Twin (conifer) creeks. Bars indicate standard error. Different letters indicate that alder is significantly higher than conifer ($p < 0.05$).

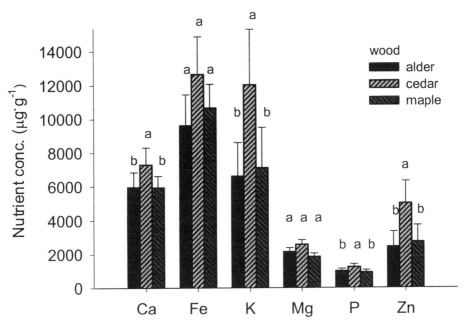

FIGURE 7. Macro- and micronutrient concentrations in periphyton collected from wood blocks. Wood block data from both Lindner Creek and West Twin Creek were averaged for wood type comparisons. Bars indicate standard error. For each element, bars followed by different letters are significantly different ($p <$ 0.05).

ent resources with increased growth rather than increased nutrient richness. The increased availability of either N or P could have stimulated algal growth (Ghosh and Gaur 1994), although specific responses can only be determined from N and P enrichment studies. Low chlorophyll a content may also suggest nutrient deficiencies in both stream types. In this case, available N and P provided by alder forests would quickly be used by organisms, increasing the productivity and turnover of nutrients within the stream ecosystem.

Alder, cedar, and maple wood blocks were used to determine if substrate composition could affect periphyton biomass and nutrient concentration. We expected the nutrient contribution from alder blocks to stimulate periphyton growth; cedar and maple blocks were selected as comparable substrata. Higher levels of macronutrients in periphyton from cedar blocks, compared with alder and maple, was unexpected; the firmer cedar blocks did not slough off as much woody material as alder and maple blocks dur-

TABLE 3. Mean monthly Cu, Na, Zn, and K concentrations, µg/g. Standard error is shown in parentheses. (leaf litter: Sept. 1999–Dec. 2000; seston: Jan. 2000–Dec. 2000; periphyton (tiles): June 1999–Dec. 2000; periphyton (wood): May 2000–April 2001). RA = red alder streams, C = conifer streams.

Material	Cu		Na		Zn		K	
	RA	C	RA	C	RA	C	RA	C
Leaf litter	10[a]	6[b]	247[a]	225[a]	24[a]	19[b]	3,429[a]	902[b]
	(0.2)	(0.6)	(14)	(15)	(0.6)	(2)	(220)	(93)
Seston	138[a]	102[a]	125,303[a]	114,813[b]	12,107[a]	13,802[a]	33,447[a]	30,037[a]
	(42)	(10)	(48,419)	(22,800)	(4,137)	(1,556)	(11,987)	(6471)
Periphyton (tiles)	130[a]	141[a]	253[a]	235[a]	4,715[a]	4,178[a]	8,315[a]	8,496[a]
	(22)	(10)	(23)	(96)	(925)	(912)	(592)	(821)
Periphyton (wood)	34[a]	32[b]	46,060[a]	23,778[b]	4,477[a]	2,329[b]	10,689[a]	5,713[b]
	(8)	(8)	(9,069)	(5,315)	(938)	(683)	(1,504)	(781)

[a, b] For each element, stream values followed by a different letter are significantly different ($p< 0.05$)

ing sampling events. As a result, cedar periphyton sample composition was primarily algae, while alder and maple periphyton samples had a much higher proportion of woody material, diluting the concentration of algal nutrients.

Our reported alder leaf litterfall N concentration, 2.37%, is comparable to the 2.45% reported by Luken and Fonda (1983). The dramatically lower C:N ratio of alder litterfall supports the well-reported evidence of the high-nutrient richness promoting the rapid decomposition and breakdown of alder litter (Irons et al. 1988). Alder litter transfers N, produced within the terrestrial ecosystem, to streams where it is broken down and utilized locally or spiraled downstream in dissolved or particulate form.

Reduced export of nutrients and organic matter from streams with declining adult salmon returns may affect production in aquatic ecosystems downstream from areas where spawning occurs (Vannote et al. 1980). Nitrogen, P, and total biomass inputs from salmon carcasses from Griffin Creek are reasonable estimates of nutrient loading for moderate to large coho salmon *Oncorhynchus kisutch* runs in the Pacific Northwest. Griffin Creek has averaged 445 coho/km over the last eighteen years (range 26–1,791 coho/km), and we estimated this to be about 1,355 kg/km coho salmon, using an average size estimate of coho in Washington of 2.83 kg (R. E. Bilby, Weyerhaeuser Inc., personal communication; Bigler et al. 1996). Bilby (from Gresh et al. 2000) has suggested that 93–155 salmon carcasses per stream kilometer are thought to be necessary to provide maximum ecological benefits from marine-derived nutrients. This indicates that run sizes from Griffin Creek are likely to play an important role in nutrient supply to the ecosystem. In the early 1970s, Richey et al. (1975) estimated that kokanee salmon *O. nerka* runs contribute between 17.3 and 44.6 kg P to Taylor Creek in California. Taylor Creek is an 8-km tributary with spawner runs of 7,000–14,000 individuals. In comparison, alder additions to an 8-km stretch of river with an influential riparian width of 20 m (10 m on either side of the stream) will contribute 40-kg P to the ecosystem, comparable to P inputs of a large kokanee escapement on Taylor Creek. However, while salmon runs can be highly variable over multiple years (Gresh et al. 2000), alder nutrient contributions will remain consistent each year, providing a stable source of nutrients to stream and terrestrial ecosystems.

The availability of nutrient resources, specifically N in streams dominated by alder, is evident in both dissolved (NH_4^+, NO_3^-) and suspended particulate matter (seston), but varies with seasonal rainfall. In California and Alaska, respectively, Triska et al. (1994) and Stottlemeyer (1992) found higher streamwater nitrate concentrations in sites with red alder than in old-growth coniferous forest. Triska et al. (1994) also found dramatic increases in NO_3^- in groundwater below alder stands after autumn rains. Transport of alder-derived nutrients to streams in groundwater or hyporheic flow also contributes to higher nutrient input. Additional macro- and micronutrients, such as Zn, K, Mg, and Ca, are also provided by alder litterfall. These nutrients are essential to the proper functioning of many pro- cesses in both plants and animals. Although it is assumed that carcass contribution of other macronutrients, such as Ca, Mg, and Zn, are also important, there is little information on their contribution to freshwater environments.

Our data support the notion that alder litter provides an important source of limiting elements to forests and streams. While nutrient inputs from salmon can be highly variable due to variable escapements and changing ocean conditions, alder can provide a steady nutrient supplement over the years (Mathisen et al. 1988; Bilby et al. 1996). Total litterfall inputs were approximately three times greater than biomass inputs from salmon carcasses on Griffin Creek, Washington (R. E. Bilby, Weyerhaeuser Inc., unpublished data) (Figure 1). Alder contributed almost twice as much total N per year into streams as salmon (Figure 8). Although salmon carcasses contribute twice as much P as alder litter, alder litter still provides significantly greater P inputs than coniferous litter (Figure 9). While degraded physical habitat and lack of suitable spawning sites with downstream barriers that block passage of spawners can limit the upstream distribution of carcasses within a watershed, alder colonizes both headwater and higher order river systems, providing nutrients throughout the channel network. Most alder litterfall occurs in autumn, but large nutrient contributions to streams are also made by catkins during the spring and steady litterfall through winter and summer months (Volk, personal observation).

Comparing salmon bearing and nonsalmon-bearing streams in Alaska, the average surface water nitrate concentration was strongly correlated with percent alder coverage in the water-

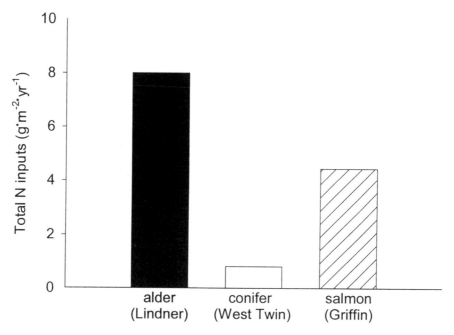

FIGURE 8. Total annual nitrogen inputs for alder and conifer streams based on litter inputs from West Twin (conifer) and Lindner (alder) creeks and salmon data from Griffin Creek (R. E. Bilby, Weyerhaeuser Inc., unpublished data). Annual input calculations were based on 2.37% N for alder, 0.77%N for conifer, and 3.03%N for salmon carcasses.

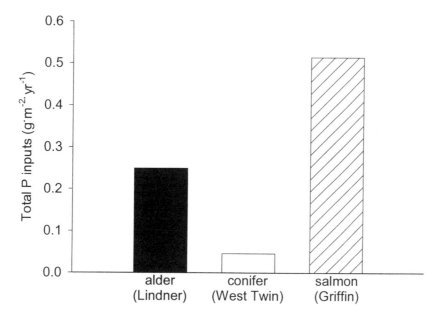

FIGURE 9. Total annual phosphorus inputs to streams based on litter inputs from West Twin (conifer) and Lindner (alder) creeks and salmon data from Griffin Creek (R. E. Bilby, Weyerhaeuser Inc., unpublished data). Annual input calculations were based on 0.35% P for salmon carcasses, 0.069% P for alder, and 0.045% P for conifer litter composition. Annual biomass inputs from West Twin (conifer), Lindner (red alder), and Griffin (salmon) creeks were used for calculations.

shed ($r^2 = 0.78$) (unpublished data, R. Edwards and T. O' Keefe, U.S.F.S., Juneau, Alaska, and University of Washington Seattle, Washington). Nitrate concentrations remained driven by the watershed coverage of alder, even when salmon bearing and nonsalmon bearing sites were compared before and during spawning events. This suggests that alder coverage may be a more important source of NO_3^- in surface water than salmon carcasses in streams where alder coverage is significant (>10% alder coverage).

Nutrient subsidies from alder forests may be important to food webs in northwest forest ecosystems facing nutrient deficiencies through reduced salmon runs. We suggest that a diverse mix of riparian vegetation is needed along streams and rivers; old growth and large conifers ensure the abundance and longevity of in-stream physical habitats, while broadleaf species, such as red alder, provide a stable and steady supply of nutrients. As a result, maintaining the heterogeneity of riparian forests, which supply important materials to streams and rivers, in conjunction with inputs of salmon carcasses from the ocean, is crucial for maintaining the diversity and productivity of Pacific Northwest watersheds.

Conclusions

Red alder provides a significant source of macronutrients to aquatic ecosystems. Our comparison of streams dominated by red alder and old-growth conifer riparian forests suggests that selective macro- and micronutrient differences in water chemistry, suspended particulate matter, and periphyton resources occur in these streams. Nutrient and organic matter resources transported from red alder-dominated riparian areas into freshwater ecosystems may temporarily replace those lost due to salmon declines and supplement those nutrients derived from fish carcasses, in areas with healthy populations. Moreover, maintaining alder forests may be critical to the recovery efforts of depressed salmon populations in the Pacific Northwest. We suggest that alder be regarded as an integral component of the riparian landscape, as it provides essential subsidies of limiting elements to stream and forest food webs while salmonid populations recover.

Acknowledgments

We give many thanks to Laurel Coe for invaluable field and laboratory assistance. Bill Baccus and other staff at Olympic National Park provided essential logistical support for this project. We also thank Bob Bilby for sharing comparative salmon data and review comments. Funding was provided through the U.S. Forest Service and Olympic Natural Resources Center (ONRC) in Forks, Washington, and the Northwest Fisheries Science Center, National Marine Fisheries Service, Seattle, Washington.

References

Barlocher, F. 1992. Community organization. Pages 38–76 *in* F. Barlocher, editor. The ecology of aquatic hyphomycetes. Springer-Verlag, Berlin.

Bilby, R. E., and P. A. Bisson. 1992. Allochthonous versus autochthonous organic matter contributions to the trophic support of fish populations in clear-cut and old-growth forested streams. Canadian Journal of Fisheries and Aquatic Sciences 49:540–551.

Bilby, R. E., B. R. Fransen, and P. A. Bisson. 1996. Incorporation of nitrogen and carbon from spawning coho salmon into the trophic system of small streams: evidence from stable isotopes. Canadian Journal of Fisheries and Aquatic Sciences 53:164–173.

Binkley, D., R. Bell, and P. Sollins. 1992. Comparison of methods for estimating soil nitrogen transformations in adjacent conifer and alder-conifer stands. Canadian Journal of Forest Research 22:858–863.

Bigler, B. S., D. W. Welch, and J. H. Helle. 1996. A review of size trends among north pacific salmon (*Oncorhynchus* spp.). Canadian Journal of Fisheries and Aquatic Sciences 53:455–465.

Bormann, B. T., K. Cromack, and W. O. Russell. 1994. Influences of red alder on soils and long-term ecosystem productivity. Pages 47–56 *in* D. E. Hibbs, D. S. DeBell, and R. F. Tarrant, editors. The biology and management of red alder. Oregon State University Press, Corvallis, Oregon.

Connolly, P. J. 1997. Influence of stream characteristics and age-class interactions on populations of coastal cutthroat trout. Pages 173–174 *in* P. A. Bisson and R. E. Gresswell, editors. American Fisheries Society, Oregon Chapter, Corvallis, Oregon.

Cummins, K. W. 1974. Structure and function of stream ecosystems. BioScience 24:631–641.

Edmonds, R. L., R. D. Blew, J. L. Marra, J. Blew, A. K. Barg, G. Murray, and T. D. Thomas. Vegetation patterns, hydrology, and water chemistry in small watersheds in the Hoh River Valley, Olympic National Park. Scientific Monograph NPSD/NRUSGS/NRSM-98/02, U.S. Department of the Interior, National Park Service.

Ghosh, M., and J. P. Gaur. 1994. Algal periphyton of an unshaded stream in relation to in situ nutrient enrichment and current velocity. Aquatic Botany 47:185–189.

Goldman, C. R. 1961. The contribution of alder trees (*Alnus tenuifolia*) to the primary productivity of Castle Lake, California. Ecology 42:282–288.

Gresh, T., J. Lichatowich, and P. Schoonmaker. 2000. An estimation of historic, and current levels of salmon production in the northeast Pacific ecosystem: evidence of a nutrient deficit in the freshwater systems of the Pacific Northwest. Fisheries 25:15–21.

Irons, J. G. III, M. W. Oswood, and J. P. Bryant. 1988. Consumption of leaf detritus by a stream shredder: influence of tree species and nutrient status. Hydrobiologia 160:53–61.

Luken, J. O., and R. W. Fonda. 1983. Nitrogen accumulation in a chronosequence of red alder communities along the Hoh River, Olympic National Park, Washington. Canadian Journal of Forest Research 13:1228–1237.

Mathisen, O. A., P. L. Parker, J. J. Goering, T. C. Kline, P. H. Poe, and R. S. Scalan. 1988. Recycling of marine elements transported into freshwater systems by anadromous salmon. Proceedings, Congress in New Zealand 23:2249–2258.

Perrin, C. J., and J. S. Richardson. 1997. N and P limitation of benthos abundance in the Nechako River, British Columbia. Canadian Journal of Fisheries and Aquatic Sciences 54:2574–2583.

Richey, J. E., M. A. Perkins, and C. R. Goldman. 1975. Effects of Kokanee salmon (*Oncorhynchus nerka*) decomposition on the ecology of a subalpine stream. Journal of the Fisheries Research Board of Canada 32:817–820.

Stottlemeyer, R. 1992. Nitrogen mineralization and streamwater chemistry, Rock Creek Watershed, Denali National Park, Alaska, U.S.A. Arctic and Alpine Research 24:291–303.

Tarrant, R. F., and E. F. Miller. 1983. Accumulation of organic matter and soil nitrogen beneath a plantation of red alder and Douglas-fir. Soil Science Society of America Proceedings 27:231–234.

Triska, F. J., A. P. Jackman, et al. 1994. Ammonium sorption to channel and riparian sediments: a transient storage pool for dissolved inorganic nitrogen. Biogeochemistry 26:67–83.

UNESCO. 1994. Protocols for the Joint Global Ocean Flux Study (JGOFS) Core Measurements. IOC Manual and Guides 29.

Valderrama, J. C. 1981. The simultaneous analysis of total nitrogen and total phosphorus on natural waters. Marine Chemistry 10:109–122.

Vannote, R. L. G. Minshall, K. W. Cummins, J. R. Sedell, and C. E. Cushing. 1980. The river continuum concept. Canadian Journal of Fisheries and Aquatic Sciences 37:130–137.

Webster, J. R., and J. L. Meyer. 1997. Stream organic matter budgets. Journal of the North American Benthological Society 16:3–161.

Worona, M, A., and C. Whitlock. 1995. Late quaternary vegetation and climate history near Little Lake, central coast range, Oregon. Geological Society of America Bulletin 107:867–876.

Method Refinement

American Fisheries Society Symposium 34:229–236, 2003

Trophic Level Implications When Using Natural Stable Isotope Abundance to Determine Effects of Salmon-Derived Nutrients on Juvenile Sockeye Salmon Ecology

Thomas C. Kline, Jr.

Prince William Sound Science Center, P.O. Box 705, Cordova, Alaska 99574, USA

Abstract.—The amount of nitrogen contributed by anadromous and semelparous Pacific salmon *Oncorhynchus* spp., marine-derived nitrogen (MDN), relative to other sources, was estimated for sockeye salmon *O. nerka* juveniles rearing in nursery lakes of the Karluk and Kvichak rivers (Alaska) from their nitrogen stable isotope abundance using an isotope mixing model (IMM). Because trophic level (TL) as well as MDN can lead to nitrogen-15 enrichment, it is critical to know, for the IMM, the TL of juvenile sockeye salmon (JSS) during their lacustrine life history phase. The initial a priori TL of 3.0 overestimated MDN. Regressing salmon escapement with stable isotope ratio and incorporating an updated herbivore isotope fractionation factor suggested that the TL of Kvichak JSS was 3.7. This TL value and the difference in carbon and nitrogen stable isotope ratios between JSS and net zooplankton suggested that the TL of net zooplankton was 2.6. Using TL = 2.6 for net zooplankton and the difference in stable isotope ratios between Karluk JSS and net zooplankton suggested that JSS TL was 4.3. These latter TL values suggested that the mean MDN for the Karluk system during the late 1980s and early 1990s was 67%, which was approximately half of that predicted using earlier fractionation and TL values. Sample isotopic variation and variation due to instrument error were minor in comparison to TL uncertainty involved in data modeling. Nonetheless, nitrogen stable isotope data provide a means for assessing MDN that can range significantly within and among systems.

Introduction

Stable isotope natural abundance data are useful for evidencing that marine-derived nutrients transported and released via the spawning migration and subsequent death of semelparous and anadromous Pacific salmon *Oncorhynchus* spp. provide a significant nutrient subsidy to freshwater (Kline 1991; Kline et al. 1990, 1993; Bilby et al. 1996) and adjacent terrestrial ecosystems (Hilderbrand et al. 1996; Ben-David et al. 1997). The method is based on the fact that nitrogen delivered by these salmon is enriched in the 'heavy' stable isotope, ^{15}N, compared with atmospheric N_2, the primary nitrogen source that is otherwise available. Because matter, and thus stable isotopic composition, is conserved, a wide range of biota within the reach of migrating salmon has been found to be ^{15}N-enriched compared with adjacent nonsalmon control areas (Kline et al. 1990; Kline et al. 1993; Ben-David et al. 1997).

Because nitrogen stable isotope ratio, $^{15}N/^{14}N$, of sockeye salmon offspring of a particular brood was correlated to the number of adult salmon returning to spawn (brood size) in the Kvichak River (Alaska) system, where brood size normally varies cyclically by at least an order of magnitude (Kline et al. 1993), and because the nitrogen stable isotope ratios of sockeye salmon *O. nerka* smolts, zooplankton, and sediment nitrogen were correlated to the numbers of salmon spawning per unit area of lake across several systems (Finney et al. 2000), nitrogen stable isotope ratios are useful for measuring the relative quantity of nitrogen delivered by salmon to their freshwater habitats (i.e., marine-derived nitrogen or MDN; Kline et al. 1990). However, two feeding steps or trophic levels enrich $^{15}N/^{14}N$ by 6.8 delta units (i.e., 2×3.4; delta units defined in materials and methods section), which is approximately the 7.0 delta unit difference between 0 and 100% MDN at a given trophic level (TL). Kline et al. (1990, 1993) developed an isotope-mixing model (IMM) to incorporate the effects of trophic enrichment when computing MDN from $^{15}N/^{14}N$ data (Kline 1991). The IMM functioned by subtracting the $^{15}N/^{14}N$ value for a given TL when MDN = 0 from the observed $^{15}N/^{14}N$ value (of same TL) and then dividing by the empirically determined constant 7.0. The $^{15}N/^{14}N$ value for a given TL when MDN = 0 was thus the critical parameter needed for interpreting isotope data.

Kline et al. (1993) used a $^{15}N/^{14}N$ delta value of 6.8 as the critical parameter for juvenile sockeye salmon (JSS). This was based on the observation that sockeye salmon fry feed selectively on smaller size classes of the cladoceran (*Bosmina*) in Iliamna Lake, the principal Kvichak System nursery lake (Hoag 1972), and assuming a simple three-step food chain of phytoplankton to zooplankton to JSS and a constant $^{15}N/^{14}N$ enrichment of 3.4 delta units per food chain step. Recently, Vander Zanden and Rasmussen (2001) suggested that while carnivore enrichment is 3.4 delta units per food chain step, herbivore enrichment is 2.5. Furthermore, Vander Zanden and Rasmussen (2001) reported that while the standard deviation for carnivore $^{15}N/^{14}N$ enrichment was 0.4 delta units, which is much less than 1.1 reported by Minagawa and Wada (1984) in the classic nitrogen isotopic trophic fractionation reference, there was a much greater herbivore standard deviation of 2.5. To overcome this uncertainty, they suggested using herbivores or a higher TL as the reference (baseline) rather than primary producers. Using the lower $^{15}N/^{14}N$ herbivore enrichment factor in the IMM and assuming the TL of JSS = 3.0 has the effect of increasing MDN to untenable values. The purpose of this paper was, thus, to revise the IMM for JSS of the Kvichak River and Karluk River systems by (1) developing alternative estimates for what the $^{15}N/^{14}N$ content of JSS should be when MDN = 0 (the critical parameter) and (2) using net zooplankton as the reference.

Methods

Collections

Sockeye salmon smolts from the outlet of Karluk Lake (Karluk River; 1988, 1991, and 1992) and Iliamna Lake (Kvichak River; 1985 and 1986) and sockeye salmon fry from Karluk Lake (1986 and 1988 through 1991) were collected by the Alaska Department of Fish and Game. Kvichak system fry were collected from Iliamna Lake in 1986 and 1987 (Kline et al. 1993). Smolts were collected during their spring out-migration, while fry were collected during the summer ice-free period. Zooplankton were collected at both lakes using 153-μm mesh, 0.5-m diameter ring nets that were towed obliquely from as deep as 100 m, depending on sampling station depth, to the surface and saved as bulk samples. Iliamna Lake zooplankton were collected during 1986 and 1987 (Kline et al. 1993), while Karluk Lake zooplankton were collected from 1988 to 1990 (within-year sampling periods are given in the results). Location of Karluk system zooplankton sampling stations were shown by Schmidt et al. 1998, while those from the Kvichak system were shown by Kline et al. 1993.

Laboratory Preparation and Analysis

Samples were generally frozen (–20°C; the exceptions were that Karluk fry from 1991 and 1992 were preserved in alcohol; Kline and Goering 1994) and processed in the laboratory for isotopic analysis (Kline et al. 1990, 1993, 1998). Laboratory processing included measuring fork length to the nearest millimeter. Final stages of isotopic preparation varied, according to instrumentation, by year. Sealed-tube combustion and manual cryogenic distillation was applied to samples collected from 1985 to 1991. These samples were analyzed with either a VG SIRA-9 or VG Series II mass spectrometer. Automated combustion via a Europa RoboPrep unit coupled to a Europa 20/20 was used for later samples. Stable isotope data are reported as delta values, defined by the following relationship:

$$\delta^{15}N \text{ or } \delta^{13}C = \left(\frac{R_{sample}}{R_{standard}} - 1 \right) \times 1,000\%,$$

where $R = {}^{15}N/^{14}N$ or $^{13}C/^{12}C$, $R_{standard}$ for N is air, and $R_{standard}$ for C is Vienna Peedee belemnite

(VPDB). By definition, the isotope standards have delta values of zero (i.e., $\delta^{15}N$ = 0.0 for atmospheric N_2. Typically, instrument replication is less than 0.2 ‰.

Data Modeling

Fry determined to have a natal signature were excluded from analyses based on fry length (Kline et al. 1993). The general form of the IMM model (Kline et al. 1993) can be written as follows:

$$\%MDN_i = \frac{OBS_{TL_i} - TEM_{TL_i}}{MEM_{TL_i} - TEM_{TL_i}},$$

where TEM_{TL_i} (terrestrial end-member) is the $\delta^{15}N$ value when MDN is 0%, and MEM_{TL_i} (marine end-member) is the $\delta^{15}N$ value when the MDN is 100% for TL value i (TL = i). OBS_{TL_i} is the observed $\delta^{15}N$ value of TL = i. The denominator value (i.e., the end-member difference) was determined empirically to be 7.0 ‰ based on observations of primary producers (i.e., TL = 1.0; Kline et al. 1990, 1993). TL = JSS is thus the trophic level of lacustrine juvenile sockeye salmon. The value for TEM_{JSS} is thus needed to calculate the MDN from OBS_{JSS}.

Estimating TEM$_{JSS}$

Finney et al. (2000) found a linear relationship between the $\delta^{15}N$ values of lake biota and salmon escapement, especially when escapement density was less than ~20,000 salmon per km^2 of lake surface area. A criterion of 20,000 salmon per km^2 of lake surface area would be met when considering the surface area of just the primary Kvichak nursery lake, Iliamna Lake, for escapements of less than 52 million, which is more than twice the highest Kvichak escapement ever recorded (1965). Because of the large surface area, $\delta^{15}N$ values of Kvichak system biota most likely to reflect a linear relationship with escapement size, which varies in a five-year cycle by at least an order of magnitude. Kvichak sockeye salmon fry and smolt $\delta^{15}N$ data from Table 7 of Kline et al. (1993) were plotted to extrapolate the $\delta^{15}N$ value for zero escapement (i.e., the TEM_{JSS}). Karluk sockeye salmon runs vary only by about 2:1, precluding extrapolation. Therefore, TEM_{JSS} was estimated by ascertaining differences in food chain length between JSS and the net zooplankton reference. Bulk net zooplankton samples (e.g., Kline

et al. 1993), which were initially defined as herbivores, were used because of mass spectrometry size requirements. Net samples may include large chain diatoms as well as potential carnivores (e.g., *Cyclops* copepods). Therefore, net zooplankton TL was revised according to their isotopic relationship with JSS, assumption that the TL of Karluk and Kvichak net zooplankton was the same, and that the $\delta^{15}N$ value of phytoplankton in the absence of MDN was zero.

In the absence of salmon, N_2 fixation within a drainage basin can deliver significant quantities of nitrogen to Alaskan salmonid ecosystems (Gunther 1989). The $\delta^{15}N$ of $TEM_{phytoplankton}$ should, thus, be around zero because primary producers tend toward this value in systems where the primary nitrogen input is N_2 fixation (Minagawa and Wada 1984; Owens 1987). This assuming was verified by periphyton $\delta^{15}N$ from anadromous salmon-free parts of watersheds used as controls (Kline et al. 1990, 1993). TL differences were calculated based on a trophic fractionation factor of 3.4 for $\delta^{15}N$ and 1.0 for $\delta^{13}C$ (DeNiro and Epstein 1978, 1981; Fry and Sherr 1984; Minagawa and Wada 1984) for TL greater than net zooplankton (Vander Zanden and Rasmussen 2001). Trophic fractionation factors of 2.5 and 1.0 for $\delta^{15}N$ and $\delta^{13}C$, respectively, were used for 'net zooplankton' (Vander Zanden and Rasmussen 2001).

Results

Kvichak System TEM$_{JSS}$

The TEM_{JSS} was 8.4‰ (Figure 1). The TEM_{JSS} confidence interval was around ±1.2. The value 8.4 ‰ was, thus, significantly greater than the a priori TEM_{JSS} of 6.8. The $\delta^{15}N$ difference of 1.6 ‰, which is the equivalent $\delta^{15}N$ increase due to ~0.5 TL, systematically overestimated MDN by about 23%.

Karluk System TEM$_{JSS}$

The data suggested inconsistencies in the TL difference between zooplankton and JSS (>35 mm) and MDN difference between the Kvichak and Karluk systems (Figure 2). Karluk zooplankton were $\delta^{15}N$ enriched on average by about 2‰ compared with Kvichak zooplankton. The between-system JSS $\delta^{15}N$ difference was greater, about 5‰. There was, thus, a greater $\delta^{15}N$ increase for Karluk

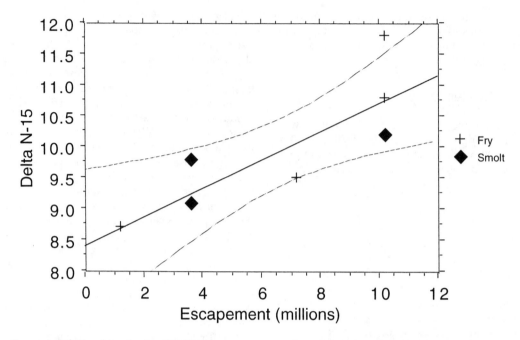

FIGURE 1. Relationship of cohort MDN to escapement number. Regression plot with 95% confidence intervals relating the $\delta^{15}N$ of sockeye salmon offspring to brood year escapement number using data from Table 7 of Kline et al. (1993); $p < 0.0001$, $r^2 = 0.66$. Each point represents the mean of $n = 5$ to $n = 52$ individual salmon collected at different sampling seasons. The y-intercept value suggested a TEM_{JSS} value of 8.4.

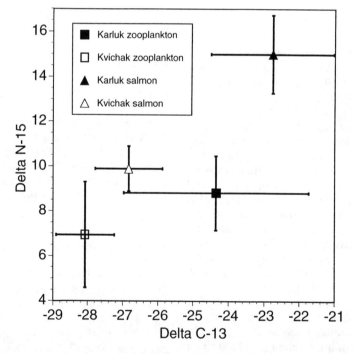

FIGURE 2. Dual-isotope plot comparing mean $\delta^{15}N$ and $\delta^{13}C$ of zooplankton and juvenile sockeye salmon >35 mm from the Karluk and Kvichak systems. Error bars indicate ±1 standard deviation.

JSS relative to Karluk zooplankton compared with the Kvichak system. The $\delta^{13}C$ increase for Karluk JSS was also greater than the Kvichak. TL differences based on stable isotopes of each element isotopic were consistent (Table 1). However, the TL difference between zooplankton and JSS for the Kvichak system was 1.1 ± 0.2 TL, while that of the Karluk system was 1.7 ± 0.1 TL. Assuming that net zooplankton sample had a mean TL of 2.0, then, TL of JSS would be estimated to be 3.7 from adding 2.0 to the JSS-zooplankton TL difference. The Karluk TEM_{JSS} would, thus, be 8.3 and MDN, thus, 96%, which would compare favorably with MDN = 117%, based on TL = 3. Alternatively, Kvichak zooplankton were estimated to be TL = 2.6, using the salmon TL = 3.7 from the extrapolation (Figure 1) and the isotope-based Kvichak JSS-zooplankton TL difference. If the TL of Karluk net zooplankton was also 2.6, then the TL of JSS would be 4.3, which would make the Karluk TEM_{JSS} = 10.3. The MDN of Karluk would then be 67%.

Karluk Interannual and Ontogenetic Isotopic Variability

Box plots for Karluk sockeye fry larger than 35 mm (Kline et al. 1993) and smolt by year suggested a gradual increase in $\delta^{15}N$ and a gradual decrease in $\delta^{13}C$ over time (Figure 3). Karluk smolts were more positive in $\delta^{15}N$ than fry from the previous year. Karluk smolts were more negative in $\delta^{13}C$ than fry from the previous year. While

Karluk zooplankton also appear to have shifted downwards in $\delta^{13}C$ over time, seasonal variability within 1988 exceeded interannual differences. With the exception of early 1988, the $\delta^{15}N$ of zooplankton increased in 1989 and 1990, relative to 1988.

Discussion

Assumptions of TL or 'food-chain length' profoundly affected $\delta^{15}N$-based MDN calculations. While isotopic signatures of Karluk JSS tracked those of zooplankton, confirming that shifts were due to prey, trophic relationships between predators, salmon, and their prey, zooplankton, in terms of number of food chain steps, differed markedly from the Kvichak system. More trophic steps in Karluk salmon fry food webs, in part, led to higher $\delta^{15}N$ values. Although the TEM_{JSS} parameter compensated for trophic fractionation effects, different approaches or assumptions for estimating TEM_{JSS} produced different estimates of MDN. Assuming a prior or a consistent TL for JSS among systems is, thus, inappropriate, except possibly as a starting point.

TL and trophic isotopic enrichment factors are critical considerations for estimating TEM_{JSS} when salmon run size is generally consistent and cannot be used to extrapolate TEM_{JSS}. The herbivore fractionation reported by Vander Zanden and Rasmussen (2001), alone, systematically lowered TEM_{JSS} by 0.9‰, necessitating an increase in JSS TL to maintain previous MDN estimates.

TABLE 1. Estimations of trophic level (TL) difference between net zooplankton and juvenile sockeye salmon larger than 35mm from the Karluk and Kvichak systems based on nitrogen and carbon stable isotope analysis.

Karluk	n	$\delta^{15}N$	SE	n	$\delta^{13}C$	SE	Mean TL difference
Zooplankton	60	8.8	0.2	75	−24.4	0.3	
Salmon > 35mm	152	15.0	0.1	161	−22.8	0.1	
Salmon-zooplankton		6.2			1.6		
		TL			TL		
TL difference		1.8			1.6		1.7

Kvichak	n	$\delta^{15}N$	SE	n	$\delta^{13}C$	SE	
Zooplankton	19	6.9	0.5	6	−28.1	0.2	
Salmon > 35mm	169	9.9	0.1	180	−26.8	0.1	
Salmon-zooplankton		3.0			1.2		
		TL			TL		
TL difference		0.9			1.2		1.1

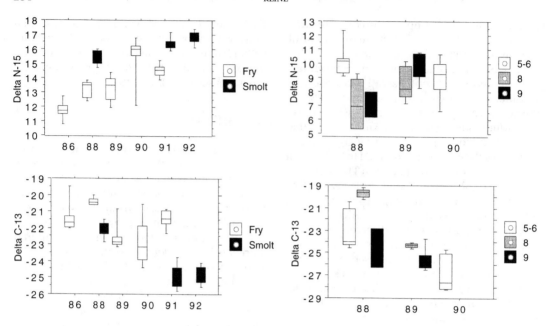

FIGURE 3. Box plots of $\delta^{15}N$ (upper panels) and $\delta^{13}C$ (lower panels) over time for Karluk sockeye fry larger than 35 mm and smolt by year (left panels) and zooplankton by month and year (right panels).

Increases in food chain length (e.g., ~3.7, compared with a prior TL = 3) imply additional *carnivore* fractionation effects, thus avoiding the isotopic fractionation uncertainty due to the trophic link between primary produces and herbivores. Therefore, developing a better understanding of the trophic relationships *within* the zooplankton community is key to enhancing use of $\delta^{15}N$ to quantify MDN.

The relatively high $\delta^{15}N$ of Karluk JSS may have been, in part, ontogenetic. Karluk smolts are older and larger than those from the Kvichak system (e.g., lengths of 96–152 mm versus 80–122 mm, respectively; Burgner 1991). Because Karluk smolt $\delta^{15}N$ values were greater than fry, they could have fed at a higher TL or MDN increased during winter. In contrast, year-to-year differences among life history stages of Kvichak JSS were much greater than ontogenetic differences, other than natal effects (fry < 35 mm in length; Kline et al. 1993). Contrasting with the Karluk system, Mathisen et al. (2000) showed virtually no change in the $\delta^{15}N$ values of Egegik sockeye salmon smolts as a function of length of 85–145 mm for observations made during 1993–1997.

Although Karluk sockeye salmon runs do not vary in size to the same extent as those in the Kvichak, the study period coincided with an extraordinarily large 1.1 million sockeye salmon spawning run resulting from curtailment of all fishing in the region subsequent to the T/V *Exxon Valdez* oil spill (commercial fishing was halted for 1989 in order to ensure that no Alaska salmon would be sold contaminated by oil). Therefore, an increase in $\delta^{15}N$ due to increased MDN was expected. The zooplankton $\delta^{15}N$ increase in August and September 1989 compared with August and September of 1988 was, thus, most likely due to this extraordinary run. The observed delay in transference of the zooplankton $\delta^{15}N$ increase to JSS was probably a sampling artifact, since fry were sampled prior to the peak of spawning and smolts were not collected during spring 1990. The high $\delta^{15}N$ and low $\delta^{13}C$ values observed until the end of the study may have been due to the prolonged effects of the 1989 carcass loading.

There were similar patterns in the qualitative aspects of Karluk zooplankton and JSS $\delta^{13}C$ and $\delta^{15}N$ shifts. The highest within-year $\delta^{13}C$ values coincided with the lowest $\delta^{15}N$ values during August 1988, which was consistent with the general inverse relationship of the $\delta^{13}C$ and $\delta^{15}N$ year-to-year trends for both zooplankton and JSS. The large change in Karluk $\delta^{13}C$ values is suggestive of multiple or changing carbon sources within the lake. Very negative $\delta^{13}C$ values (e.g., less than –26) were found in about half of the smolts of both systems. Low $\delta^{13}C$ is not uncommon in lake food webs and is indicative of respired carbon (see Kline et al. 1990). Salmon carcasses as well as other carbon sources could play a role in supplying carbon that is respired. Systems without MDN can also have significant respired carbon input. For example, the nonanadromous salmon section of Sashin Creek, including Sashin Lake, contained low $\delta^{13}C$, indicating respired carbon (Kline et al. 1990). Marine and terrestrial carbon sources, when respired, may, thus, not be distinguishable in food webs based on $\delta^{13}C$ alone.

The possible range in TL used for the IMM is a greater source of error than the uncertainty due to instrumentation or to the sample. A TL uncertainty of less than 0.1 TL, based on standard error, was due to instrumentation (Kline 2001). The sample standard errors were no more than about twice instrument uncertainty. The greatest standard error-based TL confidence interval found here was for Kvichak zooplankton, which was ±0.3 TL. The standard error for the JSS suggested a narrower TL confidence interval of less than ±0.1 TL. Thus, assumptions used to model $\delta^{15}N$ data have a greater impact on the interpretation of results than the measurements themselves. Instrumentation uncertainty was also less than temporal isotopic variability in both systems, confirming that temporal variability of MDN was measured. However, one would have to assume a consistent TL, since $\delta^{15}N$ fluctuation could be interpreted as change in TL, if MDN was assumed to be constant. However, isotopic shifts among years suggest generally consistent within-system TL differences between zooplankton and JSS. Recent improvement in mass spectrometric capability enables isotopic analysis of individual zooplankters (e.g., Kline 1999), which could potentially improve understanding of trophic structure and, by extension, the role of MDN in JSS food webs.

Differences suggested for food web structure, 'food-chain length' in particular, between the Kvichak and Karluk systems have broader implications than this study. Stockner (1987) suggested that food-chain length of coastal sockeye salmon nursery lakes can be longer than those of interior lakes by one to two trophic levels. The longer food chain length suggested for Karluk JSS compared with the Kvichak system is, thus, consistent with Stockner (1987), since the former is located on Kodiak Island within the North Pacific Ocean, whereas the Kvichak system is located inland, situated mostly within a continental climate regime (Williamson and Peyton 1962).

Mathisen and Sands (1999) determined that JSS of Becharof Lake, like Iliamna Lake a Bristol Bay nursery lake, had a trophic level of 3.1 using a mass-balance modeling approach in conjunction with $\delta^{15}N$ measurements. They were aided, in part, because Egegik River (the Becharof Lake outlet) mean annual sockeye salmon smolt $\delta^{15}N$ values varied by no more than 0.7‰ during five years (Mathisen et al. 2000), suggesting a lesser MDN variance than either the Kvichak or Karluk systems. Thus, IMM parameters must be developed and applied on a system-by-system basis.

Acknowledgments

I am grateful to the following for their many years of advice and collaboration: John J. Goering, Ole A. Mathisen, Patrick L. Parker, Patrick H. Poe, Jeffrey P. Koenings, Dana C. Schmidt, Donald M. Schell, and Bruce P. Finney. The data presented in this paper represent the product of a number of past projects that were funded by the National Science Foundation Division of Polar Programs, the Alaska Sea Grant College Program, the Bristol Bay Borough, the Alaska Department of Fish and Game, and the *Exxon Valdez* Oil Spill Trustee Council. This manuscript benefited from suggestions made by an anonymous reviewer and the volume editor, John Stockner.

References

Ben-David, M. T., A. Hanley, D. R. Klein, and D. M. Schell. 1997. Seasonal changes in diets of coastal and riverine mink: the role of spawning pacific salmon. Canadian Journal of Zoology 75:803–811.

Bilby, R. E., B. R. Fransen, and P. A. Bisson. 1996. Incorporation of nitrogen and carbon from spawning coho salmon into the trophic system of small streams: evidence from stable isotopes. Canadian Journal of Fisheries and Aquatic Sciences 53:164–173.

Burgner, R. L. 1991. Life history of sockeye salmon (*Oncorhynchus nerka*). Pages 3–117 *in* C. Groot and L. Margolis, editors. Pacific salmon life histories. UBC Press, Vancouver.

DeNiro, M. J., and S. Epstein. 1978. Influence of diet on the distribution of carbon isotopes in animals. Geochimica et Cosmochimica Acta 42:495–506.

DeNiro, M. J., and S. Epstein. 1981. Influence of diet on the distribution of nitrogen isotopes in animals. Geochimica et Cosmochimica Acta 45:341–353.

Finney, B. P., I. Gregory-Eaves, J. Sweetman, M. S. V. Douglas, and J. P. Smol. 2000. Impacts of climatic change and fishing on Pacific salmon over the past 300 years. Science 290:795–799.

Fry, B., and E. B. Sherr. 1984. $\delta^{13}C$ measurements as indicators of carbon flow in marine and freshwater ecosystems. Contributions in Marine Science 27:13–47.

Gunther, A. J. 1989. Nitrogen fixation by lichen in a subarctic Alaskan watershed. The Bryologist 92:202–208.

Hilderbrand, G. V., S. D. Farley, C. T. Robbins, T. A. Hanley, K. Titus, and C. Servheen. 1996. Use of stable isotopes to determine diets of living and extinct bears. Canadian Journal of Zoology 74:2080–2088.

Kline, T. C., Jr. 1991. The significance of marine-derived biogenic nitrogen in anadromous Pacific salmon freshwater food webs. Doctoral dissertation, University of Alaska Fairbanks, Fairbanks, Alaska.

Kline, T. C., Jr. 1999. Temporal and spatial variability of $^{13}C/^{12}C$ and $^{15}N/^{14}N$ in pelagic biota of Prince William Sound, Alaska. Canadian Journal of Fisheries and Aquatic Sciences 56(Supplement 1):94–117.

Kline Jr., T. C. 2001. Trophic position of Pacific herring in Prince William Sound, Alaska, based on their stable isotope abundance. Pages 69–80 *in* F. Funk, J. Blackburn, D. Hay, A. J. Paul, R. Stephenson, R. Toresen, and D. Witherell, editors. Herring: expectations for a new millennium. University of Alaska Sea Grant, AK-SG-01–04, Fairbanks, Alaska.

Kline, T. C., Jr., J. J. Goering, O. A. Mathisen, P. H. Poe and P. L. Parker. 1990. Recycling of elements transported upstream by runs of Pacific salmon: I. $\delta^{15}N$ and $\delta^{13}C$ evidence in Sashin Creek, southeastern Alaska. Canadian Journal of Fisheries and Aquatic Sciences 47:136–144.

Kline, T. C. Jr., J. J. Goering, O. A. Mathisen, P. H. Poe, P. L. Parker, and R. S. Scalan. 1993. Recycling of elements transported upstream by runs of Pacific salmon: II. $\delta^{15}N$ and $\delta^{13}C$ evidence in the Kvichak River Watershed, Bristol Bay, southwestern Alaska. Canadian Journal of Fisheries and Aquatic Sciences 50:2350–2365.

Kline, T. C. Jr., and J. J. Goering. 1994. Stable isotope analysis of juvenile sockeye salmon #2. Final Report produced for the Alaska Department of Fish and Game. University of Alaska Institute of Marine Science, Fairbanks, Alaska.

Mathisen, O. A., and N. J. Sands. 1999. Ecosystem modeling of Becharof Lake, a sockeye salmon nursery lake in southwestern Alaska. Pages 685–703 *in* Ecosystem approaches for fisheries management. Alaska Sea Grant College Program. AK-SG-99–01.

Mathisen, O. A., J. J. Goering and E. V. Farley. 2000. Nitrogen and carbon isotope ratios in sockeye salmon smolts. Verhandlungen Internationale Vereinigung Limnologie 27:3121–3124.

Minagawa, M., and E. Wada. 1984. Stepwise enrichment of ^{15}N along food chains: further evidence and the relation between $\delta^{15}N$ and animal age. Geochimica et Cosmochimica Acta 48:1135–1140.

Owens, N. J. P. 1987. Natural variations in ^{15}N in the marine environment. Advances in Marine Biology 24:389–451.

Schmidt, D. C., S. R. Carlson, G. B. Kyle, and J. A. Edmundson. 1998. Influence of carcass-derived nutrients on sockeye salmon productivity of Karluk Lake, Alaska: importance in the assessment of an escapement goal. North American Journal of Fisheries Management 18:743–763.

Stockner, J. G. 1987. Lake fertilization: the enrichment cycle and lake sockeye salmon (*Oncorhynchus nerka*) production. Pages 198–251 *in* H. D. Smith, L. Margolis, and C. C. Wood, editors. Sockeye salmon (*Oncorhynchus nerka*) population and future management. Canadian Special Publication in Fisheries and Aquatic Science 96.

Vander Zanden, M. J., and J. B. Rasmussen. 2001. Variation in ^{15}N and ^{13}C trophic fractionation: implications for aquatic food web studies. Limnology and Oceanography 46:2061–2066.

Williamson, F. S. L., and L. J. Peyton. 1962. Faunal relationships of birds in the Iliamna Lake area, Alaska. Biological Papers of the University of Alaska, Number 5.

American Fisheries Society Symposium 34:237–243, 2003

Evaluations of Slow-Release Fertilizer for Rehabilitating Oligotrophic Streams

MEGAN S. STERLING

B.C. Conservation Foundation, #206-17564
56A Avenue, Surrey, B.C. V3S 1G3, Canada

KENNETH I. ASHLEY

Research and Development Section, British Columbia Ministry of Fisheries
2204 Main Mall, Vancouver, B.C. V6T 1Z4, Canada

Abstract.—A solid briquette fertilizer for use in the Pacific Northwest streams and elsewhere was identified from a variety of slow-release formulations (26 were tested with varying $N:P_2O_5:K_2O$ ratios and binders) using indoor trough and controlled field experiments. The use of a slow-release fertilizer is an innovative method for adding inorganic nutrients to nutrient-poor (oligotrophic) streams to increase autotrophic production and aid in the restoration of salmonid populations. A series of indoor trough experiments demonstrated that the majority of samples containing binders of molasses, hydrated lime, vegetable oil, bentonite, starch, acrawax, candle wax, and Daratak® XB-3631 (unpolymerized Saran™) dissolved too slowly. The fastest dissolution rates occurred with fertilizer briquettes having no binder or vegetable oil. Further trough and field studies using fertilizer with no binder and vegetable oil as binder examined the effects of varying $N:P_2O_5:K_2O$ ratios. Dissolution rates were varied by using different percentages of magnesium ammonium phosphate (MagAmP; its formula 7:40:0 $N:P_2O_5:K_2O$) and urea (46:0:0). Optimal continual nutrient release for a period of four months was achieved with a fertilizer formulation of 17:30:0 (percent by weight $N:P_2O_5:K_2O$), with a ratio of 75% MagAmP to 25% urea, and containing no binder. The dissolution rate for this product ranged from 4.6% to 6.6% per week (for field and trough experiments, respectively) in water of 0.15 m/s average velocity. These studies indicate that a slow-release fertilizer product can be manufactured to last approximately four months when applied in the spring to stimulate autotrophic production in nutrient deficient streams, thereby increasing forage and salmonid production.

Introduction

Pacific salmon accumulate nutrients while feeding and growing during their ocean rearing life stage. Marine-derived nitrogen, carbon and phosphorus, and organic matter of high nutritional value contained in eggs and carcasses are transferred to the freshwater environment by adult salmon returning to spawn (Bilby et al. 1996; Gresh et al. 2000). The return of spawning salmon and associated marine-derived nutrients (MDN) to freshwater ecosystems are important for sustaining primary productivity, salmon populations, and nontarget species (e.g., riparian vegetation, carnivores, and scavengers) in the Pacific Northwest's N- and P-limited freshwater ecosystems (Stockner 1987; Ashley and Slaney 1997; Cederholm et al. 2000).

The current decreased return of spawners and declining input of MDN to the Pacific Northwest's freshwater environment results from a number of factors, including overfishing, loss of freshwater and estuarine habitat, construction of dams, and water pollution from industrial activities (Slaney et al. 1996; Stockner and MacIsaac 1996). Generally, fewer salmon carcasses results in reduced primary productivity in nutrient limited systems and, hence, less food available for the next generation of salmon (Larkin and Slaney 1996). Smaller and weaker fish may have reduced ocean survival and lose their opportunity to spawn in their natal stream (Ashley and Slaney 1997; Gresh et al. 2000).

In order to counter the "negative feedback loop" of salmon productivity, nutrient additions to oligotrophic streams have been shown to effectively enhance ecosystem productivity, including growth and survival of juvenile salmonids (Perrin et al. 1987; Slaney and Ward 1993; Bilby et al. 1996; Ashley and Slaney 1997; Larkin and Slaney 1997). Liquid fertilizers traditionally have been the product of choice for stimulating the base of the food chain, but their use is limited to more accessible streams and rivers, and application is expensive due to the high cost of maintenance that is required (Ashley and Slaney 1997). Slow-release fertilizers have the advantage that a once-per-year or per-season application is much more operationally efficient than continuous drip or monthly applications of solid granular fertilizers.

Target Slow-Release Fertilizer Characteristics

The ideal slow-release fertilizer briquette should consistently and uniformly release a chosen nutrient concentration at the appropriate N:P ratio. Briquette size should be large enough to avoid fluvial transport or burial in sand, yet dissolve over a period of approximately four months. Binders should be natural or biodegradable and strong enough for aerial application, and the briquette should resemble stream substrate to avoid vandalism. Phosphorus quality must be food grade to ensure that trace metal concentrations meet the most stringent water quality criteria.

Slow-Release Fertilizer Development

The first slow-release fertilizers used in British Columbia were introduced to the Keogh River on northern Vancouver Island. They consisted of crushed barley and agricultural fertilizer pellets. Barley was less effective than the agricultural fertilizer pellets and was labor-intensive to introduce (Perrin et al. 1987). In 1983, a solid prill, slow-release fertilizer with a soybean resin coating (Osmocote™, Sierra Chemical Ltd., Milpitas, California) was used, but the briquettes dissolved too

quickly, releasing the nutrients immediately after application, even with the thickest coating. They also fractured during aerial application, and the cost was 2–4 times higher than conventional granular agricultural blends (Johnston et al. 1990).

In 1994, slow-release fertilizers developed by I.M.C. Vigoro (Winter Haven, Florida), Cominco Fertilizers (Calgary, Alberta) and Sierra Chemical (Milpitas, California) were tested (Pons 1995). I.M.C. Vigoro's product, using MagAmP (magnesium ammonium phosphate) and Daratak® XB-3631 (unpolymerized Saran™: vinylidene chloride-acrylic acid-2-ethylhexyl acrylate polymer) as a binder, proved to be the most suitable for stream fertilization, based on these trials. Chemical and physical factors affecting phosphorus bioavail-ability (as PO_4^{3-}), as well as the response of periphyton growth to nutrient additions, were determined for I.M.C. Vigoro's product (Sterling 1997; Sterling et al. 2000).

Successful aerial and hand application of I.M.C. Vigoro's slow-release fertilizer (3 µg/L dissolved inorganic phosphorus) occurred from 1995 to 1997 in a variety of B.C. streams (Mouldey and Ashley 1996). Diatom and invertebrate production was enhanced in a matter of weeks and lasted 3–12 months, as anticipated. However, I.M.C. Vigoro discontinued manufacturing the fertilizer in 1997.

In 1999, another fertilizer company (Lesco Inc., Rocky River, Ohio) was identified as capable of manufacturing slow-release fertilizer briquettes with characteristics similar to I.M.C. Vigoro's product. This paper examines the dissolution rate characteristics of Lesco's products in order to determine an optimal slow-release fertilizer for use in candidate Pacific Northwest streams chosen for nutrient supplementation to aid in salmon restoration.

Methods

The dissolution rates of 26 formulations supplied by Lesco Inc. were evaluated during exposure to a range of water temperatures and velocities in indoor troughs and a constructed side channel. Four key characteristics were considered: binder type, duration of nutrient addition, N:P ratio, and metal concentrations.

1. Binder Type

An ideal binder will not fracture during aerial application and will release nutrients uniformly over time. Binder formulations tested ranged from no binder to combinations of molasses, hydrated lime, vegetable oil, bentonite, starch, water, acrawax, candle wax, methocel cellulose, and Daratak®.

2. Duration of Nutrient Addition

Ideally, the fertilizer should last approximately four months when applied in late spring or early summer in the Pacific Northwest. Dissolution rate of the briquettes was altered by varying the magnesium ammonium phosphate (MagAmP; $7:40:0$ $N:P_2O_5:K_2O$) and urea (46:0:0) proportions, which ranged from 85.75% MagAmP and 14.25% urea to 75% MagAmP and 25% urea. Urea dissolves quickly upon contact with water and produces a "Swiss cheese" effect in the briquette that enhances the dissolution rate.

3. N:P Ratio (for Application in Both N- and P-Limited Streams).

Streams are considered N-limited when the N:P atomic weight ratio is less than 10:1, co-limited when N:P is between 10:1–20:1, and P-limited when N:P is greater than 20:1 (Borchardt 1996). The formulations that were tested had N:P ratios ranging from 7:40 to 17:30.

Metal Concentrations. The presence of metals in the manufactured fertilizer product is based on the purity of the phosphoric acid source. Some metals of concern are lead, nickel, cadmium, arsenic, magnesium, and mercury. Their concentrations were closely monitored by analytical laboratory analyses before the fertilizer products were tested in the field.

4. Indoor Trough Studies to Determine Dissolution Rates

Indoor channels located at a trout hatchery in Abbotsford, B.C., were used to determine the dissolution rates of a variety of fertilizer briquettes. Fertilizer supplied by Lesco Inc. contained 12% magnesium, 7% nitrogen, and 40% P_2O_5 by weight, existing as the $MgNH_4PO_4 \cdot H_2O$ compound. Briquettes were formed by compressing ~9 g of fertilizer with a variety of binders.

Hatchery-heated water (14.0°C) and well water (9.5°C) were used but had a flow restriction, limiting water temperature of 13.0 ± 0.5°C to a velocity of 0.30 ± 0.03 m/s. Variations in temperature and velocity were obtained by mixing heated water and groundwater sources, as well as adjusting the trough slopes. Water velocity was measured using a Marsh McBirney, Inc. Model 2000 Portable Flowmeter. Temperature gradients across the troughs were eliminated by water hose positioning.

Plexiglas troughs, modeled after Bothwell (1983, 1988), were equipped with various dams at the head of the troughs to reduce visible turbulence. A total of three troughs were used, each containing four to six wires strung with six to eight fertilizer briquettes. The briquettes were drilled, individually weighed, and strung, separated by 5-mm diameter plastic beads, onto galvanized wire. Extra beads were strung on each end of the wires to keep the briquettes from the slower-moving water at the trough edges. Each sampling day, the briquettes furthest downstream were removed, air-dried for two weeks at 17.5°C, desiccated, and weighed to determine dissolution rate. Sampling varied according to the number of briquettes available but took place over a period of two months and occurred 1, 2, 3, 4, 6, and 8 weeks after the briquettes were introduced to the flowing water.

Initial Screening of Fertilizer Samples

Initially, 18 samples were provided in two batches and tested in June 1999. The first trial (samples A–J; Table 1) contained two briquettes per sample (sampled at 4th and 8th week). A second trial[1] (samples K–R) contained six briquettes per sample and were sampled at 1, 2, 3, 4, 6, and 8 weeks.

Dissolution Rates of Fertilizer Samples

A third trial of slow-release fertilizer samples involved 16 combinations of nutrients and binders. These briquettes were sampled from the troughs at 1, 2, 3, 4, 6, and 8 weeks. Variations in fertilizer formulation (A0 to D3) were achieved by using different percentages of magnesium ammonium phosphate (MagAmP; 7:40:0) and urea (46:0:0). The letter in the fertilizer identification represents the binder (A = none; B = Daratak® and vegetable oil; C = vegetable oil; and D = mo-

---

[1]The fertilizer binders and N:P ratios were withheld for the second trial in order to conduct a blind study.

lasses, hydrated lime, and vegetable oil), and the number indicates the proportion of MagAmP and urea as $N:P_2O_5:K_2O$ (0 = 12.55: 34.3: 0; 1 = 13.44: 33.4: 0; 2 = 14.80: 32.0: 0; and 3 = 16.75: 30.0: 0).

Controlled Field and Indoor Trough Studies

Griffin Channel, a man-made side channel of North Vancouver's Mosquito Creek, was used for the field testing (trial four). The three trials of indoor trough dissolution rate experiments reduced the number of fertilizer samples to be tested in the field to six types. All four fertilizer samples with no binder (A0, A1, A2, A3) and two with vegetable oil binder containing the highest concentrations of urea (C2 and C3) were selected and tested simultaneously in the field and troughs to determine if briquette dissolution in the controlled environment was similar to the field environment.

The trough experiments were set up as in previous studies (Sterling 1997; Sterling et al. 2000). For the field studies, the briquettes were drilled, individually weighed, and labeled with a colored and numbered tag attached by galvanized wire. Approximately 1,000 individually-labeled briquettes were placed in riffle sections of the stream with a velocity of 0.15 ± 0.05 m/s and a temperature range of 3.6 ± 0.1°C to 5.2 ± 0.1°C; trough water velocities were set at 0.15 ± 0.04 m/s to match the field conditions, and temperature was 9.5 ± 0.1°C. Riffle velocities greater than 0.25 m/s were avoided because the briquettes are transported downstream where they settle in pools. Sterling et al. (2000) determined that temperature did not have a significant effect on dissolution rate of the fertilizer briquettes.

Eight briquettes were removed from the trough and thirty were randomly removed from the stream every two weeks. Sample numbers for the field study decreased near the end of the experiment because of difficulty locating the briquettes (some were buried and others were very well camouflaged). Sampling occurred for both trough and field studies at 2, 4, 6, and 8 weeks.

Results

Initial Screening of Fertilizer Samples

Ideally, after eight weeks, the fertilizer briquettes should dissolve by approximately 60%. In trial one, the majority of samples A–J had very slow, average release rates after eight weeks in the trough (13–32%). Sample G dissolved too quickly and fell off the wire before the first sampling at four weeks. None of these slow-release fertilizer samples were deemed promising.

In trial two, the majority of samples (K, L, N, O, P, Q, and R) had dissolution rates that were too slow (12–18%) with the exception of sample M (formulation withheld), which showed the most promise since 42% dissolved after eight weeks. The results from these two trials were provided to Lesco Inc. and were used to develop further samples that were tested.

Dissolution Rates of Fertilizer Samples

The average percent weight lost in trial three of the 16 different briquettes formulated from combinations of four binder types and four combinations of urea and MagAmP after eight weeks ranged from 17% to 55%. The slowest dissolution occurred with the Daratak™ and vegetable oil binder (B series), followed by molasses, hydrated lime, and vegetable oil binder (D series). The fastest occurred with no binder (A series) and vegetable oil binder (C series).

The dissolution rate of the briquettes was increased by increasing the proportions of highly soluble urea in the fertilizer (fertilizer identification numbers 2 and 3). Upon contact with the water, the urea dissolves creating a more porous briquette and increases the surface area in contact with the water. An initial 'pulse' of urea should not be a concern because urea is a long-chain molecule that takes time to break down (via bacterial decomposition) to nitrate, and previous experiments using urea in fertilizer have produced positive results because of its effective bacterial stimulation (Stockner and MacIsaac 1996).

Controlled Field and Indoor Trough Studies

Four fertilizer samples with no binder (A0, A1, A2, A3) and two with vegetable oil containing the highest concentrations of urea (C2 and C3) were tested simultaneously in the field and trough experiments during trial four. These compositions had the highest dissolution rates of the 16 samples tested in the previous batch and were also ideal because of their natural ingredients:

magnesium, ammonia, phosphate, and vegetable oil (canola oil).

In both the field and trough studies (Figures 1 and 2), the briquettes without binder (A series) had slower, more consistent release rates, as demonstrated by the linear dissolution rates compared with briquettes with vegetable oil binder (C series). A consistent release rate is favored for a slow-release fertilizer product. As with trial three, the dissolution rate of the fertilizer briquettes was proportionate to urea concentration.

Briquette dissolution rate was found to be similar in both the field and trough environments. The slow-release fertilizer that lost approximately 60% of its weight after eight weeks and had the most consistent dissolution in the field and trough was sample A3. Its dissolution rate (determined by slope calculation) ranged from 4.6% per week to 6.6% per week (53.3% to 63.6% after eight weeks) for field and trough experiments, respectively, in water of constant velocity (0.15 m/s). The increase in dissolution rate of the C2 and C3 products after six weeks (Figure 2) was potentially due to structural weakening of the briquette.

Discussion

Indoor trough and outdoor field testing of proprietary slow-release fertilizer products (Lesco Inc.) suggests that a formulation of 75% MagAmP and 25% urea with no binder (sample A3) is acceptable for instream use. It possesses characteristics that make it suitable for nutrient rehabilitation of the Pacific Northwest's oligotrophic streams. The briquette dissolves uniformly, and after eight weeks exposure, approximately 60% of the initial weight is lost, which is within the target dissolution rate.

The highest urea concentrations resulted in briquettes with the fastest dissolution rate. In addition, the 9-g briquette size is adequate for providing nutrient release over four to five months without being washed downstream by average summer flows in smaller streams. They can be

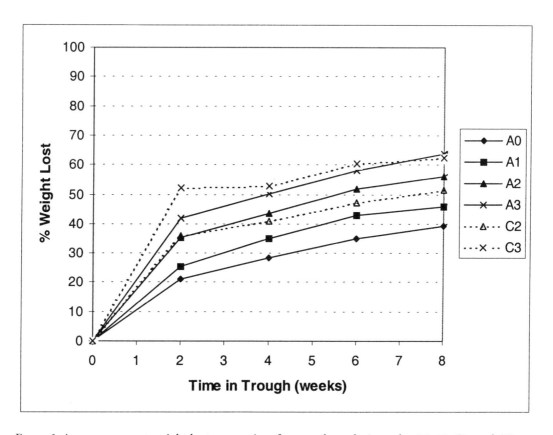

FIGURE 1. Average percent weight lost versus time for trough study (samples A0–A3, C2, and C3).

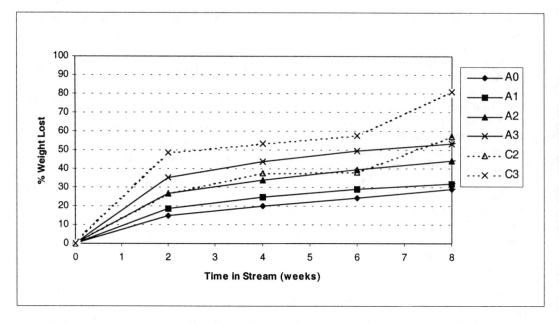

FIGURE 2. Average percent weight lost versus time for field study (samples A0–A3, C2, and C3).

hand-placed or distributed by aerial application in more remote systems.

These field experiments also demonstrated that the ideal location for briquette placement is around similar or slightly smaller-sized cobble substrate. This ensures that the briquettes are not buried in sand, nor washed away by larger flow events, since they are placed with substrate of similar size ensuring their perseverance at that stream location.

After the fertilizer briquettes are in contact with water for a few weeks, they become very well camouflaged due to a thin layer of biofilm, and they become darker from water saturation. This feature is advantageous because there is no concern of vandalism or alterations to the nutrient addition regime (i.e., frequent replacement of briquettes).

Based on the four considerations described in "Methods," the following is a summary of research findings to date:

1. The preferred fertilizer type is without any binder;
2. To achieve nutrients lasting approximately four months, the highest urea concentration (25%) is preferred, with the briquette dissolving at a rate of approximately 4.6% per week to 6.6% per week for field and trough experiments, respectively;
3. The preferred N:P ratio for P-limited streams is 7:40% by weight. A high nitrogen product (i.e., 40:7:0) is currently under development;
4. To ensure that there are no metal concentrations that would be of concern for drinking water and aquatic life purposes, a food grade phosphoric acid source (used for making the fertilizer product and often the source of metal contamination) should be used.

The results of this research pose several avenues for future investigations: 1) develop high nitrogen briquette for nitrogen limited river systems; 2) confirm that N and P release is constant over time to ensure that N or P does not become limited by uneven dissolution rates; 3) conduct a toxicity bioassay to verify that the briquettes are an environmentally safe product; and 4) paired carcass and slow-release fertilizer study, to compare if inorganic N and P additions are adequate for stimulating primary production or if the addition of organic minerals, vitamins, and lipids from carcasses, are also required.

Acknowledgments

Financial assistance for this project was provided by Forest Renewal B.C.'s Watershed Restoration Program. Thanks to the Fraser Valley Trout Hatchery staff, Abbotsford, for use of their troughs and technical assistance. We are especially grateful to Pat Slaney for initially suggesting the slow-release fertilizer concept and to Bob Land for his assistance in setting up the trough studies. Comments on this manuscript by Vic Palermo and two anonymous referees were greatly appreciated.

References

Ashley, K. I., and P. A. Slaney. 1997. Accelerating recovery of stream, river and pond productivity by low-level nutrient replacement. Chapter 13 *in* P. A. Slaney and D. A. Zaldokas, editors. Fish habitat rehabilitation procedures. Watershed Restoration Technicular Circular No. 9.

Bilby, R. E., B. R. Fransen, and P. A. Bisson. 1996. Incorporation of nitrogen and carbon from spawning coho salmon into the trophic system of small streams: evidence from stable isotopes. Canadian Journal of Fisheries and Aquatic Sciences 53:164–173.

Borchardt, M. A. 1996. Nutrients. Pages 183–227 *in* R. J. Stevenson, M. L. Bothwell, and R. L. Lowe, editors. Algal ecology–freshwater benthic ecosystems. Academic Press Inc., San Diego, California.

Bothwell, M. L. 1983. All-weather groughs for periphyton studies. Water Research 17:1735–1741.

Bothwell, M. L. 1988. Growth rate responses of lotic periphytic diatoms to experimental phosphorus enrichment: the influence of temperature and light. Canadian Journal of Fisheries and Aquatic Sciences 48:261–270.

Cederholm, C. J., D. H. Johnson, R. E. Bilby, L. G. Dominguez, A. M. Garrett, W. H. Graeber, E. L. Greda, M. D. Kunze, B. G. Marcot, J. F. Palmisano, R. W. Plotnikoff, W. G. Pearcy, C. A. Simenstad, and P. C. Trotter. 2000. Pacific salmon and wildlife–ecological context, relationships and implications for management. Special Edition Technical Report, prepared for D. H. Johnson and T. A. O'Neil, managing directors. Wildlife–Habitat Relationships in Oregon and Washington. Washington Department of Fish and Wildlife, Olympia, Washington.

Gresh, T., J. Lichatowich, and P. Schoonmaker. 2000. An estimation of historic and current levels of salmon production on the Northeast Pacific ecosystem: evidence of a nutrient deficit in the freshwater systems of the Pacific Northwest. Fisheries 25(1):15–21.

Johnston, N. T., C. J. Perrin, P. A. Slaney, and B. R. Ward. 1990. Increased juvenile salmonid growth by whole-river fertilization. Canadian Journal of Fisheries and Aquatic Sciences 47:863–872.

Larkin, G. A., and P. A. Slaney. 1996. Trends in marine-derived nutrient sources to south coastal British Columbia streams: impending implications to salmonid production. B.C. Ministry of Environment, Lands and Parks, and Ministry of Forests. Watershed Restoration Management Report No. 3.

Larkin, G. A., and P. A. Slaney. 1997. Implications of trends in marine-derived nutrients flow to south coastal British Columbia salmonid production. Fisheries 22(11):16–24.

Mouldey Ewing, S. E., and K. I. Ashley. 1996. Development and testing of a slow-release fertilizer for restoring salmonid habitat, 1995 progress report. B.C. Ministry of Environment, Lands and Parks, Fisheries Project Report No. RD 54, Vancouver, B.C.

Perrin, C. J., M. L. Bothwell, and P. A. Slaney. 1987. Experimental enrichment of a coastal stream in British Columbia: effects of organic and inorganic additions on autotrophic periphyton production. Canadian Journal of Fisheries and Aquatic Sciences 44:1247–1256.

Pons, A. 1995. Study on slow release fertilizers. Master's of Engineering project, University of British Columbia, Vancouver, B.C.

Slaney, P. A., and B. R. Ward. 1993. Experimental fertilization of nutrient deficient streams in British Columbia. Pages 128–141 *in* G. Shooner and S. Asselin, editors. Le développement du saumon Atlantique au Québec: connaître les règles du jeu pour réussir. Colloque international de la Fédé-ration Québécoise pour le saumon Atlantique. Québec, décembre 1992. Collection *Salmo salar* nº1.

Slaney, T. L., K. D. Hyatt, T. G. Northcote, and R. J. Fielden. 1996. Status of anadromous salmon and trout in British Columbia and Yukon. Fisheries 21:20–35.

Sterling, M. S. 1997. Phosphorus release from a slow-release fertilizer under simulated stream conditions. Master's thesis, University of British Columbia, Vancouver, B.C.

Sterling, M. S., K. I. Ashley, and A. B. Bautista. 2000. Slow-release fertilizer for rehabilitating oligotrophic streams: a physical characterization. Water Quality Research Journal of Canada 35(1):73–94.

Stockner, J. G. 1987. Lake fertilization: the enrichment cycle and lake sockeye salmon Oncorhynchus nerka production. Pages 198–215 *in* H. D. Smith, L. Margolis, and C. C. Woods, editors. Sockeye salmon Oncorhynchus nerka population biology and future management. Canadian Special Publication of Fisheries and Aquatic Sciences 96.

Stockner, J. G., and E. A. MacIsaac. 1996. British Columbia lake enrichment programme: two decades of habitat enhancement for sockeye salmon. Regulated Rivers Research and Management 12:547–561.

American Fisheries Society Symposium 34:245–258, 2003

Protocol for Applying Limiting Nutrients to Inland Waters

KENNETH I. ASHLEY

Fisheries Research and Development Section, Ministry of Fisheries
2204 Main Mall, University of British Columbia, Vancouver, British Columbia, Canada V6T 1Z4

JOHN G. STOCKNER

Fisheries Centre, University of British Columbia, Vancouver, British Columbia, Canada V6T 1Z4
and
Eco-Logic Ltd., 2614 Mathers Avenue, West Vancouver, British Columbia, Canada V7V 2J4

Abstract. The depressed status of many Pacific Northwest (PNW) salmonid stocks has focused considerable attention on the role of marine-derived nutrients (MDN) in maintaining the productivity of salmonid ecosystems and created a strong interest in stream and lake enrichment as an important salmon restoration technique. This paper reviews some of the technical and more applied aspects of stream, river, and lake enrichment as currently practiced in British Columbia and elsewhere in the world. The first step when considering potential stream and lake enrichment is to determine the ambient nutrient concentrations, stock of biogenic biomass, and trophic status of the candidate ecosystem by conducting nutrient bioassays, synoptic surveys, low-level nutrient analyses, and qualitative assessments of the ecosystems. Phosphorus is considered limiting when concentrations in composite stream or epilimnetic lake samples during the growing season are less than 1 µg/L SRP and less than 2–3 µg/L TDP. Nitrogen is considered limiting in streams when dissolved inorganic nitrogen (DIN) concentrations during the growing season are less than 20 µg/L and in lakes when spring epilimnetic concentrations are less than 30 µg/L. At minimum, a 1–2 year pre-treatment study is required to determine the nutrient status and requirements of the ecosystem. Water users and regulatory agencies must be notified in advance of plans to add nutrients to rivers, lakes, or streams, and provincial, state, and/or federal permitting processes and guidelines should be followed. All nutrient enrichment programs must consider seven key variables: (1) desired concentration of nutrients, (2) type of nutrients, (3) seasonal timing of application, (4) frequency of nutrient addition, (5) location of application sites, (6) DIN:TDP (total dissolved phosphorus) ratio of nutrients to be added, and (7) application technique. Enrichment programs should attempt to mimic the anadromous salmon 'nutrient pump' where applicable and implement a nutrient prescription that assures the production of edible phytoplankton/periphyton and avoids the occurrence of nuisance algae. In addition, sufficient funds should be secured to monitor the ecosystem responses.

Introduction

The depressed status of many Pacific Northwest (PNW) salmonid stocks (Nehlsen et al. 1991) has recently focused a considerable amount of attention on the role of marine-derived nutrients (MDN) in maintaining the productivity of salmonid ecosystems. The Returning Nutrients to Salmonid Eco- systems conference held in Eugene, Oregon, on 24–26 April 2001 attracted nearly 400 delegates from Japan to Scandinavia, clearly demonstrating the growing interest in this topic. The emerging recognition that salmonid carcasses are ecologically important sources of marine-derived organic carbon (C), nitrogen (N), and phosphorus (P) for aquatic and terrestrial ecosystems provides a compelling argument for abandoning single-species stock–recruitment-based fisheries and adopting holistic ecosystem-based resource management models (Schuldt and Hershey 1995; Willson and Halupka 1995; Bilby et al. 1996; Michael, this volume).

Recent quantitative estimates of the 'nutrient deficit' in the PNW have created a strong interest in the efficacy of stream and lake enrichment (fertilization) as a salmon restoration technique (Larkin and Slaney 1997; Gresh et al. 2000; Stockner et al. 2000). The goal of stream and lake enrichment is to rebuild salmonid escapement to historical levels via temporary supplementations of limiting nutrients using organic and/or inorganic formulations. Stream and lake enrichment should not be used as a 'techno-fix' to perpetuate the existing mismanagement of salmonids when there is any possibility of re-establishing self-sustaining wild populations through harvest reductions and restoration of salmonid habitat. Therefore, fertilization should be viewed as an interim restorative measure that is most effective if all components of ecosystem recovery and key external factors (e.g., overfishing) are cooperatively achieved and coordinated. This paper reviews some of the technical and more applied aspects of stream, river, and lake enrichment as currently practiced in British Columbia and elsewhere. As a caveat, the discussion assumes that salmonid stock status of candidate lakes and streams has been quantified and classified as significantly depressed and that additional limiting factors (e.g., habitat/water quality and quantity) have been addressed and/or incorporated into an integrated basin or lake 'restoration' plan. It also assumes that salmonid harvest/exploitation rates have been previously reduced to near zero and that the stock is not recovering naturally due to severe nutrient loss (oligotrophication), reduced habitat, or nonaddressable external factors (e.g., reduced ocean survivals).

Nutrient Limitation

Phosphorus and nitrogen are the primary limiting macronutrients in most freshwater ecosystems in the PNW and elsewhere (Wetzel 1975). The first step when considering potential candidates for enrichment is to determine the trophic status of each stream and/or lake by examining seasonal concentrations of P and N and standing stock and abundance of phytoplankton, zooplankton, and fish. There are essentially four nutrient assessment techniques available:

(1) Run bioassays to determine nutrient limitation (i.e., floating or streamside mesocosms in which limiting nutrients are applied over several weeks or months at known rates);

(2) Conduct synoptic surveys so that comparisons of community composition and biomass of periphyton/phytoplankton and benthic invertebrate/zooplankton can be made and nutrient/trophic standards established (e.g. ultra-oligo, oligo-, meso-, and eutrophic);

(3) Obtain samples for low-level (detection level required: <1 µg/L SRP; 1–3 µg/L TDP; 4–5 µg/L DIN) water chemistry analyses for soluble reactive and total dissolved phosphorus (SRP and TDP) and dissolved inorganic nitrogen ($DIN = NO_3\text{-}N + NO_2\text{-}N + NH_3\text{-}N$) during the summer growing season to determine ambient nutrient status;

(4) A strictly qualitative assessment of the general 'slippery feel' and relative abundance of periphyton on natural substrates and density of aquatic insects beneath stones in streams during the growing season (lotic ecosystems only).

The last technique is quite basic, but when conducted by an experienced stream ecologist, it can be surprisingly informative and reliable. Techniques 2 and 3 will likely form the basis of most nutrient assessments, owing to their relatively low cost and quantitative nature, while qualified individuals typically will use technique 4 during preliminary stream reconnaissance surveys.

Phosphorus is considered the limiting nutrient when concentrations in composite stream or epilimnetic lake samples during the growing season are routinely at limits of detection (less than 1 µg/L SRP; less than 2–3 µg/L TDP). Lotic ecosystems are remarkably efficient at removing phosphorus at low concentrations, and experimental studies have demonstrated that SRP concentrations as low as 0.3–0.6 µg/L are sufficient to saturate specific growth rates of unicellular periphytic diatoms (Bothwell 1988). However, biomass accrual continues to increase with increasing SRP as the relationship shifts from cellular- to community-controlled growth rates (Bothwell 1989; Quamme and Slaney, this volume). In streams, DIN concentrations less than 20 µg/L may become limiting (Bothwell 1988), and in lakes, spring epilimnetic concentrations less than 30 µg/L usually signal N-limitation of phytoplankton by mid-summer (Stockner and Shortreed 1985). Most of the background DIN will be in the form of NO_3-N, as NO_2-N is ephemeral and, like ammonium, is usually found under anoxic conditions. Ammonia (NH_3-N) is not as mobile as NO_3-N in groundwater and is generally undetectable in well-oxygenated lake and stream water. As in lakes, additional nitrogen is generally not required in streams if the background concentration of DIN is between 30–50 µg/L. However, in some situations, DIN concentrations near the low range (<30 µg/L) can become co-limiting during enrichment experiments due to the increased biological uptake of DIN caused by addition of P. The form of DIN most rapidly assimilated by both attached algae and phytoplankters is NH_3-N rather than NO_3-N. Organic forms of N are ubiquitous in freshwaters, but most compounds are refractory (e.g., tannins, lignin, humates) and require a slow microbial reduction before their N components can be utilized. However, urea is the exception to the above and is an excellent nutrient source readily assimilated after reduction by phytoplankters and bacteria.

Legal Application and Notification Requirements

The addition of limiting nutrients, either in the form of salmon carcasses, organic nutrient analogues, or inorganic nutrients, to lakes, rivers, and streams initially appears at odds with more than four decades of efforts to reduce nutrient discharges and can be interpreted by provincial, state, and federal authorities as being in violation of water pollution control laws (e.g., Clean Water Act). Hence, water users and regulatory agencies must be notified in advance, and provincial, state, and/or federal permitting processes and guidelines should be followed. Since nutrient enrichment is a relatively new procedure, existing guidelines are now being modified, or new guidelines developed, to address the issue. In Washington State, a National Pollutant Discharge Elimination System (NPDES) Waste Discharge Permit is being modified to allow temporary water quality modification for nutrient restoration (H. Michael, Washington Department of Fish and Wildlife, Olympia, Washington, personal communication). In British Columbia, draft guidelines for instream placement of hatchery salmon carcasses have been developed and

are currently being reviewed by field staff and hatchery managers (A Fedorenko, Canada Department Fisheries and Oceans, Vancouver, British Columbia, personal communication). Similar guidelines are being developed in Oregon to facilitate application of surplus hatchery carcasses in culturally oligotrophic streams (D. Shively, U.S. Forest Service, Mt. Hood National Forest, personal communication).

In addition to the formal water quality regulatory agencies, it is important to determine which additional agencies and individuals should to be notified. In British Columbia, under the Water Act, downstream water users must be notified of any activities that may impact the water quality of their licensed withdrawals. Accordingly, water licensees on treatment streams must be notified in advance in order to avoid complaints of water quality degradation and health issues (C. Cross, Fisheries and Oceans Canada, Vancouver, British Columbia, personal communication). Since nutrient addition to waters is a novel concept in many areas, it is often advisable to post notices and conduct public meetings to explain the rationale and risks/benefits of the proposed treatments. Within the fisheries agencies, it is important to notify stock assessment personnel, area management staff, stewardship groups, and First Nations fisheries officers, particularly if salmon carcasses are used as the carbon and nutrient source. In British Columbia, provincial fisheries staff meet with regional Public Medical Health Officers, as required, to discuss planned treatments and nutrient formulations to alleviate concerns about potential nitrate and heavy metal addition to potable water sources.

Project Planning

One of the most important aspects of conducting a successful nutrient enrichment program is detailed project planning, which should start 1–2 years prior to nutrient treatment. This typically involves collection and analysis of background physical, chemical, and biological data from the candidate stream or lake, analysis of discharge patterns (rivers and streams), examination of epilimnetic and whole lake residence times, compensation depth (1% light level), and the duration and depth of thermal stratification (lakes and reservoirs). After these data are in hand, the final process is to develop an agency and public notification plan, preparing a permit application strategy (if required) and a well-designed monitoring plan. At least one full season of pre-fertilization data must be collected in order to characterize the nutrient status of the ecosystem in question. For project planning purposes, most nutrient enrichment programs can be described in terms of seven key variables:

1. Desired concentration of nutrients;
2. Nutrient formulation of fertilizer;
3. Seasonal timing of application;
4. Frequency of nutrient addition;
5. Location of application sites;
6. DIN:TDP ratio of nutrients to be added;
7. Application technique.

1. Desired Concentration of Nutrients

In streams and rivers, excessive periphyton biomass is reported to occur when SRP concentrations exceed 10 µg/L; therefore, target concentrations of SRP for stream and river fertilization (background plus nutrient additions) are in the 3–5 µg/L (ppb—parts per billion) range, or approximately one-third to one-half of potential nuisance concentrations, but high enough to be effective over several kilometers of stream. Uptake of SRP by attached bacteria and algae is very rapid, and concentrations can fall to below 1 µg/L within a kilometer of the addition source. Since nutrients are rapidly transformed into biomass accrual and will spiral to lower stream reaches, the actual concentration often cannot be measured in the water, and care must be taken to accurately apply P only at the pre-determined loading rate and not exceed it. Minimum target DIN concentrations for streams and rivers (background plus nutrient additions) are ~30–50 µg/L to ensure that DIN:TDP ratios remain ~10:1 on a weight:weight basis.

Because many oligotrophic lakes show co-limitation of N and P (Stockner 1987), river or stream ecosystems that originate from N-limited lakes may require additional N to prevent stream N-limitation. Fortunately, many river systems contain sufficient ambient concentrations of DIN, often originating from dense alder stands in riparian corridors (Volk et al., this volume), that they do not require additional nitrogen loading, thus significantly reducing fertilizer costs. In some cases, the concentration of DIN will vary during the season as the runoff gradually shifts from snowmelt to base groundwater flows. This reinforces the prerequisite for at least one year of pre-enrichment data collection to adequately characterize the temporal variation in ambient nutrient concentration and develop a site-specific enrichment strategy. Special attention should be directed towards not exceeding government regulatory agency standards for algal biomass. For example, in British Columbia streams and rivers, 50 mg/m² chlorophyll a (CHL) is the maximum concentration permitted under aesthetic considerations, and 100 mg/m² CHL is the maximum without detriment to aquatic life in streams (Nordin 1985).

When using salmon carcasses as a carbon and nutrient source, nutrient-loading density is often based solely on the availability of carcasses. More scientific approaches are recommended in which carcass nutrient loading is determined through quantitative estimation procedures. Methods to determine the carcass loading density include (1) analysis of historical escapement records, (2) back-calculation of desired in-situ nutrient concentration, (3) stable isotope analysis of lake and/or tree ring cores, or (4) comparison to stream systems in terms of fish per km of stream length. A promising new technique is the areal loading (kg of carcass per m²) approach based on ^{15}N stable isotope saturation curves for juvenile salmonids (Bilby et al. 2001). This approach has been adopted in Washington State and results in the following maximum carcass density guidelines (Table 1).

Although this is a preliminary estimate based on a limited number of streams, it represents a sound ecological approach that can be experimentally derived for most river systems.

In lakes and reservoirs, the target concentration of P should be derived from a Vollen-weider-type loading model that incorporates mean depth and flushing rate and predicts the trophic state that results from various P loads (Vollenweider 1976, Stephens and Stockner 1983). Given the large literature on eutrophication and P loading to lakes,

TABLE 1. Draft Washington State NPDES carcasses loading guidelines.

Salmon species	Carcass loading
Coho/steelhead/cutthroat	0.15 kg m² bank full width
Pink/chum/sockeye	0.78 kg m² bank full width
Chinook	0.39 kg m² bank full width

it is not difficult to estimate the desired P load (nutrients plus background watershed loading) to ensure that the lake or reservoir remains within the permissible loading range. Nitrogen is then applied at sufficient rates to ensure that the epilimnetic DIN:TDP ratio remains greater than 10:1 on a weight:weight basis throughout the growing season. For example, in Kootenay Lake, British Columbia, the annual concentration of nutrients that were applied during the April–August treatment season (assuming a 0–20 m epilimnetic mixing depth) was 271 mg·m^2 (13.6 µg/L) of P and 1,191 mg·m^2 (59.5 µg/L) of N. This loading was sufficient to rebuild kokanee Oncorhynchus nerka escapement while maintaining excellent water quality conditions (Ashley et al. 1997). In the Federal Lake Enrichment Program (LEP), weekly phosphorus loads averaged 3.0 to 4.5 mg P·m^{-2}·week^{-1} and yielded a weekly epilimnetic P enrichment of 0.2 to 0.7 µg/L over a 16–22 week growing season (Stephens and Stockner 1983; Stockner and MacIsaac 1996).

2. Nutrient Formulation

Salmon carcasses represent the ideal nutrient source as they contain a complex array of macro- and micronutrients, vitamins, and organic compounds, including highly unsaturated fatty acids or HUFAs. In terms of macronutrient analysis, most salmonids are between 0.3–0.4% by wet weight as P and 3.0–3.5% by wet weight as N and, hence, have close to a 10:1 TN:TP ratio on a weight:weight basis (Stansby and Hall 1965). The advantages of salmon carcasses as nutrient source is that they provide multiple pathways for transferring nutrients and energy into ecosystems (Wipfli et al. 1999), including direct consumption by numerous fish, amphibians, and terrestrial vertebrates (Cederholm et al. 2000; Jauquet et al., this volume). In addition, adult spawners distribute themselves freely throughout the watershed, a basic but underappreciated fact that becomes very evident when examining the logistics of redistributing thousands of kilograms of salmon carcasses in a drainage basin.

The reality of the current salmon crisis in the PNW is that sufficient numbers of salmon carcasses are not always available for distribution, particularly in basins where salmon runs have been severely depressed for many years. Under these conditions, the only option open to 'kick-start' population growth and restore ecosystem production is to examine alternate sources of nutrients. This is an important scientific and psychological step that often causes biologists to re-examine their basic understanding of the freshwater ecology and early life history of salmonids. Inorganic nutrients, while far from being a complete nutrient package, can increase salmonid production by stimulating autotrophic production at the base of the food web (Stockner and MacIsaac 1996; Ward et al., this volume). This bias against inorganic nutrients likely arises from confusion about the relative roles of allochthonous versus autochthonous carbon sources and resultant energy flows in forested stream ecosystems (Minshall 1978; Johnston et al. 1990).

A variety of inorganic nutrient formulations are suitable for lake and stream enrichment. Most formulations have been manufactured for agricultural use; hence, the accepted convention is to express the macronutrient content in terms of three numbers (e.g. 10-34-0 [ammonium polyphosphate]). These numbers refer to the percentage by weight of N, P_2O_5, and K_2O in the product. It is very important to note that phosphorus is expressed as percentage by weight as P_2O_5 and not as P or PO_4. This has caused much confusion when designing an enrichment program! To convert from percentage by weight of P_2O_5 to percentage by weight of P, one simply divides the percent P_2O_5 by 2.29 to obtain the percent P by weight. For example, 10-34-0 (ammonium polyphosphate) contains 34% P_2O_5 by weight and 14.8% P by weight (i.e., 34/2.29). Therefore, 10 kg of liquid 10-34-0 fertilizer contains 1.48 kg of P.

The molecular formulation that the P and N occur in can also vary among fertilizers. The P always exists in a phosphate molecule (PO_4^{-3}), as elemental phosphorus does not occur naturally on earth (Emsley 2000). The P can also occur in long chains as polyphosphate (as in 10-34-0), and bioassay experiments indicate that polyphosphate is a better P source for lake and stream fertilization, as the time required for hydrolysis of the poly-P bonds acts as a slow-release agent that favors small-sized phytoplankton with rapid uptake capabilities (Suttle et al. 1988, 1991). Nitrogen in inorganic fertilizers can be obtained in a variety of formulations including nitrate alone (e.g., granular $CaNO_3$), as ammonia-nitrate blends (e.g., granular 34.5-0-0 ammonium nitrate), as urea alone, or as urea-ammonium nitrate blends (e.g., liquid 32-0-0 and 28-0-0). Most phytoplankton and periphyton must synthesize the enzyme nitrogenase before NO_3^- can be utilized, but ammonium can be directly utilized and, hence, is the preferred form of N for aquatic ecosystems.

One of the most frequently asked questions by biologists and the public regarding the use of inorganic nutrients is the concern about heavy metal contamination of fertilizer products. The phosphorus in inorganic fertilizers is derived from phosphate rock that is mined from several principal phosphate deposits around the Earth. Each ore body has a characteristic signature of heavy metals that is unique to the geology of the ore deposit. An emerging concern is that all of the Earth's high quality phosphate rock deposits have already been mined and that the concentration of heavy metals is increasing in the remaining deposits as the phosphate industry extracts lower quality ore (Driver et al. 1999). For example, the concentration of mercury is highest in Chinese ore, whereas cadmium and chromium tend to be highest in Idaho phosphate deposits (Table 2).

Therefore, careful scrutiny of the ore source can significantly reduce heavy metal concentrations in the phosphate fertilizer. An alternate but more expensive approach for reducing heavy metal concentrations is to specify food grade (human consumption) or feed grade (animal consumption) phosphate in the fertilizer. The slow-release stream fertilizer used in British Columbia is manufactured with food grade phosphate (Sterling and Ashley, this volume). Pharmaceutical grade phosphate is the purest type of phosphate; however it so expensive that it is suitable only for small mesocosms or laboratory scale experiments.

Storage and Handling

Fertilizers. Solid fertilizers absorb moisture; hence, they need to be stored in a cool, dry place to prevent caking. The nutrients in liquid fertilizers (e.g., 10-34-0) will precipitate or 'salt out' in cold weather when mixed with higher concentrations of nitrogen fertilizer (e.g., 32-0-0). The resultant jelly-like precipitate will clog pumps and small orifices, and it is a troublesome problem to rectify. In practice, 28-0-0 has proven to be less prone to precipitate when blended with 10-34-0. Ideally, supplies of fertilizer should not exceed seasonal requirements so that all liquid fertilizer is used during the treatment season and winter storage is not required. Most solid and liquid fertilizers are quite corrosive, and standard safety precautions should be taken when handling the various products. Most metallic and ferrous compounds corrode very quickly when exposed to fertilizer (e.g. phosphoric acid and ammonium polyphosphate), and care must be taken to thoroughly clean equipment soon after use. Ammonium nitrate is extremely explosive if exposed to sparks or open flames and fuel oil and should be handled very carefully and never transported or stored near fuel oil or an ignition source.

Carcasses. Salmon carcasses have a limited 'shelf life' due to exponential mass loss and must be applied to lake, stream, and riparian habitat as soon as they become available; hence, the need for good project planning and close attention to

TABLE 2. Concentration of heavy metals in various phosphate ore deposits. Note: table taken from Driver et al. 1999.

Country	Deposit	P_2O_5	As	Cd	Cr	Hg	U	V
		wt%	mg/g	µg/g	mg/g	µ/kg	mg/g	mg/g
Israel		32	5	25	227	130	150	200
Jordan		32	8	5	92	48	78	70
Morocco	Bu Craa	35.1	Nr	37.5	Nr	Nr	75	Nr
	Louribga	32.6	13.3	15.1	200	855	88	106
	Youssoufia	31.2	9.2	29.2	255	120	97	200
Togo		36.7	10	58.4	101	365	94	60
USA	Florida	31.9	11.3	9.1	60	199	141	108
	Idaho	31.7	23.7	92.3	290	107	107	769
	N. Carolina	29.9	11.2	38.2	158	233	65	26
South Africa		39.5	11	<2	Nr	Nr	9	17
Tunisia		29.3	4.5	39.5	144	Nr	44	27
Senegal		35.9	17.4	86.7	140	270	67	523
Australia		28.9	14	4	35	75	84	63
Syria		31.9	4	3	105	28	75	140
China		31	26	2.5	33	4,990	22.8	80

Nr = not recorded

logistics are keys to a successful carcass treatment plan. Decomposition rates for salmon, derived from a single exponential regression, range from k = ~0.033/day to k = ~0.061/day (Chaloner et al. 2002). Rainbow trout decompose at 1.5%/day at 4.2°C and 4.9%/day at 8.6°C (Minshall et al. 1991). If carcass distribution is delayed, the carcasses can be frozen for application at a later date; however, each should be individually frozen on racks and not be frozen in aggregate or in plastic bags, as they will be difficult to separate for later use. Commercial freezing is relatively inexpensive and is a plausible alternative if adequate freezer capacity is un- available.

3. Seasonal Timing of Application

The seasonal timing of inorganic nutrient application in temperate lakes corresponds to the normal ice-free growing season that coincides with the period of stable thermal stratification in dimictic and warm-monomictic lakes. A 20–22 week application window from late April to early September is standard for most lakes and reservoirs in southern British Columbia (Stephens and Stockner 1983; Stockner and Ashley, this volume). This period would be reduced accordingly at higher elevations or latitudes as the growing season shortens. Nutrients can be added at a constant application rate throughout the growing season or 'front-end' loaded to apply more phosphorus and less nitrogen during the early part of the season when concentrations of DIN in most systems are at maximum levels. The 'front end loading' concept is intended to simulate spring freshet conditions for phosphorus loading and substantially increase spring production on the tail of the 'freshet' P-input. Ever increasing loads of N, as the season progresses, compensates for the rapid spring biological uptake and gradual depletion of epilimnetic DIN; this regimen also matches phytoplankton production to the seasonal patterns of the early copepod and later cladoceran population increases (Stockner and MacIsaac 1996). This loading pattern results in a late spring peak in P input, which then declines to a constant summer loading and eventually to a reduced late summer loading (Figure 1). If sufficient ambient epilimnetic DIN concentrations are present to sustain production through the growing season without periods of depletion, then nitrogen applications can start at very low rates in the spring, with only slightly higher rates through-

out the summer. This strategy is designed to prevent DIN limitation and decrease the likelihood of colonial cyanobacteria (blue-green algae) blooms that are often associated with N depletion or low N:P ratios (Smith 1983; Pick and Lean 1987).

In rivers and streams, the seasonal timing of application depends on the nutrient source being considered. If salmon carcasses are used, the general rule is to apply them at the same time as the historic salmon runs (i.e., mimic nature). If inorganic nutrients are being used, the principle is to apply the nutrients during the summer growing season, which will vary depending on latitude and elevation. In British Columbia, the standard practice is to begin applying nutrients on the descending limb of the hydrograph. In southern rivers, such as the Keogh River on northern Vancouver Island, this can be as early as late April. In more northern systems that exhibit snow-melt freshets in late May and June (e.g., Mesilinka River), nutrients are typically applied in early July and sometimes as late as mid-July depending on the magnitude and duration of the freshet period.

4. Frequency of Nutrient Addition

Lakes. There is a paucity of information on the 'optimal' or best frequency of nutrient addition to rivers (Ashley and Slaney 1997), but there have been some studies on application frequency to lakes to optimize production (Stephens and Stockner 1983). The basic principle is to add nutrients as often as technically feasible without exceeding economic or logistic constraints (resources). In lakes, laboratory experiments have demonstrated that more frequent pulses of light nutrient loads favor smaller-sized phytoplankton (e.g., picoplankton), as their greater surface area to volume ratio permits rapid nutrient uptake (Suttle et al. 1987). Less frequent weekly loadings with higher loads initially stimulate picoplankters but gradually tend to favor larger-sized nano- and micro-phytoplankton that have slower uptake rates but larger internal P storage capabilities (Suttle et al. 1987). After several decades of lake enrichment, weekly application rates have provided the best community production responses, and these have proven to be logistically the most feasible application frequency for lake fertilization (Stockner 1987; Stephens and Stockner 1983; Stockner and MacIsaac 1996; Ashley et al. 1999). In some cases, due to unique

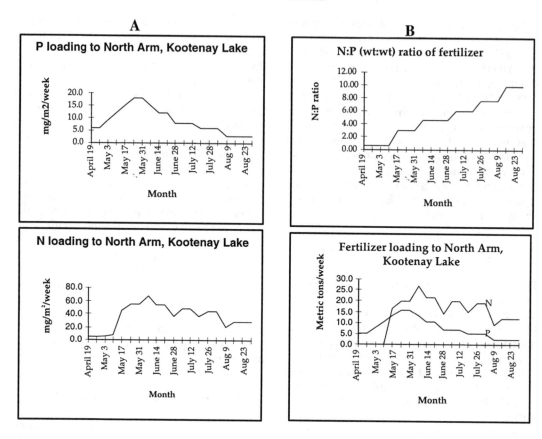

FIGURE 1. Example of a 'front end' nutrient-loading schedule for Kootenay Lake, British Columbia. A. Weekly areal P and N loading rates; B. Variation in weekly N:P ratio and weight (tonnes) of fertilizer added.

application opportunities, nutrient additions have been made several times per day from regularly scheduled ferry runs with a positive plankton response (e.g., Arrow Reservoir; Pieters et al., this volume). Innovative low-cost techniques for continuous nutrient loading to small lakes or embayments of large lakes have included placing bags of granular fertilizer in tributary streams to slowly dissolve (Milbrink and Holmgren 1981) or by using floating screen bottomed boxes near the lake center and allowing wave action to gradually dissolve solid granular fertilizer and distribute the nutrients throughout the lake (Ashley and Johnson 1989). The temperature and turbidity of inflowing streams must be examined first to determine if the resulting density will enter the epilimnion or plunge to an intermediate depth with a resultant loss in effectiveness of nutrient delivery.

Streams. In streams, the frequency of application depends primarily on the predominant nutrient sources (e.g., groundwater, carcasses, and alder). Ideally, salmon carcasses should be added at the same frequency as they once occurred in the river system, mimicking natural events. Historically, many rivers received multiple escapements that could start as early as April and last until late fall. Economics, logistics, and availability will likely determine the best frequency for carcass application. When applying inorganic nutrients to streams, the same rule applies as additions to lakes (i.e., more frequent, weekly applications are preferred). This is intended to prevent accumulation of nuisance algae and also to avoid large doses of fertilizer where the ammonia component could reach concentrations potentially toxic to fish.

In practice, simple gravity-fed drip systems have proven difficult to regulate due to constant clogging of the fine orifice valves with fertilizer precipitate. In addition, daily variations in air temperature affected fertilizer drip rates, thus under or overapplying nutrients. Three innovative application systems have been developed to facilitate nutrient addition to streams:

(1) Flow proportional fertilizer injection systems that use a pressure sensor to determine real-time stage-discharge information; programmable peristaltic pumps then inject the exact amount of fertilzer to attain the desired concentration, thus providing constant application rates. These systems were accurate and reliable but energy intensive; hence, photovoltaic pannels should be incorporated into the system to extend the operating time of the pump batteries;

(2) Pre-programmed units similar to (1) above, designed for metering fertilizer into snowmelt dominated river systems to which fertilizer was added at 20-minute intervals following a pre-programmed exponential decay curve for nutrient loading (Wilson et al., this volume);

(3) The most promising technique for constant application has been the development of slow-release inorganic nutrient briquettes (Sterling et al. 2000). Briquettes are added annually by hand or helicopter, thus allowing once-per-year treatments that are particularly useful in remote regions (Sterling and Ashley, this volume).

5. Location of Application Sites

Streams. The location of application sites depends mainly on the nutrient source(s) being applied. In anadromous salmon ecosystems, carcass applications should cover as much of the adult spawning habitat as feasible, and most intensive applications should be well away from stream mouths and estuaries so that nutrient spiraling works effectively throughout the length of the anadromous salmon use zone. The presence of large woody debris (LWD) will significantly improve carcass retention (Cederholm et al. 1988); hence, application zones can be modified somewhat to take advantage of differential LWD availability in logged and unlogged sections of the same river system. In areas where agricultural or anthropogenic input of nutrients has raised ambient concentrations of nutrients above limiting values, carcasses can be applied in riparian zones, thus enriching the terrestrial portion of the nutrient shadow without contributing to excessive enrichment of the aquatic ecosystem.

When using inorganic nutrients, the principle factors influencing the location of nutrient addition are the logistics of delivering nutrients to the application site(s) and the nutrient spiraling length

of the ecosystem. In practice, these two factors should be integrated whenever possible to optimize the treatment plan. In remote regions, the cost and logistics of delivering large quantities of liquid fertilizer is often the critical factor when deciding whether to proceed with a nutrient enrichment project. If there are adequate sites for liquid fertilizer tank storage, then the application sites should be located to function in concert with the inherent nutrient spiraling characteristics of the stream or river to provide the most ecologically effective nutrient enrichment. If the geography of the site location precludes establishment of liquid fertilizer tank farms, slow-release fertilizer, although more expensive, can be used in a manner consistent with nutrient spiraling distances. If the increased cost of the slow-release fertilizer exceeds the project budget, then it is preferable to defer the project until additional funds are obtained or logistical constraints removed, rather than proceeding with a precarious and ecologically risky treatment plan.

In streams, the gravitational flow of water downhill displaces nutrients considerable distances downstream as nutrients are taken up by autotrophic and microbial biomass and recycled or 'spiraled' through the biota and back to the water (Mulholland 1996). Experiments involving radioactive $^{32}PO_4$ applications to streams have confirmed that spiraling does occur and that the distance traveled is dominated by the water component (i.e., water velocity). Increasing the uptake of nutrients from the water may reduce spiraling distance. For example, filter-feeding invertebrates, through capture of seston, may impede downstream transport of organic matter and effectively reduce spiraling distance (Minshall et al. 1985). In addition, some nutrient cycling does take place within the boundary zones created by benthic algae that does not involve downstream displacement and, hence, is an alternative pathway to nutrient spiraling (Mulholland 1996). Evidence from river fertilization experiments indicates that increased periphyton and presumably heterotrophic microbial biomass can extract sufficient nutrients from the water to shift P-limited systems to N and P co-limitation; hence, spiraling length has likely been reduced by increasing the biomass and effective nutrient uptake capacity of the biological community (Slaney et al. 1994; Wilson et al., this volume). An example of an integrated treatment plan is the Keogh River that flows for 30 km from source to ocean (Ward et al., this volume). The prescription for the Keogh required ~1,000 kg of slow release fertilizer, and previous enrichment experiments (Slaney et al., this volume) indicated a spiraling distance of ~6 km. Therefore, 200 kg of slow-release fertilizer was applied at the start of the Keogh River, and four additional 200-kg treatments applied at 6-km intervals moving downstream towards the mouth of the river. This approach avoids excessive single-site enrichment effects by distributing nutrients in a manner that is ecologically consistent with each river's inherent spiraling distance. Additional research is required to further our understanding of nutrient spiraling and enrichment practices.

Lakes. Nutrient application to most lakes targets pelagic phytoplankton and ultimately the zooplankton forage-base of sockeye salmon or land-locked kokanee. Therefore, on larger water bodies (>100 ha), nutrient application is on transect lines toward the center of the lake and well away from lake littoral margins (>500 m from shorelines) and outflow river mouths (e.g., Ashley et al. 1999). If shore spawning is a prevalent feature of the salmon run, then treatment can include application over the littoral zone as well as near shore pelagic. It is important to disperse the nutrients over as wide an area as possible so that dilution by epilimnetic water prevents 'pooling' and sinking of concentrated fertilizer into the metalimnion. Dye studies have confirmed that horizontal dispersion in small lakes is consistent with previous observations in oceans and large lakes (Lawrence et al. 1995); hence, wind-driven circulation will distribute nutrients over a large area, albeit at a rate considerably slower than the biological uptake of nutrients in the water column. Shore-based water pumps have been successfully used in small lakes to spray a dilute liquid fertilizer mixture ~10 m offshore; however, this must be done frequently enough to avoid harmful concentrations of ammonia in the treatment zone (Johnson et al. 1999). Again, a trade-off between logistics, cost, and ecological principles will determine the most effective location for nutrient application.

6. N:P Ratio of Nutrient Blend

Once the desired concentration of N and P has been determined, the ratio of ambient nitrogen to phosphorus (i.e., N:P ratio) must be calculated to determine whether the system is limited by more than one macronutrient. The Redfield ratio, which is the cellular atomic ratio of C, N, and P in marine phytoplankton, provides a benchmark for assessing nutrient limitation, most commonly between N and P (Borchardt 1996). N:P ratios can be calculated as total nitrogen divided by total phosphorus (e.g., TN/TP); however, the utility of this calculation is limited due to the large percentage of refractory N and P incorporated in the TN and TP analyses. It is much more informative to compare the N to P ratios of biologically available nutrient, and the best approximation for this is the DIN/TDP ratio (Stockner and MacIsaac 1996).

Ambient N:P atomic ratios greater than 20:1 are considered P limiting, less than 10:1 is N limiting, and between 10 and 20:1, the distinction is equivocal (Borchardt 1996). Atomic weight ratios can be converted to weight:weight ratios by multiplying by the atomic weight of the element in question. For example, a 10:1 N:P atomic weight ratio is equivalent to a 4.5:1 N:P weight:weight ratio (e.g., $10 \times 14/1 \times 31 = 4.5$, where 14 = atomic weight N, 31 = atomic weight P). Minimum target N:P ratios (weight:weight) should be at least 7.5:1 (i.e., 30 μg/L NO_3-N + NO_2-N + NH_3-N/4 μg/L SRP; ambient concentration plus added nutrients) to ensure the system does not become co-limited by N.

The ambient N:P ratio will vary as a function of the drainage basin's underlying bedrock geology, as modified by the existing topography and precipitation regime. As a general rule, productivity and nutrients tend to be lower in coastal waters where the underlying geology is mainly erosion resistant granites and rainfall is high (Stockner 1981). In British Columbia, the interior plains, except for the northeast, are composed mainly of nonmetamorphosed sedimentary and volcanic rocks; hence, interior lakes, rivers, and streams usually have a higher concentration of dissolved ions (TDS) and higher productivities and ambient nutrient concentrations (Stockner 1987), although many examples of nutrient deficient interior streams are known as well (Slaney et al., this volume). In parts of Washington and Oregon, the geology has been heavily influenced by volcanic activity that often results in higher concentrations of phosphorus but low concentrations of dissolved inorganic nitrogen. Many of these systems are naturally nitrogen-limited (e.g., Sandy and Clackamas rivers, Mt. Hood area; D. Shively, U.S. Forest Service, Mt. Hood National Forest, unpublished data).

In British Columbia, many coastal streams (e.g., Adams River, Big Silver Creek, Keogh River) usually have soluble reactive phosphate (i.e., SRP) concentrations less than 1 μg/L and adequate dissolved inorganic nitrogen (i.e., DIN) greater than 30 μg/L, whereas some interior streams (e.g., Blackwater River) have 27 μg/L P and less than 5 μg/L DIN. Rivers that span two or more biophysiographic regions may exhibit blended nutrient regimes as a ratio of their respective watershed areas and water yields. Thus, it is possible to have a productive system on the coast (e.g., Dean River) because the majority of the nutrients are derived from an interior basin. Similarly, lake-headed river systems can significantly modify downstream nutrient regimes, owing to the uptake, retention, and bioassimilation of nutrients within the lake, although to some extent this is compensated for in the immediate outlet zone due to washout of lake seston. For example, the Nechako River, which flows across the B.C. interior, is both N- and P-limited due to its large coastal drainage basin and large headwater lakes, whereas the Nation River is N-limited due to the presence of headwater lakes.

7. Application Techniques

The topic of nutrient application often receives the least amount of research attention, yet is one of the most important aspects of an effective nutrient enrichment program. A scientifically correct program can fail if the logistical aspects of nutrient application have been improperly planned. Conversely, a logistically correct application program may be ineffective if it is not ecologically sensible. Hence, the application technique must be appropriate for the specific characteristics of each treatment project. Tables 3 and 4 summarize some of the general observations to date, gathered from projects that have

been successful and those that have not. Two general rules emerge: (1) attempt to mimic nature whenever possible; (2) be cognizant of the density differential between the nutrients being added and the water body in question. Slight differences in density will cause nutrients, either in the form of liquid fertilizer or dissolved from solid granular fertilizer to rapidly sink; hence, it is important to dilute the fertilizer to avoid its sinking through the epilimnion. Dilutions in the order of 10,000:1 have been used to avoid this problem (G. Lawrence, University of British Columbia, Vancouver, personal communication). Finally, be creative; nutrient enrichment is a relatively new field and many new techniques have yet to be discovered. Just ensure that ecological principles and logistical constraints receive equal consideration and are not at odds with each other.

Once the specifics of the application technique has been resolved, a summary table of the seven key variables should be developed and reviewed to ensure that the plan is enrichment plan is technically sound (Table 5).

Conclusions

There are a variety of application techniques available to fisheries managers seeking to enhance the production of salmonid rearing habitat. After a minimum 1–2 year pre-treatment study, one must carefully consider the specific requirements of the ecosystem, N or P or co- limitation of autotrophic production, and then select the technique that is best suited for the ecosystem. Be creative; try to mimic the arrival of the anadromous salmon 'nutrient pump' where applicable, and proceed to write the nutrient prescription so as to assure a well-balanced seasonal N:P ratio in receiving wa-

TABLE 3. Summary of nutrient application techniques for lakes and reservoirs.

Nutrient source	Application techniques	Issues
Salmon carcasses	Manual or aerial application in littoral zones	Logistics of transport and application, transplant permits, seasonal availability of carcasses
Granular fertilizer	Aerial (fixed or rotary wing), tug-barge, shore based spray, lake center dispersion	Logistics of transport, delivery, mixing, storage and application, density differences
Liquid fertilizer	Aerial (fixed or rotary wing), tug-barge, shore based spray, lake center dispersion	Logistics of transport, delivery, storage, spill containment and application, density differences
Slow-release solid fertilizer	Manual or aerial (rotary wing) application in littoral or reservoir drawdown zones	Logistics of transport and application, density differences, seasonality of reservoir drawdown

TABLE 4. Summary of nutrient application techniques for streams and rivers.

Nutrient source	Application techniques	Issues
Salmon carcasses	Manual or aerial (rotary wing) application	Logistics of transport and application, transplant permits, seasonal availability of carcasses, public and agency notification
Granular fertilizer	Automatic application stations	Logistics of transport, delivery, mixing, storage and application, nutrient spiraling distance, public and agency notification, energy sources
Liquid fertilizer	Manual drip stations, flow proportional or pre-programmed (snow-melt systems only) injection systems	Logistics of transport, delivery, storage, spill containment and application, nutrient spiraling distance, public and agency notification, energy sources
Slow-release solid fertilizer	Manual or aerial (rotary wing) application	Logistics of transport and application, nutrient spiraling distances, cost, public and agency notification

ters that have sufficient dissolved N to assure the production of edible phytoplankton/periphyton and to avoid the occurrence of nuisance colonial cyanobacteria in lakes or mats of colonial greens in streams. One must develop a prudent application strategy that insures that nutrient additions are well dispersed in stream or within the epilimnion and are applied at an appropriate frequency extending over a time period sufficient to illicit a response (e.g., weekly additions for lakes over a 22-week period). Finally, one must proceed to notify appropriate authorities well in advance of first nutrient applications and secure the necessary permits, which should include a requirement to monitor the ecosystem responses throughout the duration of the application period and for one year after cessation of supplementation.

References

Ashley, K. I., and N. T. Johnson. 1989. Habitat conservation fund progress report (1988–1989): Salsbury Lake fertilization. Fisheries Project Report No. RD 19. Ministry of Environment, Province of British Columbia.

TABLE 5. Examples from the Kootenay Lake and Keogh River fertilization programs listing the seven key variables of nutrient enrichment.

Key variable	Kootenay Lake	Keogh River
1. Concentration of applied nutrients	P = 271 mg/m^2 (13.6 µg/L); N = 1,191 mg/m^2 (59.5 µg/L) in 0–20 m epilimnion	5 µg/L P, 3.7 µg/L N
2. Nutrient formulation	Blend of 10-34-0 and 28-0-0 liquid agricultural fertilizer	7-40-0 slow release fertilizer
3. Seasonal timing of application	3rd week in April to end of August	Late spring
4. Frequency of nutrient addition	Weekly, Monday morning	Single application in late spring
5. Location of application sites	10-km zone in the center of the North Arm	River source and 6-km intervals
6. N:P ratio of nutrient blend	Seasonally adjusted at 3–4 week intervals from 0.67:1 to 7.5:1 (wt:wt basis)	0.4:1
7. Application technique	Tug/barge, surface spray + propeller mising travelling at 5 km/hr	

Ashley, K. I., and P. A. Slaney. 1997. Accelerating recovery of stream, river and pond productivity by low-level nutrient replacement. Chapter 13 *in* P. A. Slaney and D. Zaldokas, editors. Fish habitat rehabilitation procedures. Province of B.C., Ministry of Environment, Lands and Parks, and Ministry of Forests. Watershed Restoration Technical Circular No. 9.

Ashley, K. I., L. C. Thompson, D. C. Lasenby, L. McEachern, K. E. Smokorowski, and D. Sebastian. 1997. Restoration of an interior lake ecosystem: the Kootenay Lake fertilization experiment. Canadian Journal of Water Quality Research 32:192–212.

Ashley, K. I., L. C.Thompson, D. Sebastian, D. C. Lasenby, K. E. Smokorowski, and H. Andrusak. 1999. Restoration of kokanee salmon in Kootenay Lake, a large inter-montage lake, by controlled seasonal application of limiting nutrients. Pages 127–169 *in* T. Murphy and M. Munawar, editors. Aquatic restoration in Canada ecovision. World Monograph Series, Backhuys Publishers, Leiden, Netherlands.

Bilby, R. E., B. R. Fransen, and P. A. Bisson. 1996. Incorporation of nitrogen and carbon from spawning coho salmon into the trophic system of small streams: evidence from stable isotopes. Canadian Journal Fisheries and Aquatic Sciences 53:164–173.

Bilby, R. E., B. R. Fransen, J. K. Walter, C. J. Cederholm, and W. J. Scarlett. 2001. Preliminary evaluation of nitrogen stable isotope ratios to establish escapement levels for Pacific salmon. Fisheries 26:6–14

Borchardt, M. A. 1996. Nutrients. Pages 183–227 *in* R. J. Stevenson, M. L. Bothwell, and R. L. Lowe, editors. Algal ecology: freshwater benthic ecosystems. Academic Press Inc., San Diego, California.

Bothwell, M. L. 1988. Growth rate responses of lotic periphyton diatoms to experimental phosphorus enrichment: the influence of temperature and light. Canadian Journal of Fisheries and Aquatic Sciences 45:261–270.

Bothwell, M. L. 1989. Phosphorus-limited growth dynamics of lotic periphyton diatom communities: areal biomass and cellular growth rate responses. Canadian Journal of Fisheries and Aquatic Sciences 46:1293–1301.

Cederholm, C. J., D. B. Houston, D. L. Cole, and W. J. Scarlett. 1988. Fate of coho salmon (*Oncorhynchus kisutch*) carcasses in spawning streams. Canadian Journal of Fisheries and Aquatic Sciences 46:1347–1355.

Cederholm, C. J., M. D. Kunze, T. Murota, and A. Sibatani. 2000. Pacific salmon carcasses. Fisheries 24:6–15.

Chaloner, D. T., M. S. Wipfli, and J. P. Caouette. 2002. Mass loss and macro invertebrate colonization of pacific salmon carcasses in south-eastern Alaskan streams. Freshwater Biology 47:263–273.

Driver, J., D. Lijmbach, and I. Steen. 1999 Why recover phosphorus for recycling and how? Environmental Technology 20:651–662.

Emsley, J. 2000. The shocking history of phosphorus–a biography of the devil's element. Pan Books, London, England.

Gresh, T. J., J. Lichatowich, J. and P. Schoonmaker. 2000. An estimation of historic and current levels of salmon production in the Northeast Pacific ecosystem: evidence of a nutrient deficit in the freshwater systems of the Pacific Northwest. Fisheries 25:15–21.

Johnston, N. T., C. J. Perrin, P. A. Slaney, and B. R. Ward. 1990. Increased juvenile growth by whole-river fertilization. Canadian Journal of Fisheries and Aquatic Sciences 47:862–872.

Johnston, N. T., M. D. Stamford, K. I Ashley, and K. Tsumura. 1999. Responses of rainbow trout (*Oncorhynchus mykiss*) and their prey to inorganic fertilization of an oligotrophic montane lake. Canadian Journal of Fisheries and Aquatic Sciences 56:1011–1025.

Larkin, G. A., and P. A. Slaney. 1997. Implications of trends in marine-derived nutrient influx to south coastal British Columbia salmonid production. Fisheries 22:16–23.

Lawrence, G. A., K. I. Ashley, N. Yonemitsu, and J. R. Ellis. 1995. Natural dispersion and the fertilization of small lakes. Limnology and Oceanography 40:1519–1526.

Milbrink, G., and S. Holmgren. 1981. Fish species interactions in a fertilized reservoir. Report Institute of Freshwater Research, Drottningholm, Sweden 59:121–127.

Minshall, G. W. 1978. Autotrophy in stream ecosystems. Bioscience 28:767–771.

Minshall, G. W., K. W. Cummins, R. C. Petersen, C. E. Cushing, D. A. Bruns, J. R. Sedell, and R. L. Vannote. 1985. Developments in stream ecosystem theory. Canadian Journal of Fisheries and Aquatic Sciences 42:1045–1055.

Minshall, G. W., E. Hitchcock, and J. R. Barnes. 1991. Decomposition of rainbow trout (*Oncorhynchus mykiss*) carcasses in a forest stream ecosystem inhabited only by non-anadromous fish populations. Canadian Journal of Fisheries and Aquatic Sciences 48:191–195.

Mulholland, P. J. 1996. Role in nutrient cycling in streams. Pages 609–639 *in* R. J. Stevenson, M. L. Bothwell, and R. L. Lowe, editors. Benthic Algal ecology in freshwater benthic ecosystems. Academic Press, New York.

Nehlsen, W., J. E. Williams, and J. A. Lichatowich. 1991. Pacific salmon at the crossroads: stocks at risk from California, Oregon, Idaho and Washington. Fisheries 16:4–21.

Nordin, R. L. 1985. Water quality criteria for nutrients and algae. British Columbia Ministry for the Environment, Water Quality Unit, Resource Quality Section, Water Management Branch, Victoria.

Pick, F. R., and D. R. S. Lean. 1987. The role of macronutrients (C,N,P) in controlling cyanobacterial dominance in temperate lakes. New Zealand Journal of Marine and Freshwater Research 21:425–434.

Schuldt J. A., and AE. Hershey. 1995. Effect of salmon carcass decomposition on Lake Superior tributary streams. Journal of the North American Benthological Society 14:259–268.

Slaney, P. A., W. O. Rublee, C. J. Perrin, and H. Goldberg. 1994. Debris structure placements and whole-river fertilization for salmonids in a large regulated stream in British Columbia. Fifth International Conference on Aquatic Habitat Enhancement, Long Beach, California. November 1991. Bulletin of Marine Sciences 55(2–3):1160–1180.

Smith, V. H. 1983. Low nitrogen to phosphorus ratios favor dominance by blue-green algae in lake phytoplankton. Science 221:669–671.

Stansby, M. E., and A. S. Hall. 1965. Chemical composition of commercially important fish of the United States. Fish. Ind. Research 3:29–46.

Stephens, K., and J. G. Stockner. 1983. The Lake Enrichment Program: methods for the fertilization of lakes in British Columbia 1970-1982. Canadian Technical Report of Fisheries and Aquatic Sciences No. 1192.

Sterling, M. S., K. I. Ashley and A. B. Bautista. 2000. Slow-release fertilizer for rehabilitating oligotrophic streams: a physical characterization. Canadian Journal of Water Quality Research 35:73–94.

Stockner, J. G. 1981. Whole-lake fertilization for the enhancement of sockeye salmon (Oncorhynchus nerka) in British Columbia, Canada. Verhandlungen Internationale Vereinigung Limnologie 21:293–299.

Stockner, J. G. 1987. Lake fertilization: the enrichment cycle and lake sockeye salmon (Oncorhynchus nerka) production. Pages 198–215 in H. D. Smith, L. Margolis, and C. C. Wood, editors. Sockeye salmon (Oncorhynchus nerka) population biology and future management. Canadian Special Publication of Fisheries and Aquatic Sciences 96.

Stockner, J. G., and K. S. Shortreed. 1985. Whole-lake fertilization experiments in coastal British Columbia: empirical relationships between nutrient inputs and phytoplankton biomass and production. Canadian Journal of Fisheries and Aquatic Sciences 42:649–658.

Stockner, J. G., and E. A. MacIsaac. 1996. The British Columbia Lake fertilization program: overview after two decades of salmon enhancement. Regulated Rivers 12:344–356.

Stockner, J. G., E. Rydin, and P. Hyenstrand. 2000. Cultural oligotrophication: causes and consequences for fisheries resources. Fisheries 25:7–14.

Suttle, C. A., J. G. Stockner, and P. J. Harrison. 1987. Effects of nutrient pulses on community structure and cell size of a freshwater phytoplankton assemblage in culture. Canadian Journal of Fisheries and Aquatic Sciences 44:1768–1774.

Suttle, C. A., J. G. Stockner, K. S. Shortreed, and P. J. Harrison. 1988. Time-course studies of size-fractionated phosphate uptake: are larger cells better competitors for pulses of phosphate than smaller cells? Oecologia 74:571–576.

Suttle, C. A., W. P. Cochlan and J. G. Stockner. 1991. Size-dependent ammonium and phosphate uptake, and N:P supply ratios in an oligotrophic lake. Canadian Journal of Fisheries and Aquatic Sciences 48:1226–1234.

Vollenweider, R. A. 1976. Advances in defining critical loading levels for phosphorus in lake eutrophication. Memoirs Istituto Italiano Idrobiologie 33:53–83.

Wetzel, R. G. 1975. Limnology. W.B. Saunders and Co., Philadelphia.

Willson, M. F., and K. C. Halupka. 1995. Anadromous fish as keystone species in vertebrate communities. Conservation Biology 9:489–497.

Wipfli, M. S., J. P. Hudson, D. T. Chaloner, and J.P Caouette. 1999. Influence of salmon spawner densities on stream productivity in Southeast Alaska. Canadian Journal of Fisheries and Aquatic Sciences 56:1600–1611

Innovative Ecosystem Management

American Fisheries Society Symposium 34:261–276, 2003

Searching for a Life History Approach to Salmon Escapement Management

E. Eric Knudsen

USGS, Alaska Biological Science Center, 1011 Tudor Road, Anchorage, Alaska 99503, USA

Eric W. Symmes and F. Joseph Margraf

USGS, Alaska Cooperative Fish and Wildlife Research Unit
University of Alaska, Fairbanks, Alaska 99775-7020, USA

Abstract.—A number of Pacific salmon populations have already been lost and many others throughout the range are in various states of decline. Recent research has documented that Pacific salmon carcasses serve as a key delivery vector of marine-derived nutrients into the freshwater portions of their ecosystems. This nutrient supply plays a critical biological feedback role in salmon sustainability by supporting juvenile salmon production. We first demonstrate how nutrient feedback potential to juvenile production may be unaccounted for in spawner-recruit models of populations under long-term exploitation. We then present a heuristic, life history-based, spreadsheet survival model that incorporates salmon carcass-driven nutrient feedback to the freshwater components of the salmon ecosystem. The productivity of a hypothetical coho salmon population was simulated using rates from the literature for survival from spawner to egg, egg to fry, fry to smolt, and smolt to adult. The effects of climate variation and nutrient feedback on survival were incorporated, as were density-dependent effects of the numbers of spawners and fry on freshwater survival of eggs and juveniles. The unexploited equilibrium population was subjected to 100 years of 20, 40, 60, and 80% harvest. Each harvest scenario greater than 20% brought the population to a reduced steady state, regardless of generous compensatory survival at low population sizes. Increasing harvest reduced the positive effects of nutrient contributions to population growth. Salmon researchers should further explore this modeling approach for establishing escapement goals. Given the importance of nutrient feedback, managers should strive for generous escapements that support nutrient rebuilding, as well as egg deposition, to ensure strong future salmon production.

Introduction

No longer is it news that Pacific salmon *Oncorhynchus* spp. populations are declining and, in some cases, disappearing. The critical questions now are whether, and to what extent, the Pacific Northwest populations can recover and whether apparently healthy populations in Alaska and British Columbia can be protected from further declines. Much of this book focuses on the science of nutrient cycling in freshwater ecosystems. There are clear ecological links between salmon carcass-derived nutrients and aquatic ecosystem health including subsequent salmon production (e.g., Kline et al. 1990; Bilby et al. 1996; Cederholm et al. 1999). Although awareness of a nutrient deficit in freshwater ecosystems is rapidly growing (e.g. Gresh et al. 2000; Stockner et al. 2000), there are few quantified relationships between the biomass of spawners entering aquatic habitats and resultant future run sizes (Bilby et al. 2001). This chapter evaluates a new paradigm wherein salmon escapement management includes life history-based production limits and nutrient feedback.

Reduced nutrients in the freshwater ecosystem, due to diminished spawning escapements, is just one of many causes interacting to deplete salmon runs. While a salmon population may sometimes decline due to an obvious cause, such as overfishing, dams, or loss of estuarine intertidal habitats to development, in most cases, the decline is attributable to a complex, negative synergism of anthropogenic and natural assaults (see NRC 1996, Stouder et al. 1997; Knudsen et al. 2000). Although sorting out the role of reduced nutrients from other harmful factors may be impossible, the topic warrants specific attention. The relative importance of nutrient cycles in the southern part of the Pacific salmon range is obscured by habitat alteration. However, there are a number of relatively pristine watersheds that have limited runs. If the science on nutrient cycling is correct, lack of salmon in these apparently healthy stream systems may indicate that overfishing has been the primary cause of run reduction. In the northern portion of the range, where many habitats are intact, the effects of potential reductions in nutrients may be more difficult to detect but could be contributing to recent declines in some areas.

The enormous scientific attention focused on Pacific salmon management practices over the years makes the pervasive population declines difficult to reconcile and accept. Existing management practices clearly lack some important elements. The primary weakness is likely the absence of an integrated approach that accounts for all the major factors impinging on salmon populations throughout their ecosystem (Lichatowich et al. 1995; Mobrand et al. 1997), including nutrient cycling (Williams et al. 1999). Nutrient cycling has been alluded to in several previous reconsiderations of carrying capacity and salmonid ecosystems (Spence et al. 1996; Mobrand et al. 1997; Williams et al. 1999). While these new studies set the stage for fully integrating nutrient cycles into management modeling, they have only considered nutrients in a limited contemporary context, rather than striving to assess the full biological capacity of aquatic ecosystems when optimally fertilized by salmon carcasses. Therefore, this chapter will 1) reinforce why previous approaches to salmon escapement management have been less than successful, 2) propose a new way of thinking about escapement management that accounts for critical life history characteristics and nutrient feedback loops, and 3) make research and management recommendations that support salmon biological productivity.

True Salmonid Carrying Capacity

A central unknown in salmon population dynamics is the *true* carrying capacity. Some have referred to this concept as "pristine carrying capacity." We use the term "true carrying capacity" to acknowledge that many populations may never return to the pristine conditions that occurred prior to non-indigenous human settlement. However, even in altered habitats, salmon populations have an intrinsic capacity for colonization and rebuilding (e.g., Milner et al. 2001) that should be maximized. Regardless of the habitat condition, the challenge is to understand how many salmon a given population can sustainably produce (Mobrand et al. 1997).

The spawner-recruit model (e.g., Ricker 1975) adequately describes the number of offspring produced from a given number of spawners if all the assumptions are met; however, such models often incorrectly estimate escapement at maximum sustainable yield (MSY) and results in an inappropriate harvest rate (Hilborn and Walters 1992; Needle, in press). This can result from measurement error, time series bias due to lack of independence, and nonstationarity of the spawner-recruit relationship (Hilborn and Walters 1992).

The spawner-recruit model can also underestimate the true production capacity and, particularly, the unexploited equilibrium replacement point in an exploited population (Knudsen 2000, in press). When the model is fit to contemporary data, there is rarely any information to judge the assumption that the population is currently performing at full production potential. For example, recent core analyses of historic marine-derived nitrogen in Alaskan sockeye lakes demonstrate that some populations in unaltered habitats are producing less salmon than they did before heavy exploitation (Schmidt et al.1998; Finney et al. 2000). These data provide a rare surrogate for historic, pristine escapement that can be compared to contemporary escapements. We mimicked these concepts and generated hypothetical run size data for a generic salmon population before and after exploitation (Figure 1, top panel). Extended exploitation reduces both the number of spawners at MSY estimated by the spawner-recruit model, relative to the system's potential (Figure 1, middle panel), and the equilibrium replacement point, which is drastically

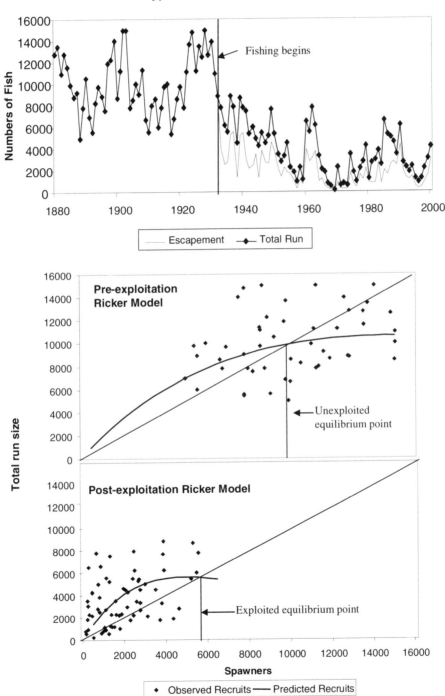

FIGURE 1. Hypothetical coho salmon population total run size before exploitation and total run and escapement after exploitation (top panel). Ricker spawner-recruit plots of the pre-exploitation data (middle panel) and post-exploitation data (bottom panel) from the same habitat. Note that the equilibrium population replacement point has shifted to dramatically fewer spawners under exploitation even though the habitat has not changed.

reduced under exploitation (Figure 1, bottom panel). If the system were performing to its full biological capacity, the exploited equilibrium point would be the same as in the unexploited state. Any harvested production that is truly "excess" should not reduce the ability of the population to replace itself at its full production capacity.

The effectiveness of spawner-recruit models is further compromised by the inconsistencies and dynamics of the real world. The spawner-recruit model is a composite of all the factors that influence salmon production, "averaging" all historic observations into one relationship. Yet those factors are highly variable from year to year, and the limiting factors can change annually. Because of the drawbacks to salmon spawner-recruit modeling, a new model accounting for the multiple and variable limitations to survival, including nutrient cycling, will be required for successful future management. Admittedly, application of such an analytical system to salmon management is a long way off, but we encourage thought in that direction and offer the following preliminary model as a step in the right direction.

A Proposed Life History Approach to Escapement Management

Life history approaches to managing Pacific salmon have been proposed previously (e.g., Lichatowich et al. 1995; Mobrand et al. 1997; Nickelson and Lawson 1998). Nickelson (1998) and Bradford et al. (2000) estimated escapement needs by focusing on life-history and habitat-oriented modeling, but they assessed capacity using recent observations (i.e., from populations normally exploited) and did not explicitly include nutrients in their models. Our approach is based on a stepwise accounting of mortality throughout the salmon's life, attempting to account for all major mortality sources, as generally illustrated in Figure 2.

The new approach was evaluated using a heuristic spreadsheet model to simulate the life history of a simplified coho salmon *O. kisutch* population (coho were selected because they mostly return at the same age and they depend on nutrients during freshwater rearing). We estimated relationships at each life history step and

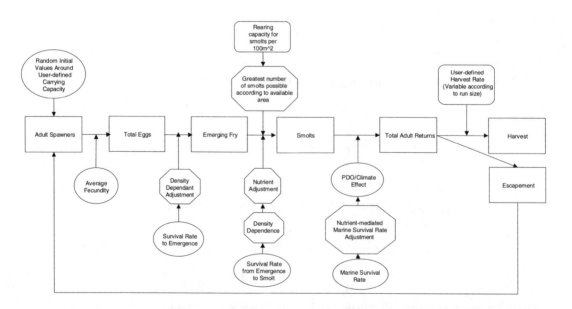

FIGURE 2. Flow chart illustrating the modeled coho salmon life cycle. Rectangles indicate life history stages where population numbers are calculated. Ovals represent stochastically varied user inputs. Rounded rectangles include user inputs that are not directly stochastically varied. Octagons are stochastically varied density-dependent survival adjustments.

included nutrient and density dependent feed-back, as well as appropriate stochasticity, where relevant. Ideally, the model would be parameter-ized based on empirical observations for any population of interest. However, our first genera-tion model is based on a hypothetical coho salmon population for which we assume we know the appropriate parameters (not the same data illustrated in Figure 1). We estimated mor-tality rates and their variation, based on infor-mal meta-analysis from the literature or edu-cated guesses of reasonable values based on coho salmon ecology.

A key feature of this preliminary investiga-tion is the assertion that we know the true popu-lation equilibrium replacement point. If a popu-lation was not exploited and did not experience major perturbations or long-term climatic trends, it would exhibit interannual escapements always varying around the true equilibrium re-placement point (for example, see Figure 1, middle panel). A predefined, unexploited equi-librium point is our standard reference point for assessing population performance under various scenarios of nutrient feedback and harvest rate.

Compensatory survival following exploita-tion is accounted for in the model by increasing intragravel survival and freshwater rearing sur-vival when spawner densities are less than the equilibrium number of spawners. Incubation and rearing survivals were likewise reduced when spawners or fry were above average. When spawners were above the unexploited equilib-rium, we included positive nutrient-derived ad-justments to rearing survival (Quinn and Peter-son 1996) and marine survival (Bilby et al. 1998) because of larger smolt size resulting from im-proved food production.

Model Assumptions

Our coho salmon life history model functions under several important assumptions.

- The population equilibrium replacement carrying capacity is known.
- The population does not experience cata-strophic perturbations lasting more than one generation.
- There is no nutrient effect from other salmon species.
- The nutrient effect comes only from the parental escapement.
- There is no freshwater or marine compe-tition with other runs or species.

- The male:female ratio is 1:1.
- There is no effect from jacks.
- Natural mortality between harvest and spawning is negligible.
- There is neither a genetically based del-eterious effect at small population size nor compensatory genetic effects for ex-tremely small populations.
- Fish do not stray from or into the popula-tion.

Model Steps

Each row in the spreadsheet represents one an-nual cohort. Survival rates and associated varia-tions for each life history stage are computed in the columns. The escapement resulting at the last step (column) in the model feeds the number of spawners for the beginning of the resulting co-hort three years (rows) later. There are 100 an-nual cohorts in the model. The model begins de-terministically in that sex ratio, fecundity, egg to fry survival, fry to smolt survival, and marine sur-vival balance to the original number of spawn-ers in the unexploited state. Survival rates are sto-chastically modified based on variations re-ported in the literature. Carcass-derived nutrient feedback and marine environmental variation simulations further modified survival but only to the extent that the unexploited population re-mained approximately balanced over model it-erations.

The model allows the user to input certain values for the population of interest: equilibrium carrying capacity (number of spawners), stream area (m^2), maximum smolt production (per $100m^2$), the maximum expected fry to smolt sur-vival rate (used only to calculate a reference point for fry density dependence), and the intended harvest rate (Figure 2). At the start of each model run, the initial spawners for years 1, 2, and 3 were generated randomly using a normal distribution with a mean of the user-input equilibrium spawner carrying capacity and a standard devia-tion of 10%.

Fecundity values were randomly generated using a normal distribution with a mean of 4,500 eggs (Groot and Margolis 1991) and standard de-viation of 500. Assuming a spawner sex ratio of 1:1, the total potential number of eggs was equal to the number of spawners divided by 2 and mul-tiplied by fecundity.

To calculate the adjusted egg to emergence survival rate, we multiplied the spawning to emergence survival rate, randomly generated using a normal distribution with a mean of 0.3 and standard deviation equal to 0.07 (Groot and Margolis 1991, modified by Bradford et al. 2000), by a density dependent adjustment factor regulated by the number of spawners present. That relationship is theoretically controlled by limited spawning area. When spawners were at equilibrium carrying capacity, there was no density dependent effect. Otherwise, the effect was described by a modified Richards 3-parameter model where incubation survival was gradually adjusted downward as spawners exceeded the equilibrium level or upward when spawners were less than equilibrium (Figure 3). Finally, we multiplied the adjusted egg to emergence survival rate by the potential number of eggs to generate the number of emerging fry.

The basic survival rate from emergence to smoltification was randomly generated using a normal distribution with a mean of 0.029 and standard deviation of 0.0029 (Groot and Margolis 1991, modified by Bradford et al. 2000). A density dependent pre-smolt survival adjustment factor was described by a modified Richards 3-parameter model, such that when the number of calculated fry was less than expected, the survival was gradually adjusted up to 2.0 times, but when the calculated fry number was greater than expected, survival was adjusted downward to a minimum of 0.33 (Figure 4).

A nutrient-related pre-smolt survival adjustment factor was regulated according to the number of spawners relative to the equilibrium carrying capacity. A logistic equation described the relationship between the number of spawners and the nutrient input to the system (Figure 5). When the number of spawners was greater than the equilibrium carrying capacity, the survival rate was gradually adjusted upward to 2.0 times. When the number of spawners was less than or equal to the equilibrium carrying capacity, the nutrient adjustment had no effect on the emergence to smolt survival rate. The number of potential smolts was calculated by multiplying the emergence to smoltification survival rate by the density dependent adjustment and the nutrient adjustment.

Since coho salmon smolt production is apparently limited by available habitat (e.g., Nickelson 1998; Bradford et al. 2000), we compared the survival-based estimate of potential smolts to an estimate of the maximum expected smolts. The maximum smolt production was calculated from the user-input maximum smolts per 100 m² from which the model randomly gen-

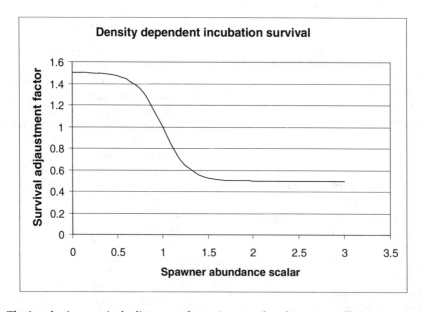

FIGURE 3. The incubation survival adjustment factor is set so that there is no effect when spawners are at the equilibrium carrying capacity. Incubation survival is adjusted according to the factor on the *y*-axis: reduced gradually to 50% as spawners increase above equilibrium or increased gradually to a maximum of 125% when spawners are less than equilibrium.

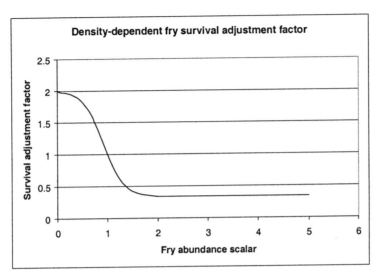

FIGURE 4. The fry density-dependent survival adjustment factor was 1 (no effect) when fry densities were equal to the maximum expected fry carrying capacity. When fry exceeded that point, the adjustment factor reduced fry survival down to 33%. When fry were less than the expected carrying capacity, survival was increased up to 2X.

erated a normal distribution of expected maximum smolts per area. The maximum number of smolts per area was then multiplied by the user-input available stream rearing area. The results were used as an upper cap on smolt production if the survival-based estimate exceeded this area-based maximum smolt production.

The basic marine survival rate was randomly generated using a normal distribution with a mean of 0.05, standard deviation equal to 0.01 (Groot and Margolis 1991; Coronado and Hilborn

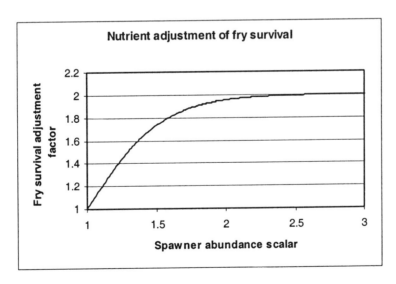

FIGURE 5. The nutrient-related fry survival adjustment factor: when the number of spawners was greater than the equilibrium carrying capacity, fry survival was increased up to 2.0 times; when the number of spawners was less than or equal to the equilibrium carrying capacity, the nutrient adjustment had no effect on the emergence to smolt survival rate.

1998). The marine survival rate was then adjusted by the nutrient-mediated growth factor, which was described by a logistic equation controlled by the number of spawners (Figure 6). When the number of spawners was less than or equal to the equilibrium carrying capacity, there was no adjustment to the marine survival rate. When the number of spawners was greater than the equilibrium carrying capacity the marine survival rate was adjusted by up to 1.75 times.

The overall effect of climate and environmental variability was incorporated with an adjustment factor that was based on a sine function having a randomly generated period ranging between 10 and 20 years, with a mean of 15 years (to approximately mimic patterns described by Beamish and Boullion (1993) and Hare et al. (1999). The periodicity and starting point of the cycle were randomly recalculated for each model iteration. The amplitude of the cycle ranged from 0 to 2. Each annual value was also stochastically adjusted to mimic the variation that is observed on the decadal oscillation (Figure 7). The climatic factor was then used to adjust coho salmon marine survival up or down. Marine survival rates were ultimately constrained so that they were never less than 2% nor greater than 20%, realistic bounds as reported in many populations by Coronado and Hilborn (1998).

Total adult returns were then calculated by multiplying the number of smolts by the adjusted marine survival rate. The user-input harvest level was taken as a percentage of the total return. To simulate a basic harvest conservation strategy, when the total run was less than 20% of the equilibrium carrying capacity escapement, the harvest rate was zero. If the run size was greater than 20% of equilibrium, the specified harvest rate was applied to the entire run.

The escapement was the difference between the total return and the harvest. Escapements completed the life cycle and were fed back into the next generation in the model. To help evaluate population performance, a nutrient factor was calculated by multiplying the two nutrient adjustments. The number of spawners relative to the carrying capacity regulated this factor.

Trials

We modeled the population 100 years into the future to observe performance under various scenarios. We used 100 iterations to dampen the sometimes extreme variation within individual model runs and to explore the "average" effects of the various density dependent and nutrient feedback loops. For this paper, we explored the effects of five different harvest rates (100 itera-

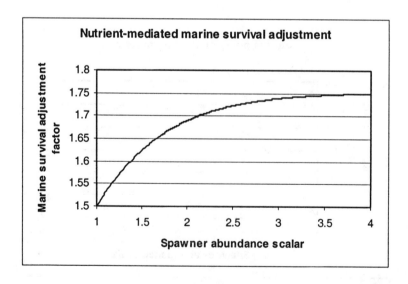

FIGURE 6. The nutrient-mediated marine survival adjustment increased survival gradually up to 1.75 times, as the number of spawners increased above the equilibrium carrying capacity. If the number of spawners was less than or equal to the equilibrium carrying capacity, there was no adjustment to the marine survival rate.

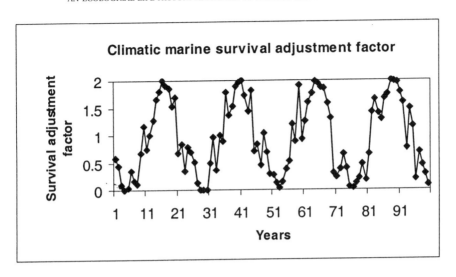

FIGURE 7. An example of the stochastically varied, decadal-oscillating marine survival adjustment factor.

tions each) on total run size, harvest, escapement, and nutrients. We used the following values as user inputs:

Spawner carrying capacity	5,000
Smolts per 100m^2	100
Stream rearing area (m^2)	95,000
Maximum fry to smolt survival	0.05
Harvest rates	0, 0.2, 0.4, 0.6, 0.8

Results and Discussion

Model Performance

The model appears to provide reasonable patterns when all the iterations are averaged (Figure 8). Because the model was developed to first simulate the unexploited equilibrium replacement, the unexploited total run size maintains itself around the 5,000-spawner equilibrium carrying capacity identified a priori for the system (Figure 8, top panel). The slight, gradual decay in the total returns with no exploitation is likely an artifact of the interrelationship between the survival rates, nutrient feedback, and the marine environmental variation.

Total run size was diminished by exploitation rates of 40, 60, and 80%, but there was not much apparent effect of 20% harvest. The results indicate that harvest rates greater than 20% tend to reduce the population over the first 20 years and then impose a persistent and relatively constant reduction in production (Figure 8). At first glance, this raised concerns that the model may be oversimplified. However, performance of individual model runs indicates that the various density dependent or nutrient-related survival and growth adjustments are operating as expected; they tend to rebuild the population, sometimes dramatically, after it has been reduced. For example, in years when egg to fry survival was reduced due to high spawner densities, fry to smolt survival was compensatorily increased because the number of emerging fry was less than average, but then the number of potential smolts and/or the marine survival rate (influenced by smolt size) were adjusted upward because of carcass-derived nutrient input. Many times the model produced adults far exceeding the equilibrium replacement, as expected, but harvest eventually drove the population back down after several generations.

The performance observed in our simulations is logically reminiscent of the ecological performance of a natural population. The model is intended to mimic nature. Keeping in mind that an unexploited population would have evolved numerous compensatory mechanisms to replace itself and to normally realize a productive "surplus" to hedge against ecological downturns and catastrophes (e.g., Mobrand et al. 1997), we have included five conditions under which the population would expand, and some of those are quite generous depending on population levels. Without exploitation, the popula-

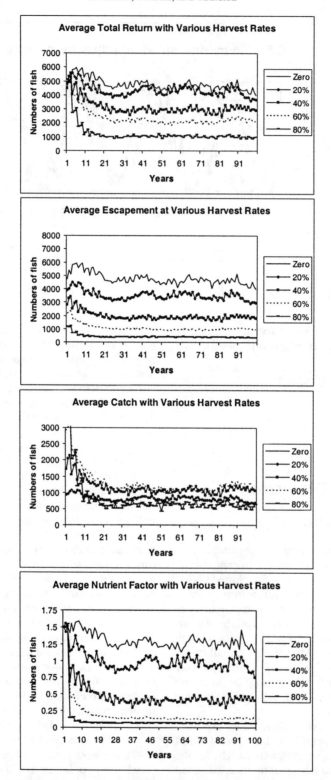

FIGURE 8. Model outcomes of an average of 100 iterations under 0, 20, 40, 60, and 80% harvest scenarios. Top panel, total run size; second panel, escapement; third panel, harvest; and bottom panel, nutrient factor.

tion maintained long-term equilibrium. The eventual reduction to a diminished steady replacement state under exploitation may indicate that a salmon population's innate production capacity can only rebuild the population over the short run, but that continued exploitation will, on average, depress the population according to the harvest rate.

Strengths and Weaknesses of the Model

We see four major benefits of this heuristic model. The first is that it provides an intuitive basis for thinking about how a salmon population functions. It therefore aligns management-oriented modeling with the animals' life history. In that sense, this life-history-based approach holds significant promise for restoration and sustainability because it accounts for most critical factors impinging on salmon population productivity. Previous work by Nickelson and Lawson (1998) followed this intuitive pathway, although they emphasized the viability of small populations rather than the sustainability of healthy populations.

Second, the modeling approach is exceedingly specific in its configuration of the life history and could conceivably include more terms than it does, thereby capturing most of the complexity and dynamics of salmon in their environment, as recommended by Mobrand et al. (1997). For example, we were able to reasonably incorporate several terms for the effects of marine-derived nutrients into our model. This approach is in sharp contrast to the highly generalized spawner-recruit models that are statistical expressions based on observed parental and resultant offspring run sizes. While statistical models must have few terms to accommodate the principle of parsimony (Hilborn and Liermann 1998), the life cycle approach is improved with additional terms.

Third, the model is organized in a clear, stepwise order that parallels the life history in a straightforward manner. Rather than depend on one primary mathematical or statistical expression, with a few terms added for influential variables, the model can incorporate as many steps as necessary, each having its literature-based biological function, with stochasticity as appropriate. While our approach is very similar to that of Nickelson and Lawson (1998), the use of a spreadsheet rather than computer coding makes

our model very accessible and understandable to a wide audience of potential users.

Fourth, this model allows examination and evaluation of various management scenarios. Once the model has been acceptably stabilized and appears to simulate the species and population of concern, it can be used to test the population's sensitivity to alterations in climate, nutrient inputs, harvest, or other relevant factors.

We recognize three drawbacks of our model. First, this model is very preliminary. Thus far, the model is theoretical and completely hypothetical, although based on realistic assumptions as well as means and standard deviations from the extensive available literature. Progress will require applying the concepts to some empirical case studies. We also recognize the need for incorporating an evaluation of uncertainty and risk associated with sensitivity analysis for management scenarios. Future refinement should include formal meta analysis to both build on previous knowledge and incorporate variation and uncertainty (Hilborn and Liermann 1998). Additionally, the spreadsheet model needs to be mathematically formalized as described by Prager and Mohr (2001).

Second, the model as configured uses 100 iterations to simulate the "average" outcome of the population, based on our estimated input parameters. In a practical application to a given population, many of the variables would be better known for that particular population. The model would then be used to assess how the population performs under a range of possible scenarios. This model is a generalization of real populations because it is based on 100 iterations of individual runs. The averaged iterations obscure the variation among individual model runs. Examination of individual model runs indicates a relatively wide range of outcomes. We caution that each natural population has only one outcome per generation and that outcome depends on the actual conditions experienced. However, once the model is based on empirical data, as recommended below, it should be useful in evaluating various projected outcomes for a given population. As an example, Nickelson and Lawson (1998) based their similar model on habitat quality in three specific coho-producing basins, an important step necessary for further development of our model.

Third, we realize our assumption of steady state conditions does not offer any new solutions to the problem of predictability. For example, advances using traditional statistical approaches are gradually revealing some of the important environmental factors driving salmon marine survival, such as sea surface temperatures and upwelling (e.g., Hare et al. 1999; Pyper and Peterman 1999). While concepts based on the nature and extent of climatic changes and environmental variability have been incorporated into our model, they have yet to be cast in a predictive sense to account for future uncertainty. Likewise, direct links between environmental variation and survival have not yet been made in this model. On the other hand, specifying environmental fluctuation, as we have in this hypothetical situation, is like a natural experiment where the unknown environmental variation is controlled so that sensitivity to the effects of nutrients and harvest can be examined.

The Role of Nutrients in Escapement Management

We included a relatively simplistic accounting of the carcass-derived nutrient effects in this model. Nutrients had only positive effects; when escapement exceeded equilibrium carrying capacity, increased numbers of fry survived, they grew bigger and therefore survived better in the ocean. There were no imputed negative effects of reduced nutrients. Figure 8 (bottom panel) clearly indicates that the role of nutrients is diminished with harvest in this model, and we believe this may substantially explain the reduced population sustainability with increased exploitation.

We are unaware of any previous mechanistic models that have explicitly included the role of nutrients in the sustainability of salmon populations, although both Larkin and Slaney (1997) and Bilby et al. (2001) demonstrated the relationship between carcass-derived nutrients and salmon production. Nickelson and Lawson (1998), whose model was similar to ours and in some ways better developed, did not include specific consideration of nutrient feedback in their model. While no one has directly addressed the role of nutrients in escapement management directly, Stockner and MacIsaac (1996) and Bilby et al. (2001) recommend that nutrient enrichment should be accounted for in escapement management. Some important next steps for studying the role of nutrients using life history-based models include incorporating multi-year and multi-species effects of marine-derived nutrients and the effects of nutrients on estuarine productivity.

True Salmon Carrying Capacity

Accurately assessing true biological carrying capacity may be untenable but, we believe, a worthy goal to strive for. In a line of many previous attempts to estimate target production for coho salmon, Bradford et al. (2000) used the hockey stick model to estimate carrying capacity and escapement targets. However, their model, like their predecessors, was based on smolt production per female spawner and used contemporary data from exploited populations. It is possible that smolt production may be greater if watersheds were fully supplied with marine-derived nutrients and sufficient eggs resulted in enough fry to fully utilize the nutrient-enriched food base in the physical habitat. Furthermore, increased nutrients may result in larger smolts that apparently have better average survival than smaller smolts (e.g., Holtby et al. 1990).

For the present exercise, we assumed we knew true carrying capacity. Without empirical evidence, carrying capacity is difficult if not impossible to determine when the population is under exploitation. We suggest that one way to approach the estimation of carrying capacity is to use a model similar to ours, populated with empirical survival data, especially if those data are from populations that have been allowed to experience "overescapement" or nutrient enrichment, as well as a range of freshwater and marine survival conditions, and analyze the array of outcomes with various estimated equilibrium spawner numbers.

Salmon Escapement Management

Our life history-based model appears to provide some insight into why spawner-recruit models have not always resulted in thriving fisheries. First, we see no obvious evidence that salmon populations should consistently be expected to produce dramatic surpluses beyond their equilibrium capacity once they are under exploitation (a basic tenant of surplus production models, e.g., Ricker 1975). Even though our model includes many generous compensatory survival opportunities, the populations remained depressed under long-term exploitation. Generally, as the harvest rate increased, the model indicated that continued exploitation brings the population to a "steady state" production level less than its inherent capacity (Figure 8). Interestingly, catch appeared to be maximized at 40–60% harvest, but 80% harvest resulted in the smallest catches (Figure 8, third panel). Although catch was greatest at 40–60% harvest in this model, the selection of alternative survival rates and nutrient feedback and environmental variation adjustments (i.e., a population with different compensatory capacity) would result in catch being maximized at a different harvest rate. Furthermore, at 40–60% harvest, the total run and escapement (Figure 8) are noticeably reduced, which may have important implications to the aquatic ecosystem and associated wildlife needs (Cederholm et al. 1999).

Second, if any of the data from model runs under exploitation were plotted with a standard spawner-recruit model, the conclusion would be that the population was in a "steady state" and the spawner-recruit model would result in an underestimate of the true equilibrium replacement point and an overestimate of the sustainable harvest rate.

In terms of direct application of this modeling approach to escapement management, several critical steps, described below, will be required before managers can use it to decide how many spawners should be allowed to escape the fishery to maximize productivity of a specific population. In the meantime, increasing evidence indicates that setting escapement goals at a fixed point based on traditional spawner-recruit models may result in underutilization of habitat capacity and may diminish nutrient supply (Cramer 2000). For example, Myers and Barrowman (1996) concluded that recruitment overfishing was pervasive but difficult to detect because so many populations were at low levels. Gilbert (1997) used similar analyses to conclude that spawner-recruit derivations of harvest and escapement reference points were valid for salmonids. Myers (1997) reanalyzed the same data and concluded that recruitment was indeed dependent on spawners. However, none of this work has differentiated the relative importance of spawners as delivery vectors of eggs into the gravel versus supplying nutrients for supporting future recruitment. Research by Bilby et al. (2001) provides a strong argument that allowance for nutrient replenishment in setting escapement goals will likely improve productivity. Cramer (2000) demonstrated that fishing at a level about two-thirds less than that predicted through traditional spawner-recruit modeling could provide maximum harvests, while allowing the spawning stock to double. Until further research discerns the relative roles of spawners in delivering nutrients as well as eggs, and the amounts of each necessary for maximum production, the watchword should be generous escapements.

Recommendations

This model and other similar approaches (e.g., Nickelson and Lawson 1998) hold substantial promise for testing the sensitivity of salmon populations to a wide variety of both limiting and favorable factors that together influence population size. Custom configurations of this model should help test effects like climate, catastrophic events, spawning population size, straying rates, hatchery supplementation, restoration alternatives, harvest scenarios, interspecific nutrient supplementation, or unique life history strategies on the various aspects of compensatory or depensatory survival. It can be used to study the population's resilience to perturbations, relative to various management options. With further refinement, the model can also interrelate multiple populations having unique survival rates but subject to the same fisheries or multiple fisheries with variable harvest rates.

Before this approach can be practically implemented, though, it must be evaluated relative to real, case history populations. As a first step, model performance should be evaluated by hind-casting run sizes for well-documented case history populations. This would require incorporating empirical survival data into the model from populations under exploitation but for which there is a long data record. To bring the model to its full utility, however, will require incorporating information on true carrying capacity. While there are no known, extant populations that are at unexploited equilibrium carrying capacity, it is essential that further research be conducted on equilibrium potential, rather than assuming that contemporary freshwater survival and productivity represent the population's potential. One way to do this is to stop fishing on some experimental populations having relatively unaltered habitat and observe production of smolts and adults as the population gradually resets itself to the suspected higher equilibrium point. An alternative approach to evaluating the model, as well as equilibrium production, might include simulating smolt production and survival when carcass deposition reaches 0.15 kg/m², as suggested by Bilby et al. (2001).

Based on the outcomes observed in this model, taken in context with previous research, we make the following recommendations for Pacific salmon escapement research and management.

Research

- Continue modeling, as done here, testing various scenarios of harvest, survival, environmental variation, and other influences.
- Continue data collection on all aspects of survival, run sizes, smolt production, marine nutrient composition, and so on, for as many populations as possible, with an increased focus on marine and estuarine survival and production.
- Integrate this model with migration models and ocean condition models (e.g., Hinch et al. 1995).
- Conduct bioenergetic and feeding studies as they pertain to survival.
- Relate both physical habitat and nutrient enrichment to productive carrying capacity by
  - using historic records before harvest as compared with contemporary production,
  - evaluating contemporary nutrient contributions in a variety of streams having a range of escapements and harvest rates,
  - implementing intentional "overescapement" on several study streams to observe and understand true equilibrium replacement, and
  - continuing existing and establishing new, intensive study streams and expanding as necessary to assess production potential and capacity.
- Apply sensitivity analyses to life history population models to evaluate outcomes when environmental, nutrient, and survival rates are varied.
- Apply these and other related models to specific case study populations for which there is a rich data history (e.g., Puget Sound or Oregon coastal coho).

Management

- Ensure generous escapements (Larkin and Slaney 1997; NRC 1996; Bilby et al. 2001) by reducing or closing fisheries when necessary for long-term population health.
- Explore alternative methods of estimating escapement goals.
- Reduce direct reliance on spawner-recruit models—use only as one source of information in a precautionary approach that includes other considerations for sustainability, like those of Michael (1998), Cederholm et al. (1999), and Bilby et al. (2001).
- Consider replenishing nutrients to fresh waters where appropriate (Larkin and Slaney 1997; Stockner et al. 2000; Bilby et al. 2001).

Acknowledgements

We greatly appreciate quantitative assistance from Jeff Bromaghin. Nick Hughes provided spirited strategic consultation. The reviews of Jeff Bromaghin, Hal Michael, Jennifer Nielsen, Joel Reynolds, Carol Ann Woody, and several anonymous reviewers helped improve this manuscript.

References

Beamish, R. J., and D. R. Bouillon. 1993. Pacific salmon production trends in relation to climate. Canadian Journal of Fisheries and Aquatic Sciences 50:1002–1016.

Bilby, R. E., B. R. Fransen, and P. A. Bisson. 1996. Incorporation of nitrogen and carbon from spawning coho salmon into the trophic system of small streams. Canadian Journal of Fisheries and Aquatic Sciences 53:164–173.

Bilby, R. E., B. R. Fransen, P. A. Bisson, and J. K. Walter. 1998. Response of juvenile coho salmon (*Oncorhynchus kisutch*) and steelhead (*Oncorhynchus mykiss*) to the addition of salmon carcasses to two streams in southwestern Washington, U.S.A. Canadian Journal of Fisheries and Aquatic Sciences 55:1909–1918.

Bilby, R. E., B. R. Fransen, J. K. Walter, J. K., C. J. Cederholm, and W. J. Scarlett. 2001. Preliminary evaluation of the use of nitrogen stable isotope ratios to establish escapement levels for Pacific salmon. Fisheries 26:6–14.

Bradford, M. J., R. A. Myers, and J. R. Irvine. 2000. Reference points for coho salmon (*Oncorhynchus kisutch*) harvest rates and escapement goals based on freshwater production. Canadian Journal of Fisheries and Aquatic Sciences 57:677–686.

Cederholm, C. J., M. D. Kunze, T. Murota, and A. Sibatani. 1999. Pacific salmon carcasses: essential contributions of nutrients and energy for aquatic and terrestrial ecosystems. Fisheries 24:6–15.

Coronado, C., and R. Hilborn. 1998. Spatial and temporal factors affecting survival in coho salmon (*Oncorhynchus kisutch*) in the Pacific Northwest. Canadian Journal of Fisheries and Aquatic Sciences 55:2067–2077.

Cramer, S. P. 2000. The effect of environmentally-driven recruitment variation on sustainable yield from salmon populations. Pages 485–503 *in* E. E. Knudsen, C. R. Steward, D. D. MacDonald, J. E. Williams, and D. W. Reiser, editors. Sustainable fisheries management: Pacific salmon. Lewis Publishers, Boca Raton, Florida.

Finney, B. P., I. Gregory-Eaves, J. Sweetman, M. Douglas, and J. P. Smol. 2000. Impacts of climatic change and fishing on Pacific salmon abundance over the past three hundred years. Science 290:795–799.

Gilbert, D. J. 1997. Towards a new recruitment paradigm for fish stocks. Canadian Journal of Fisheries and Aquatic Sciences 54:979–977.

Gresh, T., J. Lichatowich, and P. Schoonmaker. 2000. An estimation of historic and current levels of salmon production in the Northwest Pacific ecosystem: evidence of a nutrient deficit in the freshwater systems of the Pacific Northwest. Fisheries 25:15–21.

Groot, C., and L. Margolis, editors. 1991. Pacific salmon life histories. University of British Columbia Press, Vancouver, British Columbia.

Hare, S. R., N. J. Mantua, and R. C. Francis. 1999. Inverse production regimes: Alaska and West Coast Pacific salmon. Fisheries 24:6–14.

Hilborn, R., and M. Liermann. 1998. Standing on the shoulders of giants: learning from experience in fisheries. Reviews in Fish Biology and Fisheries 8:273–283.

Hilborn, R. C., and C. J. Walters. 1992. Quantitative fisheries stock assessment. Chapman and Hall, New York.

Hinch, S. G., M. C. Healey, R. E. Diewert, and M. A. Henderson. 1995. Climate change and ocean energetics of Fraser River sockeye (*Oncorhynchus nerka*). Pages 439–445 *in* R. J. Beamish, editor. Climate change and fish populations. Canadian Special Publication in Fisheries and Aquatic Sciences 121.

Holtby, L. B., B. C. Andersen, and R. K. Kadowaki. 1990. Importance of smolt size and early ocean growth to interannual variability in marine survival of coho salmon (*Oncorhynchus kisutch*).

Canadian Journal of Fisheries and Aquatic Sciences 47:2181–2194.

Kline, Jr., T. C., J. J. Goering, O. A. Mathisen, P. H. Poe, and P. L. Parker. 1990. Recycling of elements transported upstream by runs of Pacific salmon: I. 15N and 13C evidence in Sashin Creek, Southeastern Alaska. Canadian Journal of Fisheries and Aquatic Sciences 47:136–144.

Knudsen, E. E. 2002. Ecological perspectives on Pacific salmon: can we sustain biodiversity and fisheries? Pages 277–320 *in* M. L. Jones and K. D. Lynch, editors. Sustaining North American salmon: perspectives across regions and disciplines. American Fisheries Society, Bethesda, Maryland.

Knudsen, E. E. 2000. Managing Pacific salmon escapements: the gaps between theory and reality. Pages 237–272 *in* E. E. Knudsen, C. S. Steward, D. D. MacDonald, J. E. Williams, and D. W. Reiser, editors. Sustainable fisheries management: Pacific salmon. Lewis Publishers, Boca Raton, Florida

Knudsen, E. E., C. R. Steward, D. D. MacDonald, J. E. Williams, and D. W. Reiser, editors. Sustainable fisheries management: Pacific salmon. 2000. Lewis Publishers, Boca Raton, Florida.

Larkin, G. A., and P. A. Slaney. 1997. Implications of trends in marine-derived nutrient influx to south coastal British Columbia salmonid production. Fisheries 22:16–24.

Lichatowich, J., L. Mobrand, L. Lestelle, and T. Vogel. 1995. An approach to the diagnosis and treatment of depleted Pacific salmon populations in Pacific Northwest watersheds. Fisheries 20:10–18.

Michael, J. H. 1998. Pacific salmon spawner escapement goals for the Skagit River watershed as determined by nutrient cycling considerations. Northwest Science 72(4):239–248.

Milner, A. M., E. E. Knudsen, C. Soiseth, A. L. Robertson, D. Schell, I. T. Phillips, and K. Magnusson. 2001. Colonization and development of stream communities across a two hundred year gradient in Glacier Bay National Park, Alaska, USA. Canadian Journal of Fisheries and Aquatic Sciences 57:2319–2335.

Mobrand, L. E., J. A. Lichatowich, L. C. Lestelle, and T. S. Vogel. 1997. An approach to describing ecosystem performance "through the eyes of salmon". Canadian Journal of Fisheries and Aquatic Sciences 54:2964–2973.

Myers, R. A. 1997. Comment and reanalysis: paradigms for recruitment studies. Canadian Journal of Fisheries and Aquatic Sciences 54:978–981.

Myers, R. A., and N. J. Barrowman. 1996. Is fish recruitment related to spawner abundance? Fishery Bulletin 94:707–724.

Needle, C. L. In Press. Recruitment models; diagnosis and prognosis. Reviews in Fish and Fisheries.

Nickelson, T. E. 1998. A habitat-based assessment of coho salmon production potential and spawner escapement needs for Oregon coastal streams. Oregon Department of Fish and Wildlife, Portland.

Nickelson, T. E., and P. W. Lawson. 1998. Population viability of coho salmon, *Oncorhynchus kisutch*, in Oregon coastal basins: application of a habitat-based life cycle model. Canadian Journal of Fisheries and Aquatic Sciences 55:2382–2392.

NRC (National Research Council). 1996. Upstream: salmon and society in the Pacific Northwest. National Academy Press, Washington, D.C.

Prager, M. H., and M. S. Mohr. 2001. The harvest rate model for Klamath River fall chinook salmon, with management applications and comments on model development and documentation. North American Journal of Fisheries Management 21:533–547.

Pyper, B. J., and R. M. Peterman. 1999. Relationship among adult body length, abundance, and ocean temperature for British Columbia and Alaska sockeye salmon (*Oncorhynchus nerka*), 1967-1997. Canadian Journal of Fisheries and Aquatic Sciences 56:1716–1720.

Quinn, T. P., and N. P. Peterson. 1996. The influence of habitat complexity and fish size on over-winter survival and growth of individually marked juvenile coho salmon (*Oncorhynchus kisutch*) in Big Beef Creek, Washington. Canadian Journal of Fisheries and Aquatic Sciences 53:1555–1564.

Ricker, W. E. 1975. Computation and interpretation of biological statistics of fish populations. Fisheries Research Board of Canada Bulletin 191. Ottawa, Canada.

Schmidt, D. C., S. R. Carlson, G. B. Kyle, and B. P. Finney. 1998. Influence of carcass-derived nutrients on sockeye salmon productivity of Karluk Lake, Alaska: importance in the assessment of an escapement goal. North American Journal of Fisheries Management 18:743–763.

Spence, B. G., Lomnicky, G. A., Hughes. R. M., and R. P. Novitski. 1996. An ecosystem approach to salmonid conservation. Mantech Environmental, Inc. Report Number 21TR-4501-96-6057.

Stockner, J. G., and E. A. MacIsaac. 1996. The British Columbia Lake fertilization program: overview after two decades of salmon enhancement. Regulated Rivers 12:344–356.

Stockner, J. G., E. Rydin, and P. Hyenstrand. 2000. Cultural oligotrophication: causes and consequences for fisheries resources. Fisheries 25:7–14.

Stouder, D. J., P. A. Bisson, and R. J. Naiman, editors. 1997. Pacific salmon and their ecosystems: status and future options. Chapman & Hall, New York.

Williams, R. N., P. A. Bisson, D. L. Bottom, L. D. Calvin, C. C. Coutant, M. W. Erho, Jr., C. A. Frissell, J. A. Lichatowich, W. J. Liss, W. E. McConnaha, J. A. Stanford, and R. R. Whitney. 1999. Scientific issues in the restoration of salmonid fishes in the Columbia River. Fisheries 24:10–19.

American Fisheries Society Symposium 34:277–282, 2003

Toward New Escapement Goals: Integrating Ecosystem and Fisheries Management Goals

JOHN H. MICHAEL, JR.

Washington Department of Fish and Wildlife, Fish Program/Hatcheries Division
600 Capitol Way N., Olympia, Washington 98501-1091, USA

Abstract.—Based on the information presented at the Restoring Nutrients to Salmonid Ecosystems conference in Eugene, Oregon, in April of 2001, it will be necessary to substantially increase and achieve salmon spawner escapement goals in order to meet ecosystem productivity potential. Modeling of recovery rates shows that achievement of even the currently identified spawner escapement goals (much less ecosystem recovery) in less than 50–100 years is unlikely, unless there are substantial shifts in management thought and practice. To speed recovery, it is necessary to achieve consistent rates of increase in spawning escapement not seen in current management activities. Until actual spawner escapements approach levels necessary to support ecosystem function, it will be necessary to utilize alternative methods such as the distribution of salmon carcasses, carcass analogs, or the use of fertilizer to provide the nutrients needed to assist its salmonid population recovery. In addition to restoring absolute numbers, the size and age structures of the fish populations need to be restored in order to successfully utilize the available environment. Simply increasing escapements and resultant nutrient levels, however, is insufficient. Stream flows, whether average, flood, or low, need to be stabilized. Instream and riparian habitats need to be stabilized and restored; this would include allowing normal flood paths to be followed.

Introduction

Management of Pacific salmon *Oncorhynchus* spp. has reached critical status in the contiguous United States. Regardless of what measure is used, whether Endangered Species Act (ESA) listings, analyses of stock health, or simply a decline in number of fish landed in sport and commercial fisheries, the perspective is the same: as a resource believed to be capable of sustaining intense levels of consumptive use, salmon are in trouble (Nehlson et al. 1991). The decline in the number of spawning salmon has led to the depletion of nutrient supply in the ecosystems that once nurtured them (Cederholm et al. 1999; Gresh et al. 2000). Restoring the historic nutrient levels, temporal, and spatial distribution through natural processes will require restoring salmon populations to the levels of escapement seen in the paleontological and historic record (Munn et al. 1998; Gresh et al. 2000). If this becomes a societal goal, it will re-

quire large changes in how anadromous salmonids are perceived and managed.

Restoring Nutrient Levels in Ecosystems

Restoration of salmonid populations to historical levels will necessitate restoring the productivity of the ecosystems upon which they depend. Increasing nutrient levels in the freshwater environments that are used for early rearing represents an important step toward restoring the productive capacity of these systems. In order to provide the justification for fundamental changes in salmon management, it will be necessary to understand preEuropean contact abundance and causes for cycles of abundance.

Paleontological evidence from lakes shows that the abundance of sockeye salmon *O. nerka* dramatically varied over time in what appear to be responses to climate (Finney et al. 2000). However, even the lowest levels of spawner abundance seen in the paleontological record appear to be higher than recent escapement levels. These glances into the past also show that salmon runs do not need to be stable in order to sustain the run and the associated ecosystem. Rather than being a biological necessity or even a biological occurrence, population stability stems from economic and social needs relative to the consumptive use of the resource.

Increasing Spawner Escapement

In addition to being substantially lower than historic levels, current levels of spawning escapement are generally lower than established salmon management escapement goals. This represents a significant concern because such established salmon management goals are unlikely to result in the delivery of requisite nutrients to freshwater systems, even if the goals are achieved. The present goals in Puget Sound, Washington, were developed in the late 1960s and early 1970s. For Skagit River chinook salmon *O. tshawytscha*, the goal was set at 17,900 spawners. In defining chinook salmon escapement goals, the Washington Department of Fisheries noted that escapement goals have been primarily dependant on past escapement levels: "the spawning area available to chinook greatly exceeds the amount needed to support rational spawning escapements" (Ames and Phinney 1977). However, the term rational was not defined. Ames and Phinney (1977) noted that fisheries managers defined escapement goal as the adult spawning population that would, on average, maximize the biomass of juvenile out-migrants under average environmental conditions. Using this definition, managers need not consider the broader values delivered by aquatic and riparian ecosystems, nor the inter- or intra-species connections that make such ecosystems function, unless they directly result in more juvenile outmigrants. By way of comparison, Michael (1998) developed a chinook salmon spawner escapement goal for the Skagit River based on the biomass of spawners needed to meet the nutritional needs of rearing salmonids, nesting insectivorous birds, and wintering eagles. The number of spawners needed was estimated as 121,600. Cederholm (Washington Department of Natural Resources biologist, personal communication), basing his estimate on spawner biomass densities developed by Bilby et al. (2001), estimated a spawner need of 270,348 chinook salmon. The two ecosystem-based escapement goals represent an increase of 6.8 to 15.1 times the current goal.

Broadly speaking, salmon spawner escapement goals are not consistently being met in Washington State or elsewhere in the Pacific Northwest. Current escapement goals for Skagit River spring, summer, and fall chinook salmon (17,900), Dungeness River chinook salmon (925), and Cedar River chinook salmon (1,200) runs in Washington State serve as examples. The combined escapement goal for all Skagit River chinook salmon stocks has been met twice during the period 1974–2000; the Dungeness River chinook salmon escapement goal has not been met even once in the years 1986–2000, while the escapement goal for Cedar River chinook salmon has been met only six times between 1974 and 2000. The fact that even modest escapement goals are consistently not met suggests that the likelihood of achieving these goals is consistently low. Over the same time periods, assuming that chinook are on a four-year return cycle, the average percent change from brood year escapement, for each of the four brood-year cycles, is +8% for the Skagit River, –6% for the Dungeness River, and +2% for the Cedar River. That very little progress has been made in achieving even modest escapement goals suggests that the likelihood of achievement of the goals under the present management institutions is low.

Throughout the late 1970s to mid-1990s, the prevailing management scheme for Puget Sound chinook salmon was to subtract the designated spawner escapement goal from the estimated total run size. This identified the harvestable number to be taken by the combined commercial, native, and sport fisheries. However, this management approach created difficulties, particularly with the management of chinook salmon and coho salmon *O. kisutch* in mixed stock fisheries, because the total run size of many stocks was less than the escapement goal, so these stocks should not be fished. Pressure to maintain fishing industry infrastructure, to balance inter- and intra-group allocations to meet user group needs have all led to a collective desire to fish when identified harvestable surplus did not exist. The new management scheme is to apply overall conservative exploitation rates to each stock and to assume that these rates are low enough to allow for some level of rebuilding of each stock. The comprehensive chinook management plan, developed by WDFW and the Puget Sound Indian Tribes that has been accepted by the National Marine Fisheries Service as meeting the requirements of the ESA, called for an overall exploitation of 52% for Skagit chinook. In the Klamath River, California, managers set what are called optimal harvest levels for managing chinook salmon. These harvest levels are defined as the highest levels attainable within current management policy (Prager and Mohr 2001). It is important to note that both of these schemes are premised on the assumption that some level of harvesting is appropriate.

The results of recent research on the delivery and consumption of anadromous salmonid derived nutrients in ecosystems demonstrate that the escapement goals currently in use in Puget Sound are substantially lower than the levels that would meet ecosystem nutrient needs (Cederholm et al. 2000; Gresh et al. 2000). This means that, for the systems in question (and probably all Puget Sound chinook watersheds), the ecosystems and reliant food webs are being deprived of essential nutrients.

To evaluate how long it would take to reach current escapement goals, increasing the actual cyclic (based on 4-year cycles of maturity) chinook salmon spawner escapements achieved in 1997–2000 by 10%, 25%, and 100% annually was evaluated (Table 1). For example, the 1997 escapement would return in 2001, 2005, 2009, and so on. Restoration is considered to occur when the identified escapement goal is achieved for four consecutive years. This would mean that each cycle had achieved its escapement goal.

If annual escapement increased 10% above the brood year escapement, it is estimated that the current combined escapement goal for the Skagit River would be achieved in four successive years during 2048–2052. By comparison, current escapement goals for the Dungeness River and Cedar River would be achieved in 2118–2121 and 2076–2079, respectively. If the brood year escapement were increased by 25% each year, the escapement goal for the Skagit River would be achieved in four successive years in 2020–2023. For the Dungeness River, the escapement goal would be first achieved in four successive years in 2050–2053, while the Cedar River escapement goal would be achieved in four successive years in 2032–2035. Even with an increase in brood year escapement of 10–25% per cycle year, rebuilding will be a long process under any scenario that seeks to allow even modest levels of consumptive fisheries. Placing extreme restrictions on harvest so that escapement doubles with each brood year return (100% increase) would result in achieving the escapement goal for four successive years in 2004–2007 for the Skagit River, in 2014–2017 for Dungeness River, and in 2013–2016 for the Cedar River. These scenarios are based on making the specific increase (10%, 25%, or 100%) in escapement each year. In the three river systems examined, the longest streak of annual increases of any level was four years; which occurred once in each system. Even at the slowest rate of recovery modeled (10%), the rate of recovery exceeds the average rate of escapement increase that has occurred on any of the three systems since 1974. As such, it is unlikely that recovery (four consecutive years achieving the escapement goal) for any of these systems would be achieved within 20 years under the current management approach (Table 1).

Michael's (1998) ecosystem-based escapement goal for the Skagit River chinook salmon stocks of 121,600 would be achieved for four successive years in 2128–2031 at the 10% rate of increase and in 2052–2055 at the 25% increase rate. The goal of 270,348, proposed by Cederholm (DNR biologist, personal communication), would take even longer. In summary, if we rely on harvest restrictions alone to restore nutrient

TABLE 1. Estimated time (yrs) for achievement of chinook salmon spawner escapement goals if achieved escapement was 10%, 25% or 100% greater than brood year escapement for Skagit, Dungeness, and Cedar rivers, Washington State.

River	Goal	Years at		
		110%	125%	200%
Skagit-WDFW	17,900	46–50	18–21	2–5
Skagit-Michael	121,600	126–129	50–53	14–17
Skagit-Cederholm	270,350	162–165	62–65	18–21
Dungeness	950	116–119	48–51	12–15
Cedar	1,200	74–77	30–33	12–14

delivery rates, the three watersheds are nutrient deficient to such an extent that over a century would be required to achieve ecosystem restoration goals.

Therefore, it is apparent that additional nutrient supplementation, such as the application of carcasses, carcass analogs, or fertilizer, will be needed if the productive capacity of these salmonid ecosystems is to be restored in any reasonable period of time. The use of these artificial applications of nutrients, though, should be viewed only as an interim measure to be used until natural spawning and carcass deposition can take over nutrient delivery.

Artificial Means of Increasing Nutrients

The most technological solution for restoring nutrient levels is the application of fertilizer with specific formulations of nitrogen and phosphorus at predetermined rates (Stockner et al. 2000). They enhance lacustrine food chains through the phytoplankton-zooplankton-fish food chain while in streams they pass through the epilithic algae to grazing invertebrates to predators that may be fish or insects (Bilby et al. 1996). In both situations, the food chain does not directly support aquatic scavengers or any of the terrestrial animals. The application level is controlled, can be easily monitored, can be modified if conditions require, and can be easily terminated. It is an easily quantifiable restoration technique that results in demonstrable improvement in fish populations in short order (Stockner and Mac-Isaac 1996).

The application of carcass analogs, essentially fish carcasses and processing waste that is treated to kill pathogens and formed into cakes of some shape, is a step toward a more natural delivery of nutrients to ecosystems that is currently being developed by fish food processors. The analogs contain most of the constituents found in carcasses. Absence of pathogens following heat treatment allows analogs to be distributed in watersheds where carcasses are not allowed due to concerns of pathogen transmission. Analogs differ from fertilizers in that they are consumed by a variety of animals (Todd Pearsons, WDFW biologist, personal communication) and thereby increase the number of pathways by which nutrients enter the ecosystem.

A third source of nutrients is from carcasses obtained from fish hatcheries. The Washington Department of Fish and Wildlife (WDFW) has been making carcasses available for this purpose for about a decade. In brood year 2000 (fall 2000–spring 2001) approximately 160,000 carcasses were distributed to streams throughout the state. In brood year 2001 this has increased to more that 180,000 carcasses. Current practice is to limit carcass distribution to streams currently accessible to anadromous salmonids. The nutrients from carcasses enter the food chain through the same pathways described for natural spawners (Cederholm et al. 2000). Naturally spawned carcasses tend to be distributed more widely in the system, often including reaches of streams that are not easily accessible.

Although all these methods of delivering nutrients can be effective, they represent technological fixes that deal with the symptom but not the root cause of the problem, the lack of natural spawners. In the past, adult salmon contributed more than just their bodies to the ecosystem. The very act of spawning cleaned sediment from gravel, deposited eggs into the intragravel ecosystem, and in many situations physically changed the streambed contours which actually provided an additional protection against extreme flows during freshet events (Montgomery et al. 1996). In order to bring the ecosystem back to productivity, it is necessary to let the fish themselves return the nutrients, deposit the eggs, and provide carcasses for all of the organisms in the ecosystem (Cederholm et al. 2000).

Spawner size and spawn timing may be as critical to population recovery as simple numbers. For example, the removal of two dams on the Elwha River represents a unique opportunity to restore a fully functional wild salmon-based ecosystem in the lower 48 states. Once the dams are removed, salmon will have the opportunity to reinvade the best quality contiguous salmonid habitat remaining in Washington. The expectation, at least in the public's mind, will be that once the dams are gone, fish populations will start to immediately rebuild. The habitat, most of which is protected in Olympic National Park, is relatively intact; there will be no hydroelectric projects, the impact of hatcheries will be minimized; it is a perfect situation.

Historically, Elwha River chinook salmon were huge, averaging 30–40 kg (Munn et al. 1998). Current weights average 10–20 kg, although some of the fish still exceed 30+ kg. The presence of such individuals suggests that the potential for producing large fish is still there. Why were the chinook so large? The fish were that size because they needed to be large to successfully reproduce in the Elwha (Quinn et al. 2001). Given that the habitat base that provided the selective forces that culminated in such large fish remains intact, it will be necessary to return big fish to the river. To do this, fisheries that remove chinook salmon before they have had a chance to achieve maximum size and maturity will need to be constrained so that the fisheries will have a negligible total impact on Elwha River chinook salmon. These fisheries are the marine, mixed stock, hook-and-line fisheries that target immature, aggressively feeding chinook salmon.

The restoration of Fraser River sockeye salmon shows the importance of spawn timing in optimizing reproductive success. Problems, such as excessive pre-spawning mortalities, complicated recovery efforts. To date, the more successfully recovered populations are those that have adapted to the existing environmental conditions. In many cases, the remnant population was not returning at the optimum time for that particular system (Roos 1991).

The same reasoning can be applied to other salmonid restoration projects. Fish need to be physically capable of successful reproduction. This includes abundance, but also includes return and spawning timing, size and age of spawners, and the other physical characteristics of the populations that allow them to successfully reproduce.

Hydrological and Habitat Considerations in Salmonid Recovery

The restoration of nutrient levels to ecosystems is only one part of the puzzle of salmonid population restoration. Fixing only one part of the total problem will not, ultimately, achieve ecosystem restoration. Ultimately, if the goal is to restore ecosystem functionality, then all of the many components need to be considered. For example, dam construction, diversion of water for agriculture, industrial, and domestic uses, logging, and flood plain management to protect human infrastructure development have all altered the quantity and quality of water present in streams. Salmon are the product of their environment. They are adapted to the hydrologic cycle, freshet pattern, temperature cycles, and water quality of their watershed of origin. Activities in watersheds that

change the relationship between precipitation and stream flow can have severe consequences for fish. Until the issues related to flood flows and associated floodplain management are addressed, the addition of more spawners will not result in the recovery of affected salmon populations.

Puget Sound did not exist 15,000 years ago. It was covered by glacial ice. The salmon populations present when the first people arrived had colonized the area after the glaciers retreated. Puget Sound is currently undergoing another glaciation, this time instead of ice it is one of asphalt and concrete. For the ecosystems to be restored, it will be necessary for that glacier to retreat.

Summary

Based on the past record, management practices of today are not likely to restore salmonid ecosystems to historic productivity levels through natural reproduction in less than 50 years, more likely it will take centuries. It has taken 150 to 200 years of concerted effort to reduce the health of salmon populations and associated ecosystems to current levels; it should be expected that recovery will take some time. The artificial addition of nutrients, increases in spawning escapements, removal of dams, restoration of instream and riparian habitats, restoration of fish age and size at maturity, and restoration of natural hydrologic cycles must all occur. Addressing only one of the factors that have contributed to low salmon abundance will not result in recovery.

Acknowledgments

This paper is the result of conversations and discussion with aquatic and terrestrial biologists concerned with restoration of ecosystems, whose nutrient base was provided by spawning salmon. Their input, ideas, comments, and criticism have shaped the ideas presented. The review and comment provided by R. Bugert, C. Drivdahl, D. MacDonald, P. Michael, J. Stockner, and an anonymous reviewer substantially focused the manuscript. Their input is sincerely appreciated.

References

Ames, J., and D. E. Phinney. 1977. 1977 Puget Sound summer-fall chinook methodology: escapement estimates and goals, runs size forecasts, and in-season run size updates. Washington Department of Fisheries Technical Report 29, Olympia, Washington.

Bilby, R. E., B. R. Fransen, and P. A. Bisson. 1996. Incorporation of nitrogen and carbon from spawning coho salmon into the trophic system of small streams: evidence from stable isotopes. Canadian Journal of Fisheries and Aquatic Sciences 53:164–173.

Bilby, R. E., B. R. Fransen, J. K. Walter, C. J. Cederholm, and W. J. Scarlett. 2001. Preliminary evaluation of the use of nitrogen stable isotope ratios to establish escapement levels for Pacific salmon. Fisheries 26:6–14.

Cederholm, C. J., M. D. Kunze, T. Murota, and A. Sibatani. 1999. Pacific salmon carcasses: Essential contribution of nutrients and energy for aquatic and terrestrial ecosystems. Fisheries 24(10):6–15.

Cederholm, C. J., D. H. Johnson, R. E. Bilby, L. G. Dominguez, A. M. Garrett, W. H. Graeber, E. L. Greda, M. D. Kunze, B. G. Marcot, J. F. Palmisano, R. W. Plotnikoff, W. G. Pearcy, C. A. Simenstad, and P. C. Trotter. 2000. Pacific salmon and wildlife-ecological contexts, relationships, and implications for management. Special Edition Technical Report, prepared by D. H. Johnson and T. A. O'Neil (Managing Directors), Wildlife-Habitat Relationships in Oregon and Washington. Washington Department of Fish and Wildlife.

Finney, B. P., I. Gregory-Eaves, J. Sweetman, M. S.V. Douglas, and J. P. Smol. 2000. Impacts of climatic change and fishing abundance on Pacific salmon abundance over the past 300 years. Science 290:795–798.

Maser, C., R. F. Tarrant, J. M. Trappe, and J. F. Franklin, editors. 1988. From the forest to the sea: a story of fallen trees. General Technical Report PNW-GTR-229. Pacific Northwest Research Station, United States Department of Agriculture, Portland, Oregon.

Michael, J. H. Jr. 1998. Pacific salmon spawner escapement goals for the Skagit River watershed as determined by nutrient cycling considerations. Northwest Science 72:239–248.

Montgomery, D. R., J. M. Buffington, N. P. Peterson, D. Shuett-Hames, and T. P. Quinn. 1996. Stream-bed scour, egg burial depths, and the influence of salmonid spawning on bed surface mobility and embryo survival. Canadian Journal of Fisheries and Aquatic Sciences 53:1061–1070.

Munn, M. D., R. W. Black, A. L. Haggland, M. A. Hummling, and R. L. Huffman. 1998. An assessment of stream habitat and nutrients in the Elwha River basin: implications for restoration. USGS Water-Resources Investigations Report 98–4223. United States Geological Survey, Tacoma, Washington.

Nehlson, W., J. E. Williams, and J. A. Lichatowich. 1991. Pacific salmon at the crossroads: stocks at risk from California, Oregon, Idaho, and Washington. Fisheries 16:2–21.

Prager, M. H., and M. S. Mohr. 2001. The harvest rate model for Klamath River fall chinook salmon, with management applications and comments on model development and documentation. North American Journal of Fisheries Management 21:533–547.

Quinn, T. P., L. Wetzel, S. Bishop, K. Overberg, D. E. Rogers. 2001. Influence of breeding habitat on bear predation and age at maturity and sexual dimorphism of sockeye salmon populations. Canadian Journal of Zoology 79:1782–1793.

Roos, J. F. 1991. Restoring Fraser River salmon. Pacific Salmon Commission, Vancouver, British Columbia.

Stockner, J. G., E. Rydin, and P. Hyenstrand. 2000. Cultural oligotrophication. Fisheries 25:7–14.

Stockner, J. G., and E. A. MacIsaac. 1996. The British Columbia lake fertilization program: overview after 2 decades of salmon enhancement. Regulated Rivers 12:344–356.

American Fisheries Society Symposium 34:283–285, 2003

Nutrient Addition to Restore Salmon Runs: Considerations for Developing Environmental Protection Policies and Regulations

ROBERT T. LACKEY

National Health and Environmental Effects Research Laboratory
USEPA, 200 SW 35th Street, Corvallis, Oregon 97333, USA

One scheme to help restore salmon to the Pacific Northwest is the addition of nutrients (i.e., raw or processed salmon carcasses and commercially-produced organic or inorganic fertilizers) to headwaters (e.g., lake or stream salmon spawning and rearing habitat) that are now nutrient deficient because of inadequate replenishment from oceanic or other sources. The rationale is as follows:

> Salmon are a vector by which marine nutrients are captured and conveyed against the force of gravity into freshwater ecosystems. Especially in the upper reaches of watersheds where salmon are able to spawn and their offspring spend their early lives, these nutrients, in both organic and inorganic forms, play an important, perhaps essential, role in maintaining viable salmon runs along with numerous other ecosystem components. For example, a substantial proportion of the nitrogen in plants and animals in streams where salmon are abundant is undoubtedly derived from decomposed spawned salmon. This "anadromous nutrient pump" has been attenuated considerably because salmon runs have been reduced substantially in the Pacific Northwest for decades and, in some places, for more than a century. Thus, the addition of nutrients to watersheds, lakes, or streams where salmon runs are now much reduced would replace, at least partially, the "missing" marine-derived nutrients and would likely enhance salmon runs and overall aquatic productivity.

There are many scientific uncertainties with assessing the efficacy of nutrient addition. For example, is it *possible* for salmon runs in the Pacific Northwest to be restored without somehow compensating for diminished nutrient inputs? When and where is it most effective to add nutrients to improve spawning and rearing success, thus enhancing salmon runs? Is it feasible to add nutrients to nutrient-poor headwater streams without degrading downstream water quality where nutrient levels already are too high due to agricultural or other land/human activities? What form of nutrient addition is the most effective? Is there any significant difference in how organic and inorganic forms of nutrients perform in salmon enhancement? If salmon carcasses are used, what is the risk associated with disease transmission? How important is the carcass substrate, itself, as compared with the role of the nutrients themselves? How important is the effect of spawning *activity* on the physical attributes of channels compared with the biological effect of elevated *nutrients* from salmon runs? Are there ecological consequences from spawning fish (e.g., aerating gravel) that are not realized with carcasses or other forms of nutrient addition? What is the contribution of salmon eggs as a nutrient source, or as food for other animals? How do human-caused changes in stream hydrology and riparian habitat interact with nutrient addition to influence salmon runs? To what extent do salmon accumulate toxins in marine waters and then transport them to fresh waters? Apart from potential effects on salmon populations, what are the broader ecological consequences of nutrient addition on streams, rivers, riparian zones, and estuaries? Perhaps the most crucial scientific uncertainty hindering salmon recovery is answering the century old question of knowing the *relative* contribution of nutrient shortages, fishing, dams, water withdrawal, forest and agricultural practices, pollution, hatchery operations, predators, competitors, ocean conditions, and climatic changes.

Answers to these and similar questions *can* be addressed with a comprehensive, sustained research effort.

However, equally important are the many important questions *not* amenable to scientific evaluation. For example, is the use of nutrients just the latest techno-fix in attempts to restore salmon and will it fail, as have the others, because it does not address the root cause of the decline? Because it is a relatively painless way for society to address the salmon decline issue, will nutrient addition become the tool of choice to avoid the important societal actions that must be implemented if salmon are to be restored? What criteria should regulatory agencies use to decide which proposals for nutrient addition to approve? How should a government agency justify forcing some members of society (i.e., farmers, ranchers, forest managers, golf course owners, and suburbanites) to reduce their addition of nutrients to streams and lakes, while simultaneously condoning requests from fisheries managers to add nutrients?

The specific policy questions that should be answered, at least implicitly, by the relevant regulatory agencies are

- Fundamentally, even assuming that rigorous field tests demonstrate that nutrient addition has the capability of restoring wild salmon runs, is it an appropriate tool for restoration?
- Is there an inherent policy conflict between adding nutrients to watersheds to enhance salmon runs and other societal values such as protecting or enhancing water quality, given that society wants both?
- Intended or not, will fisheries technocrats lead society again down the track of a quick-fix solution rather than addressing

the fundamental causes of the salmon decline?
- Is there a regulatory bias toward achieving "distilled water" in lakes and streams such that the important beneficial role of waterborne nutrients will not be appropriately understood and considered?
- Should regulatory agencies categorically reject large-scale requests for nutrient addition until its efficacy is adequately documented in scientifically validated field tests?
- How should regulatory agencies balance the universally supported but apparently conflicting goals of enhancing water quality and restoring salmon through nutrient addition?
- If nutrient additions are approved, what level of monitoring should be required to evaluate effects on water quality, and which agency or organization should be responsible for the stipulated monitoring and evaluation?
- How much latitude will various levels of government (and society) be granted in deciding to what extent nutrient addition will be permitted, given that local, state provincial, and national environmental and natural resources priorities often differ markedly?

Beyond the relatively narrow constraints of restoring *salmon* runs and maintaining water quality, there are other important policy and scientific issues to consider. For example, is it desirable (perhaps even essential) to add nutrients specifically to rehabilitate key wildlife species (e.g., bears and eagles), vegetation (e.g., to restore the growth rates of trees), and scavengers (e.g., aquatic invertebrates and small mammals). Although policy and scientific assessments of the desirability of nutrient addition are generally limited to concerns about restoring salmon runs, concurrent with maintaining water quality, other ecological considerations are also important.

There are many concerns that need to be evaluated carefully before environmental protection agencies develop general policies or promulgate specific regulations on granting requests for permits to add salmon carcasses, processed fish products, or inorganic fertilizers to rivers and lakes in the Pacific Northwest. It is easy to be diverted with arguments of the scientific merits of proposals to add nutrients, but there remains, even with *complete* scientific knowledge, explicit policy choices and clashes of competing values that society will adjudicate through the bureaucracy of the regulatory agencies or the courts.

Given the intense public commitment to restore runs of wild salmon and the likelihood that nutrient addition of some sort will be seriously considered in recovery efforts, the policy challenge for environmental protection agencies will be to craft policies that carefully balance the apparent need for nutrient *removal* (at some locations) to enhance water quality with nutrient *addition* (at other locations) to help restore salmon runs.

Acknowledgements

Summary of a panel and audience discussion at the International Conference on Restoring Nutrients to Salmonid Ecosystems, Eugene, Oregon, 24–26 April 2001. Special thanks are due to panelists Xan Augerot, Don Dodds, Dave Peeler, and Mitch Wolgamott for presenting and defending their personal views on this contentious issue. The views and opinions expressed here, however, are those of the author and do not necessarily reflect those of the panelists or any organization.